AF717869

Automating the Office

Automating the Office

Office Systems and End-User Computing

Elizabeth A. Regan

Massachusetts Mutual Life Insurance Co.

Bridget N. O'Connor

New York University

MACMILLAN PUBLISHING COMPANY
New York
COLLIER MACMILLAN PUBLISHERS
London

Copyright © 1989 Macmillan Publishing Company, a division of Macmillan, Inc.

Printed in the United States of America

All rights reserved. No part of this book may be reproduced or transmitted in any form or by any means, electronic or mechanical, including photocopying, recording, or any information storage and retrieval system, without permission in writing from the publisher.

Macmillan Publishing Company
866 Third Avenue, New York, New York 10022

Collier Macmillan Canada, Inc.

Library of Congress Cataloging-in-Publication Data

Regan, Elizabeth Ann.
Automating the office.

Includes bibliographies and index.
1. Office practice—Automation. 2. End-user computing. I. O'Connor, Bridget N. II. Title.
HF5548.R37 1989 651.8 88-37271
ISBN 0-02-399165-8

Printing: 3 4 5 Year: 1 2 3

Acknowledgments

Figure and photo credits appear on page 853.

Pages 82 and 84: The narrative examples of information systems career paths are adapted from Addie Mattox and Janice McCollum, "How To Create a Career Path in Information Processing," *Papers and Proceedings of Syntopticon VII* (Willow Grove, Pa.: Association of Information Systems Professionals, 1980), pp. 413–417. Reprinted with permission of the Association of Information Systems Professionals, 104 Wilmot Road, Suite 201, Deerfield, IL 60015-5195.

Pages 236–237: The narrative example of the use of Videotex technology is adapted from Elizabeth M. Ferrarini, "Videotex: The Race To Plug In," from *Computerworld Extra* (18 March 1981). © 1981 by *Computerworld* magazine. Used with permission.

Page 312: The narrative example of an organization's use of spreadsheet software is adapted from "PC Users Rediscovering Mainframes," *Software News* (April 1986), p. 29. © 1986 by Century Publishing Company, Westborough, Mass. Used with permission.

Page 343: The narrative example of the applications of office automation in a legal office is adapted from Bill Dooley, "Computerization Is Beginning To Permeate the Legal Profession," *MIS Week* (3 Feb. 1986), p. 12. © 1986 by Fairchild Publications. Used with permission.

(continued on page 858)

To my husband Charles, my children Keith, Meredith, and Deanne, and my family, friends, and associates who have encouraged me throughout this endeavor.

Elizabeth A. Regan

To my father Thomas and in memory of my mother Helen, to Michael, Dennis, Loretta, and Rita, and to my students, for whom this book was written.

Bridget N. O'Connor

CONTENTS

PREFACE

We have written this text for a specific purpose: to bring fresh perspectives and insight to the field of office systems, with special emphasis on the end-user applications of office technologies. What does the individual who is responsible for planning and implementing new office work tools need to know about this dynamic field? How can automated technologies improve office operations to meet specific business objectives? What issues are involved in the introduction and use of office automation systems? How are companies handling the internal organization of new technologies? What does one need to know to ensure that the right technologies are used in the right way by the right people?

Throughout the text, we emphasize the need to *improve business performance,* not merely to automate existing procedures. We believe that technology is best used when it supports people rather than replaces them. Toward this end, office automation is viewed as a catalyst for innovative problem solving. Thus this text is designed to develop an understanding of business applications and organizational development as well as technology.

As both practitioners and academics in the field of office systems and end-user computing, we bring together the best of two worlds: a strong conceptual framework and good, practical know-how. Our combined years of experience and study of the field have resulted in a unique textbook that addresses the need for more effective use and management of information at all levels of the organization.

The purpose of this book is to provide a basic understanding of the technologies, applications, problems, and opportunities related to the introduction of office systems into an organization. Office automation is not a one-shot solution but an evolving, continuous process. This text acknowledges that process and identifies not only the technology but the *appropriate use* of the technology. The text also addresses the need for office systems professionals to understand the corporate culture and business requirements of the organization as well as technology and its effective application.

Automating the Office: Office Systems and End-User Computing meets the requirements for courses in both the Office Systems Research Association (OSRA) Model Curriculum for Office Systems Education (Office Systems and Technologies; Office Systems Planning/Implementation) and the Data Processing Management Association (DPMA) Model Curriculum (Advanced Office Systems).

CONCEPTUAL FRAMEWORK

The text is divided into six parts and twenty-five chapters. The parts and chapters are presented in a logical conceptual order, but each unit can be used alone as needed to meet specific instructional objectives.

Part 1, "Automating the Business Office: An Overview," presents an historical review of office technologies, office systems, and the evolution of end-user computing. Part 1 also includes a perspective on how office systems are planned and managed today, thus setting the stage for subsequent chapters.

Part 2, "Office Systems Technologies: The Hardware," covers the hardware components of office systems. The chapters in Part 2 present historical, current, and futuristic perspectives on office technologies. These chapters develop the reader's understanding of the basic terminology used to describe technologies ranging from computer systems to artificial intelligence systems.

Part 3, "Applications for Office Systems and End-User Computing," emphasizes how specific technologies are used by various office workers. Software applications appropriate for managers, professional and technical workers, sales and marketing personnel, and administrative support staff are discussed in detail.

Part 4, "Productivity: The Impact of Automation on Work," covers the theory and practice vital to understanding the impact of office automation on both the individual and the organization. Productivity is defined, and suggestions for measuring productivity are offered. Ergonomic concerns related to new technologies are also discussed. The importance of job design and redesign is stressed, and theory-related aspects of managing change are reviewed.

Part 5, "Planning and Implementing Office Systems," describes the office systems analysis process and covers both the theory and practice related to the science of designing and implementing effective office systems. Part 5 emphasizes issues involved in planning and implementing office systems and offers practical solutions to problems encountered in the systems analysis process.

Part 6, "Automating the Office: Epilog" examines current trends and future directions in office automation and office systems to orient readers to the changes that lie ahead.

FEATURES OF THE TEXT

Automating the Office has been written and designed with a wide range of features to facilitate coverage of important topics and ensure readers' understanding.

1. *Objectives.* Each chapter begins by identifying specific behavioral objectives to help the reader focus on key information presented in the chapter.
2. *Key Terms.* Each chapter opening also presents a list of key terms used within the chapter. These terms are italicized where they are defined in the text and are defined in full in the Glossary in the back of the book.
3. *Discussion Questions.* Each chapter concludes with questions appropriate for generating classroom discussion. The questions require readers to integrate and apply the knowledge gained in each chapter.
4. *Application Exercises.* Each chapter also concludes with enrichment exercises that ask the reader to interview a vendor or end user, investigate an identified problem, or develop a solution to a specific problem. Such activities suggest appropriate field work or library research.
5. *Suggested Readings.* To build on or expand the concepts presented in the chapter, each chapter concludes with a list of Suggested Readings that the reader may pursue for additional information or study.
6. *Research-Based Approach.* Throughout the text, we've attempted to offer the latest research findings on office systems and end-user computing.
7. *Supplementary Information.* Topics discussed in the text are often supplemented with additional information such as examples, historical perspectives, technical details, or special case studies. This supplementary information is included as part of the chapter text and is identified by a vertical line in the left margin.
8. *Useful Appendixes and Case Studies.* The text includes three useful and informative Appendixes. Appendix 1 presents a list of major professional organizations related to office systems and end-user computing.

   Appendix 2 is a list of professional, trade, and research journals of interest to office systems students and professionals.These resources provide additional up-to-date information about office systems technologies and identify career options and research opportunities.

   Appendix 3 presents six comprehensive case studies that allow the reader to apply concepts from the text to actual business experiences. Each case includes specific questions, recommended role plays, and writing assignments related to evaluating each case.
9. *Attractive format.* An attractive format and extensive charts, diagrams, photographs, and illustrations enhance the readability of the text and promote readers' understanding of the material.

10. *Special chapters.* The text includes special chapters on "Artificial Intelligence," "Sales and Marketing Applications," "Job Design," "Organizational Change," and other important topics seldom covered in data processing or office systems introductory texts. New topics mean a new definition of what the office systems analyst should know!

SUMMARY

Automating the Office: Office Systems and End-User Computing offers a comprehensive overview of office automation in organizations and the evolving role of the office systems analyst. The text explains office systems and end-user computing in a style and format that make technology and the opportunities and risks it presents understandable to the reader. At the same time, the text challenges readers to learn more about this dynamic field and the many career opportunities it provides.

Elizabeth A. Regan
Bridget N. O'Connor

ACKNOWLEDGMENTS

We wish to thank the following individuals for reviewing the manuscript, making useful suggestions, or providing other assistance for the development and production of the text:

Terry Ardel, Catonsville Community College, Baltimore, MD
Dr. James Bennett, California State University, Northridge, CA
Dr. Michael Bronner, New York University, New York, NY
Jeanette Dostourian, Cypress College, Cypress, CA
Marsha Ellis, Texas Instruments, Austin, TX
Dr. Blanche Ettinger, Bronx Community College, New York, NY
Michael Garber, Massachusetts Mutual Life Insurance Company, Springfield, MA
Joan Giansante, Photo Researcher, New York, NY
Edward Harrison, Massachusetts Mutual Life Insurance Company, Springfield, MA
Don Johnson, *Administrative Management* magazine, New York, NY
Dr. Dean Malsbary, University of Connecticut, Storrs, CN
Dr. Connie Masson, UNISYS Corporation, Dallas, TX
Dr. Larry Penwell, General Electric Company, Cincinnati, OH
William Wellsteadt, Massachusetts Mutual Life Insurance Company, Springfield, MA

Elizabeth A. Regan
Bridget N. O'Connor

AUTOMATING THE OFFICE: An Overview

PART 1

Part 1 presents a general overview of office automation. Computer-based technologies popularly referred to as "office automation" provide effective new ways for people to manage and use information. The growing economic importance of information in modern society demands more productive ways of handling information. Office automation addresses those needs.

Office automation encompasses the areas also known as "office systems" and "end-user computing." In effect, office automation has moved computer technology from secluded backroom technical environments into the front office next to potted rubber trees and onto desk tops. People at all levels of organizations are discovering not only more productive work methods but innovative ways to use technology in the development and delivery of goods and services. Without the aid of office automation, business and government offices could not provide the diversity of products and services our complex society demands.

An understanding of this specialized field of computer-based technology is important for individuals considering careers in business management, computer science, information systems, administrative services, or business education, as well as those preparing for careers in office systems analysis or office systems management. Individuals charged with responsibility for automating the business office require broad technical skills combined with an understanding of organizational dynamics, management practice, and business requirements.

Part 1 is divided into three chapters. Chapter 1, "Automation in Perspective: Technology," discusses the office automation process and the impact of computer technology on business operations. It offers a historical perspective and relates technology and office productivity.

Chapter 2, "The Office Work Environment: End Users," provides a foundation for understanding the office environment. It explains the purposes that business offices serve and how people work within the office.

Chapter 3, "The Office Systems Organization: Implementers," describes the role of office systems management and the organizational roles and responsibilities of office systems analysts. Chapter 3 also introduces the concept of information management and discusses the importance of adequate planning for successful office automation.

CHAPTER 1
AUTOMATION IN PERSPECTIVE: Technology

OBJECTIVES

After completing this chapter, the reader should be able to meet the following objectives:

- Define office automation.
- Explain why office automation can be described most appropriately as a *process*.
- Identify the benefits of office automation.
- Understand how office automation relates to the historical evolution of computer technologies.
- Describe the impact of office automation on the modern business office.
- Understand the relationship between productivity and technology in an office environment.

KEY TERMS

office automation
data
information
information processing
application
process
efficiency
effectiveness
business office
productivity
Information Age

INTRODUCTION

Office automation is essential to the operation of today's offices. Automation is achieved through the application of computer-based technologies and provides effective new ways for people to manage and use information. Information is crucial to the operation of business and government enterprises. It is the raw material for decision making and the foundation for producing products and providing services. People create information; people use information; people control information.

In fact, approximately half of today's work force is employed in offices, compared to less than 20 percent thirty years ago. The growing economic importance of information in modern society has led sociologists such as Alvin Toffler and John Naisbit to characterize our society as the Information Age.

Computer technology has been applied to the processing of information for approximately the past 30 years. Early data processing technology enabled organizations to speed up repetitive, high-volume, transaction-oriented tasks. It primarily affected the jobs of clerical-level people. Today, however, office automation is having a major impact on the way people work at *all* levels in the organization. Office automation brings change in job responsibilities, task content, work procedures, and human interactions. It also brings new opportunities for individuals with the foresight and understanding to apply it effectively.

Today, office automation offers solutions for a wide range of information processing requirements. The business office is in transition, and office technology is still evolving. Many find it exciting; others find it threatening. Most business people are just beginning to understand automation technology. Most students graduating from school and entering the business world today have had an opportunity to study and use computers. Technology is changing so rapidly, however, that even current graduates find their knowledge becoming rapidly outdated unless they continue to read and keep abreast of new developments.

Thus this textbook about automating the office is actually about an ongoing *process* of applying technology to improve information handling, meet business requirements, and create safe, productive work environments. The Miriam-Webster *Ninth New Collegiate Dictionary* defines *process* as "a systematic series of actions directed to some end."[1] Office automation is a process that requires understanding technology, business, and the needs and behavior of people at work.

To understand the past and future impact of technology on office operations, one must view the office as a *total system*. The term *system* indicates some combination of interrelating parts that form a unitary whole. The *office* is the system that supports an enterprise's operations. One cannot treat units of that system in isolation; a change in one component of the system necessarily affects other components. An understanding of systems concepts is important to office automation and is discussed in Chapter 20.

Viewing the office as a system underscores the fact that automating the business office involves much more than selecting the right technology. The technology must help organizations achieve their business goals by enabling people to work creatively and productively. People, not technology, are the most important variable in the success of office automation. The ultimate impact of office automation on our working environment, economy, and life-style will depend on how well the technology can be adapted to help people—managers, secretaries, professionals, clerks, technicians, and all other office workers—accomplish business goals more efficiently and effectively.

HISTORICAL PERSPECTIVE

A brief look at the historical evolution of computer technology illustrates the relationship between technology and needs. Readers should note how technology has developed in response to specific needs for processing information more quickly. This phenomenon of user needs spurring technical development is still characteristic of the computer industry today and is called *market-driven* development.

Computer technology has advanced significantly since it was first introduced to the business world in 1951. Its origins, however, go back far before 1951. Early applications of the concepts on which computers are based date back as early as 1642 to a mechanical adding machine invented by Blaise Pascal. He built it to ease the task of keeping his father's business accounts. This early computing machine, pictured in Figure 1-1, was a digital device that made computations by a process of integer counting. The device could add and subtract numbers of up to eight significant digits.

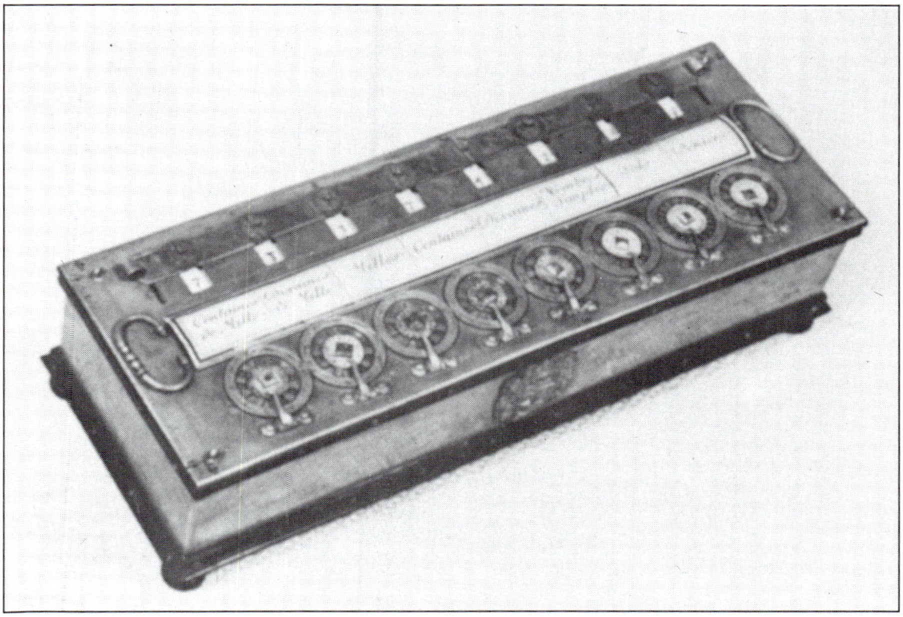

FIGURE 1-1. Pascal's adding machine (1642). The first successful calculating machine.

Almost two centuries later, in 1822 Charles Babbage developed a device he called the difference engine (see Figure 1-2) that could compute mathematical tables with results up to five significant digits. In 1835, Babbage extended this idea to develop a second device he called an analytical engine (see Figure 1-3), that was capable of addition, subtraction, multiplication, division, and storage of intermediate results in a memory unit. The analytical engine was to be a hand-operated, mechanical device. Several features that Babbage planned to incorporate into his analytical engine are used in modern computer systems, including an arithmetic unit (which he called a *mill*) to perform computations, a punched-card input system, an external storage unit, and printed output. Unfortunately, these devices were too advanced for their time. Parts for Babbage's analytical engine could not be produced by the manual methods of that day with tolerances sufficiently precise for the required accuracy. These early devices were rediscovered only after their basic concepts were applied by other people.

FIGURE 1-2. Babbage's difference engine (1822) computed mathematical tables up to five significant digits.

FIGURE 1-3. Babbage's analytical engine (1835) was capable of addition, subtraction, division, multiplication, and intermediate memory storage.

Dr. Herman Hollerith, a U.S. statistician, developed an early forerunner of modern computers as his response to a contest sponsored by the U.S. government. The U.S. Census Bureau sought a better way of compiling the 1890 census because the 1880 census had taken more than seven years to compile. Hollerith was inspired by the technology of the weaving looms of that period. In the early 1800s, Joseph-Marie Jacquard of France had devised a system of using punched holes in cards to represent numbers and control the loom's operation. Hollerith conceived the idea of using holes in cards to represent data. The data would be sensed by a machine that could then sort and manipulate the arithmetic sums represented by the holes. He combined these punched cards with electromagnetic inventions to sort 250 cards in one minute. By employing Hollerith's device during compilation of the 1890 census data, statisticians completed the census in two and a half years rather than seven and a half years. Hollerith's ingenuity has won him fame as a primary developer of modern computers. In 1896, Hollerith founded the Tabulating Machine Company to produce and market punched-card equipment for commercial use. This company merged fifteen years later with twelve other companies to form International Business Machines (IBM).

Computer technology evolved during the first half of the twentieth century through various stages of electromechanical devices. These devices were based on the concepts of binary number systems and symbolic logic (today known as Boolean algebra). Development was driven primarily by the requirements for scientific research and government applications such as compiling census data for a rapidly growing population. In 1946, the first all-purpose, all-electronic digital computer was developed at the University of Pennsylvania by J. Presper Eckert and John W. Mauchly. It was called ENIAC, an acronym for Electronic Numerical Integrator And Calculator. ENIAC, illustrated in Figure 1-4, marked the beginning of a new era in electronic computing because it had speeds more than 1,000 times faster than those of the electromechanical machines that preceded it. Its introduction seemed truly revolutionary. Shortly after its installation, scientists estimated that 100 engineers would have needed an entire year to perform the nuclear physics calculations performed on ENIAC in just two hours.

FIGURE 1-4. The ENIAC Electronic Numerical Integrator and Intermediate Calculator (1946) was the first all-purpose electronic digital calculator.

Computers made their debut in the business office in the early 1950s. The first commercial electronic computer, UNIVAC I (Universal Automatic Computer), illustrated in Figure 1-5, was purchased by the U.S. Census Bureau in 1951. The second was installed at General Electric's Appliance Park in Louisville, Kentucky, in 1954. Soon thereafter, IBM installed its first commercial electronic computer, an IBM 650, in Boston, Massachusetts.

FIGURE 1-5. The UNIVAC I Universal Automatic Computer (1951) was the first commercial electronic computer.

Computer Development Spurred by Need

As technology has evolved over the years, computers have delivered more and more calculating power at lower prices, and their use has increased tremendously. No one foresaw the extent of computer applications, which pervade almost every industry: building construction, the military, medicine, publishing, transportation, education, aerospace technology, engineering, farming, financial services, and manufacturing. It is hard to think of an occupation that does not require some type of computer device. Computers are used in products as diverse as spacecraft, automobiles, home appliances, toys, medical equipment, educational materials, and office equipment. Yet futurists tell us that computer technology is still at a developmental stage, as primitive as World War I flying technology in comparison to today's advanced spacecraft. Although commonalities exist among computer technologies, each application has its unique aspects. Computer application development is becoming less of a specialty in its own right and more of a specialization within each occupational field.

Changing Focus

Originally, operating computers was the exclusive domain of highly trained technical personnel. As computers have become more powerful and less expensive, however, they have also become easier to use. Word processors, microcomputers, and small business computers are designed for operation by nontechnical personnel. Thus a whole new aspect of computing has evolved for office automation and end-user computing.

End user refers to individuals or departments that actually work with or use the computers themselves. The interface between users and computers is a major focus today, and the term *user-friendly* has been popularized to describe the ease with which nontechnical people can learn to use a particular computer system. In the past, computers were often associated with boring standardization and repetitive functions, but today's technologies enable people to do things in new ways, to do more in less time, and to do new things that were previously infeasible. A threshold of new opportunities is emerging as the focus of computerization changes from maximizing equipment to expanding human potential.

Changing established methods and procedures in the office, however, can be difficult and complex. Implementing change has two facets: the technology side and the behavioral side. Both are equally important in the office, and both are discussed in this text.

APPLYING TECHNOLOGY TO INFORMATION PROCESSING

Processing information is essential to the operation of every enterprise. But what is information processing? *Information processing* involves the creation and capture, processing, reproduction, distribution, use, storage, retrieval, and ultimate destruction of information.

Creation and capture The creation and capture of information involves originating, collecting, and inputting data into systems. Data may originate from the ideas or decisions of managers and knowledge workers, be generated as a by-product of operations, already exist in various forms within the organization, or come from sources outside the organization. The most common way to capture data in a system is by keyboarding. Original data may first need to be captured in an intermediate format such as dictation or longhand. Pre-existing data may be captured through rekeying, electronic communications, or image scanning such as optical character recognition (OCR) or computer input microfilm (CIM). Early office automation technologies primarily served needs for capturing information, but new technologies also support the creation of information.

Processing or transformation Transforming data includes sorting, calculating, comparing, graphing, analyzing, collating, correcting, editing, and formatting. Processing transforms information from source data, or input, into forms of information suitable for use by people for an intended purpose.

Reproduction Reproduction is the transfer of already processed information into another form. Reproduction includes photocopying, printing, microfilming, phototypesetting, and voice response.

Distribution Distribution is moving or communicating one source to another. Distribution methods include hand carrying, mail services, messenger or courier, electronic mail, facsimile, telex, videotext, and teleconferencing. Distribution may be either internal or external to the organization. Business information is typically distributed or communicated in the form of letters, memos, reports, wires (Telex and TWX), manuals, catalogs, brochures, and oral instructions.

Storage and retrieval Storage is the systematic preservation of information, and retrieval is the systematic recalling of that information for reuse. Formal records management systems also provide for the systematic storage and retrieval of information. They are also used for archiving valuable records and destroying outdated information. The responsibility for storage and retrieval of corporate information is usually divided, depending upon the form of storage. Most large organizations have a centralized records management department that is responsible for protecting vital corporate information stored on paper or microfilm. As a practical matter, departmental information is often maintained in decentralized locations that are generally under control of department management. Electronic data storage is generally managed by computer data centers, office systems administrators, or end users themselves. Storage and retrieval are beginning to take on new meaning with office automation. Until recently, little attention has been paid to opportunities to use computers for more than storing and indexing information. One of the greatest challenges facing office automation is finding ways to provide more effective ways to locate, access, and condense information. New tools in this area are just beginning to emerge.

Over the years, as offices became mechanized and grew in size, many of these steps in the information processing cycle came to be organized as separate support functions or departments. Although the division of work provided efficiency, it also created problems of coordination and duplication of effort. Today's office automation calls for re-examining old organizational structures. To achieve the full potential of office automation technologies, organizations need to integrate all information processing functions more effectively.

OFFICE AUTOMATION

Office automation is the application of computer technology to *processing and using information in the office.* Office automation provides more efficient and effective use of information, as well as faster processing of information, and it puts tools in the hands of workers *in* the office. Thus office automation tools are for managers, professionals, and technical workers as much as they are for clerical workers.

Some tools generally included under office automation are listed in Figure 1-6 and explained in Chapters 4 through 14. Office automation is more than a computer system or a specific software program, however. Office automation offers new ways of organizing people, tasks, and technology to meet business objectives. It also involves *implementing* (putting into use) various tools that solve specific business problems.

FIGURE 1-6. Some office automation tools.

Text handling tools	electronic typewriters, dictation/transcription systems, word processing, desktop publishing, electronic file and retrieval, optical character recognition (OCR), printers, copiers
Data handling computing tools	calculators, electronic spreadsheets, statistical packages, databases, decision support systems
Graphics tools	computer graphics packages, computer-aided design, plotters, digitizers
Communication tools	telephones, local area networks, electronic mail and messaging, voice mail and messaging, teleconferencing, facsimile, Telex and TWX, communicating word processors, Videotex
Image processing tools	micrographics, computer output microfile (COM), computer-aided retrieval (CAR), optical disks
Time management tools	electronic calendars, project management software, electronic notebooks and tracking systems, electronic "to do" lists, directories
Artificial intelligence tools	natural language interfaces, expert systems, voice recognition/synthesis

Office automation is continually evolving and has virtually revolutionized office operations. For most organizations, however, office automation is a gradual, evolutionary process of change. The changes are implemented in response to *specific business needs* and not merely for the sake of introducing the most modern equipment.

Change must be an educational process that enables individuals to assimilate new technologies. Implementing new technologies requires new procedures and new problem-solving skills. It disturbs the way people work and disrupts accustomed patterns of handling and using information. New opportunities associated with the technology may not always be evident immediately.

The complexity of introducing office automation increases with the size and complexity of the organization. Just attempting to stay informed about technological changes and the wide range of available alternatives is almost overwhelming. To be manageable, office automation must address specific needs and solve specific business problems. Questions such as which equipment is best, which software should be used, and what capabilities are most important can only be answered in relation to the specific objectives one wants to accomplish.

Successful office automation projects focus on *the need to accomplish a business objective*. Office automation projects frequently go a step further by providing additional benefits, such as making it easier to get a job done. These efficiency-related benefits are significant, but they are not the *reason* for automating. Even if these benefits resulted from an office automation project, the project could not be considered successful if the overall business objective had not been met.

For example, early word processing centers were implemented to produce documents in a more timely manner and at a volume and cost that would enable the organization to compete in the marketplace. This word processing system, when well implemented, also brought additional benefits to the organization and the staff. It reduced the repetitive, routine aspects of document production for clerical personnel and improved the professional appearance of documents. The company would not have considered the project successful, however, if it had achieved only the latter two benefits and not the prime objective of reducing the cost and improving the timeliness of documents.

Integration of Technologies

Office automation combines a number of computer technologies, including data processing, word processing, graphics and image processing, voice processing, and communications. Ultimately, office automation will help to break down artificial barriers that exist today because of the various *formats* in which data and information are contained. These barriers are arbitrary and based on yesterday's technologies. For example, when a handwritten report must go to a word-processing department to be entered into a system, to a data processing department for its figures to be computed, to a graphics department for its illustrations to be created, to a reprographics department to be duplicated and assembled, back to the originator for checking, and finally to the mail room for transmittal, the process is slow, complex, and prone to error.

Unfortunately, when existing tasks are automated in isolation, these inefficiencies may be perpetuated instead of eliminated. Ideally, individuals who originate documents should be able to use one tool to create the text, perform calculations, and create illustrations, just as they can using paper and pencil. Thinking about or employing computer technology to fit the way we do things in organizations *today* limits the potential of computer technology.

To fully appreciate the potential of office automation, it is important to understand that most established office procedures and departments have evolved around yesterday's technologies. Thus offices have typing or word-processing departments, data-processing departments, graphics departments, mailing departments, photocopying departments, printing shops, filing departments, telephone services, wire services, and other such functional departments. Each department is organized, based on the technology used, to perform its portion of the information-processing task as quickly and easily as possible. These divisions may no longer make sense today. Why try to fit new technologies to old ways of organizing an office? Why not change the organization in ways that will provide the most benefit from computer technologies? Office automation technologies do not have the same limitations as earlier mechanical technologies. With automation, offices can integrate processing tasks that were previously handled within separate departments.

To illustrate the integration of functions, consider the following example of how a complex document would have been produced just a few years ago (and in some companies would still be produced) in comparison to how it can be produced today with the aid of office automation.

> When an insurance company provides a group life and health insurance plan for a client firm, each employee in that firm receives a booklet describing his or her insurance benefits. The procedure to produce these benefit booklets previously involved several separate departments. To create the copy, an underwriter might use a reference book containing samples of wording for various standard paragraphs of text. The underwriter would dictate or write out the entire text and, where appropriate, indicate the identification number of standard paragraphs to be incorporated into the text.
>
> The document instructions would then go to the typing pool, where a typist would key the entire document. Typing involved keying both the new text and copying the previously typed standard text. After carefully proofreading every word, the typist would send the document back to the underwriter. The underwriter proofread every word again, made any needed revisions, and sent the document back to the typist. The typist then retyped any pages with changes. If text had been added or deleted, several pages or even the entire document might need to be retyped in order to align the text properly on the pages. The typist carefully proofread the document again and returned it to the underwriter, who also proofread the entire document to ensure that it was accurate. Then the document was ready for approval by the department manager. If no further changes were required, the approved text was sent to the printing department.
>
> In the printing department, the entire document was rekeyed into a phototypesetting machine. The rekeyed document was carefully

proofread, errors were corrected, and it was proofread again. Typeset text was produced in the form of a galley proof (continuous text not cut into pages). This galley would go back to the underwriter to be proofread again for accuracy before it was returned to the printing department, pasted up in page format, and photographed to produce the printing plates. After printing, assembling, and binding, the booklet went through a final quality control check before being delivered to the underwriter. The underwriter then proofread the entire booklet one last time before authorizing delivery of the printed product to the client firm.

With office automation, this entire process is streamlined.* By using word processing to compose the document, the underwriter him/herself can input information and also indicate what standard text already stored in the computer should be included in the new document. After composing the entire document, the underwriter needs to proofread only the sections of variable text (or run them through a computerized dictionary to identify misspellings or typographical errors), make any necessary corrections, and print out the document. The underwriter then submits the document for department approval. If no additional changes are required, the document is ready for phototypesetting.

In the composition process, the underwriter keyed typesetting commands directly into the document. Submitting the document for printing then requires only keying in some special instructions. A computer program translates the typed commands in the text into instructions for the laser printer. The document is printed at a speed of two pages per second. The booklet is assembled and bound automatically and returned to the underwriter.

Thus a process that previously took two weeks can now be accomplished in two days! The print shop has not been eliminated. It does other types of higher-quality printing work, with photographs and colors, that cannot be done on the laser printer. The print shop staff has not grown as rapidly or added the additional equipment that would have been necessary to keep pace with the growing volume of group insurance business.

With the aid of computers, professionals such as underwriters have greater control over the information processing tasks required to perform their jobs. Automation is more efficient than the old method because the number of steps required to complete tasks is reduced, and it is more effective because the work passes through fewer hands, thus reducing the chance for errors.

**Note:* Terminology and systems discussed in this example are thoroughly defined in subsequent chapters.

The Relationship Between Office Automation and Productivity

Productivity, which is discussed in more detail in Part 4, is a measure of the *quantity and quality of work.* The idea of using technology to improve productivity is far from new, of course. In fact, history shows that people constantly strive to improve their ability to get things done by using technology. They strive to do more work faster and better with less effort—in short, to be more productive. This generalization applies whether one considers the primitive tools of early civilizations, the advances of ancient Middle Eastern and Roman societies, mechanization during the Industrial Revolution, or any other historical period.

Although history bears witness to humanity's ongoing efforts to improve productivity, the individuals on whom technological improvements are imposed frequently resist the advances or changes that technology brings. No one knows if early cave people protested when the first bow and arrow was fashioned or the first wheel invented, but historians recount many instances of resistance to new technologies.

One of the best-known instances of resistance to technology was the Luddites' protest against industrialization in the weaving mills of England during the early 1800s. Organized bands of masked English handicraft workers rioted and tried to destroy the textile machinery that was displacing them from their traditional jobs (see Figure 1-7). But advances in one area of technology often lead to major technological advances in other areas. The same Jacquard weaving looms that the Luddites opposed later inspired Hollerith's invention of punched cards for data processing.

FIGURE 1-7. Luddites rioting in weaving mills.

As one might expect, office workers have not always welcomed new technologies either. When typewriters were introduced in the mid 1800s, some businesspeople rejected typed correspondence as too impersonal. Thus many eighteenth-century businessmen continued to handwrite their letters long after typewriters became available. Typewriters often were used to create drafts of documents, and the final copy was then carefully handwritten. Gradually, the need for efficiency forced businesses to change.

Typing machines precipitated other rather revolutionary changes in the nineteenth-century business world. They brought women into the business world in large numbers for the first time. In 1881, the New York City YWCA began teaching typing to its first class of eight young women. Those who were trained to operate typing machines were called *typewriters*. These typing course graduates were in high demand. Eager to gain employment, thousands of women soon discovered that skill as a "typewriter" provided entry into the business world (see Figure 1-8). Proprietary business schools sprang up to train eager students. The secretarial and clerical jobs previously held by men became dominated by women. Jobs multiplied rapidly as the size and number of industrial organizations exploded during the Industrial Revolution.

FIGURE 1-8. Early typewriters.

a. A young woman working with a Sholes-Glidden-Soule typewriter (1872).

FIGURE 1-8.

b. An early Hammond typewriter.

Resistance to change often manifests itself in more subtle ways. The impact of change in the workplace is an important consideration in the implementation of office automation. A detailed discussion of organizational change is provided in Chapter 20.

Many organizations are racing to implement new office technologies; others are proceeding more slowly with decidedly less enthusiasm. Whereas some offices have barely begun to use computers, many progressive companies have been using office automation technologies for ten to twenty years. Most have realized substantial benefits. Today, many of these companies are in the forefront of installing a computer workstation on the desk of every office worker.

In addition to significant productivity gains, office automation technology has brought changes in the nature of people's jobs and in the organization of responsibilities within the enterprise.

Office automation technology should not be viewed, however, as the magic answer to improving office productivity. Instead, office automation should be recognized as a set of new tools that offer tremendous potential for facilitating work. This potential can be realized, however, only when office automation is implemented as part of a carefully planned program for productivity improvement. Such a program requires a systems approach that gives adequate attention to business requirements, job design, work procedures, and technology. *People* make technology work; the inverse cannot be taken for granted. In and of itself, technology does not make people more productive.

In reality, worker productivity results from the interdynamics of several factors. These factors include management practices, skill variety, task significance, task identity, autonomy, and feedback on the job. Understanding the nature of productivity is important to successful implementation of office automation. If one is to improve productivity in the office—the prime objective—one must first understand what factors contribute to productivity.

Historically, increases in productivity have been attributed to increases in capital investment. Thus when productivity figures dipped in the 1970s (Figure 1-9), economists pointed to the comparatively low capital investment for white-collar workers (Figure 1-10), who represented a growing proportion of the total work force. Huge investments in office automation, however, did not initially slow the demand for clerical employees, casting doubt on the value of these technologies as labor-saving devices. Recent evidence suggests that unit labor costs have begun to drop, and the labor-saving effects of office automation are expected to become more apparent in the future. The delayed impact has been attributed to the lack of experience with these new technologies and the time needed to reorganize the work flow and labor force.

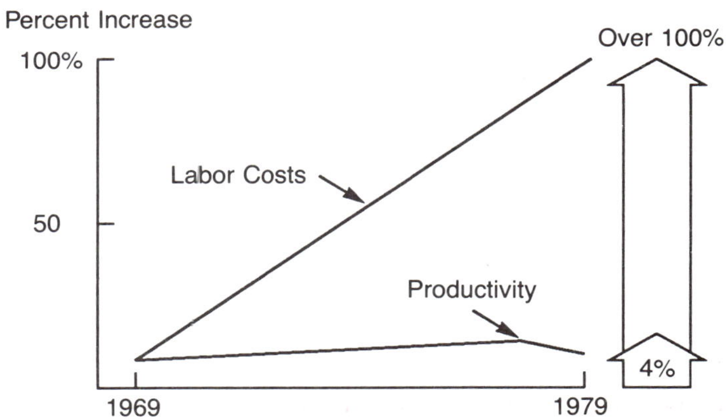

FIGURE 1-9. The state of the office.

Farm Worker	\$53,000
Factory Worker	\$35,000
House Worker	\$ 5,000
Office Worker	\$ 3,000

FIGURE 1-10. Average capital investment per worker.

For several years, however, economists have been modifying the idea that capital investment produces gains in national wealth. They have been moving toward a theory of human capital, recognizing that people and human behavior also affect productivity. These ideas are reflected in the growing emphasis on productivity improvement programs such as quality circles, work group participation, and other worker-centered efforts to improve the quality of work life. Technology is important because it extends what people can do. Technology facilitates work. Chapter 15 on "Measuring Productivity: Cost Justification" addresses the issues and complexities of quantifying and measuring the effects of office automation.

How Automation Facilitates Work in the Office

Automation facilitates office work in several ways:

1. Automation can perform routine, repetitive tasks that were formerly done by manual methods.
2. Automation provides tools to improve manual methods by making them more efficient or effective.
3. Automation provides tools to accomplish new tasks that are infeasible by manual methods.
4. Automation makes information more readily available to all who need it.
5. Automation can enable an enterprise to restructure entire operations in new ways.
6. Automation can be used by industries to gain strategic advantage over competitors through innovations in products and services.

SUMMARY

Information is crucial to the operation of business and government enterprises. The hub of the enterprise that processes and provides that essential information is the business office. Computer-based technologies, popularly referred to as "office automation" and "end-user computing," provide new ways to manage and handle information. Without automation, institutions could not provide the diversity of products and services today's complex society demands.

Office automation is defined as the *application* of computer technologies to processing and *using* information in the office. The use of information is emphasized because office automation allows information to be processed more quickly than earlier mechanical technologies and introduces many new possibilities for helping individuals to work with information and use it effectively.

Automating the office may be viewed as an ongoing process of applying technology to improve information processing, meet business requirements, and create safe, productive work environments. It is a process that requires understanding technology, business, and people at work. Automation is much more than selecting the right technology; the technology must help organizations to achieve their business goals.

Office automation technologies should not be viewed as a magic answer to improving productivity. The potential offered by these tools can be realized only when office automation is implemented as part of a carefully planned program for increased productivity. Adequate attention must be given to business requirements, job design, and work procedures, in addition to technology. In and of itself, technology does not make people more productive.

Computer technology has evolved over the past century in response to specific needs to resolve problems and perform more work in less time, a phenomenon referred to as *market-driven development.* During this evolutionary process, computer technologies have become much more powerful, less expensive, and easier to use. Whereas only highly trained technicians could operate early computers, today nontechnical office personnel (end users) use computers regularly to aid them with their work.

To take full advantage of new office technologies, organizations must change old ways of doing things. Change must be a learning process that enables individuals to assimilate new technologies. Change disturbs the way people work and disrupts accustomed behavior patterns. New opportunities associated with technology often are not evident immediately.

The ultimate impact of office automation on our working environment is not fully understood. It will depend on how well the technology can be adapted to help people—the managers, secretaries, professionals, clerks, technicians, and all other office workers—perform their jobs more efficiently and effectively.

The chapters ahead present detailed discussions of the technologies available today and on the horizon for tomorrow. Topics include methods for analyzing business requirements, developing solutions, and implementing technological changes in organizations. First, however, it is important to have a clear understanding of the business office, how it functions as a system, and how people work in the office environment. These topics are the subject of Chapter 2.

DISCUSSION QUESTIONS

1. What is office automation? Why is office automation best defined as a process?
2. The development of computers and office automation has been described as "market driven." Explain. Do you expect this premise to be more or less true in the future?
3. Who is the end user? How have developments in office automation been directed to the end-user?

4. List six categories of office automation tools used in offices today.
5. What is the focus of office automation? How does it facilitate office work?
6. Summarize the relationship between productivity and office automation.

APPLICATION EXERCISES

1. Visit your city or school library to identify books and periodicals about office automation to supplement this text. Use the card catalog to develop a listing of references.
2. Review several textbooks on Management Information Systems (MIS) and Computer Information Systems (CIS). How do these texts address the subject of office automation?

SUGGESTED READINGS

Greenia, Mark W. "Redefining the Scope of Office Automation," *Proceedings of the 1987 Office Automation Society International Conference,* pp. 63–67.

Toffler, Alvin. *The Third Wave* (New York: Bantam Books, 1980).

THE OFFICE WORK ENVIRONMENT: End Users

CHAPTER 2

OBJECTIVES

After completing this chapter, the reader should be able to meet the following objectives:

- Understand the unique characteristics of the office environment.
- Describe the kinds of work activities performed in an office environment.
- Describe how technology is changing the way people work in the office environment.
- Compare and contrast the characteristics of traditional versus automated office environments.

KEY TERMS

administrative support
end-user computing
function
information systems
integrated systems
line and staff
office support
overhead
principal
support function
support personnel
traditional office
work flow

INTRODUCTION

The office work environment reflects the nature of the activities conducted within it. Other types of workplaces such as factories, farms, mines, and schools are characterized by activities that likewise distinguish them as distinct types of workplaces. Yet each office, factory, farm, or mine is also unique unto itself. This uniqueness reflects the particular personalities, equipment, tasks, and resources that encompass its operation. All office work and office environments have some features in common, but it is important to remember that every office has a culture and set of business requirements that are different from any other.

In any work environment, people, tasks, equipment, and resources are organized to facilitate the accomplishment of specific objectives. In most cases, these objectives generate some type of product. In the office, the product is information. Information may take the form of decisions, directives, or documents. The way in which work is organized into the functions performed by people within an office depends on three factors: (1) the nature of the tasks, (2) the knowledge and skills of the staff, and (3) the equipment and resources available to accomplish those tasks. The role of equipment, or *technology,* is to help accomplish required tasks. In performing that role, the technology influences how people and tasks are organized within the office. Each office is not only unique, it is also dynamic. The ways in which technology, resources, tasks, and people are organized into specific functions change over time in response to changing business requirements.

THE ROLE OF ORGANIZATION

Whenever two or more people attempt to work together to accomplish specific objectives, some form of organization is necessary. Organization is required to coordinate the efforts of the various people so that each individual and each group contributes to the overall goals. To be purposeful and personally satisfying, work must contribute to organizational goals. Organization also brings other necessary resources such as materials, equipment, capital, and markets together in a practical format to accomplish organizational goals.

Through organization, people can accomplish more work than individuals working alone. Activities are organized into manageable units in which the work can be planned and controlled effectively. Group goals are defined, and individuals are assigned specific responsibilities. Through team effort to accomplish defined organizational goals, the value of each member's contribution is increased. Confusion about who is to do what work is avoided. A supportive work environment is provided. A good organization creates synergy: 2 + 2 produces 5, not just 4.

The organizational framework, as reflected in a formal organization chart, defines who does what in an enterprise. How are responsibilities divided, coordinated, and linked together? Who should report to whom? Who should make what decisions? Which members should be in which groups? What amounts of what basic resources should be used, and by whom? What work environment should be provided? An effective organization should facilitate the exchange of information and minimize duplication of effort. Figure 2-1 depicts how one large firm elected to organize support functions within the office. Notice the number of functions, such as telephone services, graphic services, photocopying, records management, and word processing, that are organized around specific technologies.

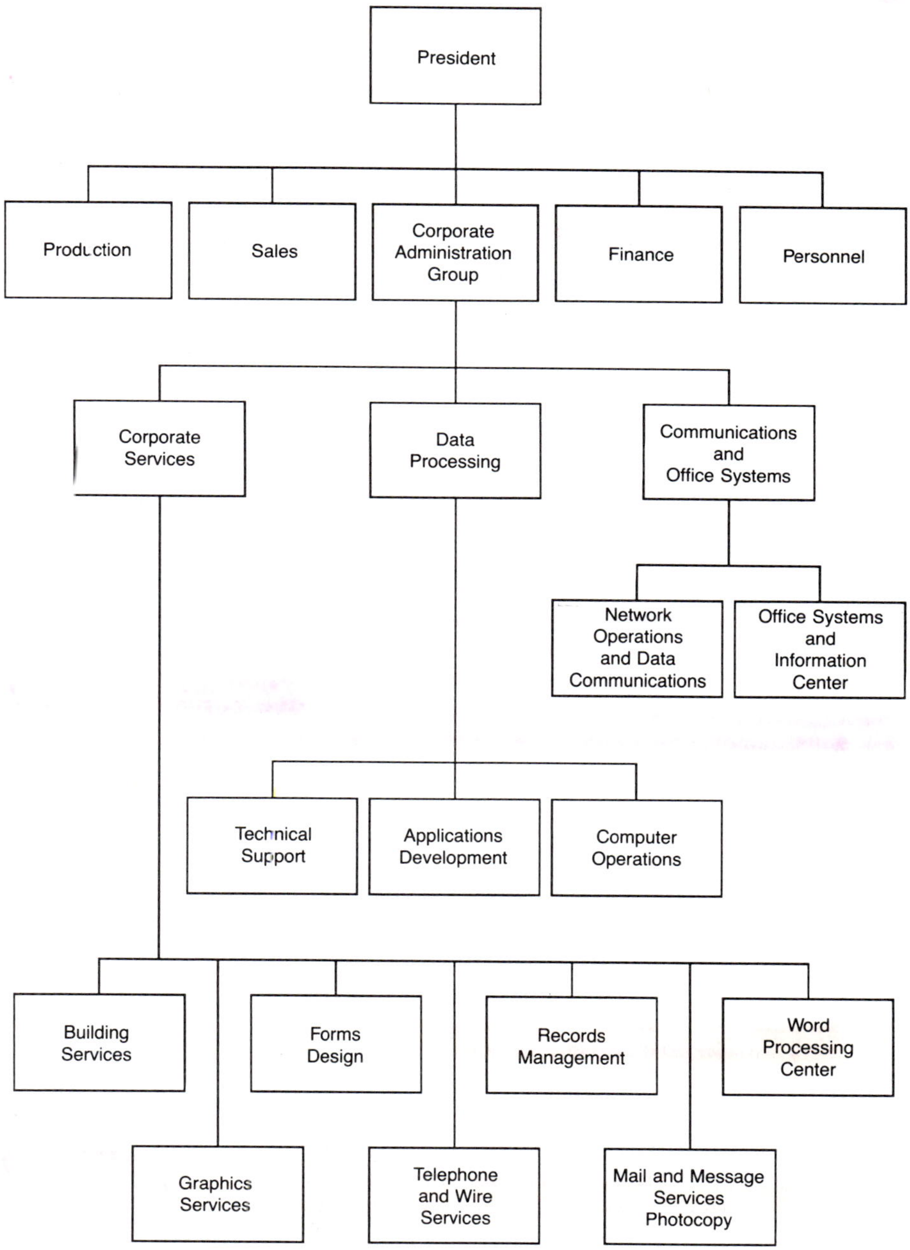

FIGURE 2-1. Organization of support functions in a large firm.

HISTORICAL ORGANIZATION OF THE OFFICE

Historically, the office has been considered *overhead*, that is, a necessary cost of doing business. The office provided ancillary services to support the main operations of the business, which took place on the factory floor.

In the *traditional office*, secretaries and clerical workers support people who manage or supervise the operations of the enterprise. Senior and middle managers usually have full-time secretaries on a one-to-one basis. The boss/secretary team has been the basic organizational structure for offices in both the private and the public sectors. These full-time support assignments are generally justified on the basis of the manager's position rather than the volume of work. In fact, a private secretary is often considered the classic "status symbol" of a high-level management position.

In addition to secretaries, organizations employ clerical workers in a wide variety of roles. Groups of clerical personnel usually are assigned to specific tasks, such as invoice processing, billing, and bookkeeping. Other office support functions exist as separate, independent operations such as mail services, telephone and wire services, printing services, filing and records administration, and facilities management.

Moreover, large enterprises are comprised of multiple business units, each of which is organized with one or more managers. Each unit usually plans, organizes, staffs, and controls its own resources. Senior management personnel work together to coordinate these business units to accomplish the organization's basic goals. The requirements for shared information often result in considerable duplication of effort and additional costs associated with handling and storing information. For example, duplicate copies of documents are made and stored within each unit.

As the volume of paperwork processed by enterprises has grown, more and more secretarial and clerical employees have been required. When salaries earned by clerical employees were low, costs for processing information were absorbed as necessary overhead. Secretarial and clerical salary levels have risen in recent years, however, and organizations can no longer continue to add personnel to keep up with the expanding volumes of information.

For a growing number of enterprises, moreover, the main operations now take place in the office itself. The products of the enterprise are produced in the office, not on a factory floor. Examples include the insurance industry, banking and other financial industries, law firms, publishing houses, and government agencies. In addition, a growing percentage of the office work force consists of professional and technical knowledge workers rather than low-level clerical employees.

As information management costs have risen, the costs of computer technology during the same period have been falling at equally dramatic rates. Consequently, organizations have turned to office automation to increase productivity.

HISTORICAL EVOLUTION OF OFFICE AUTOMATION

In one sense, office automation is a process that started with the Industrial Revolution. The typewriter was first introduced in the office in the 1840s and was followed by stenotype machines, duplicators, mail-handling equipment, dictaphones, teletypes, tabulating machines, and many other devices. The term *office automation,* however, originated in reference to the application of computer technology to office activities such as document processing, copying, and distribution.

In many ways, the evolution of office automation parallels the evolution of data processing. Both have evolved primarily in response to three factors: advancements in computer technology, experience in using the technology, and changing business and market conditions. This evolutionary process can be broken into four developmental periods based on the kinds of applications addressed:

1. Automation of repetitive tasks
2. Administrative support
3. End-user computing
4. Integrated systems

These four periods are discussed in the next sections.

Period 1: Automation of Repetitive Tasks

Early applications of office automation, like those of data processing, were directed at reducing the time and effort required to perform repetitive, labor-intensive tasks, especially typing. This era began with the automated typewriter and ended with display word processors.

The introduction of automatic typewriters in the 1930s to process repetitive form letters and documents paralleled the use of tabulating machines to calculate data in accounting departments. Automatic typewriters used "storage" mechanisms of punched-paper rolls similar to those used in player pianos and weaving looms. The keystrokes for a form letter were coded as holes punched on a paper tape. As the typist sat at the typewriter, the keystrokes played back like a player piano, pausing where indicated to allow the typist to manually insert variables such as a date, name, or address. The playback speed of approximately 100 words a minute was about twice the speed of an average typist and eliminated errors. Enhancements included five- or eight-channel punched-paper tape and electromechanical logic to allow switching between two tape readers. This allowed a master form to be recorded on one tape and lists of variables to merge with it on the other. The typist could then do other tasks while each letter was typed, returning only to remove the completed letter and insert the next piece of paper.

Then, in 1964 IBM introduced the Magnetic Tape Selectric Typewriter (MT/ST). The use of magnetic tape allowed recorded information to be erased, corrected, or rerecorded. Magnetic tape also provided greater storage capacity and durability. The availability of magnetic storage and recording media fueled the explosion of computer technologies. Magnetic tape was soon replaced by magnetic cards, which were easier to handle. Magnetic cards were followed by the introduction of display-screen word processors with floppy disks and increasingly powerful systems.

IBM Germany coined the term *Textverarbeitung*, which was translated into English as *word processing*. As with data processing, early word-processing technology was best suited for repetitive, high-volume tasks. To offset its high cost in comparison to typewriters, word-processing equipment had to be used to its full capacity. This meant keeping it in operation constantly for a full eight-hour day, an additional evening shift, or even around the clock. Thus word processors were first purchased primarily by very large companies to replace typewriters and reduce staff in typing or stenographic pools. The result was high-volume document production.

Such centers, however, did not address the typing that secretaries and typists performed as part of their general office responsibilities, which in aggregate represented a significant portion of an organization's total typing volume. Because the typical secretary spent only 30 percent of the day typing, early word processors could not be financially justified as replacements for typewriters. To address this problem and promote the marketing of word-processing equipment, vendors advocated the concept known as word processing/administrative support (WP/AS). The WP/AS concept promotes organizing office support personnel into centralized teams of specialists. Typing is done by word processing operators on word processing equipment, and nontyping tasks are handled by administrative assistants supporting groups of *principals*, a term that replaced "boss." The traditional one-to-one relationship between secretary and boss was eliminated. Organizational charts, career paths, and professional management were introduced to office support. Some proponents of WP/AS advocated production-oriented techniques, such as work measurement and incentive pay based on lines of copy typed.

While some firms successfully adopted the WP/AS concept, in most cases the concept was modified to satisfy managers who were unwilling to give up their private secretaries. Most organizations implemented specialized positions for word processing operators (also called *correspondence secretaries* or *document specialists*), who were centralized in one location or in several clusters. The few organizations that implemented the administrative support concept typically continued to employ generalist secretaries for higher-level managers, with WP/AS teams handling requirements for professionals and supervisors. Thus these higher-level secretaries continued to perform much the same tasks as always but with a lower volume of typing. They were expected to use the word-processing center for handling longer or more complex documents. Some progressive firms restructured jobs and improved career opportunities by shifting appropriate tasks from principals to their administrative assistants or secretaries.

Early definitions of word processing reflected a very production-oriented philosophy. The official U.S. government definition of word processing is a good example: "Word processing is the efficient and effective production of written communications at the lowest possible cost through the combined use of systems management procedures, automated technology, and accomplished personnel." An early word-processing text defined word processing as "a planned interrelationship of personnel, procedures, and equipment within an office of work specialization and controls to facilitate the production of typed documents in a cost-effective manner."[1]

To justify the high cost of equipment, word-processing analysts, like their data-processing counterparts, borrowed methods from industrial engineering. They needed to be able to measure production in order to demonstrate that the costs of word-processing equipment would be offset by reductions in other operating expenses, usually salaries. If two people using word processors could do the work of four people using typewriters, the cost of purchasing the new equipment would be offset by reduced salary dollars within one or two years, and the company's salary expenditures would be reduced thereafter. The emphasis on measuring results encouraged the creation of routine, repetitive jobs with easily measured outputs.

The application of work simplification techniques, work measurement, and standardization advocated by early proponents of word processing centers was effective in some cases, but in other cases it failed or met with resistance. Organizations in which these efforts failed had often overemphasized production line procedures, limited the scope of jobs, and used the computer to monitor every keystroke. These practices often led to poor employee morale and high turnover and drew the wrath of women's advocate groups, which charged that the office of the future would become a re-creation of the factory assembly line. In some cases, clerical personnel turned to unions to regain control over their work environments.

Period 2: Administrative Support

The second period of development in data processing and office automation extended computer applications to activities that were less structured than word processing. The office automation concept of *administrative support* (AS) emerged along with the data-processing concept of *management information systems* (MIS). (MIS refers to mainframe computer systems designed to support management decision making.) The objective was to use computers to support administrative and management activities such as maintaining appointment calendars, scheduling meetings, handling telephone calls, tracking activities, arranging travel, handling mail, and receiving visitors. Early AS implementations met with limited success. The concepts of MIS and AS are sound, but the implementation of systems was ahead of the technology. Only real technology buffs had the inclination and patience to master the idiosyncracies of the systems, which were far from user-friendly. In short, both MIS and AS fell far short of envisioned goals for various reasons, including the following:

1. Existing systems had technological limitations.
2. The technology was still too complex for most users.
3. Technical people did not understand enough about how individuals work in the office.
4. Technical people lacked sufficient understanding of how decision makers arrive at their decisions and what information plays the key role.
5. Managers and other office personnel (users) resisted the technology.

Gradually, more useful and user-friendly systems evolved. Three that were introduced at this time and have continued to evolve are the IBM PROFS system for centralized mainframe computers and the Wang OFFICE and Digital Equipment Corporation's All-in-One systems for minicomputers. These systems are shown in Figures 2-2a, b, and c.

FIGURE 2-2. Three systems that provide administrative support.

a. The IBM PROFS system for large, centralized mainframe computers.

b. A user of a Wang Integrated Image System (WIIS) running VS OFFICE (foreground) can review a document created in another department on a microcomputer local area network.

c. The Digital Equipment Corporation's All-in-One system for minicomputers.

Period 3: End-User Computing

As business personnel became increasingly dependent on computer support systems, they demanded greater flexibility and control. The movement to end-user computing marked the beginning of a major change in philosophy about computing. The term *end user* evolved from data-processing terminology in reference to individuals who actually *use* the reports or other output produced by a computer system. Even when computer systems operate very efficiently from the perspective of technical specialists, the information they produce sometimes falls short of the result desired by the end-user. In addition, business requirements often change. End-user computing puts computer tools directly into the hands of the individual with the problem. End-user computing ushered in the following revolutionary concepts:

1. Nontechnical personnel can operate computers.
2. Individuals should process their own information.
3. Computers can be effective personal productivity tools.
4. End-users want more computing power.
5. Users should have greater control over computing resources.

End-user computing has resulted in many changes for both data-processing and office automation personnel. Programmers and systems analysts are frequently accused of being insensitive to the needs of people on the user end of computer systems. Word-processing operators and other suppliers of office services are also sometimes guilty of a similar insensitivity toward users. Users require certain information or material to perform their jobs. They may have specific procedural requirements and deadlines. When they cannot meet requirements because of problems with information systems, they become frustrated, resentful, and angry—perhaps justifiably. When forms or procedures require information in one format but the system produces it in another, results must be redone manually. This is a wasteful duplication of effort. When exceptions arise or business requirements demand changes on short notice, computer systems seem terribly inflexible. When the results produced from a computer report do not match manual records, personnel must expend time and energy cross-checking information, retracing calculations, and verifying accuracy. Growing demands on computing resources often created backlogs of a year or more.

Arbitrary Boundaries Between Processors and Users of Information

As mentioned in Chapter 1, a notable characteristic of the historical office organization was the separation of information processing from its actual use. Support personnel process information by capturing, collecting, transforming, sorting, organizing, retrieving, filing, duplicating, and transmitting it. Managers and professionals then use the information to take actions or make decisions. This artificial separation between processing and using information became necessary because individuals could not possibly process all the information required to perform their jobs using early twentieth-century mechanical technologies. Thus delegation was necessary, and various tasks were pushed down the organizational hierarchy to the lowest level capable of performing them. Despite its obvious effectiveness, however, this approach involves several disadvantages:

1. Mistakes are more likely to occur when work is performed out of context. Those performing the work do not necessarily understand the information. Often they do not receive direct feedback about the accuracy of their work, and they are therefore unable to correct their own errors.
2. Work can become fragmented. Coordination between activities can become complex and inefficient.
3. When activities are broken down into a number of smaller, specialized tasks, the resulting jobs are often repetitive and boring. Increased errors, low morale, and high turnover can become problems.

New Opportunities for Integrating Tasks

Today, office technology provides the capability to do things differently. End-user computing tools allow the actual user of the information to also manipulate it. This approach is ultimately more effective and efficient. According to one management consultant, "In the long-run, the manager will be able to handle more functions and will need less people, less layers. Many bureaucratic functions can be replaced by technology."[2]

Five major factors have spurred the movement toward end-user computing:

1. *Introduction of microcomputers.* Radio Shack, Apple, Commodore, and other vendors pioneered the use of microcomputers, or personal computers, for home, hobby, and educational use. These devices were not taken seriously in the computer world at first, but they quickly began to find their way into the business environment. Small businesses that could not afford large computers and technical staffs began to use them. Microcomputers began to appear in corporate departments. Corporate data-processing departments could not seem to stamp them out. Their low prices made it easy for managers to slip a few devices into departmental budgets.
2. *Fourth-generation languages.* New, easy-to-use, English-like programming languages were developed for large mainframe computers. These less structured languages allowed nontechnical individuals to use mainframe computers effectively.

3. *Merging of DP and WP.* The worlds of data processing and word processing began to overlap. Text-processing systems were developed for large mainframe computers, and data processing capabilities were added to office word processors. Word-processing programs became available for microcomputers. Users demanded the capability to interchange information between data-processing and word-processing applications.

4. *Increased computer literacy.* Computer education was expanded in the schools. Informative features about computer technologies began to appear in the media. The computer industry initiated activities to educate the public about computer technology. Vendors began to advertise on television and in general-readership publications. Computer trade shows and professional education seminars and workshops mushroomed. In addition, more and more people were using computers at work and at home.

5. *DP application development backlogs.* Data processing departments were unable to keep up with growing demands for computer applications. The waiting list for computer applications often exceeded two years.

Period 4: Integrated Systems

Many companies have now entered the period of *integrated systems.* This period is marked by two major changes in focus:

- A shift in emphasis from addressing separate applications to integrating systems.
- A shift from technological imperatives to meeting business objectives.

Organizations are developing computer systems as an inherent part of their plans to meet business objectives, improve service, expand markets, and change the overall mission of the organization. Computer systems have become an integral part of providing products and services. A good example is the Cash Management Account (CMA)™ first introduced by Merrill-Lynch to provide clients with comprehensive banking and investment services. This service is made possible by a very sophisticated computer system for managing customer account information.

A subtle but important change has occurred in the way organizations think about information. Information is viewed as an important resource that has both monetary and strategic value. The *monetary* value of information relates to the cost of obtaining or producing it. Its *strategic* value relates to the important role that accurate, timely information plays in helping an organization to introduce successful products in the marketplace.

Organizational barriers to change are breaking down. Instead of trying to adapt the technology to existing procedures, companies are seeking ways to use computer technologies to perform new tasks and to perform existing tasks more effectively.

Systems are being linked together, or *networked,* to provide greater access to information resources both inside and outside the corporation.

Communications and compatibility among devices are the overriding technical concerns. Technicians strive to integrate voice, data, and graphics technologies.

Technologies in the research laboratories suggest directions for continued change. The emergence of technologies such as supercomputers and optical storage devices indicates that computers will continue to become more powerful and less expensive. Artificial intelligence will increase the flexibility of computers to deal with unstructured tasks. The ultimate outcome is still speculative, of course, but it appears that office automation will continue to provide more flexibility and integration at lower prices.

OFFICE WORK IN THE INFORMATION AGE

The rapid increase in the percentage of the total population that works in offices has led several observers to characterize our society as the "Information Age." According to the Automatic Data Processing Reorganization Project, the information industry now accounts for more than half of the Gross National Product (GNP). In 1955, the information industry represented only a quarter of the GNP.

According to the U.S. Bureau of Labor Statistics, the white-collar work force constituted 55 percent of adult employees in the United States in 1980 (see Figure 2-3). About 70 percent of salaries and wages are paid to this white-collar work force. Some observers predict that by the year 2000 the white-collar work force will include 90 percent of the total work force. The office work force includes the following employment categories:

1. Managerial personnel
2. Professional and technical knowledge workers
3. Sales and marketing personnel
4. Clerical and administrative personnel

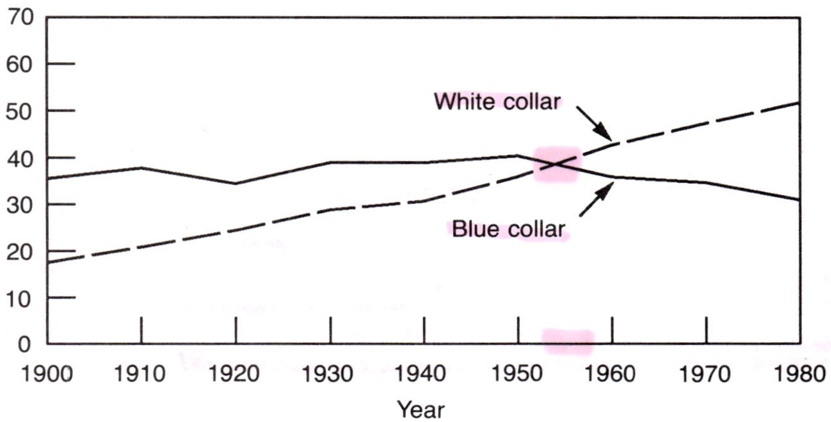

FIGURE 2-3. Changing white-collar/blue-collar percents of work force: 1900-1980.

A definition of office work in the Information Age must include all four of these employment categories. It must also include activities beyond the boundaries of a physical location termed "an office." Office work is increasingly transacted at home, in a car, on a plane, in a hotel room, or wherever the conduct of business takes an individual. Some sources are using the terms *knowledge workers* or *information workers* as more inclusive of the range of workers represented in office work. Whatever terms are preferred, this office work force is the target population for office automation and productivity improvement efforts.

The Office Work Force

In the past, the study of office administration or office management generally focused on support services performed by clerical and administrative personnel. These personnel serve in staff roles that are designed to support management in meeting its goals.

The term *support system* suggests a planned structure for integrating all support services under centralized supervision and control. Only through a *systems approach* can organizations provide the most cost-effective combination of hardware, software, and people and reduce costly duplication of effort. The objective of a support system is to support management in achieving organizational goals. To meet this objective, the system must provide accurate, timely information for decision making.

Support services are generally divided into three classifications: document production, administrative support, and office services. A detailed list of tasks that fall into each of these classifications is shown in Figure 2-4.

Before the advent of office automation, services such as typing, mail processing, reprographics, records management, data processing, communications, and information retrieval were conducted as separate functions. Today, however, the lines between functional departments are breaking down. Support functions are more likely to be viewed from a systems perspective as an interrelated group of services with a common objective. This systems approach requires new procedures, structures, and methods of working.

The concept of support systems, however, does not sufficiently identify the information processing requirements of the business office. In today's Information Age, limiting the concept of office work to clerical activities conducted in support of management decision making overlooks a significant portion of information processing. Of growing significance to office automation is the multitude of information-processing tasks that are performed in the office by professional, technical, sales, supervisory, and managerial personnel. Although the *volume* of information processing performed by clerical-level personnel is higher, the *cost* to the organization of the information processing performed at professional and managerial levels is almost eight times higher. Interpersonal communications, analysis, and decision making, which are primarily managerial functions, comprise a hefty 47.2 percent of all office functions. Obviously, the potential savings at the managerial and professional levels are significantly greater than at clerical levels. As indicated in Figure 2-5, labor costs for managers, technical, and professional workers constitute 68 percent of total white-collar labor costs. The potential benefits in terms of improved products and services are also considerably greater.

Document Production

- Transcribe dictated work
- Proofreading
- Collating
- Type memos and letters
- Type reports
- Type statistical data
- Compose large, complex documents
- Photocopying
- Maintain mailing lists
- Prepare envelopes, labels, or lists
- List and record processing
- WP system administration
- Backup of WP system storage
- Inserting photo composition commands in text
- Operating OCR equipment
- Routine equipment maintenance, such as changing ribbons, cleaning printer platens, etc.
- Electronic document distribution

Admin. Support

- Greeting visitors
- Making appointments
- Telephone messages
- Travel arrangements
- Taking shorthand
- Opening and sorting mail
- Errands and deliveries
- Photocopying and collating
- Proofreading
- Taking and giving instructions
- Typing or word processing
- Budget tracking
- Problem resolution
- Filing
- Maintaining departmental records
- Requisitioning and maintaining office supplies
- Assigned research
- Processing forms
- Writing reports or informational materials
- Composing correspondence
- Assisting in planning, assigning, and supervising work
- Tracking and following up activities

Office Services

- Mail and messenger services
  - Sorting and distributing incoming mail
  - Sorting, weighing, and stamping outgoing mail
  - Processing bulk mailings
  - Express mail services
  - Errands and messages
  - Courier service
- Telephone services
  - Receiving and routing incoming calls
  - Placing outgoing calls
  - Providing directory assistance
  - Maintaining directory listings
  - Installing and maintaining internal telephone equipment
  - Operating PBX equipment
- Records management
  - Establishing retention schedules
  - Filing and retrieving information
  - Safeguarding critical records (archives)
  - Maintaining active records
  - Storing inactive records
  - Purging obsolete files
  - Creating and maintaining microfilm files
  - Operating CAR equipment
  - Looking for misplaced files
- Building services
  - Building maintenance and repair
  - Grounds maintenance
  - Equipment maintenance and repair
  - Moving furniture and equipment
  - Building security
  - Fleet maintenance and service
- Space planning and design
  - Designing office floor plans
  - Selecting and ordering furniture, fixtures, and accessories
  - Decorating and furnishing office
  - Coordinating relocations of offices and personnel
- Forms design
  - Designing forms
  - Maintaining inventory of all company forms
  - Designing special projects
- Reprographics
  - Photocopying
  - Phototypesetting
  - In-house printing
  - Collating
  - Binding
  - Graphic layout and design
- Wire services
  - Facsimile operations
  - Telex and TWX operations
- Food services
- Warehouse operations
- Supplies management
- Travel services for company business

FIGURE 2-4. Support services: Document production, administrative support, and office services.

FIGURE 2-5. Distribution of white-collar labor costs.

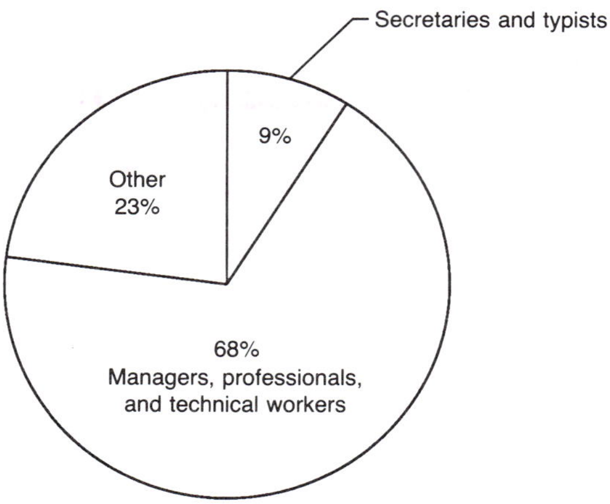

Changing Management Attitudes

Managerial practices have also been changing. In many organizations, management is becoming less authoritarian and more participative. Traditionally, planning and decision making were done at the top of the organization. Today, however, authority is frequently accorded by expertise as well as by position. The participative management movement is pushing responsibility down the organizational hierarchy. The people who perform a job have greater autonomy and control over the results of their work. In addition, office automation makes middle managers more effective, thereby decreasing the number of middle managers needed. Thus the number of middle management positions, which had grown significantly since World War II, is beginning to decline. Because of the growth in information-based industries, however, the overall number of middle management jobs is still increasing even though their relative percentage in organizations is decreasing.

As more responsibility is "pushed down" in the organization, offices are experiencing an increase in technical/professional positions and a decline in clerical positions. Until 1980, clerical jobs increased at a rate faster than the national employment growth rate. Since then, however, growth in clerical positions has eased to 2 percent below the national employment growth rate. According to one study, the number of jobs for secretaries, stenographers, and typists has declined by 100,000 since 1980. Researchers attribute this decline to office automation, job loss in industrial areas resulting from the shift away from manufacturing toward a service-based economy, and drops in government employment levels.

Joseph V. Brophy, Senior Vice-President of Data Processing of the Travelers Insurance Company, says that the personal computer is instrumental to a "fundamental demographic transformation in our company." In 1970, two thirds of Travelers' 30,000 employees were clerical and one-third were professional. According to Brophy, by 1990 that ratio will be reversed.[3]

The typical representation of an organizational hierarchy is shaped like a pyramid, as shown in Figure 2-6. The purpose of the hierarchical structure is *control*. Computers are diminishing the need for this hierarchical structure by providing direct access to information. In view of the recent statistics on the office work force, a truer characterization of the organizational hierarchy today would be diamond-shaped (see Figure 2-7).

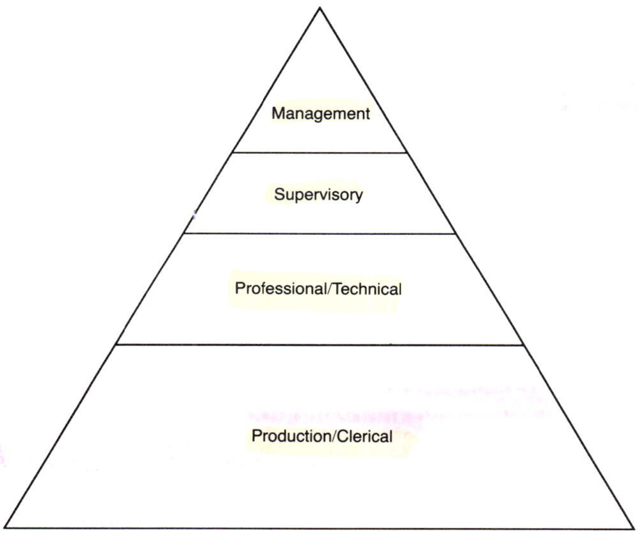

FIGURE 2-6. Historical organizational hierarchy. Historically, organizational hierarchy has been represented by a triangle with a broad base of low-level employees and a much smaller number of professional, technical, supervisory, and managerial personnel.

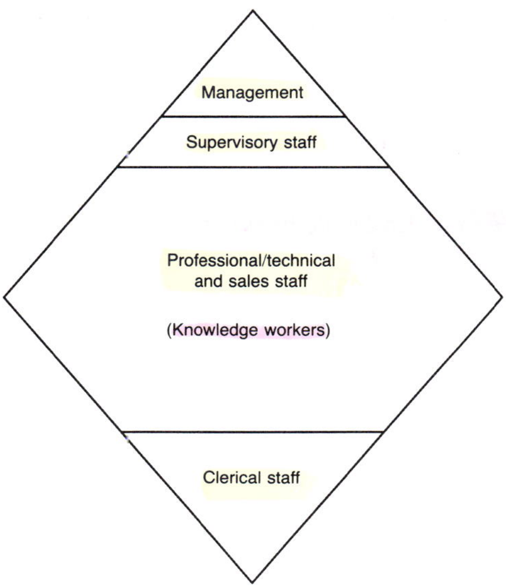

FIGURE 2-7. Organizational hierarchy in the Information Age. Today, the typical organizational hierarchy is more accurately represented as a diamond than as the traditional triangle of the past.

The Nature of Office Work

Although identifying lists of tasks is quite easy, little is known about the nature of office work from the standpoint of *information processing,* that is, how people interact with their work in the office. How do they identify information that is critical to their tasks or decision making? How do they go about locating or researching this information? How do they organize it, use it, store it, and assimilate it? How do they interact and interface with other information-processing functions in the office? What information-processing tasks do professional, technical, sales, supervisory, and managerial personnel do themselves, and what do they delegate to support personnel? Are these tasks based on the nature of the work or on personal preference?

Much more is known about what kinds of tasks are performed by the office work force than is known about *how* they perform these tasks. Yet the questions about how work is performed in the office are crucial to efforts to improve productivity. When systems analysts deliver a tool, it quickly falls into disuse when it does not match the task that needs to be performed. For example, a follow-up or tracking system that does not allow administrative assistants to look up information in all the ways that it is needed would lead them to keep and use their old manual system as a cross-reference. In all likelihood, maintaining two separate systems would soon become cumbersome, and the new automated tracking system would fall into disuse. It has become apparent that the developers of office automation must understand more about the nature of work performed at all levels of an organization if automation is to effectively serve information-processing needs at those levels.

Work flow analysis is an industrial engineering technique that has been frequently applied to job design for clerical personnel and factory production workers. At higher levels, however, work flow techniques are seldom applied. In fact, until fairly recently few people were concerned about the productivity of professionals and managers. Lagging productivity, the transition in the United States to an information-based economy, and the opportunities afforded by office automation are now changing that attitude.

The nature of information processing performed by professional, technical, and managerial personnel is closely aligned to the functional areas in which they work. Functions such as finance, legal services, marketing, production, research and development, and personnel administration have information requirements unique to their operations. Information may be used for planning, maintaining operations, evaluating results, reporting to executive management, and complying with government regulations. Typical functional divisions in large organizations and examples of information relating to their operations are depicted in Figure 2-8.

Descriptions of office work often depict clerical support personnel as processors of information for managers who use the information for decision making. There is a tendency to think of the office as an information factory that produces correspondence, reports, and other information products. These descriptions are somewhat misleading, however, and conceptualizing the office in these ways poses several risks for designing effective office systems.

First, professional, technical, sales, supervisory, and managerial personnel process a great deal of information themselves in addition to the information that is processed by clerical staff. Determining how technology can provide support for these professional information-processing tasks is a prime challenge for office automation.

Second, the focus on highly visible products of the office such as reports, correspondence, transactions, and decisions leads analysts to focus on product *quantity* rather than *quality.* Computer systems tend to be

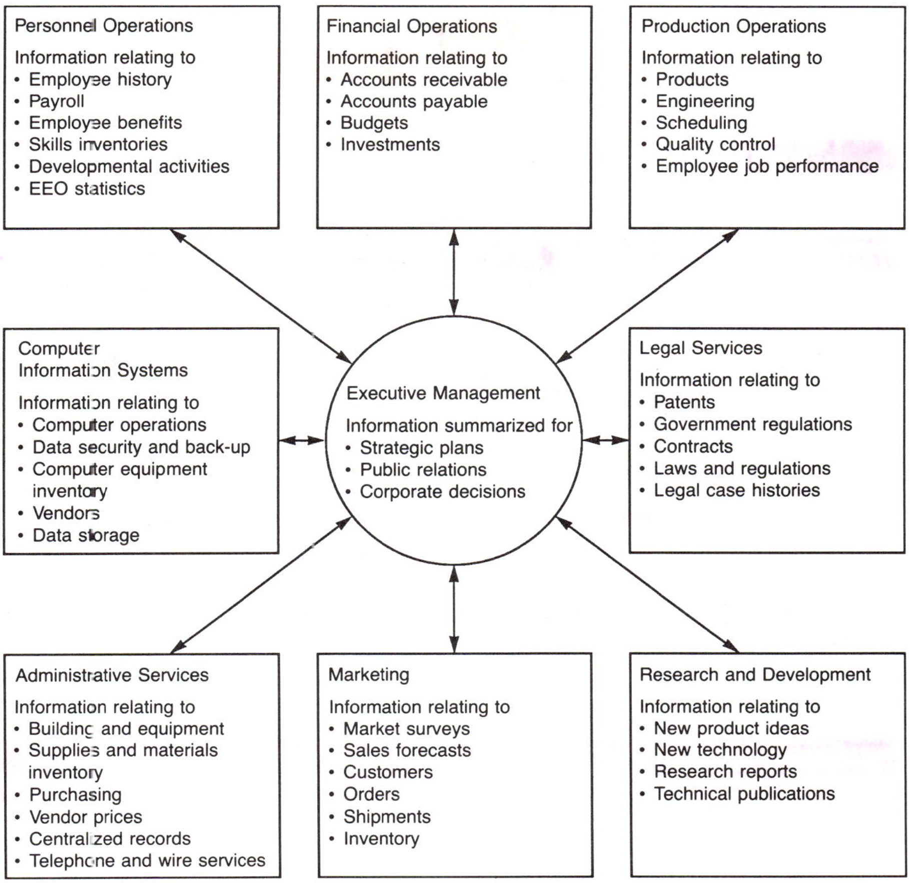

FIGURE 2-8. Typical functional divisions and related information requirements in a large enterprise.

based on the inherent structure of these products instead of on the processes people use to create them.

Third, the true objective of information processing activities generally is to *filter* information rather than *produce* information. The office serves to capture information and reduce it to a form that is useful for decision making. In this sense, the filtering process of the office resembles the filtering process of the human mind. The office also serves as a collective memory for the organization, documenting results of past actions and maintaining resources that may be useful for future actions.

The best source of information about how end users perform their jobs and the tools they need is the end users themselves. Thus information systems professionals, working alone, will never be able to devise systems that truly meet individual needs. New tools and procedures, if they are to evolve, will evolve out of a joint effort. The concept of end-user computing is a first step in this direction. Office automation, therefore, must be driven by business needs, not by technology. Solutions must focus on enhancing the capacity of end users to perform their jobs. In order for office automation to serve information processing needs effectively at all levels, it is crucial to understand more about the nature of work performed at those levels.

How People Work in the Office

Analyzing how people work in the office has an immediate pitfall because we are looking at *individuals,* not groups. The ways in which the work methods of a group or classification of persons are identified does not necessarily reflect the work style of a particular end user. Yet the process of providing office automation tools in the workplace, or on the desktop, usually attempts to do precisely that: tailor tools to the needs of individual workers. In considering managers as a group, for example, requirements would vary among managers in different roles such as factory supervisors, sales managers, or hospital administrators.

Realizing that individual differences must always be taken into account, the following section summarizes some characteristics of office workers in four job categories: (1) managerial, (2) professional and technical knowledge, (3) sales and marketing, and (4) clerical and administrative.

Managerial Personnel

Most management studies have focused on the decision and information *requirements* of managers rather than on the communication *process* by which information is obtained and decisions are translated into actions to achieve results. Management science has little to say about how the physical limitations of communications restrict the complexity of management tasks that an organization can accomplish.

As part of a comprehensive, one-year, $1.5 million study of managerial productivity in 1980, Booz, Allen and Hamilton provided a number of insights into how "knowledge workers" (managers, supervisors, professionals, and technical workers) perform in the office. The study involved 300 professionals in 15 major U.S. corporations. The series of in-depth case studies consisted of hundreds of personal interviews and a careful recording of each manager's use of time within a company. Participants in the study carried a wallet-like folder containing a device that beeped at 20-minute intervals. Each time the device beeped, managers recorded what they were doing at the time and rated its importance on a scale from one to ten. The participants also recorded other factors relating to work output, activities, and habits. The purpose of the study was to determine how automated office support systems are justified in terms of managerial/professional performance. Investigators used productivity and quality as the two principal criteria by which to analyze that performance. The results of the study provided interesting insights into work habits of knowledge workers. Booz, Allen and Hamilton concluded that most organizations could save 20 percent or more of operating costs by taking advantage of office automation. Office automation systems could reduce office support costs and improve managerial and professional productivity at the same time.

Specific findings regarding how managers work include the following:

1. Top management makes little use of available computer tools. They spend less than 2 to 3 percent of their time looking at computer printouts or dealing with information retrieval machines such as terminals or intelligent workstations.

2. Management spends too much time on nonproductive activities, such as looking for information and incomplete telephone calls, and not enough time on analytical and planning activities, updating professional skills, or taking part in decision making processes.

3. Roughly 90 percent of all hardcopy activity involves words:
   - Graphics is involved in only 5 percent of all hardcopy activities.
   - A combination of words and numbers occurs in almost 50 percent of hardcopy activities.
   - Numbers account for only 7 percent of all hardcopy activities.
   - Nonmanagers use computer printouts twice as often as managers.

4. Telephone use was rated low as a good use of time, except for outgoing external calls, because of a combination of the disruptive nature of incoming calls and the less productive time spent seeking people on outgoing calls.

Since managers accomplish tasks through other people, good communication of information is extremely important for effective management. Managers need the right information at the right time. Simply providing *more* information is not necessarily the answer. A major problem for most managers is filtering through vast amounts of information to find what they need. Unfortunately, automation often simply provides more information more quickly. Automated systems are most beneficial when they help sort and condense information so that managers receive only the information they need to perform their jobs effectively, at the right time and place and in the right format. In short, office automation can facilitate communication.

Henry Mintzberg conducted some of the most useful research regarding the work of managers, in terms of what they do and how they do it. His research indicated that the classic description of management as planning, organizing, coordinating, and controlling does not actually reflect how managers spend their time or what they actually do. Familiarity with Mintzberg's work and that of other researchers who have studied management behavior is important to office systems analysts and consultants charged with providing tools to assist managers. Some highlights of Mintzberg's findings that are especially relevant to office automation are summarized here:

1. Managers work at an unrelenting pace. Their activities are characterized by brevity, variety, and discontinuity. They are action-oriented, and dislike reflective activities.

2. Managers play a key role in securing "soft" external information (much of it available to them because of their status) and in passing it along to subordinates.

3. Managers' prime media for dealing with information are verbal: telephone calls, meetings, and observational tours. Managers spend 65 to 75 percent of their time communicating orally. Mail provides only 13 percent of information of specific or immediate use. A small percentage of the manager's information comes from formal reports or documents or computer printouts. Mintzberg suggests this fact as the main reason why MIS systems are rarely used by managers.

4. Because of its reliance on verbal information, according to Mintzberg, the chief strategic data bank of the organization is not in the memory of its computers but in the minds of its managers.

5. Manager reliance on verbal media also helps explain why it is frequently difficult for them to delegate many tasks. In order to delegate, managers have to "dump memory": tell everything they know about the subject.[4]

Mintzberg described the manager's job in terms of various roles or organized sets of behaviors identified with position. Formal authority gives rise to three interpersonal roles, which in turn give rise to three informational roles. The first two roles then enable the manager to play the four decisional roles. Mintzberg's description of these ten roles is shown in Figure 2-9. These roles are closely integrated and inseparable.

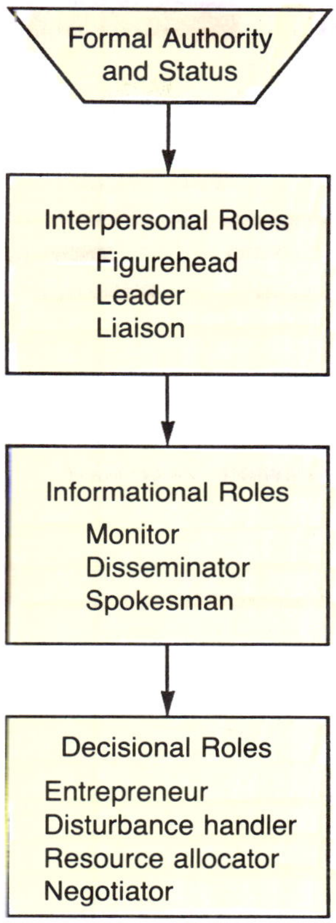

FIGURE 2-9. Managerial roles stemming from formal authority and status.

Professional and Technical Knowledge Workers

Factual information about how professional and technical personnel—the so-called *knowledge workers*—work is even sketchier than that about managers. Little research has been done in this area. The work of professional and technical knowledge workers shares several commonalities with the work of managers. Their work, however, is more information-intensive than that of their managers. They generally serve as specialists in one or more aspects of the business. Examples include business analysts, marketing researchers, government policy researchers, public relations specialists, legal advisers, and many others. Although information about knowledge workers is limited, the following generalizations can be made:

- The knowledge worker spends considerable time probing complex problems.
- The knowledge worker depends on accurate, timely information and decisions by managers.

- Managers are coming to rely more and more on knowledge workers, such as staff specialists and business analysts, for detailed computer analyses of information.
- Knowledge workers spend most of their time in informational roles. They are the experts who are supposed to have the facts. Other people and parts of the organization look to them for advice.
- Knowledge workers spend considerable time analyzing, manipulating, and summarizing information. They need to look at information and organize it in different ways. They frequently require different views of the same information.

Access to information is critical for professional and technical knowledge workers. Office information processing for these specialists included the following:

1. *Tracking systems.* Knowledge workers often have to track the status of events or actions related to their organization. For example, public affairs specialists may track legislation that relates to the business.

2. *Forecasting.* Knowledge workers may play a role in trying to estimate future trends or happenings that pertain to their firm or industry. Business forecasts might include short- and long-term forecasts of sales, price forecasts for important raw materials and equipment, market demand for new products, and a host of other matters of specific interest.

3. *Modeling.* Knowledge workers use models to explain phenomena, clarify certain aspects of problems, or help analyze constraints and potentials. Models represent an abstraction of reality: what things *were* like, what they *are* like, what they *could* be like, or what they *should* be like. The objective is to highlight certain important relationships and key interactions.

4. *Statistical analysis.* Knowledge workers often need to analyze information with various statistical techniques.

5. *Graph production.* Knowledge workers frequently use graphs and charts to analyze trends, illustrate statistical information, or clarify data.

6. *Report generation.* Information must be summarized in written format so that it can be disseminated. Often, various forms of media are needed.

7. *Access to corporate information resources.* Availability of accurate, timely corporate information, such as sales figures, manufacturing costs, budgets, and other data, is essential for knowledge workers to do their jobs.

8. *Access to outside reference sources.* Knowledge workers require business information such as economic data, stock quotations, interest rates,

demographic information, technical information, or any of hundreds of topics.

9. *"What if" analysis.* Knowledge workers often need to look at information in different ways, changing one factor while holding other factors constant. For example, a business analyst may study the effect of various interest rates on a business investment decision.

In summary, knowledge workers make up a growing percentage of the office work force. Their work is very information-intensive. They spend considerable time researching, analyzing, manipulating, and summarizing information related to products, services, or other business requirements. As indicated by the preceding list, office automation provides a variety of tools that can be helpful for knowledge workers. In fact, the value of this group to organizations has increased as computers have improved their ability to deliver detailed, accurate, timely information. The office systems analyst must have an accurate understanding of the knowledge worker's business needs as a basis for selecting the most appropriate tools.

Sales and Marketing Personnel

A sales professional is usually responsible for achieving sales results for a defined territory. The size of an appropriate territory varies widely with the nature of products. Within the norms of a particular industry, the size of a salesperson's territory is based on the convergence of two factors:

1. Salespeople want their territory to be as large as possible. Obviously, the larger the potential customer base, the higher the salesperson's potential earnings.

2. Time constraints limit the size of a territory that a salesperson can cover. It is in the best interest of a company to ensure that territories are small enough to service thoroughly.

For the salesperson, then, managing a territory is a balancing act between ambition and available time. It requires effective use of time. The salesperson must spend as much time as possible selling and as little time as possible on administrative tasks. Ideally, sales representatives spend minimum time at their desks and maximum time in clients' offices. In reality, a sales representative's "office" is often a car or hotel room.

Most sales representatives spend only 35 percent of their time actually selling and another 35 percent traveling. Monthly sales reports require an average of four to six hours of preparation. Any time savings that can be translated into additional selling opportunities can directly affect earnings.

Efficient and effective information processing is important for good time management. Typical sales representatives use card files of contacts, appointment books, and folders of good prospects. Office information processing for sales representatives includes the following:

1. *Prospect management*. Salespeople, obviously, must have a procedure for identifying and maintaining lists of potential clients. Effective time management depends on the ability to discern those prospective customers who are most likely to purchase a particular product. This process, referred to as *qualifying prospects*, is a valuable method for targeting sales calls.

2. *Client information and purchasing history*. The ability to understand clients and a client's product needs enables a salesperson to service that client more effectively.

3. *Sales presentation materials*. The most effective way to convince potential customers that a product meets their needs is to tailor the sales presentation to their requirements. Individually tailored sales materials can be powerful selling tools.

4. *Product information and prices*. Information must be accurate, current, and readily accessible.

5. *Communications*. Both telephone and written correspondence are essential for establishing contacts and appointments and following up on sales calls.

6. *Paperwork*. Purchase orders and various other paperwork must be submitted, depending on the nature of the product. When salespeople use manual methods to send follow-up correspondence after completing a call, they must sit down and write a letter in longhand (or dictate it), give it to a secretary upon returning to the office, wait for it to be typed, and then proofread and sign it. The process could take three or four days.

7. *Client services*. A good salesperson keeps careful track of the status of customer orders and follows up to ensure that the customer is completely satisfied. Salespeople must avoid walking into a client's office with a big smile when the client is "waiting with a baseball bat," angered about overdue orders.

In summary, sales personnel can benefit from office automation tools that enable them to reduce time spent on administrative tasks and to increase the time available for selling. Office automation can help sales personnel identify and manage prospects, make effective sales presentations, and follow up on orders and deliveries.

Clerical and Administrative Personnel

The U.S. Department of Labor identifies clerical personnel as including "a wide range of office occupations from messenger to the highly-skilled positions . . . of executive secretary, or office manager with professional certification."[5]

Use of the term *clerical worker* has declined as specialization has led to many new titles. It is estimated that two-thirds of all jobs within the clerical and administrative category are held by women.

As with the preceding three categories of office workers, much more is known about what clerical and administrative personnel do than about how they do it. Here, too, the *how* is as important as the *what* for designing effective office systems. Far too many systems are underutilized because they missed the target of being truly useful to the personnel for whom they were designed.

The following generalizations can be made about clerical and administrative personnel:

1. *No standard job description*. The make-up of clerical and administrative jobs varies from one office to another depending on the type of enterprise, its size, and the assignments involved. Many clerical jobs are routine and repetitive in nature. Others are extremely diverse and include a wide variety of duties and responsibilities. One employee in a small office may perform a variety of duties that are divided among several specialized jobs in a large office. Many office jobs require teamwork. The ability to see another employee's problem and to help whenever possible is important. Staying with a task until it is finished, adaptability, and tact are often requirements. Office work may require working under pressure. Clerical workers frequently have deadlines to meet. Reports must be ready for an upcoming meeting, or contracts have to be in the mail by the first day of the month.

2. *Direct interface with clients and business associates*. Clerical and administrative personnel may represent the official company face to the public in positions such as receptionist, bank teller, or sales order clerks. They may need to locate information, resolve problems, handle exceptions, and smooth the ruffled feathers of irate customers.

3. *Various levels of authority*. High-level administrative or executive secretarial positions entail considerable responsibility and authority. An executive secretary may have great latitude in screening mail and visitors, handling administrative details, and keeping an office running when the executive is away. Initiative and good judgment are required. Administrative personnel sometimes hire, train, and supervise junior-level personnel. They may be authorized to respond to and sign correspondence. Because they have access to confidential materials, loyalty is often a requirement. An effective secretary functions in a close team relationship with the executive to anticipate requirements and to work with minimum direction. Otherwise, much of the potential time the executive can gain by delegating responsibilities is lost. An effective team relationship with an administrative assistant or secretary can be an executive's most valuable means for leveraging time.

4. *Line and staff structures of organizations.* Administrative and clerical personnel may work in either line or staff relationships. "Line and staff," the reader will recall from management texts, indicates whether departments in an organization have direct responsibility for operations (line) or provide ancillary services (staff). Most often, administrative and clerical personnel are part of a department and report to department management. Less frequently, clerical personnel are organized as service groups in a staff relationship. As a staff service group, clerical personnel have their own reporting structure and management. Examples include word processing centers, administrative support groups, and mail services (see Figure 2-10).

Information processing requirements of clerical and administrative personnel include the following:

1. *Text processing.* Clerical personnel produce documents, ranging from simple notes and one-page memoranda to complex statistical reports and manuals several hundred pages in length.
2. *Dictation.* Since ancient times, when early stenographers recorded the words of Greek orators, one of the information processing tasks of clerical workers has been to record the spoken word.
3. *Copying and duplicating information.* Multiple copies of documents are frequently required to communicate information to all who need to be informed.
4. *Arranging meetings.* Setting up meetings frequently involves numerous telephone calls to check availability of participants and agree on a time and place.
5. *Handling telephone calls.* Handling telephone calls may be the major portion of a clerical person's job or only one of numerous responsibilities. Telephone calls can be a source of constant interruption. Clerical personnel must screen calls, determining which inquiries to handle themselves and which to direct to others. If the intended recipient is not available, they must take accurate messages and deliver them to the appropriate party. Since telephone calls may be the major (or only) contact clients or customers have with an organization, good telephone etiquette is important to building good will and a good public image. The telephone is a major tool for securing or transmitting information. Formerly, clerical personnel spent much time placing telephone calls for others; today it is common for individuals to place their own calls.
6. *Handling visitors.* Clerical personnel frequently greet and assist visitors, sometimes screening those who wish to meet with principals.
7. *Calendaring.* Clerical personnel are usually responsible for scheduling time and making appointments for managers and professionals.

FIGURE 2-10.
Line and staff reporting relationships for clerical/administrative personnel.

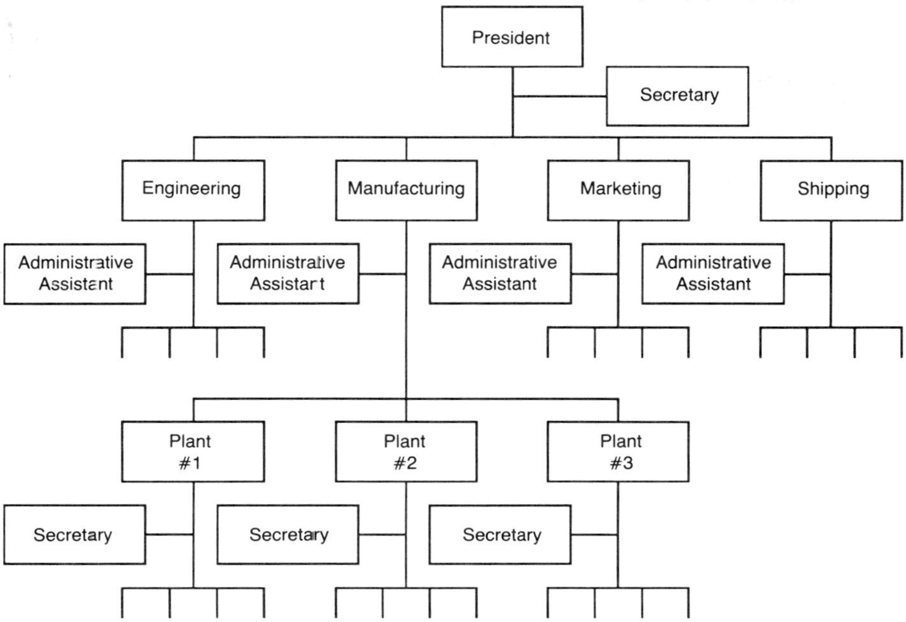

a. Typical line-reporting relationship for office support. Office support personnel are usually part of a department and report directly to department managers.

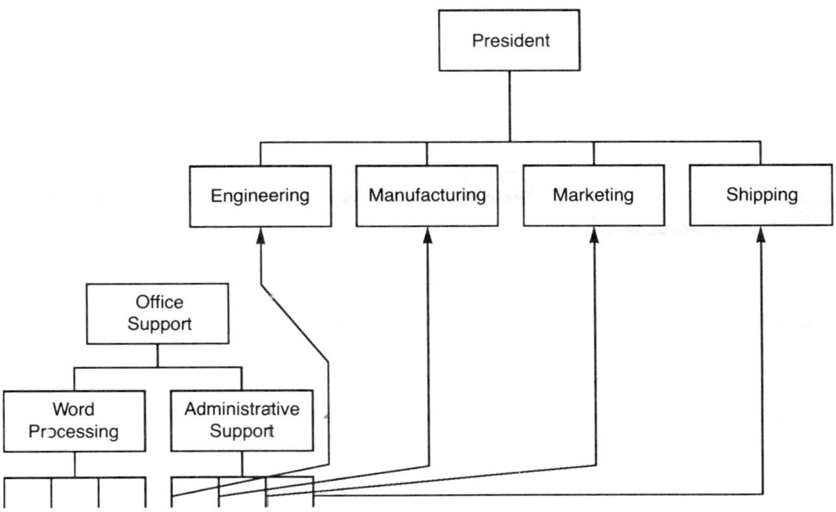

b. Typical staff-reporting relationship for office support. When organized as a staff service group, office support personnel have their own reporting structure and management.

8. *Tracking and follow-up.* Clerical personnel must track and follow up on activities such as responses to inquiries, replies to correspondence, renewal dates, delivery dates, invoices, and the like.

9. *Filing and retrieving information.* In large organizations, records management is a full-time responsibility with specialized personnel. In small organizations and for departments and individual offices, filing and retrieving information may be one of many responsibilities of a clerical person. Centralized record departments follow generally accepted practices for categorizing and indexing records. Formal procedures are employed to safeguard records and periodically dispose of outdated materials. Departmental and individual files are more often than not organized intuitively rather than according to formal rules.

10. *Travel arrangements.* Clerical personnel make travel arrangements, organize itineraries, and submit travel expense reports. These activities require the clerical person to be thoroughly familiar with the principal's preferences or to work closely with the principal. Large corporations may have their own travel departments.

11. *Budgeting.* Clerical personnel generally track expenditures against projected expense allocations. They may be involved in developing department budgets, although the principal or department manager would be accountable for the budget. Clerical personnel frequently maintain petty cash accounts.

The activities identified above are representative of the myriad duties likely to be handled by clerical personnel. Clerical personnel also perform tasks such as billing, invoicing, shipping, data entry, mail handling, transmitting wires and facsimiles, order processing, scheduling conference rooms, and many other tasks. It should be evident to the reader that typing or document production makes up a minor portion of the responsibilities of most clerical personnel. Because of the broad diversity of clerical tasks, each situation must be considered individually when office automation systems are developed.

SUMMARY

In any work environment, people, tasks, equipment (technology), and resources are organized to accomplish specific objectives, generating some type of product. In the office, the product is information. Information may take the form of decisions, directives, or documents.

The role of technology is to help accomplish required tasks. In performing that role, the technology influences how people and tasks are organized within the office. Not only is each office unique, it is also dynamic. The ways in which technology, resources, tasks, and people are organized into functions change over time, in response to changing business requirements.

Some form of organization is required to coordinate the efforts of the various members of a group so that each member contributes to the goals of the group. Through organization, people can accomplish more work than individuals working alone. The organizational framework of an enterprise, as reflected in a formal organization chart, defines who does what. The organizational framework of today's offices has changed and evolved over time.

Technology has played a part in how office organization has evolved. In the past few decades, office automation has had a major impact on people and organizations. In many ways the evolution of office automation parallels that of data processing. Both have evolved in response to three major factors: advancements in computer technology, experience using the technology, and changing business (market) conditions. Chapter 2 suggests four periods that summarize major stages in the evolution of office automation:

1. Automation of repetitive tasks
2. Administrative support
3. End-user computing
4. Integrated systems

The text uses four major employment categories to classify the office work force:

1. Managerial personnel
2. Professional and technical knowledge workers
3. Sales and marketing personnel
4. Clerical and administrative personnel

The composition of the office work force is changing. The typical representation of an organizational hierarchy as a triangle—with a broad base of clerical positions, a smaller number of professional technical workers, and a few executives at the top—no longer fits many of today's information-based industries, such as insurance, finance, and law. The organizational hierarchy in these organizations can be represented more accurately as a diamond, with the majority of employees falling within a wide middle range of professional and technical knowledge workers, with much smaller numbers of employees at the high and low ends of the hierarchy.

Much more is known about what kinds of tasks are performed by the office work force than how they perform these tasks. Yet the questions of how work is performed in the office are at the heart of efforts to improve productivity. When systems analysts deliver a tool (the "what"), it quickly falls into disuse when it does not match how the task needs to be performed. It has become apparent that for OA to serve the information processing needs effectively at all levels, it is crucial to understand more about the nature of work performed at those levels.

Managerial-level personnel work at an unrelenting pace. Their activities are characterized by brevity, variety, and discontinuity. Their prime media for dealing with information are verbal (oral); they make minimum use of computer reports. Much of their information is kept in their head, which often makes delegation of work difficult. Studies indicate, however, that managers spend considerable time on nonproductive activities. This limits their time for analytical and planning activities.

Professional and technical knowledge workers spend most of their time in information roles: analyzing, manipulating, and summarizing information. Access to information is critical for knowledge workers.

Sales personnel constantly try to spend as much time as possible selling and as little time as possible on administrative tasks. They need efficient and effective procedures for identifying and qualifying sales leads, maintaining accurate sales records, obtaining customer and product information, and making effective sales presentations to clients.

Clerical and administrative personnel play a support role in creating, distributing, storing, and retrieving information both inside and outside the organization. They perform a broad diversity of tasks.

When office automation systems are developed, each situation must be considered individually to address the processing requirements and business needs.

DISCUSSION QUESTIONS

1. Summarize the developments in each of the four periods of office automation as described in this text. Is it important to have an understanding of how office automation has evolved/is evolving? Why?
2. What is the WP/AS concept? Who in the organization was instrumental in the decline of this practice?
3. Identify four reasons why the end-user computing movement has grown.
4. Why is office work so difficult to describe?
5. Describe, in general terms, the activities of the following categories of office workers:
   a. Managerial personnel
   b. Professional and technical workers
   c. Sales and marketing personnel
   d. Clerical and administrative personnel

6. What is meant by the term "integration"? Can one office system support the activities of all four categories of office workers? Explain.

APPLICATION EXERCISES

1. Select one category of office worker: manager, professional, sales, or clerical. Interview five people in such a position, asking them to describe the work they do and the office automation tools that support them. What are the workers' attitudes toward the technology? Discuss your interview results with others in the class.
2. In anticipation of future chapters, make a list of tasks that all categories of office workers have in common.

SUGGESTED READINGS

Galitz, Wilbert O. *The Office Environment: Automation's Impact on Tomorrow's Workplace*. (Willow Grove, Pa.: Administrative Management Society, 1984). Second of a four-part study called *Managing the Office: 1990 and Beyond* conducted by the AMS Foundation.

Millman, Zeeva, and Hartwick, Jon. "The Impact of Automated Office Systems on Middle Managers and Their Work," *MIS Quarterly* (December 1987), pp. 479–491.

THE OFFICE SYSTEMS ORGANIZATION: Implementers

CHAPTER **3**

OBJECTIVES

After completing this chapter, the reader should be able to meet the following objectives:

- Describe how typical organizations delegate responsibility for office automation.
- Differentiate between office automation and data processing environments.
- Identify various career opportunities in office systems.
- Describe the role of office systems management in typical business enterprises.
- Explain why a broad, corporate management perspective is essential for office automation planning.
- Explain the concept of information as a resource.

KEY TERMS

communications
computer information systems
data processing
data processing department
decision support systems (DSS)
end users
information management (IM)
information resource management (IRM)
information systems (IS)
line authority
management information systems (MIS)
management support systems
office automation (OA)
office systems
office automation systems
automated office systems
office automation department
office systems department
office systems analyst
staff authority

INTRODUCTION

Among enterprises that were early office automation innovators, leadership tended to be self-selected; that is, some individual within the organization learned about the technology and took responsibility for introducing it into the organization. For example, an accounting manager may have been the catalyst for bringing microcomputers with spreadsheets into the company. An innovative secretary may have recommended and implemented the first word processing system. Now that office automation has gained wide acceptance in both business and public-sector enterprises, however, office automation responsibility is generally a management function within the formal organizational structure.

Chapter 2 discussed the role of organization and how office automation has evolved in the business office. Chapter 3 explains how responsibility for office automation is delegated and managed within an organization. How do organizations plan for office automation? How are organizations changing their view of information management? The chapter begins by describing how authority and responsibility for office automation are delegated. Then it clarifies office automation terminology in relation to data processing and information systems in general.

DELEGATING RESPONSIBILITY FOR OFFICE AUTOMATION

As readers may recall from their study of management texts, *delegation* is the granting of responsibility and authority by one manager to another within an organization. *Responsibility* is the obligation to carry out assigned duties or tasks, and *authority* is the right to decide, take action, or direct the actions of others in carrying out those responsibilities. When managers are granted responsibility and authority, they are *accountable* to the delegator for accomplishing the assigned tasks and objectives.

Managers may have either *line authority* or *staff authority,* or both, depending on their relationship to other managers within the organization. Line authority is used to carry out the major goals of an enterprise, whereas staff authority is used to provide support or special expertise to aid line authority. *Line managers* have direct authority over personnel and resources within their organizational unit. Personnel and line managers report in superior-subordinate authority relationships, forming a *line,* or *chain of command,* from the top to the bottom of the organization. *Staff managers,* on the other hand, usually operate in advisory or adjunct roles, contributing indirectly to the accomplishment of major goals. The indirect authority relationship of staff managers is generally designated on an organization chart by a horizontal or dotted line.

Authority and responsibility for planning and implementing office automation vary from one organization to another. In a small company or agency, responsibility for office automation may be only part of the accountability of one individual or department. In a large organization, responsibility is usually assigned to a specialized technical group.

Office systems groups are generally considered to perform a staff function, along with data processing, administrative services, personnel services, and financial services. Office automation groups provide specialized technical services to aid line managers in accomplishing the major objectives of the enterprise, usually producing the products and services through which the enterprise earns its revenues or justifies its existence. Thus office systems groups make recommendations regarding appropriate use of technologies, but the line managers retain the authority to decide whether or not to implement the recommendations.

As reflected by formal organization charts, the way in which responsibility for office systems is delegated varies depending on several factors:

1. The overall centralization or decentralization of office operations.
2. The importance of information processing to the enterprise.
3. The stage of office automation development.
4. The placement of other related functions, such as data processing.
5. The political climate for change within the organization.

The broad scope of office automation requires managers to collaborate with other relevant staff functions. The manager with responsibility for automating the business office requires strong leadership skills to orchestrate change and innovation.

DEFINITIONS

Within an enterprise, the department that has responsibility for office automation may be called an *office automation department*, *office systems department*, or something similar. As suggested in Chapter 1, the process of categorizing is rather arbitrary. Pitfalls exist in trying to define office automation in relation to other areas of computer technology. Although some clear distinctions can be made, emphasizing the differences tends to obscure the similarities. In the business world, boundary lines are not as clear as a textbook discussion might suggest. This fluidity is especially apparent during an evolutionary stage of technology. Ultimately, when an organization is addressing real problems, it does not make any difference whether the solution would be classified academically as word processing, data processing, communications, or anything else. Frequently, in fact, the solution may be some combination of these technologies. As suggested by Figure 3-1, information technologies are becoming more integrated over time.

As a starting point for learning, however, it is important to have some clear definitions and concepts on which to build one's knowledge and experience. Definitions, even if tentative, provide a basis for conceptualizing the logic of theoretical constructs. Definitions help develop a frame of reference for clarifying, understanding, or criticizing the perspective offered by the writer. One should not forget that, in the workaday world, computer technologies do not fit neatly into the cubbyholes that a textbook might suggest.

Terminology is discussed in two senses: (1) as general classifications and (2) as names for departments or staff functions within an organization. Little consensus exists on precise definitions or on practical usage. Usage evolves along with the technology; early dividing lines blur as technologies

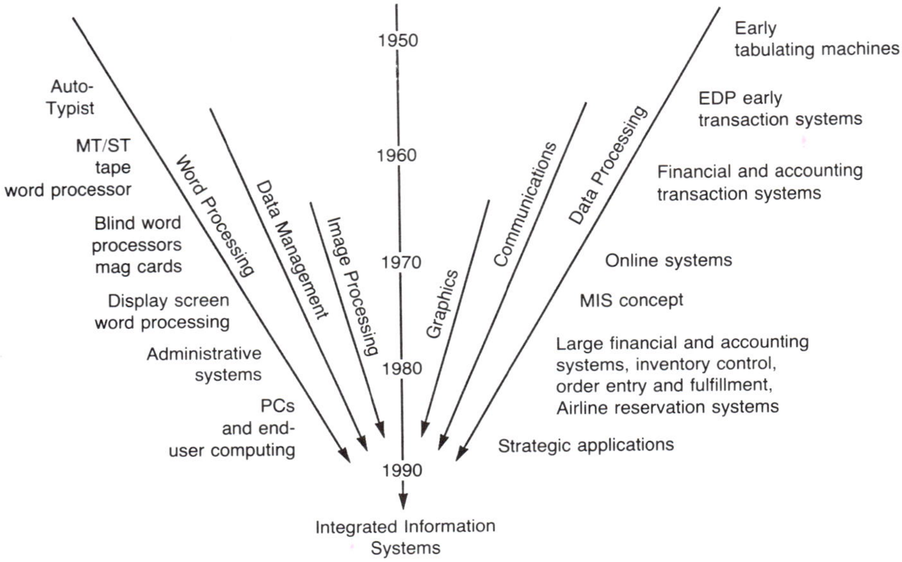

FIGURE 3-1. Converging information technologies.

converge. Thus the discussion reflects the general trends in current usage rather than authoritative definitions. It is intended to serve as a framework for coherence rather than an exhaustive listing.

The terms *office automation (OA), office systems (OS), office information systems (OIS), office automation systems (OAS),* and *automated office systems (AOS)* are used interchangeably to refer to computer systems designed for office applications and end-user computing. Office automation technologies include word processing, end-user computing tools such as spreadsheets, database, and fourth-generation languages, computer graphics, decision support, electronic mail, copiers, image processing, electronic storage and retrieval, and printers, to name only a few (refer to Figure 1–6 for a more complete list). These computer solutions may be based on mainframe, minicomputer, or microcomputer technologies. An *Office Systems Department* or *Office Automation Department* would be charged with accountability for planning and implementing these technologies to meet organizational requirements.

Data processing (DP) also refers to the application of computer technologies to business applications. Data processing has been defined as a systematic set of techniques for collecting, manipulating, and disseminating data to achieve specified objectives. Both OA and DP process data and information. Both automate routine, repetitive tasks. The focus and orientation of data processing and office automation differ in a number of important ways, however (as discussed in the next section).

Another term sometimes used in place of data processing is *computer information systems (CIS).* Within an organization, the *Data Processing Department* would be accountable for planning, implementing, and maintaining computer applications and operations. Data Processing Departments may also be called *Management Information Systems (MIS) Departments.* (The term MIS also has other meanings, which will be explained shortly.) Because they have been in existence for over twenty years, data processing departments are generally much more established in organizations than are office automation departments. The size and organization of data processing departments have grown dramatically, of course, with the growth of computer use.

Both data processing and office automation can be viewed as specializations within the realm of computer technologies. Other specializations include computer-aided manufacture (CAM), computer-aided design (CAD), and scientific research. One additional area of importance to both office automation and data processing is *communications.* Some view communications as a specialization, while others consider it part of office automation or data processing. Communications refers to the electronic transfer of data between computer devices. A detailed discussion of communications is included in Chapter 8. This text treats communications as a specialized area of prime importance to office automation.

It has become accepted practice to view the role of computers in business from a global perspective, with the emphasis on managing information rather than on managing technology. Current terminology reflects this perspective. In this global sense, the terms *information systems (IS), management information systems (MIS),* and *information management (IM)* are often used interchangeably. Originally, the terms referred only to mainframe-oriented operations (as indicated in the previous paragraph, where MIS was an alternative term for data processing department). With the growing importance of office automation and communications technologies, however, it is becoming common practice to use IS, MIS, and IM as umbrella terms to encompass office automation, data processing, and communications.

Management information systems (MIS) sometimes has a more specialized meaning. MIS originally referred to the data processing concept of mainframe systems designed to support management decision making. Implementing such systems met with limited success. Even when systems delivered accurate, timely information, they were seldom accepted and used by the managers for whom they were intended. In spite of early failures, the concept of computer systems to support management decision making persists. Today, it has become more common to use the terms *decision support systems (DSS)* or *management support systems (MSS), executive information systems (EIS),* or *executive support systems* (ESS) when referring to these tools. New technologies hold promise for successful implementation of this concept.

OA VERSUS DP ENVIRONMENTS

In the application of computer technologies, important distinctions exist between the office automation and data processing environments. The distinctions are helpful for understanding the office automation process. Office automation and data processing differ primarily in their orientation and approach to problems. This distinction might best be characterized as a business orientation in office automation, in contrast to a technical orientation in data processing.

In more specific terms, data processing's approach is to create systems that process information *for* people, generally replacing manual systems. In essence, the DP approach is to remove information processing from the office environment, manipulate it in a "magical" black box, and return the results in the form of printed reports or *output*. Accordingly, DP operates in an isolated, technical environment. *Endusers* are passive participants. They are the individuals who key data into keypunch machines, enter data at terminals, and receive output. Endusers explain their requirements to DP personnel, who have the technical expertise to create systems to process it. DP personnel control the information processing environment.

Office automation, in contrast, introduces computer technologies directly into the workplace as tools to help process information. Endusers are involved as participants in performing the information processing themselves. Users develop skills to operate the computer tools and process their own work. Thus tools that are easy for a nontechnical person to understand and use, or *user-friendly* tools, are important. Users frequently are involved in defining requirements, evaluating alternatives, and designing solutions. Office automation personnel serve in technical advisory roles.

Data processing is suited for well-defined processes, such as those in accounting and manufacturing. Applications include transaction-oriented, numerical applications such as payroll, inventory, order entry, and accounts receivable and payable. Processing volumes must warrant the high cost of developing systems. Changes are expensive to implement. Many DP applications lend themselves to batch processing (hold and process together at one time), rather than the interactive processing required for office automation. Office automation has evolved primarily in response to loosely structured text, data analysis, and communications requirements. OA addresses applications that require flexibility for handling exceptions and making changes. Applications include word processing, spreadsheet analysis, tracking and filing systems, project management, graphics, and forms design. Office automation is appropriate for individual and departmental processing. It meets a need for quick response and offers cost-effective solutions for applications that do not have volumes high enough to warrant the expense of developing mainframe systems. Some of the key distinctions between data processing and office automation are summarized in Figure 3-2.

Data Processing	Office Automation
Numeric-oriented	Text-oriented
Takes work out of office	Brings tools into office
Converts data into information	Assists people as they process information
Technical, production-oriented	Consistent, friendly, user interface
Repetitive, well-defined processes	Flexible, less well-defined activities
Formal development cycle	Quick response
Formal control and security procedures	User responsible for control and security of data
Batch processing	Interactive processing
Transaction-oriented	Nonprocedural
Practical for high-volume applications	Practical for small applications
Optimizes equipment	Optimizes people
Systems analysts address software solutions (technical environment is a given)	Office systems analysts deal with hardware and software solutions

FIGURE 3-2. **Contrast of office automation and data processing environments.**

OFFICE AUTOMATION ACCOUNTABILITY

Office automation has had a profound impact on the way organizations are structured. Responsibility for introducing new technologies is often shifted to technical departments. Organizations that are most advanced in their use of office automation generally have a full-time manager accountable for office automation. According to a recent research study of office automation, the median level of those managers was three steps down from the chief operating officer and typically had the job title of "director."

Within organizations, the reporting structure for OA and DP varies. Where does office automation fit into the organizational structure? The answer is not clear-cut; moreover, all OA technologies do not always fall within the scope of a single department. The best way to illustrate this occurrence is by examining organizational charts. Note particularly the placement of OA and DP in Figures 3-3 to 3-8.

The obvious problem is determining who should have responsibility for office automation. Data processing departments have earned greater prominence than office automation departments in most organizations. DP has recognized technical expertise. As office automation has taken on new importance in organizations and as dividing lines between DP and OA have blurred, questions of appropriate reporting structures arise. A number of management concerns have arisen, such as incompatibilities among equipment, wasteful duplication, and the need to safeguard corporate information. The need to coordinate an organization's computing resources becomes obvious. The building of an appropriate reporting structure, however, is not always easy.

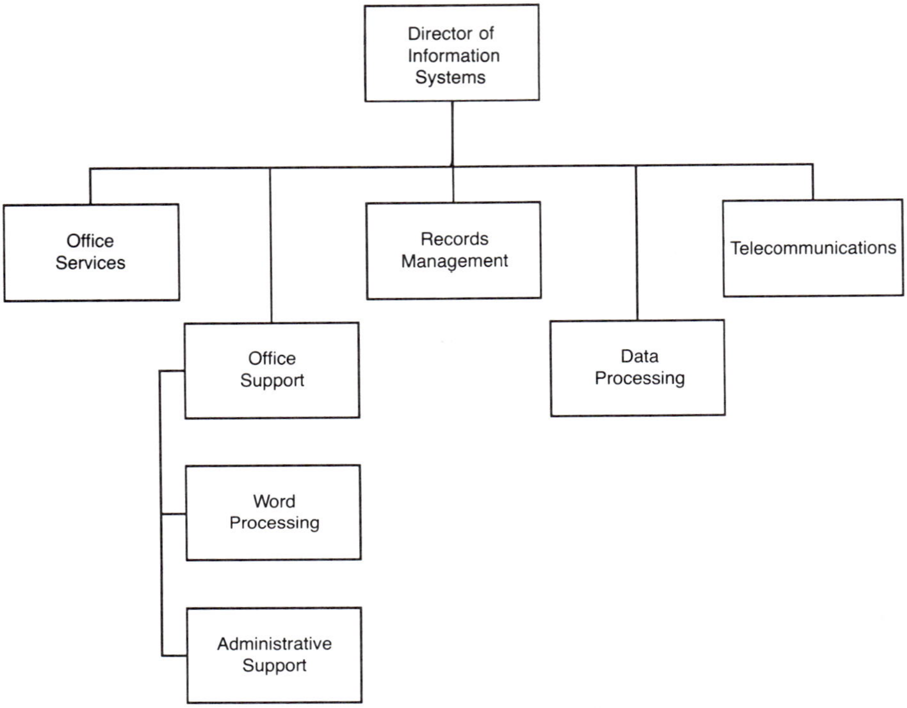

FIGURE 3-3. Sample organization chart for a large law firm depicting a team approach to office support.

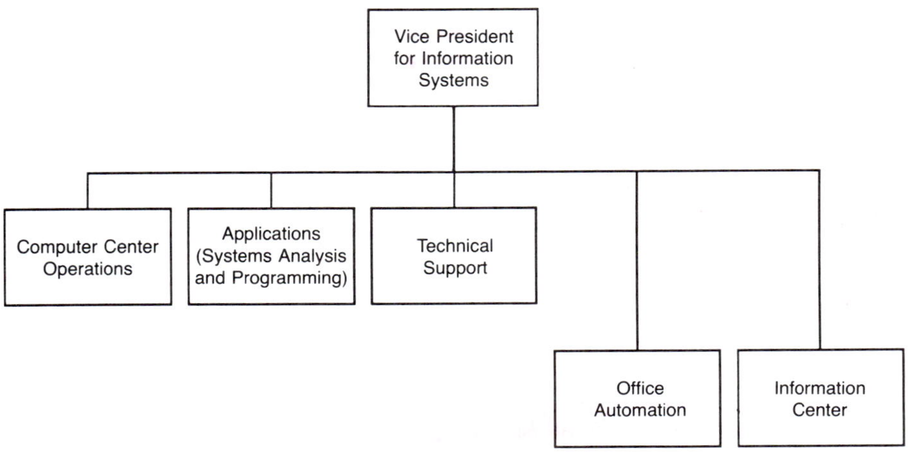

FIGURE 3-4. Sample organization chart for a public utility.

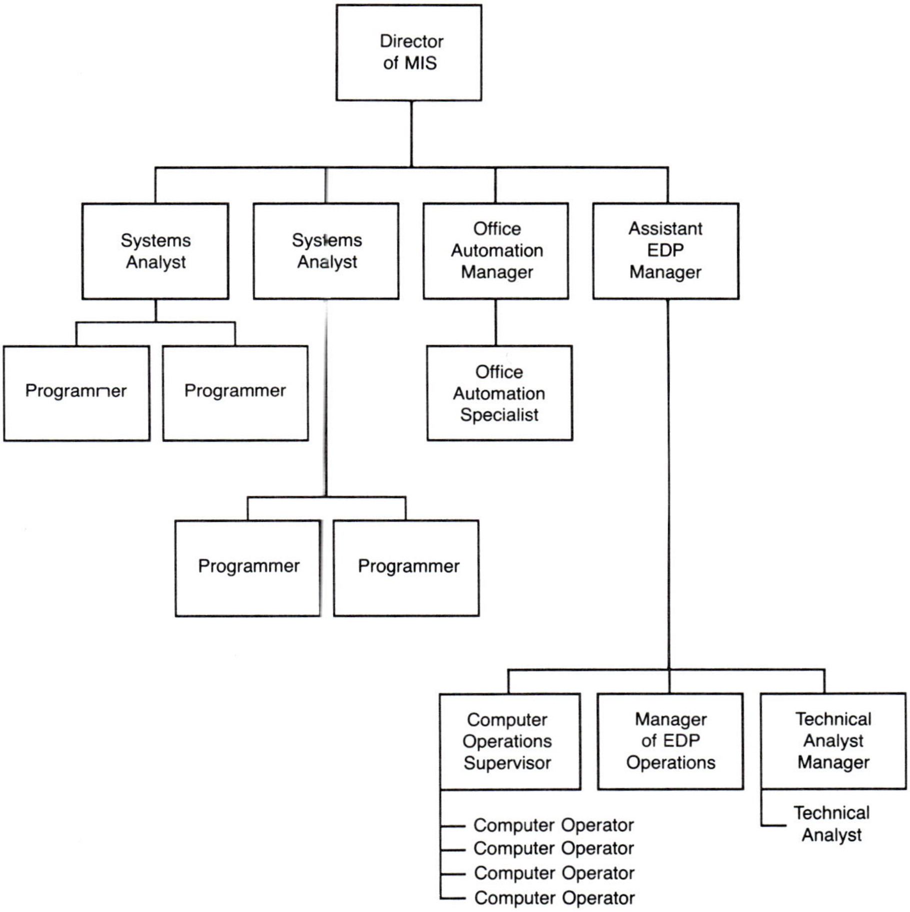

FIGURE 3-5. Sample organization chart for a small business.

Some organizations assume that data processing personnel have superior technical knowledge and, therefore, are best qualified to take responsibility for office automation. Office systems analysts who did not go through the traditional DP programming ranks may be viewed as technically unqualified to deal with data processing. This viewpoint often is based on a lack of understanding of the differences between the two fields. Office automation requires its own set of specialized technical skills, which do not necessarily qualify one to be a DP programmer, any more than DP programming skills necessarily qualify one to be an office systems analyst. In fact, some would argue that office automation requires a much broader knowledge of computing technologies than does data processing. In reality, much of the argument depends on how broadly or narrowly one defines terms.

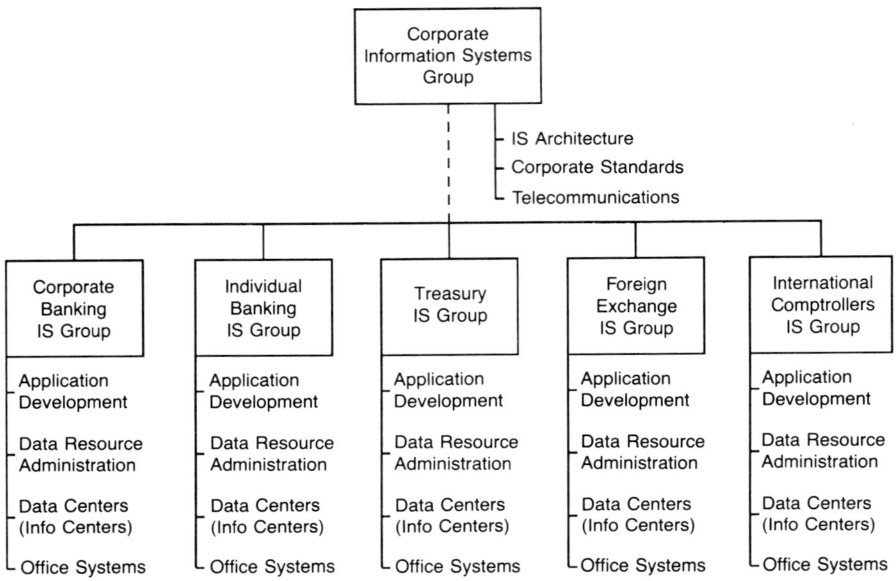

FIGURE 3-6. Information systems organization in a large bank. In the classic matrix organization, the central group is typically responsible for IS architecture, telecommunications, and corporate standards, and other functions are decentralized in each division.

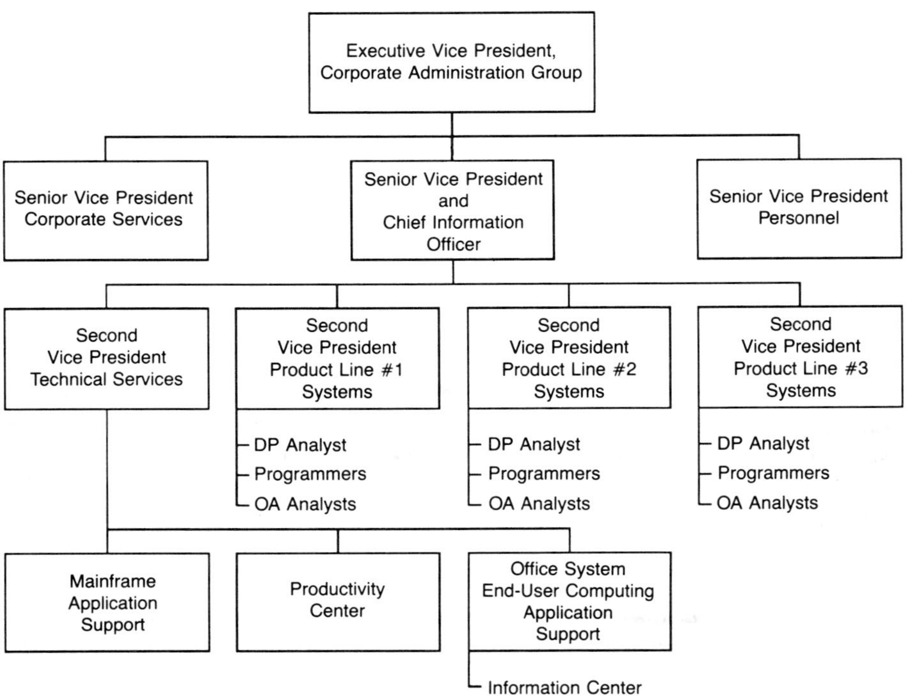

FIGURE 3-7. Sample organization chart for an insurance company.

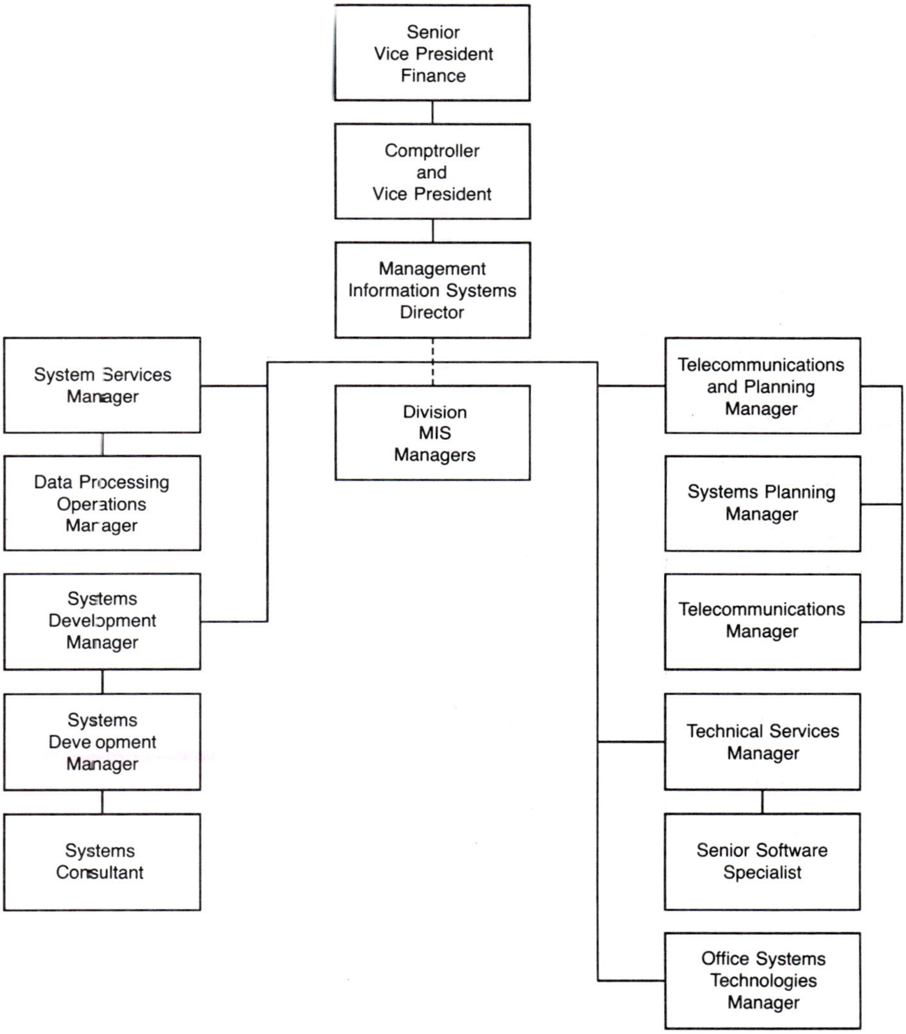

FIGURE 3-8. **Sample organization chart for a typical manufacturer.**

Many companies have resolved the issues by merging data processing and office automation into one department. These departments may have titles such as Information Systems (IS), Management Information Systems (MIS), or Information Management (IM). In 46 percent of the organizations participating in a 1980 research study on management strategies for office automation, OA reported through an IS department. Forty-two percent reported to a corporate administrative department, and 10 percent reported to other parts of the organization. One year later in the 1981 follow-up study, 60 percent of the OA groups were reporting through IS departments.

The level at which the manager of such an umbrella IS department reports has moved upward in the organization structure in recent years:

> The trend of promoting senior IS executives to top corporate positions is most conspicuous in industries that rely heavily on information or information technologies—such as insurance and other financial institutions. Other industries are also beginning to accord more importance to IS in the organization. In service, retail, and industrial corporations, top IS executives are becoming more directly involved in corporate planning or research. While it may not be essential that they be in the corporate upper echelon, IS managers should have direct access to their companies' top managers.[1]

THE CONCEPT OF INFORMATION MANAGEMENT

The concept of *information as a resource* has been gaining acceptance in the business world and has prime relevance for office automation. This concept reflects the increased value placed on information in today's competitive, international economy.

Information Resource Management (IRM) is defined as the systematic management (through organization, policy, and procedures) of information. The concept originated from the work of the President's Commission on Federal Paperwork. The commission made 770 recommendations to reduce governmental information overload. A key element of the report was that government bureaucrats should stop regarding data and information as a *free good* and should carefully consider the costs associated with developing, maintaining, processing, and storing data. The major focus of the approach was that information should be treated as a valuable resource that must be managed and conserved.

The true costs of information processing in organizations far exceed the operating costs of data processing, office processing, and records management operations.

- IRM recognizes that data and information are important resources to the organization and that they need corporate control.
- The IRM concept calls for centralized coordination of the automation and systematization of information, as differentiated from data.
- IRM advocates better support of corporate goals through a high level of coherent and useful management of information achieved through information technology, systematic analysis, policies, and procedures.

Basically, this means the following:

- Management should establish policies based on its information needs and use technology to meet those needs.
- Information management should be based on business needs rather than technology.

- Emphasis should shift from managing technology to managing information.
- Management should *plan for* technology rather than *respond to* technology.[2]

To implement information management concepts, most organizations need someone who understands that a long-term strategy is needed to integrate electronic communications, office technology, and data processing into the future workplace. Information is more than the historical by-product of an enterprise's affairs; it is the lifeblood of operations and management. David Vincent, general manager of the Institute for Information Management (IIM), a California-based educational service organization for information managers, predicted that by the end of this decade, every "enlightened" corporation will include the information asset in its financial reports. He believes that competitive pressures will force organizations to optimize the value of information. "Many companies need to create chief information officers (CIOs), just as they have created a chief financial officer." Wells Fargo and the World Bank are among leading organizations that have created the position of CIO.[3]

The Role of the Chief Information Officer (CIO)

The concept of a Chief Information Officer is still relatively new. Indeed, the acronym CIO has not yet caught on as an actual title the way CEO (Chief Executive Officer) has. The CIO is generally defined as "the highest ranking executive at the corporate, business unit, or functional division level with primary responsibility for information systems."[4] Perspectives on what has led to the emergence of this new executive role vary. John P. Imlay, Jr., chairman and CEO of Management Science America, Inc., writing in *FE: The Magazine for Financial Executives*, linked the rise of the CIO to the growing importance of information technology:

> All of this implies a changing role for the information manager. He or she will now aspire to being CEO, because in automating administration, in automating mail, in automating the standard computing functions, and tying in communication, he becomes the heartbeat of the company. And the computer is his tool. Do you doubt a new title is forthcoming? You've seen him [or her] go from data processing manager to MIS director. Now you're going to see all this coming together as he becomes a new officer in the firm and is called the chief information officer.[5]

Although most companies do not have a CIO, the role of the CIO is emerging in response to the increased importance of information technologies:

> By centralizing information management in the hands of a CIO, business can coherently manage increased office automation, the proliferation of PC's, and

> the expanding use of communications technology. . . . Furthermore, the CIO offers a focal point for determining how to control access to data, what types of end-user support are needed most, how to integrate data and telecommunications systems effectively, and what impact the implementation of new technologies will have on corporate culture. The CIO can also be a leader in strengthening his or her company's current and future competitive position by using technology wisely.[6]

STAFFING THE OFFICE AUTOMATION ORGANIZATION

Selecting the right individual to lead office automation is important. Research on strategic planning for office automation indicates that the personality of the office automation manager was more significant in achieving success than the location of the function within the organization. "This manager must assume an active role as pioneer, must create a collaborative environment that melds the mix of skills on the office automation team, and must be respected by both users and staff groups."[7]

Careful staffing of the office automation team is essential. Implementing the wide variety of OA technologies requires a wide range of skills. Evidence indicates that the most effective teams combine expertise in technology, administration, and business skills. Skills in dealing with people are a valuable asset. The work of the OA team requires collaboration with individuals in other staff functions, including data processing, administrative services, operations research, finance, and personnel departments. The OA group should be an integrating focal point rather than a competing technology group in the organization.

PLANNING FOR OFFICE AUTOMATION

To achieve maximum benefit from office automation systems, organizations need to link their systems planning to a long-range strategic plan based on business requirements. All too often, acquisition and implementation of office automation technologies are disjointed and unmanaged. In such cases, the potential for substantial benefits is unrealized. While specific applications may be effective, the overall impact of office automation in the organization may be short-changed. Achieving substantial gains in productivity, as well as information processing support, requires more than simply building and installing computer-based systems. Organizations need a business framework to guide selection among the dizzying array of mainframe, minicomputer, and microcomputer hardware and software. Addressing requirements on an application-by-application basis will not necessarily add up to office automation systems that produce significant business benefits. To be confident that their firm is addressing the appropriate applications and spending automation dollars effectively, management must develop a strategy based on business objectives. (A comprehensive discussion of planning is provided in Chapter 19 on "Strategic Planning and Office Automation.")

Moreover, the use of office automation tools in the workplace requires changes in the work behavior of people; managers, professionals, salespeople, and secretaries may need to change their habits, thinking, and values. To effect permanent changes in work behavior requires more than training in the use of a system. Patterns in the flow of work may need to be altered. Reporting relationships may shift. New standards and procedures may need to be established. Jobs may have to be redesigned and performance criteria revamped. Before managers rush out to buy the latest in office automation gadgetry and software, they must take a long, hard look at organizational and work changes that will be required to achieve intended results with the new systems. (A comprehensive discussion of organizational change theory is provided in Chapter 18.)

Cost Justification for Office Automation

The traditional return on investment (ROI), the model applied to most capital expenditures, is not always applicable to the office. The concept that the office must receive a measurable increase in output for dollars invested is not easily adapted to office functions (occasionally, word processing may be an exception). The costs of technology and automation have been dropping dramatically, while human labor costs are escalating. Consequently, the criteria applicable to the justification of projects involving automation have changed. A system that 10 years ago would have required cost-avoidance equivalent to many clerical positions, today may be easily justified by improving the productivity of relatively few individuals. Therefore, if justification is required, alternative methods are used. Among them are measures of increased quality and timeliness of products, improved service to customers, and increased quality of worklife for employees. (Cost justification plans are discussed in detail in Chapter 15 on "Measuring Productivity: Cost Justification."

CAREERS IN OFFICE AUTOMATION AND INFORMATION SYSTEMS

Many career opportunities are available in the growing field of office automation. Opportunities include (1) technical careers implementing and operating computer technology for office automation, (2) managing and operating automated office support services, and (3) related fields. Because of the similarity in technologies, lines between office automation and data processing careers are quite fluid. Individuals who have strong technical skills and strong human relations skills commonly move back and forth between these two fields. A career path that has combined experience in both office automation and data processing provides especially strong preparation for higher-level Information Systems positions. The resulting breadth of experience provides the broad perspective required for high-level information systems management.

Technical Careers

Technical careers in office automation include programmers, systems analysts, computer operators, and telecommunications specialists. A growing need also exists for office automation managers. Technical careers in office automation require a combination of training and experience in computer skills, systems analysis, organizational behavior, and business knowledge. Courses of study appropriate for the student pursuing a technical career in office automation include the following:

- Data processing concepts.
- Basic and COBOL programming languages.
- Fourth-generation languages, such as FOCUS, Statistical Analysis System (SAS), Easytrieve, RAMIS, APL, QBE, ADR Data Query and Data Reporter, and others.
- Data communications and telecommunications.
- Systems analysis.
- Project management.
- Business management.
- Organizational behavior.
- Business communications.
- Office automation or office systems.
- Administrative management or automated office systems management.
- Ergonomics or human factors.
- Microcomputer applications (spreadsheets, graphics, database, project management).
- Word processing.

Figure 3-9 presents a sampling of technical job titles for individuals with office automation skills.

Addressing the need for professional careers in office systems, the Office Systems Research Association (OSRA) developed a model curriculum for undergraduate office systems programs. This model curriculum is outlined in Figure 3-10a. Core courses for the model curriculum are described in Figure 3-10b, and optional courses are described in Figure 3-10c.

FIGURE 3-9. Sampling of job titles for individuals with office automation skills.

High-Level Positions

1. Vice-President, Information Systems
2. Information Resource Manager or Director, Information Resource Management
3. Director of Office Automation
4. Information Center Manager
5. Information Database Manager
6. Training Director for Information Systems
7. Information Systems/Library Administrator
8. Professor of Information Systems or Office Systems
9. President, Office Systems Consulting Firm
10. Research Associate

FIGURE 3-9.
(continued)

Mid- and Entry-Level Positions

1. Office Automation Project Manager
2. Office Systems Analyst
3. Office Systems Programmer Analyst
4. Office Systems Programmer
5. Office Automation Consultant
6. Image Processing Specialist
7. Office Environment Specialist
8. Technical Support Specialist
    - Local Area Networks
    - Storage/Retrieval (optical disks)
    - Video Conferencing and Computer Conferencing
    - Decision Support Systems
    - Graphic Display Systems
    - Electronic Mail
    - Voice Processing
    - Tracking Systems
    - Database Integrity
    - Micrographics
    - Reprographics
9. Security Specialist
10. System Trainer/Course Designer
11. Computer-Based Training Author
12. Information Center Consultant
13. Microcomputer Training Specialist
14. Product Support Manager
15. Desktop Publishing Center Manager
16. Word Processing Operations Manager
17. End-User Support Specialist
18. Vendor Sales Representative

FIGURE 3-10. Office Systems Research Association (OSRA) Model Curriculum: Undergraduate programs for office systems.

Core Courses

OS-1	Office Systems and Technologies
OS-2	Office Systems Planning
OS-3	Office Systems Implementation
OS-4	Office Systems Applications
OS-5	Integrated Office Systems

Elective Courses

OS-6	Telecommunications
OS-7	Administrative Communication
OS-8	Training and Development in Office Systems
OS-9	Special Topics in Office Systems
OS-10	Professional Practice in Office Systems

FIGURE 3-10. (continued)

a. Model curriculum structure for office systems education.

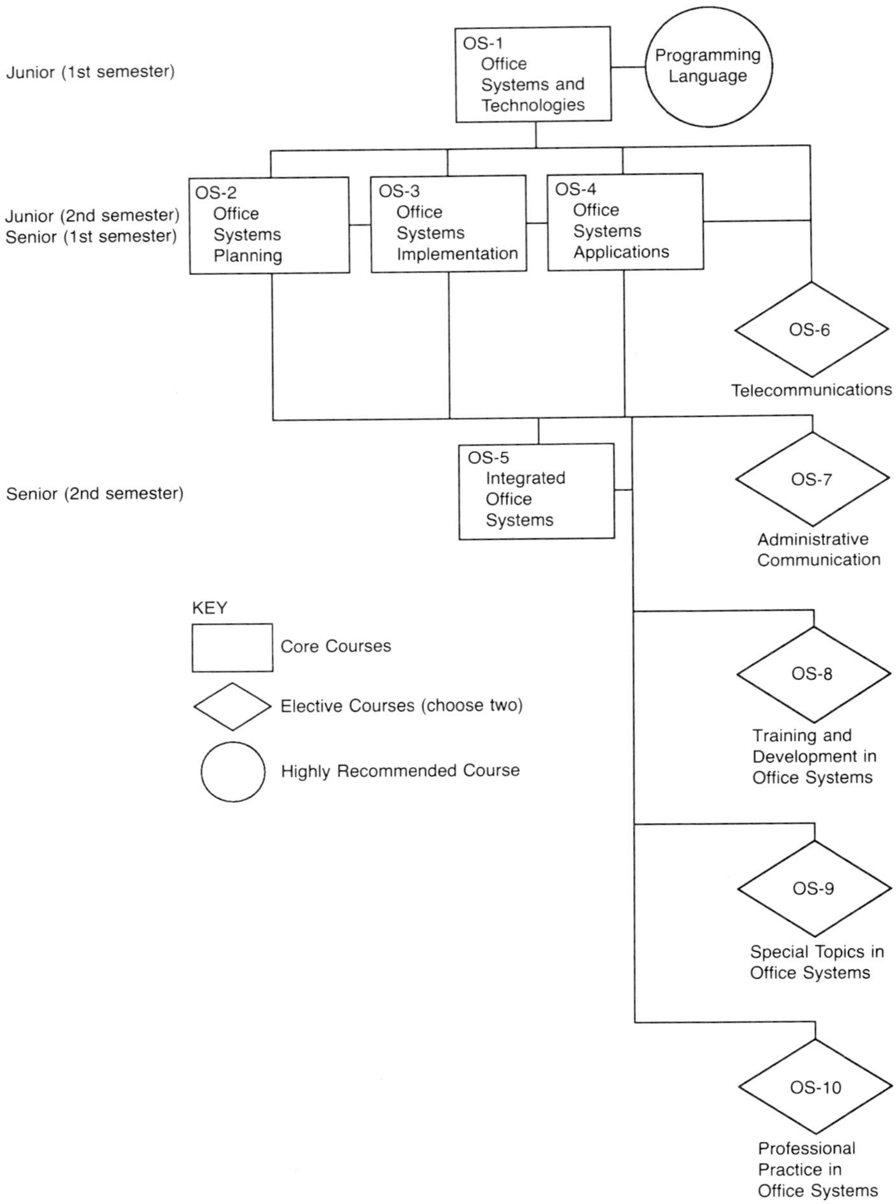

b. Office systems core courses.

OS-1 Office Systems and Technologies

An overview of office systems—technology, people, and procedures—within organizational and environmental contexts. Improvement of productivity through appropriate application of office tools and techniques (manual or electronic) is stressed. Major hardware and software that support information creation, storage, retrieval, manipulation, and distribution are covered.

OS-2 Office Systems Planning

Planning for office systems development with particular emphasis upon employee and work group interactions. Application of proven methodologies through case or field-based projects. Office systems productivity assessment. Special attention to intergroup needs as related to end-user, departmental, divisional, organizational goals. Prerequisite: Office Systems and Technologies (OS-1)

OS-3 Office Systems Implementation

The study of development and implementation processes, tactics, and strategies based upon office systems planning results. Application of tested methodologies through case or field-based projects. Particular attention is devoted to development of end-user office support systems. Prerequisite: Office Systems and Technologies (OS-1)

OS-4 Office Systems Applications

Applications of office automation technologies from the user perspective to enhance productivity of office employees— executive/managerial, professional, and support personnel. Relationship of automated technologies and corporate goals. Comparison and evaluation techniques for appropriate selection of hardware and software. An introduction to telecommunications. Prerequisite: Office Systems and Technologies (OS-1)

OS-5 Integrated Office Systems

Capstone course of the Office Systems curriculum. Synthesis and application of concepts related to current office systems topics. Prerequisites: Office Systems Planning (OS-2), Office Systems Implementation (OS-3), and Office Systems Applications (OS-4)

c. Office systems optional courses.

OS-6 Telecommunications

An introduction to telecommunications in office systems. Topics include telephony, data codes, protocols, network architectures, local area networks, communications media, hardware, and software. Management issues and practical applications are an integral part of this course. Emphasis will be on the application of telecommunications to facilitate information interchange in whatever form the information takes: voice, data, text, or image. Prerequisite: Office Systems Applications (OS-4)

OS-7 Administrative Communication

Applications of communication theory, human relations concepts, research methods, and information technology to the internal communi-

FIGURE 3-10.

c. Office systems optional courses (continued).

cation of professionals who work in environments with automated information and communication systems. Survey of organizational communication climate; analysis of communication tasks and audiences; problem/decision definition and analysis; primary and secondary research methodology; oral and written reporting; applications; oral and written reports, system-related documents (reports, proposals, procedures), systems documentation for users; human factors of communication in a technological environment.

OS-8 Training and Development in Office Systems

Application of theories of learning and instructional development to the education and training of employees in office systems. Topics include instructional design; strategy; technology; and the implementation, evaluation, and management of training in an organizational environment.

OS-9 Special Topics in Office Systems

The study of advanced concepts and issues relative to office systems. Content will vary according to the needs and interests of the students, keeping in mind current technological advancements and office systems management concerns.

OS-10 Professional Practice in Office Systems

An internship or cooperative work experience supervised by a faculty member. Provides an opportunity for students to gain practical work experience while working in a private business or government agency.

Office Support Careers

Careers in office administration and office support also include a broad range of options in word processing, administrative support, and secretarial, records management, and office services. Some of these career opportunities are listed in Figure 3-11. Individuals preparing for careers in these areas should take courses in some or all of the following areas:

- Data processing concepts
- Word processing
- Administrative management or automated office systems management
- Office automation systems
- Records management and forms design
- Stenography or machine transcription
- Accounting
- Business law
- Business communications
- General business operations and management

Office Services Manager
Manager of Word Processing Systems
Supervisor of Word Processing
Word Processing Specialist
Manager, Administrative Support
Administrative Assistant
Secretary
Marketing Service Representative
Records Manager
Records Clerk/Trainee
Micrographics Supervisor
Micrographics Technician
Telecommunications Manager
Electronic Mail Supervisor

FIGURE 3-11. Careers in office and administrative services.

Careers in Related Fields

Careers in fields related to office automation are also increasing. Various career opportunities are available in firms that offer products and services for the office automation marketplace. Positions are available with equipment vendors, furniture companies, supplies dealers, software vendors, and management consulting groups. Some of these career opportunities are described in Figure 3-12.

Sales Manager for computer or office products firm
Market Support Manager
Sales Representative of OA hardware, software, and services
Office automation software programming
Teacher/Instructor of Office Systems

FIGURE 3-12. Office automation-related fields: Typical job opportunities.

An excellent way to learn more about jobs in the office systems field is to monitor the job advertisements in newspapers. Figure 3-13 provides a composite of some recent job openings advertised in newspapers in the Northeast.

FIGURE 3-13.
A sampling of advertisements for jobs in the office systems field.

SYSTEMS ANALYST

We're one of the oldest, largest and most progressive trade associations in the world. More than that, we're a sophisticated research organization, a storehouse of statistical information, a consulting organization, a human resource development firm, and we operate on a worldwide basis.

If you have a working knowledge of DEC VAX/VMS and DEC software, along with strong written and oral communication skills, then this could be the position for you. This position requires analysis of diverse office environments and designing, programming, implementing and maintaining systems developed. Knowledge of All-In-One software would be highly desirable.

We offer a pleasant working environment in a park-like setting, a competitive salary and benefit package including medical, dental and vision, tuition reimbursement and a company-paid pension plan along with the opportunity to use your creativity within a professional setting.

To explore this opportunity further, send resume with salary requirement in confidence, to:

Paul D. Martin, Employment Coordinator

LIMRA INTERNATIONAL

8 Farm Springs Road, Farmington, CT 06032

an equal opportunity employer m/f/h

INSURANCE

Business Automation Analyst

Hanover Insurance, one of the top 40 companies in the Property/Casualty industry, offers an opportunity for an experienced insurance professional to join our National Office Systems Department.

A Business Automation Analyst is needed to work on the Management Reporting Systems Project. Responsibilities will include coordination of data processing related projects and work as a user liaison between systems development and the functional insurance departments within the company.

The ideal candidate will have a college degree, 3+ years experience in the insurance industry, and a desire to become part of an automation development team. Prior experience with management reporting systems is a plus.

Hanover offers a unique working environment that places emphasis on the individual contribution to the continuing development and success of our company.

Please send your resume and salary history to:

Kathleen T. Kilcoyne.

HANOVER INSURANCE

MANAGER OFFICE TECHNOLOGY

Local, well established company with successful track record has experienced half a decade of continuous growth. Currently seeking professional to effectively recommend and carry out R&D projects within PC/office automation area, develop, publish and enforce standards and policies, training programs nationwide and set direction and manage support staff. BS or BA plus 3-5 years managing PC function in DP or equivalent years of experience required. We ask for your commitment to success and we will give you individual recognition and reward. Submit resume and salary history in confidence to:

COURANT BOX 03845M
Hartford, CT 06115

Equal Opportunity Employer M/F

FIGURE 3-13. (continued)

INFORMATION CENTER PROFESSIONALS

Hamilton Standard is seeking highly motivated professionals to work in its well-established Information Center. Professionals experienced in FOCUS, SQL, microcomputer and/or office automation technology will be working in a state-of-the-art environment.

You will be using hardware that includes IBM, DEC, and WANG. Join us in exploring networking, document handling and decision support for a variety of users. A BS in Computer Science or related field is desirable. Equivalent experience will also be considered.

Find out more about the advantages waiting for you at Hamilton Standard. We offer a salary commensurate with experience, outstanding company benefits and advancement potential. Send your resume with salary history to: Mr. William Podrasky, Hamilton Standard, Windsor Locks, CT 06096.

UNITED TECHNOLOGIES
HAMILTON STANDARD

Extraordinary achievements . . .
through hands-on creativity

An Equal Opportunity Employer
U.S. Citizenship Required

SR. MICROCOMPUTER SYSTEMS ANALYST

Applicant will design and implement foundation software/hardware req. applications for use in countries served by Carribbean, Central & South America banking group including ML/CITIACCESS eletronic banking applications and CITIMARKETS info systems. Applicants will review, analyze, evaluate and recommend microcomputer systems operations systems and special routines for specific applications, design new applications and collaborate in their programming; & train microcomputer technical staff. Bachelor's of Engr. in electrical/electronics. 2 yrs exp or related exp as Software Engineer developing systems software on microcomputers using "C" and assembler languages. $34,240/yr.; 40 hrs/wk. Send resume to: Job Service of Florida, 105 E. Broward Blvd, Ft Lauderdale, FL 33301. Attn: J.O. #FL 5748213.

ASSOCIATE INFORMATION CENTER CONSULTANT

Reporting to the Information Center/Office Systems Manager, you'll become part of a team advising management and project teams on the best use of hardware/software in the area of personal computing and timesharing.

You'll be expected to maintain an in-depth working knowledge of technology, including software/hardware, communications, database management and distributed processing techniques. You will also support and develop end-user computer applications.

This position requires an undergraduate degree and 4 years of Information Systems experience, with 2 years working with personal computer hardware, software and communications. Experience in the design, development and implementation of new systems in the IBM environment and working with local area networks would be a plus. This includes on-line and database systems using IBM PC, FOCUS, and VM/CMS. The selected candidate should have excellent interpersonal skills and the ability to work independently.

PROFESSIONAL DEVELOPMENT IN OFFICE SYSTEMS

Technology changes quickly. Keeping up with technological developments in the office automation field can be a full-time job. Likewise, keeping informed about issues related to organizing and managing this volatile function is a challenge.

Appendixes 1 and 2 of this text present lists of resources that the reader can use to keep abreast of state-of-the-art developments in office automation and office systems. Appendix 1 is a list of office systems professional organizations where one can find professionals to share and exchange ideas and information. Many of these organizations have local chapters or student divisions, and many also sponsor seminars, have guest lecturers at meetings, and organize annual conferences at which leaders in the organizations' specialties discuss their work and ideas with conference attendees. Annual conferences frequently result in a compendium of useful reports on the various presentations.

Appendix 2 presents a list of the titles and subscription addresses major periodical publications related to office systems and automation. The list includes both business publications and academic journals that can be used to keep informed of new issues and developments.

Keeping informed of new developments is an important responsibility for anyone in the field of office automation. The reader can use Appendix A as a starting point for places to go in search of new ideas and information.

THE PLANNED CAREER PATH

The table of information processing career paths in Figure 3-14 illustrates typical career paths in various functional areas within the category of information systems. The right-hand column lists the salary range for the job classification on a national average.

A career can generally progress up one or even two levels, laterally along any of the functional levels, and even down one level while still showing a strong career growth.

Two hypothetical career paths in information systems are described and charted in the following pages. The career path of Tom Green (fictitious name) is a classic example of a career path that could lead to a position as a director of information systems. Tom's career path is charted in Figure 3-15.[8]

INFORMATION PROCESSING CAREER PATH											
Word Processing	**Systems Analysis**	**Application Programming**	**Systems Programming**	**Computer Operations**	**Telecom-munication**	**Micro-graphics**	**Production Control**	**Data Entry**	**Database Administrator**	**Related Fields**	**Annual Salary Ranges**
	Manager Systems Analysis		Operating Systems Manager		Manager Telecom-munication				Manager	Sales Manager	$40,000–$65,000
	Lead Systems Analyst	Manager Programming	Lead Systems Programmer			Manager Micro-graphics			Database Administrator	Market Support Manager	$30,000–$45,000
	Senior Systems Analyst		Senior Systems Programmer	Manager Computer Operations	Analyst Telecom-munication					Sales Representative	$25,000–$35,000
	Systems Analyst	Lead Programmer	Programmer	Manager of Operations						Teacher / Instructor OS	$20,000–$30,000
WP Manager	Trainee Analyst	Senior Programmer	Trainee Systems		Technical Control Specialist					Customary Support Representative	$20,000–$25,000
		Programmer		Lead Operator		Shift Supervisor	Supervisor Production Control				$18,000–$22,000
Supervisor / Trainee		Trainee		Senior Operator	Analyst Trainee	Senior Equipment Operator		Supervisor Data Entry			$16,000–$20,000
Specialist / Photosetting			Program Librarian	Operator / Trainee	Internship	Micro-graphic Technician	Lead Production Control	Lead Data Entry			$14,000–$18,000
Proofreader / Operator		Team Librarian		Librarian / Proc. Post Clerk		Production Technician	Clerk / Trainee	Operator / Trainee			$12,000–$16,000
WP Trainee											$10,000–$14,000

FIGURE 3-14. Information processing career paths.

Tom started his career at the City Municipal Authority as a keypunch trainee. He was promoted to operator after six months. He worked as an operator for approximately one year. He then asked for a transfer to the Word Processing Department.

Organizationally, Tom had to take a step backward, but the opportunity to learn the technology was worth it to him. There he was promoted quickly, and over a three-year period he became an operator, proofreader, and second-shift supervisor. Realizing that his boss would never quit or be promoted, he began looking for other opportunities in the company. He took a Programmer Aptitude Test, passed it with a top score, and was placed in the programmer training program.

Training took more than one year. His new assignment as Programmer was challenging, but after two years Tom realized that he could make more money if he changed jobs. For a 20 percent increase, he left the City Municipal Authority and went to work for the Food Warehouse Company. At Food Warehouse, he quickly learned new applications but realized his interest was in systems programming. No openings were available in his company for a systems programmer, but his old company offered him a job as systems programmer trainee if he would return.

When Tom returned to the City Municipal Authority, he soon discovered that decision was a mistake. It is difficult to go back to an old company. Tom stayed for one year but never adjusted to the changed environment. He left the company once again, this time as an entry-level telecommunications specialist for Smith and Company.

Tom's years in word processing helped him to get this position because of his exposure to data communications. At Smith and Company, he has spent the last five years in several different jobs. As Manager of the Telecommunications Department, he is promoting the reorganization of several functional areas under the information systems umbrella. He sees duplication of resources at every level. He has met with the president of the company many times on the subject. The reorganization is anticipated for the first quarter of 1990, and Tom is expected to be the Director.

INFORMATION PROCESSING CAREER PATH

Word Processing	Systems Analysis	Application Programming	Systems Programming	Computer Operations	Telecommunication (13)	Micrographics	Production Control	Data Entry	Database Administrator	Related Fields	Annual Salary Ranges
	Manager Systems Analysis		Operating Systems Manager		Manager Telecommunication (12)				Manager	Sales Manager	\$40,000–\$65,000
	Lead Systems Analyst	Manager Programming	Lead Systems Programmer			Manager Micrographics			Database Administrator	Market Support Manager	\$30,000–\$45,000
	Senior Systems Analyst		Senior Systems Programmer	Manager Computer Operations	Analyst Telecommunication (11)					Sales Representative	\$25,000–\$35,000
	Systems Analyst	Lead Programmer	Programmer	Manager of Operations						Teacher / Instructor OS	\$20,000–\$30,000
WP Manager	Trainee Analyst	Senior Programmer	Trainee Systems (9)		Technical Control Specialist (10)					Customary Support Representative	\$20,000–\$25,000
		Programmer (8)		Lead Operator		Shift Supervisor	Supervisor Production Control				\$18,000–\$22,000
(6) Supervisor / Trainee		Trainee (7)		Senior Operator	Analyst Trainee	Senior Equipment Operator		Supervisor Data Entry			\$16,000–\$20,000
Specialist / Photosetting			Program Librarian	Operator / Trainee	Internship	Micrographic Technician	Lead Production Control	Lead Data Entry			\$14,000–\$18,000
Proofreader (5) (4) / Operator		Team Librarian		Librarian / Proc. Post Clerk		Production Technician	Clerk / Trainee	Operator (2) (1) / Trainee			\$12,000–\$16,000
WP Trainee (3)											\$10,000–\$14,000

FIGURE 3-15. Example of a career path in information systems.

The career path of Susan Andrews (fictitious name) is a second example of a career path in information systems. Susan's career path is charted in Figure 3-16.

While completing her bachelor's degree in Office Systems at New York University, Susan accepted an internship at the local telephone company, where she worked on the Telenet project. Telenet is a voice and data network that connects many colleges and businesses in the Northeast. Susan's responsibilities were to work with those colleges and businesses to identify and implement appropriate applications.

When she received her degree, Susan accepted a permanent position with the telephone company as a Telecommunications Analyst Trainee. After two years, however, she wanted to try programming. Though successful, Susan soon discovered that this job was not for her; she wanted to work more directly with customers. She learned of a new opportunity at Voicenet for a Customer Service Representative. In this position, Susan worked with clients, assessing their telecommunications requirements and recommending voice-mail networks. She became more interested in expanding the scope of the technologies with which she was working. When the company announced an opening for a Systems Analyst, Susan applied and was hired for the job.

In her job as Systems Analyst, she worked with Voicenet sales staff, helping them to identify customer telecommunications needs. She developed considerable expertise in microcomputer applications and local area networks. She was promoted to Senior Systems Analyst and continued working on customer service projects for four years. At this point she had to make a decision to either stay on the technical career path or move into management. Susan opted for management and was offered an opportunity to manage a new office automation project within the company. She decided to accept the offer.

As a Project Manager, Susan was responsible for implementing the new office system for the Sales Department. As part of this project, she had a staff of four people, including two analysts and two trainers. Her next project assignment was to establish an information center to meet the needs of the growing number of microcomputer uses and mainframe end-user computing tools.

Knowing that the potential for promotion was limited, after several years Susan began to look for opportunities outside the company. When a friend told her of an opening at a large manufacturing firm for a Director of Office Systems, Susan applied. Her broad background with data communications, microcomputers, and mainframes gave her the experience she needed to succeed in this position. Currently, she has three project managers reporting to her: one for office systems, one for communications, and one for the Information Center.

INFORMATION PROCESSING CAREER PATH

Word Processing	Systems Analysis	(9) Application Programming	Systems Programming	Computer Operations	Telecommunication	Micrographics	Production Control	Data Entry	Database Administrator	Related Fields	Annual Salary Ranges
	Manager Systems Analysis (8)		Operating Systems Manager		Manager Telecommunication				Manager	Sales Manager	\$40,000–\$65,000
	Lead Systems Analyst (7)	Manager Programming	Lead Systems Programmer			Manager Micrographics			Database Administrator	Market Support Manager	\$30,000–\$45,000
	Senior Systems Analyst (6)		Senior Systems Programmer	Manager Computer Operations	Analyst Telecommunication					Sales Representative	\$25,000–\$35,000
	Systems Analyst (5)	Lead Programmer	Programmer	Manager of Operations						Teacher / Instructor OS	\$20,000–\$30,000
WP Manager	Trainee Analyst	Senior Programmer	Trainee Systems		Technical Control Specialist					Customary Support Representative (4)	\$20,000–\$25,000
		(3) Programmer		Lead Operator		Shift Supervisor	Supervisor Production Control				\$18,000–\$22,000
Supervisor / Trainee		Trainee		Senior Operator	Analyst Trainee (2)	Senior Equipment Operator		Supervisor Data Entry			\$16,000–\$20,000
Specialist / Photosetting			Program Librarian	Operator / Trainee	Internship (1)	Micrographic Technician	Lead Production Control	Lead Data Entry			\$14,000–\$18,000
Proofreader / Operator		Team Librarian		Librarian / Proc. Post Clerk		Production Technician	Clerk / Trainee	Operator / Trainee			\$12,000–\$16,000
WP Trainee											\$10,000–\$14,000

FIGURE 3-16. Example of a career path in information systems.

SUMMARY

Chapter 3 discussed how responsibility for office automation systems is delegated and managed within an organization. The terms office automation (OA), office systems (OS), office automation systems (OAS), and automated office systems (AOS) are frequently used interchangeably when referring to computer systems designed for office applications and end-user computing. Tools that come under the office automation umbrella generally include word processing, end-user computing (spreadsheets, database, fourth-generation languages, etc.), computer graphics, decision support, electronic mail and messages, copiers, image processing, storage and retrieval, and printer technologies. The department within an enterprise that has responsibility for office automation may be called an *office automation department*, an *office systems department*, or similar terminologies.

Office automation can be distinguished from data processing primarily by orientation and approach to business problems, rather than by differences among technologies. Office automation introduces computer technology directly into the office work environment as a tool to employees in working with the information they need in carrying out their jobs. In contrast, data processing transfers responsibility for information processing to a technical data center. Office automation emphasizes flexibility, practicality, and quick responses to problems. Objectives focus on optimizing people rather than technologies. The differences between the two environments are summarized in Figure 3-2.

Practices for delegating responsibility for office automation vary among organizations. The predominant trend is to create a separate technical department that, along with data processing and communications, reports to an information systems executive. The level at which that executive reports within the organization structure has been moving upward in recent years as the role of information systems in organizations has grown more significant.

The right individual to lead office automation is more important than the location of the function within the organization. The OA manager must assume an active role as a change agent, collaborate effectively with various staff groups, coordinate the skills of the office automation team, and understand the business requirements.

To achieve maximum benefit from office automation systems, organizations need to develop long-range strategic plans based on business requirements. Traditional return-on-investment (ROI) methodologies for justifying capital expenditures are not always applicable to office automation because many of the benefits for office work are difficult to quantify.

The concept of information as a resource has been gaining acceptance in the business world. This concept recognizes the increased value placed on information in today's competitive, international economy. It also recognizes the costs associated with developing, processing, maintaining, storing, and using that information.

Various career opportunities are available in the growing field of office systems. Opportunities include (1) technical careers, such as office systems analysts, project managers, programmers, and trainers; (2) careers in office support services, such as administrative managers, records managers, word processing supervisors, administrative assistants, and secretaries; and (3) related careers, such as marketing support representative or sales manager for an office products firm.

DISCUSSION QUESTIONS

1. Compare and contrast the functions of data processing and office systems in an organization.
2. Is office automation typically a line or a staff function? Explain.
3. "MIS is to DP as OS is to WP." Do you agree or disagree with this statement?
4. Which key areas of study make an office systems degree program different from a data processing degree program?
5. Most OS managers and others on an OS career path have had little formal education in office systems. Why? How are colleges and universities responding to this situation?
6. Describe the concept of information management. Of what importance is this concept to office automation?
7. Discuss the role of the CIO. In which types of organizations does one see such a position?
8. Using the list of careers on pages 72–73, develop a career ladder that an office systems graduate could follow.

APPLICATION EXERCISES

1. Interview the office systems manager (or equivalent) in a local organization. Ask that person to describe his or her career path. Exchange this biography with others in your class. What characteristics (if any) do the various career paths have in common?
2. Select one of the OS-related organizations listed in Appendix 1. Write a short paper describing the history of the organization and profiling its current membership.

SUGGESTED READINGS

Cardinali, Richard. "Business School Graduates: Do They Meet the Needs of MIS Professionals?" *Words* (March–April 1988), pp. 33–35.

Office Systems Research Journal (Fall 1986). Special Curriculum Issue.

Stitt, Wanda. "An Investigation of Office Automation and Office Systems in Leading California Companies," *Proceedings of the Seventh Annual Office Systems Research Conference* (1988), pp. 196–197.

Thomas, Edward, and O'Connor, Bridget. "PhD Meets OIS," *Words* (August–September 1986), pp. 19–21, 38.

OFFICE SYSTEMS TECHNOLOGIES: The Hardware

PART **2**

If the automobile industry had made as much progress in the past 25 years as the computer industry, one writer has theorized that you could "buy a Rolls-Royce for $2.75, it would drive three million miles to the gallon, and it would deliver enough power to drive the Queen Elizabeth II. And, if you were interested in miniaturization, you could place half a dozen of them on a pinhead."[1]

Progress in the computer industry has had far-reaching effects in the office. Advancements in microcircuitry chips, originally designed for science and engineering, have led to computer applications far surpassing their original purpose of performing rapid calculations. Basic office functions, including word processing, records management, and communications services, have changed markedly as a result of progress in computer technologies and their integration into viable office systems.

One also needs to know where one is to know where one is going. This unit provides the reader with basic information on the wide spectrum of technologies known as "office technologies" or "office automation" and discusses their evolution—past, present, and future.

Chapter 4, "Computer Systems," examines the basics of computer systems. This chapter gives the reader a basic understanding of how computers operate. Included in Chapter 4 is a discussion of computers by category, purpose, and size. Operating systems, applications software, and magnetic storage media are also covered.

Chapter 5, "Peripherals: Input Devices," examines alternative ways of entering information into a computer system. This chapter discusses three categories of input media: (1) visual display terminal technologies such as the mouse and light pen, (2) typewriters used in conjunction with character recognition technologies, and (3) dictation equipment.

Chapter 6, "Peripherals: Image Technologies," discusses alternatives to magnetic storage media. Micrographics and the optical digital data disk are highlighted in this chapter.

Chapter 7, "Peripherals: Printers and Copiers," provides the "paper connection" for system output and distribution. Despite predictions of the paperless office, paper continues to be an essential output medium, and its use actually increases year to year. Technological considerations related to understanding how the technologies work, as well as listings of what to look for in selecting printers and copiers, are also discussed.

Chapter 8, "Communications Technologies," shows how office technologies can be linked to establish integrated office systems. Topics in this chapter include telephone systems, local area networks, satellite communications, and teleconferencing systems.

Chapter 9, "Artificial Intelligence," explains the concept of artificial intelligence (AI). This chapter explains what artificial intelligence is and describes how AI is being applied today and how it may be used in the future.

When studying these chapters, the reader should keep in mind that a given technology may logically fit into more than one chapter, but its location in the text has been chosen to highlight the technology and, at the same time, show its relationship to other technologies.

COMPUTER SYSTEMS

CHAPTER

4

OBJECTIVES

After completing this chapter, the reader should be able to meet the following objectives:

- Define a computer by its purpose, category, and size.
- Distinguish between ROM and RAM.
- List characteristics that make a terminal "intelligent."
- Compare vector, raster-scan, and shadow-mask VDT technologies.
- Appraise the potential for flat screen displays.
- Label the four sections of a keyboard.
- Explain the difference between serial and parallel interfaces.
- Differentiate systems programs from applications programs.
- Contrast magnetic tape with magnetic disk storage media.
- List characteristics of disk packs, floppy disks, and hard disks.
- Select an appropriate computer systems classification for an identified processing need of a given organization.
- Summarize the differences between mainframe computers and minicomputers, and between minicomputers and microcomputers.
- Understand the role of the standalone word processor in organizations today.
- Describe features of integrated office systems (IOS) products.

KEY TERMS

computer
general-purpose computer
special-purpose computer
mainframe computer
minicomputer
microcomputer
digital computer
analog computer
hybrid computer
computer hardware
central processing unit (CPU)
assembly language
assembler
low-level language
high-level language
code
statement
syntax
compiler
interpreter
systems program
documentation

arithmetic logic unit (ALU)
control unit
architecture
read only memory (ROM)
random access memory (RAM)
visual display terminal
dumb terminal
smart terminal
intelligent terminal
vector display
raster-scan display
shadow-mask display
liquid crystal display (LCD)
gas plasma display
electroluminescent display
computer software
programming language
machine language
batch processing
interactive processing
real-time processing
processing program
utility program
applications program
magnetic tape
disk pack
hard sectoring
soft sectoring
initialization
formatting
floppy disk
hard disk
standalone word processor
shared-logic word processor
integrated office systems

INTRODUCTION

Computer systems are the heart of office automation (OA). Understanding computer systems is the basis for identifying office automation needs and for selecting the appropriate equipment to meet those needs. While the OA professional does not necessarily have to be a technical guru, knowledge of basic computer technology is essential.

After a brief overview, this chapter describes major computer system components. Next, it explains software programs and magnetic storage media. Finally, details are given on three general-purpose computers—the mainframe, the minicomputer, and the microcomputer—and one special-purpose computer, the word processor. For those who have studied computers, Chapter 4 should serve as a review to clarify concepts and put facts into perspective.

COMPUTERS TODAY

A computer, very simply, is a machine that uses electrical signals to perform work. Work may consist of calculating numbers, producing text, drawing pictures, operating machinery, or a host of other tasks. Computers are often classified by purpose, category, and size.

Business offices primarily use *general-purpose* digital computers and some special-purpose computers. A general-purpose computer is capable of performing a wide variety of applications. The same computer may be capable of performing payroll, billing, inventory control, word processing, and many other tasks. A *special-purpose* computer, as its name implies, is designed to process one specific application. Dedicated word processors, discussed later in this chapter, are one type of special-purpose computer.

Its category identifies the types of applications the computer is capable of doing. Generally, when people use the term *computer,* they assume a specific category: the *digital computer.* Digital computers count discrete units, such as numbers, and are generally used for processing business data. The less familiar *analog computers,* on the other hand, record and process continuous values such as voltages, temperatures, and speeds. Analog computers are used as measuring devices by the scientific community and in manufacturing operations. A *hybrid computer* combines the digital and the analog—it is capable of processing both discrete and continuous forms of data. Because digital computers are generally used for processing business data, the term computer is used synonymously with digital computer throughout this text.

The various sizes of computers will be discussed in detail later in this chapter, but a brief description of mainframes, minis, and micros will be presented at this point. *Mainframes* are large, expensive, and extremely powerful. Generally housed in specially designed rooms, mainframes require highly trained personnel for programming and operation. *Minicomputers* (minis) are smaller, less expensive, and less powerful than mainframes. Manufacturers dubbed them *minicomputers* when they were introduced in the 1960s because of their size, relative to mainframes. *Microcomputers* (micros), also called *personal computers* (PCs) or *home computers,* are even smaller, much less expensive desktop machines. Introduced in the 1970s, they are called *microcomputers* because of their small size.

COMPUTER HARDWARE

A computer system consists of physical equipment, called *hardware,* and the instructions, or *programs,* that make the computer work; these are called *software.* The component referred to as the *computer* is actually the *central processing unit* (CPU), or "system unit" or "processor." The *data* that goes into a computer is called *input.* Input is *processed,* or manipulated, to produce *output.* Anything that comes out of the computer is called *output.*

To be used, the CPU must be connected to computer *peripherals,* which are the input and output devices. Peripherals allow the user to put data into the central processing unit in order to view or record the results of processing. The main peripheral components of every computer system are the *media* used for storage, the *storage unit(s),* the *video display terminal,* and the *keyboard.* The connection, or *channel,* between the CPU and a peripheral is called an *interface.*

The Central Processing Unit

The central processing unit (CPU) is the "brain" of a computer system. It controls the activities of the computer and consists of three components: the *arithmetic logic unit,* the *control unit,* and the *internal memory.* Figure 4-1 illustrates how the components interrelate. The internal construction of the CPU, the connection and organization of the internal circuitry, is called the *architecture.* In large computers, the central processing unit is comprised of many processors and circuits; in a microcomputer, the central processing unit is contained on one chip, or *microprocessor.* The architecture of the components differs from one model of computer to another, but the components' functions are always the same.

FIGURE 4-1. Components of the central processing unit.

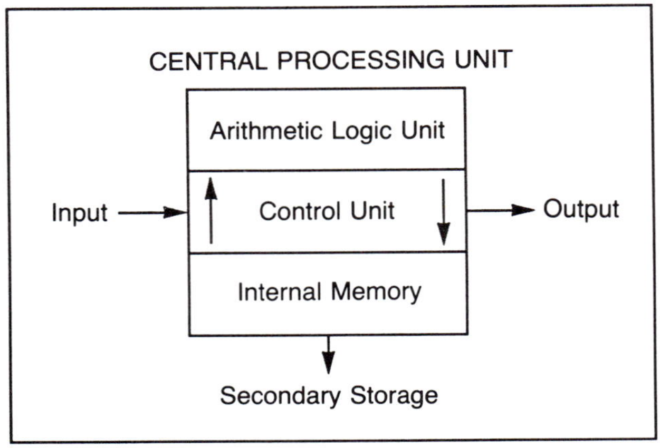

The Arithmetic Logic Unit

The arithmetic logic unit (ALU) performs arithmetic computations (addition, subtraction, multiplication, division) and logical operations (comparisons) to determine if one number is equal to, greater than, or less than another number. While the ALU can perform only one calculation at a time, it works at an incredibly fast speed. Since most internal processing involves calculations or comparisons, the capabilities of a computer generally depend upon the design and capabilities of the ALU. It should be noted that the ALU only performs calculations; it does not store data.

The Control Unit

The control unit directs the activities in the CPU. Acting much like a traffic cop, it sequences operations and directs the flow of data to and from input and output devices. The control unit interprets the instructions of a stored software program and produces signals, or commands, to circuits to perform the instructions. In mainframes and minicomputers, the control unit is an integrated collection of subsystems, each consisting of programs that perform specific duties.

Internal Memory

A computer's internal memory (also known as internal storage, main storage, or primary storage) stores software programs and data during processing by the ALU and control unit. Data is transferred from an input device to internal memory, where it is held for processing. During processing, internal memory holds intermediate and final results of ALU calculations and data manipulations. These results are then passed by the control unit to an output device (discussed later in this chapter).

The internal memory of most late-model computers consists of miniature integrated circuits. These integrated circuits are built into tiny chips of semiconductor material through a complex manufacturing process. They are referred to as *semiconductor random access memory* (RAM). RAM is volatile: if the power goes off, data in RAM is erased. Therefore, RAM is sometimes also referred to as *temporary memory.* RAM offers more speed, smaller size, and lower cost than earlier storage technologies.

Many large computers still use a form of internal memory called *magnetic core storage,* a series of donut-shaped rings that are negatively or positively charged. Unlike the volatile RAM semiconductor memory, magnetic core storage retains its magnetism indefinitely, until deliberately changed, even when the power is off.

In addition to their RAM internal memory, microcomputers generally have a permanent *read only memory (ROM)* chip, which stores initial start-up instructions and other routines for the CPU. The ROM microprogramming is supplied by the computer manufacturer, and typically cannot be altered by users. ROM is *nonvolatile,* meaning that when the electric power is off, its contents remain.

Two special kinds of ROM *can* be modified by a programmer to meet special requirements: *programmable* and *erasable.* While programmable ROM (PROM) can be modified only once, erasable PROM (EPROM) can be erased with ultraviolet light and then reprogrammed any number of times.

The amount of memory the computer has depends upon the CPU's architecture. The size of a computer's internal memory is identified by the number of its discrete, uniquely addressable memory locations. These locations are measured in *bytes* (pronounced *bites*) or, more conveniently, *kilobytes* (K) or *megabytes* (M). A kilobyte is approximately 1000 bytes, or precisely 1024 bytes (2 to the 10th power). Generally, 1000 is used as an approximation for expressing memory capacity. Thus one refers to "64K of memory" even though the exact figure is 65,536, or 256K, which is actually 262,144 bytes. A megabyte is approximately 1000K (i.e., 1024K) bytes, or 1,048,576 storage locations. Internal memory ranges from 16K in microcomputers to 128 megabytes in mainframe computers, to a gigabyte (approximately 1 billion bytes) in a supercomputer.

Bytes also come in different sizes, or word lengths, that are measured in bits. (A *bit* is an acronym for *b*inary dig*it*, the smallest unit of data in binary representation.) A byte may consist of a word length of 4 bits, 8 bits, 16 bits, 32 bits, or 64 bits, depending on the architecture of the computer. Thus it is important to know the unit of measure when talking about amounts of storage. For example, 256K of 32-bit memory has twice the capacity of 256K of 16-bit memory.

When more capacity is needed for processing than is available in the computer's internal memory, the data or instructions are stored on *secondary,* or *auxiliary, storage units.* The data is retrieved from secondary storage when needed and is then returned. This process is considerably slower than working with data in internal memory.

Interfaces

To be used, the CPU must be connected to peripheral devices, used for input and output (I/O), by a channel, the interface. Binary data from the CPU travels through the interface to the peripheral device. This data must be in a prescribed format for the peripheral to "understand" what it is to do.

Each interface requires a *port,* where data enters and exits the processor. The peripheral is connected to the port by a cable. Two common interfaces are *serial* and *parallel.* Serial interfaces, such as the commonly used RS232, transfer data as a series of bits, one after the other. Parallel interfaces, on the other hand, transfer groups of bits simultaneously. Figure 4-2 shows the back of a personal computer with an exposed printer port (interface). (More detail is included about connecting devices to computers in Chapter 8, "Communications Technologies.")

FIGURE 4-2. Printer port on a personal computer.

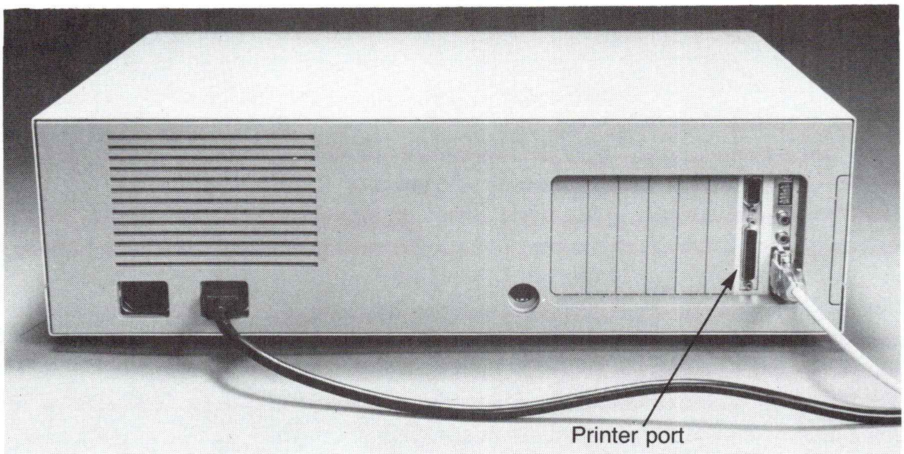

Visual Display Terminals

The term *visual display terminal* (VDT), or simply *terminal,* is generally applied to the combination of a *monitor* and a *keyboard,* although the keyboard is usually a separate unit, connected by cable. (The keyboard is discussed later in this chapter.) The VDT monitor, or *screen,* is a device that electronically displays text or graphics. VDTs provide the visual medium for reviewing, editing, and manipulating data that is entered or stored in a computer system. The VDT is an input device and a "soft" output device; that is, it produces electronic output rather than printed output, which is called *hardcopy* output. When a key on the keyboard is pressed, the character is displayed on the monitor and, when directed, transmitted to the processor. Likewise, when the processor has data to present or requires additional data, the data or messages are displayed on the monitor.

A particular computer system may be limited to specific VDT models. In this case, the VDTs are *proprietary,* or vendor-specific. Older-model VDTs or special-purpose models often are built into one-piece cabinets that incorporate the keyboard. However, newer VDT models are usually designed with separate keyboards and have ergonomically designed features, such as adjustable brightness and contrast controls, adjustable heights, and tilt and swivel pedestals (see Chapter 16, "Ergonomics").

Intelligence of Terminals

VDTs are differentiated by the amount of *intelligence* they contain. A VDT may be *dumb, smart,* or *intelligent.* Intelligence refers to the ability of a VDT to be programmed to perform functions such as data editing, data conversion, or communicating with other devices before data on the display screen is transmitted to the CPU. (Usually data is transmitted by pressing the enter key on the keyboard.)

A dumb terminal has no intelligence built into it. Data is transmitted from the display screen to the processor one character at a time. Editing is limited to the ability to delete a line or a character. A smart terminal, on the other hand, transmits a full line of data to the processor at a time. Other features of smart terminals include the following:

- *A full complement of editing features that are controlled through special keys on the keyboard.* Editing includes capabilities such as tabulation; changing, inserting, or deleting characters or lines; and clearing the screen.
- *Cursor movement up, down, right, left, and home.* Home is the top left-hand corner of the screen.
- *Scrolling, or the ability to move the displayed data up, down, right, and left.*
- *Visual attributes such as highlighting and reverse video display.* Highlighting displays characters with brighter intensity. In reverse video display, the color of the characters is reversed with the color of the background.

An intelligent terminal has a built-in microprocessor that allows text displayed on the screen to be edited and manipulated. As with the smart terminal, data can be transmitted to the processor a screenful or page at a time. Typical features beyond those of smart terminals include the following:

- A *memory buffer,* or built-in memory to store data before transmission to the processor.
- *Special character sets,* such as mathematical symbols or foreign alphabets.
- A *protected fields* feature that allows certain areas of the screen to be "frozen" so that data in those areas cannot be changed.
- *Line graphics* to produce simple line drawings.
- *Function keys* (usually labeled F1, F2, etc.) that can be defined by the user. Also called *program function keys* (PF keys), they can be assigned a certain task or sequence of keystrokes. For example, a function key might be assigned to bring up "help screens" or to send a program to print with a single keystroke.

Many VDTs used for word processing have 32K or 64K of memory built into the terminal and are, therefore, considered intelligent. Users can enter and edit one or more pages of text before transmitting the document to the processor. More advanced word processing features, such as moving or copying text from one document to another or automatically checking the spelling of a document, usually require a terminal model with a minimum 64K intelligence.

Types of VDT Displays

The most common type of VDT employs cathode ray tube (CRT) technology and is similar to the display in home television sets. In fact, with the proper connections, television sets can double as VDTs; their quality, however, is generally inferior to that provided by VDTs. Diagonal screen size ranges from 9 to 24 inches. A VDT may be monochrome (white and black, green, or amber) or color. Typical VDT resolution is 300 to 800 lines, displaying 25 lines of 80 characters each, for a total of 2,000 characters. Some inexpensive displays for personal computers and television sets may be limited to line widths of 40 characters.

Video Display for Microcomputers

Three components are required to view output on a microcomputer:

1. Software drivers, which convert the application data to a format that can be used by the adapter board.
2. An adapter (controller) board, which converts the data from the way the computer works with it to the way it can be displayed on a VDT screen.
3. A video display monitor (VDT), which displays the converted data for viewing.

Software drivers are provided by the vendors with their applications packages. Their recommendations regarding proper monitor and adapter board combinations are crucial to the display and use of their product.

The number of pixels or dots on the video display screen, along with screen intensity and refresh rate, are important considerations in choosing the right monitor. The greater the number of pixels, the more finite the screen detail.

Think of the adapter board as the main support for the monitor. The type of board depends upon the type of monitor desired. If the user wants to display text on a monochrome monitor, a simple monochrome display adapter is needed. If the user needs to display text and graphics on a monochrome display screen, then a graphics adapter board is required. If the user wants to display color and graphics, a color graphics adapter and color monitor are required. Various types of color adapter boards provide varying degrees of graphics support. The types of applications, along with the level of resolution required, will dictate the proper board and monitor. An Enhanced Graphics Adapter (EGA) and monitor will satisfy most color requirements. Software vendors specify the minimum and recommended requirements to run their products.

The result that the user sees on the screen reflects the combination of the components. An improper combination of the board and monitor will provide an undesirable display or no display at all. Various types of adapter boards and the level of support provided for graphics and color are given below.

- Color Graphics Adapter (CGA) supports 640 × 200 pixels, with 4 of 16 possible colors displayed simultaneously.
- Hercules Graphics Adapter supports 720 × 350 pixels for monochrome display.
- Enhanced Graphics Adapter (EGA) supports 640 × 350 pixels, with 16 of 64 possible colors displayed simultaneously.
- MultiColor Graphics Array (MCGA) supports 640 × 480 pixels, with 256 colors simultaneously. The MCGA is built into the "mother board" on the IBM PS/2 Model 30.
- Video Graphics Adapter (VGA), for the IBM PS/2 Models 50, 60, and 80, supports 640 × 480 pixels and 250 colors from a palette of 256,000, or 720 × 400 pixel monochrome display with 17 graphics modes and 64 shades of gray. VGA will also support EGA and CGA products. As new software evolves, the VGA may set the standard for color and graphics.

Traditional VDT technologies Familiar VDTs, based on cathode ray technology (CRT), are *vector, raster-scan,* and *shadow-mask.* These VDTs differ in the way the electronic gun aims its beams from the back of the display unit.

The electronic beam in *vector displays* is aimed at the image only, not at the entire screen. *Raster-scan beams* project top to bottom and display each element of an image repetitively many times per second; this is called the *refresh rate.* The refresh rate determines the amount of flicker noticeable on the screen and, consequently, determines viewing comfort. Recommended refresh rate is a minimum of 60 times per second (60 hertz). *Shadow-mask VDTs* use three electronic light guns to emit the beam rather than the single gun in the vector and raster-scan displays.

CRT-based VDTs offer dependability and low cost. On the plus side, their brightness can be easily adjusted for viewing under varying light conditions, and they are readable from a wide range of viewing angles. Unfortunately, the technology is rather large and bulky, and results in a noticeable flicker. In addition, overall CRT quality is poor, and CRTs can display graphics but not images or pictures from digital data. Because of their low cost and dependability, however, these devices will likely dominate as the major display technology for the office, at least into the early 1990s.

A special type of cathode ray display, the bit-mapped display, improves on the limitations of most CRTs. Bit-mapped displays incorporate thousands of *pixels* (picture elements), which can be turned on and off individually. The bit-mapped display provides much sharper characters, excellent graphics, and reduced flicker. The bit-mapped monitor is used in the Apple Macintosh computer and in expensive VDT models intended for high-quality graphics display.

The high-resolution VDT The resolution of a character on a monitor is considered high if the character is clear, easy to read, and highly distinguishable from other characters on the screen. A subcategory of VDT monitor referred to as *high-res* is the newest option on the VDT market.

Figure 4-3 shows an example of a high-res screen. This screen is larger than its counterparts and typically supports the upper-end graphics array cards. The advantages of this monitor will be discussed more fully in Chapter 16, "Ergonomics." As the price of the high-res screen falls, office systems specialists are finding it easier to cost justify the larger, easier-to-read screen.

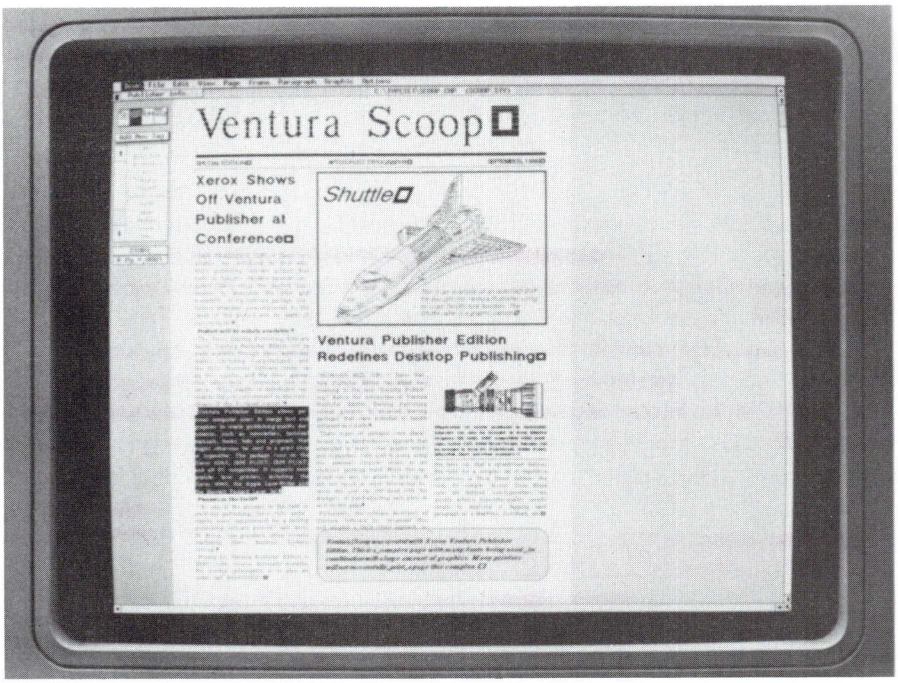

FIGURE 4-3.
A high-resolution screen: The Viking I Monitor displaying Ventura Publisher software.

Flat display technologies In addition to the standard VDT technologies, many others are being developed. The VDTs discussed above are of relatively low quality. Also, they are not appropriate for the portable computer market; they are too large and require considerable amounts of energy—too much for a single battery pack. To address quality needs and the needs of the portable computer, flat VDTs are being developed. Flat screens operate quite differently than "electronic beam" screens. Besides being smaller, flat panel displays are clearer than the standard VDT screens because they eliminate distortion around the edge of the screen. The display actually looks like a backlit slide. Because of their size and quality, flat screens are especially appealing for work stations designed for desktop use. In the future, such panels may actually be designed into desk units. Currently, their cost is several times that of standard CRTs, so their applications are limited. Some that appear to have the greatest applicability to the office market are liquid crystal, plasma panel, electroluminescent, and projection displays.

Liquid crystal displays (LCDs) Based on technologies first used in watches and clocks, LCDs are currently the leaders in flat displays, primarily because of their price; they cost one-third as much as other types of flat displays. A 9-inch liquid crystal display can be purchased for as little as $120. LCDs are cost-effective and lightweight. Battery packs may last three to four times longer on LCD technology than with other flat display technologies. Thus LCDs are considered by many experts to have the most potential for the future. Their disadvantages are primarily low contrast, narrow viewing angles, and slow responses to electrical signals. Currently, LCDs are monochrome and their display capacity is limited to 16 lines by 80 characters. However, more than 20 vendors are working on improving the quality and color capabilities of liquid crystal displays.

Gas plasma displays Also known as plasma panel or matrix display units, gas plasma offers a sharp monochrome graphics display with a longer life than the traditional VDT. IBM and other vendors are incorporating them into their high-performance data terminals. For large screen transmission, however, gas plasma displays are inappropriate; because they glow at full intensity or not at all, they cannot produce the shades required for lifelike color.

Electroluminescent displays (EDSs) Often referred to as *projection displays*, EDSs have become available for commercial use in the past few years. Their major use is for group presentations; the screen is large enough for many people to see simultaneously. EDSs, however, require much more energy than other flat panel display technologies, and cost as much as four times the cost of typical LCDs.

The Keyboard

Keyboard designs vary from one brand of computer system to another. Figure 4-4 shows an IBM keyboard, which, like many vendors' models, consists of four sections:

- Standard typewriter layout of alphabetic, numeric, and symbol keys.
- Special action keys and cursor keys.
- Function keys (or program function keys).
- Numeric keypad similar to a standard 10-key calculator.

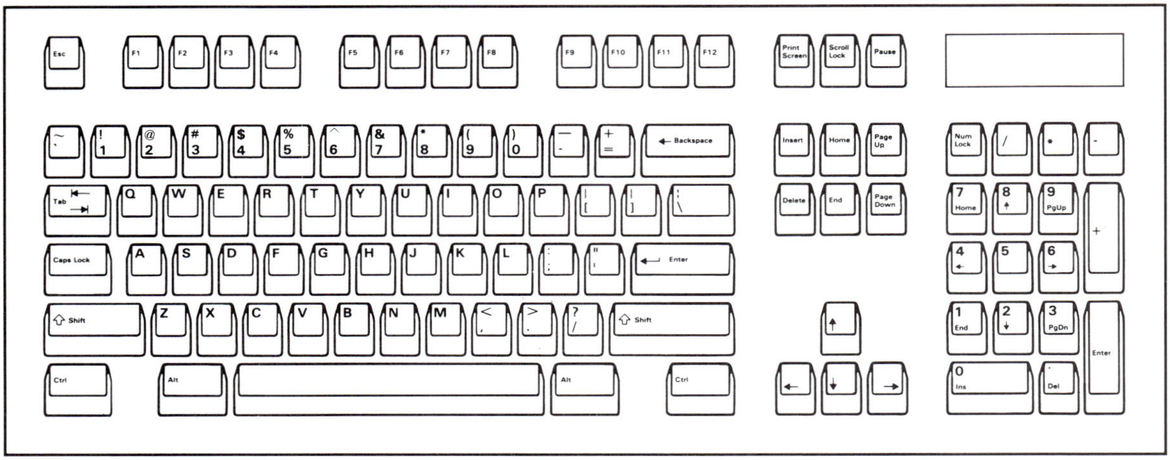

FIGURE 4-4. The IBM keyboard.

Alphanumeric and Symbol Key Layout

The standard typewriter layout is termed QWERTY, for the first six letters of the top row of the alphabet keys. QWERTY is the standard layout for English-language typewriters. Another layout, ASK (American Simplified Keyboard), is discussed in Chapter 16, "Ergonomics." The keyboard discussed in the following section is QWERTY, with numbers and symbols comprising the top row, as in the standard typewriter.

Special Action Keys and Cursor Keys

The most common special action keys are the *Control key*, the *Alternate key*, the *Carriage Return*, and the *Escape key*. The Control (CTRL) and Alternate (ALT) keys are used in combination with other keys to enter special instructions. They operate much like the Shift key on the typewriter keyboard in that they are held down while a second key is pressed. The Carriage Return (CR) or Enter key, which ends a line of data, moves the cursor down and to the left margin of the screen. It also serves to send data to the processor and to *enter* instructions to the processor. The Escape key is used to undo or cancel an instruction.

The cursor, or point of type, on a VDT is controlled in many ways. The 10-key pad on many terminals doubles as a cursor control medium. Not only can the cursor be moved from left to right and up and down, but special keys will take the cursor automatically to the top or bottom of a screen, or actually "scroll" (move the entire page up or down). Note the captions under the numbers on the ten-key pad in Figure 4-4: Home, PgUp, End, and PgDn. These keys allow the user to move the cursor efficiently.

Function Keys

Use of the function keys was described in the previous section on intelligent terminals. Not all function keys are used in every application. Various programs use function keys in different ways, but key usage is explained in the documentation for each particular software package. F1 on WORDSTAR, for example, may be programmed to mean "Save File"; F2 may mean "Reformat Paragraph." Function keys are software-specific.

Numeric Keypad

Some keyboard models combine the cursor keys on the same keys as the numeric keypad. The keyboard for the new IBM PS/2 microcomputer line has an additional set of keys that allow the user to control the cursor independently of the numeric pad. This enables users who work primarily with numbers to use the "num lock" key for entering numbers and the additional set for controlling the cursor. This also eliminates the need for constant "toggling" (moving from one function back to another by the same command).

The keyboard generates characters on the screen by accessing a special *character generator ROM* in the terminal or microcomputer system unit. When a key is depressed, it accesses the corresponding character pattern stored in ROM, and the character is displayed on the screen. The characters in ROM can be interchanged to provide alternative character sets.

Because of the programmability of the computer, many video display terminals and keyboards offer alternative keyboard character sets. The user can select a keyboard option such as ASK, or the computer output can be designed to conform with the standards of foreign countries. For example, the operator could elect to display the British pound sign instead of the dollar sign and reverse the period and comma conventions for numbers and decimals (£28.000,50 instead of $28,000.50) to conform to European usage.

SOFTWARE

Software programs provide step-by-step instructions that the computer follows to process data. Software programs are discussed first in terms of how they are written—programming languages—and then in terms of how they are used—types of programs.

Programming Languages

Programs are written in special programming languages, or predefined sets of words and symbols that can be converted to the *machine language.* The CPU's machine language or *native language* is binary code, expressed as a series of zeros and ones. Because writing programs in machine language is extremely tedious and time-consuming, software programs are written in *assembly language.* Assembly language uses a system of three- and four-letter acronyms called mnemonics (literally, memory aids) to symbolize machine code. An *assembler* converts the mnemonic form of assembly language to the binary machine language for *execution* by the CPU.

Assembly language is categorized as a *low-level language* in contrast to more recently developed *high-level languages.* Assembly language is low-level in that it is complex; it does not resemble human language. It is nearly as complex, however, as the CPU's native language. Higher-level languages use English-like statements rather than mnemonics. In a sense, higher-level languages are a form of shorthand, referred to as *code.* A given code may be equivalent to many machine-language instructions, whereas a low-level language requires one instruction for every machine instruction.

Programs consist of a series of *statements* arranged according to a set of rules referred to as *syntax,* analogous to the syntax that governs English grammar. Once written, a program can be saved and used over and over again for similar types of problems. To use a program, one *loads* it into the internal memory of the CPU, where it can be *run* or *executed.* When a program is executed, the statements are read one after the other and carried out. If an error is encountered, the execution will either stop ("bomb") or produce unexpected results. Errors in programs are referred to as *bugs;* when programmers go through the process of correcting those errors, they are *debugging* the program.

The most common business programming languages are COBOL (*Co*mmon *B*usiness-*O*riented *L*anguage) and FORTRAN (*For*mula *Tran*slation) for large computers, and BASIC (*B*eginner's *A*ll-purpose *S*ymbolic *I*nstruction *C*ode) and C language for microcomputers. Before programs written in high-level languages can be executed by the CPU, they must go through a translation process to convert them to the machine-language instructions, or *executable program code.*

This process is done by either a compiler program or an interpreter program. A *compiler program* takes all the statements in a high-level language program, known as the *source program,* and translates them into machine code. This compiled machine code is saved for later use; it is known as the *object program.*

An interpreter program takes one statement at a time and translates it into machine code. A statement is translated and executed by the CPU, followed by the next statement to be translated and executed, and so forth. The translation is not saved. Thus each time the program is used, the machine code must be regenerated by the interpreter.

Compiled programs (object code) execute much more rapidly than interpreted programs. With short programs or programs that do not process large volumes of data, however, the advantage may not be obvious. In a data processing environment, once programmers have created complex programs and debugged them, programs are saved as compiled object code for actual use. (The source code is saved also, in case the program has to be revised at a later time.) Compilers for all programming languages are available for mainframes. Most microcomputers come with a BASIC language interpreter. Compilers are available for some micros; however, not all compilers can be used on all brands of micros.

Types of Programs

Two types of programs are used with computers: (1) *system programs*, which coordinate the operation of all computer circuitry, and (2) *application programs*, which solve specific problems, such as payroll processing, spreadsheet processing, or word processing. System programs are supplied by the computer manufacturer. Applications programs may be custom-designed by programmers to do specific tasks or may be written and marketed for general uses such as accounting, inventory control, or word processing.

System and applications programs should include *documentation*, that is, instruction manuals and system descriptions. Documentation explains the use and operation of the software on specific computer models. Good documentation is essential for both the programmer, who needs a record of how a program is designed, and for the user, who needs guidance in operating the program.

Programs manipulate *data files*—consisting of numbers, letters, and symbols—that the user creates and inputs into the CPU. Data files are organized into logical *records* containing *fields* of data elements. For example, a *data file* of customers could be organized into hundreds of separate records for each customer. Each customer record might contain separate fields for first name, middle initial, last name, address, city, state, zip code, and telephone number. Following program instructions, data files are processed and results are output.

System Programs

System programs are the internal managers of the computer; they coordinate the operation of all computer circuitry. For example, a system program allocates storage space in internal memory for data being read into the computer. System programs are written for a particular type of computer and, for the most part, cannot be used on dissimilar machines. Designed to facilitate the use of the hardware and run the computer system quickly and efficiently, system programs include *operating systems* and *processing programs*.

The operating system The operating system, or control program, provides an interface between the physical hardware and the applications program. Operating systems for mainframes and minicomputers are generally designed to allow the use of several applications programs by several users at once. The operating system allocates the computer's resources to the corresponding programs. Because this activity is done "behind the scenes," each user can proceed as if the computer were servicing only his or her needs. Mainframes and minicomputers use either *batch* or *real-time* operating systems. In batch systems, data is stored and processed, from start to finish, in one continuous stream. Real-time (online) systems process small segments interspersed over time. In other words, real-time programs are interactive with their user. For example, the user keys in a request; the program processes the request, returning output to the user's display screen within seconds; the user may then enter another request; and so on.

Many mainframes and minicomputers combine both batch and real-time operating systems. In such cases, *job-control language (JCL)* serves as the communication link between the programmer or user and the operating system. Job-control language is used to indicate required details such as the beginning and end of a program, the kind of program, the work to be done, the amount of internal memory space required, and the input and output devices required. Most microcomputer operating systems are designed to handle only one user and one application at a time (with the notable exception of the UNIX operating system and the OS/2 operating system).

Processing programs Processing programs handle system configuration, device assignments, file maintenance, and programming support. They include language-translator programs, library programs, and utility programs. A *language-translator program* translates English-like programming instructions into binary machine language (ones and zeros) that the computer can process. *Library programs* are sets of computer instructions for frequently performed tasks. To save time and effort, library programs are written once and stored so they can be used in any program when needed. *Utility programs* are specialized, self-contained programs that perform specific tasks, such as copying files from one storage device to another or merging two files.

Applications Programs

Applications programs are either written by an organization's data processing staff or purchased from a software development organization. When produced by an organization's staff, the programs are generally custom-designed for the organization's own unique applications. Banks, for example, have custom-designed systems for maintaining records of customer accounts. On the other hand, generic applications software, such as word processing, spreadsheets, and database management systems, serves a more universal need and is used by diverse organizations. (See Part 3 for an overview of applications programs currently used in business.)

STORAGE UNITS (MASS STORAGE)

Software programs and data files are generally kept on *magnetic tapes* or *disks,* external or auxiliary to the CPU's main memory. (See Chapter 6, "Peripherals: Image Technologies," for details on alternative storage media.) Instructions and data are brought into main memory by the control unit as needed for processing and then returned via the same route to auxiliary storage.

Magnetic Tape

Magnetic tape is an input/storage/output medium on which information is stored sequentially. Tape widths vary from ¼ to 3 inches, with ½ inch the most common. Magnetic tape must be mounted on a tape drive, which has a *read/write head.* The number of characters that can be stored per inch of tape is called the *density* of the tape. Density ranges from 125 to 200 characters per inch (cpi) on cassettes to 9600 cpi on powerful tape drives. The density of the tape and the speed at which it travels past the read/write head determine how fast data can be transferred between the tape and the CPU. For example, if a tape with a density of 1600 cpi is read at 112.5 inches per second, data is transferred at 180,000 characters per second (cps).

Magnetic tape is commonly used for sequential or *batch* processing on mainframe and minicomputer systems. Magnetic tape is widely used for archival storage, as its cost is relatively low, or for programs that are used only periodically. Magnetic tape also is commonly used as a back-up system for microcomputer hard disks.

Magnetic Disks

The magnetic disk is the most widely used storage medium in today's computer systems. Magnetic disks are round platters, similar to phonograph records, coated on both sides with a magnetic recording material. Disks contain concentric circles (unlike the spiral grooves of a record) called *tracks.* Data is stored by magnetizing spots on the disk's *tracks.* Magnetic disks provide *random access* (or *direct access*) capability. Random access refers to the capability to locate any track directly on the disk, without going sequentially through other tracks. The three types of magnetic disks most commonly used with office computer systems are disk packs, diskettes, and hard disks.

Disk Packs

Disk packs consist of several rigid metal magnetic disks connected by a center shaft that spins all disks in the pack at the same time. Most disk packs have one read/write head for each recording surface. These read/

write heads are positioned between the disks and controlled by an access mechanism. For example, if a disk pack contained 11 disks, it would employ 20 read/write heads, with the top and bottom disk surfaces not used for recording because of their vulnerability to damage. Most disks contain 200 tracks, numbered 0 to 199. All the outermost tracks (0 tracks) on both sides of each disk form one *cylinder,* all the 1 tracks form a second cylinder, and so on. Thus each disk pack contains 200 cylinders, one inside the other.

Each track is in turn divided into sectors of equal size. The sector divisions may be permanently fixed by holes in the hub of the disk (*hard sectoring*), or they may be identified by codes written on the disk (*soft sectoring*), as shown in Figure 4-5. The process of creating soft sectors is called *initialization* or *formatting*. One or more sector's worth of information can be sent back and forth between the computer and a disk at one time.

The disk pack is positioned in a disk drive that rotates all platters in unison at speeds up to 3600 revolutions per second (rps). The density at which data is stored and the speed at which the disk pack rotates determine the time required to transfer data between the disk and the internal memory of the CPU. Disk packs are used with most mainframes, minicomputers, and large office systems.

FIGURE 4-5. Hard-sector and soft-sector modes.

Using small sector holes to locate the beginning of each sector is called the "hard sector" method. This is little used any more. Rather, the "soft sector" method is standard. This method locates the position of each sector on a track by using software and the ID field (where the sector numbers are written).

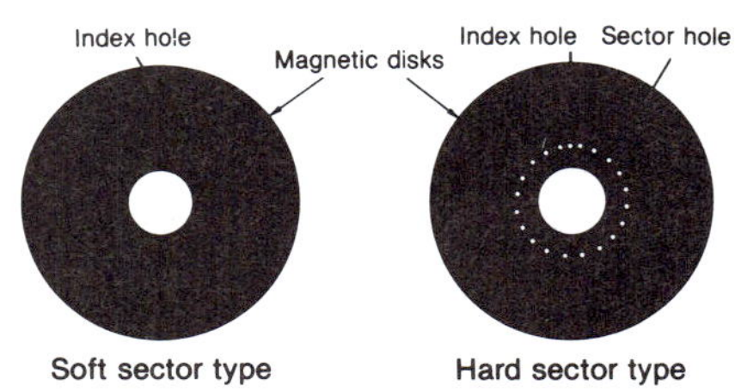

Diskettes

The most widely used type of diskettes are *floppy diskettes,* which derive their name from the flexible plastic material of which they are made. A permanent protective jacket holds the diskette, which is coated with a magnetic substance. The most popular variety resembles a 45 rpm record inserted into a square plastic envelope. When inserted into a floppy disk drive, the diskette spins inside the jacket. The read/write head comes into contact with the recording surface through a long hole in the protective jacket called the *head slot* or *head window.*

Originally, diskettes were 8 inches square; most diskettes are now 5.25 inches or even smaller, such as the 3.5-inch size used by Apple's Macintosh, the IBM PS/2, and many portable microcomputer models. The 8-inch floppy diskettes continue to be used, however, with word processing and other office systems. The 5.25-inch floppy is widely used on microcomputers. Floppy diskettes must be handled carefully. Figure 4-6 presents tips on handling floppy disks.

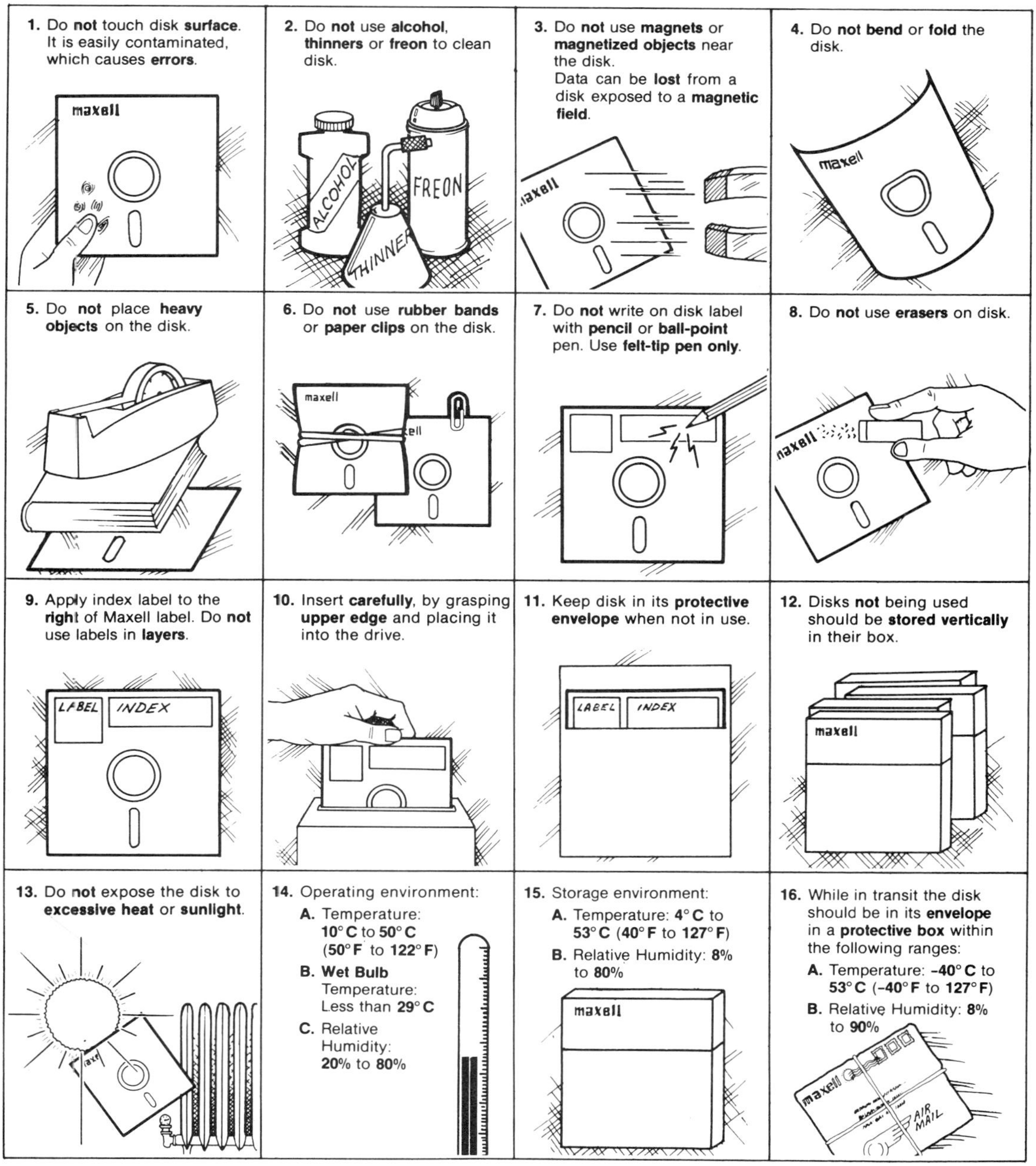

FIGURE 4-6. Procedures for storing and handling floppy disks.

The newer 3.5-inch diskette, which is encased in a hard plastic envelope, is gaining popularity for microcomputers because its case makes it easier to handle and less prone to physical damage. Data capacity of these smaller diskettes goes up to 800K, as opposed to the 360K of the standard 5.25-inch technology. Figure 4-7 illustrates these three popular diskette sizes. Because of the industry's acceptance of the 3.5-inch disk drive for IBM's new PS/2 series microcomputers, this size will probably become the industry standard.

FIGURE 4-7.
Floppy disk sizes: Large, medium, and small.

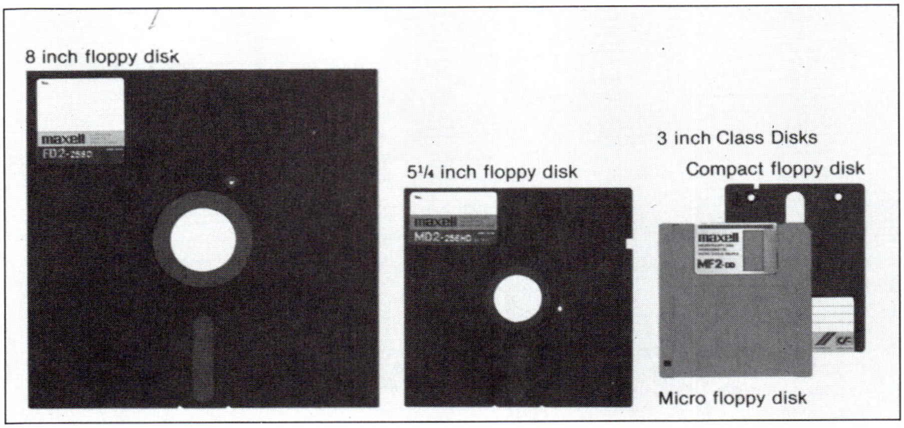

Diskettes may be either single-sided or double-sided. A standard 5.25-inch double-sided floppy contains 80 tracks (40 on each side) that are numbered 0 to 39 or 0 to 79. As in the computer's memory, space on the diskette is measured in bytes. Each byte may be considered equivalent to one character. Most floppy diskettes are *soft-sectored.* The amount of data they can store is determined by the type of computer system and disk drive involved. Floppy disks must be initialized, or formatted, before they can be used to store information. One popular format is provided by the MS/DOS operating system, used on IBM microcomputers and compatibles. MS/DOS divides the diskette into nine sectors, each of which is 512 bytes long, as shown in Figure 4-8. Such a format provides 184,320 characters on single-sided diskettes and twice that, or 368,640 characters, on double-sided diskettes. In round numbers, that is 360K (360,000 characters), or about 120 pages of text on a single-sided diskette and 240 pages on a double-sided diskette.

New *high-capacity* 5.25-inch floppy diskettes and drives use a 15-sector, 80-track format that provides 1.2 megabytes of storage. Also sometimes referred to as *high-density* or *ultrahigh-resolution* diskettes, they store three times as much information as the 360K diskettes, or approximately 600 pages of text.

Format structure (FD2–256D)	
The configuration of the tracks	
Track 00	Index track
Tracks 01–74	Data recording tracks
Tracks 75–76	Tracks to substitute for faulty tracks
The structure of index tracks	
Sectors 01–04	Reserve sectors
Sector 05	Sector for determining the existence of faulty tracks. If a faulty track appears during use, the track number is recorded.
Sector 06	Reserve sector
Sector 07	Manufacturer's name (for instance, Maxell)
Sectors 08–26	Data label, data beginning and ending, end of recorded data, and record length (256 bytes) are recorded)

FIGURE 4-8. **IBM disk format structure.**

Hard Disks

Hard disks, or *fixed disks*, provide high-speed, high-capacity storage for microcomputers. Hard disks combine characteristics of floppy diskettes and disk packs. Hard disk systems use a technology first code-named Winchester during its development at IBM. In contrast to the flexible plastic floppy, the hard disk employs a rigid metal platter enclosed in a permanently sealed case. The tightly controlled environment of the Winchester technology enables data to be stored at a much higher density than floppy disks; the hard disk also spins faster, thus providing faster data access. The mechanism of many hard disk drives is the same size as the standard floppy disk drive, so it can fit into the same location of the microcomputer system unit. Other models of hard disks are self-contained units that require their own power supply. They sit next to or under a microcomputer and are connected by a cable attached to the computer system unit. The terms hard disk, fixed disk, and Winchester disk are often used interchangeably. Although some technical differences exist, all three types provide high-speed, high-capacity disk storage for microcomputers.

Whereas floppy disk systems can access unlimited amounts of data by changing disks, the hard disk has *fixed capacity.* The capacity of hard disks depends on the number of disk surfaces used; the range of their recording density varies from 5 megabytes (5,000,000 bytes) to hundreds of megabytes. The 10-megabyte IBM Winchester fixed disk contains two platters, providing four recording surfaces. The fixed disk has 306 tracks with 17 sectors on each track. Its sector size, 512 bytes, is the same as a floppy's. New half-height hard disk drives use a single platter.

Because they are sealed, the disks on a Winchester system cannot be removed. One type of hard disk system called a *cartridge system* has exchangeable storage cartridges. Cartridge systems combine most of the advantages of floppies and hard disks: high capacity, high speed, and unlimited storage (by interchanging cartridges).

A more recent innovation is a hard disk on a single expansion board that simply slides into a slot inside a personal computer. This new device eliminates the need to replace one of the standard floppy disk drives with a hard disk or to place an extra hard disk unit next to the microcomputer. Plus Development Corporation, a subsidiary of Quantum Corporation, introduced the first such product in 1985. Called a Hardcard, it can cost much less than a traditional hard disk. Among other new entries are Mountain Computer's Drive Card, Tandon Corporation's Diskard, and Western Digital Corporation's FileCard. The development and price-cutting in this part of the hard disk market are fast and furious. This trend toward more megabytes in a smaller space for a lower price will undoubtedly continue.

CLASSIFICATIONS OF COMPUTER SYSTEMS

If one were to categorize applications for mainframes, minicomputers, microcomputers, and dedicated word processors, the following generalizations might be made:

- Mainframes are most appropriate for corporate applications and large networks.
- Minicomputers meet the needs of small organizations, departmental requirements in large organizations, distributed processing applications, and special applications.
- Microcomputers meet many needs for individuals, small departments, regional offices, small businesses, and special applications.
- Dedicated word processing equipment meets high-volume document production needs and other specialized text-processing applications.

One should keep in mind, however, that these generalizations are useful only for comparison. Applications always should be considered on their individual merit.

The following is a discussion of each of these computer systems, with special reference to their respective roles in office automation.

Mainframe Computers

Mainframe computers are the largest, fastest, and most sophisticated computers. They are capable of processing massive amounts of data at extremely high speeds. Operation and maintenance of mainframe computer systems is highly technical and complex and requires specialized training. Mainframes require a special environment where the buildup of heat, dust, dirt, and static electricity can be controlled.

Security is equally important. Today's data centers provide tight security to protect the huge investment in equipment and information. Most data centers have formal disaster-recovery plans, which may include duplicate processing facilities at another location or reciprocal exchange arrangements with other companies. Backup copies of records and critical programs are often secured at remote sites to protect computer operations.

While selection and implementation of mainframe equipment fall within the purview of the data processing department, many issues and concerns directly affect those charged with office automation accountability. In large organizations, the mainframe may provide integrated office systems (see IOS, the final section of this chapter).

Current mainframe design offers greater processing capacity and speeds at lower costs than ever before. Processing power of the mainframe CPU is measured in *millions of instructions per second* (MIPS). Mainframes range in power from 1 to 25 MIPS. Their architecture designs offer flexibility in customizing hardware and operating environments. Mainframe memory sizes range from 1 to 64 megabytes. The speed of operation for the more powerful computers is approximately 500 nanoseconds (a nanosecond is one billionth of a second). Prices range from $100,000 to almost $5 million. Computer "mainframe" generally refers specifically to the CPU (control unit, ALU, and internal storage) of a full-scale computer. The business mainframe computer market is largely dominated by IBM. Other manufacturers include Control Data Corporation (CDC), Fujitsu (Amdahl), Honeywell Information Systems (see Figure 4-9), UNISYS Corporation, and the National Cash Register (NCR) Corporation.

FIGURE 4-9. The Honeywell DPS 88.

Mainframes can support many peripheral devices. Hundreds of terminals can be connected through *controller* interface devices. Mainframes generally use dumb or smart (but not intelligent) terminals. They can also be connected to a number of smaller computers to do distributed processing. In addition to the CPU, a mainframe computer system would include operator consoles, tape and disk drives, printers, and video display terminals. All this equipment may be manufactured by the same vendor, or include *compatible* equipment from several vendors. So-called Plug Compatible Manufacturers (PCMs) offer many options in the peripheral equipment marketplace.

Mainframe computers meet a need for high-volume applications coupled with fast processing. They are most suitable for applications that require massive amounts of data online for immediate updating or applications with complex numerical iterations. A major feature of mainframes is their ability to handle many tasks simultaneously. Mainframes have multiple data paths and/or pipelined architecture. Most support all programming languages and multiword processing. Most software programs for specific applications are written in-house by the data processing department. A trend exists, however, toward purchased mainframe applications packages. This trend might be attributed to the availability of quality products and the increased complexity of mainframe applications. Mainframes are also used as central hosts for communications networks. This use of the mainframe is discussed in Chapter 8, "Communications Technologies."

Supercomputers

Supercomputers are designed for handling extremely large number-crunching operations, such as those for certain engineering simulations and scientific studies. Supercomputers incorporate a feature called *vector processing,* also referred to as *array processing,* designed for efficient mathematical calculations involving tables of numbers (arrays or vectors). Supercomputers operate above 50 million instructions per second (MIPS). Prices range from $4 million to $12 million. The high cost of these supercomputers has limited their application primarily to scientific research facilities. Improved technology and declining prices are bringing supercomputers into the realm of consideration by large corporations for the first time.

Minicomputers

Minicomputers possess a wide range of computing capabilities. Many are more powerful than the mainframe computers of just 10 years ago. They have less main storage capacity than large systems, yet they feature similar capabilities. Minicomputers can be divided into two convenient classifications: high-end minicomputers and traditional minicomputers.

High-end minicomputers feature 32-bit or larger words, as do mainframes, but lack the overall throughput of the physically larger mainframes because of architectural constraints. They operate in less stringent environmental conditions than the mainframes. In terms of pure processing power (MIPS), they are not always distinguishable from the larger systems. The larger minisystems, such as the Wang VS100 or the Hewlett-Packard 3000, require a controlled environment and can support as many as 120 terminals, printers, and other peripherals.

Traditional minicomputers have 12-, 16-, or 24-bit word sizes. They are less powerful than the high-end minicomputers. Minis are sold in configurations from processor-only dedicated computers to fully configured, expanded standalone systems. Because of their favorable price and performance, they are used for diverse office automation applications. In fact, for certain applications, minis offer the performance of a mainframe without the disadvantages of a mainframe's complexity. Smaller minisystems can operate satisfactorily in the normal air-conditioned office environment.

Generally, minicomputers support a limited number of programming languages. Minicomputers feature interactive (real-time) processing, suitable for many office processing applications. A number of vendors offer *turnkey software packages* for minis. Designed as a complete solution for specific business needs, turnkey systems offer both operating system and applications software optimized to run on a particular minicomputer configuration. Turnkey software is often *proprietary* in nature, that is, supplied by the computer vendor and run only on that vendor's equipment. The availability of turnkey software makes minicomputers especially appealing to small organizations that cannot afford to support data processing staffs. In large organizations with professional programming staffs, turnkey software contributes to the cost effectiveness of special applications.

Minicomputers frequently serve as *front ends* for the input or output of larger central computer systems. Used in this way, minicomputers can speed slower input and output processes to meet the fast calculating speeds of the mainframe.

Combined minicomputers are sometimes used instead of one larger machine. This approach offers flexibility, lower cost, and expandability. This grow-as-you-go approach can be practical. Multiple minicomputers provide backup for each other so that if one mini fails, an identical machine is available to take over, and for some applications they may be less expensive than one large computer. Factors such as the type and volume of processing and the company's processing needs must be considered.

Leading manufacturers in the minicomputer market are Digital Equipment Corporation (DEC), Wang Laboratories, Hewlett-Packard, Data General, Honeywell Information Systems, International Business Machines (IBM; see Figure 4-10), Texas Instruments, Prime Computer, and UNISYS Corporation. Prices range between $10,000 and $500,000.

FIGURE 4-10. An IBM minicomputer: The IBM System 36.

Microcomputers

Microcomputers have had a profound impact on the automated office environment. They have taken data processing out of data centers and put it on the users' desktops.

The least expensive source of computer power, the microcomputer has scaled-down characteristics of its larger counterparts, the mainframe and the minicomputer. Yet micros, such as the Compaq Deskpro 386, DEC Rainbow, and Macintosh Plus Computer (see Figures 4-11, 4-12, and 4-13), can be used by nontechnical personnel for a wide range of activities. Micros are limited only by slower processing speeds, a smaller memory, and application-specific software.

Because of the importance of the microcomputer to office automation, the prospective user, analyst, or manager of office systems must understand the microcomputer's unique operating systems. The microcomputer's operating system is the software that controls the way the computer processes data. The most widely used operating systems include the following:

- OS/2 Operating System/2 (International Business Machines Corp.)
- CP/M Control Program for Microprocessors (Digital Research Corp.)
- MS-DOS Microsoft/Disk Operating System (Microsoft Corp.)
- PC-DOS Personal Computer Disk Operating System (IBM's proprietary version of MS-DOS)
- p-System (Softech Microsystems)
- UNIX (Bell Laboratories)

FIGURE 4-11. The Compaq Deskpro 386.

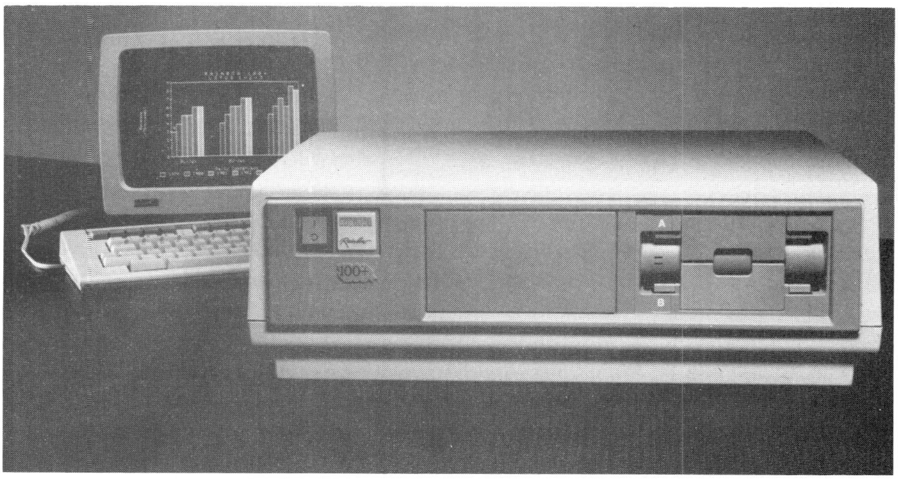

FIGURE 4-12. The DEC Rainbow.

FIGURE 4-13.
The Macintosh Plus.

Each of these systems runs software through its CPU by directions unique to the system. This is one reason why Apple computer software, for example, is incompatible with an IBM microcomputer.

Most microcomputer systems operate on two disk drives; one drive is reserved for the software, and the other is reserved for data files. While two disk drives may be the norm, microcomputers are capable of operating with multiple floppy and hard disk drives. In fact, hard disks are rapidly becoming standard equipment. When the microcomputer is used in connection with a local area network (see Chapter 8), the network file server acts as an additional drive. If the system is connected to multiple local area networks, any number of disk drives may be accessible. In addition, a microcomputer may operate with only one disk drive. In this case, the user loads the software disk, and after the software disk is read into the internal RAM memory, the data disk can be inserted. The single disk drive requires "diskette shuffling" by the user.

Portable Personal Computers

The *portable personal computer,* sometimes referred to as a *PC* or *laptop computer,* is perhaps best described as a subcategory of microcomputers. Smaller and lighter than their microcomputer counterparts, they typically offer both the power and speed of microcomputers. Portable computers are totally self-contained and easily carried. Their light weight is in part attributable to its LCD screen. Most use high-density 3.5-inch disk drives; some may include a hard disk. Figures 4-14 and 4-15 depict the Compaq Portable II and the Zenith Z-181, two popular portable computers on the market today.

Different portable computers can be compared by size, weight, type of screen, computer power and size, power requirements and battery life, and screen resolution and size. Newer models also offer an adapter for operating the computer or charging its battery from an automobile cigarette lighter.

FIGURE 4-14. The Compaq Portable II personal computer.

FIGURE 4-15. The Zenith Z-181 Portable personal computer.

The Future of Microcomputers

John Roach, president of Tandy Corporation/Radio Shack, has claimed that "microcomputers will be more prevalent than typewriters and as pervasive as calculators."[2] According to Roach and other vendors, as the cost of the microcomputer falls and its processing power increases, by the mid 1990s the ratio of users to workstations will be 1 to 2—two terminals for each knowledge worker. Users concur.

For example, the Travelers Insurance Company promotes the idea that everyone should use a PC both at work and at home. Because Travelers employs 30,000 people, that would amount to 60,000 microcomputers. Independent agents who sell Travelers Insurance policies were among the first to purchase personal computers. Another industry leader, John Mayo,

Executive Vice President of AT & T, has suggested that the three basic types of computers will "all achieve the same level of power sometime in the 1990s." Mayo has also forecast the development of computer chips with as much as "100 million components and dimensions of one ten-millionth of a meter and operating at speeds of 10 trillionths of a second."[3]

In other words, the office may no longer be dependent upon mainframe processing, thus leaving the door open for microcomputers as the dominant processing method. For the present, however, the mainframe computer remains an important source for complex programming needs and fast applications. Moreover, as portable units increase in capabilities and decrease in price, the microcomputer has the potential to create the global office, allowing information to be processed in virtually any location. Thus the personal portable computer has a very bright future.

Dedicated Word Processors

A computer system that is capable of doing only word processing is a *dedicated* word processor. Dedicated word processors are designed to provide the greatest flexibility, capability, and ease of use in processing words (text). Although word processing packages have been available on mainframes, minicomputers, and microcomputers for several years, only in recent years have their editing and document-handling capabilities approached those of dedicated word processors.

Historical Perspective

In his book *The Office Technologies,* Alan Purchase offered the following historical perspective on the development of word processors:

> Office automation effectively got its start during the 1970s, with the advent of "word processors." In the early 1970s, word processors were complicated, printer-based systems using magnetic cards or tape cassettes for their memory capability. Word processing systems such as the IBM MT/ST or the Redactron system were typically used by word processing operators who were often organized into "word processing centers." However, by the end of the 1970s, word processors had developed into display-based systems using floppy diskettes for memories. Examples of such systems are the IBM System 6, the Lanier/AES "No-Problem," and the Wang System 25. By the end of the 1970s, the growth of word processing centers had reached its peak, and a trend began to decentralize to provide word processing capability to individual secretaries at their desks.
>
> In the 1970s, each of the word processing vendors had its own operating systems and application software so that, in the tradition of the data processing industry, the systems were sold complete with hardware, software, training, and ongoing support. The suppliers provided complete solutions. Users, of necessity, developed a high degree of loyalty to their vendors and felt protective of their systems.

> The proliferation and improvement of word processing systems continued strongly during the early 1980s so that by 1982, about 25 percent of the secretaries in large organizations were equipped with word processing systems. By 1984, the number was approximately 50 percent, and this statistic is expected to reach 75 percent by 1988. However, more and more of the newer word processing units will be multifunction workstations rather than dedicated word processing systems.[4]

Dedicated word processors remain a viable alternative for meeting high-volume text processing needs. The three main types of dedicated word processors are standalone, shared-logic, and distributed logic. A discussion of these three systems is followed by an overview of integrated office systems (IOS).

Standalone Word Processors

When a self-contained computer system is dedicated to word processing applications and supports a single operator, the system is called a *standalone*.

The standalone's relatively large internal memory is an important system feature. Memory size dictates the speed at which the word processor operates, as well as the number of commands that will be necessary for a given function. The faster the response and the fewer the commands, the easier the system is to use. Figure 4-16 shows the keyboard of a Wang word processor; note the word processing commands on the function keys. Figure 4-17 depicts the Wang screen the way a user would see it.

FIGURE 4-16. Wang word processor keyboard.

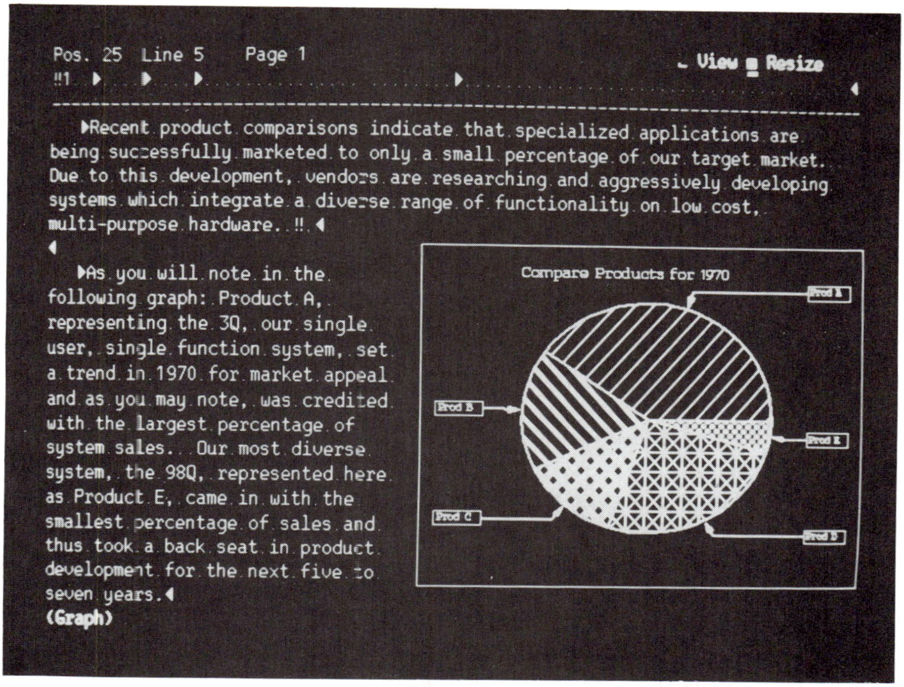

FIGURE 4-17. Wang screen as viewed by a user.

Because of their speed and ease of operation, standalone word processors with dedicated software currently have an edge over microcomputer technology. As the power of the microcomputer increases, it may provide a low-cost alternative to the standalone with little sacrifice of speed or ease of use.

The components of a standalone system are the same as those of any computer system. Indeed, most standalone word processing systems include a printer. (Chapter 7 explains printers in detail.) Currently, approximately 30 vendors of standalone systems remain in the market. Whether or not the standalone system will continue to be part of the electronic office may depend on its ability to adapt to standards that will integrate it with other technologies.

Shared Logic Systems

Systems with multiple terminals attached to a single central processor are called *shared-logic systems*. It is relatively inexpensive to expand shared-logic systems because a limited number of low-cost dumb terminals can be added to build multiterminal configurations. The main disadvantage of sharing a processor is that, since all terminals are dependent upon the processing power of the central computer, the whole system is shut down if the central processor shuts down.

Shared-Resource Systems

When a word processing system is designed so that each terminal has its own local memory and software capabilities, yet may access common resources on a networked system, it is called a *shared-resource system.* Shared-resource systems usually offer greater capacity to add terminals, but they are more costly than shared-logic systems. In a shared-resource system, each workstation has its own processor, so the individual workstations are less subject to problems elsewhere on the system.

Integrated Office Systems

Integrated office systems (IOS), also called *office automation systems* (ADS), are systems that perform a variety of office and data processing functions with a standard or consistent user interface. A number of vendors offer products in this category. Some are dedicated hardware systems and others are software packages designed for general-purpose minicomputers. Examples in the first category include the Barrister Law Office Information Management System and Wang Alliance 250 System. Examples in the second category include the Wang OFFICE product for the Wang VS100 and VS300 series minicomputers and the Digital Equipment Corporation's ALL-IN-ONE Office Information System.

In its most basic form, an IOS offers integrated word processing, electronic mail/message distribution, and electronic filing functions. More advanced forms integrate these functions with records or file processing, electronic calendar (administrative support), spreadsheet and graphics (decision support), and even voice store-and-forward (voice mail) functions. IOSs may also be configured to handle teleconferencing, PBX-type voice telephone operations, access-security and time-attendance monitoring, composition and printing, and other office-related functions.

The objective of IOS systems is to connect different office automation capabilities together on one system so that they are readily accessible to a large number of users. At present, no IOS system on the market offers the solution of a complete set of office automation functions, nor consistent integration in terms of user interface throughout the functions provided. *User interface* refers to universal (standard), easy-to-learn menu structures; command sets; "help" aids; system prompts; and text editors. It also involves the ability to move documents or files easily from one function into another.

Despite their advantages, relatively few IOSs under the above definition are on order or have been implemented in the corporate community. Office systems task groups and committees are certainly discussing such systems, and major vendors are racing to introduce their particular versions. Several factors are presently restraining implementation of full-blown integrated systems. These factors include high cost, lack of consistent user interface (which limits ease of use), lack of compatibility in transmission media and configurations, and—far from a minor concern—a wide set of unknown factors regarding how people will actually work with these systems. Changes in work procedures and habits can certainly be expected. As experience is gained from the IOSs now in place and as integrated technology is modified, widespread acceptance and use of IOSs can be expected throughout the coming years, particularly in the medium-to-large corporate environment.

Most if not all of the systems now on the market are in a phase of growth and development as user feedback and competitive product introductions lead to systems enhancements. New vendors will certainly join the list of companies now in the market, and some will surely drop out.

SUMMARY

The purpose of this chapter was to acquaint the reader with the major components of computer systems.

Computers are classified by their purpose, category, and size. General-purpose computers can be used for a myriad of applications; special purpose computers, such as standalone word processors, are application-specific.

Computer hardware includes the central processing unit (CPU), interfaces, the video display unit, and the keyboard (or alternative input device). The CPU consists of the arithmetic logic unit, the control unit, and memory. CRT-based VDTs are described in terms of the way the light beam is emitted through the screen: in vector, the light is aimed at the image only; in raster-scan, the light is rapidly flashed from top to bottom; and in shadow-mask, three light guns, not one, emit the beam. Flat display technologies are growing in popularity, as both their smaller size and higher quality make them attractive alternatives to CRT-based technologies. Examples of flat display technologies are liquid crystal displays (LCDs), gas plasma displays, and electroluminescent displays.

Keyboards differ from computer to computer; however, nearly all have alphanumeric keys, special action keys, function keys, and a ten-key keypad.

Software programs are instructions a computer follows to process information. Software is written in a programming language. System programs (operating systems) control the operation of the computer, while applications programs perform specific tasks, such as word processing, budgeting, or accounting.

External storage for computer systems is provided by magnetic tape, disk packs, diskettes, and hard disks. Magnetic tape is mounted on a tape drive with a read/write head and is typically used with batch processing on mainframe and minicomputer systems. Disk packs are rigid metal disks connected by a central shaft. They are typically used in mainframe and minicomputer processing. Magnetic disk media offer random access capabilities; one can locate data on any track without sequentially scanning through other tracks, as on magnetic tape. Diskettes are made from flexible plastic materials that spin inside a square protective envelope. Diskettes come in a variety of sizes, including 8-, 5.25-, and 3.5-inch. Eight-inch disks are commonly used in standalone word processing systems; 5.25- and 3.5-inch diskettes are typically used in microcomputers and portable computers.

The final section of this chapter described the three main classifications of computers: mainframes, minicomputers, and microcomputers, including the special-purpose word processor. Mainframes are the fastest and most sophisticated computers, followed by minicomputers and microcomputers. An organization chooses a system that serves its processing needs.

Technological developments are certain to increase capabilities and decrease costs. In the future, the distinctions among computer categories may fade. Computer technology is complex; for more detail about how computers process data, the reader should consult a book on computer information systems or data processing. The next chapter delves into alternative input media for computer systems.

DISCUSSION QUESTIONS

1. A computer can be defined by its purpose, its category, and its size. Using these criteria, describe the following computers: mainframe computer, minicomputer, microcomputer, and standalone word processor.
2. What is the role of computer memory? Distinguish between ROM and RAM.
3. What are characteristics of a "smart" terminal? How does one measure the "intelligence" of equipment?
4. Compare vector, raster-scan, and shadow-mask VDT technologies. Why do these technologies remain so popular?
5. Appraise the potential for flat screen displays. What is their value over the more traditional VDT technologies?
6. What are the four sections of a keyboard? Which of the sections can be programmed by the user?
7. What is the role of the interface? Explain the difference between serial and parallel interfaces.

8. Differentiate systems programs from applications programs, giving examples of each.
9. Define the following programming languages: machine language, assembly language, low-level language, and high-level language.
10. Identify the tasks of a compiler and an interpreter program.
11. Describe magnetic tape. What are the major applications of magnetic tape today?
12. Describe each of the following magnetic disks: disk packs, diskettes, and hard disks. Which categories of magnetic disks have the most potential for future use?
13. For each of the following applications, identify an appropriate computer system:
    a. A three-person law firm needs a system to prepare documents.
    b. A large manufacturing organization needs a system to prepare its monthly payroll and offer electronic mail to its multisite offices.
    c. A free-lance writer needs a system to compose and edit her articles.
    d. A major bank needs a system to record its customers' banking transactions.
14. Explain the differences among mainframe computers, minicomputers, and microcomputers.
15. Discuss the history of the standalone word processor. What features make it attractive—and not attractive—to organizations today?

APPLICATION EXERCISES

1. Select three trade publications—one for the mainframe market, the second for the minicomputer market, and the third for the microcomputer market. Browse through them and compare the discussions of hardware, software, and applications. Identify articles that demonstrate different issues, perspectives, or applications.
2. Lisa Bond is an office systems analyst for State University. She is responsible for controlling costs related to the operation of the campus mainframe computer system. Lately, professors and students have been using the mainframe computer for word processing. The result is that the computer is heavily used for word processing. With your classmates, brainstorm how Lisa may solve this problem.
3. Visit a computer store and compare the speeds of three models of microcomputers. What factors, other than speed, differentiate the models? Discuss your findings in an oral report to the class.

SUGGESTED READINGS

Hirschheim, R. A. *Office Automation: Concepts, Technologies, and Issues* (Reading, Mass.: Addison-Wesley, 1985), Chapter 5.

Leeson, Marjorie. *Computer Operations* (Chicago: Science Research Associates, 1987).

O'Connor, Bridget N. "High-Res Monitors Demystified," *Administrative Management* (December 1987), pp. 41-43.

Purchase, Alan. *The Office Technologies* (Willow Grove, Pa.: Administrative Management Society, 1985), Chapters 1-2.

PERIPHERALS: Input Devices

CHAPTER 5

OBJECTIVES

After completing this chapter, the reader should be able to meet the following objectives:

- Describe the purpose and use of a wide range of input devices used in conjunction with visual display terminals: mouse, light pen, touch-sensitive screen, joystick, paddle, trackball, and interactive tablet.
- Given a specific application, identify an appropriate input device.
- Explain the history and role of the typewriter and the electronic typewriter in the automated office.
- Appraise the potential of optical recognition technologies: optical character readers, magnetic ink character recognition, and point-of-sale terminals.
- Describe features of popular optical character readers.
- Give three examples of how bar codes are used in offices.
- Identify the purposes, uses, and types of various dictation/transcription equipment.
- Summarize the differences among categories of dictation devices.

KEY TERMS

cursor
mouse
light pen
touch-sensitive screen
joystick
paddle
trackball
interactive tablet
electronic typewriter
optical character reader
magnetic ink character recognition
point-of-sale terminal
bar code
portable dictation unit
desktop dictation unit
central dictation system
transcription unit
capture rate
throughput
reject rate
self diagnostics
digital dictation device
integrated dictation/transcription/word processing technology

INTRODUCTION

Input is the first step in any systems operation. Creating and entering data into the system for further processing is facilitated by a number of technologies. Chapter 4 discussed tape drives, disk drives, and video display terminals (including the keyboard), all of which play important roles in data input. Input can also be accomplished by other devices. This chapter is outlined around three common types of input technologies: (1) visual display terminal technologies, (2) typewriters used in conjunction with character recognition technologies, and (3) dictation equipment used for recording voice input for later transcription.

VISUAL DISPLAY TERMINAL TECHNOLOGIES

While the keyboard is the primary alphanumeric input device for a computer system, several instruments are available that enable the user to enter data by positioning the cursor (point of type) at various locations on the screen. The mouse, popularized by Apple Computer, and the joystick, familiar to all who have played electronic games, are two examples. These and other input devices are called *visual display terminal* technologies.

Mouse

The *mouse,* shown in Figure 5-1, is a small object that fits into the palm of the hand. It is connected to the computer via a wire (the tail). The user operates the mouse by rolling it around the desktop on a ball bearing in its base. As the mouse moves, the cursor on the display screen moves in the corresponding directions: up or down, left or right. Individuals with little keyboarding skills find the mouse easy to use. It allows the user to manipulate data on the screen and enter instructions by pointing to options and then "clicking" (pushing down on the keys on the mouse), rather than by keying special codes or special function keys.

FIGURE 5-1. **Input device: The IBM mouse.**

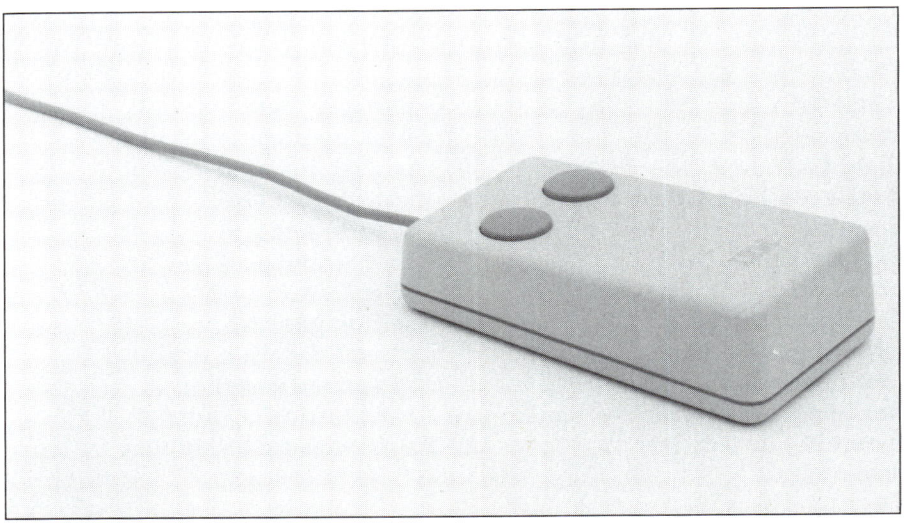

Light Pen

A *light pen,* such as the one pictured in Figure 5-2, allows the user to control the cursor by touching the screen with an instrument that resembles a small pen, with a light for an eraser. Special filaments in the light pen cause the cursor to move when the pen is applied to the screen.

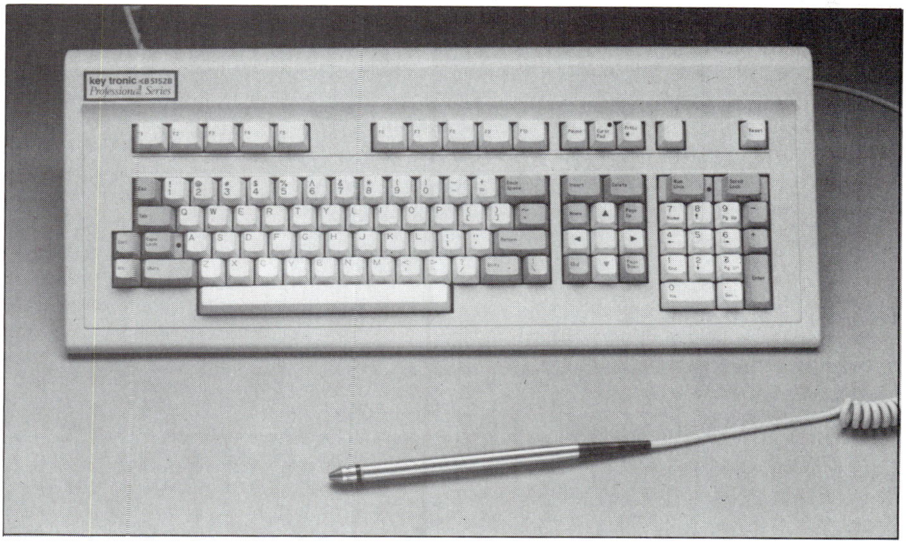

FIGURE 5-2. The Key tronic light pen.

Touch-Sensitive Screens

Touch-sensitive screens are based on the same concept as the light pen: heat applied to the screen. Rather than requiring a special instrument, however, touch-sensitive screens respond to the warmth of the user's fingertip. Touch-sensitive screens are easy to use and are a popular option for inputting data when ease of use is critical.

Joystick

A short rod extending from a rubber base that resembles a gear shift, the *joystick* permits the user to move the cursor quickly in any direction—horizontally, vertically, diagonally, or circularly (see Figure 5-3). Joysticks are used not only in video games but also for graphics, special design, and business software such as spreadsheets. They allow the user to move the cursor quickly to menu selections, edits, and entries.

Paddle

The *paddle* is an instrument that resembles a boat or ping-pong paddle mounted on a universal joint. Using a paddle, one can move the cursor in two directions at the same time (left/right or forward/backward). Like the joystick, the paddle is often used in creating graphics or playing video games.

FIGURE 5-3. Kraft joystick.

Trackball

The purpose of the *trackball* is to move the cursor very quickly through large amounts of data. Unlike the joystick, however, the trackball may be mounted directly on the display unit or off to the side of the computer. Users operate it by spinning the ball in the direction they want it to move. One popular use of the trackball is in conjunction with special function keys, to move the cursor quickly through spreadsheets. Such a combination allows extremely fast movement through columns and rows.

Interactive Tablet

The *interactive tablet* resembles a small blackboard. An individual uses a special stylus to draw the intended object on the "tablet." The interactive tablet, such as the one in Figure 5-4, is often built into the keyboard, although detachable interactive tablets are on the market. The image drawn on the tablet appears on the VDT.

TYPEWRITER

Typewriters are the oldest technology for direct document output and are also used for systems input in conjunction with character recognition

FIGURE 5-4. A Key tronic interactive tablet.

devices. This machine revolutionized office work when it was first introduced by Christopher Latham Sholes in 1868, and it remains an important technology in the office even today. Today's typewriters, however, hardly resemble early models, which looked like a treadle sewing machine. In fact, Sholes's original machine required foot action by the user to return the carriage!

At first, changes in the design of the typewriter were slow; the most obvious change was the gradual flattening of the keyboard. Beginning in the 1960s, however, change came quickly.

The first change powered the typewriter with electricity. For decades, office workers had used manual machines that required strong fingers and well-paced strokes. Then the remarkable electric typewriter (sometimes referred to as the electromechanical typewriter), introduced in the 1920s, eliminated the physical strain, enabling the keyboarding task to be done much more easily.

Perhaps the most important breakthrough in electromechanical technology was the development of the ball typing element, in 1962. This golfball-size element eliminated the need for the entire typewriter carriage to move, and solved the problem of jamming keys (more than one key hitting the platen at the same time).

While technologically a minor advancement, the "correcting" typewriter has virtually eliminated the mess related to correcting errors on the original page of type. Corrections are made by backspacing, using a special key to remove the error, and retyping the correct letter or letters. High-quality corrections are made in seconds, not minutes.

Electronic Typewriter

The most recent development in typewriter technologies has been the *electronic typewriter* (ET). With its microchip technology, the ET bridges the transition between the electric typewriter and the word processor (see Chapter 4). Many electronic typewriters have features similar to those of more powerful word processors. Some models have "windows"—small screens that range in size from five characters to an entire line of type, such as the Xerox model shown in Figure 5-5. Nearly all are equipped with memory. Generally, memory is internal (ROM) to the operating system of an electronic typewriter and may be limited to no more than 1K, but some models have external storage devices.

An electronic typewriter is defined as an input/output device with the following components:

- Alphanumeric keyboard.
- Recording and storage capabilities (internal or magnetic cards, tape, or disk).
- Printing device (the typewriter itself), generally a daisywheel or ball element with speeds capable of 12 to 22 characters per second.
- Logic/intelligence (automatic centering, underscore, boldface, carriage return, etc.).

FIGURE 5-5. A Xerox electronic typewriter.

Some electronic typewriters have interfaces to microcomputers that enable them to be used as printing devices. Printing options are limited, however, as the electronic typewriter is relatively slow and the interface technology is often unreliable.

The role of the electronic typewriter in the office of the future has mixed forecasts. Some critics describe it as an overpriced typewriter; its editing features are limited, and for very little extra money one can purchase a word processor.

ET advocates, on the other hand, stress the efficiencies of the ET as a paper handling device. They claim that a secretary will always need a typewriter to perform such functions as filling forms, typing envelopes, labels, and the like. Some typists find an ET more efficient than a word processor for short letters, memos, and other items that require minimum editing. Market analysts such as Venture Development Corporation expect sales of electronic typewriters to grow from the 480,000 units sold in 1983 and the 1.3 million sold in 1986 to 2.8 million in 1990. Of particular importance to manufacturers and buyers, this represents 1990 sales dollars of $2.4 billion.

OPTICAL RECOGNITION TECHNOLOGY

Optical recognition devices eliminate the laborious task of rekeying data. Such technology electronically scans data from paper and converts it to digital format for direct input to a computer. Character recognition devices include (1) optical character recognition (OCR), (2) magnetic ink character recognition (MICR), (3) point of sale (POS), and (4) bar codes.

Optical Character Recognition (OCR)

Credit card companies and utilities have used OCR as an input medium for decades. Remitting to such organizations, the customer returns a specific form with the payment, which the organization's computer can "read." The form eliminates the need for a computer operator to manually enter payment information, such as customer name, address, account number, and so forth.

Only in recent years, however, have OCR readers become sophisticated enough to read typefaces other than the uniquely sized and shaped OCR characters on such billings. Many OCRs are microcomputer compatible and can read a variety of standard typefaces, such as IBM Selectric 10-pitch and 12-pitch Courier or Prestige elite, 10-pitch Prestige pica, 12-pitch Letter Gothic, and Bookface Academic. Depending on the model, an OCR may be able to read alphanumeric handprinting that conforms to a standard acceptable to the OCR's memory unit. *Intelligent* OCRs (to be described later in this chapter) have even more capabilities and features.

Prices of OCR readers vary, depending primarily on their capacity to read different type fonts (character shapes) and their scan speed. An OCR reader, such as the CompuScan reader in Figure 5-6, has a throughput of 120 pages per hour (30 seconds for and 8-1/2 × 11-inch page) and can range in price from $7000 to $20,000.

OCRs that read multiple fonts at approximately 400 characters per second (cps) range in price from $10,000 to $40,000. The most complex readers, which scan multiple fonts and handprints at rates of 200 to 7500 cps, cost between $30,000 and $175,000. Figure 5-7 outlines what to look for in comparing OCR features.

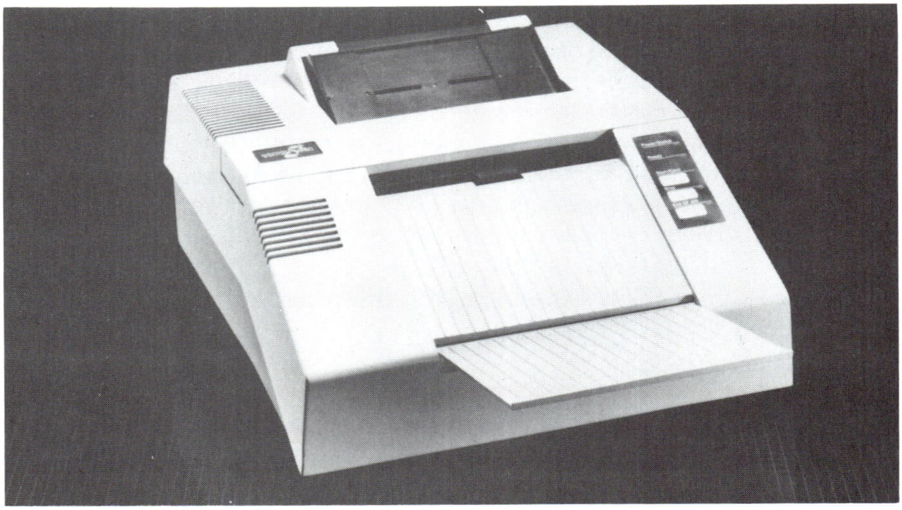

FIGURE 5-6. The CompuScan optical character recognition (OCR) reader.

How an Optical Character Reader Works

Optical character readers recognize and interpret characters in one of two ways. One type of reader employs a detector that analyzes the light reflected by characters on a white field. Characters are distinguished by their topology: shapes, loops, line directions, and position. The other type employs matrix matching. As characters are scanned, they form patterns in grids, or matrixes, consisting of hundreds of tiny squares. Each character is represented as a distinct pattern of squares.

The translation of printed text to digitized text is, at present, not 100 percent accurate. However, new optical character readers are much more accurate than early models, which had high error rates. As shown in Figure 5-7, reject (error) rates, reported by vendors, range from 1 in 20,000 to 1 in 100,000 characters.

How the Optical Character Reader Is Used

An optical character reader can literally turn every typewriter in an organization into an input terminal for text processing. Any material prepared on a relatively inexpensive typewriter can be read by the reader into a word processing system for later editing or processing by anyone

FIGURE 5-7. Factors to consider when shopping for an OCR.

Model: Is it a floor, desktop, or hand-held model?

Dimensions and weight: Does it fit where you intend to place it?

Operating temperature and relative humidity: How does your office environment compare with system requirements?

Power requirements and dissipation: Is your office adequately wired?

Compatibility: Is the unit compatible with your automated equipment?

Readable fonts: Can the OCR read fonts that correspond with existing documents and typewriters?

Paper handling: Will the paper transport handle your paper's type, size, and weight?

Input requirements: How do your needs for margins, pitch, line spacing, ink colors, and tabs compare with model specifications?

Capture rate: The range is 25 to 7500 characters per second. How many cps can the OCR handle?

Throughput: The average is 50 to 300 pages per hour: How many pages per hour can the OCR handle?

Reject (error) rate: The range is 1:20,000 to 1:100,000. What is the error rate for the OCR?

Editing capabilities: Is there a keyboard and display?

User programming: Does the model offer it? Do you need it?

Self-diagnostics: Does the model offer self-diagnostics?

Maintenance: How prompt and reliable is vendor service?

(anywhere) with access to a terminal on that system. OCR readers are often used to convert from one word processing system to another, to input manuscripts into phototypesetting equipment, and to eliminate rekeying at Telex terminals.

Because it digitizes data, the optical character reader is particularly useful for electronic distribution of incoming paper documents and the development of databases. Any document that arrives from outside the organization can be scanned and sent electronically to whomever needs to see it. Used to create databases, the optical character reader can digitize paper documents—correspondence, reports, or records—that were created outside the organization or prior to the organization's use of electronic storage media. The reader eliminates the need to rekey documents for distribution or for storage.

The Intelligent Optical Character Reader

The intelligent OCR, such as the Kurzweil DISCOVER 7320 System pictured in Figure 5-8, was developed to help the blind to access materials not yet published in Braille. The intelligence in the Kurzweil OCR enables it to analyze the shape of each printed character, identifying it as either a letter, number, or symbol. (See Chapter 9 for more information on artificial intelligence.) Figure 5-9 shows how the character is analyzed. The built-in intelligence of the Kurzweil system enables it to enter a variety of texts, including handwriting, line art, graphics, and documents with multiple fonts. Using this OCR, text can be entered ten times faster than the fastest typist could input it by hand.

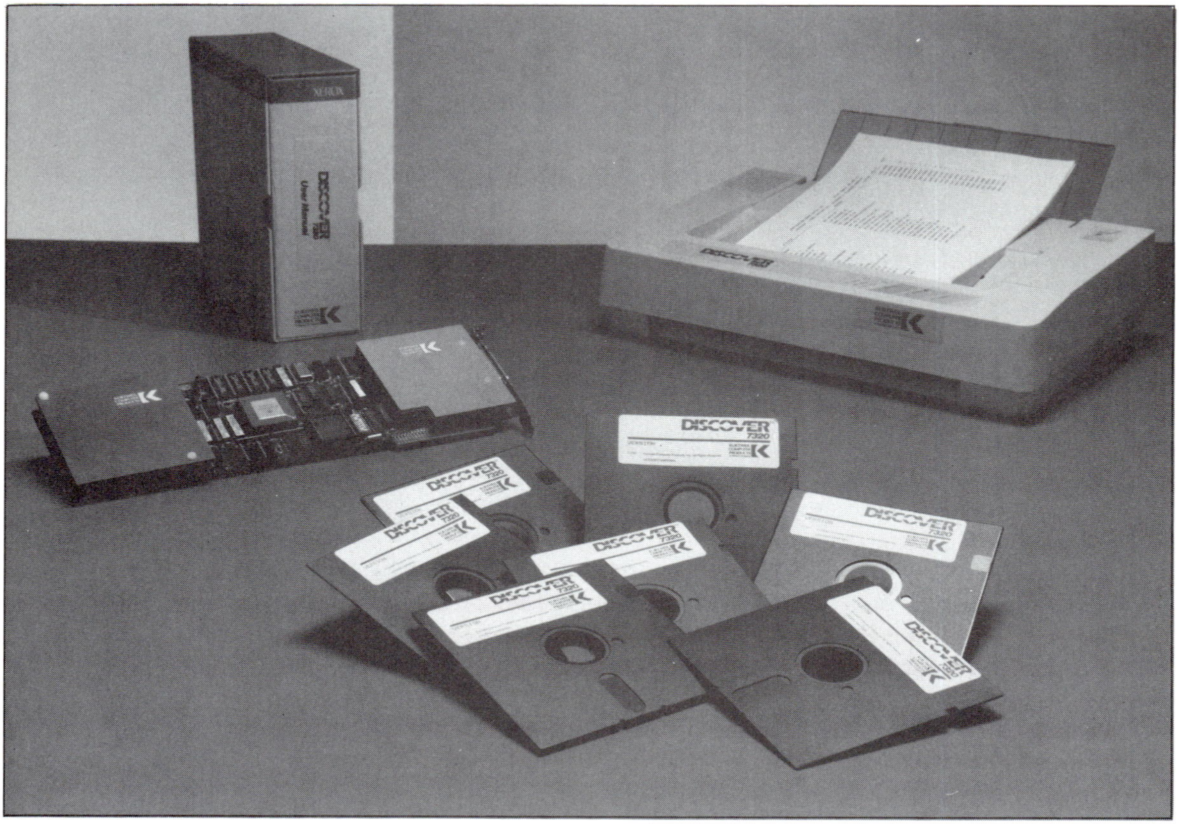

FIGURE 5-8. The DISCOVER 7320 Model 20 from Kurzweil Computer Products is a PC-based intelligent scanning system that automatically inputs text and graphics documents in five languages. The system includes 4 MB of random access memory and a desktop scanner.

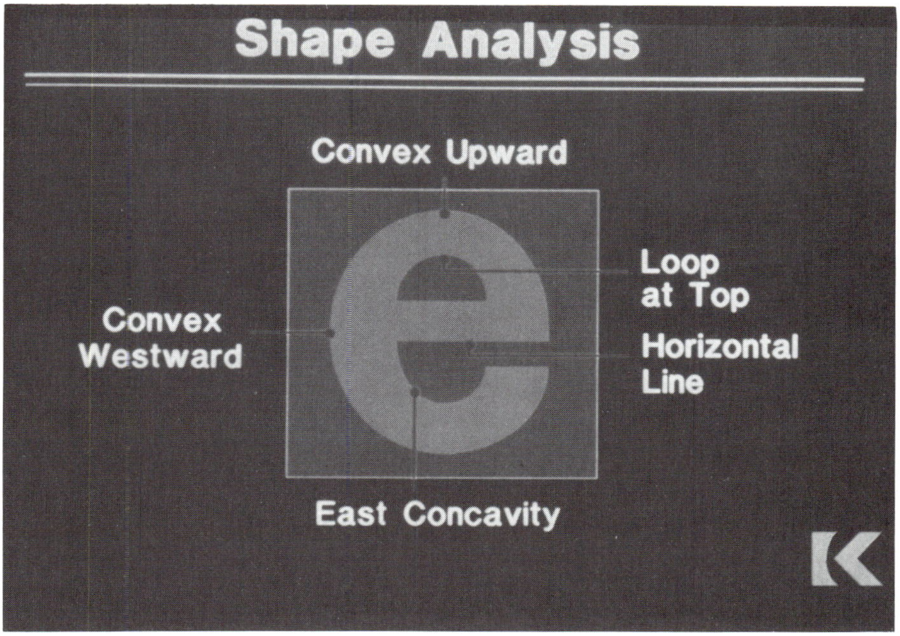

FIGURE 5-9. Intelligent OCRs read characters by analyzing their shapes.

What's Next for the OCR?

OCR technology is being continually refined to offer increased accuracy, speed, and flexibility. The OCR is being integrated with office technologies such as electronic mail, magnetic ink character recognition, micrographics, facsimile, and communications. OCR can be networked with small business computers and word processors. In the future, OCR technologies will probably offer voice response and voice recognition and be linked to optical disk storage and file management systems.

Magnetic Ink Character Recognition (MICR)

MICR is used almost exclusively in the banking industry. Figure 5-10 shows a bank check in which the fields of data at the bottom of the check are identified. These numbers are written in special *magnetic ink* characters and enable the check to be entered into the bank's system for processing. MICR not only saves data entry time but also reduces the possibilities of error; note that the only column that must be entered by the bank is the amount of the check. Because of its limited scope (14 figures and symbols), MICR is currently limited to the banking industry.

Point-of-Sale Terminals

Chances are that the last time the reader was in a major department store, such as Sears, the salesclerk's cash register was operated not by punching numbers but by a *point-of-sale* (POS) terminal, which resembles a small pencil with a light for an eraser. The light scanned the price ticket, which

F-66(REV.12/79)
FIRST TENNESSEE BANK 1st
N.A. MEMPHIS MEMPHIS, TENNESSEE
®Registered Service Mark owned and licensed by First Tennessee National Corporation
19____ NO.____
26-2 / 840
PAY TO THE ORDER OF ____ $____
____ DOLLARS
PLEASE INSERT ACCOUNT NUMBER BEFORE SIGNING
CHECKING ACCOUNT NUMBER
FOR ____
⑆084000026⑆

FIGURE 5-10. Fields of data on a bank check.

was written in a special OCR font, and the price of the item was automatically recorded. Another popular POS terminal is frequently found in grocery stores; the checkout person simply passes the merchandise over a special device that reads the uniform product code on the merchandise. Both devices are considered point-of-sale terminals.

POS terminals provide the following advantages:

- *Errors are limited.* Even the best sales clerk can make an error on a cash register. When correctly programmed, however, POS terminals are virtually error-free.
- *Prices, including regular and sale prices, can be adjusted.* Each item does not have to be retagged for a price update or special promotion.
- *Inventory records can be updated automatically.* The system can automatically reorder stock when supplies reach a predetermined level.

POS applications are not limited to department and grocery stores. In the automated office, any application whereby inventory records are kept is a potential application for a POS terminal.

Bar Codes

Today one can frequently find bar codes in the grocery store. Bar code readers scan bars of varying thickness and convert them to alphanumerics. A universal product code identifies a specific product by manufacturer and by item. When the bar code is read by a special scanner, called the *bar code reader,* a listing of the item, which may include additional descriptive information (e.g., brand name, price, and so on), is recorded. The advantages of the bar code are identical to those of the POS terminal; only the entry device differs.

Bar codes are also found on library books and borrowers' cards. An office application is the use of bar codes to group documents for filing or processing. Many companies use bar codes on return envelopes to expedite the sorting of incoming mail (see Figure 5-11). Figure 5-12 is a label

FIGURE 5-11. Return postcard/envelope bar code.

for Lowell Systems. Such labels aid the mail room or the storage room in swiftly handling packages.

Bar codes can also help speed and control the process when a document must be handled by more than one person or department. For example, Symbol Technologies has a laser scanning bar code-reading system in the Registry in Australia, which handles 500,000 inquiries a year. Each inquiry is assigned a sequential number, which is translated into a bar code symbol on the recording form. Scanning systems then check each document as it moves from department to department. Anyone can learn the status of the inquiry by accessing the microcomputer-based control file. Thus the bar code system keeps track of inquiries and helps to ensure that they are handled promptly and are not lost.[1]

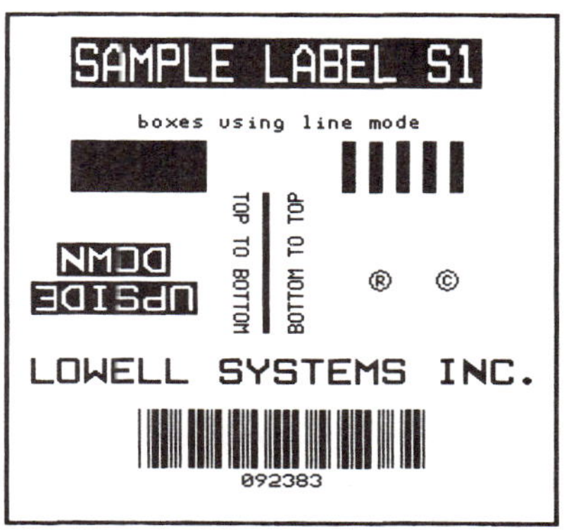

FIGURE 5-12. Label bar codes.

DICTATION/TRANSCRIPTION SYSTEMS

Probably one of the most cost-effective yet underused and time-saving devices for facilitating input to word processing systems is dictation equipment. Traditional input methods of preparing copy for processing or distribution—longhand (writing with pen or pencil on paper) and shorthand (dictating to another person, who writes in shorthand)—are time-consuming activities. Handwriting speed is generally 15 to 30 words per minute (wpm), and a good stenographer can take dictation at 120 to 140 wpm. However, people speak at 180 to 250 wpm. The dictation machine speeds the creation process. Dictation is limited only by the skill of the dictator.

The Dartnell Institute of Business Research, a Chicago-based research group, found the 1984 cost of preparing an average letter by traditional input methods to be $8.10. When dictation/transcription equipment was used, however, the cost of that same letter fell to $6.08. The $2.02 savings was attributed to the time saved by using dictation technology.

Dictation devices for the office have been available since the 1800s. The history of dictation technology and media is tied to the phonograph industry. Dictation devices have evolved from Thomas Edison's wax cylinders, to phonograph records, to magnetic tapes, and now to digital devices. Dictation devices offer several "extra" features that aid the dictation process, including pause buttons, volume controls, and instant, easy-to-use playback controls.

The recording medium may be magnetic belts, magnetic tape cassettes (in standard, mini, or micro sizes), or magnetic disks. Tapes used for dictation need not be of the high quality used for music recordings, which often require multiple tracks. Moreover, the dictation cassette is designed to be erased and used over and over again.

Because developments in technology are often market-driven, the dictation equipment described in this section reflects efforts by the industry to tailor these devices to fit a diversity of needs for both "dictators" and transcribers. *Portable* units are small, easy-to-carry devices that offer mobility and flexibility. Durable *desktop* units offer quality features, and *central systems* can provide high quality and high accessibility.

When selecting dictation/transcription equipment, the office systems specialist should first carefully assess the organization's dictation requirements. Then the task is to choose among the standard operational features and special options in various categories of equipment. Benefits to both dictators and transcribers should be considered.

Portable Dictation Units

Portable, hand-held dictation units have caught a growing segment of the market. Battery operated so that they may be used in virtually any location (plane, car, or home), these lightweight, inexpensive instruments record 30 to 120 minutes per cassette tape. The units and their tapes are inexpensive, easy to use, easy to carry, and reusable, and the tapes can be mailed from the point of creation back to the office for transcription. An organization with many occasional dictators might consider establishing a loan bank of portable units. Portable units serve individuals who have light dictation needs. It should also be noted that the portable unit has a low life span, compared to desktop models.

One of the smallest portable devices is Dictaphone Corporation's Dictamite II dictation/transcription system, pictured in Figure 5-13. This microcassette recorder, as small as a hand-held calculator, offers flexibility and ease of use.

FIGURE 5-13. The Dictaphone Dictamite II micro-cassette portable recorder.

Desktop Dictation Units

Desktop units remain the most popular because of their ease of use, high-quality recording, high speed, and durability. These relatively stationary units (see Figure 5-14) are used by authors at their desks. The completed (but reusable) dictation tapes are physically transferred to the transcriber. Tapes vary in length; 1- or 2-hour tapes offer longer playtime than tapes used in portable units.

Useful features of desktop units include one-button controls on the microphone for record, stop, rewind, and playback; end-of-text indexing; and an instruction cue to enable the transcriptionist to identify and listen to the author's instructions before beginning transcription. The office with distributed word processing services benefits most from desktop dictation units.

FIGURE 5-14. A desktop recorder: Dictaphone's Exec-Talk Plus voice processing system.

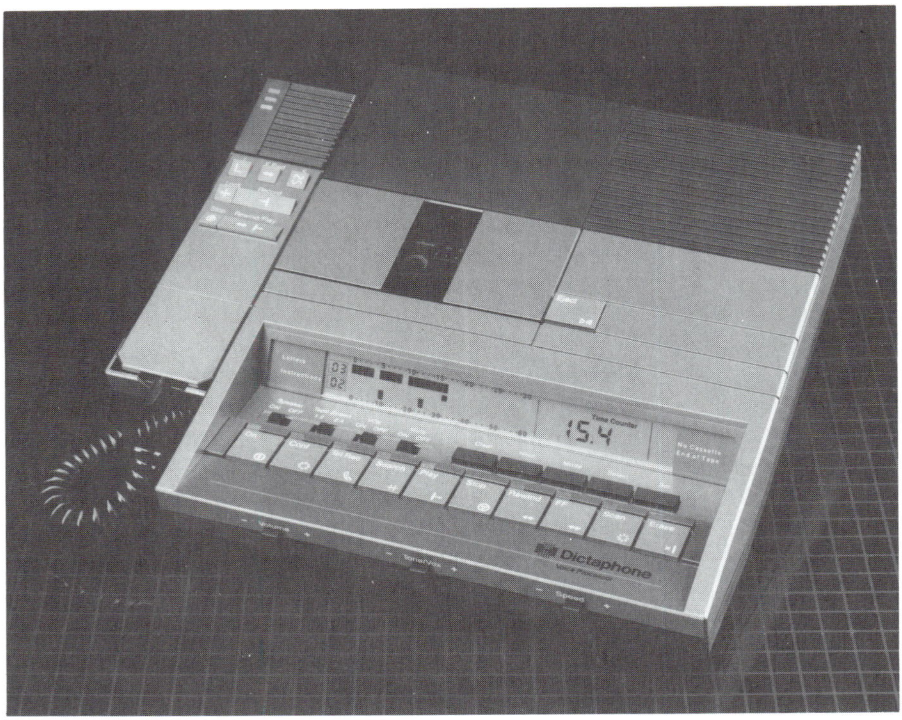

Central Dictation Systems

Central dictation systems are often used in organizations with central word processing facilities. The author "dials up" the system from within the office, via a direct wire or through the internal telephone system. The direct-wire dictation device in a central system often resembles a telephone and includes the features on desktop units. The information is available for transcription virtually immediately, eliminating the need for physical transfer of tapes. The value of central dictation units is increased through off-premise access, so that an individual can dictate into a central system from any telephone in the world.

Central units employ either discrete (removable) media or an endless loop, which is permanently contained in a recording "tank" to which both the dictation and transcribing units are connected. Many systems offer sophisticated management capabilities to provide logging and tracking of dictation activity, from time of entry to completion, and to produce statistical summaries, such as type of work, production totals, cost allocations and billing, and turnaround time.

Transcription Units

Transcription units are used by the transcriber, who keys the voice dictation into a word processing system. A transcription unit enables the transcriber to control the rate of speech and the audio level, as well as to repeat sections of dictation upon demand. Depending upon their features, transcribing units range in cost from $300 to $750.

The Dictaphone MVP microcassette dictation/communication system is a small dictation/transcription system that has four separate voice paths. This separation of paths allows four people to use the system at one time. Figure 5-15 shows the four-way dictation terminal, the record/play deck, and the transcription headset.

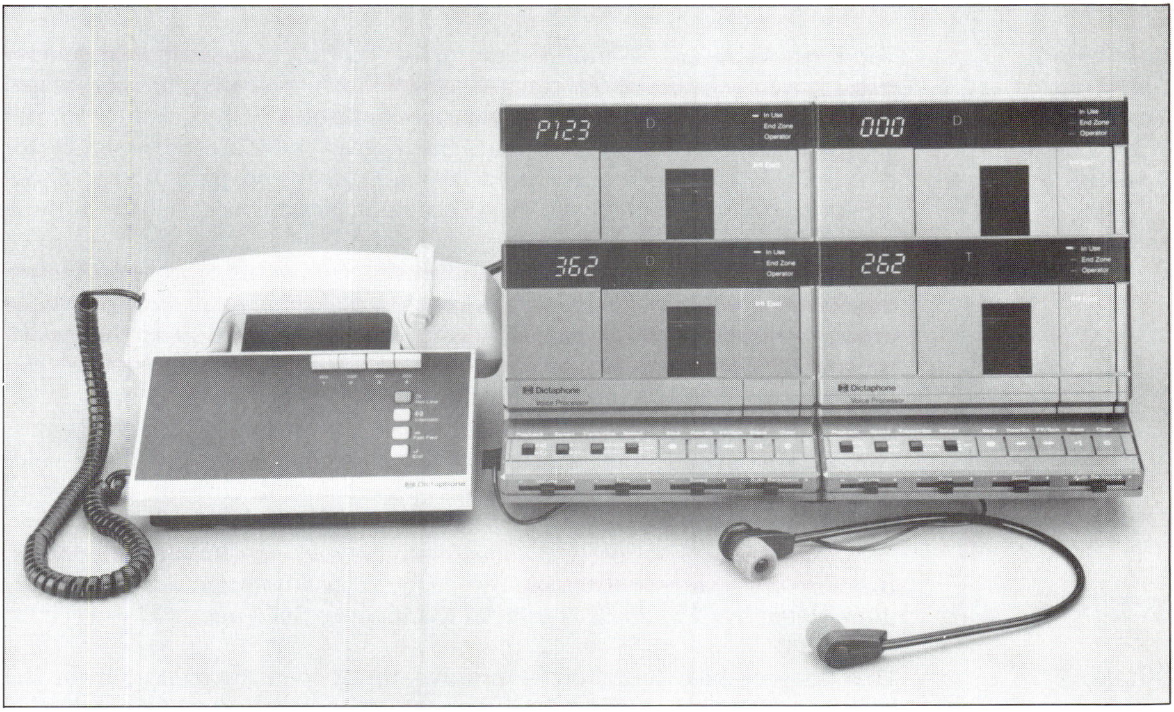

FIGURE 5-15. The Dictaphone MVP microcassette dictation/communication system.

Digital Dictation Devices

The dictation devices previously described for recording voice patterns on magnetic tape are based on *analog* technologies. To find a specific recording, one must search through the tape in a sequential fashion. Once recorded, revisions of dictated material are difficult, if not impossible; there is no room to "squeeze" new information into the text of the message. Any revised message will erase previously recorded material.

To address the problem of accessibility, and the need for updating (revising) dictated text, the industry offers *digital dictation devices*. Digital devices record sound waves and store them as binary units on disks or in solid-state memory banks. Using digital dictation technology, a dictator can quickly find and add to (or change) previously stored data.

Because of its high price and large size (Dictaphone's digital recording system costs $2000 per hour of recording and is the size of a refrigerator), use of such systems is currently limited to industries with large, central dictation systems. For instance, in hospitals, users (in this case, physicians) can read and update patient information even before it is transcribed. Industry leaders expect the price and size of digital dictation units to decrease. Digital dictation is seen by many as the next step in the evolution of dictation technology.

Integrated Dictation/Transcription/Word Processing Systems

Vendors such as Wang Laboratories market integrated dictation/transcription/word processing systems. These systems provide visual feedback on a VDT screen as information is dictated. While authors do not see their actual words on the screen, they see a symbolic representation for each second of speech, structured into sentences and paragraphs. These screen symbols provide visual reinforcement, making it easier for authors to visualize the context of dictated material.

Because the integrated dictation/transcription/word processing system digitizes the voice and stores it in random access memory, dictators easily can edit the dictation because they can stop at any point or move back to previously dictated text, using the screen symbols to locate the text. Dictators can quickly replay text, and edit—insert, delete, or move sentences or paragraphs. When dictation is completed, the document is stored. To transcribe the document, a transcriber plays back the voice recording and creates a new word processing document at a word processing terminal.

The next step for voice technologies—users "talking" to their computers—is available today. Digital voice technologies are covered in more detail in Chapter 9, "Artificial Intelligence Systems."

SUMMARY

This chapter has described alternative input media, ranging from the traditional typewriter to the voice technologies of the future. Visual display terminal technologies include the mouse, the light pen, touch-sensitive screens, the joystick, the paddle, the trackball, and the interactive tablet.

Each of these devices offers distinct advantages over a standard keyboard for specific applications.

Any typewriter is an input device when it is used in conjunction with optical character recognition devices. The electronic typewriter of today only vaguely resembles Christopher Sholes's 1868 model. This electronic device bridges the gap between the typewriter and the word processor; many of its features are characteristic of word processing systems.

Optical character recognition technologies scan data from paper, converting it to a digital format. These technologies include OCR, MICR, POS, and bar codes. The all-purpose OCR transforms paper data to digital data; MICR is used almost exclusively by banks to read checks; POS reads numbers; and bar code readers are used to identify, sort, catalog, or record prices of products and items that can be prelabeled, such as grocery items and office envelopes.

Workers in the office of today, as well as workers in the office of the future, have a wide variety of input devices from which to choose. Selection of the most appropriate applications depends on two interrelated considerations: the application and the user's preference.

DISCUSSION QUESTIONS

1. Identify the seven input devices discussed in this chapter that can be used in lieu of a keyboard. For each input device, suggest an application.

2. Select an appropriate input device for the following:
   a. An accountant who must work with long spreadsheets.
   b. An engineer who works with graphic drawings.
   c. An advertising artist who designs layouts for publication.
   d. A company newsletter editor.

3. Do you agree or disagree with the following statement: The typewriter is on its way out of the automated office; it has outlived its usefulness.

4. What are optical recognition technologies? Which have the most potential for office applications?

5. Describe dictation/transcription systems in the following categories: portable, desktop, and central.

6. Choose dictation/transcription systems for use in the following locations, and justify your selection:
   a. A 20-person law office.
   b. The office of the president of your university.
   c. A hospital.
   d. A large insurance company.

APPLICATION EXERCISES

1. Visit computer stores and ask to see the array of input devices for their products. If possible, use the devices. In interviewing the salespeople, ask for a profile of who would benefit from the devices they sell.
2. Visit a company that uses an optical character reader, then describe the capabilities of their system. What (if any) drawbacks are there to using the OCR?
3. Obtain an article in the popular press that describes voice recognition technologies. Critique the article, offering a summary of it and your reactions to the author's ideas.

SUGGESTED READINGS

Finlay, Douglas. "Electronic Typewriters: The Next Steps," *Administrative Management* (January 1987), pp. 34–40.

Gillespie, Karen R. "Computer Technology and Its Impact on Marketing/Retailing," *Business Education Association of Metropolitan New York Journal* (Spring 1987), pp. 9–21.

Paznik, M. Jill. "Optical Character Readers and Image Scanners Can Reduce Workload," *Administrative Management* (July 1986), pp. 23–28.

Williams, Charles M., and Senn, James A. "Introduction of Images into Automated Office Systems." In *Proceedings of the Sixth Annual Office Systems Research Conference* (Cleveland, Ohio: OSRA, 1987), pp. 64–74.

CHAPTER 6

PERIPHERALS: Image Technologies

OBJECTIVES

After completing this chapter, the reader should be able to meet the following objectives:

- Discuss the role of image technologies in the automated office.
- List characteristics of the following microforms: roll film, microfiche. microfilm jackets, aperture cards, and computer output microfilm.
- Justify the use of microfilm as a computer input/output medium.
- Given an image storage requirement, determine the best way to store the image.
- Identify three types of cameras used in micrographic systems.
- Explain the basic concepts of computer-assisted retrieval (CAR) systems.
- Give examples of the use of optical disk technology in the automated office.
- Appraise the outlook for both micrographics and the optical digital data disk in the automated office.

KEY TERMS

micrographics
rotary camera
planetary camera
step-and-repeat camera
index
blip coding
microform reader
microform reader/printer
reduction ratio
magnification ratio
roll film
microfiche
ultrafiche
microfilm jacket
aperture cards
computer output microfilm (COM)
computer input microfilm (CIM)
microfilm chip
computer-assisted retrieval (CAR)
optical disk
read-only disk
write-once/read-only disk
erasable disk
optical digital data disk (OD3)
optical videodisk
compact disk (CD-ROM)

INTRODUCTION

Chapter 5 described input peripherals; this chapter is about image storage peripherals. These technologies are capable of capturing information in any form—text, numbers, and/or graphics (including pictures)—and storing that information on an easily accessible medium. Unlike magnetic disk technologies, image technologies store a picture of the document, not just the data that is on the document.

Despite the infusion of technology, most offices today remain paper-based. To respond to the needs of offices for document storage media other than paper filing cabinets and for retrieval methods other than manual searches, vendors are developing and refining image technologies. Image technologies have the potential to redefine the ways information is stored. In fact, the emphasis of office systems is beginning to center on ways to manage and retrieve documents that are compatible with existing systems.

Office documents are one of two types: intelligence or evidentiary. Intelligence documents hold data that records what has been done—recordkeeping, forecasting, etc. Evidentiary documents (from the root word *evidence*) are proof that something happened. Examples are contracts, signed delivery slips, shipping documents, and invoices. While intelligence documents are not always kept for long periods of time (the computer can store their data; there is no need for the document itself), evidentiary documents must often be preserved in their original form.

For example, a marketing manager might want to know the quantity of merchandise shipped to a particular store for the past three years. The marketing manager needs numbers (intelligence documents), not the invoices (evidentiary documents). The adjustments manager, on the other hand, needs copies of original bills of lading (evidentiary documents) to process purchasers' claims that goods were missing or received in damaged condition.

Image technologies are changing the way evidentiary documents, which are typically paper-based, are saved. Image technology was limited to micrographics until just a few years ago. Today, another technology, the optical disk, is a contender in that market. Both of these technologies are discussed in detail in this chapter.

Facsimile systems are also considered to be image technology. However, because of facsimile's role in electronic transmission rather than in storage and retrieval, facsimile is discussed in Chapter 8, "Communications Technologies."

MICROGRAPHICS: TECHNOLOGY AND MEDIA

In 1839, John Dancer reduced a 20-inch document to 1/8 inch and read that document under a 100-power microscope. This was the beginning of micrographics. Micrographics was first used extensively in banks for maintaining records of check transactions. Micrographic applications have grown steadily since then, particularly as the technology related to micrographics enables it to be used in conjunction with other office technologies as part of an office system.

Traditionally, *micrographics* has been defined as technology that is used to reduce information to microminiature size and to capture that information on microforms. The definition has been updated, however, to include not only the creation but also the storage and retrieval of all types of microforms. Micrographic systems include cameras, indexing methods, readers or reader/printers, and computer-assisted retrieval. Today's micrographic systems can reduce storage space, and computer-assisted retrieval (CAR) can greatly increase retrieval speed. Computer output microfilm (COM) not only reduces paper use but also facilitates input. No longer a standalone technology, micrographics has the potential to play an important role in the integrated office.

This chapter discusses five micrographic media, or microforms: roll film, microfiche, jackets, aperture cards, and computer output microfilm. Next it describes the hardware technology of micrographics, including cameras and reader/printers. Computer-assisted retrieval systems, which enable a user to retrieve a microform via a computer system, are the last topic in this section.

Microform Media

Basic to an understanding of microform media are the terms *reduction ratio* and *magnification ratio*. *Reduction ratio* refers to the ratio between the size of the source document and the microform. For example, a system that reduces 48× has a reduction ratio of 48. *Magnification ratio* is the number of times the microform is to be enlarged in the viewing process.

The choice of a microform media depends on the following factors:

- The number of records to be filmed.
- The frequency of access needed.
- The need for a unit record card.
- The extent to which a microform is to be updated.

The office systems planner should be able to answer such questions before deciding upon a micrographic media/system. Five basic micrographic media are available: roll film, microfiche (''fiche''), jackets, aperture cards, and computer output microfilm (COM). Each medium has features that give it advantages over other media for certain types of applications. These features are discussed as each medium is described in the following section.

Roll Film (Microfilm)

Roll film, or microfilm, is frequently the medium of micrographic systems designed to store historical documents. One roll of 16mm, 35mm, or 105mm microfilm can contain as many as 2700 frames. Figure 6-1 pictures a roll of microfilm on top of a stack of papers. A microimage of all these papers is contained on the microfilm. The sequential roll film offers both

FIGURE 6-1. The small roll of microfilm stores all the data in this entire stack of papers.

file integrity and a simple means of indexing. However, scanning through roll film to retrieve documents may be time-consuming; therefore, high-speed readers (discussed later) are often part of a roll film micrographic system.

Microfiche

When the user needs to update microrecords easily, microfiche (shortened by the industry to "fiche"; pronounced "feesh") is often chosen. Fiche is a microfilm image cut and slipped into a 4 × 6 inch plastic holder. This holder acts as a unit record card, containing 60, 72, or 98 microimages. Because of its design, the fiche can be replaced or updated. Figure 6-2 includes an illustration of microfiche. Another advantage is that fiche readers are less expensive than high-speed roll film readers.

Ultrafiche stores records as fiche but at much higher reduction ratios that range from 90× to 400×. One ultrafiche card can hold up to 400 documents. Because of ultrafiche's extremely small size, an ultrafiche document requires a more powerful reader than the traditional fiche reader.

Microfilm Jacket

Another easily updated microform medium is the microfilm jacket (see Figure 6-2). A jacket is formed by two plastic sheets fused together, with the microform in between. The plastic sheets are divided horizontally into five rows, with 12 images in each row. To create or update, the user places a new piece of the roll film or fiche into the jacket.

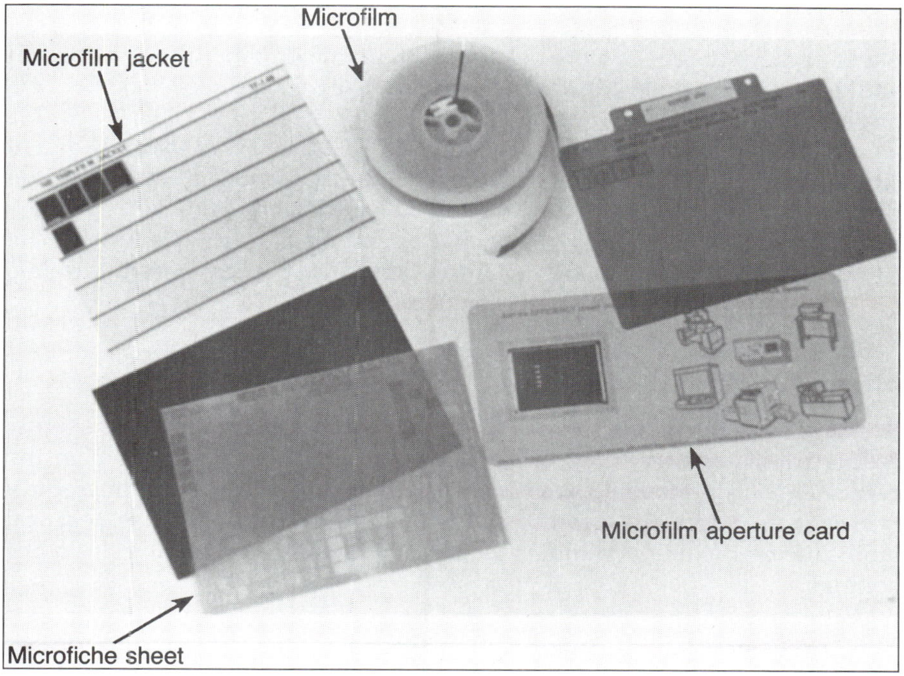

FIGURE 6-2. Roll microfilm, microfilm jacket, microfiche, and microfiche aperture card.

Aperture Cards

An aperture card (see Figure 6-2) is a keypunch card with a special insert for a piece of roll film. The aperture card thus combines a means of providing a unit record and a means of storing additional data for, perhaps, indexing or design specifications. Aperture cards are frequently used in engineering and design applications.

Computer Output Microfilm (COM)

Computer output microfilm (COM) transfers electronically stored data onto magnetic media without the need for a paper output stage. The COM system is capable of recording information either from magnetic tape or directly from a computer at extremely high speeds. As a rule of thumb, one cubic foot of COM fiche at 48× reduction will replace about 512 cubic feet of 11 × 14-inch computer printout paper.

Obvious advantages of COM are its ease of use and low cost of duplication and distribution. COM is extremely fast because no paper is required; output speeds can reach 26,000 lines per minute. COM becomes Computer Input Microfilm (CIM) when it is used as input for a processing system.

CIM permits data to be input directly from the microform, thus increasing throughput speed and data accuracy. CIM jams less often than paper because its size is more consistent than that of paper input media. In addition, the computer can read CIM more easily because its characters are more uniform.

In 1967, experts predicted the demise of COM/CIM in favor of digital storage media—optical disks (discussed later in this chapter). However, the prediction has not come true. In 1967, 50 COM units were sold; in 1983, over 700 were sold, bringing the total operating base to 7400 units. The future of COM is tied to the future of micrographics in general. Today, COM is a very viable storage/retrieval medium.

Microfilm Chip

A microfilm chip is an extremely small piece of microfilm with highly reduced images stored in a retrieval device. Because it is encased in the retrieval device, retrieval speed is extremely fast. The casing for microfilm, however, is extremely expensive; for this reason, and because practical applications do not abound, the technology has limited use in office settings.

Cameras

The three types of cameras used in micrographic systems are *rotary, planetary,* and *step-and-repeat.* The type of camera chosen is directly related to the type of media used. For example, rotary cameras or planetary cameras are used for microfilm or microfilm jackets; step-and-repeat cameras are required for microfiche and COM.

A *rotary camera,* such as the ALOS Simplex Recorder shown in Figure 6-3, operates much like a photocopier, with the source document "fed" into the camera unit. The speed of the film is synchronized to the speed of the conveyor belt. Once filmed, the unit stacks both the source documents and the newly created microimages.

On the other hand, a *planetary camera* is a stationary camera. A manual planetary camera requires an operator to place a source document (of almost any size) on the work surface, select the reduction ratio, and control the lighting. A semiautomatic planetary camera positions the source document, adjusts the light, and ejects the original document after it is filmed (see Figure 6-4).

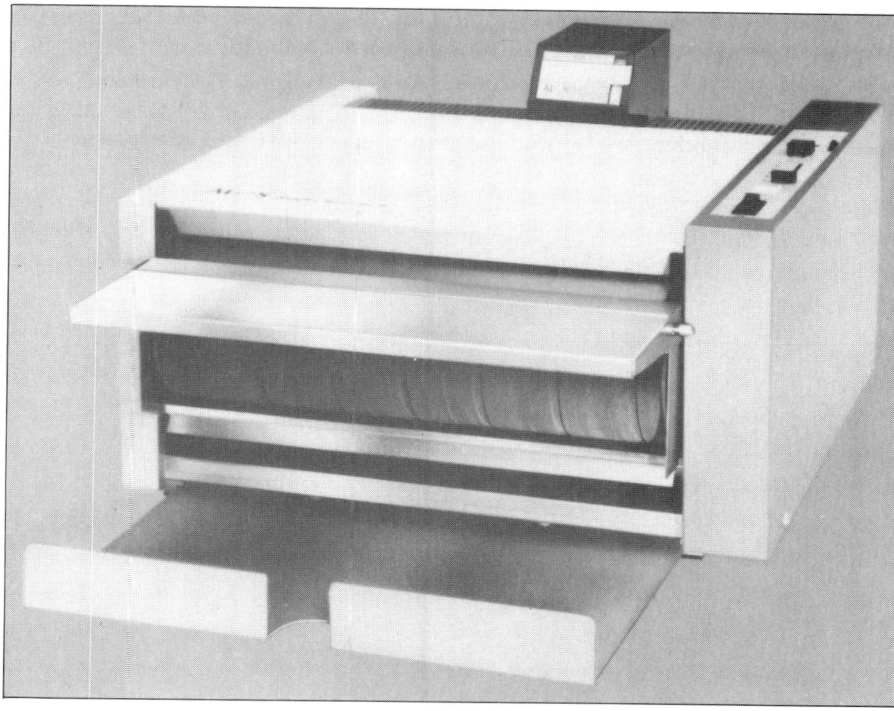

FIGURE 6-3.
A rotary camera:
The ALOS Simplex
Recorder 16.

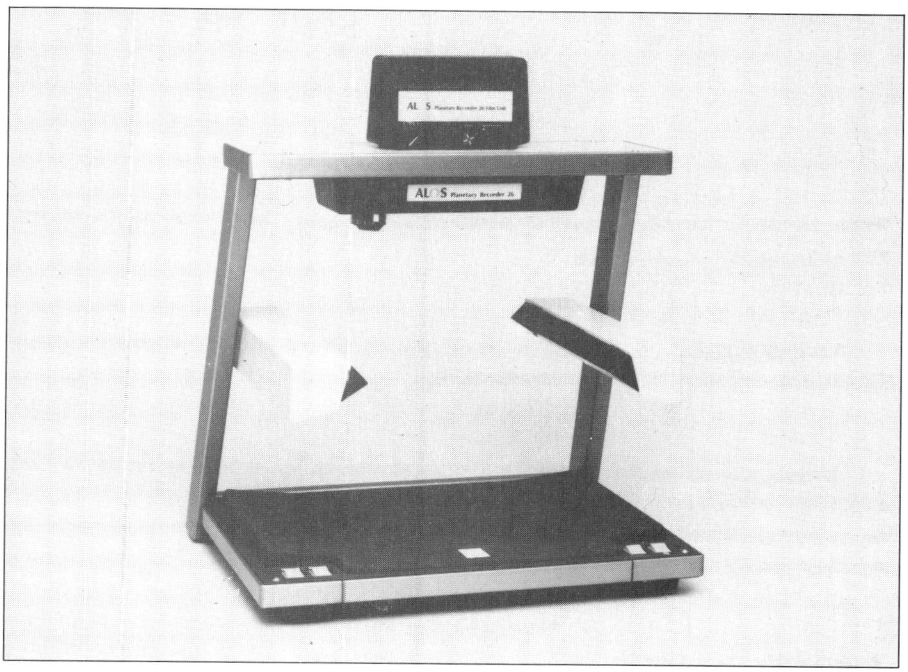

FIGURE 6-4.
A planetary camera:
The ALOS Planetary
Recorder 26.

A *step-and-repeat camera* is used to film small documents, and may also facilitate the updating of both fiche and COM. Because of the special film employed in the process, documents can be added to fiche or COM without damaging the original microforms. These very versatile cameras can capture both sides of a document at rates up to 5000 an hour; COM camera systems typically operate at speeds of 10,000 to 30,000 documents per hour. The Duplex Camera 15 illustrated in Figure 6-5 is a step-and-repeat camera used to microfilm checks and other small documents up to 5-1/2 inches wide.

FIGURE 6-5.
A step-and-repeat camera: The ALOS Duplex Camera 15.

Indexing Methods

To be useful, a microform must be easily retrieved. An *index* is the address of a particular microform. Imagine the difficulty of finding a particular microformed document among the thousands of images stored if an index were not available!

Only microfilm jackets and aperture cards have a means of indexing that is external to the microform itself. The other microform media rely on cameras that either number documents automatically or have a blip-coding mechanism.

Cameras that number documents automatically require the operator to manually create an index of the documents after the filming is completed. The operator lists the key words or document titles that correspond to the number on the microimage. Cameras that offer a blip-coding mechanism require the operator to first batch and index the documents. Then, as the documents are filmed, the blip-coding mechanism creates a small square mark on the film frame that can be read to retrieve a particular frame based on the pre-established index.

Microform Readers and Reader/Printers

Two basic types of microform readers are on the market: a unit that projects light from the front and a unit that projects light from the rear. Readers with light projected from the front are typically considered superior to readers with light projected from the rear. The front-light reader provides the following advantages:

- The lens projects directly onto a matte surface; no mirrors are needed.
- The shielding design prevents ceiling light obstruction.
- The viewing glass deflects glare.
- Bifocal wearers can easily view images.
- The design is simple and less expensive than the rear-light design.

Readers come in various sizes. The *stationary reader* is a large, generally high-resolution reader. The *portable reader*, such as the Elite II pictured in Figure 6-6, is lightweight and easy to use. The *lap reader* is very small and very inexpensive (many readers in this category cost less than $100). A final

FIGURE 6-6. A portable microform reader: The Elite II.

category of readers is the *reader/printer,* which enables the user to have the document output on paper at the time it is retrieved. Top-of-the-line reader/printers, including the Canon 80 (see Figure 6-7) and the Minolta

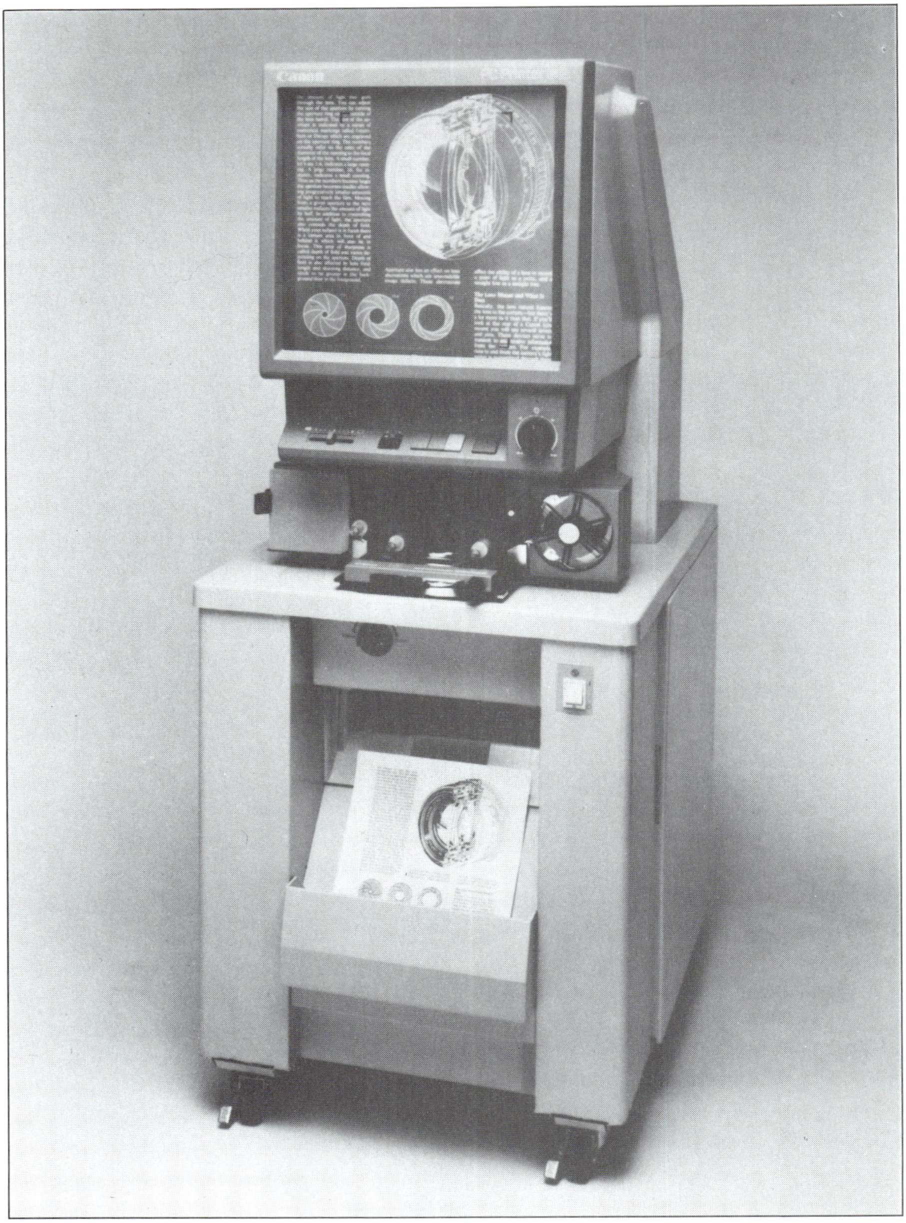

FIGURE 6-7. The Canon 80 reader/printer.

RP509 (see Figure 6-8), have many features that resemble copier features (see Chapter 7). Available features include the following:

- A motorized zoom lens that allows the user to view and print at the preferred magnification ratio.
- Automatic paper feed and high-speed printing.
- Bimodal printing, which allows the reader/printer to produce positive prints from either negative or positive microfilm images.
- Partial printing, which allows the operator to make prints of only selected portions of an image rather than the entire document.
- Book format printing, which allows the user to print side-by-side images (as in a book) on separate sheets of paper.

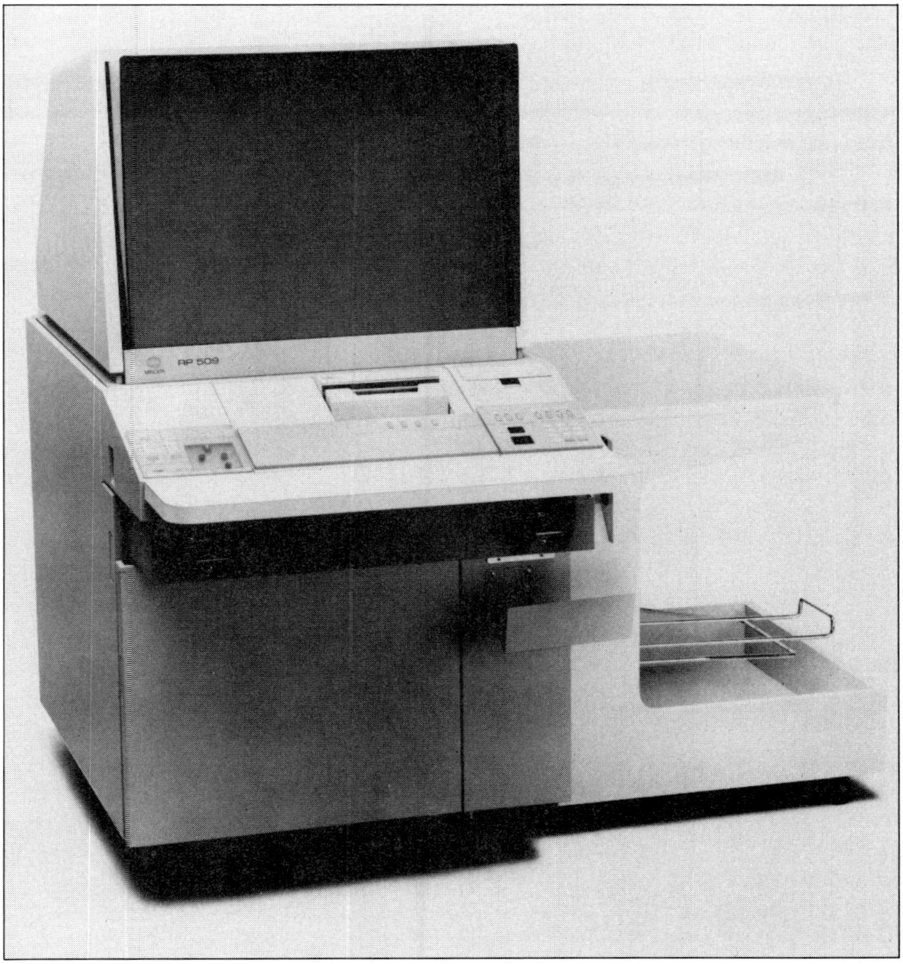

FIGURE 6-8.
The Minolta RP 509 reader/printer.

Computer-Assisted Retrieval

Computer-assisted retrieval (CAR) combines the ability of computers to store and manipulate index data with the space-saving and other advantages of microforms. By storing records on microfilm and using a computer to index storage addresses and summary information, control and retrieval of records can be improved at reduced cost. CAR systems such as the system shown in Figure 6-9 can provide fast indexing, easy cross-referencing, and quick and easy retrieval.

A CAR system requires the user first to establish a central database. This database can be on roll film, cassette film, cartridge film, or fiche. For example, individual records are retrieved from microfiche systems as the retrieval device moves to a specific slot that holds the fiche. Each fiche has a unique identifier (code) that was imprinted on the fiche at the time of filming. The code may be in numbers or letters, or both. Some fiche systems generate indexes while filming. Others operate with metal strips attached to the bottom of the fiche, providing unique identification for the fiche.

A CAR system consists of the following equipment: a computer with a disk storage device (for the index), VDT and keyboard, microfilm access file, microimage reader, and printer.

The user keys into the computer a retrieval code or relevant information to locate the required information. Summary information about the document or its storage location is displayed on the VDT screen. Depending on the means by which the document is physically retrieved, CAR systems operate on one of three basic systems:

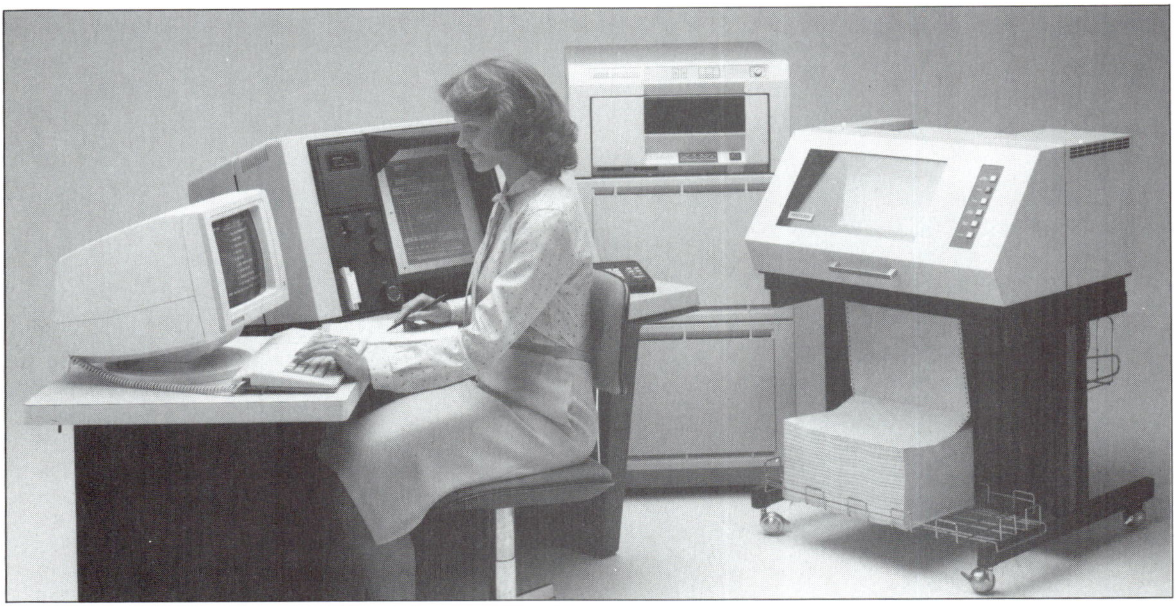

FIGURE 6-9. A computer-assisted retrieval system: The Kodak KAR-4400.

1. *Manual retrieval and display of the microform.* After the user locates the desired document(s) on the index, the user manually retrieves the film/fiche/jacket, loading the microform on the reader by hand.

2. *Automated retrieval of the microform.* After locating the documents, a mechanized retrieval system locates the appropriate microform and automatically displays it on the microimage reader for viewing or printing.

3. *Electronic image delivery.* This is the most sophisticated of the CAR delivery systems. Here the requested microimage is located automatically, digitized, and sent directly to the user's VDT for viewing or printing. For such an operation, a high-resolution VDT is required. Electronic image delivery systems provide the integration and ease of use necessary for an office system to operate efficiently. Moreover, such retrieval ensures file integrity (the records are never removed from the central file) and, in addition, a single database can support a number of remote users.

At one time, CAR systems relied on roll film because of the ease of handling cassettes and cartridges. Today, however, many systems incorporate microfiche as the microform medium of choice. To remain competitive, microform manufacturers will need to continue to develop their CAR systems. Figure 6-10 depicts a CAR system that links microimage terminals with the IBM PC/AT, the PC/XT, or compatible microcomputers through special software and hardware. This system is designed for use in small businesses and in departments where there is a need for fast access to documents.

FIGURE 6-10. **A computer-assisted retrieval (CAR) system that links microimage terminals with a microcomputer: The Kodak KAR-1500 PC information system.**

The Role of Micrographics

The success of micrographics in the automated office largely depends on how the technology coexists with paper systems and digital systems. Ideally, one could convert any of the information transfer media—paper, digital data, or micrographics—from one media to another, "going from paper to microforms, enlarging back to paper when needed, and going from digital to microforms using computer-output microfilm (COM) technology."[1] This process is diagrammed in Figure 6-11; note the inclusion

FIGURE 6-11. Format options for information: The paper/digital conversion process.

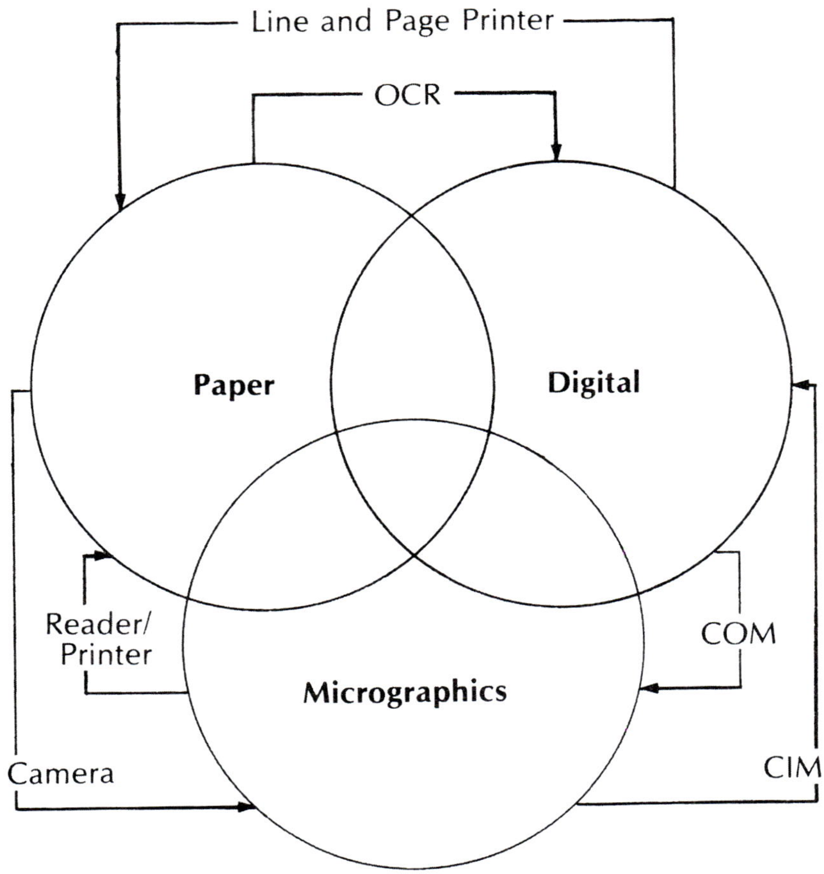

OCR – Optical Character Reader

CIM – Computer-Input Microfilm

COM – Computer-Output Microfilm

of printers. Line and page printers (discussed in Chapter 7) are fast enough to compete with COM units (a page printer can produce 18,000 lines per minute; a COM recorder can produce 32,000 lines per minute). Such systems serve the user by providing output on the most convenient medium.

Microforms as storage media are considerably less expensive than magnetic tape and today are much more operable than optical disks, which are discussed in the following section.

OPTICAL DISKS

Magnetic disks, discussed in Chapter 4, store digital data. Microforms store microminiature pictures of a document. The optical disk combines the digital capabilities of the magnetic disk with the graphic capabilities of microforms It can even offer audio capabilities. Because optical disk technology provides a means of storing graphics as digits, a document can be retrieved electronically and displayed on a video monitor.

To understand optical disk technology, one needs to differentiate between *digital* and *digitized* data. When information is keyed or entered into a system via an OCR device, that information is digital. Digital information is stored as distinct characters ("a," "33," "income statement") and can be read, accessed, changed, and stored.

Digital data can be stored as single digits, but photographs and charts (images) cannot. The computer cannot find a single, identifiable character within an image. Because a single element cannot be found, a photograph or chart must be stored as a unit record. What this means to image-storage technologies is that the photograph or chart must first be *digitized*. Digitized data may require from 10 to 100 times more storage space than digital data. To be read, digitized data also requires a high-resolution terminal. It cannot be printed out on conventional data or word processing printers.[2]

The Optical Disk: How Does It Work?

The optical disk is also known as a *laser disk*. (*Laser* and *optics* both mean *light*.) Data is recorded by the presence or absence of holes. The diagram of the optical disk system shown in Figure 6-12 shows how the laser light writes and reads data.

In *The Office Technologies*, Alan Purchase described optical disk technology as follows:

> The input signal modulates a semiconductor diode-write laser. This then sends binary "0" or "1" signals through a beam combiner and mirror to the objective lens that focuses the coherent light, marking for "1's" and not marking for "0's." On readback, the pattern marked on the disk modulates the beam of a helium-neon read laser. The read beam is returned to an optical detector that converts the optical pattern to the binary bit-pattern output signal.[3]

FIGURE 6-12. The optical disk system.

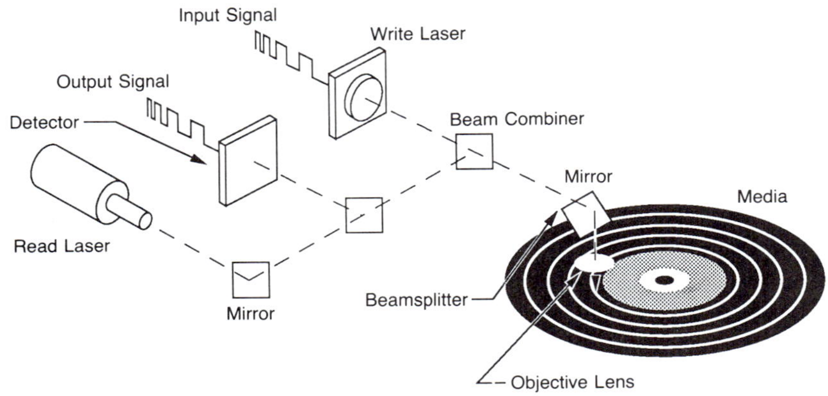

An optical disk drive differs from a magnetic disk drive in that the optical read/write head is a laser; other components are similar. Optical disk technologies on the market today fall into one of the following three categories:

1. *Read-only disks,* which are prerecorded. Examples include disks offered by electronic publishing companies (the entire *Encyclopaedia Britannica* can be purchased on CD-ROM) and suppliers of databases.
2. *Write-once/read-only disks,* which record information once for retrieval later.
3. *Erasable disks,* which have limited availability today. This technology is expected to grow in the future.

Generally, these disk types are used as descriptors for three varieties of optical disk technologies: the optical digital data disk (OD3), the optical videodisk, and the compact disk (CD). The following section describes each of these disks and gives examples of their roles in the automated office.

Optical Digital Data Disk (OD3)

The optical digital data disk (OD3) works much like magnetic storage but is read-only. The OD3, a thin, silver disk, offers long archival life and extremely quick retrieval time. While the OD3 is not erasable, it is updatable when tracks are left open. A practical use of the OD3 is for telephone directories; items can be either added or coded "no longer in service." Because of its expense, the OD3 is limited to large-scale document filing by organizations such as the United States Army, NASA, and the Library of Congress.

The future of the OD3 will largely depend on its degree of standardization, the development of necessary operational software, and the lowering of its price.

Optical Video Disk

The optical video disk, like the OD3, is a thin, silver 8- or 12-inch disk that can store up to 54,000 unique, digitized images. What is unique about the video disk is that it can store graphics and full-motion video, and can even include two audio tracks. The video disk can stand on its own with a TV monitor or be interfaced with a computer, at which point it is considered an interactive video disk. Of special interest, graphics can be imposed, offering instructions, questions, or updating. The system can also permit one image to remain on the monitor while the narration continues, allowing for more audio information.

The future of the optical video disk will depend upon the development of practical applications. Currently, the optical video disk is touted as an extemely valuable training tool. Wang, for example, has developed a computer-controlled video disk tutorial to train word processing operators. Called the Wang Interactive Learning System (WILS), it instructs operators in the use of Wang word processing equipment. Research interest in the video disk as a training tool remains high, with manufacturers investing in research ventures, such as the Japan Victor Corporation–New York University interactive video disk project.

Compact Disk

The compact disk, which is also known as CD-ROM (compact disk, read-only memory), was introduced in 1983. This is the disk found in the consumer market for extremely high-quality audio and video. It can store digital, digitized, and video data and is small enough to fit in a standard floppy disk drive (although it requires a special laser disk drive). The CD-ROM can store more than 550 megabytes of compressed digital data.

Like its two optical counterparts, the growth of CD-ROM depends upon the development of standards. When manufacturers produce file formats and hardware interface standards, CD-ROM will have an effect on the automated office. However, pioneers exist; for example, Information Storage has introduced a desktop optical disk system with 100 megabytes of memory.

Figure 6-13, an article entitled "Newsreel of Fortune," describes an application of CD-ROM technology—the storage and retrieval of newsreels that ran between 1929 and 1967.

FIGURE 6-13.
A CD-ROM application.

Newsreel of Fortune

When Jonathan Pollard was an associate producer for the ABC documentary *'45/'85,* he spent months riffling through index cards that summarized old movie house newsreels, "searching for the 9,001st story that was undoubtedly the gem." He figured there had to be a better way to keep track of all that footage. So he invented one.

Today, sitting in his brand-new home office, 26-year-old Pollard holds up a compact disc encoded with thousands of newsreel summaries. "With this," he says, "I will save the media thousands of dollars, hours of tedious research, and a *lot* of angst."

Pollard's new company, Newsreel Access Systems, will offer networks and other clients some 200,000 synopses of newsreels that ran between 1929 and 1967. The footage—a "21" Club manager unveiling thousands of dollars' worth of bootleg booze in 1935, an Air Force pilot flying loops over San Francisco in 1929—has been gathering dust in libraries in New York, California, and Washington, D.C., too scattered and unorganized for harried researchers to exploit fully.

Using a "full text retrieval" system, Pollard's computer indexes every word of the newsreel summaries; users type in key words, and the computer spits out stories. Pollard, who broke into television as a 23-year-old assistant to ABC News Executive Vice-President David Burke, will lease his discs to heavy users such as ABC and have his own research staff track down stories for his lighter users. Producers for ABC's documentary series, *Our World,* are hoping that Pollard's discs will lead them to fresh, offbeat stories.

Uses of Optical Disk Storage Technologies

Figure 6-14 gives some guidelines for determining which of the three formats—videodisk, OD3, or CD-ROM—would be most appropriate in a given situation.

The future of optical disk technology depends upon how quickly and cheaply vendors can respond to market demand for the technology. At the time of this writing, at least 40 companies are developing optical media, and 30 others are building appropriate hardware. Yet another driving force to the development of such an image storage system is the need for such technology in Japan, where 70 percent of all stored information consists of documents handwritten in Kanji. In the United States and Western Europe, information is stored in alphanumeric characters, represented by an ASCII code. Given Japan's interest and success in developing other information technologies, one can only expect the region-specific demand for optical disk technology to spur its development.

When retrieving information, the office worker of the near future will be able to see the series of pictures, hear the speech, or read the table. The concept of the optical disk is "leading the way for the next series of changes in the automated office—not just more storage capacity, but toward greater storage of more appropriate data."[4]

FORMAT	VIDEO DISK	OPTICAL DIGITAL DATA DISK	COMPACT DISK (ROM)
When to consider When there is a need for. . .	Mass delivery of prepared multimedia information	Mass storage of digital data	Mass distribution of data bases, application and operating system software
Criteria for use When user population is. . .	Geographically dispersed	In discrete locations	Geographically dispersed
When the data is. . .	Multimedia material	Documents, records, transactions, logs, operating system software	Databases, application software, operating system software
When the situation calls for . .	Individual or group training, practice, or information gathering	Mass storage, individual retrieval of permanently stored data	Individual manipulation of data or application software
When data is needed for the successful completion of. . .	Processes, procedures, problem-solving, decision-making	Document retrieval and manipulation	Data searches and computer programs
Similarities among the three formats of optical storage technologies: random access; high-density storage; durability of the media; consistent, error-free data; cost-effectiveness per unit of storage; ten+ year life span of the data.			

FIGURE 6-14. Guidelines for choosing video disk, optical digital data disk, or compact disk (ROM).

SUMMARY

This chapter described image storage technologies: micrographics and optical disks. In an effort to kill the "paper tiger," organizations are looking to ways of storing documents that must be saved (evidentiary documents) on media other than paper.

Micrographics is the technology related to the creation, retrieval, and use of microforms, the media on which the miniature picture of the document rests. The cameras required for capturing the document are the rotary (moving), planetary (stationary), and step-and-repeat (for updating fiche and COM) cameras.

While microfilm jackets and aperture cards are indexed external to the microfilm itself (on the jacket or card), other microforms are indexed by a blip-coding mechanism. To index by using a blip-coding mechanism, one must first compile an index. Then, when documents are entered in the order of the index, the blip-coding mechanism creates a small square mark that records the index code. The code can be used later to retrieve the microform.

Microform readers operate either with light projected from the front or with light projected from the rear. The size and quality of readers vary; reader/printers enable the user to make a paper copy of the image on the reader screen.

Microforms come in five basic forms or media: roll film, microfiche, microfilm jackets, aperture cards, and computer output microfilm.

Roll film (microfilm) is the medium of choice for historical documents. (For example, libraries often use roll film for storing documents.) The main disadvantage of roll film is that it must be accessed sequentially; therefore, high-speed readers are often necessary.

Microfiche is the medium of choice when documents are best accessed as a unit record or must be updated. Fiche is roll film that has been cut and slipped into a plastic holder. To update it, one simply replaces the old film with a revised film.

Microfilm jackets are formed by two plastic sheets fused together, with a piece of roll film in between. The plastic sheets hold 60 microimages, enabling large numbers of documents to be filed and kept together.

Aperture cards are keypunch cards with a special insert for a piece of roll film. The keypunch cards enable indexing and specifications to be recorded with the microform.

Computer output microfilm (COM) stores computer output on micrographic media without going through a paper stage. COM is easy to use. When used as input for a computer system (computer input microfilm), CIM enables data to be input at extremely high speeds.

Computer-assisted retrieval (CAR) systems aid the microform retrieval process. CAR systems may be manual, automatic, or electronic. CAR systems may ensure the future of micrographics as a key player in the automated office.

Like microforms, the optical disk stores graphic data; however, the OD first digitizes the document. Three varieties of the OD are on the market today: (1) The *optical digital data disk* (OD3) is typically not erasable and can be updated only by leaving tracks open. The OD3 is expensive and is now used only for large-scale document filing. (2) The *optical video disk* can store full-motion video as well as audio tracks. The video disk has applications beyond storage; popular applications are in the field of training. (3) The *compact disk* (CD-ROM) can store digital, digitized, and video/audio data.

Never before has there been such a variety of ways to store documents. In the effort to reach the "paperless office," organizations will turn to either micrographics or the optical disk. Which medium is chosen will depend on the technology that makes it compatible with existing office systems, a price range that makes it feasible, and a perceived need for the quality or features that define the medium.

DISCUSSION QUESTIONS

1. Why is micrographics making a comeback as a technology appropriate for the automated office?
2. List the six micrographics media discussed in this chapter and state the advantages and disadvantages of each.
3. Describe the technologies that constitute a micrographics system.
4. What are the three ways in which computer-assisted retrieval (CAR) systems may operate?
5. What is the outlook for applications of the optical disk (OD)? What factors are encouraging OD developments? What factors are currently hindering OD development?
6. Suggest image storage media for the following cases:
   a. An insurance company that has copies of customer policies dating back to 1960.
   b. A law firm that has case records for 20 attorneys for 10 years.
   c. The public library's archival division.
   d. "Directory assistance" for the telephone company.
   e. City University, which has records of its graduates since its founding in 1878.
   f. A three-person CPA office in your community.

APPLICATION EXERCISES

1. Interview the director of micrographics (or an individual with a similar title) in his or her work location. Which technologies does that person use? Why? What are the department's plans for the future?
2. Read several recent articles on optical disk technology. Summarize the technical developments and compare the authors' outlooks on the potential of optical disks in the automated office.

SUGGESTED READINGS

"Advantages of Data Aperture Cards over Punched Aperture Cards," *IMC Journal* (March–April 1987), pp. 17–19.

Fidoten, Robert E. "A Prototype Interactive Video Disc System," *Office Systems Research Journal* (Spring 1988), pp. 27–29.

Records Management Quarterly. The official journal of the Association of Records Managers and Administrators.

Williams, Robert F. *Legality of Microfilm* (New York: Association of Records Managers and Administrators, 1987).

PERIPHERALS: Printers and Copiers

CHAPTER

7

OBJECTIVES

After completing this chapter, the reader should be able to meet the following objectives:

- Categorize both printers and copiers according to their various operating technologies.
- Develop a list of technological considerations important in the selection of a printer.
- Understand the concept of printer speed and the terms that describe the rate at which a printer produces paper output.
- Given a specific printing application, select an appropriate printer category.
- Describe various types of impact and nonimpact printers and their prospective effect on the printer market.
- List at least four printer accessories that may increase the cost of a printer.
- Develop a list of copier features for use in comparing various copier models.
- Understand the concept of copier speed and use the terms that describe the rate at which a copier produces paper output.
- Discuss the potential of the intelligent copier.
- Define photocomposition and differentiate among desktop publishing, workstation publishing, and photocomposition systems.
- List the components of a desktop publishing system.
- Describe printing and copying technologies of the future.

KEY TERMS

impact printer
nonimpact printer
compatible
speed
font
pitch
resolution
thermal printer
ion printer
magnetic printer
feeder
plain paper copier (ppc)
coated paper copier (cpc)
thermal copier

bit-mapped graphics
block mode graphics
dot matrix printer
daisy wheel printer
ball element printer
thimble printer
band printer
laser printer
ink-jet printer
dual spectrum copier
console copier
desktop copier
personal copier
intelligent copier
computer-aided publishing
desktop publishing system
workstation publishing system
electronic photocomposition

INTRODUCTION

Despite electronic storage and transmission technology, predictions of the paperless office have not come true. In fact, paper usage is expected to increase 10 percent per year through the end of the 1980s. Printers and copiers remain in demand because people need to see their thoughts on paper and to distribute "hard copy" from location to location. Fortunately, the development of computer systems has been paralleled by the rapid development and refinement of printer and copier technologies. Today's printers and copiers provide quality that was unimaginable a decade ago and within price ranges affordable by every office.

This chapter is divided into two main sections. The first section describes printer technologies, and the second section describes copier technologies. Within each section is an overview of criteria the office systems planner must consider in selecting the technology appropriate for a given work environment. This overview includes a categorization of each technology's functional operation, available accessories, operating costs, and special operating requirements. Each part concludes with a discussion of new developments that may emerge in the industry.

PRINTERS

Printers are categorized as *impact* or *nonimpact* printers depending on how they work. Impact printers require a typebar, element, hammer, or other striking device to transfer ink from the ribbon to the paper, much like a traditional typewriter. In fact, as discussed in Chapter 5, electronic typewriters sometimes double as printers. Impact printers are based on typewriter technologies. Nonimpact printers, on the other hand, use a variety of other techniques and technologies to create images on paper. Nonimpact printers are based on the same technologies used in the copying process.

Technological Considerations

Several technological considerations transcend both impact and nonimpact categories of printers. These considerations include speed, software compatibility, communications parameters, print size, resolution, noise, maintenance, and color and graphics capabilities.

Software Compatibility

The application software used for data or word processing must be compatible with the printer because the printing process is controlled by the computer program. Various printer models use different control codes. For example, a carriage return instruction might be indicated by !! on one brand of printer and by /r on another brand of printer. Some printers cannot be used unless the printer has been modified; others work equally well with a wide variety of software programs. In selecting a printer, one must ensure that the printer accepts the application software or can be modified to do so.

To enable application software to be used on a variety of printers, many software programs include a variety of Printer Action (or Attribute) Tables (PATs) designed for use with specific brands and models of printers. These PATs for each printer model are generally listed in the software manual

Communications Parameters

The printer must also be given *parameters*, that is, a description of how it is to communicate with the computer. The hardware interface must be compatible with the computer. This interface is either *serial* or *parallel*. Serial interfaces transmit data one piece at a time; parallel interfaces, which are much faster, send packets of data simultaneously. In the case of microcomputers, the printer card determines whether the computer requires a serial or parallel interface. By changing the printer card, the user can control whether the computer operates with a serial or parallel interface.

Speed

In describing speeds of printers, the phrases *characters per second* (cps), *lines per minute* (lpm), and *pages per minute* (ppm) are used. Industry standards specify that 70 characters equal one line and 54 lines equal one page. A ppm standard is a valid measurement only for nonimpact printers, which run at extremely high speeds, some up to 120 ppm.

A second speed consideration is *skip speed*, or the time it takes the printer to leave white (empty) space on a page of output. Skip speeds are generally given only for nonimpact printers. Skip speed is a very important consideration, for example, when only one or two items are printed per invoice. With a high skip speed, the printer can skip from invoice to invoice very quickly. This ability to sense the end of the line or blank space on a page is especially important for unidirectional impact printers.

Size of Print

As they relate to size, two terms are important: *font* and *pitch.*

Font Type *font* refers to the shape or style of the printed character (see Figure 7-1). For example, Palatino and Lubalin fonts are used in this text. More than 200 fonts are available from which to choose. Even the least expensive printer is capable of multiple pitch and font variations. The number of available fonts generally increases with the sophistication and cost of the printer, and most fonts are built into the printer itself. Legibility, clarity, emphasis, and serif (the short line stemming from the main stroke of a letter: e.g., 1, not l) are important considerations in selecting a font.

Pitch *Pitch* refers to both the size of a letter and the spacing between the letters of the font. Familiar pitch terms are 10 (*pica*), 12 (*elite*), 15 (*condensed*), and *proportional* spacing. These numbers refer to the number of characters in a horizontal inch of type. Proportional spacing allows each letter to

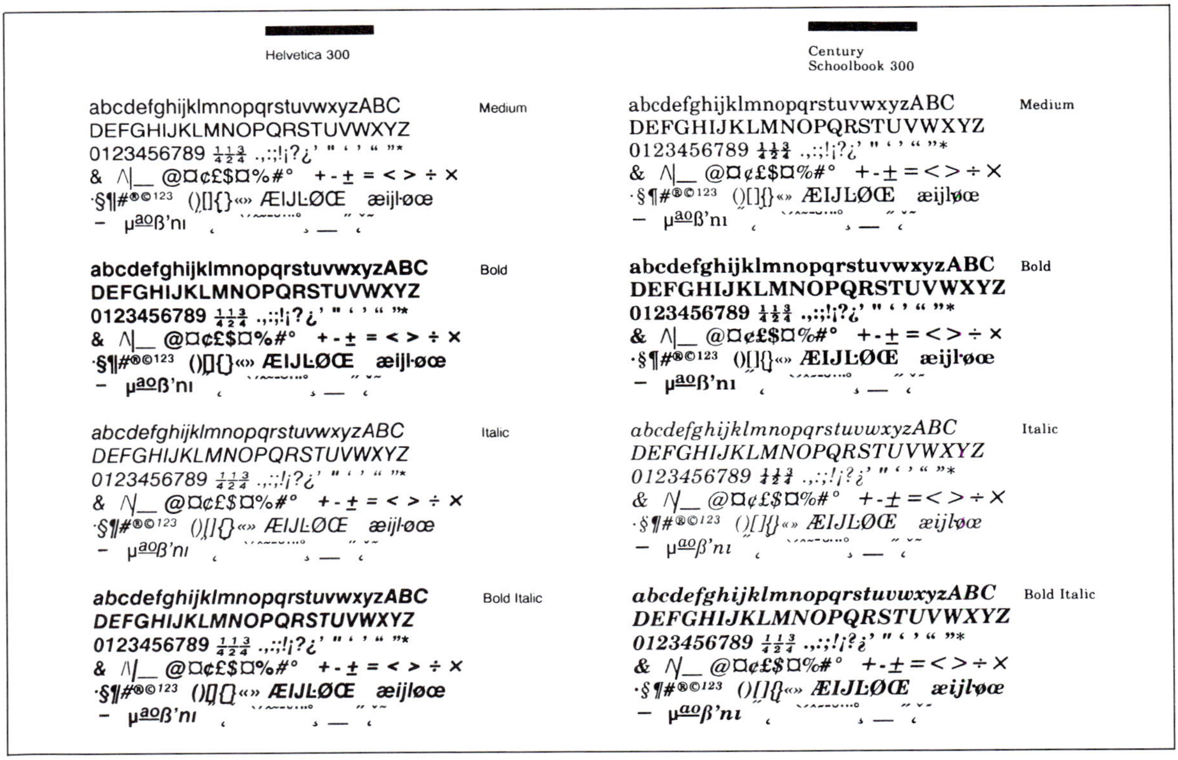

FIGURE 7-1. Examples of different fonts. The Helvetica 300 typeface is a very popular sans serif face noted for its readability. The Century Schoolbook 300 typeface is a serif design that provides maximum readability.

occupy a horizontal space in accordance with its width. For example, the letter *i* takes much less space than the letter *m;* the letter *f* takes less space than the letter *o*. Capitals also occupy more space than lower-case letters.

Another measure of print size is *point,* which refers to the size of the characters as measured in picas (a printer's measure). The larger the character, the higher the point size (which ranges from very tiny to headline sizes). In addition, point size may be emphasized or minimized by the thickness of letters; a character may be very thin, as in italics, or very thick, as in boldface. The headings and titles of this book illustrate how the appearance of one type font can be altered by changing point size. Figure 7-2 shows Helvetica 300 boldface type in six different point sizes.

Helvetica 300

Typography is a servant, the servant of thought and language to which it gives visible existence. Type gives body and voice to silent thought. The speaking page carries it through the centuries. To read means to obtain meaning from words, and legibility is that quality which enables words to be read.	6 point
Typography is a servant, the servant of thought and language to which it gives visible existence. Type gives body and voice to silent thought. The speaking page carries it through the centuries. To read means to obtain meaning from words.	7 point
Typography is a servant, the servant of thought and language to which it gives visible existence. Type give body and voice to silent thought. The speaking page carries it through the centuries. To read means to obtain meaning from words.	8 point
Typography is a servant, the servant of thought and language to which it gives visible existence. Type gives body and voice to silent thought. The speaking page carries it through the centuries.	9 point
Typography is a servant, the servant of thought and language to which it gives visible existence. Type gives body and voice to silent thought. The speaking page carries it through the centuries.	10 point
Typography is a servant, the servant of thought and language to which it gives visible existence. Type gives body and voice to silent thought. The speaking page carries it through the centuries. Typography is art.	11 point

FIGURE 7-2. Helvetica 300 boldface type in six different point sizes.

Resolution

Resolution describes the quality of print. The higher the resolution, the clearer, more readable the copy. Manufacturers often classify impact printers by the *resolution* of their output. Office systems analysts frequently refer to resolution in comparison to typewriter print quality: draft quality (DQ), near-letter quality (NLQ), or letter quality (LQ). Nevertheless, care must be exercised in using these classifications as true indicators of output quality; neither manufacturers nor consumers agree on standards that differentiate draft from near letter quality or near letter quality from letter quality.

Noise

A printer can add 80 or more sound decibels to an office environment. The Occupational Safety and Health Administration (OSHA) reports that exposure to levels above 75 decibels for eight hours can be dangerous. Nonimpact printers are noticeably quieter than impact models because they have no typebar and, therefore, make no contact with a platen. To mask the noise of a printer, sound-resistant hoods are available.

Maintenance

The degree to which a printer requires upkeep and repair is considered its reliability, which is commonly measured by the mean time between failures (MTBF). MTBF is the average time a device can be expected to run without a breakdown.

Because nonimpact printers are still in a developmental stage, they may break down more frequently than impact printers. However, because nonimpact printers have fewer moving parts than impact printers and because of continually improving technologies, maintainability as a selection factor may favor the nonimpact printer in the near future.

Color

Both impact and nonimpact printers can provide output in a variety of colors, but quality of color is not consistent among the models. Impact printers use multicolor ribbons. Some nonimpact printers, such as ink-jet printers, use various color inks in printing. Other nonimpact printers, such as the laser printer, are limited to monochrome. As the capabilities of laser printers increase, this limitation may soon be eliminated.

Graphics

Nonimpact printers are capable of graphic output, whereas not all impact printers are. Two types of graphic printing are most commonly used with impact models that have graphic compatibility: bit-mapped and block-mode. Bit-mapped graphics, often found on dot matrix printers, are capable of producing acceptable graphics; the image, however, may be jagged, as the dot matrix cannot make true curves. As Figure 7-3 shows, dots can be used to design special characters. Block-mode graphics, on the other hand, are made by repeating regular characters (see Figure 7-4). Block mode is often inappropriate, however, for business needs.

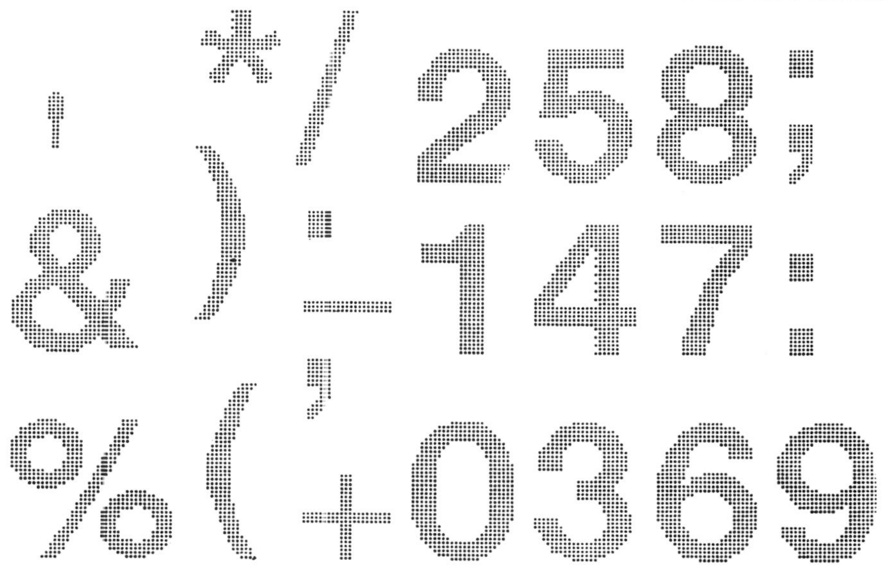

FIGURE 7-3. Bit maps of a font digitized at 240 dots per inch. Note the extraneous dots along the left edge of the vertical line in the character 4. The font designer introduced these dots for visual effect. Larger sizes of the same characters would not incorporate these dots.

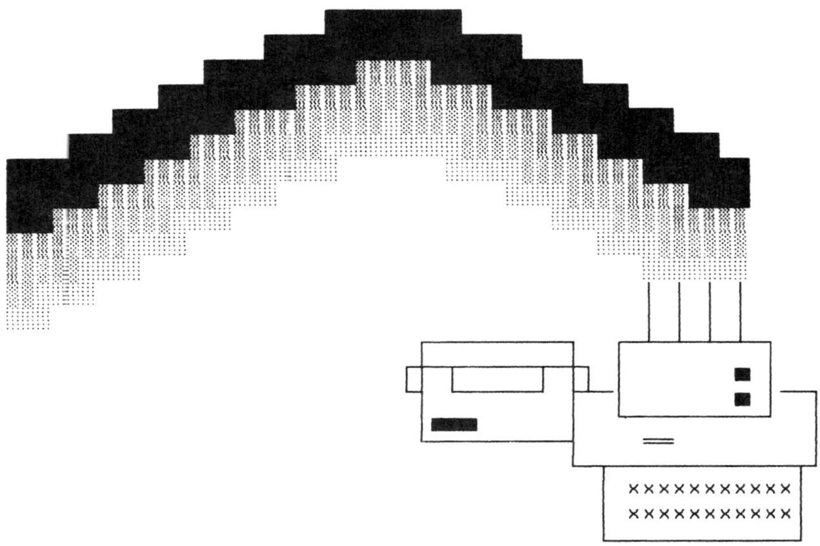

FIGURE 7-4. Block mode graphics.

When an impact printer is advertised as capable of producing graphics, the purchaser should inquire if the graphics are block- or bit-mode. Again, on the other hand, all nonimpact printers are capable of graphic output, depending upon the specific graphics software program.

Impact Printers

Impact printers are much slower than nonimpact printers. In an age when time is so important, why would an analyst choose an impact over a nonimpact printer? Price is the first factor; impact printers are less expensive than nonimpact printers. Second, an impact printer can make multiple copies. Third, impact printers are generally more reliable than nonimpact printers (at least at this time).

The types of impact printers to be discussed here are the dot matrix, daisy wheel, ball, thimble, and band.

Dot Matrix

Dot matrix technologies get their name from how their characters are shaped. Individual needles or wires striking a ribbon produce a pattern of strategically placed dots that, when assembled, produce the shape of a specific character (see Figure 7-5). The more dots stored in a given area, called a *matrix,* the higher the resolution. Dot matrix printers differ in quality, depending on the number of dots that produce a character, the size of the dots, and the character font. For the most part, dot matrix printers are considered to be only draft quality. Their technology, however, is improving. For example, when the number of dots increases from 8 per letter to 16, the dot matrix is frequently considered near-letter quality.

The price of dot matrix printers makes them very attractive and gives them the lion's share of the printer market. According to John Greitzer, "The low-cost dot matrix printer industry is about to go the way of the wristwatch and stereo industries before it: products are becoming less expensive and more Japanese."[1]

FIGURE 7-5. **Magnified dot matrix character.**

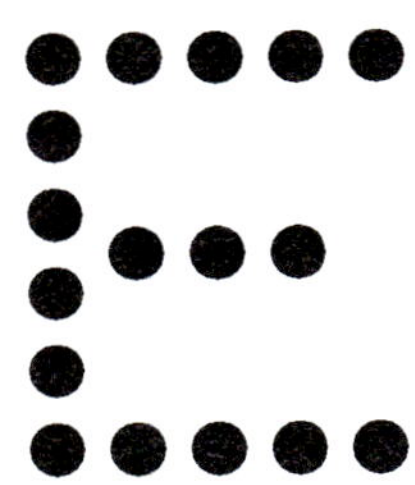

The following advancements are improving the output of dot matrix printers to the near-letter quality level:

1. Fujutsu American, Inc. and NEC Information Systems have improved the quality of the dot matrix printer by increasing the number of needles or wires on the printhead from 9 to 24. This produces a much sharper character on the page and, according to many experts, advances the dot matrix into the letter-quality category. Twenty-four-wire printers were priced as low as $700 in 1987 and can produce output at twice the speed of the 9-wire dot matrix.

2. To combat noise, some dot matrix printers are moving into the nonimpact category. Unlike regular impact dot matrix printers, thermal transfer printers use a ribbon that, when heated, transfers ink onto the page in a dot format.
3. Color may soon be standard on dot matrix printers. Three primary colors on the ribbon mix to provide a very desirable enhancement—graphics or script in color.
4. Many dot matrix printers have both draft-quality (DQ) and near-letter quality (NLQ) modes. At draft speeds, the mechanism makes only a minimum number of dots to construct the characters; the NLQ mode, however, makes more dots, thus producing a sharper image. These modes may be controlled either by software or by the flick of a switch. It is expected that dot matrix printers will soon be able to run 800–900 cps in draft mode and up to 300 cps in NLQ mode.

Daisy Wheel

As its name implies, the daisy wheel printer uses a round printwheel approximately four inches in diameter with spokes similar to a daisy's petals radiating from the center (see Figure 7-6). At the tip of each spoke are one or more characters. The daisy wheel is positioned upright (horizontally) in the printer and spins to the proper location, where a small hammer moves up or down to strike the back of the character. This action pushes the character to the ribbon and onto the paper, creating the printed image. This concept is similar to a typewriter typebar, except that the entire range of characters is on one wheel, rather than individual typebars, and no "key clash" can occur. Made of high-impact plastic or metal, daisy wheels come in a variety of fonts, at a reasonable cost, and can be interchanged easily.

FIGURE 7-6. Daisy wheels and ball elements.

Ball Element Printers

Ball element printers use an element the shape and size of a golf ball and are similar to the elements used in many electronic typewriters. The "golf ball," which may contain up to 98 characters, rotates at a very high speed to a specific character location and strikes the ribbon to produce that character on paper. With appropriate connections, electronic typewriters with ball elements or daisy wheels may double as printers.

Thimble Printers

Thimble printers, which are patented by NEC, closely resemble the ball element. Although these plastic, thimble-shaped elements can produce graphic output, critics agree that while the thimble can be used for bar charts, line graphics, and pie charts, the quality of their output is not very high. Thimble elements generally hold 88 characters and, like the other elements described, can be purchased in a variety of fonts and pitches.

Band Printers

Band printers have a band, a loop of metal with characters, that is pressed against a ribbon to produce print images. The band spins at a high speed, and when the desired character arrives at the proper position, it is struck, leaving an inked impression on the paper. According to some experts, band technology offers lower cost, fewer moving parts, more reliability, more flexibility, and higher speeds than other impact printers. Bands such as the one available on the IBM 3800 printer cost from $200 to $300; with constant use, a band will last three months. Bands currently contain 48 characters; more characters may be added, but increasing the number of characters slows the band down. Band printers are generally used with mainframes and minicomputers.

Nonimpact Printers

Nonimpact printers require no direct or mechanical pressure for transference of the character onto paper. For this reason, they operate at high speeds and low noise levels. These high-quality, versatile printers are revolutionizing printing processes. Three major nonimpact technologies are available: laser, ink jet, and thermal. Two more technologies are in the developmental stage: ion and magnetic.

Laser Printers

Laser printers were introduced by Xerox in the mid 1970s. Using light as the transfer medium, the laser beam writes an image in light in much the same way that a television image is created with a myriad of dots. The image is drawn on the photoconducting drum and is replicated as the drum picks up toner particles and transfers the image to a sheet of paper.

Laser printers are comparable to photocopiers that print from an electronic or digital signal rather than from paper.

Laser printers are often described as belonging to one of four categories: (1) high-speed, mainframe printers, (2) medium-speed printers that support numerous users, (3) extremely high-quality printers that produce typographic-quality images (at least 1000 pixels per inch to avoid the ragged edge seen on circles and diagonal lines), and (4) desktop or low-speed printers that support a single computer or local area network.

Laser printers produce letter-quality, multiple font, and graphic output of incredibly high quality at increasingly low costs. The "letter quality" varies, however. Some laser printers operate at 240 pixels (or dots) per inch (ppi), others at 300 ppi, and yet others (typographic) at 1000 ppi. All are considered letter quality and can deliver better graphic output than their impact counterparts. In addition, different fonts can be used on the same page because the font is controlled by software, not by a mechanical bar or element.

Technology that once cost $100,000 can now be bought for less than $5000. In fact, in 1988 Canon's LaserJet printer (a desktop model) could output at up to 8 pages per minute (ppm) and was priced at less than $3500. At the other end of the scale, the Xerox 9700 listed for $390,000, was capable of producing two pages per second (pps), and could be used for photocomposition. With optional software/hardware, the Xerox 8700 and 9700 series offer an array of publishing functions. The Xerox 9790/8790 laser printing system shown in Figure 7-7 has an interface for full-line editing, and the user may manipulate either a mouse or IBM PC-compatible keyboard with special programmable function keys to enter specific commands.

Figure 7-8 shows how user control of printers is changing. Instead of pushing buttons, operators of the Xerox 5700 electronic system merely touch the screen to control the system.

Desktop laser printers used with microcomputers are often more expensive than the computers they support. Additional expenses are for cartridge drums (comparable in durability to ribbons on an impact printer) and high power requirements. In addition, like all nonimpact printers, the laser cannot produce multiple copies. The laser printer can, however, make more than one run of a print job at incredibly fast speeds, thus negating this drawback. Today, laser printers do not produce color graphics and can operate only on nontextured, low-quality paper. Nevertheless, the graphic capabilities and speed of the laser printer make it a cost-effective option. Figure 7-9 depicts the Apple Computer LaserWriter Plus, which can provide 11 different fonts.

The laser printer's success in the automated office depends on how quickly its cost comes down, its integration as part of a network, and overcoming a few technological drawbacks. Even at current costs, the laser printer, connected to a telecommunications medium, may make the laser more cost effective inasmuch as one unit may replace multiple lower-

FIGURE 7-7. The Xerox 9790/8790 laser printing system.

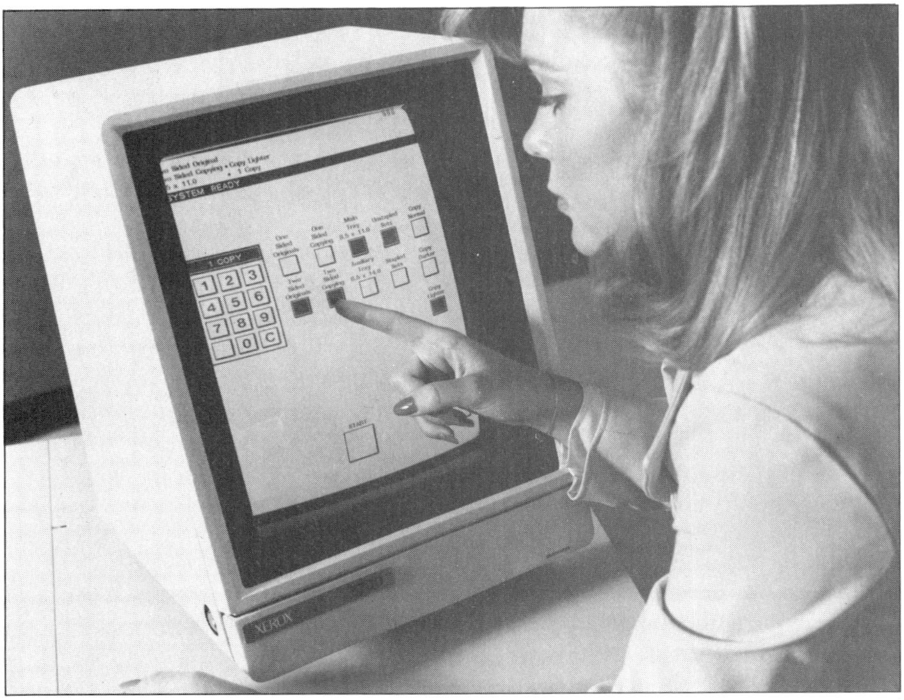

FIGURE 7-8. The Xerox 5700 electronic printing system features touch control instead of pushbuttons.

FIGURE 7-9. Apple Computer's LaserWriter Plus printer.

speed, lower-quality printers. For example, the cost per user of one $5000 laser printer, shared by five users, is $1000. It is much easier to cost-justify the laser on the basis of sharing.

Ink-Jet Printers

Ink-jet printers aim a tiny stream of electrostatically charged ink drops at the paper to create characters. They are based on dot matrix printing principles, and the ink-jet stream is ejected from a matrix of strategically placed dots. For example, the IBM 6640 ink-jet printer has a single jet nozzle that spans the width of the page and electric field deflectors direct the placement of dots on the paper. Color may be an option on this printer.

The speed of ink-jet printers depends upon the size and shape of the jet nozzle and the mechanism that advances the line of type. Because ink cannot be squirted faster than laser rays can be aimed at the paper, ink-jet printers are slower than laser printers. However, high-resolution ink-jet printers are capable of speeds up to 400 cps. They can produce beautiful, seven-color printouts and are quieter than impact printers. Also, newer models are overcoming problems related to ink clogs by using replaceable ink cartridges. The future may be bright for the ink-jet printer.

Thermal Printers

Thermal printers are the oldest of the nonimpact technologies. Thermal (heat-process-based) printers use a ribbon that passes between the paper and the flat printhead, which has "heater dots." When a dot is turned on, a bit of wax on the ribbon melts, creating ink, which is absorbed by chemically treated paper.

Thermal printers provide a sharp, very legible image. Because they need relatively little energy, they are used increasingly for portable, lap-top printers. A thermal ribbon can have four colors and, depending upon the paper, color quality can be high. The feel and quality of thermal paper, however, does not lend itself to copy quality, and images sometimes tend to fade.

Ion Printers

Ion printers differ greatly from other nonimpact printers in that they require no heat or light and have 75 percent fewer parts. Ion printers use charged air molecules to create charged patterns on the drum, and these jets of ions create the image. Ion printers use many electrodes to create images; however, some firms are experimenting with copying methods that employ scanning as the image transfer method.

Although they have only a small percentage of the market, ion printers may increase this share as their cost decreases below that of the laser, ink-jet, and thermal printer. The ion printer's most important features are its extremely high speeds (more than 60 ppm) and reliability.

Magnetic Printers

Conceptually, magnetic printers are very similar to magnetic copiers (discussed later in this chapter) and employ magnetic coil heads similar to those in disk drives (Chapter 5). Rather than light (laser) or ink or ions, the magnetic printer uses magnetic pull to attract toner to the drum to produce the copy. At this point, the process resembles the process of other nonimpact printers, as the toner forms a permanent image.

Although it is not a strong contender in the market, the magnetic printer has potential because of its low power requirements and quiet operations.

Printer Accessories

An often overlooked but important consideration in purchasing a printer is the accessories that enable it to be efficiently used. Just as the car with a sticker price of $6,888 costs $10,000 when a radio, air conditioner, floor mats, and other accessories are added, the "sticker price" of a printer increases when options are added. Some of the most frequently used accessories are discussed in this section.

1. *Paper-feed mechanisms.* Inexpensive printers often provide manual friction feed; in other words, the paper must be inserted by hand for each page of print, thus slowing the printing process. Solutions to this problem include adding a continuous forms-tractor feeder or an automatic single-sheet feeder. While the cost of the former may be reasonable, the cost of the single-sheet feeder may be more than double the cost of the printer. If both memo and letterhead paper are used, a multiple bin feeder may be desirable, further increasing the cost of the printer. Should envelopes be a desired output, a special envelope feeder

must be added, again increasing the cost. Sheet trays or bins generally hold 200 sheets of paper and up to 60 envelopes; multipart forms may also be used.

2. *Interchangeable print devices.* The ability to change one type font for another is a desirable feature. Many fonts within the daisy wheel, ball, thimble, and band categories are interchangeable, and these elements can differ greatly in price from one manufacturer to another. Should a variety of type fonts be needed, a printer that employs a standard element should be selected. Additional elements can be purchased from office supply firms in wider variety and at lower cost. Nonimpact printers can generally support a wide range of type fonts as part of their basic design, so care should be taken to determine which fonts are standard with a particular model.

3. *Consumable items.* When choosing an impact printer, consider the type of ribbon that will be required. A good rule is that the higher the ribbon quality, the shorter its life span and the greater its cost. Nonimpact printers do not require ribbons per se, but consumables such as print bands must be replaced periodically, and ink jets require supplies of ink. In short, the cost of any part that may require replacement should be considered.

4. *Paper.* Another consumable is paper. Thermal printers, for example, require specially treated paper. This adds to the expense of using the printer and makes existing supplies of paper and forms unusable for this purpose.

Trends in Printer Technology

All printer technologies are likely to come down in price and go up in options and special features. As the technology of printers in the nonimpact category matures, its reliability and connectivity will increase. In the office of the future, printing and copying technologies may be one and the same: their technologies are similar, as the following discussion shows.

COPIERS

In the 1930s, Chester Carlson developed and patented a process for reproducing documents through an electrostatic process called *electrophotography.* Carlson had a difficult time selling his patent to office equipment manufacturers, but by 1948, when the Haloid Company had refined the original process, the first copier was ready for the consumer market. In 1950, the Haloid Company changed its name to Xerox Corporation to better describe the patented process, xerography. *Xeros* is Greek for *dry,* and *graphein* is Greek for *writing.*

Xerox has remained a dominant force in the copying industry; indeed, its name has become synonymous with photocopying—much to the company's chagrin. (One "xeroxes" only when he or she is using Xerox technology.) Figure 7-10 presents a pictorial history of xerography in the office.

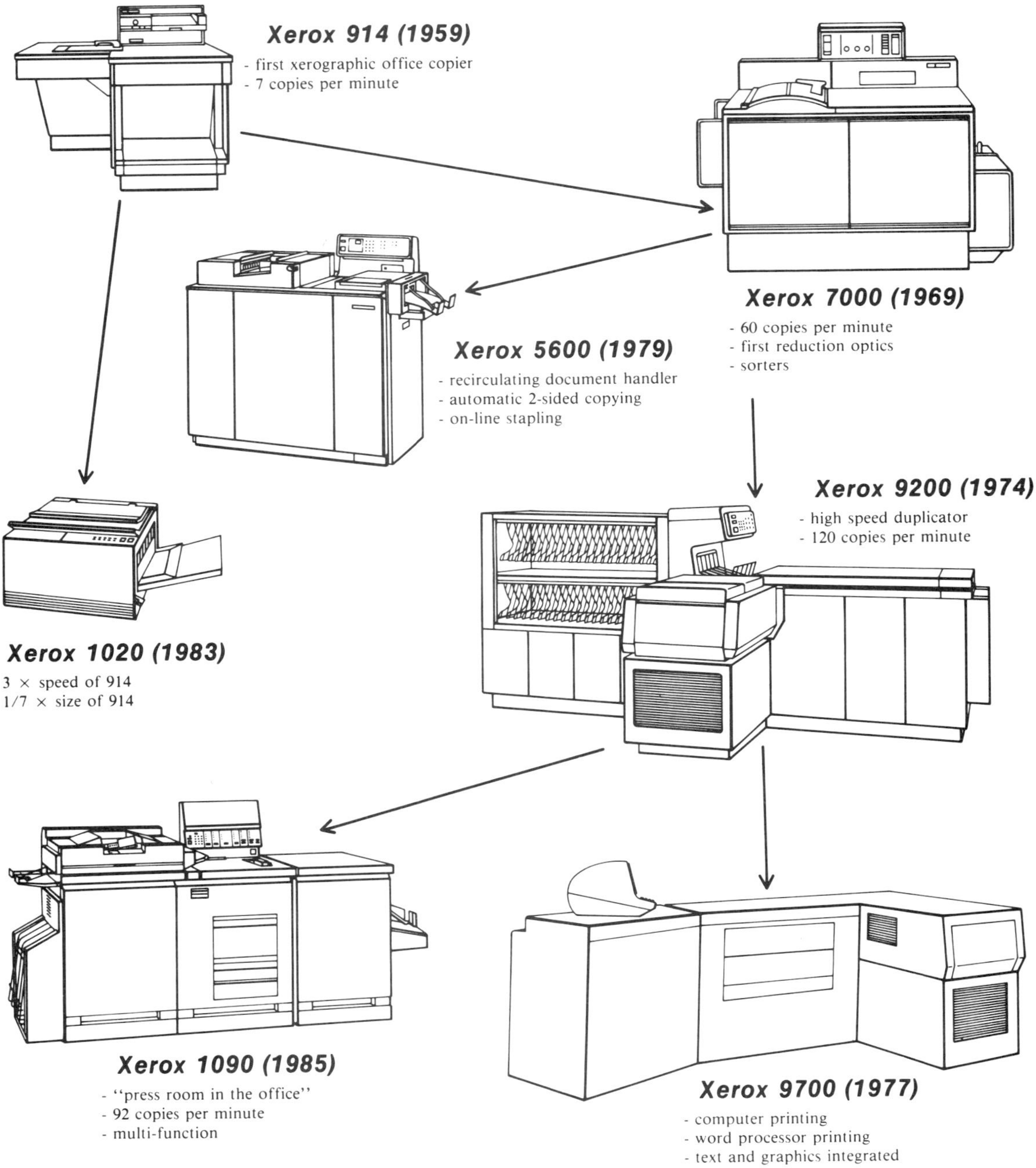

FIGURE 7-10. Twenty-five years of xerography in the office.

Xerox owned the patent for plain paper electrostatic processes until 1975. In the years since then, at least 30 other companies have captured a good share of the copier market, manufacturing more than 300 models of photocopying equipment.

Each of these 300 models relies on one of four basic types of copying technologies: plain paper, coated paper, thermal, and dual spectrum. After these copying technologies are explained, the features that differentiate models in the same category are discussed in greater detail.

Copying Technologies

Plain and coated paper copiers are for high-use, high-volume output; thermal and dual spectrum copiers are for low-use, low-volume demands. The term *reprographics,* which we frequently hear in connection with the department that is responsible for managing copier technologies, comes from *repro,* repeat, and *graphics,* image.

Plain Paper Electrostatic Copiers

Plain paper electrostatic copiers (PPCs) are the most widely used today. Following the same concepts as Carlson's, the camera throws an image of the document to be copied onto a positively charged drum, thus fixing the image.

Coated Paper Electrostatic Copiers

Coated paper electrostatic copiers (CPCs) reproduce an image on specially treated (coated) paper. Many consider this type of image contrast to be superior to the quality of copies made on PPCs.

Thermal Copiers

Thermal copiers, as their name implies, rely on heat in the transfer process. With the original document beneath a heat-sensitive copy sheet, light is beamed through both the document and the copy sheet, turning the sheet dark in the same places as the document. Thermal copiers, which produce only one copy at a time, are increasingly popular as "personal" copiers.

Dual Spectrum Copiers

Dual spectrum copiers go through two distinct steps to create an intermediate and then a final copy. First, light forms an image on one sheet of paper; in the second step, heat is applied to copy it and to transfer the image to the final copy.

Copier Features and Considerations

The more than 300 copier models come in a wide variety of sizes and shapes, with an equally great range in capacity and features such as size, automated functions, and color.

Sizes and Shapes of Copiers

Durable *console copiers* generally offer many features and are capable of high quality and high speeds. Easy-to-use *desktop copiers*, sometimes referred to as *convenience copiers*, offer "quick copy" services to those who need only one or a few copies. New on the market are inexpensive *personal copiers*, which are designed for low-end use. In choosing a copier among these categories, the purchaser should keep in mind its expected use (output). Its capacity is directly related to its size. In addition, the number and type of copier functions or features usually increase as its size increases, and the more feature-laden and faster the copier, the more it costs.

Speed

Speed of operation is an often overlooked yet very important characteristic of copiers, both in the time it takes for the first copy to be produced and the time it takes for subsequent copies. Once a machine is "warmed up," it is often capable of producing copies at much higher rates than when it was "cold." Today, Japanese machines are capable of speeds up to 40 copies per minute. American manufacturers, including Canon and Sharp, make copiers in the 50 copies per minute range.

Costs

For a realistic estimate, the prospective purchaser should consider both the purchase price of the copier and the recurring costs, including (1) the cost of special chemicals required in the process, (2) power costs, and (3) the cost of maintenance. The cost and power requirements of copiers vary markedly, and the recurring costs can considerably increase the real cost of the unit. Regular maintenance is important to avoid breakdowns, and because of their numerous parts, copiers are prone to break down. As a purchaser, one should compare not only the cost of maintenance contracts, but the servicing time. These factors are also related to an estimate of capacity: How many copies per month is the copier capable of producing?

Automatic Features

"Extra" copier features include *automatic repeat*, whereby duplicate copies can be produced without operator intervention. With *automatic document feeding*, an entire report or manuscript can be copied without need for the operator to place the individual sheets on the copier one by one. A *collator* means that as copies are made they are automatically sequenced in proper order.

Other automatic options include attachments that can staple, bind, fold, and even place the document in an envelope. Copiers can reduce and enlarge originals to a variety of ratios. Copiers with duplexing features can make copies of both sides of a document at the same time, and copiers with overlay features merge two originals on a single copy. Some copiers also offer book copying, whereby an optic assembly automatically turns the pages.

Before buying a copier, the purchaser should know what the output should look like. In addition, he or she should determine if color is required for the organization's copying needs.

Color

Color copiers are capable of reproducing documents in color. At one time, the color market was dominated by Xerox, 3M, and Canon; more and more, however, one can find color capabilities in any number of products. The quality of color varies from copier to copier. Results depend on the process by which the color is transferred. Is color dependent upon a cartridge, or can the machine produce full-color copies?

For example, some copiers operate with one black and one color toner cartridge. To obtain multiple colors, the color toner must be removed and replaced, and the document must be run through again. At the time of this writing, only Canon has a copier that can copy two colors at one time by pressing a single button.

Full-color copiers, on the other hand, offer multiple-color, high-quality copies. Copies are produced by either a thermal transfer printing process with a four-color ink ribbon or by a photographic process. Canon's NP-Color T is a full-color copier:

> The Canon NP-Color T copier uses an electrophotographic process, with cyan, magenta, and yellow toners, to produce full-color copies on plain paper. Single-color copies can also be made in red, blue, green, yellow, cyan, and magenta. Full-color copies are produced at a rate of five letter-size copies per minute, while the output speed for single-color copies is 15 per minute (yellow, magenta, and cyan) or 7.5 copies per minute (blue, green, and red). Color adjustment is achieved by an automatic color balance system or by manual adjustment. The NP-Color T retails for $52,000.[2]

Advancements in color copying technology have produced prototype digital laser copiers that can create high-resolution copies at the rate of six per minute. A Xerox model can produce color prints or enlarge color slides.

Trends in the Copying Industry

The consensus is that the future will see the continued dominance of plain paper copiers and a steady decrease in cost, coupled with attractive features. The mid- or low-volume-user market is volatile. Most offices have already purchased or are renting copiers. Because frequent trips to copy stores are inconvenient, even organizations with low-volume needs are purchasing copiers in the $800 to $2000 range. High-volume users are purchasing copiers that are "feature-rich." In some instances, copiers are replacing in-house printing operations. Intelligent copiers, desktop publishing, and photocomposition perhaps represent the next era for the copying industry.

The Intelligent Copier

Intelligent or "smart" copiers are capable of producing multiple copies directly from electronic input, thus bypassing an original paper stage. The intelligent copier, which adds to the standard photocopying mechanism a laser beam that generates characters, is controlled by computer programs. A document can be retrieved from computer memory, printed, and copied at extremely high speeds. Many experts expect the intelligent copier to be *the* output device of the automated office.

Intelligent copiers that can read paper documents and convert them to digital signals (much like an OCR) may soon be able to transmit over telephone lines (much like a facsimile machine). This means that the operator may be able to change the image of a document without affecting the original (much like a word processor). Thus the intelligent copier emulates a variety of office technologies.

Electronic Publishing

Electronic publishing enables text, graphics, and images to be integrated for printed output. These processes were formerly done only by traditional typesetters and printers. Today, however, electronic tools have brought powerful publishing capabilities directly to the end user. These tools embody all aspects of the publishing process in a single system. The creative capture tools are combined with the production tools and the outputting tools. When the computer is a mini- or mainframe computer, the arrangement is called a *workstation publishing system*. Complex, professional publishing environments are supported with more comprehensive and sophisticated *dedicated publishing systems* that break the process into three distinct stages: the creative stage, the production stage, and the delivery stage. Microcomputer-based desktop publishing systems are becoming increasingly popular with end users.

Desktop publishing Desktop publishing is defined by many vendors as "sophisticated" word processing. Desktop publishing capabilities are often characterized as WYSIWYG (pronounced *wizzy wig*). Based on Flip Wilson's famous line, "What you see is what you get," WYSIWYG is appropriate because what the viewer sees on the VDT is what the off-screen printout will look like. *Desktop publishing* is a microcomputer-based system that includes a word processing and graphics front end, page composition software, and a laser printer (see Figures 7-11 and 7-12). The basic hardware and software requirements are the same for both desktop and workstation systems except that a minicomputer is used in workstation systems.

FIGURE 7-11. A desktop publishing system: The Hewlett-Packard HP Vectra PC, software, and LaserJet 500 PLUS printer.

FIGURE 7-12. The CPT Integrated Desktop Publishing System: *(left to right)* minicomputer, full-page monitor, OCR, laser printer, and ergonomically designed keyboard.

Page composition software enables the user to create layouts by arranging printed information in multiple columns, using a variety of type pitches and fonts on the same page, and adding pictures, charts, and other elements. Page composition software also allows layouts to be easily changed. A laser printer is the standard today because of its high-quality graphic output capabilities. Figure 7-13 presents a list of terms frequently used to describe desktop publishing processes.

FIGURE 7-13. A dictionary of desktop publishing terms.

Desktop publishing has spawned its own jargon through a curious blend of typesetting terms and computer terms. Here is a brief list of terms.

Align. To line up the edge of a character, bottom, top or sides, along a single straight line.

Banner. A large headline or title, usually extending the width of the page.

Block. Style of layout that defines larger regular spaces for text and graphics.

Body. The main text as opposed to captions or headlines, or the main art as opposed to logos or letterhead.

Boldface. Copy of the same typeface but darker in tone, used for emphasis.

Camera-ready. In typesetting, copy that is ready to be made into negatives for printing; in desktop publishing it usually refers to pages that are output in a form ready for reproduction.

Caption. The text accompanying (above, below, or next to) artwork, used for explanation or context.

Column. Text running vertically less than the width of the page.

Crop. To cut down a picture or graphic element to the desired size, or to reduce or enlarge it on the screen.

Flush. Lined up vertically along a defined space (flush left or flush right).

Folio. Page number.

Font. Text all of one style and size (see typeface).

H&J. Hyphenate and justify, which means to fit text to a certain column width with proper hyphenation of split words.

Halftone. An image that contains gray values as opposed to only black and white.

Kerning. The space between characters of text on a single line.

Layout. General outline of text and graphic elements on a page or on the screen, arranged for visual effect.

Logo. A company's symbol or the stylized rendition of its name.

Page description language. Software that instructs the printer in composing the various elements of the printed page.

Page composition software. A program that allows the sophisticated merging of text and graphics on the screen.

Paste-up. In traditional typesetting, the physical act of pasting text and graphic elements on a page; in desktop publishing, the arrangement of elements on the screen.

Ragged. Uneven lines of text on the right or left side of a column (usually the right side).

Scanner. A hardware device that converts text or graphic images into digital form and transmits that information to the computer.

Spread. Two facing pages.

Typeface. A particular design or style of text (such as Times Roman or Helvetica).

WYSIWYG. "What You See Is What You Get" (pronounced "Whizzy-Wig"), which means that the way a page appears on the screen is the way it will be printed out.

Desktop publishing was created at the Xerox Corporation's Palo Alto Research Center (PARC) and was popularized in 1985 when Apple Computers introduced its relatively inexpensive LaserWriter. When they combined the LaserWriter with the outstanding graphics of the Macintosh, users could produce output that rivaled the printing industry's. Apple immediately cornered the desktop publishing market. However, vendor support of a technology is not nearly as important as the development of good applications for that technology. Therefore, desktop publishing is an easy success story for organizations of all types and sizes; all organizations produce printed output, and most are (or should be) concerned about the quality and cost of that output.

Figure 7-14 depicts the Xerox 6085 Professional Computer System, which is designed for organizations that require foreign language publish-

FIGURE 7-14. **The Xerox 6085 Professional Computer System is designed for organizations that require foreign language publishing capabilities.**

ing capabilities. Using this system, documents can be created in more than 40 languages, including dialects of Japanese, Chinese, Arabic, and Persian.

Advantages of desktop publishing The advantages of desktop publishing fall into categories of cost savings, time savings, security, and quality. Moreover, all four of these categories address the "bottom-line" needs of organizations (profit, productivity, efficiency, and effectiveness). Using desktop publishing can benefit an organization in several ways:

1. *Cost savings.* A page can be produced for $2, compared to an average cost of $14 per page by a typesetter.
2. *Time savings.* Turnaround time—the time it would take for a page to be prepared for the printer, then by the printer, and returned to the organization—is reduced (and controllable).
3. *Security.* All documents are prepared in house, thus eliminating concerns about loss or misuse.
4. *Quality.* The quality of all documents throughout the organization improves, not just those that would be scheduled for typesetting.

Although desktop systems meet many publishing needs, they are not a replacement for complex, professional printing. Desktop systems cannot reproduce high-quality graphics, high-resolution line art, or good halftones for photographs. Nor do they interface with CAD/CAM workstations, illustrator workstations, or scanners. On the output side, they usually drive only laser printers, not phototypesetting equipment. Flexible connectivity is found only in dedicated professional systems.

Electronic photocomposition This book is a perfect example of how computers are changing the publishing business. This text was typeset on a Xyvision Integrated Publishing System. The authors used their personal computers, with the appropriate software packages, to produce the manuscript. Much time and expense were saved in this manner.

Before a photocomposition system can be fully appreciated, the term *digital* must be understood. Traditional typesetting requires type to be produced, filmed, and then transferred to a (usually) metal plate before printing. Photocomposition takes digital information (information that is stored electronically or on magnetic media) and transforms it into typeset-quality output.

To be processed by photocomposition, a document may be entered into the system by an input device (such as a keyboard, CIM, or OCR), edited through the word processor, and output to a phototypesetting device. Thus photocomposition eliminates the need for the rekeying that is necessary in traditional typesetting. Photocomposition can even benefit from telecommunication services; the word processor can be linked to the photocomposition system by telephone lines. Properly enhanced word processing equipment can send information, in a common language, to a photocomposition unit.

Although photocomposition provides many advantages, the decision to purchase a photocomposition system must weigh the benefits of the system against its cost. The following is a summary of the benefits of photocomposition:

1. The need to rekey documents is eliminated.
2. Photocomposition can produce higher-quality output than printers.
3. Photocomposition provides a variety of type fonts and sizes that are not available on printers.
4. The number of pages in the final document can be reduced by one-half to two-thirds of the original document.

Electronic publishing requires careful management. It has been suggested that a desktop publishing manager must understand typography, graphics, and layout techniques. A desktop publishing manager must certainly understand computers and electronic equipment and, perhaps most importantly, must understand users' communications needs and styles.[3]

C. A. Pesko Associates, a market research firm, estimates that the market for electronic publishing will grow from the 1985 volume of 32,760 units to 561,390 units in 1990. Pesko also estimates that this translates into a sales volume of $929 million. Pesko expects that 97 percent of that market will be related to desktop publishing.

SUMMARY

Despite predictions of the "paperless office," paper output will continue to be an integral part of office operations for decades to come. The technology to produce that paper continues to evolve. The printing and copying systems described here are forerunners of systems yet to come. Like other technologies, their success is dependent on how they fit into the totally "integrated" office, as well as on their costs.

Printers are categorized as either impact or nonimpact, depending upon whether a typebar hits a ribbon or the print (character, line, etc.) is created by another means. Impact printers are described as dot matrix, daisy wheel, ball, thimble, and band. Nonimpact printer technologies are categorized as laser, ink-jet, thermal, ion, and magnetic.

Printers must be software-compatible and digitally compatible with the computers that drive them. Printers are driven by software, not keystrokes. The wires (cables) that connect the computer must also be compatible, either parallel or serial, depending upon how data flows between the technologies.

An analyst must consider speed, quality of output, and options when selecting a printer.

Speed is the rate at which a printer produces output, typically described as characters or lines per minute. Nonimpact printers that create entire lines or pages in "one swoop" are faster than impact printers, which print character by character.

Printers can produce output in a variety of type fonts and pitches. Low-priced dot matrix printers can create a wide range of fonts and pitches in both draft and near-letter quality. On impact printers such as daisy wheel, thimble, and band printers, font and pitch are controlled by changing the type element, whereas on nonimpact and dot matrix printers font and pitch are controlled by software commands. Although dot matrix printers are capable of producing graphic output, nonimpact printers typically offer higher-quality graphics.

Printer selection is a trade-off between one's needs—what the output should look like—and one's budget. As features and speeds of printers increase and as prices in all categories decrease, it is expected that the nonimpact printer will be the printer of choice in the future. Impact printers, however, are expected to remain popular because of their ease of maintenance, consistent output quality, and usefulness for the application that they do best—multiple forms.

Printer accessories include paper-feed mechanisms, interchangeable devices (for impact printers), and consumables—ribbons, toners, inks, etc., as well as the types of paper the printer can handle.

Copiers are categorized by either the paper used for output or by the process itself. Copiers for plain and coated paper are used in organizations that require frequent or high-volume copying. Thermal and dual spectrum copiers are used in organizations with low-volume needs.

The foremost considerations in copier selection are volume and quality of output. Other considerations (particularly for those who need very high quality or volume) are color options and a wide range of automated features. Copiers can collate, enlarge, reduce, copy documents on both sides, copy books, staple, and even stuff envelopes. These extra features can add considerable expense to the basic device.

Intelligent copiers (sometimes referred to as *intelligent printers*) produce multiple copies of documents from digital, not paper, input. This means that documents can be transferred, much like facsimile systems (Chapter 8). Intelligent copiers therefore combine the printer and copier with electronic transfer capabilities.

Computer-assisted publishing is an umbrella term that describes both desktop and electronic publishing. It enables a user to combine text and graphics; in other words, what the user sees on the computer screen is what appears as printed output. Requirements for desktop publishing are a microcomputer, laser printer, and special software. Electronic publishing, used in conjunction with mainframes or minicomputers, adds an additional step, a camera-related process, to produce the document. Both technologies give the creator of the document choices in terms of type fonts and page design. Organizations, departments, and individual users, when equipped with a desktop publishing system, can produce typeset-quality output at a fraction of the cost of traditional typesetting.

The paperless office is probably a pipedream. The office systems analyst can benefit from an understanding of paper-producing technologies in selecting the technologies most appropriate for hardcopy information. As the technologies mature, as in the case of the intelligent copier, they tend to become more integrated and more vital players in the automated office.

DISCUSSION QUESTIONS

1. What technical considerations must one know before selecting a printer?
2. Describe the operations of the five categories of impact and nonimpact printers discussed in this text.
3. Suggest categories of printers applicable to the needs of the following:
   a. A freelance writer who works at home and regularly submits manuscripts.
   b. A large organization that produces its own newsletter and manuals.
   c. A physician's office.
   d. The Treasury Department of a state government.
   e. A college student (a) on a limited budget and (b) without monetary restraints.
4. Identify a category of copier technology that could fit the needs of organizations that require the following:
   a. Several hundred copies a month
   b. Several thousand copies a month
   c. 10,000 to 60,000 copies a month
   d. 100,000 or more copies a month
5. List the features that add to the functionality of copiers. In your opinion, are there features you "couldn't live without"? What are they?
6. What may the future hold for copying technologies?
7. Discuss the implications of the following statement: Copying and printing technologies will soon be indistinguishable.

APPLICATION EXERCISES

1. Interview the reprographics manager of a local business. Describe the types of copiers it uses, then ask him or her "what's next" for the organization's copying needs.
2. Check consumer reports such as *DataPro* or *Auerbach Reports* for their evaluations of current printing/copying technologies. Which vendors have the best products? Do the reports concur in their evaluations?

3. Interview a local dealer (seller) of printing/copying technologies. Which products are the dealer's best sellers? Why?
4. Compare the time required to print the following documents on a letter-quality printer at 55 cps, on a dot matrix printer at 200 cps, and on a desktop laser printer at 6 ppm.
   a. A 2-page letter
   b. A 15-page letter
   c. 1000 one-page letters
   d. A 200-page report

SUGGESTED READINGS

Kleeman, Michael J. "Evaluating the Capabilities of Desktop Publishing Systems: Part I," *Administrative Management* (May 1987), pp. 31–34.

Kleeman, Michael J. "Evaluating the Capabilities of Desktop Publishing Systems: Part II," *Administrative Management* (June 1987), pp. 30–33.

"The Layout of Desktop Publishing," *Information Center* (Special Edition, June 1987).

COMMUNICATIONS TECHNOLOGY

CHAPTER

8

OBJECTIVES

After completing this chapter, the reader should be able to meet the following objectives:

- Understand what a network is and how it operates.
- Differentiate between broadband and baseband networks.
- Differentiate between analog and digital signals.
- Explain the significance of various communication variables, including type of signal, transmission medium, signaling methods, protocol, typology, access control, and coding of data.
- Compare asynchronous and synchronous transmission.
- Discuss the function of protocols.
- Use appropriate terms in describing signaling methods: simplex, full-duplex, and half-duplex.
- Appraise the role of the telephone in the automated office.
- Compare answering machines with voice mail systems.
- Summarize the important roles of the PBX, LAN, and WAN in integrating office automation.
- List examples of transmission media and the advantages and disadvantages of each.
- Differentiate among common forms of network accessing: contention CSMA/CA and CSMA/CD and noncontention polling and token passing.
- Describe facsimile technology and how it operates.
- Describe the technologies required for each of the four categories of teleconferencing.
- Describe Videotex technology and its role in business today.
- Understand a contractor's rationale in deciding to construct a "smart building."

KEY TERMS

acoustic coupler
analog
audio teleconferencing
audiographic teleconferencing
asynchronous
gateway
local area network
meet-me bridge
modem
node

baud rate
baseband network
broadband network
bus network
contention
noncontention
CBMS
CSMA/CD
CSMA/CA
polling
cable
centrex system
coaxial cable wires
coding
communications technology
computer teleconferencing
data communications
digital
duplex
electronic mail
FDM/TDM
fiber optics
full-duplex
full motion video teleconferencing
key telephone system
parallel data transfer
PBX
proprietary network
protocol
ring network
serial transfer
simplex
slow-scan video teleconference
smart building
standardized network
star network
synchronous
telecommunications
token passing
topology
twisted pair
twisted pair wires
wide area network
facsimile
Telex
TWX
teleconferencing
universal networks
Videotex
voice mail

INTRODUCTION

Communication is simply defined as the exchange of information through a common system of symbols. Communication occurs among individuals both verbally and nonverbally, directly or with the aid of devices such as pen and paper, chalkboards, sign language, or telephones. The term *communication* also refers to the exchange of information electronically from one device to another. Communication technologies include all devices that support the electronic exchange of information.

The integration of communications and computers has expanded the opportunities for office automation. Individuals seldom work in isolation; they generally need to share information. Since teamwork and departmental organization are characteristic of most enterprises, office automation, to be effective, must support not only individual productivity but communication among individuals as well. Communication technologies facilitate this information exchange, whether that exchange be "down the hall" or around the world.

The practical value of information is in its exchange; information has little value unless it is used. Because its value depends on having the *right* information in the *right* place at the *right* time, communication technologies in office automation have grown increasingly important. Experts have predicted that world expenditures on telecommunications will be over $1 trillion between 1986 and 1994. Given such a large market interest in communications, technological breakthroughs and new applications appear in the trade press almost daily.

Before launching into the specifics of communication technologies, the reader should understand the following broad terms used in this text, especially *telecommunications, data communications,* and *communications:*

- *Telecommunications. Tele* means far, and *telecommunications* describes the use of telephones, telegraphs, radio, and television via a variety of media.
- *Data communications. Data* means text or numbers, and *data communications* describes information passing from computer to computer or from computer to terminal.
- *Communications.* In office automation, communication technology facilitates the transfer of information in any form, over any distance. Communication technology, in our discussion of office automation, refers to both voice and data communications or the integration of the two.

COMMUNICATION BASICS

An office systems analyst or manager must have a basic understanding of communication technologies. Although communications is a highly technical field requiring specialized study, the basic concepts are easily understood. Using the defined terminology, the reader will proceed to a discussion of networks and various communication services. The chapter includes the technologies of teleconferencing and Videotex and the concept of "smart buildings." Advanced voice communication technologies, such as speech recognition and synthesis, will be discussed in Chapter 9, "Artificial Intelligence." Chapter 8 concludes with a discussion of criteria for evaluating and implementing communication technologies.

Communications can refer to the transmission of voice, text, data, image, or video. A communication *circuit* connects two or more communication devices in a way that allows them to exchange information. The fundamental requirements for a communication circuit include the following:

- Transmitter (source of data)
- Receiver
- Transmission medium
- Set of rules (protocols)

A communication circuit goes by many names: the path, the link, the network, the telephone line, or just line. A single communication circuit, such as that illustrated in Figure 8-1, may provide one or more communication channels. For example, a circuit of a fiber-optic medium may support over 1000 telephone calls at the same time, each on its own communication channel. A *channel* is a single path on an end-to-end communication circuit.

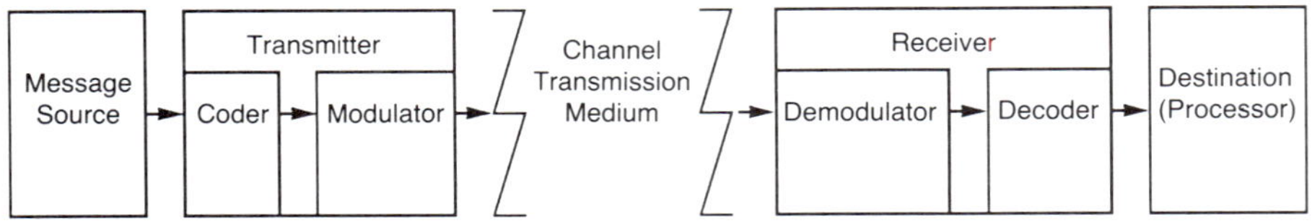

FIGURE 8-1. A typical telecommunications circuit.

When someone makes a long-distance call, his or her voice is converted to an electrical signal by the telephone mouthpiece (transmitter). The voice signal is transmitted on a copper wire circuit, called a *local loop,* to one of the telephone company's central offices. There, the voice signal may be routed to more copper wires, or it may be digitized, placed on a fiber-optic cable with over 1000 other calls, and carried to a microwave transmission system that delivers it, perhaps via satellite, to another central office near the location called. At the second telephone station, the caller's voice signal may be placed on another copper wire for delivery to the person with whom he or she wishes to speak. In this way, a single communication circuit may include several transmission media, each providing more than one data channel. The entire process is governed by prescribed rules, or *protocols,* (generally implemented in computer software) that control how the path is set up over the circuit. The person who is called hears a signal (ring) and picks up his or her telephone (receiver), which converts the electrical signal back to the caller's voice. (Typically, the same device alternates as a transmitter and receiver.)

In data communications, which is an area of growing need in office automation, computer devices become the transmitters and receivers. The transmission medium may be telephone circuits or dedicated data circuits. The set of rules (protocols) that govern how the communication takes place become complex because of the variety of ways in which different computer software programs handle information.

Several variables are involved in the transmission of signals between devices or over communication circuits. Major communication variables (discussed in the sections that follow) include type of channel, transmission media, type of signal (modulation), coding, speed, communication methods, and protocols.

Types of Communication Channels

A communication network uses one of three basic types of channels (circuits): simplex, half-duplex, or full-duplex.

In *simplex* mode, signals move in only one direction. Examples of simplex communication are conventional radio and television reception and the stock exchange ticker tapes. Simplex code is often used by teletype wire services.

In *half-duplex* mode, signals can flow in both directions but only in one direction at a time. If one machine is transmitting, the other is receiving and is temporarily prohibited from transmitting. Half-duplex is like a narrow bridge that is wide enough for only one car; cars can proceed in both directions, but traffic going in one direction must wait for the oncoming traffic to clear the bridge. Citizen band (CB) and ship-to-shore radios are examples of information that flows in half-duplex. Half-duplex is used by most asynchronous terminals. Asynchronous terminals include personal computers and are defined later in this chapter.

A *full-duplex* channel can transmit in both directions at the same time. The two simultaneous transmissions occur on separate communication channels, which combine to form a full-duplex connection. A full-duplex channel is like a two-way, multilane freeway; traffic flows in both directions, and the flows are unrelated. Full-duplex is used by intelligent synchronous terminals, multiplexers, and computers. Synchronous terminals will be explained later in this chapter.

The direction in which data flows over channels is also regulated by the set of rules (protocols) that govern the communication. The channel capacity, however, limits the options. In other words, half-duplex communication can be conducted on a full-duplex channel; however, half-duplex communication could not be conducted on a channel capable only of simplex data flow.

Transmission Media

A communication circuit or channel may include several media, such as twisted pair wire, coaxial cable, fiber-optic cable, or even air, as in microwave transmission (see Figure 8-2).

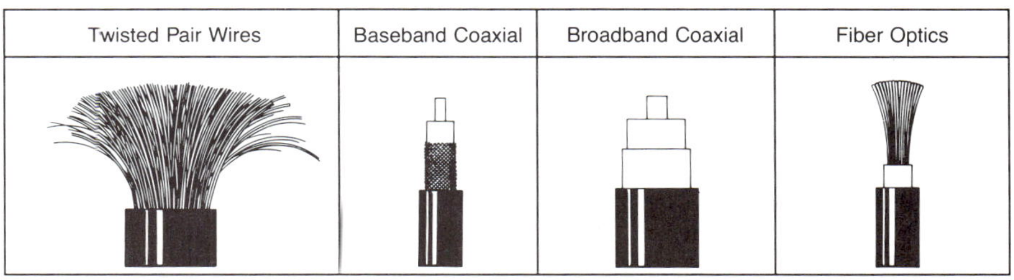

FIGURE 8-2. **Types of media.**

Twisted Pair Wires

Twisted pair wires are the simplest, most commonly used, and least expensive transmission media. A twisted pair wire consists of two pairs of plastic-sheathed copper wire twisted around one another. These wires are wrapped in an outer protective plastic tubing. Twisted pair wires have low bandwidth and are susceptible to noise and electrical interference. Electrical signals transmitted over twisted pair wire tend to decrease over extended lengths, and line amplifiers are required to boost the signals. Twisted pair wire is the medium widely used in the telephone system.

Coaxial Cable

Coaxial cables can transmit voice, data, text, and video at rapid rates. Coaxial cables consist of a conductor wire that is surrounded by insulation and then covered with a copper, aluminum, or metal jacket. They are the media of cable television transmission (CATV). Coaxial cable is more expensive than twisted pair wires, and its use can be limited because of the space required to install wires within walls and ceilings.

Fiber Optics

Fiber optics provide a high-priced yet potentially very desirable alternative to the wire-based media of twisted pair wiring and coaxial cables. Fiber-optic cable consists of a thin core of glass or plastic through which light pulses are transmitted. Data can travel through fiber optics at over 3 million characters per second, or fast enough to transmit the entire *Encyclopaedia Britannica* in less than two minutes. Perhaps the major advantage of optical fiber is its ability to withstand electrical interference. Optical fiber is more difficult to install than wires, but the primary concern is the expense of converting electrical signals to light pulses and back again.

Type of Signal (Modulation)

The term *signal* describes the physical phenomenon of data transfer—what the data streams "look like." Figure 8-3 illustrates the difference between the two types of signals: digital and analog. *Digital* signals are a stream of distinct electrical pulses transmitted in rapid succession. A device that uses a digital signal distinguishes only between the presence (on) or absence (off) of electrical pulses. The signals created by turning a current on and off are known as *bits,* the smallest "pieces" of information that can be transmitted. Binary arithmetic is an arithmetic system used for computers. In binary arithmetic, the presence of a signal is represented by a one, and the absence of a signal is represented by a zero. These binary digits, or bits, are grouped into codes that represent characters, numbers, and system commands.

Analog signals consist of continuous electrical waves. A wave has three characteristics: (1) *amplitude,* or strength, of the signal; (2) *phase,* or

FIGURE 8-3. How data flows: Analog and digital signals.

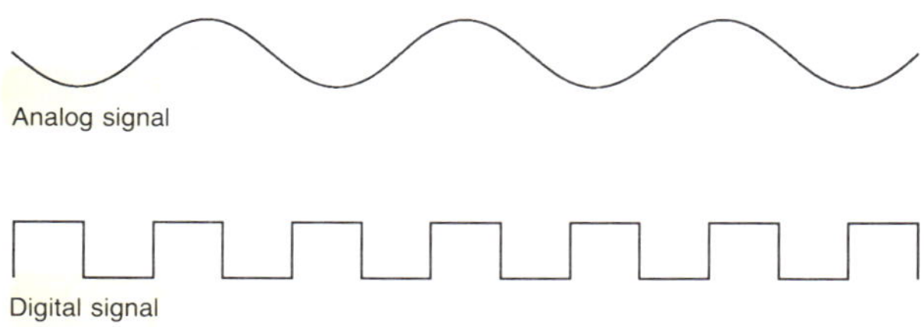

duration, of the wave; and (3) *frequency,* or number of times the wave is repeated during a certain time. Analog signals are most commonly created by the conversion of sound waves to electrical energy, as for telephone conversation and radio broadcasting.

Most voice and television communication uses analog transmission; teletypewriters and most computers use digital techniques. Through the use of *modems,* however, digital signals can be converted to analog for transmission on communication circuits, and vice versa.

Converting Signals: Modems

Because most telephone cables are capable of sending analog data only, for computers to use the same cable, their digital signal must be converted to analog. The process of changing from digital to analog is called *modulation.* Once transmitted, the data must be converted from analog back to digital, a process called *demodulation.* Devices that perform the modulation and demodulation are called *modems.*

A modem communicates in two directions, and it must be compatible with the standards used at both ends of the transmission. The modem itself may be internal or external to the computer. The external modem, such as the Hayes Smartmodem 1200* pictured in Figure 8-4a, typically connects to an asynchronous communication adapter in a PC (with an RS232C connection) and plugs into a standard telephone wall jack. A voice-data switch on the modem allows the line to be used for either voice or data transmission.

FIGURE 8-4. External and internal modems with acoustic coupler.

a. An external modem: The Hayes Smartmodem 1200.

*Hayes Smartmodem 1200 and Hayes Smartmodem 2400B are trademarks of Hayes Microcomputer Products, Inc.

Physically, the external modem may be connected directly into a modular telephone jack or *acoustically coupled* using a standard telephone handset. With an acoustic coupler, such as the one in Figure 8-4b, the connection is made by putting the handset in the rubber cups of the acoustic coupler. Acoustic couplers do not offer the transmission clarity of the direct-connect modem because background noise may interfere with the data transmission.

FIGURE 8-4.

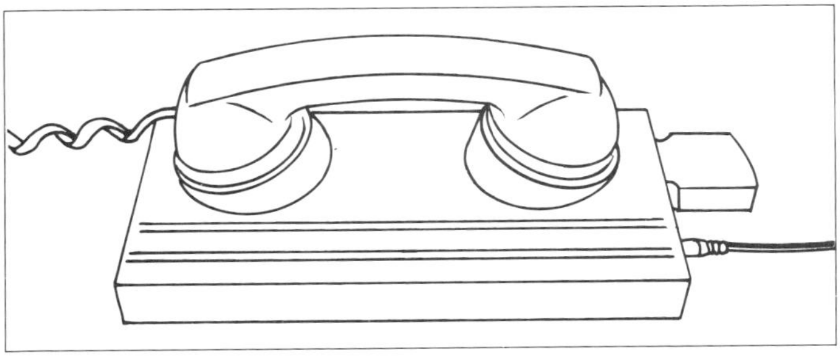

b. An acoustic coupler.

The internal modem, such as the Hayes Smartmodem 2400B shown in Figure 8-4c, is a board that is installed in a microcomputer expansion slot. The wire from the board connects the computer to the telephone wires. The internal modem saves room on the desktop, but it fills an expansion slot and could cause down time for the computer if the modem malfunctions.

c. An internal modem: The Hayes Smartmodem 2400B.

Converting signals in the other direction, from analog to digital signals, requires a device called a *codec* (from code/decoder). The technique of changing analog into digital signals is called *pulse code modulation.* Because digital can be changed into analog and vice versa, transmission between analog and digital devices can take place.

To communicate over a telephone line, both sending and receiving computers must have compatible modems. Compatibility includes coding, transmission speed, signaling methods, and protocols.

Coding

In digital transmission, various methods or codes are employed to represent letters and numbers. Binary code is the language that translates digital bits (0's and 1's) into identifiable characters. Different bit combinations represent upper- and lowercase letters, as well as special symbols, printing control codes, line advances, carriage returns, and editing codes.

The most common code is a seven-bit code referred to as *ASCII* (pronounced *as-key),* which stands for *A*merican *S*tandard *C*ode for *I*nformation *I*nterchange. IBM originated two others, *E*xtended *B*inary *C*oded *D*ecimal (EBCD), a six-bit code, and *E*xtended *B*inary *C*oded *D*ecimal *I*nterchange *C*ode (EBCDIC) (pronounced *eb-c-dic*), an eight-bit code. A six-bit code has 2(6), or 64, possible unique bit combinations. An eight-bit code has 2(8), or 256, possible representations.

Devices must use the same coding schemes to directly exchange information. When unlike coding schemes are used, a conversion procedure is required.

Transmission Rates

Data transmission rates are described by both the number of bits transmitted per second (bps) and the unit of signaling speed (baud).

Data can be sent at rates ranging from 110 bps to 56,000 bps when used with special data communication lines. Both sending and receiving devices must be set to the same speed. If, for example, one modem has the capacity to operate at 300 bps and another at 1200 bps, the transmission must be at the lower speed. Modems that operate at 1200 bps are considered adequate for most communication needs, which rely on telephone line transmission. Most modems follow the standards established by AT&T, which prior to deregulation had the exclusive right to produce modems: the 300 bps modems follow the Bell 103 standard, and the faster 1200 bps modems follow the Bell 212A standard.

Another measure associated with data transmission is the *baud* rate, which represents the number of signal elements per second. Baud rate specifies how often a signal changes state. One baud can code one or more data bits depending on the modulation scheme and the number of available states. When each signal represents only one bit condition, baud is the same as bps. Older 300 bps modems also operated at 300 baud.

Contrary to popular usage, however, bps and baud rate are different measures. The newer 1200 bps and 2400 bps modems operate at 600 baud; that is, the signals change states 600 times per second. Currently, 600 baud is the maximum rate for duplex transmission over telephone lines.

Technical information about the computer-modem dialogue is summarized in Figure 8-5.

FIGURE 8-5. The computer-modem dialog.

The RS-232C interface between the computer and modem uses a standard vocabulary. When a free-standing modem with an RS-232C port is connected by cable to the RS-232C (DCE) port on the computer (DTE), this vocabulary seems appropriate. But when the modem is on a board inside the computer, when no RS-232C port is in sight, and when the actual interface deviates from the RS-232C standard, more patience is required to unravel the signals. My math teacher from years ago would call this a clean-sheet-of-paper, cold-glass-of-lemonade, no-distractions job.

RS-232C signals fall into four groups: ground, data, control, and timing. Ground may include pins 1 and 7, but usually just 7. Data signals through pins 2 and 3 transmit and receive information. Timing signals are irrelevant here. It's the control signals we need to talk about: request to send (RTS), clear to send (CTS), data set ready (DSR), data terminal ready (DTR), ring indicator (RI), and data carrier detect (DCD).

Whether the modem is in-board or free standing, an 8250 UART (Universal Asynchronous Receiver-Transmitter) is between the modem processor and the computer's address, data, and control buses. The UART reformats bytes of data from parallel format (bits are side by side) to serial format (bits in a row) for transmitting. Each of the in-board modems has an 8250 on the printed-circuit board. A free-standing modem connects to an asynchronous communications board or multifunction board with an 8250 on it. If an 8250 or modem is to interface with the public-switched telephone net work, four signals are required by the RS-232C standard: DSR, DTR, RI, and DCD.

DSR and DTR are equipment-readiness indicators. In contrast, the RTS/CTS pair is used as a channel-readiness indicator. DTR and DSR are used with automatic dialing and automatic answering equipment. For example, after the modem has dialed the call, established the connection, and is in data-transmission mode, DSR is turned on. The modem tells the computer that it's ready to go. Similarly, if the modem is connected to the telephone network and the computer turns off DTR, the modem is disconnected from the communications channel.

That's how it's supposed to go in theory, but understanding actual practice requires close reading of the manuals. For example, the Hayes 1200B ignores RTS, CTS, and DSR. When DTR is off you completely disable the modem so that it will accept neither commands nor auto-answers. DCD indicates the presence of carrier.

The Prentice X100 has a richer, more complex instruction and register set. Like the Hayes, it doesn't use RTS. But you can set three modem modes in software to define the control lines. Dumb Terminal mode holds

FIGURE 8-5. (continued)

DSR, DCD, and CTS true, so a simple three-wire cable can be used. Smart Modem mode can set CTS false when the local phone goes off the hook, thus allowing convenient voice/data switching. Also in this mode DSR and DCD go false when carrier is lost. Bell 212 mode follows the conventions of AT&T modems, with CTS going true 200 milliseconds after carrier is detected.

The Cermetek 212PC has a hardware option switch, a jumper that chooses between normal RS-232C operation for CTS, DSR, and DCD, or having those signals forced to the same state as DTR. What's the significance of this diversity? Manufacturers are choosing slightly different ways to implement the "smart" features on their modems. Users must decide which modems have the features they want, which communications software packages support those features, and how they must set up the modem so that the software can access the signals it needs. (Crosstalk, for instance, controls the DTR line and expects to see DCD true only when carrier is actually present. Modem features such as "DTR override" and "DCD forced true" must be disabled if Crosstalk is to work. Fortunately, the modem manuals have the information you need to do this; I used Crosstalk successfully with several of the new modems and with the 1200B.)

For more technical details, see *Data Communications for Microcomputers* by E. A. Nichols, J. C. Nichols, and K. Musson (McGraw-Hill, 1982).

GLOSSARY

RTS. Request to send, an RS-232C control signal sent from the computer to the modem, asking the modem for permission to transmit data (used with clear to send, CTS).

CTS. Clear to send, an RS-232C control signal sent from the modem to the computer, saying that the modem is ready to receive data from the computer; sometimes indicates local phone is on or off hook.

DSR. Data set ready, an RS-232C control signal sent from the modem to the computer, saying whether or not the modem is connected to the (telephone) communications channel (used with data terminal ready, DTR).

DTR. Data terminal ready, an RS-232C control signal sent from the computer to the modem.

DCD. Data carrier detect, an RS-232C control signal sent from the modem to the computer, indicating that carrier is present (used with DTR).

RI. Ring indicator, an RS-232C control signal sent from the modem to the computer, indicating that the modem is receiving a ringing signal from the telephone network.

DCE. Data communication equipment, such as a modem.

DTE. Data terminal equipment, such as the IBM PC (RS-232C ports on the PC are configured as DTE).

Carrier. An analog signal sent over the telephone network.

Modulation. The process of modifying the carrier so that it varies according to changes in another analog signal (the modulating wave).

RXD. Receive data.

TXD. Transmit data.

Communication Methods

When digital pulses are assembled and transmitted over communication channels, the sending and the receiving devices must be perfectly synchronized, or "in synch" (pronounced "sink"). If they are not perfectly synchronized, the receiving device will be unable to determine where each character begins and ends, and the transmission will be incomprehensible. The communication method directly influences the speed of data transfer and, therefore, the amount of information that can be pushed through the electronic pipeline. The two main communication methods are asynchronous and synchronous.

In *asynchronous* (*async*) communications, individual characters are sent separately. Each character is bracketed by a stop-and-start bit signal, marking the beginning and the end of the character, so information does not have to be sent at a constant pace. Asynchronous communication is easy to implement but is less efficient than synchronous methods because the addition of two or more signal bits for each character slows communications. Async is the standard method of communicating for most personal computer links, including public communication networks, bulletin boards, and information utilities such as The Source or CompuServe. Many mainframes and most minicomputers support async communication for dial-up connections using modems, and sometimes for directly connected terminals.

In order for a PC to use asynchronous communication, it must have an asynchronous communication adapter, also known as a serial port. This adapter is usually inexpensive and is often part of a multifunction card. The adapter is connected to an asynchronous modem with a cable designed for this purpose. The pins and connectors on this cable follow a standard known as RS-232, so asynchronous PC communication is sometimes known simply as RS-232 communication. Unfortunately, this is a misnomer because RS-232 refers strictly to the connection, which is only a part of what is usually meant by asynchronous communication.

In *synchronous* transmission, a stream of characters is sent along the channel, and a single stop-and-start character brackets an entire block of information. Each character consists of seven or eight information bits (depending on the code structure). Timing is derived through synchronizing the characters at the beginning of each message or block of data. Once the receiving device gets the special "synch" character, it knows that every eight (or seven) bits it receives constitute a character. The reduced number of stop and start bits increases the speed of data transfer by "reducing the overhead."

The choice of communication method depends on the application. Asynchronous transmission is used mostly with human-machine interfaces (where transmission is irregular). It is the most commonly used transmission mode worldwide, especially for personal computers, computer terminals, and teletypewriters such as Telex. On the other hand, synchronous transmission offers the high speed and continuous data flow necessary for machine-to-machine communications. The deciding factor, however, for using synchronous rather than asynchronous in a PC-mainframe application may well be that many mainframes (IBM's in particular) support synchronous much better than asynchronous. Most IBM mainframes are set up to handle either bisync or SNA/SDLC, two synchronous protocols that are discussed in the next section. Figure 8-6 illustrates the two types of transmission.

FIGURE 8-6. Bit streams for asynchronous and synchronous transmission.

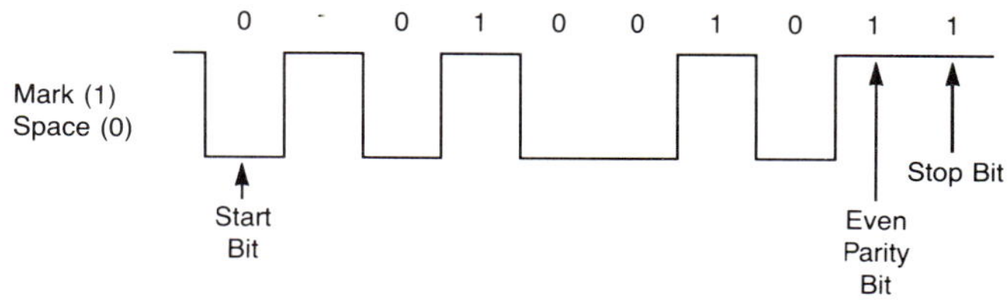

a. Asynchronous or start-stop operation.

1. Each character is preceded by a *start bit* (logical zero) and is concluded with one or more *stop bits* (logical one).
2. Zero bits are also referred to as *spaces,* and one bits as *marks.*
3. The transition from stop bits to start bits triggers the receiver's internal bit rate clock. The receiver then accepts (and discards) the start bit, accepts the number of bits appropriate to the code set, and is conditioned by the stop bit for the next character.
4. Start-stop synchronization enables characters to be sent at random, since each character carries the necessary synchronizing information with itself.

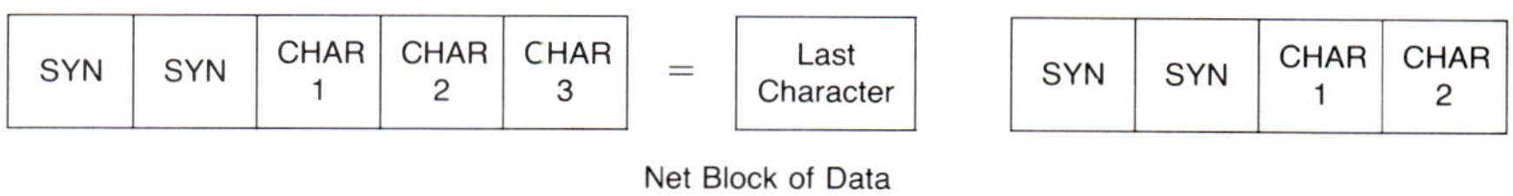

b. Synchronous or timed operation.

1. Characters are sent in blocks, with each block preceded by at least two synchronizing characters (SYN).
2. The receiver is designed to detect the SYN characters, and when it finds at least two in a row (depending on the code being used), the next group of bits will be interpreted as data characters.
3. Characters must be sent without pauses between them.

Communication Protocols

The office systems specialist must understand not only how information is sent on its way through a channel but also be aware that the sending and receiving devices must conform to the same *protocol.*

The term *protocol* comes from the word that describes the rules and procedures used by heads of state and diplomats for the official exchange of information. Likewise in communications, *protocols* are sets of rules that govern the format, timing, and sequence in which data is transmitted over communication channels or links. Protocol depends on both the type of computer equipment (hardware) and the computer program (software). Protocol has three main functions:

1. *"Handshaking."* Establishing or validating that a communication path exists and is working.
2. *Line discipline (data link control).* Control of the sequence of events, or signal exchanges, used to transfer data in a network.
3. *Error checking.* Verification of the accuracy of transmitted data and retransmission when errors occur.

Only devices with the same protocols can directly communicate. Some devices may be able to send or receive by more than one type of protocol. Devices with unlike protocols can only send or receive information through an intermediary device that translates signals (protocol converter) to a common protocol. Protocols are often associated with the devices with which they are most commonly used. The following are descriptions of common protocols and their associated devices:

Asynchronous (TTY, IBM 3101, and DEC VT-100 terminals). TTY protocol originated with teletype equipment. TTY terminals' capabilities are limited primarily to transmitting or receiving characters across an asynchronous (RS-232) interface and responding to a few simple control characters, such as line-feed, carriage return, or cancel. The IBM 3101 is an ASCII terminal (unlike the majority of IBM devices, which are EBCDIC). Digital Equipment Corporation's (DEC) VT-100, one of the most popular terminals, operates in asynchronous mode and provides 132-column display and many screen editing features.

Blocked asynchronous (microcomputers). Blocked asynchronous transmission (BLAST) is a serial asynchronous communication protocol for the IBM PC and compatibles. BLAST allows computer-to-computer file transfer between an IBM PC and any other system (micro, mini, or mainframe) for which BLAST has been implemented. The Xmodem protocol was invented by Ward Christensen and is the best known of the file transfer protocols for PCs.

Kermit is another asynchronous file transfer protocol for microcomputers. It was developed by Bill Catchings and others at Columbia University. To transfer files, each computer must have a version of the Kermit software, which is available for both IBM and DEC mainframes, as well as IBM microcomputers.

Synchronous bit (SNA/SDLC and the IBM 3270 Series). The IBM 3270 Series Computer Terminal is IBM's designation for a series of terminals, printers, and data communication controllers used mostly on its large mainframes. The most popular terminal is the 3278, which features a display that shows 24 lines of text plus an extra status line. Synchronous data link control (SDLC) is a communication protocol used by large IBM computers, especially in networks based on its systems network architecture (SNA) arrangement. SNA is a complex, layered set of rules that regulate error checking, addressing, synchronization, and many other communication chores. SDLC is a bit-oriented protocol, which means it separates the bits that constitute messages with a special flag character such as 011111110. These protocols specify that there will never be six 1 bits in a row, except for the transmission of the flag. SDLC is not compatible with IBM's older Bisynch (BSC) protocol, although many large computers are set up to support both (using completely separate and parallel software, hardware, and communication lines).

Other bit-oriented protocols include the American National Standards Institute's Advanced Data Communications Control Procedure (ADCCP) and the CCITT and International Standards Organization's High-Level Data Link Control (HDLC). Other bit-oriented protocols are offered and supported by various computer vendors.

Binary synchronous (BSC or Bisynch) (IBM 2780 or 3780 RJE terminals). Remote job entry (RJE) terminals are data-entry terminals that accumulate data and send it to a remote mainframe for batch processing. Binary synchronous is an older character-oriented protocol that uses special characters, such as SYN (synchronize the transmitter and receiver), STX (start text), and ETX (end text).

Synchronous byte (Digital Equipment Corporation's DDCMP). Synchronous byte is a byte-oriented protocol that sends data in frames marked by synchronization characters. After two synchronization characters, each frame has a start or header character, a header containing control and address information, a start-of-text character, the actual text, an end-of-text character, and a cyclic redundancy check character that serves as a "checksum."

X.25 Packet-switching protocol. The CCITT international standard protocol for public data networks, the X.25 protocol, defines how the networks operate internally and how the networks communicate with their customer's equipment. Messages to be sent across the network are chopped into packets that usually contain 128 characters (some use 256- or 512-character packets).

Error Detection

Another important factor in describing protocols is error detection. Asynchronous protocols use a method of parity checking. The *parity bit,* an optional check bit, is sent as the eighth bit after every seven-bit data character. The user must tell the computer to include the bit and define its value, either none, space (0), mark (1), odd, or even. The most common method is *even parity.* Even parity specifies that the value of the parity bit will depend on the specific character that is being transmitted and will be a binary value that will cause the total number of parity and data bits to be an even number. Synchronous protocols use primarily one of two alternative methods: synchronous byte (bisynch) protocols, devices that operate on an acknowledgment basis, and the synchronous bit (SNA/SDLC), which uses checksums.

With the acknowledgment method, the receiving device sends a negative acknowledgment (NAK) when data is not received. The checksum method adds all the bits in a block of characters and transmits the total to the receiving device. If the total matches the receiving device's count, accuracy is assumed; if not, the block of characters is retransmitted. Checksum provides the highest accuracy of the three error-checking methods.

Protocol Conversion

Microcomputers transfer data by asynchronous methods, and most large mainframe computers, most notably IBM's (which constitute 60 percent of the installed base), use synchronous methods. In order to connect micro- and mainframe computers, it is necessary to translate data back and forth between asynchronous and synchronous methods. The device designed to accomplish that is called a *protocol converter,* which is a box or card that connects a micro- (an asynchronous device) to a mainframe computer, which normally communicates with an IBM 3270-series terminal (a synchronous device).

Protocol Standards

The International Standards Organization (ISO) based in Geneva, Switzerland, is taking the lead in developing a logical model for allowing unlike equipment to communicate. Protocol standards are important to vendors and users alike. The acceptance of standards is vital, as the ultimate goal of data networks is to become as widespread as today's voice networks.

The primary concept of the ISO model is that the entire communication process can be analyzed as a few relatively independent component processes called *layers.* Layering software allows major operations to be isolated so that variables in the communication process are always defined at the same level. The objective is to make it easier to interface different kinds of software and handware.

The layers might be compared to the layers in any hierarchical organization where specific duties are assigned to prescribed levels. For example, the executive dictates a letter to a secretary, who types it, addresses the envelope, and puts the letter in the envelope. A messenger comes by at scheduled hours, picks up the envelope, and transports it to the mail room. The mail room seals and stamps the envelope and delivers it to the post office, which delivers the letter to the recipient.

The highest level of the seven ISO standards is the application layer, and the other six layers can be thought of collectively as a communication method by which the application's data is moved from one location to another. The ISO model is the framework for all networking protocol standards development. Once vendors agree to a common protocol, communications among unlike technologies will be feasible.

The ISO model, also known as the *O*pen *S*ystems *I*nterconnection (OSI) model, is made up of seven conceptual layers of protocol (see Figure 8-7). Each hierarchy in the scheme of layers provides a certain subset of

7. The Application Layer
6. The Presentation Layer
5. The Session Control Layer
4. The Transfer Layer
3. The Network Control Layer
2. The Data Link Layer
1. The Physical Link Layer

FIGURE 8-7. The open systems interconnection (OSI) seven-layer model.

service to the overall set of network functions. Standards for the first five layers have been agreed upon. In fact, the first three comprise the CCITT X.25 protocol. The remaining two (presentation and application) are being drafted. The seven layers serve the following functions:

1. The *physical link* layer controls the electrical and mechanical aspects of establishing, maintaining, and disconnecting the physical media for transmitting data. This layer includes hardware, such as modems and communication lines, as well as systems software to drive the hardware.

2. The *data link* layer sets up a communication channel between network devices and manages access to and use of that channel. The data link establishes access procedures and provides error detection, data sequencing, and data flow control.

3. The *network control* layer addresses and routes messages between communication nodes on the network and controls the flow of messages between nodes.

4. The *transfer* layer controls the communication session between devices after the channel has been established. It also performs the data manipulation required to make the network-dependent format compatible with the network-independent session layer format.
5. The *session control* layer provides the user interface for the establishment of connections. This layer coordinates the communication interchange between applications.
6. The *presentation* layer controls the display of information by terminal screens or printers and makes different data formats understandable to the user. It also provides data compaction or expansion, data encryption and decryption, data structure (for file transfer), and command translation (for virtual terminals).
7. The *application* or *user* layer offers the "window" that allows the user to access the communication services provided by the architecture. It supports user and application tasks and systems management. Examples of applications at this level include resource sharing, file transfers, remote file access, and database management.

Type of Interface

Workstations are attached to peripheral devices or networks through a connector card that may be either parallel or serial. To communicate with other devices in parallel mode (such as a printer), a *parallel interface* is required. To communicate with most networks, however, the workstation needs a *serial interface* to convert the internal parallel signal into a series of high and low voltages (corresponding to 1's and 0's) to allow the signal to be transmitted over a single data line. (For more information on interfaces, see Chapter 4.)

NETWORK BASICS

A network is simply a series of communicating devices and some control machinery, connected by cables. The telephone system is the best-known example of a network. Some networks have barebones communication capabilities; others have sophisticated capabilities. Before reading the following discussion of specific networks, the reader should understand some basic terms that describe all networks: *bandwidth, multiplexing, topology, media access,* and *connections.*

Bandwidth

Bandwidth describes the carrying capacity of a network. A network may be broadband or baseband. The major difference is that broadband networks use analog technology and baseband networks use digital technology. Coaxial cables may be either baseband or broadband. Optical fibers are broadband. Twisted pair wires are baseband.

As their name implies, analog *broadband* networks are large cables capable of dividing themselves into frequencies or bands so that more than one user can access a system at the same time. Broadband technology can carry data, text, voice, and video signals, thus taking care of all information transfer needs an organization may have. Cable TV (CATV) is the most familiar broadband network.

Digital *baseband* networks transmit one signal at a time; therefore, only one user may use the system at a given time. To allow more than one signal on a cable at the same time, a time-sharing approach (multiplexing) is necessary.

Multiplexing

A multiplexer is a combination of hardware and software that allows simultaneous transmission and reception of two or more digital data streams on a single channel. Frequency-division/time-division (FDM/TDM) multiplexers divide the baseband technology into distinct channels.

Frequency division divides the network into frequencies in much the same way that radio or television signals are divided. A user "tunes into" a particular channel. Time-division multiplexers, on the other hand, divide the channel into time divisions. A user has a specific time assigned and can transmit only in that time slot, usually in thousandths or millionths of a second. The FDM or TDM assigns channels behind the scenes; the user generally has access to the network very quickly, giving the user the impression that he or she has a private line.

Topology

Topology describes the arrangement of network stations in relation to each other. Topology is labeled by the shape of the systems on which individual workstations connect: star, ring, and bus (sometimes called tree). These configurations are illustrated in Figure 8-8.

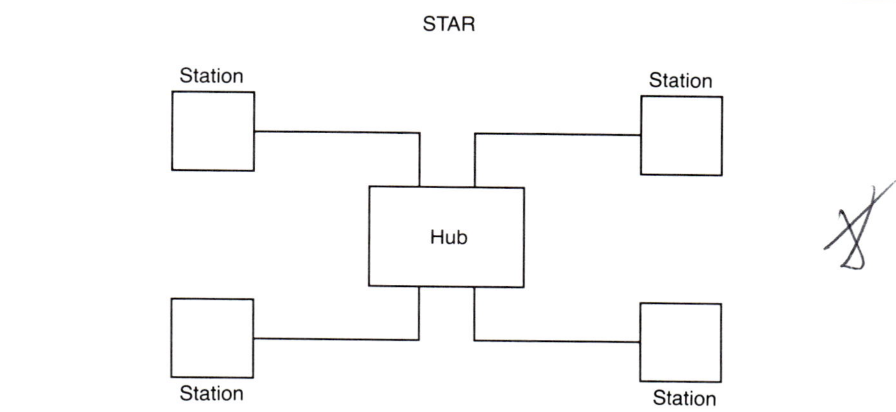

FIGURE 8-8. Network topologies: Star, ring, and bus.

a. Star network topology.

FIGURE 8-8.

b. Ring network topology.

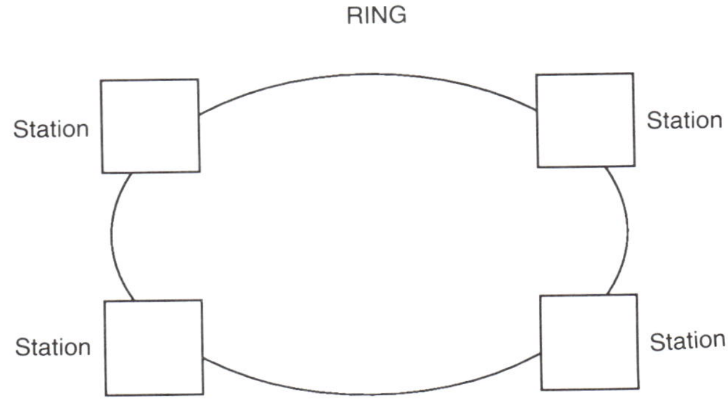

c. Bus network topology.

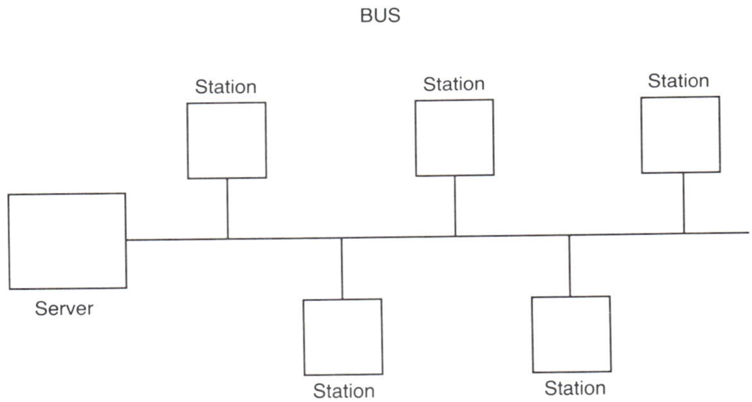

The *star* network connects all workstations to a central unit. Individual workstations (nodes) can communicate only through the central unit (or *hub*). The hub routes messages to their intended destinations. The star network, by far the easiest to understand, is commonly used to connect users via a large central computer system. The telephone company calls its hub the telephone central office (CO). Large organizations may use a central telephone switch called a private branch exchange or PBX. (There will be more discussion of COs and PBXs in a later section.) The main weakness of the star configuration is that if the central control device is down, all terminals are out of operation.

A *ring* network connects nodes (workstations) directly to a network with no central unit. All nodes have equal access to the network. Data travels in simplex flow, and individual nodes actually help push the message around the network until it reaches its intended destination. The ring network is generally used in networks where the nodes are relatively close together. An advantage of the ring node is that if one of the nodes fails, in most cases the entire ring will not be out of service.

Bus networks are similar to the ring network, except that a beginning and end point exist, and data can be transferred in more than one direction. Bus topologies enable nodes to be linked onto the cable at any point, and the number of nodes that can be part of a bus network is limited only by the length of the cable. Gateways are a means of interconnecting entire networks. When gateways are added, the network often takes the shape of a *tree.* A cable TV (CATV) network is an example of a tree network. The bus configuration provides network users with flexibility and reliability.

Media Access

Each node (workstation) that is attached to a network operates as an independent unit, allowing the user to access the network only when desired. The number of nodes sharing a network and their requirments for accessing it vary. Therefore, the concept of media access—how to get onto the network—is important.

Media access may be classified as either *contention* (the user controls access) or *noncontention* (the system decides who can access the network). The following discussion describes access methods that fit into these two categories:

1. Contention: CSMA/CA and CSMA/CD.
2. Noncontention: polling and token passing.

CSMA/CA and CSMA/CD

Carrier sense *m*ultiple *a*ccess with *c*ollision *a*voidance (CSMA/CA) or collision *d*etection (CSMA/CD) are "listen, then send" contention access methods. The concept is simple; the user "listens" to the channel to see if anyone is using the network (collision avoidance) and, if the network is free, transmits the message. If two users listen to the network at the same time, hear nothing, and send their respective messages, the messages are intercepted by collision detection, allowing neither sender to use the system until the network is clear (one user will have to wait). Some networks automatically queue the users, eliminating the need to re-send the message.

Polling

Polling is a centralized noncontention access method used on systems where a central site is responsible for controlling network access. The central site "polls" each of the network devices, in turn, to see if they require access to the network. Devices can send only when it is their turn.

Token Passing

Token passing is a distributed noncontention access method. With token passing, an electronic "packet" continually circles a ring network, passing by each node until the user puts a message into the packet and sends it to another network address. Each node along the way checks the packet to see if the message is addressed to that station. If so, the station accepts the data, and if not, sends it on its way. Token passing is considered best suited for networks with only a few nodes that require high speeds.

Types of Connections

When a workstation is connected to another workstation or computer system via a dialed telephone call, the connection is called a *switched line* or *dial-up*. Switched lines may work well for many types of communications, but line quality is unpredictable and lines are susceptible to electromagnetic interference. An alternative to a switched line is a *leased line*, a private communications line leased from a common carrier. A leased line is more predictable because the same path is used each time a call is made, and it can transmit more error-free data traffic per hour. Cost advantage depends on usage. With dial-up, users pay only for time used. As volume increases, however, there is a cross-over point where the fixed cost of leased lines (which are available twenty-four hours a day) becomes more economical. Over short distances, workstations, microcomputers, and terminals can be connected directly to each other via an in-house *direct-connect line*, which avoids the need for a common carrier.

TELEPHONE TECHNOLOGIES

The following discussion of basic voice technologies includes an overview of how the telephone system works, including the PBX (private branch exchange) and two telephone peripherals: the traditional telephone answering machine and the more recently developed voice mail systems.

The most common of all communication networks is the telephone. Telephone technology (telephony) consists of instruments, cables, switching facilities, and trunks. Everyone knows something about the telephone, but not everyone can pass the quiz in Figure 8-9. (The answers are shown in Figure 8-10.)

The instrument for telephone communication is generally a handset. However, the handset is taking on new shapes, sizes, and even mobility as the number of telephone vendors increases, addressing the demands of the entire marketplace. Figure 8-11 shows a wide variety of handsets available today.

The telephone will continue to be the most universal communication device throughout the next decades, although major changes in the instrument will be seen and many are already "smart." Telephones can be linked with a computer to initiate or receive computing functions. Some

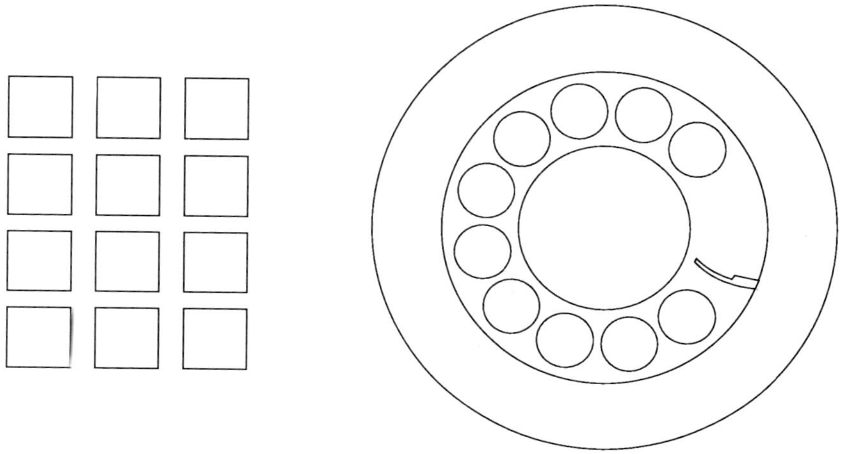

FIGURE 8-9. Complete these dials by inserting the numbers and letters exactly as they should appear.

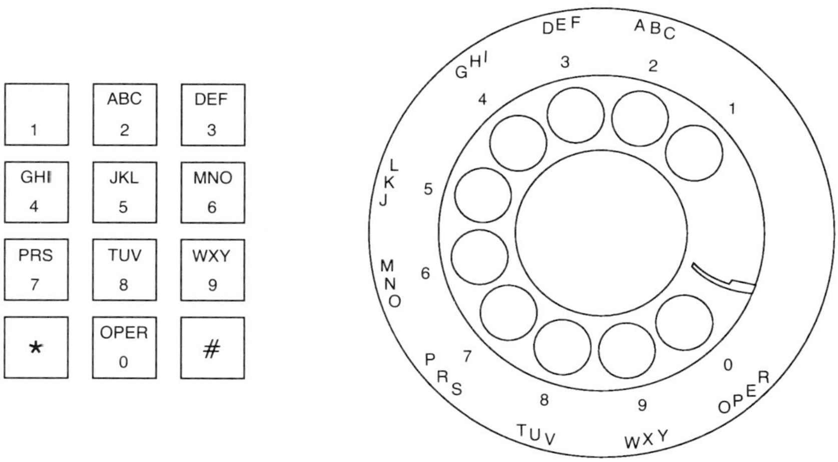

FIGURE 8-10. Here's how your telephone dials from Figure 8-9 should appear.

have internal memory; others have speakerphones; and still others, such as DataPoint Corporation's full-color, full-motion video/data teleconferencing system shown in Figure 8-12, have full video capabilities. The instrument on tomorrow's desk will be capable of providing many more services and will probably not resemble the telephone as we know it today.

a. NEC America's D-term Executive Terminal.

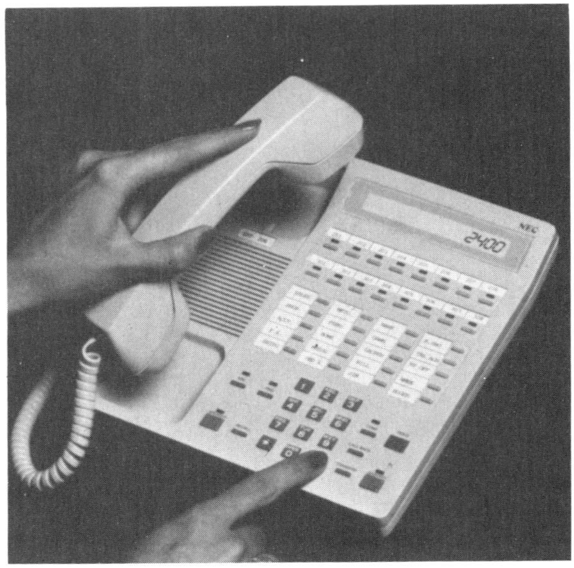

b. NEC America's D-term 16-Button Terminal.

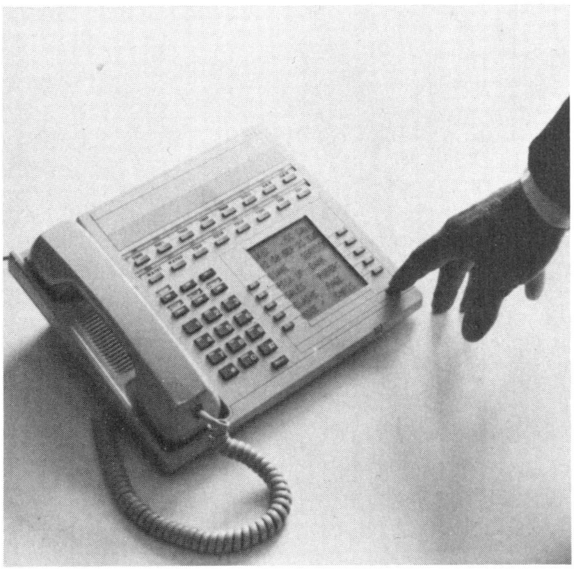

c. NEC America's 16-Line Executive Terminal.

d. NEC America's 6-Line Display Terminal.

FIGURE 8-11. Some of the many forms of telephone handsets.

FIGURE 8-12. The MINX system by DataPoint Corporation is a full-color, full-motion video/data teleconferencing system.

How the Telephone Operates

By far the most commonly used cable in the telephone industry is the twisted pair wire. These wires extend in loops that connect the subscriber to a local switching office. For long-distance service, coaxial cables and fiber optics are often used. The telephone company's central office (CO) provides switching facilities that allow a user, connected to the loop, to connect with anyone else upon demand. This is the job of the local-service telephone company. The channels that carry calls between switching offices are called *trunks*.

In locales where cables are impractical or impossible because of mountains, oceans, or great distances, alternatives to telephone cables are microwave transmission and satellite relays. A microwave system or satellite transmits the voice to the CO, which completes the phone call. For example, satellite transmission enables air travelers to make telephone calls in flight; the signal is sent to a satellite, which in turn sends the transmission to a conventional earth-bound CO.

Residential phones are connected directly to the CO. When calling from home, the user is connected via the CO directly to the line being called, without an additional connection. Large organizations, however, sometimes elect to use a private branch exchange (PBX). The PBX is actually a telephone exchange in its own right; internal telephone lines are directly connected to the PBX, which can complete calls between stations attached to the PBX, bypassing the CO. To call someone outside the PBX, however, the caller must first access the local CO. For example, "9" is dialed first, accessing the CO, and the CO completes the phone call. Because of the potential role of the PBX in linking office automation technologies, it is discussed in detail later in this chapter.

In small organizations (requiring fewer than 50 handsets), a *key telephone system* may be used. While the PBX chooses a trunk automatically, the user of a key system chooses a trunk by pressing a button. In addition, intercom facilities are typically part of a key telephone system.

With a *Centrex* system, each individual has his or her own seven-digit number. Typically found in large organizations that have thousands of handsets, the Centrex system has been described as a "PBX located at a CO." Outsiders dial the seven-digit number directly; this is called *direct inward dialing (DID)*. Insiders dial only the last four digits. Long-distance phone calls originating at these organizations are tracked to the caller by what is called *identification of outward dial (IOD)*. The Centrex system provides fast service to users.

The PBX or PABX Network

Because of the virtual universality of telephones, the private branch exchange (PBX) is a common network. Modern digital PBXs are switching stations for voice and data transmission. They operate with software programs and, consequently, can be adapted to new purposes and functions by reprogramming or new software. PBXs can be programmed to perform special functions and to assign individual access to those functions. For example, the PBX can track communication patterns and expenses. It can be linked with separate application processors to add expanded functionality such as electronic directory and message centers, communication cost-accounting systems, and voice messaging. The PBX can operate as the center for controlling calling privileges, managing circuit features, and measuring feature usage. PBX functions may include the following:

- Advanced voice functions, including automatic callback to a busy number and automatic forwarding of calls to another phone.
- Least-cost routing on long-distance calls.
- Customer control of features such as call forwarding.
- Automatic generation of reports on systems operation.
- Ability to notify security of an unlocked door.
- Hospitality services, such as wake-up calls for hotels.

As a contender for the market to link computers in the office, the PBX has a head start mainly because its cabling systems already exist in the office. Currently, however, most PBXs use twisted pair wires, which cannot transfer mass amounts of data quickly or transfer information in any other form, such as video and image.

In the future, communication experts expect to see PBXs offer more functions, including increased transmission speeds and image handling. The extent of the role that PBXs will play in creating tomorrow's office systems is not yet clear. Office system professionals should consider the advantages offered by PBXs when they evaluate communication options.

Network Peripherals: Answering Machines

Today most Americans are familiar with telephone answering machine messages such as the following:

> *Hello, this is Connie Masson. I'm away from my desk at the moment. Please leave a message when you hear a beep, and I'll get right back to you.*

An answering machine is a device that connects to the telephone handset. Using magnetic media for voice recordings, it "answers" incoming phone calls with an outgoing voice message and records incoming messages. Praised for promoting privacy and, at the same time, increasing accessibility, the answering machine is used in homes as well as offices. Rather sophisticated, yet inexpensive (low-end models sell for as little as $79), the answering machine monitors and records calls when the intended receiver is unable or unwilling to answer the phone.

Some answering machines have remote control units that allow users to obtain their recorded messages. The user can enter special codes to obtain messages and, if desired, change the outgoing voice message.

Telephone Peripherals: Voice Mail

Voice mail systems operate in conjunction with a PBX to handle multiple users simultaneously. Voice mail systems use digital technology; a computer (usually a minicomputer) holds messages until recipients call for them. Both the caller and the recipient manipulate the system by using the telephone keypad; the message can be saved, replayed, forwarded, and so on by using the keypad (rotary dials are not appropriate for this use).

Voice mail was introduced in 1976 but was not an immediate success because of special operating requirements and costs. According to one authority, "An electronic message . . . requires approximately 1,500 bytes of data for every 200 words of text. A 200-word voice message, on the other hand, requires almost 170 times that number of bytes—250,000—when digitized at a rate of approximately 25,000 bits per second of speech."[1]

The requirement of high storage capacities for digitally recording a voice message has been mitigated by the development of the 32-bit microprocessor chip. Moreover, prices have fallen; for example, the RSVP Voice Mail System by AT&E Systems shown in Figure 8-13 lists for $4,250. Figure 8-14 depicts the structure of a voice mail system.

FIGURE 8-13. The AT&E RSVP 3000 Voice Mail System.

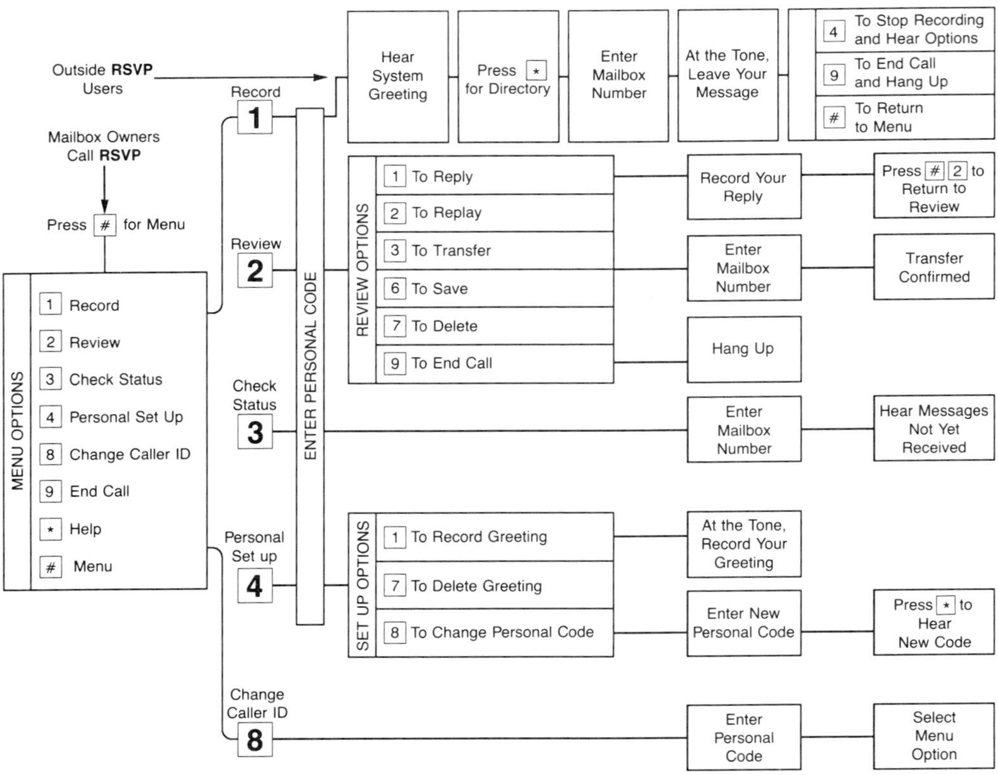

FIGURE 8-14. The structure of a voice mail system.

COMPUTER NETWORKS

Several networking options are available to organizations for data transfer. The economic incentive for networking individual microcomputers is in the form of sharing expensive peripherals, such as hard disks or printers. In addition, users can share files and send or leave messages for each other. Networks can also provide bridges between what would otherwise be incompatible computer systems and application programs.

Multiuser Systems

The least expensive networking option for microcomputers is the multiuser system. The major difference between single user and multiuser microcomputers is the complexity of the operating system. Multiuser operating systems, such as MP/M and UNIX, allow several users to work simultaneously. The maximum distance between terminals is usually 200 feet. System performance depends on the number of users and kinds of applications. The multiuser system does not allow users to communicate directly with each other, but it allows them to share files and peripherals, and leave messages.

Local Area Networks

The leading technology for sharing resources such as databases and peripheral equipment is the local area network (LAN), which is a data communication network spanning a limited geographical area, such as an office, a building, or a campus. The basic idea is easy to conceptualize; the technology, however, is not so simple. A typical LAN configuration consists of hardware such as computers (usually microcomputers) and printers, which are linked together and share software and data files. Figure 8-15 shows an office linked with the AppleTalk Personal Network.

FIGURE 8-15. The AppleTalk Personal Network and LaserWriter printer.

Definitions of LANs include the following aspects:

1. LANs are typically carriers of digital data; however, in recent years the ability to include analog data has been added.
2. LAN components include (1) computer function cards that connect the computer to the network, (2) the cabling, (3) the file server that controls the network, and (4) the operations software.
3. Most LAN installations transmit via relatively inexpensive media, such as twisted pair wires or coaxial cables.
4. LANs are generally geographically limited; they seldom span more than 10 kilometers.
5. LANs enable a user to communicate selectively with databases or with others connected to the LAN. To do this, a switching mechanism is required, commonly called a *file server.*
6. The same LAN can be accessed by users of dissimilar though compatible equipment.
7. LANs are owned by the company that uses them; they are not part of a public utility service.
8. Devices connected to a LAN operate independently of other devices on the same network. If one device goes down, the remaining units are not affected.

Basic Components of a LAN

The four basic components of a local area network include the following:

1. The cards that plug into a computer to connect it to the network.
2. The cabling and network-control hardware (file server).
3. The network-control software, which is very important because it determines what a user can and cannot do on the network.
4. Bridges and gateways that expand the network.

The network-control hardware consists of hard disks referred to as *file servers.* A network server may be dedicated or shared. Dedicated servers are microcomputers that are used only by the network; shared servers are microcomputers that serve double duty as both a computer and a file server.

A group of users can simultaneously access their portion of the file server. These individual disk segments, each of a fixed physical dimension, are preset using network software, so there is no overlap among users. The network software may be programmed to restrict users to only reading data or to give them full access to files on the disk.

Sophisticated file server software can assign shared segments on the file server. Shared access allows multiple users to access the same copy of an application or to edit the same data files simultaneously.

Generally, software that runs on microcomputers cannot be shared on a LAN because it was designed for the single-user environment. A network version of application software is required for a local area network environment. Some networks allow file access; others have restrictions.

Bridges and gateways are hardware and software that allow communication between devices on separate networks. *Bridges* connect two or more networks that use the same protocol. Two networks may be connected by a local bridge or by a remote bridge established indirectly via leased or switched circuits. *Gateways* connect LANs that use different protocols or connect LANs to mainframes.

Types of LANs

Buyers of LANs choose from three types of networks: proprietary, standardized, and universal. *Proprietary* networks are offered by manufacturers of computer systems to support their own equipment. Examples of proprietary systems include IBM's Token Ring Network and Datapoint's ARCnet.

Standardized networks are licensed by manufacturers of connecting technologies; the equipment is designed to match the standards of the network producer. Xerox's Ethernet and the DCA Corporation's 10-Net are examples of standardized networks.

The manufacturers of *universal* networks make interfaces that enable dissimilar devices to attach to a common network.

Wide Area Networks

When a LAN user at one location wants to communicate with a LAN user at another site, a wide area network (WAN) with a special gateway is used. The WAN bandwidth, which is typically smaller than the LAN bandwidth, is a public utility; it is not owned by the company. The company purchases WAN services much the same way as it purchases telephone services.

Public Data Networks

Public information services, such as The Source, CompuServe, Dow Jones News and Retrieval, and Dialog, provide news, encyclopedias, airline schedules, electronic bulletin boards, and a wealth of other information, as well as electronic mail. These services are available by subscription, with fees based on the amount of time spent on the system. Also very popular with microcomputer users is a nationwide network of dial-up bulletin boards, which provide mostly free services and are a great source of public domain software. Dial-up bulletin boards are accessed by microcomputers using special software.

For either the subscription information service or dial-up bulletin boards, the user needs a microcomputer with an asynchronous adapter and an asynchronous modem.

A popular electronic mail and bulletin board software program in the public domain is RBBS-PC. Major features include operator-defined conditions for access, user database, and a bulletin board and message system.

Microcomputer-to-Mainframe Links

The microcomputer revolution is having a great impact on the way mainframe computers are used. Although microcomputers and mainframes were originally viewed as competing technologies, many applications have evolved that are synergistic. Linking the two devices provides new opportunities to capitalize on the strengths of both devices; mainframes handle large databases and concentrate on the massive number crunching they do best, and microcomputers bring data and processing power to the desktop where it is needed.

Many new products have been designed to allow mainframes and microcomputers to communicate. Selecting the needed software and hardware is complex and requires some understanding of mainframe data communications. Special software, circuit boards, protocol devices, and controllers are required. Mainframes and microcomputers differ in word size, data transmission speed, and character structure, and appropriate translations are required in both directions to allow them to talk with each other.

Common applications for micro-to-mainframe links are (1) terminal emulation, (2) file transfer, (3) virtual disk systems, and (4) cooperative processing.

Terminal Emulation

Terminal emulation is a specialized application of micro-to-mainframe links that has grown rapidly since its introduction in 1982. *Terminal emulators* allow microcomputers to perform as dedicated terminals.

Dedicated terminals are the standard workstations connected to mainframes or minicomputers. Most terminal emulators emulate either the IBM 3270 series or the Digital Equipment Corporation (DEC) VT100 series (the two most widely used terminals). Although dedicated terminals are less expensive than microcomputers, microcomputers can do double duty as dedicated terminals. With terminal emulation, microcomputers can talk to the mainframe, do standalone computing, or work as part of a microcomputer network. With terminal emulation capability, the need for two separate devices cluttering the workplace is eliminated.

A 3270 terminal emulator usually consists of an add-on board and communication software. IBM 3270s use synchronous protocol (data is sent in blocks); this is much faster but is more complicated and expensive to emulate. Microcomputers with emulators cannot plug directly into an IBM host computer. They must be connected to a cluster controller. A cluster controller functions as a traffic cop, directing information from a number of terminals or emulators to and from the host. DEC VT100 emulators use asynchronous protocol (one character is sent at a time) on a microcomputer by using software only. If the microcomputers are in the same building as the host computer, it is possible to connect them with VT100 emulators, directly to the DEC host, using standard twisted pair wires. If microcomputers are not close enough to the host to wire them together, they can be connected by modems and telephone lines.

Some additional features that should be considered when selecting an emulator are file-transfer capability, session hold, multisession capability, and network-addressable printer support. Some emulators can transfer only ASCII files between the host and a microcomputer; others can transfer binary files, such as Lotus 1-2-3 or dBASE II. Session hold, which is available only with newer 3270 emulation, allows the microcomputer to switch between emulation and standalone work (such as word processing) without breaking the initial connection to the host. Multisession capability enables the microcomputer to switch back and forth between more than one mainframe application, without losing the initial connection to any of them. Network-addressable printer support allows any microcomputer tied into the host to request print and direct it to any printer connected to the host. Without this feature, a file can be printed only by the printer connected to the microcomputer that initiates the request.

File Transfer

File transfer refers to the ability to transfer data files between computer systems, usually between a mainframe or minicomputer and microcomputers. Most file-transfer products are included in or built around a terminal emulator. Since file structures and coding are different on mainframes than microcomputers, special protocols (Xmodem, Kermit, and BLAST are three mentioned earlier) are needed to convert file formats and coding and to control errors. Many file-transfer programs have their own proprietary protocols.

File-transfer programs may support the transfer of text that needs to be converted from ASCII to EBCDIC or vice versa, and/or binary data (such as graphic data, consisting of x-y coordinates) that do not need to be converted.

Virtual Disk Systems

Some file-transfer programs allow files to be stored on the mainframe and accessed by a microcomputer, as if the files were on a local hard disk or floppy disk. Referred to as *virtual disk,* this technique can be used to transfer files by a microcomputer copy command. One such virtual disk package is called Tempus-Link. A very different example is the IBM XT/370 PC, which runs the same operating system (VM/CMS) on the microcomputer as on the mainframe.

Remote job entry (RJE) terminals were popular in the 1970s for submitting batch jobs to mainframe computers. RJE emulation programs are used today primarily as a special means of doing file transfer. A micro emulating an RJE terminal can send files to the mainframe as virtual card decks and receive files as virtual printer files. The advantage of RJE emulation is that most mainframes already have software to support RJE workstations. Also, RJE emulation operates in bisync or SNA/SDLC protocols, which provide better error and flow control than asynchronous programs.

Cooperative Processing

Cooperative processing refers to applications where the actual processing is done jointly by a mainframe and a microcomputer. Whereas file transfer simply takes a data file and moves it from one computer to another, cooperative processing actually shares the processing of the data in one file between the microcomputer and the mainframe. The microcomputer processes part of the data, then passes it to the mainframe, which does additional processing and then passes it back to the microcomputer, and so forth. For example, in a data entry application, the microcomputer might query the operator in a user-friendly, conversational manner for required data. The data is then passed to the mainframe for processing, and the results are returned to the microcomputer.

Another application for cooperative processing is *database extraction*. In database extraction, data query and manipulation are done by the microcomputer while the database is maintained on the mainframe. On the mainframe side, data dictionaries maintain data; and on the microcomputer side, software packages provide menus and query screens to allow the user to issue instructions to extract data and download it to the microcomputer. Once on the microcomputer, the data can be converted into the proper formats for use in spreadsheets or other application programs.

Cooperative processing is the highest level of micro-mainframe application integration. Most packages that can support cooperative processing are experimental and expensive. Some communication experts predict that cooperative processing will become the normal mode of using microcomputers and mainframes together for solving problems.

ELECTRONIC MAIL SYSTEMS

Electronic mail is a means of sending messages or documents from location to location without the need for physical transfer of paper. In the category of electronic mail, the following concepts/hardware will be examined: computer-based message switching (CBMS) systems, office electronic mail systems, facsimile machines, and Telex and TWX.

Computer-Based Message Switching (CBMS) Systems

CBMS systems allow an individual on a computer network to send messages to others on that network. The software for CBMS allows a user to key a message into the system, using software controls, and send that message to any or all individuals connected to the network. For example, a manager could send a message, "Tuesday's departmental meeting canceled; please reschedule for 4 p.m. on Thursday," to an entire department or to specified individuals.

Office Electronic Mail Systems

The communication capabilities of a full-service office electronic mail system provided by office systems software such as IBM's mainframe-based PROFS, Wang's Integrated Office System (WIOS), or Digital Equipment's All-in-One (see Chapter 4) are much more extensive than those provided by a CMBS. In addition to short messages, full-service systems allow users to send and receive letters and access other documents such as mailing lists and directories. Information can be sent to multiple recipients simultaneously; documents can be annotated and forwarded, scanned into the system, and so on.

Facsimile

Facsimile machines are devices for transmitting images (as opposed to voice, data, or video). With a facsimile machine (often referred to as a FAX machine) at each end of a telephone line (or other network), images such as pictures, graphs, or charts are scanned and electronically transmitted to a receiving FAX, where the image is printed on paper. Typical applications include an organization's advertising or public relations efforts (pictures may be included), or, in an architectural firm, the transmission of design changes. Reporters use a FAX to send photos to, say, the city desk.

Facsimile systems produce a picture of a page by scanning it, much as a television camera scans a scene or a copier scans a printed page. The scanning mechanism illuminates the copy to be sent and focuses reflected light onto the photocell, which converts the image to an electronic signal that is transmitted over telephone lines. Figure 8-16 shows the features found in facsimile equipment, including autodial, autoanswer, and polling. These features eliminate the need for operators to be at either end of the transmission and allow long-distance transfers at times when transmission costs are low. Other features include self-test diagnostics, contrast control, and even paper cutting, where the output paper is automatically cut to the size of the original.

While facsimile had its origins in the 1840s, it wasn't until the twentieth century that a practical use for the technology appeared: weather maps. Today, business is finding more and more applications as facsimile transmission has become faster, easier to use, and much less costly. With the advancements in data compression technology and the availability of wideband transmission facilities, the case for the high-speed FAX will become more attractive. Increasingly, high-speed FAX will become more automated and include many of the features listed above.

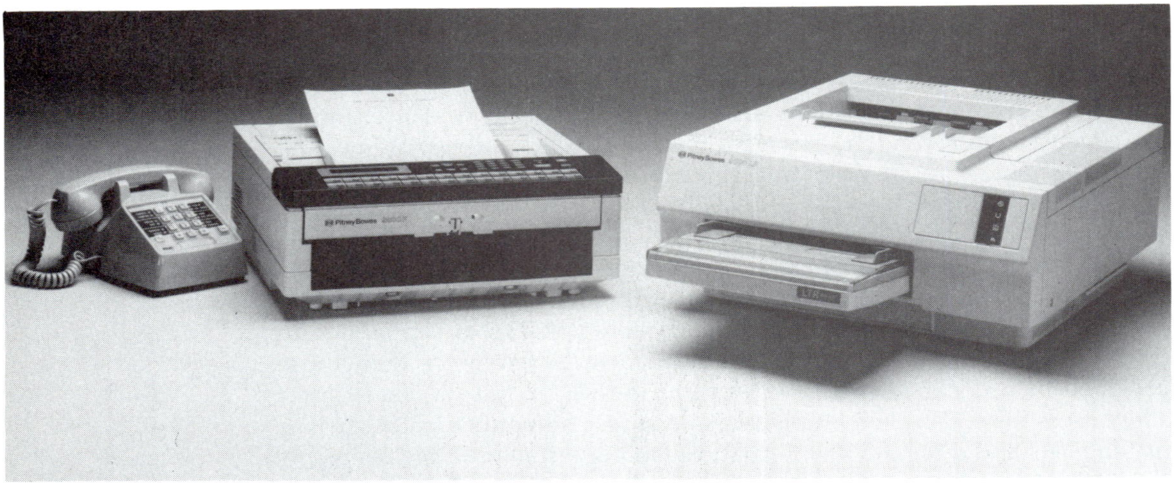

FIGURE 8-16. The Pitney Bowes Model 9200 Facsimile System allows facsimile transmission on bond paper at 11 seconds per page.

Telex and TWX

Both Telex and TWX (teleprinter exchange service) are communication networks operated by Western Union Telegraph Company. Although the two services are often referred to as Telex/TWX, there are differences between them in such matters as speed, method of transmission, and billing. Telex initially operated via telegraph lines; for years, it was *the* way for organizations to communicate. Today, Telex is a dedicated network that operates at 66.67 words per minute (50 bps) on a five-bit code. Using a teleprinter (teletypewriter) terminal rented from a designated carrier, the user types a message on paper tape, which is fed into the paper tape reader and transmitted over the Telex lines. The teleprinter at the receiving end prints the incoming message. Charges for the use of Telex are computed by the amount of transmission time and distance of transmission. In addition, Western Union charges for installation and use. Telex is an international service.

TWX, on the other hand, can operate at either 60 words per minute (150 bps) with a five-level code or at 100 words per minute (150 bps) with an eight-level ASCII code. TWX terminals may be owned by the subscriber or rented from a designated carrier. Installation charges are levied, as well as a monthly plug-in charge. TWX is available only in the United States and Canada.

As part of an office system, Telex/TWX may be incorporated as part of a microcomputer or even larger system. When traffic is not heavy, Telex/TWX provides an alternative communication system, less costly than establishing a dedicated network. In addition, Telex is geographically large, with its own directory of users.

TELECONFERENCING SYSTEMS

Teleconferencing is communication among more than two individuals through electronic media. Activities that may be conducted via a teleconference include business meetings, seminars, training sessions, public relations events, and communication ventures extending over a long time.

Teleconferencing was originally marketed as a means for lowering executive travel costs. Today, however, the teleconference's biggest selling point is the timeliness and convenience it offers: quick communication with little disruption in normal work patterns. Meetings and/or training sessions can be conducted on the spur of the moment. The four categories of teleconferencing are based on the technologies employed: audio, video, audiographic, and computer.

Audio Teleconferencing

Audio teleconferencing is voice-only interaction between individuals at two or more sites. An audio teleconference requires only a telephone device, but is notably enhanced by the use of a speakerphone or a receiving/sending device such as Darome's Convener or AT&T's Quorum. Microphones in these devices convert sound waves into electrical current; their loudspeakers reverse the process. Speakerphones differ from handsets in that the microphone in a handset is close to the participant's mouth so that the energy from the voice is enough to send the transmission on its way. Likewise, the receiver is directly over the ear, so that sound cannot "leak." Strength of signal and sound leakage are problems that teleconference receiving/sending devices must overcome. Moreover, holding a telephone handset for longer than five or ten minutes is uncomfortable. With a speakerphone or receiving/sending device, this is not a problem.

Connecting more than two sites to a telephone transmission is difficult. The channel may not be strong enough or may be prone to interference. For this reason, "bridges" are often recommended. Using a "meet-me" bridge, teleconferencing participants either call into a central service at a prearranged time or (for a higher price) the central service operator calls each participant to join the telephone connection. One can purchase bridging services from private companies such as Kellog Telephone Conferencing Service, Darome Connection, Confer Tech, and AT&T.

Video Teleconferencing

Video teleconferencing adds the technology of the television screen to the audio teleconference. Signal converters are required at both the sending and receiving end for transmission/reception of the video signals. The two forms of video teleconferencing are full-motion and slow-scan (freeze frame).

A full-motion video teleconference is similar to closed-circuit TV; slow scan is more like a slide show. Full-motion video is much more expensive than slow-scan video because full-motion video requires a much larger bandwidth. For example, a one-hour full-motion video teleconference between New York and Los Angeles could cost $120 for the transmission time alone. The same meeting conducted via slow scan could cost $30. In addition, there are special cameras and the cost of preparation, as well as site expenses. A video teleconference may be costly but may be a very cost-effective way to hold business meetings or conduct training seminars.

Audiographic Teleconferencing

As its name implies, audiographic teleconferencing combines the technology of the audio teleconference with one of the graphic technologies—perhaps a facsimile machine or an electronic blackboard. Facsimile machines, which were discussed earlier, provide a means to transfer hard copy (paper) from site to site. An electronic blackboard acts as a large electronic writing tablet. The writing originated at the sending location is transmitted over telephone lines to a television monitor at the receiving station. With multiple blackboards in use, graphic interaction can occur between or among sites.

Computer Teleconferencing

Computer teleconferencing is communication through computer terminals. Individuals on the computer network use their computer and the telephone network to exchange ideas and solutions to problems. Unlike other categories of teleconferencing, computer teleconferencing does not require participants to be "online" (although they may be). An example is a committee working to solve a problem. Because messages can be deposited into the recipient's electronic mailbox and answered at a later time, the system becomes time-independent, allowing individuals to respond at a convenient time. Computer teleconferencing requires application software much like that for electronic mail.

OTHER TECHNOLOGIES

Other communications technologies are rapidly emerging. Videotex is one example. The "smart building" integrates many of the technologies discussed in this chapter.

Videotex

The following scenario illustrates the use of Videotex technology:

> After a work day of sitting in front of a CRT terminal, Sir Toby Belch, a hypothetical British executive, returns to his London apartment. Forgetting to remove his coat, Belch mixes himself a gin and tonic and turns on the color television set. With his coat on and drink in hand, Belch steps back from the set and sinks into his Soft Wear chair. He erases thoughts of work from his head by rubbing the drink across his forehead.
>
> Bored with "The Adventures of Paddington Bear" on the BBC, Belch presses 130 on a hand-held keypad, and the program disappears. The index for today's *Financial Times* appears in four colors. "Whoever thought the BBC would deliver the *Financial Times* in color," he says to himself, chuckling.
>
> Belch remembers that he doesn't have money in his checking account for the rent. He presses another button on his keypad, and the index for the London Information Center (LIC) appears. This service

connects Belch's television set to stores, banks, and the public library via the LIC computer.

Belch types his password on the keypad. A few seconds later, an index for his bank account appears. Belch presses 2 on the keypad for "Savings to Checking." The set displays the directions for the transaction.

Sipping his drink, Belch wonders whether he wants to access the Beef Wellington recipe on the BBC. Meanwhile, a printer in the next room taps out a record of his bank transaction.[2]

Sir Belch is using Videotex. Videotex, which is very popular in Europe, is an interactive communication system that combines the technologies of broadcasting and networking. Broadcasting is the communication of one to many; networking is communication among many. Via Videotex, information bases that are broadcast through the television receptor can be accessed and, if desired, users can interact with those bases by using the network. In comparison with traditional data processing, Videotex is less expensive and much easier to use.

Additional examples of Videotex business applications are electronic newsletters or sales catalogs. Videotex has proven to be beneficial in reducing costs associated with printing a document and simplifying the distribution process. Moreover, on the receiver's end, the catalog is always available and up to date. Figure 8-17 presents examples of Videotex "pages."

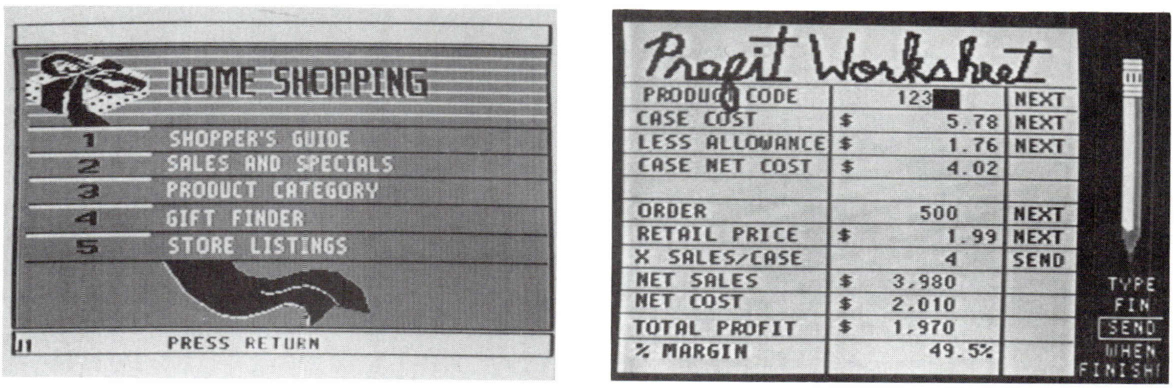

FIGURE 8-17. Videotex "pages."

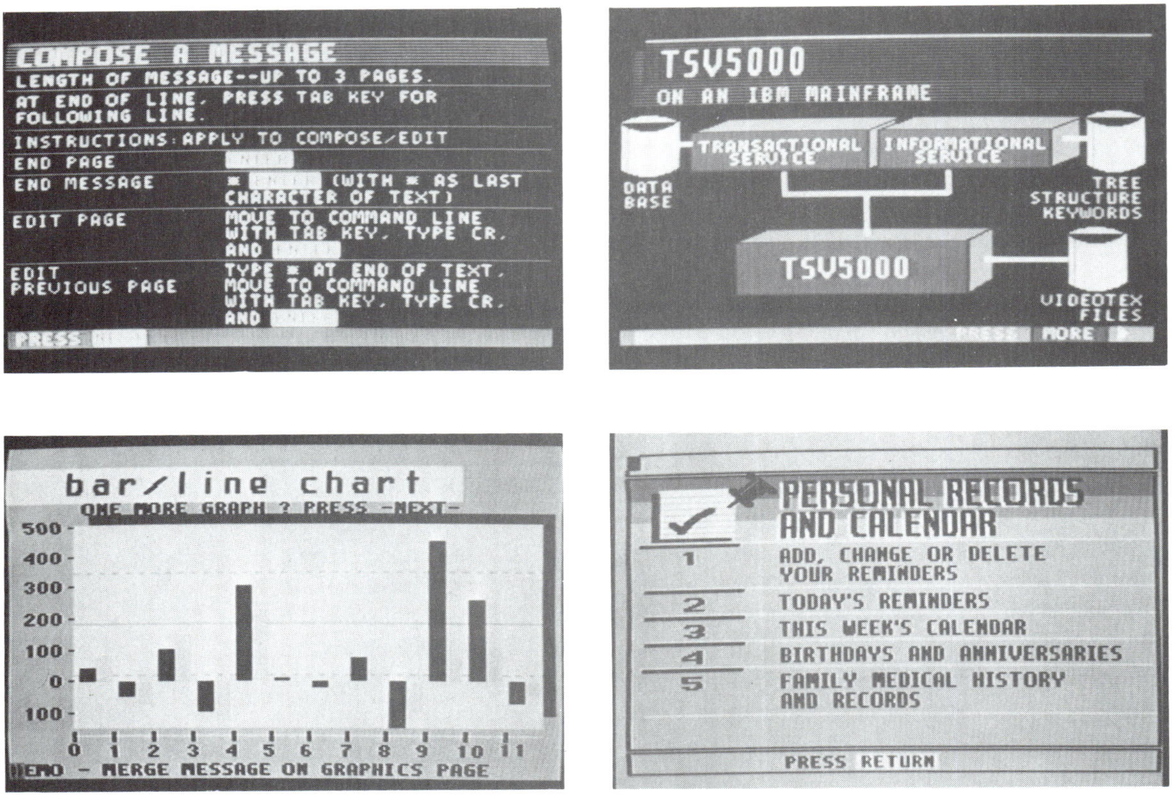

FIGURE 8-17. (continued)

The Smart Building

Many of the telecommunication services described in this chapter may be too costly for a small organization. Or a small organization may have only limited need for a large computer system. Some organizations may not wish to be concerned with the "technical side" of communication facilities. For these reasons (among others), real estate developers are offering communication services as a building utility. Included in the rent for an office or suite are charges for the "building computer."

The "smart" or "intelligent" building pictured in Figure 8-18 offers communication services and other services such as sensing the presence of an individual in a room to turn the lights on or off, automatically locking doors when workers leave the building, and automatically adjusting the heating and cooling. Thus the intelligent building offers security and energy conservation as well as a wide variety of communication services (see Figure 8-19).

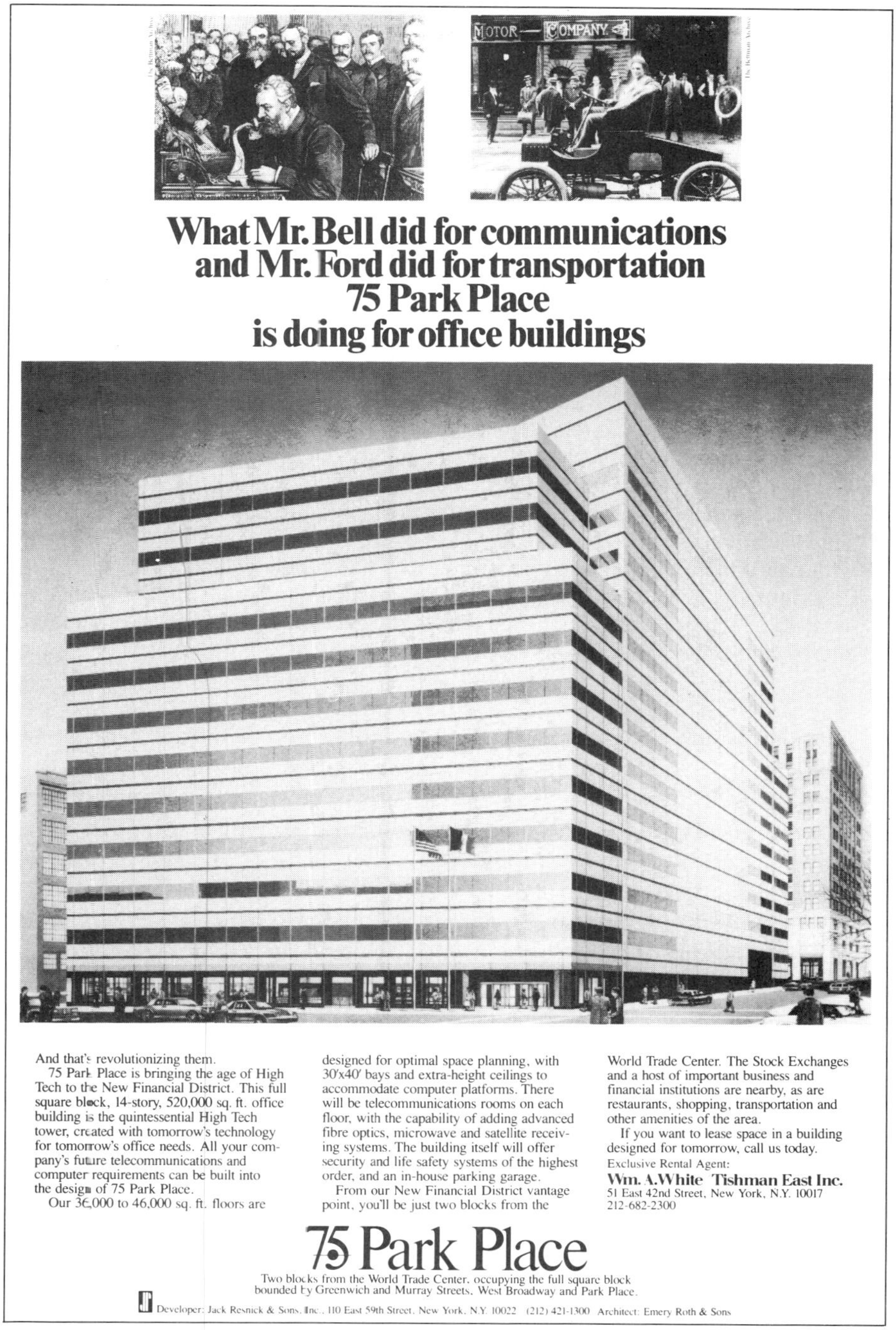

FIGURE 8-18. A smart or intelligent building.

FIGURE 8-19. Smart building services.

- Voice and data transmission capabilities.
- Least-cost routing. A pool of outgoing wide-area telecommunications services (WATS) and other common-carrier lines, governed by a software program that selects the most economical route for any given call.
- Station message detail recorder. A device that compiles cost-accounting information for tenants, including client bill-back, control of misuse and abuse of the communications system, charge-back to departmental cost centers, toll calling, and other features.
- Remote polling equipment. A feature that allows command-center personnel to do moves and changes and trouble-shooting for individual tenants and for the system as a whole.
- Building-wide message and information center. A service staffed during all business hours, with switchover to recorded announcements, if desired, during off hours.
- Dial-dictation tank. Access to tenants is through an entry code.
- Telex machines and facsimile units with operators and a word processing facility with printers and document binding.
- Message service for delivery of Telex, facsimile, word processing hard copy, and dictation tapes.
- All tenant records are kept on computer, with hard copy available.
- Environmental controls. Energy conservation units for each tenant, including automatic sensors that extinguish lights when areas are empty; separate heating and air conditioning circuits for each tenant.

It is impossible to describe a "typical" intelligent building because the services an intelligent building provides must be tailored to the needs of the building residents. The cost effectiveness of smart building systems will determine trends in the next few decades. The success of the smart building depends upon its planners.

EVALUATING AND SELECTING A NETWORK

Evaluating and implementing networks requires a skilled, broadly talented team, from within or outside the organization. Analysts must understand systems software, application software, communication protocols, networking concepts, ergonomics, and the corporate culture in which a network will operate.

Many factors must be considered when a network is selected. Basically, the analyst must first assess what kinds of services and applications are needed and who will be using them, then determine the appropriate network hardware and software. The main questions to be considered include the following:

1. How many terminals and other simple digital machines must be supported?
   - What interfaces and protocols do they use?
   - Where are they and how much will they be used?
   - How often will they be moved and how quickly must they then be connected to the network?

2. What is the speed required of the network?
   - Is there any need to support computers and workstations that need fast file transfer?
   - What about speed of resource sharing?
3. How many host computers must be supported and with what interfaces?
4. Does the overall business site need several incompatible networks in the same area?
5. Is there a need for voice/data integration?
6. What are the requirements for video communications? (Must any video communications be integrated with other communications?)
7. Are there special needs that might dictate the range of solutions that can be applied?
   - Is there need to support specific items of equipment? For example, the choice of an Apollo CAD (computer-aided design) system implies the installation of a Domain LAN.
   - Is there need for a very high network availability? This requirement can be met only by networks that can support multiple independent routes between devices with automatic re-routing.[3]

SUMMARY

Machines do not communicate, but humans do. However, humans can use communication technologies to aid interpersonal communications as well as enable office automation technologies to "speak" to each other, thus creating an office system.

Communication technology is vital to the concept of office systems; it provides the means of integrating the myriad technologies into a working system. Communication technology frees the worker from the confines of the desk, it takes computing power out of the data processing center and puts it into the hands of the end user.

Ultimately, many office automation authorities believe, corporate computing will be organized in a hierarchical fashion. Mainframe systems will maintain corporate databases. Multiuser systems or local area networks will exist in each department. Then, on the desktop, individual single-user systems will run individual applications. Applications will become more evenly distributed across the three levels, and microcomputers will talk directly to mainframes.

Communication technologies can transfer digital and analog information: numbers, words, sounds, images, and video. The challenge facing information system users and managers is choosing the appropriate means of communications: technology that can operate as part of the existing office system.

The telephone is the most common communication device. The instrument itself, however, is undergoing new development, giving users such functions as speakers and even video capabilities. Connected to the telephone company by twisted pair wires (usually), the caller is switched to the intended receiver by the local switching office. For long distance, the central office (CO) may use fiberoptics, microwave, or satellite transmission.

The PBX is a telephone network that allows organizations to switch both voice and data. PBXs are operated by software programs, allowing special functions such as automatic callback or least-cost routing of calls. The role of the PBX in the automated office may be expanded to include data capabilities, with the PBX connecting various computer systems.

The traditional answering machine and newer voice mail systems are available for handling voice communications in organizations. Using standard recording media, the answering machine offers a low-cost option for answering incoming calls. While the voice mail system provides a similar service, its potential is greater as the recording is digitized and saved on magnetic media. Digitalization allows the user to revise, forward, make multiple distribution, and so on.

Data is transmitted in bits per second (bps) in either asynchronous (individual characters sent separately) or synchronous (blocks of data) mode. Sending and receiving devices must conform to the same protocol or procedures. The start-and-stop characters used in describing modes of transmission are coding languages. Data is sent in either simplex (one direction only), full (both directions at the same time), or half-duplex flow (in both directions, but only in one direction at a time).

The local area network (LAN) is a geographically limited, user-owned network that (usually) carries digital data. Most commonly, LANs use twisted pair wires or coaxial cables; however, other media may be appropriate: microwave radio, infrared light, or fiber optics. Wide area networks (WANs) typically connect sites geographically distant from each other. WANs are often a public utility, not owned by the organization.

Network topology is a description of how nodes (access units) are arranged on the network; the terms *star, ring,* and *bus* are apt descriptors of network topology. Access to a network is provided either by contention (CSMA/CA, CSMA/CD) or noncontention (polling or token-passing).

Electronic mail is divided into four groups, each with its own technology and specialized applications. Computer-based message switching systems (CBMS) are designed for intraoffice messages. Electronic mail (EM) networks can also provide flexible inter- and intraoffice support for document and message distribution. Facsimile devices allow pictures of entire documents to be transferred over telephone lines. Telex and TWX are Western Union services that are national (Telex) and international (TWX) in scope and provide fast, reliable message service.

Teleconferencing may be conducted by audio (voice only), video (full motion or slow scan), audiographic (audio plus graphic technology, such as facsimile), or computer (communication through computers). Each of the teleconferencing technologies has its required hardware, and in the case of computer teleconferencing, required software.

Videotex allows access to information bases that are broadcast through television channels. Smart buildings are structures that have built-in communication capabilities, such as computers, security devices, and even environmental controls.

Communication technologies not only aid interpersonal communication but also facilitate access to vital databases. The databases provide a depository for information and, perhaps more important, quick access to that information. For a communication system to work correctly, however, expert planning is required. Office technologies do not generally "speak" to each other without special regard for protocols and software. An office system is not born, it is created—that is, carefully developed by communication planners.

DISCUSSION QUESTIONS

1. Why is it important for the office automation analyst to understand the difference between analog and digital signals?
2. Describe how a telephone call is completed from one's residence and from one's place of work with a PBX.
3. Contrast the following terms:
   a. asynchronous and synchronous
   b. simplex, full, and duplex
   c. modem and codec
   d. token passing, CSMA/CD, and polling
   e. star, ring, and bus
4. Discuss the role of the PBX, LAN, and WAN in the office of the future.
5. Discuss the importance of standard protocols.
6. Which of the four electronic mail systems offers the most potential for the automated office? Defend your answer.
7. Teleconferencing describes technologies that can connect two or more people in a variety of ways. Which teleconferencing category would be most appropriate in the following situations?
   a. An insurance company needs to offer training to its branch offices on new policy procedures.
   b. A doctor in San Jose wants to discuss a diagnosis with a colleague in Phoenix.
   c. A consortium of consultants needs an answer to a client's complex information processing problem.
   d. New York University offers classes in business education to students in Puerto Rico.
   e. Members of the Office Systems Research Association are working on a joint research proposal.
   f. An office automation vendor wishes to offer seminars on how to use its products to all its clients.

8. List four business applications for Videotex.
9. Discuss the following statement: Smart buildings are only a passing fad; real estate developers would do well to steer away from encouraging such developments.
10. It has been said that office systems will soon be identified not by their computer system but by their communication system. In other words, the communication system will become *the* system. Do you agree or disagree?

APPLICATION EXERCISES

1. Read and critique two recent articles on local area networks. What appear to be the main concerns of LAN implementations?
2. Prepare a one- or two-page summary of an organization's current status and future plans as they pertain to voice services.
3. Prepare a one- or two-page summary of an organization's current status and future plans in the area of data services.

SUGGESTED READINGS

Jordan, Larry. *Communications and Networking for the IBM PC* (Bowie, Md.: Robert J. Brady Co., 1983).

Schwartz, Mischa. *Telecommunication Networks: Protocols, Modeling, and Analysis* (Reading, Mass.: Addison-Wesley, 1987).

Torbett, Arlin, and Miller, Harry. "Learning to Speak Mainframe," *PC World* (May 1983), pp. 40–53.

ARTIFICIAL INTELLIGENCE

CHAPTER 9

OBJECTIVES

After completing this chapter, the reader should be able to meet the following objectives:

- List five distinct areas of artificial intelligence research.
- Define natural-language processing.
- Discuss the reasons why natural-language database inquiry systems are so difficult to develop.
- Explain how translating systems can aid text translation from one language to another.
- Explain how an artificial intelligence system can teach communication skills.
- List the components of an expert system.
- Distinguish among the three deductive reasoning techniques an expert system may use.
- Appraise the impact that expert systems can have on computer-assisted instruction.
- State four business applications appropriate for intelligent job aids.
- Describe the role of robotics in the office.
- Point out problems inherent in designing a computer with a vision system.
- Differentiate among isolated word, continuous speech, speaker-dependent, and speaker-independent voice recognition systems.
- Generalize on the potential of voice synthesis systems.
- Summarize the arguments in favor of the LISP programming language over Prolog (and vice versa).
- Discuss the legality and ethics of data ownership.
- Appraise the potential of artificial intelligence in the office.

KEY TERMS

artificial intelligence (AI)
natural-language processing
robotics
vision systems
mixed inference
computer-assisted instruction (CAI)
authoring systems

speech recognition
database inquiry
translation system
facts
rules
heuristics
inference engine
user interface
backward chaining
forward chaining
intelligent job aids
isolated word recognition system
continuous speech recognition system
speaker-independent systems
speech synthesis
LISP
Prolog
menu-based natural language

INTRODUCTION

Revolutions are sometimes measured in thousands of years (the agricultural revolution), in hundreds of years (the industrial revolution), in tens of years (the information revolution), and now in a single year (artificial intelligence). Some experts say that artificial intelligence is a fourth revolution; others say it describes a fifth generation of computers.

Artificial intelligence (AI) is included in this text as a chapter within a hardware unit; AI, however, is not necessarily hardware. AI applications are frequently software applications that require dedicated hardware; others can be done on standard mainframes, minicomputers, and microcomputers.

The underlying premise for the development of artificial intelligence is that anything that can be computed by humans can be computed by machines. In other words, AI programs emulate the thought process of human beings. Early AI efforts included checkers, chess, and tic-tac-toe. However, AI has come a long way at major research institutions and corporations, such as the Massachusetts Institute of Technology, Carnegie-Mellon University, Stanford University, Texas Instruments, Kurzweil Applied Intelligence, and any number of small software development companies. Pioneering efforts have led to greater interest in applying AI in four distinct areas:

1. Natural-language processing (giving machines people-communication skills).
2. Expert systems (giving machines problem-solving skills in a specific area).
3. Vision and speech systems (giving machines the ability to interpret what is seen or heard, then respond).
4. Robotics (enabling machines to manipulate their environment).

The purpose of this chapter is to provide a basic overview of AI in each of the four areas. An office systems analyst needs to understand the concept of AI and its impact on office work.

NATURAL-LANGUAGE PROCESSING SYSTEMS

Natural-language processing describes AI systems that enable a computer to use a natural language, such as English. Natural language is the *human* language of the user, including slang and jargon. Three applications related to natural-language processing will be discussed here: database inquiry, language translation, and text editing.

Database Inquiry Systems

An ideal database inquiry system would be able to understand its user's questions in normal, everyday language instead of responding only to well-defined commands or computer syntax. Programming a computer to respond to a natural language involves several complex problems:

1. As the example in Figure 9-1 illustrates, the meaning of human speech often depends on the context.[1]

John had a hand in the robbery.
John had a hand in the cookie jar.
John said, "Hand me a cookie."
John is an old hand.
John gave Mary a hand with her luggage.
John asked Mary for her hand.
All hands on deck!
Look Ma! No hands!

FIGURE 9-1. Defining the word "hand."

2. A very real problem is that questions are frequently hidden within questions. For example: "What time is the flight to Memphis?" (Is there a flight to Memphis?)
3. Human speech is often incomplete. For example, consider the statement, "What is the Dow Jones average?" (Is the person asking the question seeking a definition or a figure? If the person is seeking a figure, what date?)
4. Human speech often requires interpretation. For example, consider the statement, "Give me some recent inventory figures." How many is "some"? What is considered "recent"? What specific figures are being requested?

To handle such problems, natural-language interfaces require tremendous "overhead" in both computer speed and storage capacity. Therefore, analysts must evaluate whether the flexibility of a natural-language interface is worth its cost in computer resources.

Natural-language software packages that can be added on to established database systems are available for mainframes, minicomputers, and microcomputers. An example of a mainframe system is Artificial Intelligence Corporation's *Intellect*, which is custom-installed by the corporation. Once customized, *Intellect* offers flexible access to data to even the novice database user. Another example is the system used by the airline industry to make passenger reservations. When the system was first developed, it did not catch on quickly. Today, however, even the newly hired travel agent can use it. A third example, this time at the microcomputer level, is *HAL*, a natural-language interface developed for users of Lotus 1-2-3.

Menu- and Icon-Based Natural Language Query Systems

The problems inherent with natural-language inquiry include ambiguity, uncertainty, and incompleteness. A drawback of most inquiry systems is that the user does not know the limits of the system. What can be asked? What cannot be asked? *Menu-* and/or *icon-based* query systems address this problem yet maintain "natural language" as a means of interfacing with the database.

Menu-based systems allow questions to be asked by use of a menu or series of menus. As the user selects words and phrases, the menu changes, building on logical completions to the inquiry. Such a system prohibits the user from asking questions the system cannot understand or does not know. (Incidentally, it also eliminates the need for the user to be a good typist or speller.)

Icon-based query systems are similar to menu-based systems, substituting icons (pictures) for menu items. On the plus side, icons are easy to interpret and can overcome ambiguities of natural language. People also respond more quickly to icons than text. The only drawback is flexibility. Icon-based systems are limited to fairly simple inquiries.

Translation Systems

A second application for natural-language processing is translation, which translates text from one language to another, such as Spanish to English.

Although early attempts at machine translation met with failure (the computer translated "The spirit is willing, but the flesh is weak" into Russian as, "The vodka is good, but the meat is rotten"), these systems have come a long way. Today, for example, the Logos system uses its 120,000-word vocabulary to translate manuals and product literature from English to German or French. While the output still requires polishing by a translator, a human translator can handle 15 to 35 pages of computer version a day, compared with only eight pages if working from scratch. NEC and Fujitsu are working on Japanese-to-English translation systems.

The MicroCat (Computer-*a*ided-*t*ranslation) system diagrammed in Figure 9-2 shows a microcomputer-based translation system. Note that the

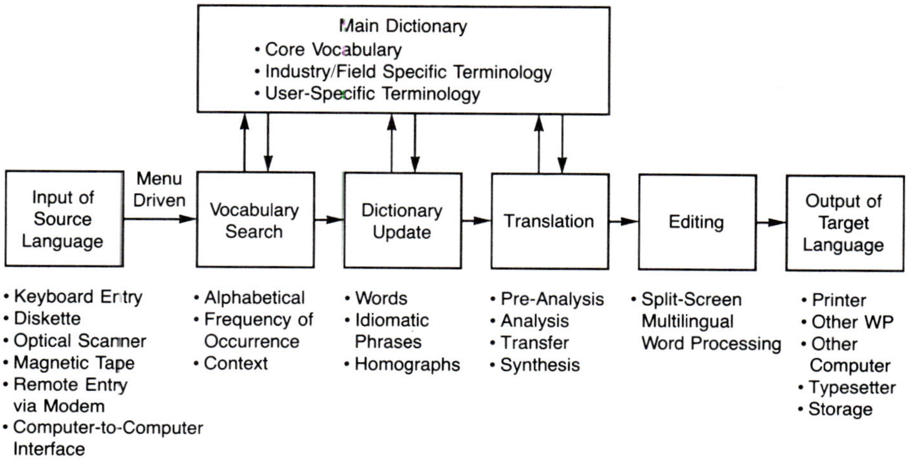

FIGURE 9-2. A computer-aided language translation process.

system's core vocabulary can be specialized by adding words and expressions unique to a given field or a given user. Such an "add-on" feature enables technical documents to be handled more efficiently.

Text Editing Systems

Text editing is a third natural-language application that checks grammar and writing style and makes corrections on written documents. Text editing systems can actually teach their users communication skills. IBM's Epistle, for example, can critique 107 elements of writing style, such as verb and subject agreement, parallel construction, and spelling, and it even offers tutorials.

EXPERT SYSTEMS

The area of AI currently receiving the most attention in the business office is *expert systems,* also known as *knowledge systems.* An expert system is a computer program that incorporates the knowledge of an expert or group of experts on a particular subject and enables the program user to systematically ask questions related to that knowledge.

The goal of an expert system is to emulate the reasoning of highly trained and experienced human experts. An expert system program dissects a process into distinct steps, understandable by a machine. It helps the user diagnose problems by accessing details long forgotten or never learned. The user needs information that will help him or her make a better decision, based on the knowledge of other people and other experiences.

Components of an Expert System

An expert system mimics human reasoning by using facts, rules, and a user interface. Expert system development requires not only a subject-matter expert (or *domain expert*) but also a *knowledge engineer:* the computer programmer who can collect the facts, identify the rules, and develop a user interface.

Facts are the knowledge base of the expert system. Computer scientists have long been struggling with ways of writing facts so that the machine can interpret them.

Rules, or *heuristics*, are the guidelines for applying facts. They are the system's means of using the facts that describe a knowledge domain. A rule is a simple clause that consists of three parts: an attribute (the subject), a predicate (action word or verb), and a value (adjective). Rules are written in an "if . . . then" format. For example, in a system with facts about employee salary schedules, the following rule could apply:

> IF the employee is a supervisor and the supervisor is paid a monthly salary,
> THEN the employee is an exempt employee.

The number of rules an expert system uses may be misleading; more does not always mean better. Systems run from 1800 to 3000 rules; with a turbine generator, however, that number could go to 20,000.

User interface is the means by which the expert system gathers data from the user about a particular situation or problem. This data is then used by the *inference engine* to reach a goal or conclusion. The inference engine is never seen by the user; it tests the rules in the knowledge base and prompts the user for information needed to prove a rule true or false. It uses one or more of three deductive reasoning techniques:

1. *Backward chaining* is a search technique that begins with the action clause of a rule and works backward through a chain of rules to find a verifiable set of condition clauses. It is often referred to as *goal-driven*. Backward-chaining systems appear to be well suited for diagnostic applications.

2. *Forward chaining* is a search technique that begins with the condition clause of a rule and works forward through a chain of rules to activate implied action clauses. It is often referred to as *data-driven*. Forward-chaining systems are well suited for data analysis and configuration systems.

3. *Mixed inference* is a search technique that establishes incremental goals and then works to reach those goals through a step-and-repeat method.

The best way to evaluate an expert system tool is to look at its knowledge representation technique and determine whether that technique fits the problem at hand. A good inference engine is characterized by an easy-to-use menu, natural-language inquiry, and a well-developed capability to explain not only the steps of the process but how or why they happened. The ability to access external data may also be vitally important for some applications.

Programming Languages for Expert Systems

Currently, LISP (*LIS*t *P*rocessor), developed at the Massachusetts Institute of Technology, and Prolog (*PRO*gramming in *LOG*ic), developed in Europe, are the leading expert system programming languages. Developers of expert systems must choose between the two languages. The Japanese have chosen Prolog as their software development language; American and European companies tend to prefer LISP.

Both Prolog and LISP are high-level languages that run on special-purpose hardware. Although LISP is more difficult to learn, it is more powerful than Prolog for the experienced user. The Japanese have added LISP-like extensions to Prolog, perhaps because Prolog's rules, or heuristics, are not as refined as LISP's. LISP, its proponents argue, has survived because it has not been a static, unchanging set of programming codes. Don Johnson, editor of *Administrative Management*, has said that LISP is favored for its symbolic processors while Prolog is gaining strength in microcomputer applications. To better understand how Prolog operates, take the one-minute course in Prolog programming presented in Figure 9-3.

The important thing to remember is that AI applications can be written in *any* language. LISP and Prolog represent a substantial portion of all expert system programming applications being developed because they offer faster processing and fewer lines of code. Expert systems allow a computer system to diagnose, monitor, predict, plan, and teach.

Recently, there has been tremendous growth in expert system shells and development languages that run on standard microcomputers. These tools cost only a fraction of the cost of tools such as LISP, and the price of the microcomputer is considerably lower than that of a special-purpose LISP machine. Moreover, from the user's perspective, expert systems running on standard microcomputers provide the same kind of autonomy and access as microcomputer spreadsheets and databases provide. In addition, the risks inherent in building expert systems on microcomputers are far less than in using specialized development environments. Market analysts predict that significant expert system activity will continue throughout the 1990s across a spectrum of hardware that includes general-purpose workstations, minicomputers, mainframes, and LISP machines. The microcomputer portion of the market is predicted to grow faster than any other segment, however.

Expert System Cases

The manager responsible for monitoring the huge soup vats at Campbell Soup Company is planning to retire. Knowledge engineers are "saving" his years of experience and expertise for his successor. Westinghouse uses an expert system to monitor steam turbines, to alert operators when something goes wrong, and to recommend solutions. General Electric uses an expert system for locomotive repair. Morgan Stanley Company uses an expert system that assesses securities market conditions and gives recommendations about trading.

FIGURE 9-3. A one-minute course in Prolog programming.

Prolog programming is based on declared facts and conditional rules that programmers can manipulate in a declarative fashion. A fact consists of a relationship or a predicate and an object or objects. Standard Prolog notation for the English statement "John is the father of Mary" would be

Father (John, Mary).

A simple query to a database with this fact stored in it of

? - father (X, Mary).

meaning "Does Mary have a father?" will produce the answer

X = John.

Once Prolog finds a fact that satisfies the desired goal, it stops searching the database unless it is asked to continue searching for additional facts that also meet the criteria. Conditional rules are declared by the notation ":-" (which can be read as "if"). The rule

Parent (X, Y) :- father (X, Y).

would mean "X is the parent of Y if X is the father of Y." Prolog can logically apply such rules to facts in the database to answer more complicated queries. For example, after a program states the following facts, Prolog can logically answer questions about relationships described in them:

Prolog statement	English meaning
Father (John, Mary).	John is the father of Mary.
Father (Paul, John).	Paul is the father of John.
Grandfather (X,Y) :- parent (Z,Y), father (X,Z).	X is grandfather of Y if some Z is parent of Y, and X is father of Z.
Parent (X, Y) :- father (X, Y).	X is the parent of Y if X is the father of Y.
When the following question is asked,	
? - grandfather (X, Mary).	Is there an X that is the grandfather of Mary?
then Prolog will answer	X = Paul

Applications that lend themselves to such declarative programming can be relatively quick and easy to write. However, it is difficult to know whether the answer the program provides is necessarily the best solution to a problem. This drawback is magnified in a large database.

Commercial artificial systems, such as MYCIN (a program that diagnoses meningitis), DENDRAL (which explains the chemical structure of complex compounds), and PROSPECTOR (which evaluates geological sites for mineral deposits) aid professionals in specific areas. Of interest to all students, Harvard University President Derek Bok has predicted an expert system that will double as a mentor; students will be able to question the "mentor" system more closely than they can question their professors.

The systems described in the previous paragraphs are relatively static, but systems that allow more "real time" are being developed. Two examples of real-time processing are ATrans and The Information Lens. Cognitive System's ATrans extracts information from unformatted Telex messages. Without ATrans, a bank's Telex operators must read unformatted messages and rekey the information into the funds transfer system. Each Telex requires four to eight minutes, and a busy bank may have as many as 2000 Telexes a day. ATrans can not only read and understand unformatted Telex messages but take appropriate action, eliminating 80 percent of Telex labor costs, reducing errors, and increasing the timeliness of the messages.

Along the same line, researchers at the Massachusetts Institute of Technology are working on an expert system for filtering electronic mail messages. The system, which is called "The Information Lens," allows the user to sift through electronic mail messages. For example, the user may program the electronic mail system to put messages with an action response code into a priority file, to delete national news items that are more than a day old, or to put messages from superiors and other "VIPs" into an urgent file. Such a system helps eliminate electronic "junk mail" and, at the same time, saves the user time by sorting, deleting, and prioritizing messages.

Intelligent Job Aids

When used to explain processes, procedures, or quality control, an expert system may be referred to as an *intelligent job aid.* The intelligent job aid helps the user make an informed decision with the computer as "coach." These job aids replace paper checklists, manuals, and one-on-one coaching with computer software. *Help menus* found within computer programs can also be classified as job aids.

For example, with an intelligent job aid programmed with the procedures for filing insurance claims, a new employee could use the aid to learn how to process the claim and, later, to handle difficult or exceptional cases. In such a situation, the goal would be to process a claim. For example, using natural-language inquiry, the employee could ask what to do if the claimant's Social Security number was not on the claim. The job aid would answer with solutions for the problem and, if asked, give the reasons why the solutions are appropriate. Such a system is particularly helpful for exceptional cases—for the new as well as the seasoned employee. How an expert system might work is illustrated in Figure 9-4.

Until recently, applications for job aids were limited because the programming was complex, expensive, and required specialized hardware. Like software breakthroughs in CAI, however, the ability of nonprogrammers to write job aids is increasing. Small expert systems, such as the Tektronix system shown in Figure 9-5, have evolved. In addition, software

FIGURE 9-4. An expert system used in insurance underwriting: An example of the decision-making process.

A publishing company in California has decided to insure its data processing facility. It hires insurance agent Smith to find the best possible policy. Mr. Smith approaches Ms. Jones of Insurance Company West to develop a policy for the data processing facility housed in a 25-year-old brick building.

Ms. Jones goes to the computer terminal and starts a file called Publishing Company Account. She then accesses the expert system to get assistance in defining the parameters of the policy. First, she must enter information about Mr. Smith, the agent. The computer system has a large database of agents the company works with, describing the type of work they do, their reliability, and the quality of the information they provide. (This database is updated quarterly by the company to enter information on new agents and update the information on old agents.) The system evaluates Mr. Smith. Uncertainty coefficients are then estimated by the computer system based on information about Mr. Smith. The expert system uses this coefficient to determine the most appropriate questions (prompts) to Ms. Jones. Any equations used in final recommendations by the system take into account the agent's uncertainty coefficient.

Ms. Jones then enters the basic information about the facility. The computer responds that in California, 20 years ago, reinforcing bars were not mandatory in brick buildings. Therefore, earthquake damage must be excluded from the policy. The system may then prompt Ms. Jones for information about smoking—is it permitted in the data processing facility, and in what rooms? The system prompts Ms. Jones about whether flammable solvents are stored in the room. A value may be assigned to designate the importance of this information. The system then combines this information with other information. It prompts Ms. Jones when necessary and comes to a decision about the policy just as an expert underwriter would.

FIGURE 9-5. The Tektronix Personal 4404 AI Development System.

programs for job aids developed and run by microcomputers are available from companies such as McGraw-Hill. With their ease of programming, use, and a drop in cost, job aids may be an invaluable means of training and updating staff (see Chapter 24, "Training").

Computer-Aided Instruction Systems

When used as a teaching aid, an expert system may fall in the computer-aided instruction (CAI) category. Computer-aided instruction systems, sometimes referred to as *computer-based instruction (CBI)* systems, originated in the early 1960s. Early CAI attempts were called *programmed instruction*. Using CAI, a trainee can control the learning process by choosing the content to be learned and self-pacing the rate at which lessons are covered. In other words, individualized instruction is obtained through computers.

The earliest CAI systems were developed to be run on dedicated systems, including Control Data's Plato and McDonnell-Douglas's AIS. Such dedicated systems were a combination of hardware and software for highly specialized instructional applications for use in schools and the military. Piggyback systems, on the other hand, do not require special hardware; examples include IBM's IIS and Boeing Computer Service's Scholar/Teach, which run on mainframe computers. Increasingly, however, CAI systems are being developed for microcomputers.

To develop *courseware* (the term used to describe CAI software) requires more than programming skills. Often, teams of subject-matter experts, artists, technicians, documentation writers, analysts, and designers work with a programmer to design the courseware. CAI development requires considerable time and effort, and it has been estimated that courseware teams spend a minimum of 200 to 300 hours to develop only one hour of instructional materials.

For microcomputer applications, some authoring systems (such as the one produced by McGraw-Hill) allow an expert/teacher to create specialized learning packages as the software "shell" is built into the system. (A shell can be compared to the framework in many database systems.) With this fill-in-the-blanks approach to developing a learning package, even the inexperienced computer user can create application-specific courseware. Authoring systems cut production costs and time. In addition, if the expert can apply principles of learning to the shell, the staff required to produce the courseware can be reduced to one.

Corporate Benefits of Expert Systems

The question that management typically raises with regard to the usefulness of expert systems pertains to appropriate applications and potential payoffs. Software developers are in the very first stages of producing expert systems. Corporations that have invested time and money in the development of expert systems typically cost-justify their investments in one of the following ways:

1. *Return on investment.* A corporation was able to show that by using an expert system, an employee saved one month of work.
2. *Conformity of results.* An insurance company, by using an expert system, helped ensure that all its adjusters would process claims the same way.
3. *Knowledge, access, and power.* A manufacturing company found it could design the floor layout for its new mainframe computer in 15 minutes by using an expert system; that same project would have taken a human engineer eight hours.
4. *Quality improvements.* A manufacturer of eyewear found it could test ten times as many lens designs as before.

In short, corporations base their investment in expert systems on the expected payoffs: productivity increases and return on investment.

Corporations also want expert systems to work within their existing computing infrastructure, not in isolation. For example, an expert system for phone company salespeople would have to access the phone company's database of products, tariffs, and restrictions to provide the correct configuration for a specific customer. An example of this type of expert system is AION, which runs on IBM mainframes. Most expert systems developers are addressing this need to work *with* the organization's current system, not in isolation. Once such compatible systems are available, organizations are likely to see benefits much more quickly.

Legality/Ethics

Who owns the information in an expert system? Is an expert system the property of the company, the creator, or the user? Does an expert system rob an expert of years of experience? Who owns the medical knowledge in MYCIN? Who owns the chemical knowledge in DENDRAL or the geological knowledge in PROSPECTOR? Do the parameters change if the expert is the manager at Campbell's Soup? After all, he is a paid employee. This individual's knowledge base of years of experience at Campbells is saved, but is his personal expertise to be rewarded on retirement? How are the experts who created such systems to be rewarded for their contributions? Or should they be?

Yet another question centers on the role of expert systems. If expert systems grow in use, what is to become of the middle manager? The middle manager may fear being made obsolete by expert systems in the same manner that secretaries feared being made obsolete by word processing systems in the 1970s.

VISION AND SPEECH SYSTEMS

Can computers see and understand? Can computers hear and understand? Can computers generate speech output? Following is an overview of the problems and possibilities in answering these questions. It describes four types of sight- and speech-related systems: vision, speech recognition, voice analysis, and voice synthesis systems.

Vision Systems

Machine vision is a robotics application that uses light sensors to allow machines to "see" objects, coupled with computer programs that interpret what is "seen," to make adjustments in a machine's movements.

It is difficult, and some say impossible, for a computer to process something that it sees. The computer sees a picture in terms of *pixels,* or small dots. To see an image requires that the computer have a very large memory. In addition, how it makes sense of those dots is a very difficult matter. Are two different photographs of one person the same person? The photographs themselves are different—and the computer has difficulty ascertaining that the two images are the same person. Again, the computer sees only dots. The "Simple Visual Experiment" in Figure 9-6 helps clarify this problem.

The multilevel nature of human vision can be observed by a series of visual tests. A subject is presented with a flash of light displaying 16 letters in a 4-by-4 array on an otherwise blank screen. Typically, he or she remembers three or four of the letters (Test 1). The experiment is then repeated with one of the letters highlighted by a circle. The subject invariably remembers *that* letter (Test 2). Now, the experiment is changed so that there are two flashes of light, the second flash appearing less than 15 msec. after the first. Because 15 msec. is the approximate image-decay time of the human retina, one would expect that images displayed less than 15 msec. apart would be perceived as a single composite image. When the first flash contains a letter and the second flash contains an arrow pointing to it, the subject does remember a composite image (Test 3). But, when the second flash contains a circle that, if overlaid, would surround the letter shown in the first flash, the subject remembers only the circle (Test 4). The circle, which the subject subconsciously recognizes as a basic visual element, erases the information—the letter from the first flash—that had been assimilated during previous levels in the visual process.

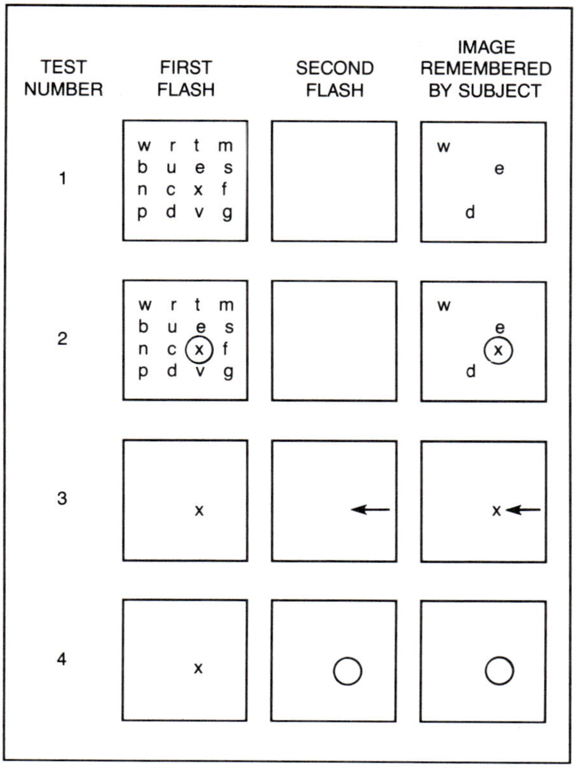

FIGURE 9-6. A simple visual experiment.

Because of the difficulty in programming a computer to see, practical applications of the research of such endeavors are limited. Nevertheless, prototype systems are used for handicapped individuals who are unable to manipulate the controls of a computer. Some systems can follow commands by eye contact with the user. For example, such a system allows the screen to go to the next frame without physical controls. The military laser/optic vision devices for weapons sighting may also be considered a form of robotic sight research.

Research is also underway at the University of Rochester's Institute of Optics, where G. Michael Morris is working on giving robots and computers more vision by giving them less light. Morris's theory is that as glass filters screen out light, the image can be simplified, allowing the computer to compare it to other images in its memory. A simplified image would mean the computer could recognize the image using less memory.

Speech Recognition Systems

Hearing is perhaps a less complex process than seeing, as a person's voice patterns can be interpreted by a computer. Yet, while speech recognition systems are less difficult than vision systems, they are far from simple. Major problems include how to filter background noise, how to have the computer understand accents, and how to understand the complexities of human speech. Most voice recognition systems available today are highly specialized and fairly limited in applications. However, some prototype models have expanded the computer's ability to interpret what is heard.

Speech recognition systems are described by variables that depict the size of the system's vocabulary and the number of people a system can understand.

Isolated Word versus Continuous Speech Systems

The first two variables defining voice recognition systems describe the number and type of voice input the computer can understand: *isolated words* or *continuous speech*. Isolated word systems recognize discrete words separated by distinct pauses. To use such a system, a user "programs" his or her voice into the computer by repeating key phrases. Continuous speech systems, on the other hand, recognize a predefined vocabulary of words spoken at a controlled pace.

Speaker-Dependent versus Speaker-Independent Systems

The second set of variables in voice recognition systems describe just *who* the system can understand. *Speaker-dependent* systems are programmed or "trained" to recognize the speech of a particular individual, and *speaker-independent* systems can recognize words spoken by any user.

Isolated Word, Speaker-Dependent Systems

Isolated word, speaker-dependent systems are the easiest to develop. Users identify themselves to the system and repeat designated words several times. This repetition provides the computer with a sample of variation in the user's voice patterns. Once the system is "trained," it recognizes words by comparing them with a stored table of prerecorded words.

Continuous Speech, Speaker-Dependent Systems

Continuous speech, speaker-dependent systems are currently under active development and testing. Continuous speech systems with limited vocabularies and acceptable accuracy are available now. To "train" a continuous speech, speaker dependent system, the user reads carefully constructed paragraphs several times into the computer. The computer records the voice patterns of the user and matches them with the corresponding commands.

Continuous Speech, Speaker-Independent Systems

The objective of voice recognition systems is to incorporate continuous speech capabilities with speaker-independence. Such systems are, for the most part, in the experimental stage. New digitizing techniques, however, are making speech recognition independent of accent, inflection, and phoneme confusion.

An example of an existing speaker-independent application is a manufacturing system in which quality control inspectors examine products with both hands while speaking classifications into a speech recognition device. Voice control of machines that require the worker to use both hands to guide the work is increasing in the manufacturing area. Another application allows handicapped persons to control machines with voice commands. However, such systems today are not totally reliable and can be quite expensive.

The application of continuous speech, speaker-independent systems is increasing in the word processing area. Early models had limited vocabularies (100 to 500 words) and difficulty identifying phonemes (such as *there, their,* and *they're*). While vocabularies are still limited and problems remain, sophisticated word processing systems are now on the market that print on the screen what the user dictates. Even more sophisticated systems are in the developmental stage. Two of the leaders in this area are Kurzweil and IBM.

Kurzweil Applied Intelligence introduced a voice-activated typewriter in 1985, with a 1000-word recognition system. A test model of a new voice-activated word processing system, called Voice Works, was introduced by Kurzweil in 1987. The latest model has a 5000- to 10,000-word vocabulary.

A speed typist who averaged 147 words per minute for an hour has lent his name to a project on speech recognition at IBM's Watson's Research Center. "Tangora" has a vocabulary of 20,000 words and can transcribe sentences, spell words correctly, and punctuate with 95 percent accuracy. Tangora uses a microprocessor chip that can perform about 30 million operations a second. The system uses a statistical model that, according to Peter Hillyer in *Think* magazine, can "differentiate the speaker's sound from background noise, identify different speakers' pronunciations, compare and evaluate the word possibilities with such criteria as frequency of use and parts of speech in context, and choose the most likely word to display. All this takes a second or two."[2] Tangora starred in a 1987 television commercial, translating *"Please write to Mr. Wright right now"* from speech to text.

Voice Analysis Systems

Voice analysis systems apply principles of speech recognition to distinguish among individual voice patterns. Voice patterns are more distinctive than fingerprints; therefore, a primary application is security systems, which verify identity by matching spoken input against a stored voice profile. According to the marketing research firm of Frost and Sullivan, voice analysis will probably replace plastic card, signature, and fingerprint identification in the 1990s.

Voice Synthesis Systems

Voice synthesis systems, referred to as *text to speech* or *synthetic voice*, enable the computer to respond in an audio fashion to input that is either keyed in or spoken. Obvious advantages are that the user would not need to read the screen, so the user's eyes could be focused elsewhere; or information from a computer file could be retrieved with a standard telephone handset. Applications for the sight-impaired are innumerable, as are applications for the traveling businessperson.

Teaching a computer to speak a natural language can be compared to teaching a person to speak a foreign language. Because the system uses phonetics, mispronunciations are common. Also, the system typically has no accent or inflection; its output is monotone.

An example of a text-to-speech unit is IBM's Voice Communication Operation Subsystem. Special software and a voice communication adapter make the microcomputer capable of voice synthesis.

ROBOTICS

Robotics is the application of computer technology to processes requiring physical labor. Robotics with applications to office work conjures up images of R2-D2's running around the office doing various tasks. However, such robots have been successfully implemented in offices. For example, a mail delivery robot has sensors that follow a chemical path laid down beneath floor coverings. Such a robot can detect obstacles in its path and can even wait for an elevator. Robotic arms, which aid in the retrieval of microforms in a CAR (computer-assisted retrieval) system, are another office application.

Robotics are having an impact on the employability of the handicapped in offices. With the help of robotic devices, handicapped workers are able to do office work.

THE FUTURE OF ARTIFICIAL INTELLIGENCE SYSTEMS

AI had its beginnings in academia and the military. Today, however, AI applications have spread to the office, now that advancements (including MS DOS v. 5, OS/2, and the 386 chip) give the microcomputer the power it needs to process AI applications. Microcomputer systems can handle 800–1000 rules; however, they are slow and their interface technologies are not as refined as those on special symbolic machines.

Once AI applications can be run using established databases so that the AI system works *with* established systems (as opposed to working beside them), applications should grow. Factors that contribute to development in AI applications include the following:

- New computer systems dedicated to AI programming.
- Lower hardware and software prices.
- Greater computer power, particularly in microcomputers.
- The development of microcomputer software tools.
- The refinement of interface technologies.

As the graph in Figure 9-7 shows, AI is expected to grow slowly at first but will eventually penetrate most or all of the computer market.

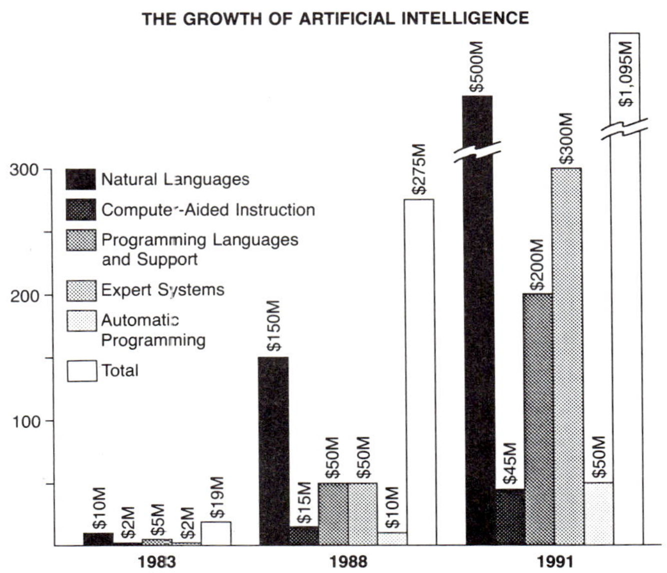

FIGURE 9-7. Artificial intelligence will grow slowly at first but will eventually penetrate most or all of the computer world.

SUMMARY

Artificial intelligence (AI) is based on the concept that anything computed by humans can be computed by machines. Applications of AI include natural-language processing, expert systems, vision and speech recognition systems, and robotics.

The success of database inquiry systems rests on the computer's understanding of human language. These systems allow the user to access the computer's database through natural-language interfaces rather than through special computer syntax. Other language-related applications include translation and text editing programs.

An expert system is a software program that has knowledge about objects, events, or situations and emulates human reasoning in a particular knowledge domain. Components of these systems are the knowledge base (facts and rules), inference engine, and user interface. Expert systems are used to diagnose problems and thereby help the user to make better decisions.

Originally, expert systems were written in either LISP or Prolog running on special hardware. LISP is favored in the United States and Europe; Prolog is used particularly in Japan. LISP is considered more flexible than Prolog but more difficult to learn. Users can now choose from a variety of expert system shells and development tools that run on standard microcomputers.

The third category of AI systems is tools for developing the computer's ability to understand what it sees and/or hears and even give it speech capabilities.

Vision systems are extremely complex; a computer sees in terms of dots, and interpreting those dots is difficult.

Speech recognition systems, which enable a computer to respond to verbal commands, are either speaker-dependent (the system recognizes the voice of one user) or speaker-independent (the system recognizes the voice of any number of users). Speech recognition systems may also be either isolated word (the system responds only to particular words or commands) or continuous speech (the system can understand large vocabularies).

Continuous speech, speaker-independent systems are currently under development and testing. Speech synthesis describes research to give the computer the ability to respond in an oral fashion to commands.

Robotics, a fourth category of AI systems, is the application of computer technology to processes requiring physical labor. Robotic applications are primarily in the manufacturing area, where robots are used on assembly lines. AI applications continue to grow as new, less expensive, and more powerful microcomputer systems evolve and as the issue of connectivity is addressed.

FIGURE 9-8. Doonesbury's encounter with artificial intelligence.

DOONESBURY. Copyright 1985 G.B. Trudeau
Reprinted with permission of Universal Press Syndicate. All rights reserved.

DISCUSSION QUESTIONS

1. List the four areas that constitute artificial intelligence.
2. Why is it difficult to develop a natural-language database inquiry system?
3. What impact could translating systems have on foreign-language translation? Could a translating system replace the translator?
4. Why is IBM's Epistle considered an artificial intelligence product?
5. Define an expert system. What are its three components? How do the components interact?
6. What is the role of the inference engine in expert systems?
7. How are authoring systems impacting computer-assisted instruction? Why are authoring systems considered expert systems?
8. What is the difference between an expert system and an intelligent job aid?
9. List three applications of robotics for office work.
10. Why is it difficult for a computer to see?
11. Differentiate between the following terms:
    a. isolated word system, continuous speech system
    b. speaker-dependent system, speaker-independent system
12. Which speech recognition system has the most potential for office applications? Why?
13. "You can't teach a machine to talk." True or false?
14. List the advantages of both LISP and Prolog as an AI programming language.
15. Discuss legality and ethics with regard to policies that outline who owns an expert system. How do you expect the courts to address this issue in the future?
16. AI applications will become commonplace only when they are designed to be run on a microcomputer. Do you agree or disagree?

APPLICATION EXERCISES

1. Interview a knowledge engineer. Where was he or she trained in AI development? What types of projects is he or she working on? What are his or her long-term plans?
2. Attend a computer or trade show where the latest in AI technologies are on exhibit. What are the applications? If possible, use the system yourself. What are your reactions?

3. Prepare a four- or five-page report on the outlook for voice technologies. Who are the leading research experts or institutions?

SUGGESTED READINGS

Bonnett, A. *Artificial Intelligence* (Englewood Cliffs, N.J.: Prentice-Hall, 1986).

Charniak, Eugene, and McDermott, Drew. *Introduction to Artificial Intelligence* (Reading, Mass.: Addison-Wesley, 1985).

Grimson, W. Eric Leifur, and Patil, Ramesh S., eds. *Artificial Intelligence in the 1980's and Beyond: An MIT Survey* (Cambridge, Mass.: Massachusetts Institute of Technology, 1987).

Kearsley,Greg. *Artificial Intelligence and Instruction: Applications and Methods* (Reading, Mass.: Addison-Wesley, 1987).

Malone, Thomas W.; Grant, Kenneth R.; Lai, Kum-Yei; Rao, Ramana; and Rosenblitt, David A. "The Information Lens: An Intelligent System for Information Sharing and Coordination." In *Technological Support for the Work Group Collaboration* (New York: New York University Graduate School of Business, 1987), pp. 97–130.

PART 3

APPLICATIONS OF OFFICE SYSTEMS AND END-USER COMPUTING

In Part 3, the emphasis is on how end users can use office technologies. The discussion of applications focuses on the needs of office personnel in four job categories:

- *Managerial*
- *Technical and professional*
- *Sales and marketing*
- *Administrative*

These categories are used by the U.S. Department of Labor for reporting purposes and provide a convenient way of grouping office workers with similar information processing needs. It may be helpful to review the discussion about these personnel in Chapter 2, "Understanding the Office Work Environment." In reality, of course, the application of computer tools is not bound by arbitrary categories. In fact, as the discussion in early chapters has indicated, the history of computer technology is replete with examples of technology that has proved to be most useful in ways quite different than originally envisioned. Where applications are similar for all office employees, they are discussed under the category where use is most prevalent. When the technology is applied with "different strokes for different folks," appropriate aspects are discussed in each category. In practice, because the categories are arbitrary, implementation of technology must fit the realities of the job.

The chapters in this section present a sampling of hardware and software tools that are currently being applied in the workplace. New tools and applications are constantly under development. The discussion is not intended to be all-inclusive, nor to suggest limitations of tools to particular personnel or tasks. As an ongoing process, office automation will probably continue in its innovative period for some time to come. The objective is to expand horizons, not to fit technology into neat categories.

Chapter 10, "Managerial Applications," focuses on concepts for increasing managerial productivity. It presents technologies in management, communication, and business applications. The concept of executive workstations is also discussed.

Chapter 11, "Professional/Technical Applications," focuses on end-user computing. It traces the development and growth of information centers and the impact of microcomputers in the office. The technologies covered include fourth-generation languages, spreadsheets, financial modeling, database management, graphics, word processing as an authoring tool, statistical analysis, and integrated software packages.

Chapter 12, "Sales and Marketing Applications," considers how office automation can help meet the unique support needs of sales personnel. It discusses support tools for client management and sales materials, and the use of portable computers.

Chapter 13, "Administrative Applications: Part 1," focuses on the changing roles of office support personnel. Special consideration is given to the needs of secretarial, word processing, paraprofessional, clerical accounting, and general clerical personnel. The chapter provides a comprehensive discussion of word processing technology, as well as document management and administrative support tools.

Chapter 14, "Administrative Applications: Part 2," discusses applications in records management, facilities management, and replication and distribution, which includes telephone and wire services, mail services, reprographics, and forms control.

CHAPTER 10
MANAGERIAL APPLICATIONS

OBJECTIVES

After completing this chapter, the reader should be able to meet the following objectives:

- Discuss the need for new managerial tools.
- List characteristics of *useful* information.
- List characteristics of effective calendar management software.
- Cite examples of managerial performance enhancers.
- Identify appropriate applications for voice mail.
- Contrast the four types of teleconferencing: computer, video, audio, and audiographic.
- Compile guidelines for running a teleconference.
- Summarize the capabilities and operations of decision modeling software.
- Describe project management software.
- Describe how managers use word processing software.
- Offer examples of managerial use of online databases.
- Discuss the concept of executive workstations.

KEY TERMS

calendar management
decision graphics
decision modeling
decision support systems (DSS)
electronic filing and retrieval
electronic notebook
executive support systems
executive workstation
key word indexing
online database
meeting scheduler
project management
to-do lists
voice annotation
voice message system
voice store and forward
word-in-text indexing
work scheduler

INTRODUCTION

Computer support tools for managerial personnel have been slow to gain widespread use—at least among the managers for whom they are intended. Although the concept of computer support for management decision making, or *decision support systems*, has been around for more than ten years, managerial use of computers is still in its infancy. A decision support system (DSS) has been defined as a group of automated tools to help managers analyze their companies' (departments', divisions') performance and to make projections for the future. The objective has been to design and integrate the tools in a way that makes them easy for nontechnical personnel to use. Analysts generally attribute the low acceptance of DDS to limitations of current technology rather than inappropriateness of the concept. Analysts believe that most of the tools have not really met management needs.

Recently, however, managerial use of computer tools has increased. According to a recent Trinet study, 34 percent of the top five officers in Fortune 500 companies use microcomputers in the office, and 23 percent use them at home. In contrast, in 1982 only 8 percent of these managers used microcomputers. The Trinet study also found that 51 percent of executives below the age of 50 use microcomputers, in contrast to 21 percent of those who are older.[1] In 1985, according to another report, analysts estimated that 30 percent of the more than 4 million business-oriented microcomputers in offices were used by upper management and top-level executives. Some office automation proponents predict that increased use of computers by executives will have a major impact on reshaping traditional management job structures.

The concept of increasing a manager's productivity through support tools is not new. The modern office has evolved on the tenet of using office support to maximize management productivity. This support has two components:

1. Delegation of work to support staff.
2. Time and activity management with personal support tools.

Support personnel to whom managers delegate work generally include some combination of secretaries, typists, stenographers, administrative assistants, technical consultants, and professional staff. In delegating tasks, managers give up a certain amount of control over precisely how the work is accomplished. They also must rely on information that is filtered through others rather than personally garnered from primary sources. The time that managers save by delegating is partially offset by the time they must devote to supervising and coordinating the work of others. Generally, as the scope of a manager's accountability expands, so does the size of the staff that supports the work.

Managers must decide which tasks to delegate and which to perform themselves. The goal is always to maximize managers' efficiency and effectiveness, which add up to *productivity*. *Efficiency* is a measure of the time and effort required to accomplish tasks whereas *effectiveness* is the ability to discern the right tasks to spend time on in the first place.

Automated tools offer further opportunities to increase managerial productivity. Traditional personal support tools include telephones, dictaphones, calculators, calendars, tickler files, and to-do lists. Improvements can be achieved in both efficiency and effectiveness, with the greatest potential benefits in the area of effectiveness. Because effectiveness is more difficult to quantify than efficiency, however, benefits are more difficult to measure. Benefits in effectiveness also take longer to realize, since they require changes in behavior in addition to new tools. For example, if a manager uses an electronic spreadsheet to produce a monthly report in two hours instead of six, the increased efficiency is obvious. If, however, the manager continues to take six hours to produce the report, but includes additional analyses and graphics, is the manager still more efficient? Is the report more effective? The evaluation now becomes more subjective.

An important way in which computer tools increase effectiveness is by changing the delegation equation: Which tasks are most productive for managers to do themselves and which should be delegated? Computers can help managers gain back some of the control over their organizations that was given up as the price of delegation. With better computer support, executives are able to extend their span of control (the number of people or departments one manager can effectively oversee). Computers can provide improved access to information, better monitoring and control of operations, and improved communications. Managers who adapt their working styles to capitalize on the new technologies stand to improve their effectiveness and efficiency.

A survey by the San Jose, California, *Mercury News* indicated that senior-level executives average a 57.5-hour workweek. Such demanding schedules underscore the need for new and better ways for managing organizations in today's fast-paced, global economy. In an age when information often equates to power, managers who have access to timely, accurate information may have the upper hand.

MANAGEMENT'S INFORMATION DILEMMA

Managers face a dilemma of growing proportion in today's information society. While they are receiving more information than ever before, that information is not necessarily useful. Information may be irrelevant, unreliable, late, incomprehensible, or contradictory. In many ways, it has become more difficult to isolate key information. Although little conclusive research is available on what constitutes the most useful information for managerial decision making, experience indicates that the following characteristics are important:

1. *Significance.* Managers need information relevant to the critical aspects of business operations. It must help them evaluate organizational performance in key areas and monitor progress toward organizational goals. For example, a marketing vice-president needs information to answer questions such as "Why have sales for Product X declined by 20 percent?" or "How much does Product X contribute to the profitability of the company?" Typical computer reports merely summarize historical results. They do not report why performance is at a certain level or what needs to be done to improve it.

2. *Reliability.* Managers need reliable information to assess organizational performance and make decisions. Data does not necessarily have to be precise by accounting standards. Data must be valid, however, and come from a source that has integrity.

3. *Consistency.* Information from various sources both inside and outside the organization should be consistent. The marketing vice-president should get sales figures from the sales force that are consistent with production figures from the manufacturing division and delivery figures from the shipping department.

4. *Timeliness.* Information is most useful when it enables managers to anticipate problems and business requirements. Receiving information after damage is done or after competition has gained the lead is ineffective.

5. *Comprehensibility.* To be useful, information must be easily understood. Managers cannot devote hours to culling essential facts from a morass of details.

6. *Action-oriented impact.* Information must help managers take action. They need to identify actions that have been completed and tasks that remain undone. Information should suggest alternative solutions. Managers need to assess what steps can or should be taken next and the probability of success for various options.

More often than not, executives receive information that is an unfocused by-product of the operational and transactional computer systems of the business. These systems contain data that support recordkeeping requirements and operational decision making. They are designed to help supervisors monitor the business on a day-by-day basis, not to help executives manage the organization. Although information summarized from these systems is usually accurate and reliable, it often is not significant, vital, and action-oriented to management. While it is apparent that managers need understandable, action-oriented information, it is unclear how to identify this information and implement support systems that provide it in an easy-to-use form.

Standard computer software, such as word processing, spreadsheets, graphics, and database managers, often go unused by executives because they assign other people to do most of what should be done. Considerable effort and research are being expended, however, on developing computer tools tailored to the needs of managers. This task is difficult because both the size and nature of the organization have bearing on the needs of any one manager. In large organizations, the needs of high-level executives differ considerably from those at lower levels (especially first-line supervisors). The failure rate among systems designed for managers has been very high. A recent study by L. F. Rothschild, Unterberg, Tobin of San Francisco found that executives spend an average of 10 percent of their day on information processing tasks. Lower-level managers may spend considerably more time. It is important to keep these differences in mind.

Technologies for management personnel will be addressed in the following categories:

- Activity Management
    - Calendar management
    - Performance enhancers
- Communications
    - Voice mail systems
    - Electronic directories (with autodialing and message management)
    - Electronic mail
    - Teleconferencing
- Business Applications
    - Decision modeling
    - Project management
    - Decision graphics
    - Word processing as a management tool
    - Data management
- The Executive Workstation
    - Executive support systems

ACTIVITY MANAGEMENT

Activity management software includes calendar management and performance enhancers such as to-do lists, electronic notebooks, and calculators. Activity management tools are designed to manage time and events.

The usefulness of activity management tools has not yet been clearly established. Results have been mixed. Sometimes tools have fallen into disuse after installation, but the reasons for this are not clear. Some believe that in order to be useful, these tools require a terminal on every desktop and a high degree of integration among systems features.

Calendar Management

Calendar management software can improve control of appointment scheduling and time management. Appointments are scheduled by date and time. Calendar entries may include location, descriptions, and agenda items. Electronic appointment calendars such as the one in Figure 10-1 offer managers or professionals several benefits over typical appointment books.

Everyone who is authorized to view a manager's calendar always sees the same version; thus the need for managers, secretaries, and administrative assistants to maintain multiple copies is eliminated. Problems such as double bookings or missed meetings when appointments are inadvertently omitted from one version of the calendar are avoided. Recurring meetings can be entered just once, with successive dates scheduled automatically. For example, a staff meeting at 9:00 a.m. every Friday needs to be entered only once. Then in one step it is copied as a weekly meeting for any duration.

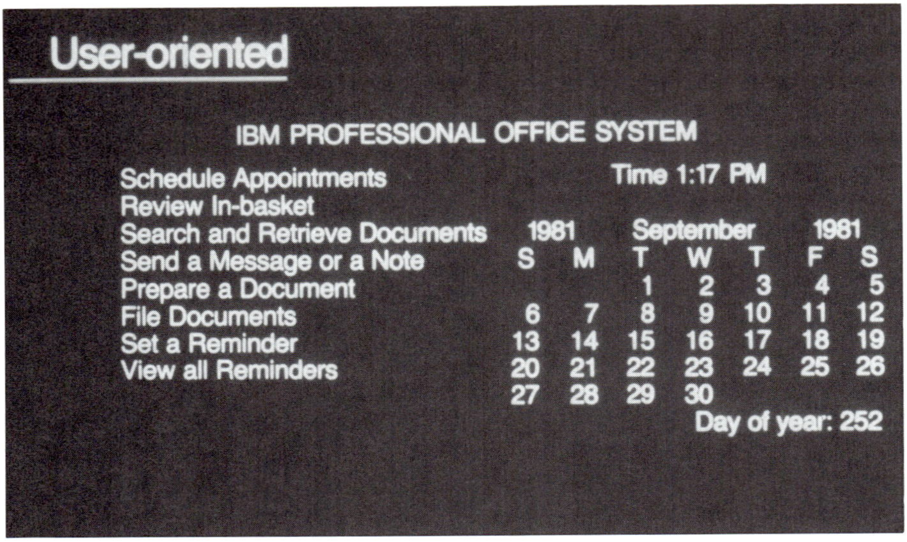

FIGURE 10-1. A typical electronic calendar: A screen display of the IBM PROFS calendar.

The same calendar may be viewed in multiple ways. An individual may view just one day at a time, a week at a time, or an entire month. Access can be controlled to permit only authorized individuals to view calendars. Even when managers grant access to others, they can schedule undesignated times or keep private notes about meetings. The calendar may be searched easily for a specific event, such as an appointment with a particular person or even a list of the days that a manager will be out of the office.

Figure 10-2 depicts the C.A.T. relational database for managing Contacts, Activities, and Time produced by Chang Labs. C.A.T. keeps track of all an individual's "events," past and present. (An "event" is an activity linked to a date. In other words, "lunch" is an activity; "lunch with Joe on Tuesday at noon" is an event.) The Events Snapshot is the way you review these. Using the "buttons" at the top, you can display only the events you want to see, such as (1) all events, (2) events involving an account, (3) events involving a person, (4) all events of a generic type (e.g., all meetings), (5) all events on a specific date past, present, or future, or (6) all events within a specific range of dates. The checkbox columns on the left allow you to further refine the selection. The little calendar window is used to help select dates.

From a manager's perspective, to be effective a calendar system must serve the following functions:

1. Provide all the scheduling information the job requires. (Otherwise, the manager will need to supplement it manually, resulting in wasteful duplication of effort.)

2. Include access to calendars of all individuals in the company with whom a manager regularly meets.
3. Offer easy access and reference.
4. Provide printed output.
5. Be easy to learn and use.
6. Work the way the users work.

For example, when secretaries manage calendars for several managers, they must be able to "flip" directly from one calendar to another. Otherwise, working with multiple calendars is so cumbersome that secretaries soon return to traditional calendar notebooks. If managers are accustomed to carrying a calendar in their pockets, they should be able to obtain a printout in a format convenient for carrying.

Features available with calendar software vary somewhat, depending on the computer model and software vendor. Calendar software is available for microcomputers, minicomputers, and mainframes, and the most appropriate choice depends primarily on the size of the organization and the need to share access to the calendar. A calendar on a standalone microcomputer meets the needs of only one individual; a calendar on a minicomputer might serve the needs of two to 100 persons; a mainframe calendar could serve several hundred or more individuals. If one secretary or administrative assistant is scheduling appointments for several individuals, shared access is essential. Shared access is also important for scheduling meetings and facilities, as explained in the next section.

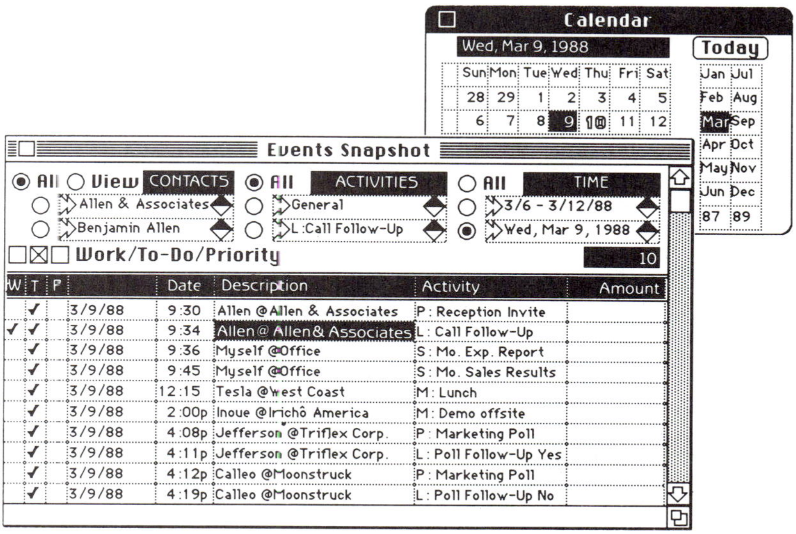

FIGURE 10-2. Chang Labs' C.A.T. relational database for managing Contacts, Activities, and Time. A calendar screen can be viewed in many ways.

Meeting Schedulers

Automated *meeting schedulers* are a major feature of most calendar management software. Meeting schedulers simplify the process of selecting meeting times and notifying attendees. They virtually eliminate the multiple phone calls required to schedule meetings with several attendees. With calendar software, a meeting for ten individuals can be scheduled as quickly as a meeting for two.

To schedule a meeting, the manager or secretary simply instructs the computer to select the times when all attendees are available. To do this, the computer needs three items of information: (1) a list of attendees, (2) the duration of the meeting, and (3) the acceptable range of meeting dates (between March 2 and March 4, for example).

Once the manager or secretary specifies these parameters, the computer reports a list of available time slots that meet the criteria. For example, a request for a one-hour meeting among six managers within the next three days might produce a list of four meeting times when all those managers would be available at the same time. The search is done completely by the computer. With some software, meetings can be assigned priorities, so that lower-priority meetings can be "bumped" for those with higher priority.

After the meeting time is selected, attendees may be notified in one of two ways. Requesters may schedule only their own calendars, then send meeting notices electronically; or the meeting may be scheduled directly on each attendee's calendar. The best way is more a matter of preference than efficiency.

With most calendar software, managers can control access by designating the individuals who are authorized to view the calendar. Administrative assistants, for example, might be authorized to access only the calendars of managers in the work group they support. Attendees who are outside the immediate group would be notified of meetings by an electronic notice.

Calendars also can be used to schedule conference rooms or other facilities. After each facility is assigned a calendar on the system, it can be scheduled, displayed, and queried. When scheduling a meeting, the requester includes the name of the meeting room, along with the list of attendees.

Electronic calendars can be very effective within departments that share a single computer system. Currently, however, they do not work effectively across departments that have different computer systems.

Performance Enhancers

Performance enhancers are designed for personal time management. They include "to-do lists" and electronic notebooks.

To-Do Lists

To-do lists, or reminder lists, are tools for prioritizing and tracking tasks. They can serve as a working scratch pad of tasks and priorities or as a permanent record of daily activities. Because to-do lists are generally linked with the calendaring feature, a manager can easily list in priority order tasks to be completed on or by a certain date. If priorities change, the manager can reorder the list at any time. When items are completed, the manager marks them complete. Unfinished items are automatically carried over to the next day. A manager can keep detailed notes about any of the items on a separate page.

Electronic Notebooks

Electronic notebooks are designed for storing random items in the format of a notepad. The user can jot down ideas, addresses, status notes, telephone messages, or other types of "notes" (see Figure 10-3). Electronic notebooks offer flexible indexing that allows the manager to store information by

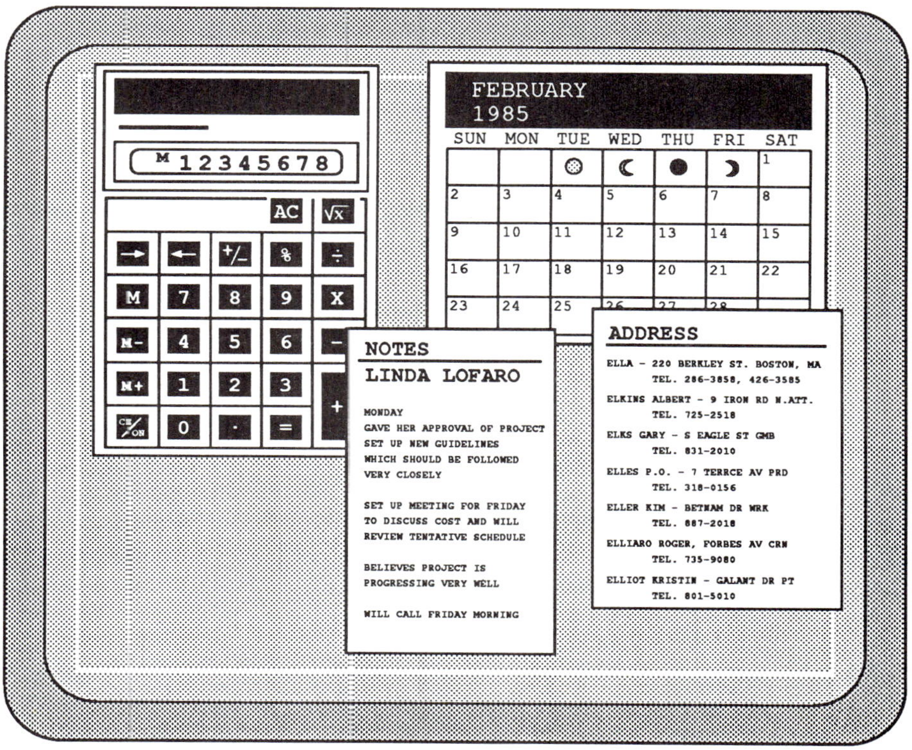

FIGURE 10-3. An electonic notebook.

categories, classes, and subjects. Information can be transferred directly from calendars, mailboxes, to-do lists, or other features to the notebook.

As substitutes for their paper cousins, electronic notebooks offer several advantages. Information is easily located simply by keying in the subject and allowing the computer to locate the information. With some electronic notebooks, a manager can search for information by any word within the note. The major disadvantage is that, unless the manager is using a portable computer, an electronic notebook cannot be carried around; retrieval requires access to a terminal. Notebook pages may be printed readily, however, for reference or transporting.

COMMUNICATIONS

Automated communication tools include voice message systems, electronic directories, electronic mail, and teleconferencing. Their usefulness depends on business requirements. For example, medium-size companies, residing in a single building, may use a voice message system much less than a large company with geographically dispersed divisions and managers who travel frequently.

Voice Mail Systems

A *voice mail system* or *voice store and forward system* allows managers to create and send digitized voice messages over standard telephone systems. These systems are also called *phone mail systems*. Managers can access messages from any tone-generating telephone at any time of day or night. An especially useful feature enables the manager to distribute a message to multiple recipients in many locations. A recipient may forward a message to someone else and preface it with an explanatory introduction. Message systems eliminate time-zone problems in communication across the country or internationally, and managers can use passwords to restrict access to their messages.

Examples of voice message systems include ROLM PhoneMail by Rolm Corporation, a subsidiary of International Business Machines, and the Wang Digital Voice Exchange (DVX) by Wang Laboratories (see Figure 10-4).

The case of a Midwestern furniture manufacturer illustrates how a voice message system may be used to improve business. Corporate management at manufacturing headquarters depended heavily on telephone communication. Decisions often had to be made quickly and required gathering information and opinions from peers and subordinates. Final signoffs for pricing decisions, contract negotiations, personnel decisions, and company reorganizations required fast input and fast distribution. Executives traveled frequently, which made coordination of meetings and telephone communication very difficult. Executives wanted to communicate the context of decisions as well as the content. Such attitudes as "We have to pursue this, but there are likely to be problems" were difficult to communicate by letter or memo. Moreover, information was often confidential. Pink-slip telephone messages or written letters were considered less than confidential.

FIGURE 10-4. The Wang Digital Voice Exchange.

After a careful analysis of its requirements, the company selected a digital voice messaging system. It developed a comprehensive implementation strategy that included careful selection of the initial users and applications, a training program, and continuing education. All upper-level management, the entire sales force, and other key departments in the sales communication network, such as the shipping and order entry departments, were given access to the voice message system.

After several months, the manufacturer reported that the system was quickly adopted and heavily used. A series of interviews assessed the impact of the voice message system on corporate management, and the research report cited the following benefits:[2]

1. *Increased corporate control*. Executives felt that the message system made it easier and faster to communicate corporate decisions, thus increasing their organizational control. For example, one executive distributed a message simultaneously to all managers about a reorganization of their division before rumors had time to spread. By receiving information through the phone mail system in advance of the official announcement, managers were prepared to handle organizational changes more calmly and efficiently. Before another executive forwarded a message to the entire sales force concerning a large contract that had implications for the industry as a whole, it was sent to the regional sales managers, who added their own introductions to indicate the local context.

2. *Increased ability to communicate context*. Executives used phone messages, instead of memos, when it was important to communicate message context as well as content. The tone of voice can indicate the level of support for a given decision, which in turn might have consequences for the strategies subordinates use to implement a decision.

3. *Increased speed of decision making*. Executives were able to participate in negotiations and to give final signoffs while they were traveling. They reported instances where complex contract negotiations, involving millions of dollars, were carried out among three or four decision makers in different cities. Because detailed messages could be communicated to the right people within a day's time, they did not have to wait for formal meetings to complete these transactions.

4. *Improved quality of information for decision making*. Executives reported being able to secure information from more people in less time, providing better-quality information for decision making. Executives reported receiving from 10 to 20 messages per day. The system proved effective even for detailed messages, several minutes in length, if they were well-organized. Consequently, executives felt that the message system provided a vehicle not previously available for making business decisions.

5. *Decreased interruptions*. Subordinates learned to use the message system to request information instead of interrupting the executives during their limited time in the office. The executives could respond to such messages while they were on the road and after hours when they were less pressured.

6. *Decreased dependence on administrative support*. Communication via a message system is a very direct process that requires no intervention

from support personnel. Thus complex negotiations could be carried out among decision makers without the support of secretaries. When meetings were desired, using the message system reduced the amount of time required to set them up. One support person reported that the average three days to set up meetings for four to twelve executives was reduced to one day.

7. *Increased control over when information is accessed.* Executives could access the digital voice message system at any time of the day or night from a telephone anywhere in the nation. They were able to carry out complex communications after hours or between meetings, which had the effect of increasing their overall efficiency.

Electronic Directories, Autodialing, and Message Management

An *electronic directory* automates the maintenance and use of telephone directories. Typical office directories include names, titles, departments, and mailing addresses. Large organizations often have duplicate directories, one arranged alphabetically by last names and the other with listings by divisions and departments.

Electronic directories offer several advantages over standard paper directories. An electronic directory is much easier to keep up to date; changes are keyed in as they occur. Everyone always has access to the current copy of the directory. The organization eliminates the need to publish and distribute periodic updates. An individual can be located in the directory simply by keying in the name. (Often, only the first two or three letters need be typed to locate the name.) If the terminal is connected with the telephone, the number can be dialed automatically after the name is selected.

The major disadvantages are that electronic directories are not readily transportable and that the manager must have access to a terminal to use the directory. These disadvantages, however, will diminish as more and more individuals have terminals on their desktops and use portable terminals when traveling.

Electronic Mail

Electronic mail systems allow a manager to send and receive messages, memos, reports, or multimedia mail packages including text files, documents, programs, data files, and databases. Images can also be sent over electronic mail but can be displayed only on a special image terminal. Electronic mail provides fast, direct communication anywhere in the world. No intermediaries—secretaries, mail clerks, postal employees—are required.

Electronic mail is used heavily by many business organizations while others are still waiting to introduce it. Some organizations have been using electronic mail for over ten years, for both internal and external communication. The Advanced Research Projects Agency of the U.S. government, for example, has been using electronic mail since the late 1950s. For many managers and administrators, electronic mail is their primary use of a computer workstation. Such organizations indicate the electronic mail identifier, along with the telephone extension, in their internal telephone directories.

Electronic mail will continue to expand rapidly as the necessary communication networks are installed. As with calendars and some other tools, its usefulness depends a great deal upon wide availability of terminals and high integration among systems features. Two major issues holding back growth of electronic mail are (1) the absence of clear directions and standards for communication networks (refer to Chapter 8, "Communications") and (2) the complexities of changing ingrained work habits.

Teleconferencing

Teleconferencing has become an effective communication medium for executives and managers. Each of the four types of teleconferencing—computer conferencing, audio conferencing, audiographic conferencing, and video conferencing—offers certain advantages for different applications. As explained in Chapter 8, audio conferencing refers to meetings conducted over voice communication lines, using either standard telephone handsets or special speakerphones. Audiographic conferencing combines audio with graphics technologies such as facsimile or electronic blackboard systems. Video conferencing refers to meetings that are conducted with special one- or two-way communication facilities. Computer conferencing refers to conducting a dialogue over computer terminals.

Teleconferencing should not be considered a replacement for other forms of communication or for travel. It is a unique medium that can supplement other media or accomplish objectives that are not possible through other media.

Computer Conferencing

In a computer conference, participants sign onto a computer at their convenience. Using the display terminal, they peruse the agenda, background information, and comments of others and then record their responses. The manager initiating the conference takes responsibility for establishing response dates, coordinating dialogue, and reaching a consensus or decision. Computer conferencing is used primarily by organizations with major international offices, such as banks and oil companies. It reduces the impact of time differences that severely limit the number of common working hours among international offices.

Audio Conferencing

Audio conferencing is a low-cost medium that, in its simplest form, permits a three-way conference with a regular telephone handset. For calls with more than one person at a site participating, a special room with microphones is more effective. Any number of sites can be included in a call, although the practical limit for discussion is probably twelve to fifteen. The average cost of an audio conference is approximately $50 per site per hour. Audio conferencing is often used in conjunction with videotapes, slides, or handouts that are prepared and distributed in advance to all conferees. When enhanced by an image transmission medium, such as electronic blackboards or facsimile machines to transmit documents, the meeting may be called an *audiographic* conference.

Project managers at the Electronics Division of the National Radio Astronomy Observatory regularly use audio conferencing to discuss projects and coordinate resources. Managers at various project sites can convene without wasting travel time or waiting until it is convenient for everyone to return to headquarters. Thus they are able to "meet" more frequently and on a more timely basis. Companies such as R. J. Reynolds have found audio conferencing effective for conflict resolution and negotiation, but some proponents caution about its use for this purpose. Executives at R. J. Reynolds and Nabisco used audio conferencing during merger negotiations. Reportedly, the final decision was made during an audio conference.

When decisions need to be made quickly, audio conferencing provides an effective medium for discussion. Generally, a conference can be arranged within one day, even when it involves executives in all parts of the world.

Video Conferencing

Several large companies, such as International Business Machines, Aetna Life and Casualty, and J. C. Penney, have full video conferencing rooms where managers around the country discuss business issues or problems and make decisions as if they were physically assembled. Aetna estimated that it saved enough money annually in travel costs between its home office facilities in downtown Hartford and satellite suburban offices to offset the cost of building the video facilities in just a few years. J. C. Penney regularly uses video conferences to display new products to help buyers at hundreds of retail sites around the country select and order merchandise.

For companies that do not have their own facilities, AT&T has established video conferencing facilities in several major cities. These facilities can be rented for business meetings. Public broadcast networks also may lease facilities for teleconferencing. Leased facilities are not as convenient for general business meetings, but since all attendees must travel to their centralized sites, they provide a forum for several applications. For example, business executives may use a leased facility to broadcast major corporate announcements, such as new products or reorganizations. Participants around the country view the broadcast on a regular television set, very much like watching any TV program. The addition of two-way audio conferencing enables participants to call in their questions.

Video conferencing is not expected to come into widespread use in business offices until the 1990s. Advances in equipment technology, as well as the installation of wide-band communication networks capable of interactive video communication, are needed before video conferencing can become cost effective. Current equipment, which is based on that developed for TV broadcast stations, is still too expensive for general use. Recent advances in video cameras, recorders, and fiber optics are expected to bring costs down.

Teleconferencing Guidelines

Teleconferencing is a unique medium. To use it effectively, managers must learn to capitalize on its strengths to convey their messages. Until an individual becomes accustomed to using teleconferencing, it is easy to be distracted by the mechanics instead of concentrating on the message. Some guidelines for using teleconferencing are provided in Figure 10-5.

FIGURE 10-5. Guidelines for conducting business meetings via teleconferencing.

1. Have clear objectives. Teleconferencing is only a means to an end, so do not be dazzled by the technology.
2. Teleconferencing is a unique medium, so you should capitalize on its uniqueness. The message remains the same; only the delivery is different.
3. Events have to be controlled by the moderator (who can control participation better than during face-to-face meetings).
4. Keep sessions short, preferably one hour and no longer than two hours. Frequent, short sessions are better than long sessions. Start and end promptly.
5. Plan very carefully. Distribute a written agenda ahead of time whenever possible and stick to it.
6. Use drama, imagination, and the unexpected to capitalize on the medium.
7. Use co-moderators at each location (if there are more than three or four participants at these locations).
8. Present information in short, clear components. Assemble support materials—graphics, slides, videotapes, written information—and distribute them in advance.
9. Someone other than the moderator should handle conference logistics. The moderator should be free to concentrate on the meeting.
10. The moderator should have a list of all participants (especially for an audio conference).
11. During audio conferences, participants should identify themselves each time they speak.
12. Participants should avoid "talking over" one another.

Benefits of Teleconferencing

Although the importance of any benefit is sometimes subjective, some tangible benefits of teleconferencing have been reported by managers as follows:

1. Teleconferencing provides a medium through which managers can introduce new policies or products to many individuals in different locations at the same time.
2. More people may be included in a teleconference than could physically travel to a meeting. Additional personnel or materials can be brought into a teleconference at the last minute.
3. Facts can be conveyed more quickly and economically than with travel or written medium.
4. Teleconferencing is by far the most convenient and comprehensive form of communication when individuals are at different locations.
5. Rapidly changing affairs can be dealt with quickly and efficiently.
6. The structured environment of a teleconference shortens meeting time, and people tend to cut down on nonessential information.
7. Teleconferencing can substitute for some business travel and can supplement other travel.

Teleconferencing also provides the following intangible benefits:

1. Both video and audio conferencing can grow to meet new corporate challenges with limitless combinations.
2. Teleconferencing is a more personal medium than the business memo for conveying messages and information.
3. Video conferencing provides a medium for increasing face-to-face contact between executives at different locations, thereby reinforcing corporate unity.
4. Teleconferencing conveys feelings and undertones that are not transmitted in written communication.

BUSINESS APPLICATIONS

Business application software for managers is designed to aid in creative tasks and decision making. Categories include decision modeling, project management, decision graphics, data management, word processing, work schedulers, public databases, and executive support systems.

Decision Modeling

Managers use *decision modeling software* to collect and organize their thoughts on a particular problem, narrow the number of alternatives, and present logical plans of action. Decision modeling software allows them—either personally or through a subordinate—to create and manipulate complex business models on an interactive basis, without the help of programming specialists. The commands that a manager keys into the terminal resemble spoken business terminology and may be phrased with great latitude. Some of the new planning software allows models to be created in a nonprocedural way; that is, managers may describe the characteristics of a model in whatever order they think of them, rather than specifying the procedure to be followed in solving the model. Simple models may be set up in a few hours, and even complex ones in a few days. Alternatives may be chosen and new solutions obtained in a few minutes, and the results may be presented in any format to suit the manager's understanding. Decision modeling programs offer guidance on many problems, from improving a subordinate's performance to locating a new branch or plant.

Models or interrelated networks of models may be set up and maintained for continuing corporate planning, forecasting, and control. Alternatively, they may be created on an ad hoc basis for decisions on specific projects. They may be manipulated as either private deliberations or group decisions. In any case, a model may become a virtual extension of an executive's mind in exploring the probable consequences of alternative decisions. As such, a model can help the decision making process, analyze raw data, enhance understanding of business relationships and alternatives, or compare the alternatives to select the best one (together with contingency plans).

Not all decision modeling software is alike; various programs take different approaches to the modeling process. Some programs provide guidance for business- or personnel-related problems, offering recommendations and options. Others use a statistical approach whereby managers compare alternatives against criteria they have defined. Results can be compared on graphs and charts. A third variety prods the manager with questions in an effort to isolate the factors that have contributed to the problem, before it offers suggestions or solutions. Representative decision modeling software products are listed in Figure 10-6.

Consider the following examples of the use of decision support software:

> An account supervisor at a San Francisco advertising agency found that using a decision modeling software package helped him convince clients of the need to change their advertising strategy. It enabled him to focus discussions with clients on objective criteria, something he was not able to do before.

For mainframes and minicomputers
- FISCAL by Applied Advanced Management Research
- EMPIRE by Applied Data Research
- System W by Comshare
- DSS1 by DeFaro Software Systems
- Express by Management Decisions System
- Decision Support System by MDCR
- Accent R, Version 7.30 by National Information Systems

For microcomputers
- Lightyear by Thoughtware
- The Management Advantage by Thoughtware
- Trigger by Thoughtware
- Trouble Shooter, Version 1.0 by Kepner-Tregoe
- Decision Aide, Version 1.2A by Kepner-Tregoe
- Decision Analyst by Executive Software
- The Decision Maker by Alamo Learning Systems
- The Idea Generator by Experience in Software
- Expert Choice by Decision Support Software

FIGURE 10-6. Representative decision modeling software.

The president of a consulting company reported using a microcomputer package called Expert Choice by Decision Support Software to help clients, primarily health care facilities, reach decisions about purchasing computer systems. The software helps consultants cut through information overload, sort out subissues, and reduce the inclination to make decisions on subjective or gut-level feelings. The consultants found that the program helped eliminate the rhetoric that frequently accompanies group decision making and helped participants to focus on the issues. It was easier to go through the process of rank ordering alternatives. According to the president, use of the decision modeling package allowed them to make decisions in about half the time it took before.

The strength of decision modeling software is primarily its organizational capabilities. It does not make final decisions; it provides information so that the manager can better determine what the solution might be. Whether or not managers could use a decision support program depends on the kinds of decisions they make on a regular basis. If they make snap judgments most of the time, they are probably not good candidates for such a package. If they need to evaluate situations and weigh alternatives, however (such as where to test-market a new product), they may find one of these programs helpful.

Project Management

In order to plan and control a large project, managers typically subdivide it into logical tasks and calculate the time and resources required to complete them. *Project management software* enables the manager to outline all required tasks, estimate starting and ending dates, assign staff resources, and analyze project costs. Key tasks and critical deadlines can be identified. Project management software automates various planning techniques such as Gantt charts, the Critical Path Method (CPM), or the Project Evaluation and Review Technique (PERT), which may be familiar to readers from business management courses.

With computerized project management tools, a manager can compare alternative strategies for completing a project, whether it is the construction of a bridge or building, designing a new product, programming a computer system, or any other large project. The manager can change the variables and assess the results, a process frequently referred to as *what-if analysis*. What-if analysis can tell the manager the effect, in both time and money, of accelerating or decelerating various activities. For example, a manager can answer questions such as the following: How much more will it cost to complete the project a week sooner? What is the best way to improve the schedule by one week? Can I save money by paying overtime for critical tasks? Figure 10-7 illustrates comparing alternative strategies with the aid of project management software.

FIGURE 10-7. Using project management software to compare alternative strategies. Project managers use Gantt charts to analyze project data and to make correct decisions for keeping projects on schedule and within budgets.

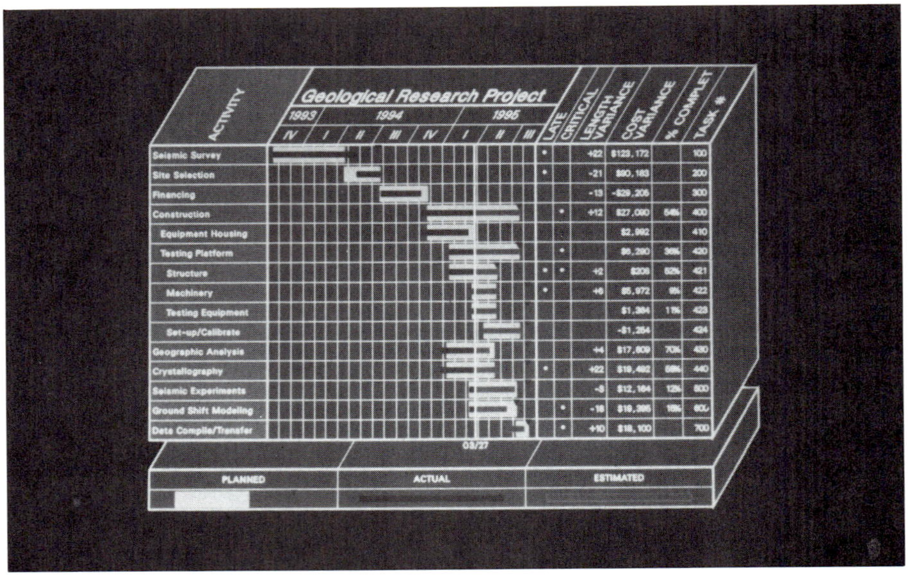

a. This overview Gantt chart created by Computer Associates' CA-TELLAPLAN Expert software shows that the project is on schedule but that senior management has requested the project manager to find a way to cut back expenditures. The project manager decides to remove some resources and equipment from Task 421 ("Structure") in order to save money. The manager will then create another Gantt chart to see the effect on cost and schedule.

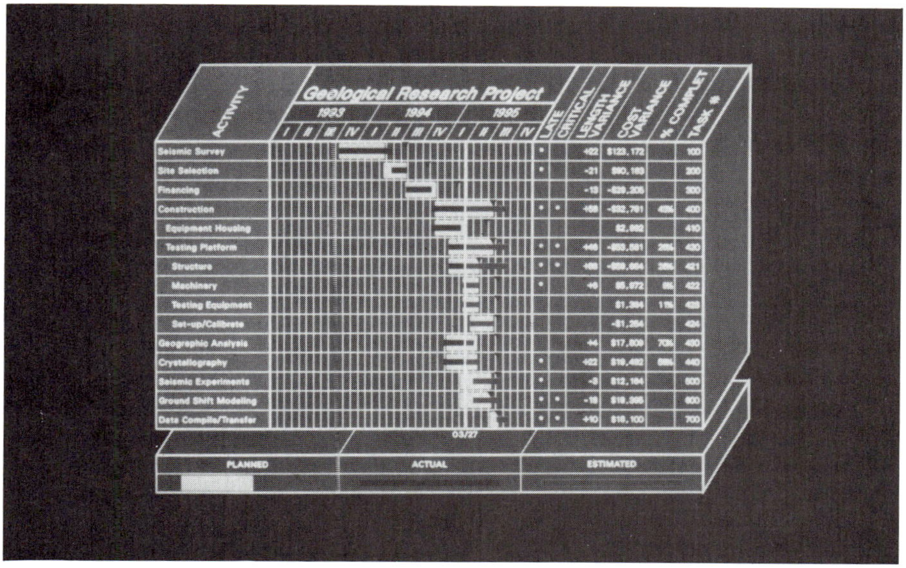

FIGURE 10-7. (continued)

b. This Gantt chart shows that Task 421 ("Structure") is taking 88 days longer than planned (Length Variance +88) because less resources and equipment are assigned to the project. The cost variance, however, is −$59,664; "Structure" will actually cost $59,664 less than it was planned to cost. This Gantt chart shows that the project manager can save the company almost $60,000, but it will cause "Structure" to take three months longer to complete. The overall project completion has also slipped; Task 700 ("Data Compile/Transfer") is now late. Thus management must decide which is more important: saving money or keeping the project on schedule.

After the project has begun, the manager can track its progress with a chart of related activities and reports of costs and resources. He or she can spot tasks that are behind schedule or whose costs exceed the budget. The manager can then assess alternatives and take corrective action based on how critical the task is and its impact on other phases of the project.

Good project management contributes to effective management of all organization resources. Once all projects are entered into a computerized database, responsibilities and strategies common to a number of projects can be identified for cost and time savings. Resource-leveling techniques can be employed to minimize costs by scheduling noncritical activities to minimize peak demands on resources.

The major advantages of project management software are their speed and capacity to handle complex projects and relationships. Project management techniques have been part of good management practices for many decades. Automating them has greatly extended their practicality and usefulness. Figure 10-8 describes the use of project management software at Magnavox Corporation.

FIGURE 10-8. Project management at Magnavox.

Like most large companies involved in government and industrial contracts, Magnavox deals with project management and reporting as an essential part of daily business. Both government and private contractors require frequent reports about the cost and status of projects, while Magnavox managers and engineers need to closely monitor project progress.

At its Ft. Wayne, Indiana facility, Magnavox uses Computer Associates' CA-TELLAPLAN project management software to manage an internal research and development program called Decision Support System Applied Center of Excellence (DACE). The goal of DACE is to disseminate decision support technology into the Magnavox corporate structure by providing the actual technology and guidance in using it. This will aid the user involved in the development of a decision support project in mapping the project structure.

"If somebody asks, 'What are the steps to organize and execute a research and development project in decision support', we can show them the basic steps," John Lianez, Magnavox engineering project planner, said. "Nobody has to re-invent the wheel."

DACE is under the supervision of the Tactical Command and Control Systems, Department 541, and its director, Don Willis. In March, 1985, Willis introduced TELLAPLAN project management and reporting software to DACE. TELLAPLAN now is the primary planning tool for project management tracking more than 450 tasks, managing four subcontractors and five internal Magnavox groups. Using a computerized approach to tracking projects replaced a cumbersome and time-consuming system of calculating schedules by hand and manually drawing Gantt charts.

"CA-TELLAPLAN is used to track progress and locate problems in on-going projects," Lianez stated. "We are finding out things we didn't expect. We can see if the original plan was correctly structured and make sure that money is spent wisely on the projects."

Lianez said work on one task was halted when tracking showed it was no longer required for completion of the overall project. The original plan indicated that storyboarding depended upon completion of two prior tasks, preliminary and final scenarios. Managers were surprised to find the storyboard task completed while work continued on the final scenario. This task was cut from the project when it was decided that it could not be tied into the project structure properly, allowing money and manpower to shift to other tasks.

"Project reporting helps keep track of the logic and feasibility of spending money so it is not spent on erroneous tasks," Lianez said. "The plan is not the king. If it is wrong the plan can, and should, be changed."

CA-TELLAPLAN also produces viewgraphs used to report project status at meetings. Although numerous details of a project can be tracked for daily work analysis, a different type of chart is required for presentations. The chart must provide an overview of the project for senior managers who may not be familiar with every detail of the project and only require an easy-to-understand status report.

"We try to keep plans shown on viewgraphs at presentations simple so we can incorporate the maximum amount of information in the simplest visual format," he said. "This makes it easier to spot trends without going through mounds of data."

Decision Graphics

Decision graphics refers to the use of graphic displays to analyze information. Data represented graphically (as in bar, line, or pie charts) is generally easier to understand than numeric summaries because patterns or trends are more apparent (see Figure 10-9). Thus graphics can help decision makers draw conclusions from data. Although the benefits are widely recognized, graphics have seldom been used in day-to-day business because of the time, cost, and complexity of preparation. With the aid of computers, however, graphics have become practical tools for decision making.

FIGURE 10-9. Trends and patterns are usually more apparent with graphic illustrations.

Hardware and software are available to produce graphic displays, ranging from simple bar or line charts to complex sales territory layouts or multidimensional maps. As assumptions are changed and decisions made, the data can be recalculated and the consequences displayed on the screen.

Graphic systems are becoming easier to use and more powerful. It has become much easier to integrate graphics with other software so that information that is stored on the computer can be used as direct input to graphs and charts. It is also possible to have group participation in graphic sessions. One approach is a computer terminal at one location and television displays at other locations.

The benefits of computer graphics include the following:

- Faster, less expensive graphic production.
- Succinct presentation of complex information.
- Easier identification of patterns or trends.
- Shorter meetings due to clearer presentation of ideas.

A research project at the Wharton School of Business demonstrated that the use of graphs on overhead projectors can significantly influence the dynamics, outcome, and even the length of meetings. Individuals, using graphics in their presentations, swayed decisions in their favor 67 percent of the time. Those who used graphics were perceived as better prepared and more professional, and meetings required approximately 28 percent less time to achieve consensus.

The use of graphics for decision making is expected to grow as software becomes easier to use and prices decline for color terminals and laser printers. Graphics will also be incorporated in executive workstations (which are discussed in a later section).

Authoring Tools

Word processing is turning out to be a major business application for managers. Originally considered a replacement for the typewriter, today managers and professionals use word processing as an authoring tool— a replacement for pen and pad. Word processing is no longer viewed as something that "real managers" don't do. Many managers draft their own letters, memos, and short documents and then let their secretaries complete them. Secretaries may also key in drafts, which managers then edit. Consequently, secretaries may do less typing than they formerly did, especially in offices where word processing is coupled with electronic mail.

The benefits of word processing as a replacement for dictation are less clear-cut. (Ultimately, it is a personal judgment.) Executives who learned to think and compose with a microphone in hand may continue to find dictation most effective. For capturing words, dictation systems are more efficient, except perhaps for the fastest keyboarders. Most dictation systems do not lend themselves to revising, however. Using word processing, on the other hand, authors can easily edit and refine their texts. Most people work in a draft-and-edit style; few people can create a final draft the first time. Many managers are discovering that they write more effectively with word processing. The ease of editing and reorganizing text encourages revision. It even changes people's approach to the writing process. With word processing, authors tend to get their key ideas down quickly and then go back to fill in the details and refine the prose.

In a 1980 pilot project, an insurance company installed a Prime minicomputer, with a terminal on each manager's desk. Word processing and electronic mail were the main applications. Soon, the executives were doing most of their own mail and other word processing; secretaries did some of the budgeting and planning, and some were lobbying for their own terminals. Memos and notes flowed freely across administrative lines. Today, microcomputers have replaced the minicomputer-terminal system, but the working environment is much the same. A manager can read a document, comment on it, and send the document and comments to one or more peers. Managers also find this capability convenient for giving instructions.

Electronic Filing, Retrieval, and Indexing

Documents or information can be filed or retrieved by keying selected words or subjects into a terminal. This helps the manager resolve the age-old problem of putting one's finger on the right information at the right time. When information is stored in paper files, it is indexed by one subject and perhaps cross-referenced by two or three others (at most). Electronic filing enables retrieval by many subjects, even by any word within a document.

There are two types of indexing:

1. *Key word indexing*, which enables a manager to retrieve documents either by key words or by categories such as title, author, department, date, or identification number.

2. *Word-in-text indexing*, which expands the search capability to every word in a document. Either all documents or only selected documents may be indexed. Word-in-text indexing requires from 10 to 20 percent more storage space than the standard filing of documents on magnetic media.

Electronic filing makes searching for documents easy. The manager simply indicates key words or categories on a selection screen, the list of documents that meet these criteria is displayed on the screen within seconds, and the desired document may be selected and displayed. Even documents that are deleted or stored offline may be retained in the index.

Data Management

Data management tools can record, store, and analyze almost any kind of data generated in today's offices. Collections of information stored on the computer are referred to as *databases*. Any information that can be broken into distinct categories is amenable to computer storage, analysis, and reporting. It makes little difference whether those items are names and addresses, dollars and cents, inventory items, dates, invoice numbers, or any other item.

Databases are a valuable source of information for executives, who tend to be "data lookers" rather than data manipulators. They depend on staff analysts and secretaries to manipulate data. They want to hit buttons and find out what is happening in their organization or business environment; they want salient information that is pertinent to the problems they must confront. Executives favor systems that are simple to operate and do not require extensive training, for which they have little time or inclination.

Tools that provide effective ways to manage information, office procedures, and resources are currently available and will continue to be refined over the next ten to twenty years. Today, the most widely used data management tools include schedulers, online databases, and executive support systems. Information about how database management systems operate is provided in Chapter 11.

Work Schedulers

Data management programs can generate work schedules for entire groups of employees. As assignments, projects, or tasks are generated, they can be logged into the computer, with assignments automatically scheduled for the next available work slot or distributed to certain employees. The manager can weigh tasks according to time required and difficulty and then spread the aggregate weightings over a large employee group.

Commercial Online Databases

Over 2650 publicly accessible online databases are available in the United States, containing over 150 million records on diverse topics. Examples include current news, stock prices, medical information, court cases, and many other subjects. Database services offer abstracts or summaries of articles and reports, financial data, bibliographies, and directory listings, as well as full-text articles and newswires. Specialized databases are available for such pursuits as law, medicine, engineering, chemistry, science, technology, education, and business. They are developed and maintained by various publishers, government agencies, corporations, and associations and are made available through service vendors. Four of the most popular database services among corporate users are the Dow Jones News/Retrieval Service, Mead Data Central's Nexis, The Source, and Dialog. Other types of organizations find different services more useful. For example, librarians and researchers frequently use ABI/Inform, and legal firms use Westlaw or Mead Data Central's Lexis. Ten popular databases that organizations find most useful for specific purposes are listed in Figure 10-10.

With online databases, managers have access to millions of pieces of information at their desktops. Using a database search, they or their staffs can obtain in minutes information that otherwise could take hours to research. The biggest advantage is a computer's ability to select, arrange, analyze, save, and update information. This also means that the information is displayed in a more usable form than on conventional paper; it can be kept current—even up to the minute—for services such as newswires and stock quotes. The researcher obtains only the requested details and does not waste time sifting through irrelevant information. Managers can devote this time to the more valuable tasks of thinking and decision making.

For example, Dow Jones News/Retrieval, a business-oriented database service, has been offering stock prices, news, and analyses of all major security and commodity markets since 1977. It also provides in-depth information relating to the financial community. The Dow Jones Financial Wire maintains an active file of all stories for the last three months. Archives can be accessed separately, and new stories and updates are

1. **Nexis.** Along with an eclectic group of 100 business publications, it contains the full text of *The New York Times* since 1980 and the *Washington Post* since 1977. Available from Mead Data Central, Dayton, Ohio.

2. **Disclosure II.** Contains SEC filings on 8,700 companies by geography, sales levels, product category. Produced by Disclosure Inc., Bethesda, Md. Available on Dialog, CompuServe, Dow Jones News/Retrieval and others.

3. **NTIS.** The National Technical Information Service indexes virtually all publicly available reports on government-sponsored research and development and engineering projects from health to robotics. Available on Dialog, SDC, BRS, and other services.

4. **International Software Data Base.** Product descriptions and published reviews of over 55,000 software packages, updated monthly. Available on Dialog.

5. **Official Airlines Guide Electronic Edition.** Daily schedule and fare updates on 650 carriers worldwide. Available on many database services.

6. **TRW Business Credit Profile.** Limited to company-approved managers, TRW offers payment information on nearly 8 million business locations in all major industries. Available through TRW Information Services Division, Orange, California.

7. **ADI/INFORM.** Indexes and abstracts more than 550 journals for "management ideas or concepts." Its 8,000-word vocabulary can be a great aid in searching. Available from several major database services.

8. **Westlaw.** Contains a full text of opinions, including headnotes and synopses covering state court cases reported in the National Reporter System from 1967 to date. Supreme Court opinions are available from 1932 to date. Produced by the West Publishing Co., St. Paul, Minnesota.

9. **SiteSselects.** A service for corporate meeting planners that describes facilities, meeting places, and surrounding areas. Available from SiteSselects, Inc., Jenkintown, Pennsylvania.

10. **Industry & International Standards.** Indexes standards in construction, communications, and packaging from over 400 technical and trade associations. Produced by Information Handling Services, Englewood, Colorado.

FIGURE 10-10. Ten popular databases that various departments within corporations find valuable for specific purposes.

available within 90 seconds after they appear on the newswire. The service is widely used in business for charting investments, analyzing trends, studying corporations, and following the news.

To use an online database, managers need a personal computer, a modem, communication software, and a subscription to the database (plus a monthly or hourly use fee). Use fees vary, depending on the database specialization, from $5 to $150 or more an hour. Many services are available almost around the clock and may offer a discount during weekends and evenings. Telephone tolls are an additional cost. Most of the major online databases offer their services through national communication networks such as Tymnet, Uninet, or Telenet. The subscriber pays for the phone call to the nearest hookup (a local call in most metropolitan areas); the network transfers this signal to the database service; and the fee is calculated into the cost of the service.

Business use of publicly accessible databases is expected to grow. In 1985, only 10 percent of American corporations were using online databases, which was attributed by some to the complexities in learning to use them. Each database has its own protocols and requires skill for efficient and effective use. Corporations are striving to develop ways for executives and key employees to access information in databases more easily. (Efforts along these lines in building *executive support systems* are described in the next section.) Until access becomes easier, it is unlikely that online databases will gain widespread use, despite their wealth of information.

When organizations use online databases, they must be careful not to violate federal copyright laws. Like printed publications and software, many databases are copyrighted, and users who transmit information retrieved from databases to other users could be violating copyright laws. This would be analogous to photocopying sections of the *New York Times* or the *Wall Street Journal* and passing them around the company. Client agreements with database firms often expressly prohibit passing on information obtained from their database. A client company can have a single account, but each user within the company must have a password. These passwords may be available at little or no additional charge, but it is illegal to send the information retrieved under any password to anyone else.

Figure 10-11 lists some of the important questions a business should answer before it selects an economic or financial database.

FIGURE 10-11. Criteria for choosing an economic/financial database service.

1. *What are the real costs?* There are many hidden costs in a subscription to an information database, so be sure you understand all the items that will end up on your bill. What are your telephone (modem) charges? Will you pay a flat subscription charge or a monthly fee? Are the rates different at various times of the day? If you will need the vendor's consultants to set up the application, what will that cost?
2. *How easy is the information database to use?* Will it require you to learn cumbersome commands or are the commands familiar English words? Will the service help if you make a mistake online? (If it doesn't, you could spend much money and valuable time trying to find where you went wrong.) Ask the vendor for hands-on experience before you make your final decision.
3. *How complete, in depth, and accurate is the service's information?* Obviously, this is one of the most important elements in selecting an economic or

FIGURE 10-11. (continued)

financial database, so research this point thoroughly, especially for forecast data. Independent organizations publish data on how accurate forecasters are, and their results should be reviewed carefully before any decision is made. Ask the vendor how often the information is updated. Do the figures come from one source or several? Does the vendor have any vested interests in the data? How far back does its historical data go?

4. *How flexible is the database?* Would you be subject to rigid program controls or free to ask questions of the database? Can you get information expressed only in quarterly terms, or can you get the component figures monthly, or weekly, or even daily? If you are searching for financial information on a particular company, will it also display nonrelated information?
5. *Does the information database allow you to update your queries?* Some databases will let you store your questions online and automatically update your files once the information has changed—and even print out a copy. But be careful; this service, though valuable, can be quite expensive.
6. *Does the information database provide for interfacing with your application programs?* Ask the vendor if you can integrate its data into application software programs (such as an electronic spreadsheet). Several information database vendors allow this convenience; the most popular interface is to Lotus 1-2-3. Be sure to determine how easy it is to accomplish integration. Several services claim they have integration, but it is often clumsy, time-consuming, and subject to error.
7. *As a final check, ask for the names of current subscribers and talk to them.* One of the best sources of accurate vendor and database information is those who are using the service.

THE EXECUTIVE WORKSTATION

An important concept in managerial support is the *executive workstation*. An executive workstation is a terminal that integrates voice and data. It is designed primarily to access information such as corporate data, online databases, electronic mail, voice mail, and other previously described capabilities that are crucial to executive decision making. Thus it must be tied into the corporate communication network. In order to fit unobtrusively into the executive office and minimize training requirements, it must be attractive, compact, and easy to use, and it must avoid the need to type commands.

A microcomputer with special software and add-on features may not be considered appropriate as an executive workstation. Moreover, many executives are not willing to spend the time necessary to learn to operate a microcomputer. "The traditional executive workstation is a secretary. There is great resistance among executives and managers to automating the office, workstation manufacturers and vendors report, and possibly to eliminating the secretary's role. There is a tendency on the part of upper-level executives to think a workstation means typing."[3]

Several vendors are currently marketing or developing executive workstation products such as the Commander Executive System by ComShare, Inc. shown in Figure 10-12. Some corporations, such as the

FIGURE 10-12. **The Commander Executive is a microcomputer-based software product for executive-level workstations.**

Travelers Insurance Company and the Hartford Insurance Group, are developing their own customized executive workstations using powerful microcomputers such as the IBM AT networked through the mainframe or Wang PCs networked through Wang minicomputers. The "smart" telephone is sometimes marketed as an executive workstation. It features a small display screen and access to both corporate and external databases, provides activity management tools, and is easy to learn. It does not provide all the functions that are considered vital to a true executive workstation, however. It is dependent upon a PBX and has no local processing.

Executive workstation technology is considered to be still in its infancy. The following features are features likely to be incorporated in the future:

1. *Voice recognition*. At first, voice recognition capability will probably be limited to vocal commands tied to specific applications, such as mail, edit, and save. Eventually, executives will be able to control the workstation by spoken commands.

2. *Expert systems*. Executive workstations of the future will include expert support systems that "learn" from experience and aid in decision making.

3. *Increased use of video*. Future workstations will include capabilities for video conferencing and videotape windows for visual aids in learning.

4. *Executive support software*. The concept of an executive workstation usually implies customized software. The efforts of some organizations to develop executive support software are discussed in the next section.

Executive Support Systems

Executive support software customizes databases to fit executives' specific needs. The objective is to provide managers "status access"—the ability to get information about the status of the corporation at a glance, in graphic form, without developing any particular computing skill. These systems are designed to collect large amounts of data from disparate sources, including mainframe databases and outside services, and put it into a format accessible on executive workstations. The systems generally are menu-driven, and using them requires only minimal keystrokes or a mouse. For example, an executive support system may be programmed to process time-series data so that the executive can review operating results at the press of a key or click of the mouse. Some analysts predict that these systems will supersede such software as modeling systems, spreadsheets, and integrated packages.

One major corporation that is trying to make the use of database information easier for its executives is the Clorox Company, of Oakland, California. At Clorox, key marketing executives use a support system that allows them to combine data from a variety of research firms with information from Clorox's internal computer systems. For instance, an executive could obtain information from outside sources, such as the marketing research unit of A. C. Nielsen Company and Time Inc.'s Selling Areas-Marketing Inc. (SAMI), and combine it with internal marketing data.

The system used by Clorox consists of four elements: an executive workstation, database server, file server, and communication server that extracts data from the company's mainframe computer systems. It also includes proprietary interactive software for information retrieval. Once retrieved, information can be viewed and incorporated into reports, or used with the available spreadsheet, graphics, or other analysis tools. To make the system easy to learn and use, it is built almost entirely on icons (pictures). Instructions are entered with a mouse. Output can be displayed graphically, and several items can be displayed simultaneously in windows on the screen. Once a manager performs a procedure manually, the system "remembers" each step and repeats it, upon request, to obtain updated information. Managers who have never used a computer can access the corporate data they need within minutes.

OTHER SYSTEM CONSIDERATIONS

Appropriate management tools or applications must be selected in conjunction with hardware considerations. When computer systems are already in place, software options will be narrowed to those designed to run on installed systems. If hardware is not a constraint, the tools that best meet business requirements are identified first, and then the appropriate hardware may be selected.

The specific features included and their operation vary among computer systems. For example, calendars for microcomputers do not provide the benefits of shared access and meeting scheduling. Even if the microcomputers are linked through local area networks (LANs), most LAN software provides only limited capability for manipulating and sharing information. Capabilities may be limited to transferring, displaying, editing, or printing information. Most LANs do not provide the integration needed for automated scheduling of meetings, although they allow a message to be sent to multiple recipients. As LAN technology evolves, these limitations may be reduced.

In large organizations with multiple computers, the selection of appropriate software is complex. Many technical considerations are involved in integrating software and hardware options. *Distributed* mainframe, minicomputer, and microcomputer strategy is an important aspect of emerging software products for managerial levels. (A distributed network links different computer systems to capitalize on the strengths of each.) Tasks the mainframe does well, such as gathering data from a variety of sources, can be performed there. Other tasks, such as graphic display of data, can be done on the microcomputer. Minicomputers may provide specialized software or serve as interfaces between the mainframes and microcomputers. Managers are thus insulated from mainframe complexity, and overall performance of the system is improved. (Identifying business needs and selecting and implementing software and hardware are covered in Part 4.)

SUMMARY

Today's fast-paced competitive world demands new and better ways for managing organizations. Executives faced with too much information must filter out the pertinent and timely facts needed for decision making. To be useful for managerial decision making, information must be significant, reliable, consistent, timely, comprehensible, and action-oriented.

Office automation tools offer new opportunities for executives and managers to improve their efficiency and effectiveness. This chapter has presented a number of such tools in activity management, communications, business applications, and executive workstations, with examples of how they are used in the business office.

Activity management software products such as calendars, to-do lists, and electronic notebooks aid in managing time and events. Automated communication tools include voice mail systems, electronic directories, electronic mail, and teleconferencing. The usefulness of some of these tools is not yet clearly established and appears to vary, based on personal preferences, business requirements, availability of terminals, and integration among systems.

Business application software for managers is designed to aid creative tasks and decision making. Software in this category includes decision modeling, project management, decision graphics, data management, word processing, work schedulers, online databases, and executive support systems.

An executive workstation is generally conceived as a terminal that integrates both voice and data. It must be tied into the corporate communication network to access corporate data, online databases, electronic mail, voice mail, and other information resources. It should be attractive, compact, and easy to use, and minimize the need to memorize keyboard commands.

In an age when information often equates to power, managers can gain a valuable advantage through improved access to information. Automation enables managers to increase their span of control, monitor operations more closely, and improve communications. The ultimate benefit is more effective control over operations.

Chapter 11 continues the discussion of office automation tools, with the focus on meeting the needs of professional and technical personnel.

DISCUSSION QUESTIONS

1. Of the tools described in this chapter, which appear to have the most potential for today's manager? Defend your answer.
2. What are the six categories of *useful* information?
3. What is calendar management software? What do users like most about it? Like least?
4. What advantages do performance enhancers have over paper and pencil? What disadvantages?
5. Voice mail will be in nearly every office by 1990. Do you agree or disagree? Why?
6. Decisions made via teleconferencing are frequently better than those made in a traditional meeting. True or false? Discuss.
7. What is decision modeling software? What are the three approaches various programs take in the decision modeling process?
8. What advantages does project management software have over paper-based techniques?

9. A picture is worth a thousand words. Do the results of reports done by graphics support this statement? How?
10. How is an executive workstation more than a computer? What features does it have?

APPLICATION EXERCISES

1. Design the ideal student workstation. Of the applications discussed in this chapter, which would you include? Would you add any others?
2. Read two articles in *PC Week* or a similar microcomputer publication related to activity management software. Identify potential uses of the software.
3. Interview a high-level manager in a local organization. Describe his or her workstation. Which features does the manager rely on most? Which could the manager do without?

SUGGESTED READINGS

Rockart, John F., and Treacy, Michael E. "The CEO Goes On-Line," *Harvard Business Review* (January–February 1982), pp. 82-88.

Rockart, John F., and DeLong, Dave W. *Executive Support Systems: The Emergence of Top Management Computer Use* (Homewood, Ill.: Dow Jones-Irwin, 1988).

Leslie, Susan. "Professional and Executive Workstations: Their Impact on Managers', Executives', and Professionals' Job Responsibilities and the Organizational Environment," *Office Systems Research Journal* (Fall 1987), pp. 19–22.

PROFESSIONAL/TECHNICAL APPLICATIONS

CHAPTER **11**

OBJECTIVES

After completing this chapter, the reader should be able to meet the following objectives:

- Discuss the concept of end-user computing, offering reasons for its growth.
- Describe the major categories of application software used by knowledge workers.
- Evaluate the impact of word processing as an authoring tool.
- Define the role of fourth-generation languages and databases.
- Explain how a database management system is set up.
- Discuss the use of computer graphics for business applications.
- List features one would look for in selecting a graphics package.
- Explain what desktop publishing is and how it is used in the business office.
- Offer examples of intelligent job aids in business offices.
- Explain how information centers evolved to support end-user computing applications.
- Discuss the role of the computer store in organizations.

KEY TERMS

database
desktop publishing
end-user computing
financial modeling
fourth-generation languages (4GL)
information center
integrated software
intelligent job aids
knowledge workers
spreadsheets

INTRODUCTION

In recent years, office automation specialists have focused on providing support for professional and technical workers, the so-called *knowledge workers* who constitute a growing proportion of the work force. This trend is generally attributed to the shift from a manufacturing- to a service- or information-based economy in the United States. The term *knowledge worker* reflects the importance of information as a resource in these jobs.

Knowledge workers are well-trained and specialized personnel who exercise considerable autonomy in carrying out their responsibilities. One source defines knowledge workers as those "whose work requires a high degree of specialized training and education and mental, rather than physical, effort."[1] Personnel departments in large organizations generally classify knowledge workers as "exempt" or "salaried" employees. Thus if overtime is required to meet job responsibilities (and it often is) knowledge workers can seldom expect additional compensation.

Knowledge workers are accountants, auditors, lawyers, computer analysts and programmers, researchers, editors, market analysts, actuaries, public relations specialists, financial analysts, engineers, and a host of others. They work primarily with information. Researching, sorting, analyzing, calculating, summarizing, and presenting information are their stock and trade. In large organizations, knowledge workers frequently serve in staff or advisory roles to managerial personnel, or they make up service organizations such as personnel departments, financial services, legal departments, and computer services, which support the main profit making operations of organizations. They also include the ranks of small business professionals and entrepreneurs.

In the broadest sense, *knowledge workers* would also include managers and executives—although generally the term applies to nonmanagerial personnel. In many ways, middle managers have information processing requirements more similar to those of knowledge workers than to senior and executive managers, because the responsibilities of first-level supervisors and operating management often require close involvement in daily business. The reader is reminded once again that business needs, rather than hard and fast rules, determine appropriate applications of office automation technologies.

Unlike executives and managers, knowledge workers generally have little secretarial and clerical support in carrying out job responsibilities. The level depends somewhat upon the organization, but the trend has been to provide one-on-one secretarial or administrative support only at senior levels. Middle managers and professional/technical personnel share clerical resources. In some organizations, knowledge workers are supported by word processing and administrative support centers. Other organizations employ departmental secretaries or clerical personnel. Most commonly, however, knowledge workers perform a number of tasks for themselves that fall into the category of clerical or administrative. The growing demand for office automation tools to meet the needs of knowledge workers is illustrated by the case of engineering workstations described in Figure 11-1.

Office Aid for Engineers

Engineering workstations perform microcomputer-like functions.

A new generation of UNIX-based office automation software for engineering workstations is helping technical professionals to become more productive office workers. The marketing alliances between UNIX software and hardware vendors that make this possible are also proliferating rapidly.

Boeing Commercial Airplane Co., a major division of the Seattle-based Boeing Co., is among the first to test Applix Inc.'s UNIX-based Alis software on 50 Apollo workstations. Alis will become the heart of a DEC VAX-based distributed office automation system. Engineers who currently submit hand drawings and use PC XTs to write reports will soon be producing integrated text and graphics for a variety of technical publications through Alis. In the future, 3,000 engineers will route finished documents to laser printers via Apollo's Domain network.

"We'll reduce the queues on secretaries' desks, the flow time on revising documents, and have the power on desktop workstations that once required a minicomputer," says Boeing computing development engineer Zaki Faraj.

"We recognize that engineers spend more than half their day dealing with myriad administrative chores," says Claudia Lukas, Senior Product Manager with Apollo Computer, Inc., which began marketing Alis late last year. Other workstation vendors that have signed on with market-leader Applix within the last year include Sun Microsystems, Masscomp, Hewlett-Packard, and Counterpoint Computers.

AT&T, in a bid to strengthen its position as a hardware supplier to vertical markets, recently became a minority investor in Counterpoint, a privately held San Jose company.

According to Joel Appelbaum, a director in AT&T's Morristown, N.J., Computer Systems Division, "Customers tell us that when they talk about high-end workstations for the CAD market, they expect workstations that support traditional office automation functions."

UNIX Universe

Hardware units shipped (in thousands)

	1985	1986	1987	1988
Science/engineering	44	72	95	121
Software development	26	35	37	41
Productivity/office automation	42	61	73	90
Business/accounting	57	77	84	99
Vertical markets	15	26	38	51

FIGURE 11-1. **A description of office automation workstations for engineers.**

THE CONCEPT OF END-USER COMPUTING

Computer support for knowledge workers is frequently referred to as *end-user computing (EUC)*, a term carried over from technical data processing terminology. People who use technology as a tool to carry out their jobs (end users) have a different perspective of information processing than people whose job is technology (e.g., programmers and analysts). Consequently, technical people are often oblivious to the plight of people on the user end and vice versa.

Computer systems often reduce the control individuals have over the information needed to do their jobs. When job demands are not met because of problems with information systems, end-users become frustrated. When forms or procedures require information in one format and a computer system produces it in another, the work must be redone manually, a wasteful duplication of effort. Likewise, incomplete information requires people to spend inordinate amounts of time tracking down missing pieces. When figures from different sources conflict, end users must cross-check information, retrace calculations, and verify accuracy—more time-consuming processes. Such inefficiencies cannot be blamed on either data processing personnel or the end users. Designers of data processing systems cannot anticipate every piece of information that individuals might need in the future. Data processing requirements often change as products, competition, and government regulations change. Moreover, since tasks performed by knowledge workers are generally unstructured, many new information needs develop along the way (ad hoc requirements).

Some of these problems have been addressed by end-user computing, which represents a holistic approach to information processing. End user computing reverses the trend of segmenting information processing tasks into discrete functions to capitalize on mechanization and automation. As pointed out in the introductory chapters, early data and word processing removed work from the front office by processing it in technical data centers; work was then returned to the users for continued processing or decision making. Although this assembly line approach provides many efficiencies, considerable coordination is required between those who use or apply the information and those who process it. Misunderstandings often arise because perspectives and priorities are different. Users want maximum flexibility; data and word processing centers want to maximize efficiency of equipment. With the decreased cost of computer memory and hardware, however, maximizing machine efficiency need no longer be a paramount priority.

The philosophy of end-user computing is that for some types of applications it is more efficient to teach businesspeople to do their own computing than to teach data processing professionals about business requirements. This philosophy is reflected in the ancient proverb, "Give a man a fish and you feed him for a day; teach a man to fish and he can feed himself for a lifetime." Applying this principle to end-user computing, an appropriate paraphrase might be, "Develop a computer application for an individual and you solve one problem; teach individuals to compute and they can solve their own business problems for a lifetime." The ideal applications for end-user computing are those that require a high level of business knowledge and understanding and a relatively low level of computing skill, as indicated in the matrix shown in Figure 11-2.

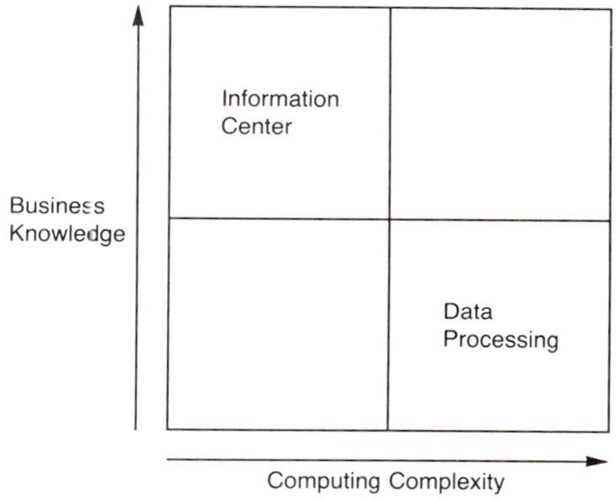

FIGURE 11-2. Matrix of computing applications.

Moreover, the volume of potential applications in the office makes it impractical for one department of computer specialists to develop all of them. Productivity improvement in the office generally results from the cumulative impact of hours saved on hundreds of small applications rather than a few major applications. Experience demonstrates that the most innovative ideas originate from business specialists who can apply technology to their own needs.

The idea that users could do some of their own computing was revolutionary in the early 1970s. Management information systems or data processing (MIS/DP) departments often resisted such efforts. Businesspeople had needs that could be met by the new technologies, however, and they used them with or without corporate approval. The match between need and new technology ushered in end-user computing, similar to the way in which mushrooming paperwork and word processors fueled the growth of clerical automation in the 1960s. The technologies that gave rise to EUC were nonprocedural fourth-generation computer languages for mainframes and easy-to-use business software for microcomputers, especially electronic spreadsheets. These and other application software for knowledge workers are discussed in the next section.

As with most grassroots efforts, implementation took various forms in different organizations. Issues of ownership and responsibility created internal conflict and organizational changes. Information centers (discussed later in this chapter) were introduced in many large organizations to promote and support end-user computing. Most organizations today consolidate support for end-user computing within the office automation department, which provides a logical point for supporting automation in the workplace.

The discussion of end-user applications is followed by background on the development and growth of information centers and microcomputers in the business office. The chapter concludes with a discussion of applications in small professional offices, such as those of lawyers and doctors.

APPLICATION SOFTWARE FOR KNOWLEDGE WORKERS

Application software for professional and technical knowledge workers is divided into the following categories:

- Financial software
  - Spreadsheet packages
  - Financial modeling packages
  - Statistical analysis packages
  - Financial management packages
- Word processing
- Fourth-generation languages (4GLs)
- Data management
- Graphics
- Desktop publishing
- Integrated software
- Intelligent job aids

Financial Software

Software for financial applications includes spreadsheets, financial modeling software, statistical analysis programs, and financial management packages. The widespread use of these programs in the business office is exemplified by the job advertisement in Figure 11-3, which lists experience

FIGURE 11-3. Many jobs require experience with application software.

Market Research Analyst

Connecticut National Bank, one of New England's strongest financial institutions, is seeking an experienced Market Research Analyst for its Marketing and Communications Division.

You will conduct competitive product pricing studies and assume responsibility for various Market Research projects that involve primary and secondary analysis.

You should have a minimum of two years Market Research experience, preferably in a financial institution. Knowledge of questionnaire development, statistical software packages, and LOTUS 1-2-3 is required. A Bachelor's degree with an emphasis on Market Research is preferred. Demonstrated written and oral communication skills are required.

We offer a competitive salary and excellent benefits, including medical/dental insurance, a thrift plan, educational assistance, and life insurance. Should your background meet our requirements, please send your resume and salary history immediately, to:

Patricia N. Howes
Manager of Administration
Connecticut National Bank
777 Main Street
Hartford, CT 06115

Connecticut National Bank

Connecticut National Bank is an Equal Opportunity Employer

with statistical software packages and Lotus 1-2-3 (a popular microcomputer spreadsheet package) among the job requirements for a market research analyst.

Spreadsheet Packages

Electronic spreadsheets help solve problems that formerly were handled with calculator, pencil, and worksheets of columns and rows (columnar accounting sheets). With spreadsheets, knowledge workers can build and edit simple or complex financial and budgetary models and test financial computations under revised conditions (what if?) with minimal effort. A sample spreadsheet is illustrated in Figure 11-4.

	A B C	D	E	F	G	H	I	J	K
1	BUDGET2: Copying Cells and Ranges								
2									
3	MONTHLY INCOME		Jan	Feb	Mar	Apr	May	Jun	Jul
4	Self		2000	2000	2000	2000	2000	2000	2000
5	Spouse		2100	2100	2100	2100	2100	2100	2100
6	Investments		200	200	200	200	200	200	250
7	Interest		150	150	150	150	160	160	160
8	Total Income ==>		4450	4450	4450	4450	4460	4460	4510
9									
10	MONTHLY EXPENSES	BUDGET							
11	Rent, Mortgage	1000	2000	2000	2000	2000	2000	2000	2000
12	Utilities	250	150	150	100	80	80	100	100
13	Food & Clothing	300	300	290	280	300	280	310	310
14	Auto	350	400	400	400	400	400	400	400
15	Misc.	200	100	150	160	200	120	210	150
16	Total Expense ==>		2100	2950	2990	2940	2980	2880	3020
17	CASH FLOW		2350	1500	1460	1510	1480	1580	1490
18	CASH FLOW YTD		2350	3850	5310	6820	8300	9880	11370
19									
20									

FIGURE 11-4. A typical electronic spreadsheet.

A spreadsheet works like this: The VDT screen serves as a window onto a blank worksheet, which resembles a large columnar accounting pad (see Figure 11-5). The worksheet is organized into a matrix of columns and rows into which the user can insert one of three types of information: words, numbers, or formulas. For example, if a knowledge worker wants to construct an annual department budget, he or she would use the keyboard to enter column headings across the top and budget categories down the side. As the knowledge worker enters numeric information and formulas, the computer manipulates the data according to instructions. For example, the worker can take a figure entered for one month's expense, such as rent, and copy it into every subsequent month for the same category.

Cell A1

	A	B	C	D	E	F	G	H	I
1									
2									
3									
4									
5									
6									
7									
8									
9									
10									
11									
12									
13									

Typical spreadsheet with *rows* numbered down the side and *columns* lettered across the top. One popular spreadsheet package has 2,048 rows and 256 columns numbered A through IV.

	A	B	C	D	E	F	G
1	DEPARTMENT BUDGET						
2		JAN	FEB	MAR	APR	MAY	JUNE
3	Sales						
4	Rent						
5	Utilities						
6	Supplies						
7	Salaries						
8	Commissions						
9							
10							
11							
12							
13							

Step 1: To construct a department budget, user would enter months of year across the top and budget categories down the side.

Sales entered as formula (B*1.05) with calculation displayed

	A	B	C	D	E	F	G
1		DEPARTMENT BUDGET					
2		JAN	FEB	MAR	APR	MAY	JUNE
3	Sales	10,000	10,500	11,025	11,576	12,155	12,763
4	Rent	1,000	1,000	1,000	1,000	1,000	1,000
5	Utilities	500	500	500	500	500	500
6	Supplies	100					
7	Salaries	6,500	6,575	6,654	6,736	6,823	6,914
8	Commissions	1,500	1,575	1,654	1,736	1,823	1,914
9	Total Expenses	8,100	8,075	8,154	8,236	8,323	8,414
10	Profit or Loss	1,900	2,425	2,871	3,340	3,832	4,348
11							
12							

Figure copied in one step into each subsequent month

Formula: (B3-B9) Profit or Loss calculated as Sales - Expense

Formula: (5000+D8) Salaries computed as base wage + commission

Formula: @sum(B4..B7) Total Expenses sums cells B4 through B7

Formula: (B3*.15) Commissions are 15% of sales

Step 2: User enters numbers, words, and formulas to project 5% sales increase per month.

	A	B	C	D	E	F	G
1		DEPARTMENT BUDGET					
2		JAN	FEB	MAR	APR	MAY	JUNE
3	Sales	10,000	11,000	12,100	13,310	14,641	16,105
4	Rent	1,000	1,000	1,000	1,000	1,000	1,000
5	Utilities	500	500	500	500	500	500
6	Supplies	100					
7	Salaries	6,500	6,650	6,815	6,997	7,196	7,416
8	Commissions	1,500	1,650	1,815	1,997	2,196	2,416
9	Total Expenses	8,100	8,150	8,315	8,497	8,696	8,916
10	Profit or Loss	1,900	2,850	3,785	4,814	5,945	7,189
11							
12							

Step 3: If sales increased by 10% instead of 5%, the spreadsheet instantly recalculates as user revises figures and tests alternatives ("what if" analysis).

FIGURE 11-5. Constructing a spreadsheet.

Vertical and horizontal totals or subtotals can be calculated simply by entering a formula that sums the intended row or column of figures. Most importantly, the worker uses formulas to calculate one figure based on others For example, the projected sales income could be entered as a formula that would increment the previous month's sales by 5 percent, then be copied into every subsequent month. Salaries might be computed as a function of base wage plus commissions, or interest might be calculated on a projected rate. It thus becomes possible to recalculate instantly, as the worker explores "what-if" assumptions. What will be the effect on salaries if sales increase 10 percent? What if interest rates decline by .5 percent? What if the utility rate increases by 7 percent instead of 4 percent? Once the budget is completed to the worker's satisfaction, it can be printed and stored for future use. It can be easily recalled to analyze new assumptions, to compare actual against projected expenses, or as a starting point for preparing the following year's budget.

Spreadsheet programs are available for microcomputers, minicomputers, and mainframes (Figure 11-6 is a representative listing). The microcomputer versions are most widely used. These programs are so popular, in fact, that they have been credited by a number of automation proponents for the rapid growth of microcomputer use in the office. While mainframe and minicomputer spreadsheets are generally not as easy to use as those on microcomputers, they offer faster calculation, integration with other data and programs, and lower cost per workstation. Although mainframe spreadsheet programs typically cost $6000 to $10,000 (in con-

Spreadsheet programs for microcomputers

- 1-2-3 by Lotus Development Corp.
- Excel by Microsoft
- Jazz by Lotus Development Corp.
- Multiplan by Microsoft Corp.
- Visicalc IV by Visicorp.
- Supercalc by Sorcim Corp.

Spreadsheet programs for mainframes or minicomputers

- Dynaplan by Dynasoft Corp.
- Maxicalc by On-Line Software
- ExecuCalc by Parallax Systems
- Electronic Spread Sheet (ESS) by Trax Softworks, Inc.
- FScalc by SAS Institute Inc.
- Omnicalc by Tower Systems International
- Graphic Outlook by Stone Mountain Computing
- Supercomp-Twenty by Access Technology Inc.
- Minitplan/36 and Minitplan/38 by Business Model Systems
- Boeing Calc by Boeing Computer Services
- Dyl-Calc by Sterling Software, DylaKor Division
- SuperCalc by Computer Associates

FIGURE 11-6. Representative spreadsheet software.

trast to $300 to $600 for microcomputers), one program on a mainframe could be made available to hundreds of users on the system.

The following example illustrates a large organization's use of spreadsheet software:

> MCI Inc., a Dallas-based telecommunications company, uses a spreadsheet called 20/20 installed on a Prime minicomputer. MCI has 300 terminals with 50 to 60 knowledge workers using 20/20, and the number is snowballing. Knowledge workers use 20/20 to analyze database data. For example, they compare several months of data using time-series analyses to determine any unusual movements or trends. Other knowledge workers use the spreadsheet to project telephone traffic needs and to plan network configurations. The 20/20 spreadsheet is also used for cost analyses, operations reporting, and forecasts of telephone company costs and operating expenses.
>
> MCI selected a minicomputer spreadsheet because standalone microcomputer packages did not interface with its established customer database and could not match the power of the minicomputer. For example, with 20/20, after each department completes monthly departmental reports, the accounting department can hit a button and the 20/20 spreadsheet gives it instant consolidation of all departmental figures on the divisional level.

Financial Modeling Packages

Financial modeling programs, although similar in purpose, work somewhat differently than spreadsheet programs. The knowledge worker creates a financial model by a series of English-like commands called a *modeling language* to enter, manipulate, and calculate data. Figure 11-7

Figure 11-7. Example of a modeling language.

a. A knowledge worker using the IFPS/Plus modeling and financial planning system.

FIGURE 11-7. (continued)

```
MODEL TEST1 VERSION OF 01/26/88 12:00
 1 COLUMNS 1-5
 2 !24 INCH TELEVISION SALES = 100,200,300,400,500
 3 !24 INCH TELEVISION UNITS = 300,400,500,600,700
 4 TRANSISTOR RADIO SALES = 1000,2000,3000,4000,5000
 5 TRANSISTOR RADIO UNITS = 3000,4000,5000,6000,7000
 6 STEREO HI FI SALES = 500,1000,1500,2000,2500
 7 STEREO HI FI UNITS = 1000,2000,3000,4000,5000
 8 GENERATE L99 FOR 24 INCH TELEVISION, TRANSISTOR
   RADIO, STEREO HI FI
99 # INVENTORY = !#UNITS - !#SALES
 END OF MODEL
```

b. This input screen displays command statements for creating a financial model using the IFPS/Plus system.

	1	2	3	4	5
24 INCH TELEVISION SALES	100	200	300	400	500
24 INCH TELEVISION UNITS	300	400	500	600	700
TRANSISTOR RADIO SALES	1000	2000	3000	4000	5000
TRANSISTOR RADIO UNITS	3000	4000	5000	6000	7000
STEREO HI FI SALES	500	1000	1500	2000	2500
STEREO HI FI UNITS	1000	2000	3000	4000	5000
24 INCH TELEVISION INVEN	200	200	200	200	200
TRANSISTOR RADIO INVENTO	2000	2000	2000	2000	2000
STEREO HI FI INVENTORY	500	1000	1500	2000	2500

c. This output screen displays the report produced by the financial model in Figure 11.7b.

illustrates the use of a modeling language. After specifying all information and instructions, the knowledge worker selects the desired report format. The computer formats the report in the selected style, which could be a row-and-column spreadsheet or one of several other options.

For example, London Life Insurance uses modeling tools to develop models for the projected five-year profit-and-loss report. Details by division and product line are simple to include, and users can forecast income and expenses based on variables such as inflation and investments (rental income, mortgages due, and stock and bond portfolios).

Many people find financial modeling software more difficult to work with than spreadsheets. Modeling requires users to conceptualize how they want the finished report to look as they create it with the English-like commands. The "what-you-see-is-what-you-get" screen display for the spreadsheet is considered easier. Financial packages have greater data capacity and are faster for large amounts of data. They have more functions than spreadsheets have, make it easier to consolidate reports, and are capable of goal-seeking and other repetitive problem-solving operations. They are most appropriate for financial planning professionals.

Statistical Analysis Packages

Statistical packages can compute statistics such as means, medians, modes, analysis of variance, and t-tests, as well as advanced factor, discriminant, cluster, and other multivariate procedures. Data can be input at the keyboard or stored in other computer programs. Statistical analysis programs also produce graphics and reports. Two statistical application packages widely used in business are the Statistical Analysis System (SAS), from the SAS Institute, and the Statistical Package for the Social Sciences (SPSS), from SPSS, Inc. Both packages were developed for the mainframe but are now available in microcomputer versions.

By automating laborious manual calculations, computers have turned statistical analysis into a practical tool for market research, survey compilation, and other business research. For example, a marketing research department within a nationwide travel agency uses the SPSS program to compile customer demographics and service patterns. Data analysis helps them to plan programs to attract and serve business travelers. In another case, a division of the U.S. Army uses SPSS to analyze data and build models from surveys, studies, and personnel data on hundreds of thousands of recruits. Analysis of their data enables the Army to improve its recruitment campaigns.

Financial Management Packages

Financial management packages, which were once strictly back-office functions, are moving to the front office. End-users are demanding and getting more control. These packages combine accounting systems (general ledger, accounts payable, accounts receivable, and payroll) with inventory systems and financial analysis. Some add functions such as fixed asset accounting, foreign currency translation, and cash and credit management to the traditional functions. They may even include database management and spreadsheets.

Most financial management packages are aimed for the *departmental computer* (minicomputer) marketplace, although increasingly sophisticated packages are also available for microcomputers. These new systems are increasingly programmed to be *hardware independent* so that they can be moved from one brand or model of computer to another.

These newer packages provide far greater flexibility than traditional mainframe accounting systems. Often these packages can run in both batch and online (real-time) mode simultaneously. This means that instead of being limited to the traditional month-end financial statements, accountants and managers can access up-to-the-minute financial information anytime and view it in a variety of ways. Sales managers can access inventory accounting systems anytime to tell immediately if a part is available or when it can be shipped. "Users are the winners in this new environment," says one software designer. "Financial systems will have the look and feel of personal computer applications because, in fact, a lot of the processing will occur on each workstation. We will marry the best of the personal computer with the power and centralized control of the mainframe."[2]

Word Processing

Word processing is the most widely used computer tool among knowledge workers. Almost every knowledge worker must summarize and communicate information in some written format, a task for which word processing is ideal. The stigma of keyboarding as a "clerical task" is slowly dissipating. Many microcomputers, justified for other purposes, end up being used most heavily for word processing. Even when it is not "accepted practice," knowledge workers will persist in keyboarding their own reports. They may, however, do it behind closed doors after hours or on their home computer rather than in the office. Users persist in doing their own keyboarding because word processing saves time and makes writing and editing easier.

The auditing department of at least one major insurance company now requires its auditors to draft their own reports using word processing. The secretary will not accept handwritten drafts. Auditors typically create their reports on a personal computer, then transfer them electronically to the secretary's workstation for editing and printing. Using word processing, auditors are able to complete field reports in an average of six days instead of ten. The quality of the reports has improved also. Once auditors become skilled enough to concentrate on their writing rather than the mechanics of word processing, they have more time to edit and refine reports than was formerly practical. As an authoring tool, word processing enables auditors to create as they go. They can start almost anywhere in the report, create sections in any order, and then insert and move material around. They can outline major points and then go back and flesh out details where required. The result is better written, more timely reports.

As portable computers improve and prices decline, knowledge workers' use of word processing will probably increase even more rapidly. They will be able to make better use of time spent in hotel rooms and traveling. Those inclined to take work home will be able to tuck a portable into their briefcase along with their papers. In February 1986, the Internal Revenue Service awarded a much-publicized contract for 15,000 portable computers to Zenith Data Corporation. These laptops were intended for Lotus 1-2-3 spreadsheet programs by field auditors and will probably be used to word process reports as well.

The use of word processing by knowledge workers will mushroom as desktop workstations or microcomputers proliferate. Word processing's growth will be fueled even more as these devices are linked together by communication networks (LANs). Knowledge workers, who formerly had no need or were reluctant to use the keyboard, will need word processing for electronic mail and messaging.

Fourth-Generation Languages

The introduction of *fourth-generation languages* (4GLs) marked a quantum leap in productivity and opened the door to computer programming by nondata processing professionals. Earlier programming languages were *procedural* in nature, meaning that the programmer had to concentrate on *how,* step by step, the computer should accomplish a task. In the late 1960s, nonprocedural 4GL programming techniques were introduced. A *nonprocedural* language enables the programmer to concentrate on *what* should be done instead of the details of how.

For example, 4GLs provide verbs like SUM or COUNT to indicate addition, rather than requiring several steps to detail how the process is to be carried out. By reducing the level of detail in a program, 4GLs significantly reduce the time required to create an application program. Their use also requires considerably less knowledge about how a computer processes data.

Although a 4GL is more productive for the programmer, it is less machine-efficient. For small applications, the difference in speed may be insignificant, but for major data processing systems it may be substantial. For this and other reasons, such as the need to maintain data processing programs, traditional programming languages, such as COBOL and FORTRAN, continue to be widely used in the data processing department. The use of 4GLs is growing, however, for developing new data processing systems and for end-user computing.

Not everyone agrees on precisely what constitutes a fourth-generation language. Generally, however, 4GLs have the following characteristics:

- They are non-procedural.
- They are appropriate for nonprogramming professionals. (Some languages, however, are too sophisticated and technical for end-users.)
- They are easy to learn and user- or programmer-friendly. (A "two-day rule" is often applied; a user must accomplish useful work after two days of training.)
- They contain built-in functions, including an integrated database management system (DBMS) and some or all of the following: query language; report generator; screen definition facility; graphics generator; decision support, financial modeling, or spreadsheet; statistical analysis.
- They are capable of generalized application development.

Examples of 4GLs appropriate for end users are RAMIS II, Focus, Nomad2, SAS, CA-Universe, and APL. Additional 4GLs that are primarily for data processing professionals include ADS/On-Line, Ideal, Mantis, and Natural

Data Management

Data management on a computer is handled through application programs called *database management systems* (DBMS). Database management systems store, sort, and retrieve information. DBMS can keep a simple name and address file or a huge database of complex records, such as an inventory. Once information is stored in the database, a knowledge worker can use it to generate reports or obtain answers to queries. DBMS can manipulate information that has been keyed directly into the program or with information stored in other programs or even other computers. DBMS are the third most popular software category among end users (after word processing and spreadsheets). The public databases described in Chapter 10 are a special commercial application.

A database is a collection of related records stored in a computer file, much like the folders in a filing cabinet. These records contain specific information, or *fields* such as names, addresses, order numbers, or part numbers (see Figure 11-8). Database management programs allow the user

Region 9 Sales Summary

REC	NAME	ADDRESS	CITY	ST	ZIP	TITLE	F. NAME	L. NAME	MO	DAY	YEAR	AMOUNT	REP	IND
1	G & H Supply Co.	1455 34th St.	Seattle	WA	98118	Mrs.	Barbara	Harden	03	01	82	16259	Willie	Mfg.
2	East Industries	455 Ross Ave.	Verdi	NV	89439	Mr.	Thomas	Brown	02	01	82	55666	Nunes	Mfg.
3	Tool Supply Co.	156 E. Elm St.	Boise	ID	90226	Mr.	David	Stevens	02	18	82	13240	Jones	Imp.
4	Davis Contractors	219 S. 13th St.	Tucson	AZ	85719	Mr.	William	Black	03	06	82	13500	West	Med.
5	Harrington Corp.	167 White St.	Chicago	IL	85001	Mr.	Buford	Heilhock	02	24	82	27400	Calder	Bld.

Character Record Field File. The entire set of a data is a file.

FIGURE 11-8. A database indicating fields, records, and files.

to create files, enter new records, update information, organize records, and produce reports. Benefits include ease of sorting records, based on any item within that record, and search, selection, and updating of records.

As shown in Figure 11-9, database management programs can be divided into two categories: flat and relational. A flat database system maintains all data in a single file. The flat database needs to be carefully thought out so that all information needed for applications is included. A flat system is best suited for simple applications, such as computerized name and address files, since complex applications can become terribly unwieldy.

FIGURE 11-9. Flat and relational database management programs showing linkage of files.

PERSONNEL DATABASE

Employee	Department	Manager	Location	Position	Hire Date
Abbott	Accounting	White	2nd floor	Accounts Receivable Clerk	05/18/86
Barns	Marketing	Green	3rd floor	Copy Editor	01/15/81
Collins	Accounting	White	2nd floor	Assistant Comptroller	11/23/72
Dolence	Marketing	Green	3rd floor	Account Representative	09/17/74

a. A flat database. All related information must be included in one table.

DEPARTMENT RELATION

Department	Manager	Location
Accounting	White	2nd floor
Marketing	Green	3rd floor
Production	Brown	1st floor

EMPLOYEE RELATION

Employee Name	Department	Position	Hire Date
Abbott	Accounting	Accounts Receivable Clerk	05/18/86
Barns	Marketing	Copy Editor	01/15/81
Collins	Accounting	Assistant Comptroller	11/23/72
Dolence	Marketing	Account Representative	09/17/74

b. A relational database. The Department Relation and the Employee Relation show possible relations in a company database. The two relations are linked to first determine which department Dolence works in and then determine who is the manager of that department.

A *relational database system,* on the other hand, allows the user to store data in more than one file and to retrieve information from several files simultaneously. The user defines interrelationships among items by *relating* or linking data elements in one file with those of other files. For example, the user might keep a customer's name and address in a *customer file* and shipments to that customer in a separate *orders file*. Resulting invoices will contain information from both files. Relational systems are recommended for information that comes from several sources and will be used in several ways. A relational database allows the data to be reduced to smaller files that can be accessed individually, with or without reference to the rest of the database. Relational DBMS can serve many needs of end-users because they can handle a wide variety of complex data entry and retrieval tasks.

Two steps are involved in setting up a database management system:

1. *Creating the database or information file.* First, the user or programmer must inform the computer how the data will be entered. During this step, the *fields* to be included in each *record* of the database are defined. If data is to be keyed in at the terminal, the user defines the fields by designing an input form (see Figure 11-10). (Each input form, which may span several display screens, will represent one record.) If the information is obtained from another program or computer, the user must define how the computer will interpret the information. This step needs to be done only once. Options for adding or changing fields after they are defined vary with different DBMS.

2. *Selecting information for retrieval and display.* To use the information in a database, the knowledge worker must tell the computer which data will be retrieved and how it will be displayed. For example, a knowledge worker might select the customer name, address, telephone number, and balance due from data in a customer file and request it to be sorted

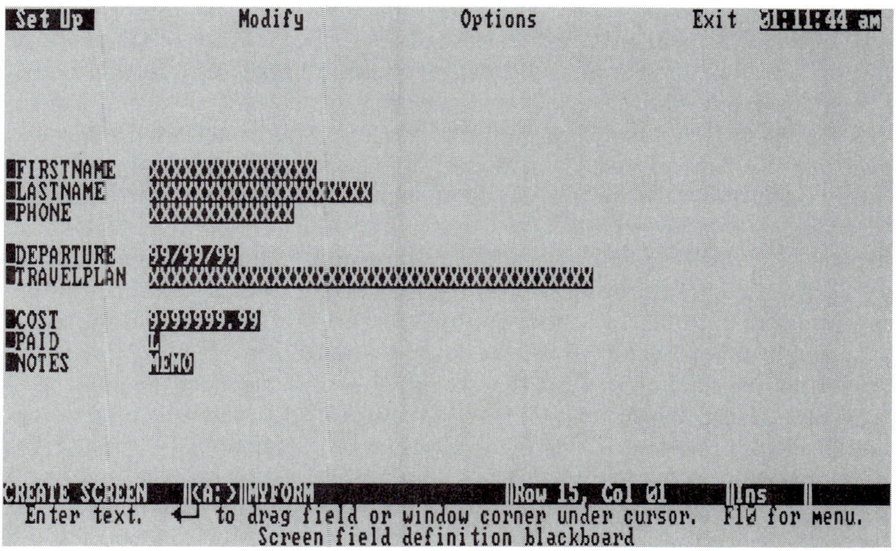

FIGURE 11-10. Designing an input form for a database management system.

a. Screen to create the form shown in Figure 11-10b.

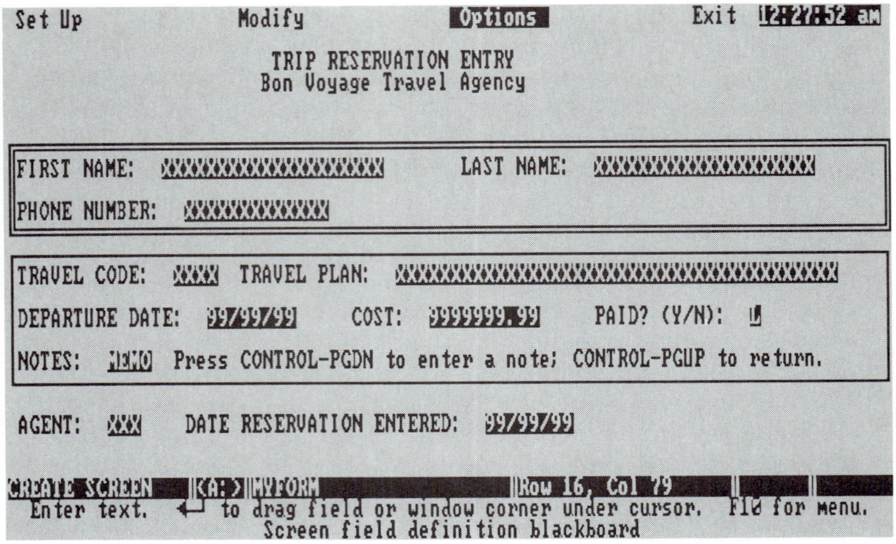

FIGURE 11-10.

b. Screen showing the created form.

by zip code and printed in a list with appropriate column headings. Instructions for retrieving and displaying information may be saved and reused at any time. No limit exists on the number of times that this step can be repeated and refined.

The simpler *flat database systems* are categorized as *file managers* rather than true database management systems. Typically, menus guide the user through data entry and retrieval. Menus are easy to use, but the predefined choices they present limit the program's flexibility. Flat microcomputer DBMS products that are popular in the business office include pfs File, pfs Report, Friday!, DayFlo, Concentric Information Processor (CIP), Nutshell, Please, and Info scope.

DBMS systems are also powerful tools in the hands of professional programmers. Most relational database management systems include a fourth-generation programming language for developing applications. Examples of relational DBMS are listed in Figure 11-11. Complex databases, especially those on mainframes and minicomputers, are generally created by professional programmers and made available to end-users through an information center. The knowledge worker accesses the database to retrieve information, analyze it, and create reports using query and reporting features provided by the 4GL. 4GLs that are popular with end-users are SAS, Focus, Nomad2, Natural, and ADR/DataQuery and DataReporter. The trend with DBMS on large computers is to insulate its many internal workings by creating easy-to-use interfaces. On microcomputers, DBMS are likely (though not always) created by the end user. The true relational DBMS with 4GLs for microcomputers are complex and difficult to learn.

Mainframe and minicomputer database management systems

- ADR/Datacom/DB by Applied Data Research (used with ADR Ideal, DataQuery, and DataReporter)
- Adabas by Software AG of North America (Natural 4GL and SuperNatural for end users)
- CA-Universe by Computer Associates
- Oracle by Oracle Corp.
- Ingres by Relational Technology
- IMS by IBM
- DB2 by IBM
- IDMS by Cullinet Software, Inc. (used with ADS/Online 4GL)
- SAS System by SAS Institute
- Ramis II by Mathematica Products
- Focus by Information Builders, Inc.
- Total by Cincom Systems, Inc. (used with Mantis and Supra 4GL's)
- PACE by Wang Laboratories

Microcomputer database management systems

- Condor 3 from Condor, Inc.
- dBaseII and dBase III by Ashton-Tate Corp.
- R:BASE Series 5000 by Microrim, Inc.
- DATAEASE by Software Solutions
- PC/Focus by Information Builders, Inc.
- Paradox by Ansa Software, Inc.
- KnowledgeMan by Micro Data Base Systems, Inc.

FIGURE 11-11. Popular relational DBMS for end-user computing.

Before microcomputers, most DBMS were on mainframe computers. Today, a diverse selection of DBMS, ranging from easy to complex, is available for minicomputers and microcomputers as well as mainframes. Many large mainframe systems provide a one-way link to transfer (download) data to microcomputer systems for analysis and reporting. Often, microcomputer database systems are used to support departmental operations independently of the mainframe database.

In general, the more features and flexibility that microcomputer DBMS provide, the more difficult they are to use. Therefore, end-users should determine which features are required for the intended applications, and then select the least powerful microcomputer database that provides them. Of course, the knowledge worker should not overlook requirements for expanded applications. Compatibility is another key concern when users share applications or when data will be transferred from other programs or computers.

Over 100 major DBMS products are available for the IBM PC alone; they range in price from $49 to $695. Many microcomputer systems require no programming and are fairly simple to set up. Of the 100 DBMS products for the IBM PC, only 25 are truly relational DBMS, and only a few include a 4GL for application programming. A current trend is toward *multi-user*

DBMS, which enable knowledge workers to share access to databases on a network of microcomputers. One of the first multi-user DBMS packages was dBaseIII Plus from Ashton-Tate.

Graphics

Computer graphics are widely used in business, engineering, manufacturing, medicine, and the arts. Business graphics packages can create a wide variety of charts (bar, pie, word, and others), graphs (line, scatter, etc.), maps, line drawings, and pictures. Computer graphics packages available for mainframes, minicomputers, and microcomputers (see Figure 11-12) offer a variety of capabilities ranging from easy to complex to use. Primary applications for knowledge workers described in this section are information analysis and presentations.

FIGURE 11-12. Representative listing of business graphics packages.

Mainframe and minicomputer business graphics packages

- GDDM Graphical Data Display Manager by IBM
- SAS/Graph by SAS Institute, Inc.
- Tell-A-Graf by ISSCO
- Mangraf by Cincom Systems, Inc.
- Deegraph by Digital Equipment Corp.
- MegaGraph by The Mega Group
- Template by Megatek Corp.
- DI-3000 by Precision Visuals
- Plot 10 Interactive Graphics Library by Tektronix

Microcomputer business graphics packages

- Chart-Master, Sign-Master, and Map-Master by Decision Resources, Inc.
- SlideWrite by IBM
- Microsoft Chart by Microsoft Corp.
- Lotus 1-2-3 Graph by Lotus Development Corp.
- Freelance by Graphic Communications
- MacDraw and MacPaint from Apple Computer, Inc.
- BPS Business Graphics by Business and Professional Software, Inc.
- Graphics Presentation Pac by Hewlett-Packard
- ShowIt by Martin Marietta Data Systems
- pfs Graph by Software Publishing
- JAZZ by Lotus Development Corp.
- Excel by Microsoft Corp.

Information Analysis

Computers have turned graphics into practical tools for business analysis. Business personnel can take advantage of inexpensive, easy-to-use graphics software to chart or graph numerical data for analysis and comparison. When data is graphed or charted, trends and patterns become obvious. Graphics are the basis for decisions; they motivate people to action. Market analysts, for example, chart sales performance of products to compare them with industry trends and forecast sales growth.

Graphics also aid in planning. Since computers create graphics so quickly, planners can play "what-if" games with different scenarios. A corporate planning department, for example, might use computer graphics to examine investment alternatives, comparing each for return on investment, return on sales, gross margins, and cash flow. Planners can project various scenarios involving different budget allocations, manpower projections, economic conditions, revenue increases, or possible acquisitions and mergers.

Presentation Graphics

Presentations include visual displays for reports or for projection during meetings. Both knowledge workers and graphic artists can benefit from computer-generated graphics. In the hands of the graphics artist, the computer provides new opportunities for creativity. Artists can produce high-quality color graphs and charts for slide presentations or publication. Work can be stored and modified for reuse. Illustrations can be printed using graphic plotters either on paper or on acetate for overhead projection. A camera device can be attached to the computer to produce 35mm slides. Special devices can project computer images directly onto a screen. Corporate trainers can easily create teaching materials for classes and seminars. Instructions can be saved, edited, and revised as needed.

Graphics software can be used to "draw" in one of several ways:

- The user "draws" directly on the screen with a hand-held device, such as a mouse or joystick (MacPaint and MacDraw).
- The user draws or traces an image on a special tablet (a *digitizer*), which transfers the image to the screen.
- The user issues commands that are translated into computer graphics (Tell-A-Graf, SAS/Graph).
- The computer automatically converts data into a graph, chart, map, or other image, based on options or commands selected by the user (Lotus 1-2-3 Graph, JAZZ, Excel).
- The image is scanned into the computer and manipulated by the user (Wang Pic PC and software).

The knowledge worker uses the computer keyboard to enter instructions, such as "draw pie," "label," and "plot," or selects from a menu of options to define the type of graph and sets of data to be displayed. The computer arranges the information in the requested format. The user generally has a variety of options for titles, scales, legends, and colors. With some systems, users can create freehand illustrations. Lines, grids, and geometric shapes, though laborious for the artist, are easily produced on a computer. Designers can think in new ways because it is easy for the computer to produce complex grids and screens that would be too time-consuming to do by hand. Digitizing tablets can be used to trace a diagram onto the computer. Once created, illustrations can be printed on graphics printers, plotters, or laser printers in either black and white or color. Linked to other equipment, the computer can produce slides and films for screen projection (see Figure 11-13).

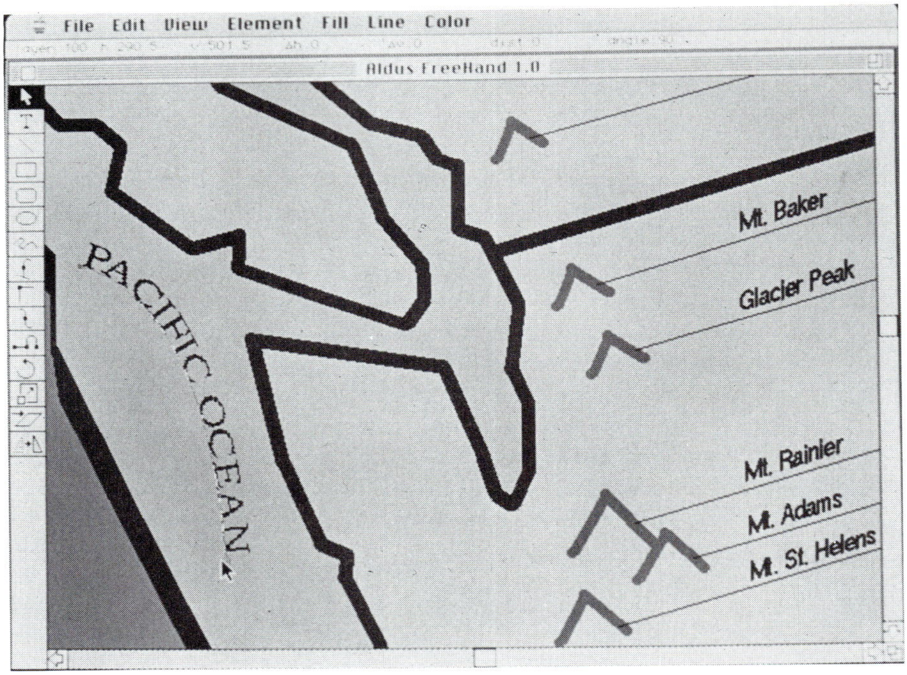

FIGURE 11-13. **An example of an illustration produced on a computer.**

Graphics packages include a variety of features. Most packages enable the user to do the following:

- Create graphs and charts (including bar charts, pie charts, scattergrams, line graphs, word charts, or even freehand drawing).
- Plot several sets of data on each graph.
- Adjust the scale of the graph to best represent data.
- Use data directly from other programs without rekeying it.
- Customize graphs with horizontal and vertical labels.
- Print in various type fonts and sizes.
- Perform statistical analysis (to determine minimum, maximum, sum, mean, standard deviation, variance, or other statistical comparisons).
- Establish data trends through fitting least squares (regression analysis) and several types of curves.
- Work with ("drive") a variety of printers and plotters.

Determining which graphics hardware and software are most appropriate depends on the user's specific needs. The Information Center Institute's checklist in Figure 11-14 can help office systems analysts select and justify graphics hardware and software.

No.	Item	Yes	No	N/A	Comments
	Management Attitudes				
1.	Is management interested in graphic rather than tabular presentations for decision-making tasks?				
2.	Is management comfortable with graphic presentations for spotting trends and making forecasts?				
3.	Is management satisfied with the quality, scale, and accuracy of graphs produced in the past?				
4.	Will management place a value on the availability of better graphics?				
	Uses of Graphics Systems				
5.	Are business graphics desired primarily for a. presenting information for discussion and decision? b. summary and display of large quantities of information?				
6.	Are graphics applications already used for a. observing statistical relationships and variable interactions? b. display of engineering results and designs?				
7.	Is there interest in image generation for a. visualization of planned objects? b. illustration of presentation slides? c. eye-catching figures to include in presentations?				
8.	Have cost comparisons been made for a. microcomputer-generated graphics? b. mainframe-generated graphics? c. graphics produced by specialized hardware? d. hand-generated graphics for comparisons?				
9.	Have costs been analyzed for downloading prepared files to minicomputers or microcomputers for graphic production?				
10.	Will the graphics costs be absorbed by information services or charged back to the users?				
11.	Have cost calculations for any software included the cost of needed modifications and extensions? Is the price of the graphics package competitive with similar packages when modifications and extensions are considered?				
12.	Are the total costs, including extra features, modifications, and maintenance, likely to remain within the budget limitations for the next three years?				
13.	Will overall costs be lowered by a. reducing graphics production expenses? b. reducing graphics maintenance expenses? c. reducing manual effort and clerical expenses? d. reducing communications expenses?				
14.	Will controlling production costs reduce operational expenses?				
15.	Will there be faster turnaround for clients at same or reduced costs?				
16.	Will certain costs be avoided by a. making personnel available for other work? b. employing fewer people for graphics production?				

FIGURE 11-14. Information Center Institute checklist for justifying business graphics hardware and software.

FIGURE 11-14. (continued)

17.	Can profit increases be estimated for a. providing graphics for management? b. providing graphics for customers/clients? c. providing faster reaction and turnaround times? d. improving the use of resources?				
18.	**Intangible Benefits** Is there value in reducing errors that result in the manual production of graphics?				
19.	Is there value in having more checks and controls on designs and displays?				
20.	Are there operational cost advantages in sharing graphical information between files?				
21.	Are there operational cost advantages in improved planning and scheduling through the use of graphics?				
22.	Can a value be estimated for the reduction of problems and complaints?				
23.	Is there a business advantage in the improved timeliness of graphics production?				
24.	Can financial benefits be estimated for a. improved business analysis? b. improved business control? c. improved responsiveness to customers?				

The use of graphics is now far more advanced in engineering and scientific applications than in business. For example, many schematics created on technical workstations are stored as images rather than text. Office automation systems have been slow to incorporate high-resolution graphics. Business graphics tend to be far lower in resolution and restricted to a few types of displays: bar charts, pie charts, and graphs. Until now, few office applications have been able to justify the cost of high-resolution equipment. Graphics use can be expected to change, however, as equipment costs decline, storage capacity expands, and image systems improve. Corporations with foresight are making images a significant part of business (as well as scientific databases).

Images require considerably more memory space and are stored differently than numbers and text on the computer. New optical disk systems, however, can provide the enormous storage needed to handle images (see Chapter 6). A single optical disk cartridge can store as much as a gigabyte of data. Image also requires special high-resolution graphics software and display terminals. The most advanced image systems can integrate image and text so that a photograph and caption can be put on a page in one process. This is an important step in creating comprehensive computer-aided publishing (CAP) systems. Engineers use software packages such as Sun's SunAlis to create manuals and other professional documentation. In the future, office workers will be able to use such technology cost effectively to prepare high-quality reports.

Desktop Publishing

Improved computer graphics and high-quality laser printers have opened the door to a new application called *desktop publishing*. With special software for page layouts and artwork, knowledge workers are combining text, graphics, and sophisticated artwork from commercially produced disks to create newsletters, advertising flyers, training materials, forms, and other types of printed materials.

U.S. companies are the biggest producers of forms, brochures, circulars, catalogs, and other printed materials. In fact, corporations are the largest segment of the U.S. publishing industry. Most of these formats are produced with offset printing by commercial printers or in-house print shops. Desktop publishing now offers a fast, low-cost alternative for printing some of these materials right in the office.

Desktop publishing uses a microcomputer to assist in all phases of producing a finished page, from text entry to composition, layout, graphics, and sometimes reproduction. The user can design and format a document on the screen, as well as pick type fonts and sizes. The display provides a what-you-see-is-what-you-get (WYSIWYG) presentation of exactly what the document will look like when it is fed into the laser printer or sent as a completed page to a commercial printer. Desktop publishing does not replace full-service corporate print shops—in-house versions of commercial printing plants—capable of producing high-resolution reproduction and color. Nor is it a substitute for corporate electronic publishing systems that start at $30,000 and can cost up to $200,000 for high-volume, complex requirements. Today, however, many applications that were previously sent to print shops can be produced quickly and economically right in the office. Desktop publishing is also a boon for small and medium-size firms that do not have big budgets to design and produce ads and public relation materials.

The Apple Macintosh computer is especially popular for desktop publishing because of its superior graphics capabilities, ease of use, and low cost. To turn a Macintosh into a desktop publisher, all that is needed is a page makeup program such as PageMaker, ReadySetGo, or MacPublisher. Products are also available for IBM PCs and compatibles with the addition of graphics hardware (see Figure 11-15). With desktop publishing software, the user can combine material from compatible word processing and graphics packages to "paste up" pages electronically on the microcomputer screen. A variety of font styles and sizes are available to design pages for professional-looking results. Unlike their expensive cousins on mainframes and minicomputers, desktop publishing software does not provide extensive editing of text and graphics. To make changes, the user returns to the individual word processing or graphics program. After the work is recombined with the publishing package and viewed on the screen, it can be printed with an electronic printer, such as the Apple Laserwriter or Hewlett-Packard Laserjet (see Figure 11-16).

FIGURE 11-15. Representative listing of desktop publishing software.

Page make-up systems. Page make-up systems are designer/layout-oriented products that automate the paste-up process. They are the least expensive run on the Macintosh. All of those listed here are software-only products. Representatives of this group (on the Apple Macintosh) include the following:

Company	Product	Price
Aldus	PageMaker	$ 495
Boston Software	MacPublisher I	$ 99
	MacPublisher II	$ 149
	Professional Publisher	$ 500
Manhattan Graphics	ReadySetGo	$ 125

Page make-up systems that run on the IBM PC include the following (all are software-only products):

Company	Product	Price
Aldus	PageMaker	$ 495
BestInfo	Typeprocessor 1	$2,695
	SuperPage	$5,000
Studio Software	DO-IT	$2,500–$3,500
Ventura Software	Ventura Publisher	$ 700
T-Maker	Personal Publisher	$ 185

Text composition systems. Text composition systems are code-oriented, typesetting-oriented products. Unlike page make-up programs, which typically output to either Hewlett-Packard or Apple Laser printers, these systems (for IBM PCs) support typesetters. This group (software only) includes the following:

Company	Product	Price
Magna	MagnaType	$8,500
(also emulates CCI)		
Modtek	PC Type	$1,995
MicroPrint-X		
(Laser Printer Version)	MP-XL	$ 494
(APS-5/Micro 5 Version)	MP-XL	$3,495

Emulators. These products mimic traditional graphic arts typesetting systems such as Compugraphic's MCS system. Like their predecessors, they are all IBM PC-based, code-oriented and support typesetters. This group includes the following:

Company	Product	Price
Cybertext	Compuwriter I & II	$ 795
(MCS Emulator)	MCS100 Emulator	$2,700
Hampstead	PC-TS	$1,900–2,400
(MCS Emulator)		
Magna	Magna Type	$8,500

FIGURE 11-16. **The Hewlett-Packard LaserJet PLUS printer is an ideal tool for graphics, business presentations, and desktop publishing.**

Desktop publishing software can also be used to produce one-part (carbonless) forms on a laser printer. These forms are easy to modify and as many as desired can be printed when needed. A laser printer can print even the most complex form in seconds. Forms produced by computer can be merged with data from a word processing document. The process is rather cumbersome, however, since typists cannot see the forms they are filling out on the word processing screen. Programs that provide this capability will soon be available.

Integrated Software

Integrated software refers to computer programs that combine applications into one package, permitting data transfer among the applications. Figure 11-17 is a representative list of available programs.

Although no single definition is universally accepted, integrated software generally offers the following features:

1. *Support for multiple applications such as word processing, spreadsheets, file management, graphics, or communications.* Integrated software offers various combinations of applications and features. The operation depends in large part upon which application is dominant.
2. *Integration among applications.* Four forms of integration are available:
   - *Compatible series.* A compatible "family" of products that share a common data format and user interface but are actually standalone packages. Examples are the *pfs* series by the Software Publishing Corporation and the Smart Software System by Innovative Software.
   - *Multifunction packages.* Multifunction packages are combined on a single disk or group of disks that are loaded simultaneously into the computer's random access memory. In such tightly integrated soft-

FIGURE 11-17. Representative listing of integrated software packages.

Compatible series

- Smart Data Manager, Smart Word Processor, and Smart Spreadsheet by Innovative Software
- InteMate, InteWord, InteCalc, and IntePlan by Schuchardt Software Systems
- pfs Graph, pfs File, pfs Report, pfs Write, pfs Plan, pfs Proof, and pfs Access by Software Publishing Corp.
- Perfect Writer, Perfect Calc, Perfect Link, and Perfect File by Thorn EMI Computer Software

Multifunction packages

- Electric Desk by Alpha Software
- Jane by Arktronics Corp.
- Framework by Ashton-Tate
- Aura by BPS Systems
- Corporate MBA by Context Management
- Goldengate by Cullinet
- Jazz by Lotus Development Corp.
- Symphony by Lotus Development Corp.
- Knowledge Man by Micro Data Base Systems
- Excel by Microsoft Corp.
- Integrated 7 by Mosaic Software, Inc.
- Decision Manager by MSA/Peachtree
- Samna Plus by Samna Corp.
- Metafile by Sensor-Based Systems
- EasyPlus by Sorcim/IUS
- Enable by Software Group
- Open Access by Software Products International
- T/Maker III by T/Maker Co.
- Deskmate by Tandy Corp.
- Ability by Xanaro Technologies

Operating environments

- Visi On by Control Data Corp.
- GEM by Digital Research Corp.
- TopView by IBM Corp.
- Windows by Microsoft Corp.
- DesQ by Quarterdeck Corp.

Desk organizers and background utilities

- Sidekick by Borland International
- Spotlight by Software Arts
- Get Organized by Electronic Arts
- Desk Organizer by Warner Software

ware, one dominant application serves as the foundation for the others. For example, the dominant module for the Lotus Symphony is its spreadsheet, for The Electronic Desk it is the database manager, and for Framework and Samna Plus it is word processing.

- *Operating environments.* An operating environment is created by a universal "manager program" that sits on top of the microcomputer operating system and acts as an integrator for otherwise independent applications. Some manager programs run only with specially designed subprograms; others are designed to work with independent, off-the-shelf microcomputer programs. Examples include Visi On, DesQ, Microsoft Windows, and GEM.
- *Desk organizers and background utilities.* Desk organizers and background utilities provide low-level integration, giving the user easy entrance and exit to application programs and adding a few simple conveniences or background utilities. These packages do not have all the features characteristic of true integrated packages. Examples include The Desk Organizer, Get Organized, Sidekick, and Spotlight.

3. *Uniform commands.* Integrated software uses consistent commands in all applications for tasks, such as inserting or deleting text and moving, printing, or saving information. Thus learning is easier because commands can be generalized from one application package to another. The user selects options from a menu with a keystroke, mouse, or lightpen. The ten most common commands are usually assigned to the function keys on the computer keyboard. Some integrated packages use pull-down menus, which are "pulled down" as one pulls down a window shade, revealing various options.

4. *Information exchange between applications.* A key feature of integrated packages is the ability to move information from one application to another. Although the need for a knowledge worker to take figures developed in a spreadsheet program and include them in a word processing report may be obvious, such capability did not exist before the advent of integrated software.

Not all integrated software has all four of these features. Sometimes "integrated" refers simply to the compatibility of different applications within a software family rather than genuine interactivity. Software that is genuinely integrated permits "swapping" of information from one application to any other. Integration may be dynamic or static. Static information swapping is more common and easier and less expensive for the software vendor to program. Static integration allows data to be identified collectively (like a snapshot) and moved back and forth between applications. It reflects the data at the moment it was transferred.

For example, an integrated package allows the user to copy several columns of figures with totals from a spreadsheet into a word processing document or to display them in a graph. If the spreadsheet is modified later, however, the data will be inconsistent. Dynamic integration, on the other hand, means that when information is altered, the revised information is automatically updated in any application in which it resides.

Other useful features, which are not unique to integrated packages, are keyboard macros and windowing. Windowing divides the video display screen into different operations or files simultaneously. Keyboard macros save time by storing frequently used keyboard sequences and can be used to automate a series of instructions within an application. For example, a macro can contain the instructions needed to format and print a monthly report. Each month, after updating the information, the user can print the report by activating the macro with a keystroke.

Integrated software has several advantages and disadvantages. Users can work more naturally, moving from one task to another; they are not restricted to performing one task at a time. Transfer of data between applications eliminates duplication of effort or manual cut-and-paste. In addition, the learning curve for multiple applications is decreased because commands are similar. On the other hand, the integration of applications adds complexity, which often means a tradeoff of functionality for separate applications. Most integrated programs lack the power needed by those with demanding or extensive uses for database, word processing, or financial programs. Future integrated software will probably make today's products look like prototypes. In the meantime, integrated software can meet the need to perform tasks simultaneously.

Intelligent Job Aids

Job aids help workers to make correct decisions. Traditional job aids include checklists, step-by-step procedures, cookbooks, reference lists, and manuals. The help screens and menus of most software packages can also be considered job aids. Unfortunately, even well-designed instructions or manuals sometimes become too complicated and cumbersome to serve the intended purpose. Now, small expert systems provide organizations new alternatives for designing job aids. When performing a complex task, a person must consider many different facts and apply many different rules (heuristics) to arrive at a correct response. Loan officers, for example, perform a complex task when they evaluate loan applications. Although loan officers could explain the rules and guidelines for their decisions, trying to proceduralize the process in a manual is impractical. Small expert systems building tools allow skilled decision makers to record and communicate their knowledge as intelligent job aids that can provide practical assistance to new employees.

Small expert systems building tools, which run on microcomputers, can be used by nonprogrammers who want to develop intelligent job aids. As explained in Chapter 9, these tools provide the overall program, which functions like a shell. The user simply enters the data, similar to filling in a spreadsheet. Instead of entering numbers and formulas, the user of an expert system shell enters facts and "if . . . then" rules. Once this knowledge base is created with the aid of the expert system shell, it is stored as a separate file. When it is needed, it is loaded back into the expert system shell, just as the numbers and formulas from a spreadsheet file are loaded back into a spreadsheet program.

Managers and senior operational people who need to communicate information to fellow employees can use expert system shells to design their own job aids. Some artificial intelligence experts now consider small expert systems tools to be a new communications medium. Experts predict that "innovative technical and operational managers will acquire small expert systems building tools and will develop expert systems to communicate decision-making information to their employees."[3] The same kind of groundswell among innovative office managers and professionals that propelled microcomputers into the office is expected to develop for expert systems tools. Users of these small expert systems will be knowledge workers who now rely on memos, checklists, procedure manuals, and personal interaction. Most likely, office systems departments and information center staff will work directly with users in creating applications.

Although available expert system building tools are quite powerful and flexible, they are still rather limited in comparison to humans' problem-solving skills. Artificial intelligence experts suggest the following guidelines for selecting problems that lend themselves to small expert system building tools:[4]

- *A human expert who can solve the problem must be available.* Expert systems must initially obtain their knowledge from a human expert. If the expert relies on a policy or procedures manual, so much the better.
- *The solution to an appropriate problem should rely on specific, formal knowledge, not on common sense.* More formalized areas such as accounting lend themselves to expert systems because people have already developed precise vocabularies in which to discuss problems. With today's tools, the most appropriate problems, according to one expert, are found in the area of diagnosis and prescription. "These problems are characterized by a limited set of possible recommendations. One or more of the possible recommendations are chosen as a result of reasoning about evidence for and against them. A physician employs this approach when diagnosing a disease and deciding what drugs to prescribe. An engineer uses the same general strategy when considering a construction problem and deciding which structural materials to employ. A senior clerk uses this approach in reviewing an application and deciding which of several agencies would review it."
- *The task should be narrowly defined.* It is much easier to develop three small systems than one with a large number of rules.
- *The user should avoid problems that require physical examination.* Since existing tools rely on typed input, the system could only ask the user to

make an examination and report the results. One artificial intelligence expert suggests that the problem should be one that a human expert could solve over the telephone by asking questions and suggesting additional things to check before suggesting how to solve the problem.

- *The solution to the problem should depend primarily on informal reasoning.* The expert should be drawing on past cases and rules of thumb to help in solving the problem. The problems should not require a large amount of mathematical calculation. Most of the small systems can handle mathematics, but they are optimized for judgmental reasoning, not mathematical calculation.

Criteria for considering whether to use an intelligent job aid or human memorization for a specific job are listed in Figure 11-18. The process of organizing data for an expert system is often called *knowledge engineering.* An overview of the expert system development and implementation process is outlined in Figure 11-19.

FIGURE 11-18. **Criteria for considering whether to use an intelligent job aid or human memorization for a specific job.**

IF	THEN
• Response speed is very important (more important than accuracy) • Task is frequently performed • Small errors won't have large consequences • Reading instructions would interfere with performance, or • Job prestige requires a memorized response	Choose human memorization
• Response speed is not as important as accuracy (small errors have large consequences) • Tasks are infrequently performed • Reading instructions won't interfere with performance, or • Tasks involve many steps or a complex decision making process	Choose job aids

In the future, expert systems tools may also impact end-user training and support for end-user computing, which are discussed in detail in Chapter 24. Incorporation of artificial intelligence into other software products will enhance the products available to support end-user computing and expand the office applications for which automation and end-user computing are appropriate. In addition, the development of large expert systems to support decision making in the office is bound to alter office work in yet unanticipated ways and to introduce new requirements for office automation and end-user computing.

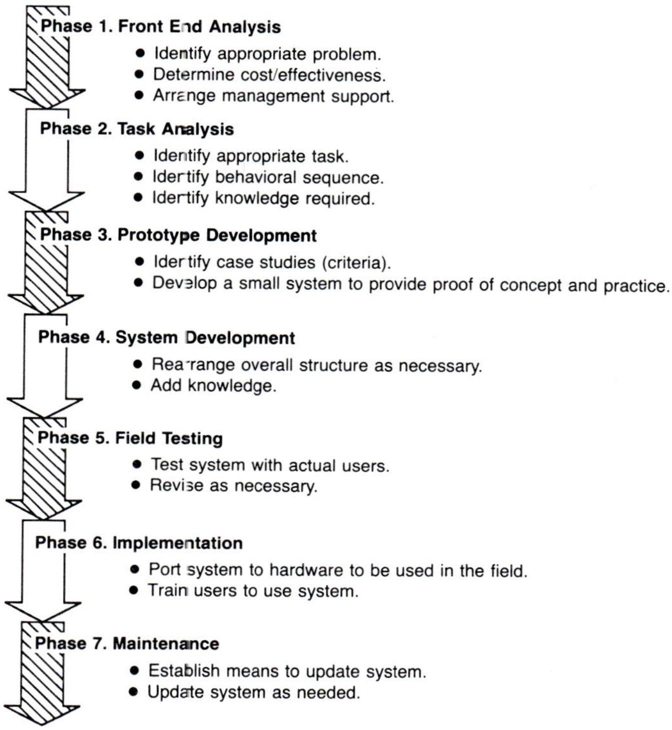

FIGURE 11-19. **Seven steps in expert system development.**

INFORMATION CENTERS

The concept of end-user computing was originally associated with information centers (ICs). These information centers helped nondata-processing personnel to interact directly with large mainframe computer facilities through new, user-friendly fourth-generation languages. Through the IC, users obtained the necessary skills and guidance to manipulate and analyze mainframe data, create and modify their own reports, produce graphs, and make ad hoc inquiries. Today, most ICs also support microcomputer applications. In fact, sometimes the IC assumes accountability for guiding and supporting acquisition of microcomputers throughout the organization. After some background on the emergence of the IC, the next section discusses their operation, services, and benefits. It concludes with some background on microcomputers in offices and the use of corporate computer stores.

Emergence of the Information Center

The concept of the information center was conceived by IBM and implemented at IBM Canada in 1974. The IC's original objective was to help reduce the application development backlog in data processing departments by allowing users to develop some of the easier applications themselves. Other changes were taking place in the data processing environment during the late 1960s and 70s that helped to set the stage for the emergence of ICs (see Figure 11-20).

FIGURE 11-20. Major factors in the growth of end-user computing.

- Development of fourth-generation computer languages.
- High demand for dp resources; large backlogs of work.
- Promotion of the concept by International Business Machines (IBM).
- Reports of early success stories.
- Introduction of low-cost microcomputers.
- Increase in computer literacy.

The need for ICs arose partly because of the centralized structure of most management information systems or data processing departments (MIS/DP). Users were required to submit requests that were then prioritized and acted on in turn. As the demand for data processing services grew, so did the list of requests. Often, high-priority requests were slipped into the queue in front of projects that had been waiting for many months. In many companies, project backlogs became two to three years long. Relationships between users and information departments deteriorated as the former realized that their work was not getting done. In addition, many organizations discovered a hidden backlog of applications desired but not requested because users knew there was a long waiting list. This situation was especially unfortunate because much of the backlog consisted of projects that were relatively simple compared to the large, complex projects that monopolized the time of the data processing professionals. Some of these simple projects were as straightforward as a one-time analyses of sales data. The IC allowed users to do for themselves some of the relatively simple tasks that MIS/DP would assign a low priority. Data processing professionals could focus on the large-scale systems development tasks.

Early ICs usually were set up as separate departments within the MIS/DP organization. The IC manager was most likely a former data processing application development manager with strong people skills. The IC was equipped with direct-access storage devices, some fourth-generation languages and packages, appropriate documentation, instructional materials, and a classroom. The computer that users accessed was either the centralized mainframe or a minicomputer system dedicated to IC operations. ICs were staffed by data processing professionals who were screened for their social and communication skills. These staff provided training, consulting, coaching, problem resolution, and other support services to users.

During the 1980s, implementation of ICs spread rapidly. A recent survey of 1080 information centers found that only 14 percent of them even existed in 1980. The number doubled to 28 percent in 1981 and increased by

25 percent in each of the following two years. The rapid growth of ICs is substantiated by other studies. Results from surveys by the American Management Association and the Diebold Group indicate that 80 percent of large companies have ICs.

Information Center Operation

The mission of an information center is to put computer technology into the hands of people who are not data processing professionals (end users). When an organization establishes an information center, the staff generally begins by "selling" the concept to end users through a series of orientation meetings. IC staff explain the center's objectives, resources, procedures, and how the IC can help users to meet some of their data processing needs. After users contact the IC, staff consult with them to obtain clear descriptions of intended projects and then help them to select and learn to use the appropriate application software.

IC staff also show users how to access needed information on computer files. First, the user must obtain authorization and a password to "sign on" to the computer system. The user must understand how the data is organized in the computer file. Generally, users are permitted to work only with copies of mainframe production files. An IC staff member generally does the work necessary to obtain ("extract") the data.

As IC users begin to work on their projects, IC staff members answer questions and troubleshoot problems, then coach and encourage as new users gain confidence. They continue to consult with experienced users regarding new applications. Generally, IC staff avoid actually programming applications for users.

Knowledge workers use ICs to access, display, sort, query, and report on data accumulated and stored on the computer. For example, marketing researchers can use data from an order processing and inventory system to assess market performance and trends. Actuaries use APL, a symbolic mathematical fourth-generation language, to compute actuarial statistics and calculate premiums for insurance products. The ten steps required to implement an IC are summarized in Figure 11-21.

FIGURE 11-21. **Ten steps required to implement an information center.**

1. Gain sponsorship for the IC from an advisory group representing management. Shared organizational support from the outset will ease the implementation process.
2. Conduct a comprehensive needs assessment. Information gathered in this way can help structure the IC plan to anticipate current and future needs.
3. Define and allocate adequate resources for implementation to avoid the "slow starvation" of insufficient funding.
4. Gain the support of end users, upper management, and MIS by directing specific marketing efforts toward these three important groups.
5. Establish a training policy early because as the IC matures, the demand for training increases.

FIGURE 11-21. (continued)

6. Select staff members carefully. Communication skills and the ability to learn and use varied computing tools are the key requirements.
7. Start with a pilot project rather than full-scale implementation. Select an enthusiastic group of users with a project that is likely to succeed.
8. Assume a partnership position with MIS to avoid conflict over boundaries and responsibilities for computing services. Communicate regularly and stress that MIS and the IC should pursue the same organizational goals.
9. Standardize the selection and evaluation processes for hardware and software, accounting for user needs as well as product quality.
10. Determine the need for a chargeback mechanism. Such a mechanism can give users and the organization a concrete way to measure the value of services and a means of tracking IC success and growth.

Information Center Services

Services provided by information centers are summarized in Figure 11-22. Note that the services offered most frequently are training, demonstrations of end-user packages and equipment, analysis of user applications, and problem resolution. Information centers may also sponsor user groups, publish newsletters and directories of microcomputer users, or initiate catalogs of IC applications.

FIGURE 11-22. A survey of services provided by information centers.

Service	1985	1987
Analyzing end-user requirements	79%	92%
Training end users	86%	86%
Selecting end-user hardware and software	67%	86%
Providing mainframe/micro link	43%	84%
Providing hotline support	78%	81%
Providing access to corporate data	58%	80%
Providing computer graphics facility	59%	68%
Providing application programming	16%	33%

Benefits of the Information Center

Information centers provide several benefits to organizations, users, and MIS/DP departments. Organizations benefit from increased computer literacy among business staff. Users gain a greater appreciation of the MIS/DP department's role in the organization and learn how to work with data processing resources. Users benefit by obtaining timely solutions to their problems. Moreover, users are free to go beyond their immediate analysis to explore additional questions as they arise. The MIS/DP department benefits from the improved rapport with users created through the cooperative atmosphere of the IC. Although the main impetus for introducing ICs was to reduce data processing backlogs, ironically this is the one benefit that organizations achieve least often. ICs are generally credited, however, in reducing the invisible backlog of low-priority applications that were previously never submitted to MIS/DP departments because of anticipated delays. Figure 11-23 presents a list of benefits that information centers provide to users.

- Timely solutions to user problems.
- Improved computer literacy.
- Increased job productivity. Routine information can be processed more quickly.
- Staff spend less time performing repetitive calculations and producing reports.
- Improved use of information.
- Improved DP/user relations.
- Reduction of DP backlog.
- Better training procedures.
- Increased standardization of microcomputer hardware.
- Increased micro/mainframe compatibility.

FIGURE 11-23. Benefits that information centers provide to users.

Application Products in Information Centers

A wide range of mainframe products are used in information centers. Figure 11-24 presents a list of the most frequently used mainframe and minicomputer products according to a recent survey of information centers. Microcomputers are also widely used in information centers, although ICs originally offered predominantly mainframe or minicomputer tools. The leading microcomputer products used in information centers are listed in Figure 11-25. Naturally, no one information center would use all the products listed. Most ICs offer several standard application products and support them with the necessary training, consulting, and assistance.

- SAS (Statistical Analysis System)
- SAS/GRAPH (Statistical Analysis System/Graphic Interface)
- ISPF (Interactive dialogue manager)
- CMS (Conversational Monitoring System)
- FOCUS (Field-Oriented Component Usage Survey)
- TELL-A-GRAF (comprehensive mainframe graphics package by ISSCO)
- SAS/FSP (Statistical Analysis System/with FS Edit, Browse, Letter, and List)
- GDDM (Graphical Data Display Manager)
- JCL (Job Control Language)
- PROFS (PRofessional OFfice System)
- IFPS (Interactive Financial Planning System)
- ADRS (A Departmental Reporting System)
- EASYTRIEVE PLUS (information retrieval and query package by Pansophic)
- SAS/OR (Statistical Analysis System/OR option)
- RAMIS (fourth-generation language)
- APL/DI (A Programming Language/Data Interface
- QBE/SQL (Query-by-Example/Structured Query Language)
- ANSWER/DB (information retrieval and query package by Sterling Software)
- INFORMATION CENTER 1 (information retrieval and query package by IBM)
- NOMAD2 (4GL marketed by Dun and Bradstreet)
- AS (Application Systems)
- INQUIRE

FIGURE 11-24. Mainframe and minicomputer products used in information centers.

FIGURE 11-25. Leading microcomputer products used in information centers.

1. **1-2-3**
   Lotus Development Corp.
2. **dBase III Plus**
   Ashton-Tate
3. **Multimate Advantage**
   Ashton-Tate
4. **Crosstalk XVI**
   Microstuf
5. **Sideways**
   Funk Software
6. **Symphony**
   Lotus Development Corp.
7. **Multimate**
   Ashton-Tate
8. **PC-DOS**
   IBM
9. **Displaywrite 3**
   IBM
10. **Norton Utilities**
    Peter Norton Computing
11. **Dataease**
    Software Solutions
12. **Chart-Master**
    Ashton-Tate
13. **Fastback**
    Fifth Generation Systems
14. **Sidekick**
    Borland International
15. **Direct Access**
    Delta Technology
16. **Officewriter**
    Office Solutions
17. **WordPerfect**
    WordPerfect Corp.
18. **pfs:Write**
    Software Publishing
19. **Fixed Disk Organizer**
    IBM
20. **Sign-Master**
    Ashton-Tate
21. **SPF-PC**
    Command Technology Corp.
22. **Relay Gold**
    VM Personal Computing
23. **Wordstar Professional**
    Micropro
24. **Rbase:5000**
    Microrim
25. **Diagram-Master**
    Ashton-Tate
26. **Spreadsheet Auditor**
    Consumers Software
27. **Superkey**
    Borland International
28. **PC/Focus**
    Information Builders
29. **Power-base**
    Compuware
30. **Project Manager Workbench**
    Applied Business Technology

Corporate Computer Stores

To guide and control the acquisition of microcomputer hardware and software by end users, some large organizations have established "computer stores" or "microcomputer centers." Computer stores may be sponsored by the IC or may be set up as a separate unit of the information systems department. Computer stores offer a limited set of carefully evaluated microcomputer hardware and software, corporate standards, and strategies. Personnel are free to browse in the store and seek advice. Potential users obtain guidance concerning the type of system that would best fulfill their needs. Personnel may experiment with various hardware and software to evaluate their appropriateness.

Organizations with computer stores leave purchase decisions to the user department. As an inducement to select from recommended equipment, companies typically provide in-house support for *only* the hardware and software offered through the computer store. The stores pass on discounts from volume purchases to the user departments. By coordinating the purchase of microcomputers, companies are able to keep records of the number of users and types of hardware and software.

The computer store works successfully in large organizations where each division operates rather autonomously. In large organizations with strong centralized management and most small organizations, the acquisition of microcomputers is controlled through the office systems department, information center, data processing department, comptrollers, or another appropriate department.

THE GROWTH OF END-USER COMPUTING: MICROCOMPUTERS IN THE OFFICE

The introduction and growth of microcomputers in the office has had a major impact on end-user computing. In fact, the term *end-user computing* is often used synonymously with the term *microcomputing*. The amount of computing power in the hands of users continues to increase dramatically. The microcomputers that first found their way into the business office in the early 1980s typically had 64K of internal memory and two 180K floppy disk drives. By the mid 1980s, however, standard microcomputer configurations in business offices were more likely to be 640K of internal memory with a 10-megabyte hard disk in addition to the two floppy drives. Today, 20- and 30-megabyte hard disks on desktops are not uncommon, and newer, more powerful microcomputers are becoming standard. By the end of the decade, every user who needs a microcomputer will probably have one at his or her desk.

As the variety and capabilities of microcomputer software programs increase, users will become more sophisticated. New employees will bring their computer skills into the workplace, and older employees will gradually gain experience. Business magazines and popular computing journals will provide new ideas for improved information processing.

Today, end-user computing is a major force shaping the workplace. Armed with computer skills, end users can increase job efficiency and improve decision making. In fact, research by MIT's Sloan School of Management projects that in the next ten years, 75 percent of business programming will be performed directly by users.

COMPUTERS IN THE PROFESSIONAL OFFICE

Professional offices such as legal and medical offices share many characteristics of business offices but have unique requirements. They are good examples of how office automation is serving the information processing needs of professionals.

Legal Offices

Law firms and legal departments within large corporations find office automation to be extremely beneficial. Originally, only large legal firms could afford computers. Now, with microcomputers and low-cost word processors, even small legal offices depend on automation tools. Legal offices are growing more innovative in using computers for a wide range of applications such as drafting laws by state and federal legislators, adjudicating cases, researching legal precedents, and managing docket calendars—not to mention the obvious need for preparing correspondence and legal documents.

A recent study of the American Bar Association (ABA) membership indicated that 57.9 percent of ABA legal firms have personal computers, 55.2 percent use dedicated word processors, 16.8 percent use minicomputers, and 6.1 percent use mainframes. Typical uses of the equipment revealed by the study are summarized in Figure 11-26. The most frequently reported applications included word processing, billing, accounts payable and receivable, docket control, litigation support, and legal research. According to the study, the three main public database services used for legal research are Lexis with 27.2 percent of the usage, Westlaw with 15.4 percent, and Nexis with 14.8 percent.

FIGURE 11-26. Common computer applications in law offices.

Application	Percent
Word processing	80.1
Billing	53.4
Accounts payable and receivable	36.7
General ledger applications	25.2
Docket control	22.0
Litigation support	19.4
Legal research	15.8

Computers are also changing the way work is done in law offices. According to Isaac Asimov, a leading science fiction writer, "Cold-blooded computers will make the United States legal systems more just and the American public less litigious over the next 70 years." Writing in the *Journal of the American Bar Association*, Asimov said, "Computers will grow more elaborate and versatile and cope better with the complexities of law, judgments, and precedents and, as a result, there will be fewer appeals, fewer delays, faster and shorter trials, more out-of-court settlements, and, most of all, fewer cases brought to court in the first place. With computers in action, there will be increasingly little chance of an egregious mistake in legal strategy or tactics and a diminishing hope of unpredictability on the part of the judge." Calling today's courts "uncivilized," Asimov explained that "competing lawyers need not consider results inevitable; they can simply wait for the opposition to make a mistake, or they can wait for a judge to make a blunder or a jury to be hoodwinked. Virtually every case, therefore, is worth trying, for it offers some hope of winning."[5]

The following example illustrates the use of office automation in a legal office:

> The legal department at Ryder Systems, a $2.8 billion transportation and business service company, is illustrative of automation in legal offices. Its legal department handles acquisitions, Securities and Exchange Commission work, contracts for the company's seven divisions, and leasing agreements, as well as general corporate legal functions. The office's integrated services provide word processing, calendaring, electronic mail and messaging, and directory service, in addition to communications to public databases and corporate mainframes.
>
> Attorneys communicate with each other through electronic messages and mail, exchanging memos and reports electronically. Attorneys can retrieve items quickly or combine new and previously created (cut-and-paste) text. Several attorneys now keep reminder lists. They keep track of billable time and print out the notes at the end of the day for the billing clerk.
>
> Paralegals find the calendaring function essential for their time-critical work of filing deadlines and tracking cases. Paralegals can research precedents for cases through legal files in public databases right at their desks.
>
> The legal department realized productivity gains in two major areas through its office automation system. First, the distributed word processing has provided much faster turnaround for documents. Documents that used to take a day to produce can now be drafted, revised, and printed in an hour, without anyone standing in line for a terminal or waiting for staff support. Second, the integrated office system has provided the legal office with much more efficient communications. Lawyers and staff can exchange information much faster, even at night or on weekends. The legal administrative assistant has estimated that the system saves her three or four hours a day by reducing the time formerly spent typing, copying, and circulating materials.

Medical Offices

Office automation can be indispensable in medical practice and research, training, hospital administration, and pharmaceutical distribution. By computerizing their patients' records and billing systems, doctors find they can maintain more detailed, accurate records and save valuable time. Less time spent on administrative chores means more time to spend with patients. Moreover, better records provide many benefits beyond good patient care. For example, a gynecologist in New Jersey used a personal computer to design and send a questionnaire to patients whose payments were delinquent. Although many patients do not pay because they cannot, he discovered that others withhold payment because they are dissatisfied. The questionnaire gave patients an opportunity to express hostility and helped the doctor better understand problems. Moreover, pressing disgruntled patients for payment can lead to unwarranted malpractice charges. Thus the gynecologist found that computerized billing helped avoid malpractice suits. For patients who could not pay, the computer made it easy to develop a payment plan to spread the costs over time.

The computer can also help doctors with decision making. For example, a doctor can analyze records to determine if a procedure is performed often enough to cover the cost of equipment or if it is more cost effective to use an independent laboratory. A doctor can also analyze patients' records to assess trends in treatment or increases in symptoms or diseases.

One innovative doctor in Connecticut has a personal computer with a modem in his home. When he receives an emergency call at home, he dials up the computer in his office to check the patient's medical record.

The medical office is another example of how computers can be used innovatively. Office automation can reduce time spent on administrative tasks and give medical professionals more time to devote to medicine.

SUMMARY

Office automation and end-user computing are proliferating to support professional and technical knowledge workers who never dreamed they would need—much less want—a computer at their fingertips. Research indicates that the growth of end-user computing is several times that of conventional systems. A growing user population is applying this new-found power to a wide range of applications, the most prevalent of which are word processing, electronic spreadsheets, database management, business graphics, desktop publishing, integrated software, fourth-generation languages, and small expert system tools. Computers in the workplace help knowledge workers increase efficiency and effectiveness, so they can devote more time to the tasks that put their expertise to best use.

Office automation and end-user computing are changing the way knowledge workers do their work. The concept of end-user computing refers to such use in the workplace by business personnel. Experience indicates that the most innovative ideas originate with specialists who can apply technology to their own business needs.

New organizational concepts, such as information centers and corporate computer stores, have developed into functional units that assist end users with applications. Information centers provide a focal point for technical assistance, training, and problem solving. In some cases, corporate computer stores are charged with guiding end users' acquisition of microcomputer hardware and software. In most organizations, the trend is to consolidate support for end-user computing within the office systems department. As microcomputers become the preferred workstations and work procedures change, responsibilities of office automation and information-center groups often overlap. Merging the two provides a logical point for supporting automation in the workplace.

DISCUSSION QUESTIONS

1. Describe the concept of end-user computing. What factors have fueled its rapid growth and acceptance in organizations?
2. The eight categories of application software described for professionals are financial software, word processing, fourth-generation languages, data management, graphics, desktop publishing, integrated software, and intelligent job aids. Explain how each application might be used by the following professionals:
   a. A certified public accountant.
   b. A college professor.
   c. A corporate attorney.
3. How do spreadsheets differ from modeling software?
4. Word processing tools have resulted in a need for everyone to know how to keyboard. Do you agree? Discuss.
5. Assume you are responsible for setting up a DBMS for the three individuals in Question 2. Describe the steps you would follow in each situation.
6. A picture is worth a thousand words. What would the originator of this statement have thought about today's graphics software?
7. Why is desktop publishing considered a growth area for office automation?
8. Integrated software packages offer various levels of integration. Compare a static with a dynamic system.
9. List three advantages and disadvantages of integrated software.
10. Describe the evolution of the information center. What factors led to its rapid growth? What role may you expect the information center of the future to play?
11. How does the corporate computer store help standardize an organization's microcomputer offerings?

APPLICATION EXERCISES

1. Ask a professional worker who uses a computer to identify the tools he or she uses. Which tools are most popular? Why?
2. Visit a software store and list the applications available. Ask for a demonstration of one or two end-user packages.
3. Learn to use the graphics package of your choice. Prepare a pie chart and a bar chart of the "Information Center Services" data presented in Figure 11-22 on page 338. Which chart presents the data more effectively? Why?

SUGGESTED READINGS

1985 AMA Report on Information Centers (New York: American Management Association, 1985).

Atre, Shaku. *Information Center: Strategies and Case Studies* (Boston: Weingarten, 1986).

Federal Office Automation Support Center. *Desktop Publishing Guide* (Falls Church, Va.: Office of Software Development and Information Technology, 1988).

SALES AND MARKETING APPLICATIONS

CHAPTER

12

OBJECTIVES

After completing this chapter, the reader should be able to meet the following objectives:

- Identify sales applications for office automation technologies.
- Explain how project management software helps a salesperson identify customers.
- Explain the concept of telemarketing and offer examples of its business applications.
- Explain how a salesperson with a portable computer can develop timely sales illustrations, proposals, and access to inventory data.
- Describe how a salesperson using office automation can improve sales follow-up.
- Identify instances in which computer-based training is appropriate for sales staff.
- List tools that aid managers in planning, managing, and evaluating sales operations.
- Compare electronic mail with voice messaging systems for handling sales applications.
- Compare teleconferencing with Videotex systems.
- Summarize the value of a portable computer to the salesperson.

KEY TERMS

direct response marketing
interactive video
kiosk
prospect management
sales illustrations
telemarketing
Videotex

INTRODUCTION

Companies have compelling financial reasons for trying to improve sales-force productivity. The average industrial products salesperson makes $36,000 a year and calls on three to eight customers daily. Excluding compensation, the average sales call costs $102. Most sales representatives spend only 35 percent of their time actually selling, 35 percent traveling, and 30 percent on paperwork. Sales managers find that selling time can be increased as much as 50 percent with better time management. More selling time generally translates into higher sales and profits. Companies can use office systems technologies to improve sales management and support. Computers help reduce paperwork, make better information available faster, focus on the best leads, and provide customer service.

Sales personnel must know their business and understand how company products and services can meet customer needs. With the diverse array of products and services offered by industries today, this is not easy. Just think of the options available to today's consumer, for example, in stereo equipment. Making an intelligent choice requires considerable time and research, and a well-informed salesperson can be very helpful. Moreover, customers often look to salespeople for product availability, shipping, invoicing, and account information. Computers can provide sales personnel a wealth of such information at their fingertips.

Until recently, computer-based sales support has been rare. One software service and consulting firm estimated that in 1986 less than 2 percent of corporate resources among Fortune 1000 companies was applied toward sales and marketing functions. Another estimate showed that in 1987 about 20 percent of all companies were using some form of sales and marketing software. Today, microcomputers, portable computers, and office automation software are providing new solutions.

Office automation software provides flexible alternatives that salespeople can adapt to personal styles. Salespeople must accurately assess customer needs and determine which combination best meets those needs. Presentation of product features or services must be tailored to the client's needs, and these demands go beyond normal data processing. Although data processing systems in service industries such as insurance often provide sales proposals and product quotations, opportunities to tailor these reports are limited. With office automation tools, however, salespersons can tailor reports to client needs. In addition, they can maintain computerized client lists, generate customized sales letters, and communicate with their offices and corporate headquarters.

In addition to providing office automation for sales support, microcomputers and portable computers provide access to mainframe systems such as inventory and order entry. To see a salesperson toting a computer can be impressive. Salespersons who can respond immediately to customer questions and demonstrate how the product meets the customer's needs have a competitive advantage. Customers are impressed because they receive better service from salespersons who are prepared to help them evaluate products and services.

Not all salespeople welcome computer tools, however; many prefer communicating by voice to typing commands. They may resent having to learn computer codes and programs. They may feel that keying in their orders is clerical work, even if it saves time and provides other advantages. Salespeople are sometimes concerned that orders will get lost in the computer.

Even management support does not guarantee acceptance. When the Life Insurance Company of Virginia announced that its agents were going to buy 2000 portable computers, only 150 brokers made the $4000 investment the first year. To avoid trauma, many companies move carefully. For example, when a top salesperson persists in making personal telephone calls instead of computer inquiries to obtain information relating to order status, it is difficult for management to be insistent.

Companies use various approaches to "sell" sales staff on the use of computers. Large companies may have professional programmers develop startup applications that are pilot-tested with enthusiastic salespeople. After establishing the benefits, the company makes computers available to all its sales staff. Some companies provide portable computers to top salespeople first, as both a reward and an incentive for others.

Some salespeople worry about losing autonomy when all their records are easily available to the manager. Even though a manager may be able to help staff identify ways to improve performance, scrutiny may not be welcomed. Concerns for privacy also arise, since most sales work is fiercely competitive.

For automation to work, sales personnel must be committed to using the system. It does not work well unless salespeople put all their customer records into the computer and keep it up to date. Salespeople may find it hard to give up paper notes and memos.

Major business objectives for sales support that office automation can help meet include the following:

1. Reducing the preparation time a salesperson spends at the office and increasing the time available for selling.
2. Expanding the territory a salesperson can handle.
3. Providing service to clients efficiently and effectively to maintain established business.
4. Developing sales expertise.

This chapter discusses how automation software can help meet these objectives. It explores specialized applications that help salespersons and their managers better manage the process. The chapter concludes with system alternatives such as portable computers, communications, and Videotex.

SALES APPLICATIONS

The types and numbers of sales applications are expanding daily. Software producers estimate that more than 50 sales-oriented programs are available for microcomputers and dozens more for large computer systems (see Figure 12-1). Some programs are flexible and can be adapted to individual sales approaches. Other programs are based on specific philosophies and methods.

FIGURE 12-1. Representative sales and marketing software.

VENDOR	PRODUCT	PRICE	RUNS ON	SALES PERSON	SALES MANAGER	TELE-MARKETING	CUSTOMER SUPPORT
Absolut Software 2001Beacon St. Boston, MA 02146	**Sales & Mktg. Management**	$8,000 +	Minis	X	X		
Adelie Corp. 125 Cambridge Pk. Dr. Cambridge, MA 02140	**Close**	$60,000 and up	Mainframe Micro	X	X	X	
Breuer & Co. 54 Middlesex Tpke. Bedford, MA 01730	**Keyword**	$5,000	Mini	X	X		
Brock Control Systems 1600 Parkwood Circle Atlanta, GA 30339	**Sales Activity Manager**	$3400/ node	All	X	X	X	X
Business Control Corp. 3–7 W. First St. Clifton, NJ 07011	**Impact**	$1,000/ intro	Mini	X		X	
Chang Labs 5300 Stevens Creek Blvd. San Jose, CA 95129	**Fileplan Sales** **CAT**	$199.95	Micro	X X	 X		
Computer Assoc. Int'l. 2195 Fortune Drive San Jose, CA 95131	**Easysales Pro**	$495	Micro	X	X		
Computer Technology Consultants, Inc. 1600 Pennsylvania Ave. York, PA 17404	**Automated Sales Info. Sys. (ASIS)**	$2,450 Micro	Mainframe Mini	X	X	X	X
Conductor Software 5215 N. O'Connor Blvd. Irving, TX 75039	**ACT**	$395	Micro	X			
Control Data Business Info Systems 1900 Market St. #501 Philadelphia, PA 19103	**Marksman**	$70,000 $500,000	Mainframe	X	X	X	X
CTek Software 30 Rockefeller Plaza New York, NY 10112	**Clientrak**	$3,000	Mainframe Mini Micro	X	X	X	
Envoy Systems Corp. 1432 Main St. Waltham, MA 02154	**Salesmate**	$100/ mo./rep.	Mainframe Micro	X	X		
Excalibur Sources P.O. Box 467220 Atlanta, GA 30346	**Excell**	$395– $1,000	Micro	X			
Executive Data Sys. 1845 The Exchange Atlanta, GA 30339	**Prospector**	$300	Micro	X	X		
High Calibur Systems 165 Madison Ave. New York, NY 10016	**Saleseye**	$89	Micro	X	X		
Integrated Marketing 6159 Executive Blvd. Rockville, MD 20852	**Market Info. Sys.**	$300/yr.	Mini	X	X		

FIGURE 12–1. (continued)

VENDOR	PRODUCT	PRICE	RUNS ON	SALES PERSON	SALES MANAGER	TELE-MARKETING	CONSUMER SUPPORT
Interactive Systems 600 Suffolk St. Lowell, MA 01854	**Omnitrac**	\$395– \$8000	Mini Micro	X	X		
Intro-Logic Inc. 24700 Northwestern Hwy. Southfield, MI 48075	**Marketing Info. System**	\$2,000	Micro	X	X		
JEB Systems 32 Daniel Webster Hwy. Merrimack, NH 03054	**Mkt. Mgmt. System**	\$595– \$3,625	Micro	X	X	X	
Key Systems 512 Executive Park Louisville, KY 40207	**Prospecting**	\$395	Micro	X	X		
KLS Inc. 862 Union St. Manchester, NH 03104	**Snap**	\$4,500	Micro	X	X		
Market Power Inc. 11780 Rough & Ready Rd. Rough & Ready, CA 95975	**Sales Manager** **Sales Wizard**	\$575– \$1,295 \$99	Micro Micro	X X	X		
Marketing Info. Systems 906 University St. Evanston, IL 60201	**MSM**	\$5,000 +	Mini Micro	X	X	X	X
Mastersoft Inc. 4621 N. 16th St. Phoenix, AZ 85016	**Sales Master**	\$695	Micro	X			
MCS Software P.O. Box 17850 Salt Lake Cy, UT 84117	**The Organizer**	—	Micro	X			
Mitchell Mgmt. Systems 2000 West Park Drive Westborough, MA 01581	**Sales & Mktg. Manager**	\$38,000	Mini Micro	X	X		
ODS Inc. 1011 E. Touhy Ave. Des Plaines, IL 60018	**Sales Consultant**	\$295	Micro	X	X		
Persoft Inc. 600 W. Cummings Park Woburn, MA 01801	**More/2**	\$375,000	Mainframe	Dir. Mail			
PLC Systems 1250 State St. Springfield, MA 01133	**Sales Link**	\$100,000+	Mainframe	X	X	X	
Portable Computer Solutions 125 Cambridge Pk. Dr. Cambridge, MA 02140	**PCS Sales Manager**	\$348– \$695	Micro	X			
Profidex Corp. 90 West St. New York, NY 10006	**Scamp**	\$695– \$100,000	Mini Micro	X	X	X	X
Prophecy Dev. Corp. Park Plaza Boston, MA 02116	**Profit Tool**	\$1,990	Micro	X			

FIGURE 12–1. (continued)

VENDOR	PRODUCT	PRICE	RUNS ON	SALES PERSON	SALES MANAGER	TELE-MARKETING	CONSUMER SUPPORT
Sales Technologies 3390 Peachtree Rd. Atlanta, GA 30326	**Salesman Software**	$200,000+	Mini Micro	X	X	X	
Scientific Mktg. 3303 Harbor Blvd. Costa Mesa, CA 92626	**Marketfax**	$695 +	Mini Micro	X	X		
Softworks Inc. 7700 Old Branch Ave. Clinton, MD 20735	**Markis**	$349	Micro	X	X		
Streamline Software 14 Perimeter Ctr. E. Atlanta, GA 30346	**Sales Repeater**	$249	Micro	X			
Systems Plus Inc. 500 Clyde Ave. Mountain VIew, CA 94043	**Lead Manager**	$350	Micro	X	X		
Target Systems Corp. 33 Boston Post Rd. W. Marlboro, MA 01752	**Target Sales**	$995	Mini	X	X	X	
Technology Developmt. P.O. Box 957 Salem, NH 03079	**Salemaker**	$70,000	Mini Micro	X	X	X	
Thomcomp Inc. 325 Chestnut St. Philadelphia, PA 19106	**Start of Sale (S.O.S.)**	$299	Micro	X	X		
Thoughtware Inc. 2699 Bayshore Dr. Coconut Grove, FL 33133	**Sell!Sell!Sell!**	$99	Micro	X	X		
Tiny Systems Inc. 634 S. Central Expwy. Richardson, TX 75080	**Track**	—	Micro	X			
Traveling Software 11050 Fifth Ave. Seattle, WA 98125	**Traveling Software**	$99	Micro	X			
Travis DataTrak Inc. 381 Elliot St. Newton, MA 02164	**Telepro**	$995	Mini Micro	X	X	X	
VanArsdale Assts. P.O. Box 12841 Raleigh, NC 27605	**Marketbase**	$5,000	Mini	X	X		

Programs may be designed for individual use, or several salespersons may share the same database. Shared programs generally include built-in security or privacy features. A number of sales management programs, designed to run on portable computers with built-in modems, provide automatic telephone dialing and other customized communication features. Programs also vary considerably in their ease of use. Sophisticated features often come at the cost of greater complexity.

As an alternative to application packages, large companies may develop their own sales-prospecting software and distribute it on diskettes to all field offices. Frequently these programs use a generic database package, such as dBase III or Paradox.

This section provides an overview of current applications and insight into what tomorrow's salesperson may find to be invaluable tools. The following specific applications are discussed:

- Sales prospecting
  - Prospect management
  - Appointment calendars and tickler files
  - Form letters and reports
- Promotional and sales materials
- Sales illustrations
- Sales proposals
- Access to inventory data
  - Order entry
  - Order status checking
- Sales follow-up
- Sales training
  - Product training
  - Sales training
  - Interactive video
- Sales management
  - Electronic mailboxes
  - Voice message systems
  - Teleconferencing
  - Videotex

Sales Prospecting

Good salespersons know who their prospective clients are. Today's technology offers a number of advantages over the notebooks and card files that have been the salesperson's stock and trade for decades.

Prospect Management Software

Prospect management software enables salespersons to keep a directory of potential clients. Using such programs, sales personnel develop databases of prospects from sources such as advertising, marketing activities, or client referrals purchased from independent firms. By specifying selection criteria, they can then generate lists of enterprises in their territories, along with names of appropriate contacts. Prospects can be selected—or *qualified*—by any appropriate set of criteria designated by the salesperson. For example, a salesperson might select firms with sales between $1 million and $5 million, employing 10 to 50 people, in oil-related industries in the Southwest. By refining the list, they can increase the likelihood that telephone calls or personal visits will produce sales. The more sophisticated programs include additional features (described below) to further reduce paperwork and information retrieval time.

Appointment Calendars and Tickler Files

Prospect management programs often incorporate an appointment calendar and tickler file to help salespeople schedule and follow up on sales calls. Appointment calendars allow sales professionals to set detailed itineraries of sales appointments and phone calls. Salespersons may be able to add extensive comments with each entry, including sales history, personal information, and tickler files concerning specific products or services. A tickler file is a *reminder* list—things that need to be done on a particular day. Some salespersons like to make notes of personal information about their prospects, such as their family, hobbies, business or social contacts in common, and product preferences. In addition, several programs provide recordkeeping to retain details of meetings and sales.

Form Letters and Reports

Comprehensive prospect management software also enables sales personnel to generate form letters and reports. Form letters contain codes to mark insertion points for variable information, such as date, name, address, product, and price. These letters can be merged with information from the prospect database to mass-produce customized letters. The prospect management program may include a word processing module to create form letters, or may work with one or more separate word processing programs. Form letter generation is useful for creating sales letters, product quotations, or follow-up letters. Some programs even provide sample letters.

Standard report formats enable salespersons to generate lists of leads, customer reports, or mailing labels. Standard reports include commission summaries, expense reports, sales transactions, sales projections, sales quota evaluations, and various sales analyses.

A typical prospect management program is described in the following example:

> A prospect name and address database stores detailed information, including company descriptions, complete contact information, product and service requirements, account potential, general comments, and followup history. Key items are *qualifiers,* which allow salespersons to categorize prospects according to criteria they define. For example, the database might be categorized into customers, prospects, and potential prospects. Such data may be classified according to industry type, region, size, or any other criteria relevant to the salesperson's market. Salespersons can then sort, select, and retrieve information in a variety of ways depending upon their needs at a specific time.

All the features of prospect management software are directed toward one goal: helping salespersons reduce the time spent in the office and increase the time available to sell products and provide customer service. With more time for selling, salespersons can cover their territories more thoroughly or expand their size. In either case, the bottom line is increased sales and profits.

Telemarketing

Telemarketing uses a telephone to perform traditional marketing activities, usually with the aid of computerized databases. Telemarketing provides opportunities for both sales prospecting and direct marketing. As a sales prospecting tool, telemarketing enables potential clients to qualify themselves and request additional information or a visit from a salesperson. A direct marketing tool, telemarketing is a substitute for the salesperson. Also referred to as *direct response marketing,* telemarketing is a technology-driven sales method.

Telemarketing is reaching a public that is increasingly receptive to advanced technology. People have grown accustomed to computers and their technological spinoffs (such as automatic teller machines) and accept direct response marketing techniques more readily than they formerly did. At one time, clients were uncomfortable unless dealing directly with a person, but today, purchasers are more willing to call a toll-free 800 number or make purchases through the mail. In fact, today's time-conscious consumers often prefer the immediacy of direct response purchasing.

With the aid of computerized databases of consumer information, automated dialers, and other tools, telemarketing can be used to qualify sales leads, provide follow-up services, supplement face-to-face selling, support customers who are too small or too distant to warrant personal visits, or provide service hotlines for customer inquiries or complaints. Using headsets to free both hands to work at the computer console, telemarketing specialists provide courteous, professional assistance to consumers.

Effective telemarketing programs must be carefully designed and implemented. Network facilities must be properly sized and configured to handle inward or outward bound telemarketing programs. Careful attention must be paid to training telemarketing specialists. Effective telemarketing programs focus on the customer and the customer's needs and avoid force-fitting structured marketing techniques.

Electronic kiosks One approach to sales prospecting that is receiving considerable attention is *kiosks.* Kiosks are an electronic adaptation of the French kiosks, the round, free-standing bulletin boards for which the streets of Paris are famous (see Figure 12-2).

The new electronic kiosks employ a combination of video and computer technologies to provide marketing information and client order entry. Attractively designed kiosks, in shopping malls, hotel lobbies, or other public places, offer information on a variety of products and services. The user selects topics of interest and receives more information. Users can tailor the desired information to their own interests by selecting from a series of menu options. A typical electronic kiosk is shown in Figure 12-3.

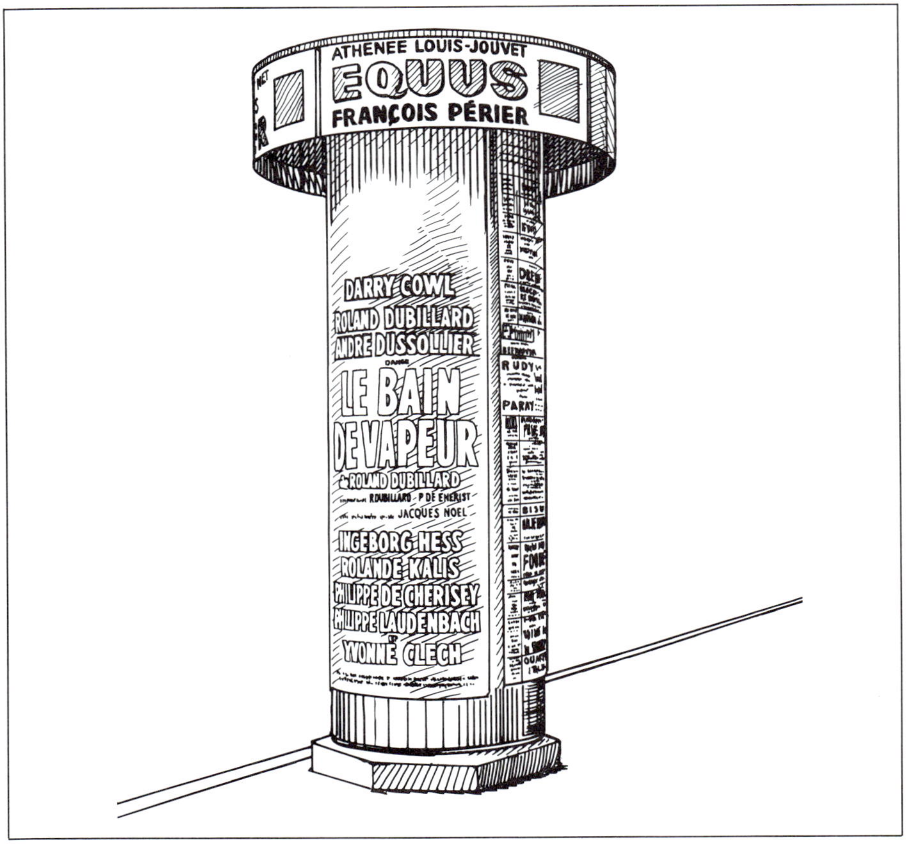

FIGURE 12-2. A typical kiosk on a street in Paris.

When employed for sales prospecting in the insurance industry, for example, kiosk technology enables clients to qualify themselves. Prospects respond to questions that are designed to analyze their financial situation, family status, investment objectives, adequacy of insurance coverage, and other pertinent information to determine which insurance products provide the best investment for their needs. If interested, prospects can request that a salesperson call on them, or perhaps (in the future) fill out an application for a policy then and there.

According to a popular insurance industry publication,

> Direct response marketers see a day coming when a totally automated insurance product will be widely accepted by the public. We would like to think that we could put up a kiosk in which an individual or family could select video presentations that would fully explain various insurance products, then contact a licensed agent at our telemarketing center via a voice-actuated phone and receive a quote or additional information based on their own situation and needs. This is something that is definitely coming in the future but will require extensive testing to ensure success.[1]

FIGURE 12-3.
An electronic kiosk.

Sales Illustrations

Comparison shopping is important to most buyers. In certain industries, such as finance and insurance, comparing products is complex and time-consuming. Using sales illustrations, however, salespeople can demonstrate the benefits of their products. For example, when purchasing financial products, customers want to know how the value of one investment compares with alternatives. How will slightly higher or lower interest rates or premiums change the accumulation of cash value in life insurance policies? Manual calculations are time-consuming and complex. When agents have to go back to the office to calculate options, they waste time and may lose the sale. By carrying portable computers with appropriate software, they can calculate alternatives in the client's office or home.

An agent for Life Insurance Company of Virginia claimed his portable computer paid for itself the very first day, when he wrote 11 policy applications. Instead of taking almost an hour to write one proposal in a face-to-face interview, he found that he could write three or four variations in 35 minutes. He claimed that the portable computer helped him earn a $15,000 commission on just one sale:

> Inquiring about a company's interest in group health insurance, he found its president studying bids for "key-man" insurance on top executives. "I went to the car and got the computer," the agent reported. "I said, would you like quotes on using our universal life at the same figure?" He closed that sale and then made successful bids for other major parts of the company's insurance.[2]

Sales Proposals

A sales proposal provides detailed written information about a product or service, tailored to the needs of a client. It is common practice for commercial and government agencies to issue a Request for Proposal (RFP) outlining their requirements and inviting suppliers to submit a sales proposal. The practice may be mandated by competitive bidding requirements. In other instances, it is considered a wise business practice for the purchase of complex or high-priced products or services, especially those that require tailoring to the client's requirements. Sales proposals are commonly used, in response to RFPs, for computer or industrial equipment and financial products (such as pension programs), to name just a few applications.

Standardized proposals can be developed using word processing software so that a sales representative or manager enters only the information that is unique to a client. A customized sales proposal can be tailored quickly to the client's needs. With word processing, even complex, multipage proposals can be prepared in less than a day. Using a portable computer with specially developed software, a sales representative can survey a prospect's needs right in a client's office and immediately produce a sales proposal.

Access to Inventory Data

By using a portable computer with modem connected by dialup to the mainframe inventory system, salespeople can determine if an item is in stock or even provide delivery information. If the item is out of stock, they can suggest an alternative. The likelihood of getting the order for an alternative item is considerably better on the spot than if the customer is not advised until a week or two later, by mail, that the item is unavailable. If an alternative is not acceptable, the salesperson can at least let the customer know how long delivery on a backorder will take.

The experience of Blue Bell Corporation's Wrangler Female and Children's Apparel division is typical of firms that have provided their sales personnel with portable microcomputers. Wrangler provided its 115 salespeople with Sharp PC-5000 computers so that they could send orders to headquarters in Greensboro, North Carolina, directly from a customer's office. The vice-president of sales reported that, as a result, salespeople who were annually selling $1 million of clothing could sell $1.1 or $1.2 million without any more work. When a Wrangler salesperson placed an order by portable computer, the mainframe computer at headquarters instantly reported whether the product was in stock. If it was not available, the salesperson could say, "We're out of green in that style. Would you like to try the blue or pink instead?" Formerly, when Wrangler salespeople mailed their orders, they might not find out for a week or two that an item was not available. By the time they followed up, the customer was likely to cancel the order. Using portable computers reportedly reduced cancellations by 90 percent.

Order Entry and Status Checking

Remote order-entry systems enable salespersons to key orders into a portable dumb terminal and transfer the data into the main order system upon return to the office. Such systems have been in use for several years. An estimated 25 to 30 percent of the food distribution industry uses this method, and it is used also in other distribution industries such as pharmacy and hospital supplies. Order entry can now be combined with other office automation features on portable microcomputers to allow sales personnel to practically carry their offices with them. Small portable computers such as the one pictured in Figure 12-4 can replace order-entry books, price lists, appointment calendars, inventory records, and delivery schedules. In addition, they can provide electronic mail, word processing, and spreadsheets. With dumb terminals, salespersons can use modems to transmit orders to the main office; with portable computers, they can download orders and receive daily price changes, corrections, messages, inventory updates, and other information.

An example of such a system is Distribution Management Systems' SalesRunner. The SalesRunner system incorporates customized software for the MicroOffice 100 portable microcomputer. The package includes 64K (kilobytes) of random access memory (RAM), a rechargeable battery pack, an RS-232 interface (for printer connection), the MicroOffice text editor, Microsoft BASIC, and special programs for order entry and electronic mail. An optional 300 bits-per-second (bps) internal modem is also available. Other options include RAM expansion modules, word processing, spreadsheets, and even game cartridges.

A typical scenario might have a sales representative starting the week in the office, where the portable computer's programmable memory cartridges have been loaded with the week's prices, inventory, delivery

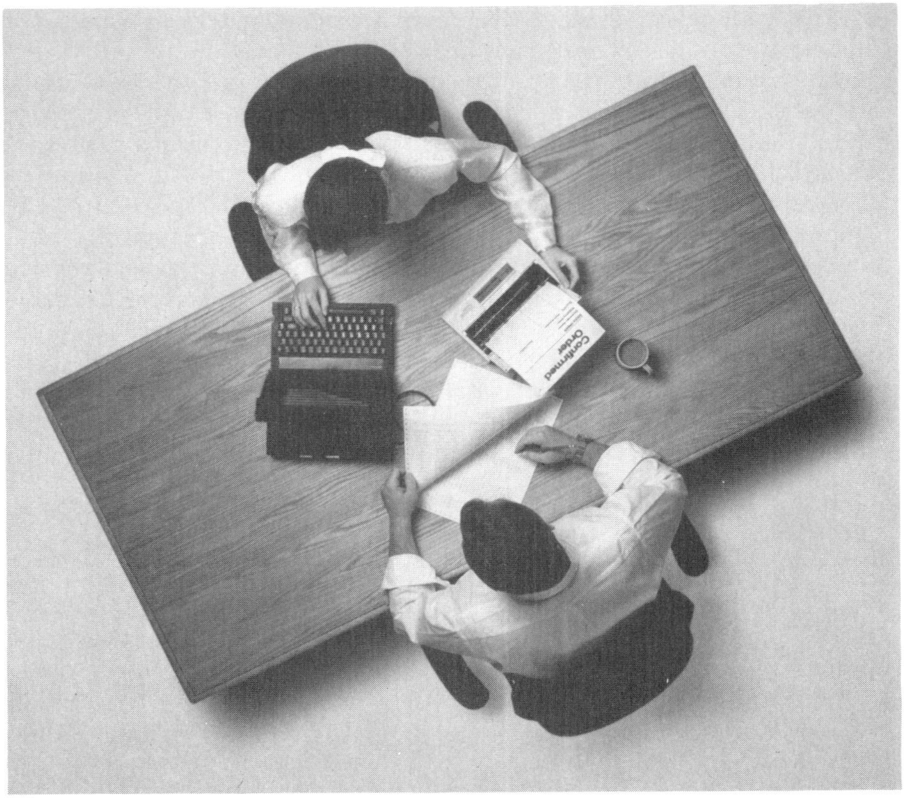

FIGURE 12-4. City Provisioners, a regional food service distributor, equips its field sales force with laptop PCs. In addition to entering and printing orders, field salespeople can dial their home office to update inventory information, transmit orders, and send or receive electronic mail.

schedules, and other sales information. A schedule for the first day's customer calls is also programmed into the system, along with details on each client: the quantity of each product usually ordered, the inventory levels of those items, and the date when further supplies are expected. In addition, valuable customer information can be entered into the portable computer, such as account balances, outstanding invoices, and whether a certain amount of money must be collected before additional orders are shipped.

In the customer's office, the sales representative can show all these items on the computer's 8-by-80 liquid crystal display (LCD) screen. With a printer connected to the portable's RS-232 port, a hardcopy price list, quotation, or order verification can be generated. The computer can be programmed to suggest alternatives for out-of-stock items, and the sales representative has discretion to override the price quotations for quantity discounts, promotions, or as an inducement.

After closing the sale, the representative goes to the next customer. If orders require immediate processing, the representative can download the orders to the main office computer by using the built-in modem and a telephone line. Whether in a motel, at a customer's office, or at home, the salesperson needs no additional equipment to transmit the data to the office and receive updates.

Portable computers, such as the MicroOffice 100, have built-in modems with autodial and autoanswer capabilities. With a built-in clock and a "wake-up mode," the system can be programmed to call the main office at an off-peak time, download the day's orders, receive updates and other data, and access the mailbox feature of the software. Sales representatives can leave messages and check their mailboxes for messages awaiting replies, storing them in the SalesRunner's memory to be read later. Electronic mail not only improves communications but can reduce telephone costs by eliminating multiple callbacks and taking advantage of off-peak rates.

Sales Follow-Up and Customer Service

Contact with customers does not end with the sale. Products of a contractual nature, such as insurance policies, require continual customer service and followup for renewals. Consumable products must be replaced, equipment must be serviced, and high-technology products must be updated. Timely follow-up and prompt, courteous service can make the difference between continued sales or lost business.

Follow-up and service require teamwork between sales and staff personnel, and consume considerable time. Office automation helps to streamline procedures, reduce costs, and improve service. Word processing replaces form letters with personalized correspondence. Customers appreciate a personal letter and usually reply more promptly. Database management programs can track anniversary or expiration dates, and even send holiday greetings. A database management system can be used to maintain notes about product requirements and personal preferences. A personalized letter, a few weeks before the renewal date of a contract, can reinforce customer rapport, help retain the client's business, and offer opportunities for new sales.

With office automation, organizations can capitalize on the reduced time required for routine, repetitive tasks to provide more personal customer service, even in a mass market.

Sales Training

Sales staff must acquire presentation skills as well as product knowledge, and office automation technologies aid training in a number of ways.

Product Training

Product training can be accomplished with the aid of computer-based training (CBT), a superior alternative to manuals for learning product information. It can reinforce key selling features and check the salesperson's product knowledge. CBT engages the salesperson in the learning process, periodically checks the learner's progress, and directs the learner to additional information or review as needed.

Computer simulations are hypothetical situations portrayed on a computer. Such simulations provide a practical way for trainees to test their product knowledge. For example, a major insurance company uses CBT to teach agents the features of new products. After reading the product manual, the agent uses a CBT program to reinforce his or her understanding of key features of the product and learn its strengths and weaknesses for meeting client needs. During the simulation, the agent must determine which product best meets a client's needs in various situations. Thus the agent must analyze the financial needs of the client in each situation and determine which product is most suitable and for what reasons. It all adds up to better-informed agents.

Presentation Training

In addition to knowing their products well, sales representatives must be able to analyze a prospect's needs, select the appropriate product, and present its features clearly and succinctly. These skills are best acquired through experience. Often sales trainees accompany experienced representatives who coach them, a slow, time-consuming process. Innovative companies are capitalizing on computer technology to improve sales training and help representatives become productive more quickly. One of the most innovative approaches is interactive video training.

Interactive video Innovative sales training programs combine CBT with interactive videotape, touch screens, and laser disks to create sales simulations. One such program is used by the Pfizer Drug Company to train sales personnel who introduce doctors to new medications. The program begins with a videotaped demonstration of an effective sales presentation to a doctor. Sales trainees are then guided into trying part of the sales presentation in response to questions posed by the doctor on the screen. As trainees practice presentations, they are videotaped. When the videotape is played back, trainees view themselves interacting with the doctor in the sales presentation. As trainees continue to practice, they receive less prompting from the system until they are doing the entire presentation themselves, interacting with the doctor on the video screen. Sales trainees can practice in a training room until they are satisfied with their presentation skills. When they are ready, their supervisors review the videotape to evaluate their performance. (More details about computer-based training are provided in Chapter 24.)

Sales Management

Sales management programs and other office automation software aid managers in planning, managing, and evaluating sales operations. With sales management software or electronic spreadsheets, salespeople and their managers can analyze how they spend time. The manager can trace the weekly progress of sales personnel or critique their performance. For example, managers can produce graphs to prove that lower sales reflect too few calls.

Computers can also help the sales manager develop annual quotas for the sales force. The variables that go into quota development are complex, tricky, and constantly changing. To prepare sales quotas, the sales manager needs information from production staff, finance staff, marketing staff, economists, and strategic planners. Although accurate decisions are important, they are extremely difficult. Artificial intelligence software can provide a new alternative. The expertise of essential staff can be captured in an expert system to aid the sales manager in producing accurate quotas by product line, time period, and sales representative, consistent with product introductions and marketing schedules.

Effective communication is important in all phases of the sales management process, but maintaining timely, accurate communications with a mobile sales force is a challenge. Electronic mail and voice mail can meet many communication needs. Teleconferencing is also effective for some applications. Videotex is a new approach to improving communication and providing other office automation features. Some firms are also experimenting with direct client communications. (These alternatives are discussed in the next several sections.)

Electronic Mailboxes

Electronic mailboxes can improve communication between headquarters and the field and save considerable time. A typical system consists of a mainframe computer that has a "mailbox" in which each salesperson can leave or receive mail. The salesperson uses a micro or portable computer linked by modem to the main computer through telephone lines. When a sales representative cannot reach someone immediately, leaving an electronic message can bring a faster reply than playing "telephone tag."

Raytheon Company's semiconductor division in Mountain View, California, lets salespeople send messages to electronic mailboxes in a central computer. People check their mailboxes periodically during the day, avoiding telephone tag. Sales representatives no longer have to go back to their office every night to collect their messages. Instead of breaking off sales calls at three in the afternoon to drive back to the office, they can make additional calls. Then they simply plug in at a phone booth or when they get home to check their messages.

Voice Mail Systems

Voice mail systems can solve many problems inherent in managing and supporting a field force. Sales managers can leave detailed voice messages for traveling sales staff, and they can access these messages from any tone-generating telephone at any time. Managers can also distribute a single message to several or even hundreds of sales representatives in various locations. An inquiry or request for information can be redirected to the appropriate salesperson with comments added by the manager.

A case study at a Midwestern furniture company demonstrated the impact of voice mail systems on the sales force and on corporate management. The sales department depended heavily on the telephone for communication. Since the sales representatives were constantly traveling, however, they found communication difficult. They often experienced repeated cycles of incomplete telephone calls, a situation referred to as "telephone tag."

In addition, sales personnel needed information from field managers and the home office about such things as product availability, contract negotiations, and personnel decisions. Timely information was also critical for providing customer support. The sales force needed to communicate frequently with the logistics and order-entry departments. Frequently, sales managers needed to distribute time-sensitive information to the sales force. Distribution of requests for information was also problematic.

The published *Research Report* summarized the impact of the voice mail system on the sales force:

> 1. *Decreased time delays.* Prior to installation of a voice mail system, delays of up to three days for communicating information were common. With the message system, most information is received within one day. Sales staff promptly receive time-sensitive information such as pricing decisions, fabric shortages, slow lead times, and cutoff times for orders. Consequently, the number of reorders that had to be written because of temporary shortages was reduced.
>
> 2. *Better quality of information.* The sales force often needed complex information from the home office, for which the voice mail system provided a new, immediate channel. Managers and sales representatives were able to transmit time-sensitive information (like contract negotiations) within a few hours, confident that messages were accurate and complete.
>
> 3. *Increased number of people receiving information.* Sales managers frequently needed to convey the same information to large groups of people. By using the message system, they could send a single message to multiple recipients in different locations.
>
> 4. *Increased ability to channel information appropriately.* Managers often redirected requests for information from home-office personnel to sales representatives. With the message system, they could forward the original request along with their comments. Sales representatives received the same detail that the managers received.
>
> 5. *Increased confidence.* Managers felt that the system was more reliable than leaving messages on slips. Although salespeople did not spend

much time at their desks, they checked their phone mail an average of twice a day. Managers felt less frustrated trying to reach people directly by telephone because they were confident their messages were received the same day.

6. *Increased support for casual communication.* Sales managers used the system to communicate personal support, much like a chance meeting in an elevator. For example, one manager left a friendly message for his staff before he went on vacation. The exchange of informal information actually increased with the message system because of the previous difficulty of getting through by telephone. A number of users reported that the system encouraged relaxed and friendly communication with people in other time zones. Casual communication from sales staff to managers also increased. When sales representatives had an idea about how to improve a plan for a new product, they felt free to send the idea to the boss on the message system. Formerly, they may have hesitated to call the manager directly for fear of interrupting and would not have taken the time to write the idea down.

7. *Increased ability to coordinate activities and resources.* Supporting the sales force required coordination among many departments, which were scattered throughout different time zones, but the logistics department coordinated materials and labor. By using the message system to communicate with manufacturing plants and warehouses in other time zones, they avoided having to schedule their calls. In some instances, the manufacturing facilities used the message system instead of memos to send reports to the logistics coordinator.[3]

Teleconferencing

Low-cost audio conferencing is an excellent medium for communicating with a field force. Among other applications, organizations use it to announce new products or product changes and for training purposes. For example, the marketing vice-president of an insurance company with 100 agencies ran five regional audio conferences to announce a new product to the sales staff.

A relatively new use of teleconferencing is microcomputer training for field representatives. When new software is distributed to the sales force, audio conferencing is a practical means of familiarizing staff with its features and answering questions.

If companies can justify the expense, they use full video conferencing. The J. C. Penney Company, for example, uses video conference centers at regional locations to introduce and demonstrate merchandise.

Videotex

Videotex involves information bases that are broadcast over television for office automation applications (see Chapter 8). Like microcomputer training for field staff, Videotex is relatively new. According to authorities, most attention has been directed toward using Videotex for home delivery of information and services such as banking and shopping. Videotex vendors have targeted their products for the masses. Growth projections are based on acceptance patterns similar to telephone and television. U.S. corporations and foreign governments have funded Videotex projects, hoping that home information will become a profitable utility. For public Videotex to become cost-effective, however, it needs a mass of subscribers. Wide acceptance will encourage advertisers to decrease subscription costs, lower the manufacturing cost and the price of components, and foster new applications and sources of information.

The success (or failure) of public Videotex systems is important to office automation planners for two primary reasons. First, a competitive Videotex industry promotes new and better uses of the technology for internal or closed user groups. Second, the acceptance of Videotex in the home will help acceptance by the work force.

Current business applications of Videotex are experimental, though the conditions under which Videotex is considered appropriate apply directly to sales management and support activities. Videotex is recommended for corporations and users who have one or more of the following characteristics:

- Casual use with infrequent access. Videotex is not for high-volume data entry, update, or retrieval. Users of these applications do not need the ease-of-use structure Videotex provides, and may even find that it slows them down.
- Geographic separation or other form of information boundary.
- Volatile information that requires frequent updates.
- Excessive information delivery costs.
- Electronic color or graphics for user appeal and acceptance.
- Information from multiple areas or need to access multiple systems.

Videotex can integrate office tools as well as address managerial, knowledge-worker, and sales productivity. Several experimental applications have addressed the management and support of sales and marketing. The following case study of a two-year Videotex pilot project in two sales divisions of a large manufacturer illustrates some of the capabilities and benefits of Videotex.

A manufacturing company with over 1000 employees in 25 locations decided to evaluate Videotex and conduct a pilot study because of the following problems:

- Problems communicating to employees in the highly decentralized company.
- Problems maintaining relationships with over 4000 dealers and the public.
- Reductions in time the sales force was spending in sales calls.

In addition, the manufacturer thought that a Videotex information system, developed for in-house use, might also have market potential as a new information product. The manufacturer used a Videotex service bureau for the pilot rather than developing its own Videotex system for the following reasons:

- It needed to leverage technical obsolescence risks.
- Internal resources were not available.
- The pilot needed to be implemented in a short time to maintain a technology advantage.
- It provided the lowest cost alternative for trying Videotex.

The project was introduced to management with a film about Videotex. Managers were asked to suggest ideas for applications and more than 110 were suggested. The applications selected for the pilot project included the following:

- Product information
- Order entry
- Diaries
- Company information
- Electronic mail

Users of the pilot system requested 20 additional applications. The company reported the following benefits from using Videotex:

- Better and wider communications.
- Increased time for sales calls (10 percent increase).
- Reduced peak-period telephone calls to the office, fewer calls at home, and reduction in other communication expenses.
- Improved morale, motivation, and efficiency in the sales force. (Before the pilot, the salesforce was within 70–80 percent of targeted sales; during the pilot, it was within 98–110 percent of target).
- Daily communication between the office and a salesperson and between the salesperson and marketing.
- Company procedure manuals were not reproduced on hardcopy or needed by pilot users.

The company reported two problems that it plans to address in the next development phase. First, several mainframe applications need to be interfaced to the Videotex system. Second, people were reluctant to use the system, and the number of system accesses was smaller than anticipated.

A consultant who specializes in strategic planning, design, and installation of Videotex projects has made the following predictions on the use of Videotex technology:

> As Videotex use grows and higher quality, lower-cost terminals are available, corporations will open internal Videotex systems for customers, potential

> customers, suppliers, accountants, lawyers, etc. These systems will have improved graphics quality through videodisc and other video interfaces. They will use expert system features and audio access and response. The placement of terminals with corporate associates and permitting associates access to these sophisticated systems will give the corporation several competitive advantages. The system will promote the corporation's technical proficiency and quality-service image. These advanced systems will help control and reduce the cost of goods purchased from suppliers and sold to customers.[4]

Consumers in Orange County, California, can use their home computers to communicate with sales representatives at a large insurance company to learn more about financial services. The 1986 pilot program was offered through the insurer's sales office in Santa Ana and was available to consumers with home computers who subscribed to a Videotex service.

To use the program, the consumer simply typed a question on the computer keyboard and sent the message electronically. A representative at the agency answered the question and sent it to the consumer's computer. Other features included a program that helped consumers develop a financial profile of their investment and savings goals, a financial newsletter with investment information, and a reference dictionary of insurance and investment products and services.

SYSTEM ALTERNATIVES

Appropriate software applications must be selected in conjunction with hardware considerations. A combined mainframe and microcomputer strategy is an important aspect of sales support. Procedures for identifying business needs and selecting and implementing software and hardware are covered in Part 5. This section notes some considerations relating to sales applications for portable computers and Videotex.

Portable Computers

Portable computers provide the power and productivity of automation independent of location. Microcomputers bring office automation to the desktop, but portable computers take it almost everywhere.

One of the most important things that a portable computer can do to increase productivity is to keep the user in contact with headquarters. A portable computer can access electronic mail, calendar, and everything else one might expect from a sophisticated office automation product. As standalone devices, portables offer several advantages, but when connected to an organization's central office automation systems, they virtually allow sales personnel to take their offices with them.

The following case study illustrates the effective use of portable computers by a large organization:

> Sales agents at Equitable Life Assurance Society of America report excellent results with laptop portables from GRiD Systems Corporation.
>
> Equitable developed customized software to produce insurance

quotations. This custom software, which took an investment of over 20 man-years to produce, was originally designed for IBM microcomputers. Generally, the insurance agent invites a client into the office to discuss his or her needs and then runs the quotation programs on the IBM microcomputer. Because not all clients were willing to come to the agent, in many cases the agent would travel to the client's location. After the meeting, the agent would return to the office to generate quotes on the microcomputer. The time frame for running this system, from initial client meeting to the closing of the sale, ranged from days to weeks. Equitable Life Assurance wanted a more efficient system, so it turned to portable computers.

Portable computers would allow insurance agents to perform several important functions during client meetings. Agents could analyze needs, make slide presentations on the portable computer, and run software to produce premium quotations on the spot. The ability to make an entire sales presentation, as well as generate quotations at the point of sale, would provide better time management and increase productivity.

After evaluating several portable computer manufacturers and their system offerings, Equitable Life Assurance chose the GRiDCase laptop. One of the first Equitable agents to purchase a GRiDCase was Bob Rea, who works in Equitable's Sacramento branch office.

Rea uses his desktop computer with customer applications. "My company and several companies that I represent provide agents with diskettes and programs that will do proposals for the various life insurance policies," Rea said. He also uses Lotus 1–2–3, Wordstar, pfs File, and a few other off-the-shelf applications.

Rea easily adapted to using computers in his daily work. Although he has been very successful with his desktop computer, he found that he still was not selling to some individuals who refused to come to the office for quotations. The need for a portable computer became evident. "Ideally," Rea explains, "I want the client to come to my office. As a matter of fact, my statement to clients is, 'Come on in and we'll play games with some numbers; we'll tailor a policy for you.' Well, a lot of people who call don't want to or can't come in."

Rea saw the GRiDCase for the first time at Equitable's Top Producers Conference in March 1985 and was impressed with the readability of the GRiDCase plasma display. Screen readability was the major reason why Rea chose GRiDCase over other popular portables that use LCD displays. "Many times I need to talk to two people, one on each side, and if they can't read the screen, then there is no use in me being there," said Rea.

Rea purchased his laptop through a special arrangement between GRiD and Equitable. He says he recovered the full cost of the laptop in his first client meeting using the computer. The personnel director of a large client firm was never, according to Rea, a great believer in personal life insurance. Rea tried several times to get him to come into his office to sit down with the IBM microcomputer, but he would not. Rea invited him to lunch one day and did not tell him he was going to bring the laptop. "We had lunch, cleared the table, and I pulled the GRiDCase out and started to run the program on a universal life policy. We got right into the feature, and I ended up selling him an insurance policy, and the commission was sufficient to pay for the GRiDCase."

Rea says that he now takes his laptop on three to five sales calls per week and that his productivity has increased considerably.[5]

SUMMARY

Office automation offers new opportunities to improve sales force productivity. More time devoted to selling generally translates directly into increased sales, yielding higher commissions for sales personnel and increased profits for the company. Office automation can also mean improved service for the customer.

Computerized sales support can help reduce preparation time that salespeople spend at the office and can increase the time available for selling, expand the size of the territory a salesperson can handle, improve service to clients, and help a sales staff develop its expertise.

More than 60 software programs are available for micro, mini, and mainframe computers to support sales and marketing activities. In addition, many large companies develop their own customized programs. Sales applications include prospecting, illustrations, proposals, access to inventory data, follow-up, and training.

Prospect management software enables salespersons to keep a directory of potential clients. The prospects can be selected—or qualified—by any appropriate set of criteria designated by the salesperson. By carefully refining the list, salespersons can increase the likelihood that telephone calls or personal visits will produce sales. The most sophisticated programs include additional features such as appointment calendars, tickler files, form letters, and reports.

Telemarketing is the use of a telephone to perform traditional marketing, usually with the aid of computerized databases. Telemarketing provides opportunities for both sales prospecting and direct marketing. The latest innovation is the electronic kiosk, which combines video and computer technologies to provide marketing information and client order entry.

Computers aid salespersons in producing illustrations and proposals. Computers also provide access to inventory data and order status. Even sales and product training can be improved with computer-based training (CBT).

Sales managers have more accurate, timely information to monitor sales performance, coach staff, and manage operations. Customers benefit from faster delivery, reduced errors, and better service.

Ironically, computers are saving the salesperson from extinction. Without the aid of computers, face-to-face sales calls would be too costly for all but the most expensive products. By reducing paperwork and weeding out uninterested prospects so as to make every call count, the impersonal computer is sustaining the personal sales system.

DISCUSSION QUESTIONS

1. Which features of the portable computer are most valuable to a salesperson?
2. Assume you are a sales manager with a sales force of 200 in five states. How would you use the following office automation applications?
   a. Telemarketing
   b. Teleconferencing
   c. Videotex
3. Getting a proposal to a company quickly can mean getting the sale. Describe how a salesperson can use office automation to prepare this document.
4. How can a portable computer help a salesperson to follow up with customers?
5. Why is it important for a sales staff to have access to inventory data? Discuss.
6. Discuss ways in which office automation can help keep a sales staff informed of new products.
7. Explain the concept behind the following office automation products and give an example of their application by sales departments:
   a. Electronic mail
   b. Voice messaging
   c. Teleconferencing
   d. Videotex

APPLICATION EXERCISES

1. Assume you are a seller of college textbooks. Make an argument to your sales manager to support your use of a portable computer.
2. Visit an insurance agency and find out how it uses telemarketing.
3. For each of the following situations, explain how a computer could help you develop a prospect list:
   a. You have been assigned to sell a photographer's services for baby pictures.
   b. You are the new owner of a sports shop in your area.
   c. You and your partner, both attorneys, are dissolving your law firm partnership.

SUGGESTED READINGS

Hildebrand, J. D. "Turning Leads into Gold," *Portable Computer* (October 1984), pp. 38–43.

Hughes, G. David. "Computerized Sales Management," *Harvard Business Review* (March–April 1983), pp. 102–113.

Marinello, Robert. "Marketing in Modern Mode," *Best's Review, Life/Health Edition* (April 1986), pp. 82–84.

Mayer, David, and Greenberg, Herbert M. "What Makes a Good Salesperson?" *Harvard Business Review* (July–August 1964), pp. 119–125.

ADMINISTRATIVE APPLICATIONS: Part 1

CHAPTER **13**

OBJECTIVES

After completing this chapter, the reader should be able to meet the following objectives:

- Understand the concepts of office support.
- Understand the diverse features available with word processing software packages and why they are important for document production.
- Differentiate between the word processing needs of clerical and administrative personnel in a production environment and those of casual users such as managers and knowledge workers.
- Identify the major administrative applications for office technologies.
- Differentiate between features of electronic mail, phone mail, spreadsheets, and other software that are most important to an administrative assistant versus a manager or knowledge worker.
- Explain how technology is changing the roles of secretaries, administrative assistants, and office clerical workers.

KEY TERMS

administrative assistant
administrative support
format
infrastructure
logbook
merge printing
principal
systems concept of office support
tickler file
total support concept
tracking and follow-up systems
word processing
word processing center
word processing/administrative support (WP/AS)

INTRODUCTION

Clerical and administrative personnel are responsible for supporting the *information processing infrastructure,* the network of services that keep information flowing into, within, and out of the enterprise. Clerical and administrative personnel perform four primary functions:

1. Processing information to support decision making.
2. Processing information to support operations.
3. Providing services (or support) to clients or customers.
4. Operating the physical facilities of the office.

As pointed out in Chapter 2, clerical and administrative services cover a broad spectrum of jobs. At one extreme, executive assistants, who are the elite of the secretaries, command salaries beyond $50,000 a year. Closely aligned with the executives for whom they work, these secretaries exercise subtle power and sometimes supervise staffs of their own. At the opposite extreme, a variety of entry-level positions require little skill and pay minimum wage.

The *Dictionary of Occupational Titles* lists the following job titles under the category of clerical support and administrative services:

1. Secretarial
2. Word processing and administrative support (WP/AS)
3. Paraprofessionals
4. Clerical accounting
5. General clerical
6. Telephone and wire services
7. Mail services
8. Records management
9. Graphic services
10. Forms design
11. Reprographics
12. Facilities management

In one sense, clerical and administrative personnel are providers as well as users of information technologies. They apply office technologies to their jobs of providing information processing support to the entire organization. Office automation (OA) is changing the services they provide. Notions about who performs what work in the office are being redefined. Data processing (DP) and OA systems now provide some of the information processing previously done manually or mechanically.

For example, office technologies make it practical for managers and knowledge workers to do some of the information processing that previously had been delegated to support staff. Electronic mail allows managers to compose and distribute their own memos. Formerly, the knowledge worker would have dictated the memo, using a dictating machine or stenographer; a transcriptionist would have typed the memo; and mail personnel would have distributed it. Although the trend is to provide office technologies that enable end users to process information themselves, a major proportion of information processing and support will probably continue to be performed by clerical and administrative personnel.

This chapter begins with a general overview of office support concepts. This overview is followed by a discussion of the needs of the first five categories of clerical and administrative personnel: secretarial, word processing, paraprofessional, clerical accounting, and general clerical personnel. The other seven categories of clerical and administrative personnel will be discussed in Chapter 14.

CONCEPTS OF OFFICE SUPPORT

Although clerical and administrative services are often considered routine and repetitive, many of these tasks are not well structured. In fact, contrary to popular perceptions, the use of computers has made many clerical positions less, rather than more, routine. Computer processing systems usually automate the routine, repetitive tasks but leave less structured tasks such as correcting errors, handling exceptions, and resolving problems to be handled by secretarial and administrative personnel. Some secretarial, administrative, and clerical jobs have been redefined, others eliminated, and new ones added.

Clerical employees often are an organization's primary interface with its customers as they receive payments, take orders, answer telephone inquiries, and handle complaints. They have a more accurate knowledge of the day-to-day operations of a business than most managers. They understand the requirements of their jobs, take pride in performing them well, and appreciate technologies that improve their performance. In a well-organized and well-managed office support system, clerical and administrative personnel are a valuable resource for aiding management in streamlining procedures, improving customer service, and controlling costs.

The way in which an enterprise organizes clerical and administrative support services depends upon the size and type of the enterprise, organizational structure, management preferences, volume of work, and technologies used. Support services may be centralized or decentralized; staff may be specialists or generalists. The staffing charts in Figure 13-1 show several alternative design options for staffing office support. In some organizations, secretaries are assigned to executives, but lower management and knowledge workers share departmental secretaries. In other organizations, executives have administrative assistants, and lower-level managers and knowledge workers share the services of administrative and word processing centers. The accounting department might employ several clerical accounting personnel, and the customer service department might employ several general clerical staff. A third alternative is the use of individual secretaries for executives and departmental secretaries for others, with one or more word processing centers for high-volume document production. Many alternatives are possible, and the best way to organize office support functions is not clearcut. Large organizations may employ hundreds, even thousands, of clerical and administrative employees.

General Job Requirements of Office Support

To meet the diverse needs of clerical and administrative personnel, office system analysts must carefully analyze each situation. Some of the general information processing requirements of clerical and administrative employees are described in the following sections, but these requirements often vary from organization to organization.

FIGURE 13-1. Design options for staffing office support.

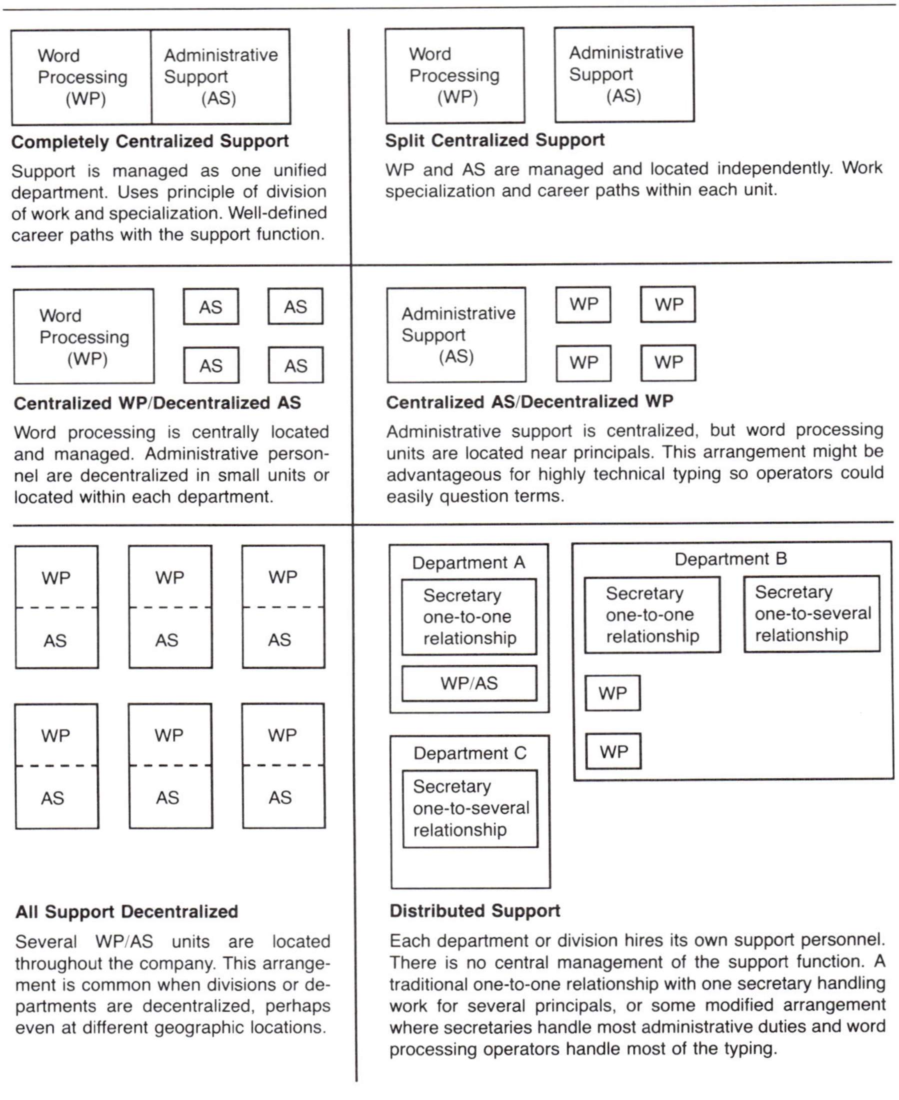

Secretaries

The *traditional secretary* supports one individual, working in a close, one-to-one relationship. The number of traditional secretarial personnel has declined since word processing was introduced. In most organizations, only officers and senior-level people have their own secretaries. Secretaries handle diverse responsibilities and channel much of the information and communication to and from the executives for whom they work. A secretary typically handles correspondence, manages the executive's calendar, screens visitors and telephone calls, plans travel itineraries, and tracks a myriad of details. High-level secretaries frequently manage special projects as well. A good secretary anticipates the needs of the executive and shares the confidences, thought processes, and sometimes the personal styles of their *principals* (the modern term, preferred to *boss*). To the frazzled chief executive who is always pressed for time, a good assistant can be invaluable. Typical duties of a secretary are listed in Figure 13-2.

Departmental secretaries, on the other hand, usually must be "jacks of all trades," doing everything for everyone. Formerly referred to as "Gal Fridays," departmental secretaries must diplomatically juggle the work of many principals. They may have to handle multiple calendars, telephone lines, and track and follow up on details. Their responsibilities may include any assignments the principals ask them to handle, plus general department administration and filing.

FIGURE 13-2. Typical duties of a professional secretary.

1. Look at the job from the executive's point of view. Be sensitive to time limits, priorities, and the need to plan and organize accordingly.
2. Maintain a schedule of the executive's time, including a calendar of meetings and projects. Keep a "to do" list for the executive and ensure that it is of workable size. Prioritize the items. Prepare folders for meetings the executive will attend, providing all the pertinent materials that he or she will need.
3. Schedule regular meetings with the executive to review office operations.
4. Keep interruptions to a minimum. Screen visitors, making an effort to handle requests or problems, and discern which ones must be handled by the executive.
5. Answer the executive's phone and handle as many calls as possible. Refer calls when necessary.
6. Open mail and answer letters when possible. Draft answers to others if possible.
7. Act as an interface between the executive and the department, writing notes and memos.
8. Attend the executive's staff meetings as part of the management team.
9. Maintain and monitor a list of general reading projects.
10. Review articles on the efficient management of office operations, especially those on time management.

Word Processing and Administrative Support Staff

In the early days of word processing, its high cost could not be justified for secretaries, who typically spend less than 25 percent of their day typing. The concept of work specialization for secretaries was introduced in the form of word processing/administrative support (WP/AS). According to the WP/AS concept, secretaries work as centralized teams of specialists rather than as individual generalists. The traditional one-to-one relationship between secretary and boss is eliminated. Clusters of word processing secretaries handle all typing assignments and document production for a group of principals who use dictation equipment linked to word processing centers. Shorthand is eliminated.

Administrative secretaries (or assistants) are also clustered to serve groups of principals. They no longer have typewriters but are assigned to handle telephone calls and visitors, schedule calendars, file documents, compose and edit correspondence, research information, and many other management-related tasks.

Document production in word processing centers Word processing centers operate as professionally managed service centers that provide services to everyone within the organizational unit they serve. Word processing support personnel handle all aspects of document production. Sample word processing job descriptions are provided in Figure 13-3. Word processing specialists may be clustered in small groups or organized in large centralized units. The size, number, and location of word processing centers depend on the following factors:

- The size of the organization.
- The degree of centralization or decentralization within the organization.
- Management philosophy.
- The type of documents processed.
- The volume of work.

FIGURE 13-3. Word processing job descriptions.

a. Corresponding Secretary.

Job Title
Corresponding Secretary

Responsibilities
- Transcribes proficiently all kinds of dictation from central recorder on word processing equipment.
- Types handwritten or other copy on word processing equipment.
- Maintains high productivity and meets established deadlines.

Relationships
- Reports to Supervisor, Word Processing Center. Supervision is of the "progress and results" type.
- Maintains frequent contact with dictators, assisting them in formatting and setting up special documents.
- Offers guidance to dictators to correct poor dictating habits and improve clarity.
- Contacts various persons and departments in regard to projects; requires tact and the ability to apply effectively knowledge of machine capability to work applications.

Specific Duties and Skills
- Performs diverse typing services requiring fundamental knowledge of company procedures and general operations, including the following:
  1. Complex statistical reports.

2. Technical reports requiring familiarity with sophisticated nomenclature.
3. Confidential material.
4. Special requests of varied nature.

- Edits copy as typed to correct grammar and provide proper punctuation.
- Proofreads finished copy.

Problems Encountered

- Works in centralized, high-pressure environment requiring interaction with others in group whose productivity is measured daily.
- Follows company procedures (e.g., following standard memo, letter, and report formats).
- Must meet deadlines.
- Must decipher poor handwriting.
- Must interpret vague instructions.
- Must establish priorities as directed by supervisor.
- Must retain records as directed by supervisor.

FIGURE 13-3. (continued)

Job Title

Composer, Corresponding Secretary

Responsibilities

- Transcribes proficiently all kinds of dictation from central recorder on word processing equipment.
- Operates composer to provide camera-ready copy for printing on photographic equipment.
- Maintains high productivity and meets established deadlines.

Relationships

- Reports to Supervisor, Word Processing Center. Supervision is of the "progress and results" type.
- Maintains frequent contact with dictators, assisting them in formatting and setting up special documents.
- Offers guidance to dictators to correct poor dictating habits and improve clarity.
- Works with Copy Center and consults with IBM on Composer-prepared copy.

Specific Duties and Skills

- Performs diverse typing services requiring fundamental knowledge of company procedures and general operations, including the following:
  1. Complex statistical reports.
  2. Technical reports requiring familiarity with sophisticated nomenclature.
  3. Confidential material.
  4. Special requests of varied nature.
- Edits copy as typed to correct grammar and provide proper punctuation.
- Proofreads finished copy.
- Prepares forms, literature, brochures, and a wide range of specialized applications on Composer, exercising judgment and a degree of artistic skill for formatting and paste-up of camera-ready copy; organizes data to conform to rigid government manual specifications.

b. Composer, Corresponding Secretary.

FIGURE 13-3.

b. Composer, Corresponding Secretary (continued).

Problems Encountered
- Works in centralized, high-pressure environment requiring interaction with others in group whose productivity is measured daily.
- Must follow company procedures (e.g., following standard memo, letter, and report formats).
- Must meet deadlines.
- Must decipher poor handwriting.
- Must interpret vague instructions.
- Must establish priorities as directed by supervisor.
- Must retain records as directed by supervisor.

c. Bilingual Secretary.

Job Title
Bilingual Secretary

Responsibilities
- Transcribes proficiently all kinds of dictation from central recorders on word processing equipment, consistently maintaining high productivity and meeting established deadlines.
- Translates Spanish, Portuguese, and Italian; serves as Spanish interpreter.

Relationships
- Reports to Supervisor, Word Processing Center. Supervision is of the "progress and results" type.
- Maintains frequent contact with dictators, assisting them in formatting and setting up special documents.
- Offers guidance to dictators to correct poor dictating habits and improve clarity.
- Translates orders, letters, etc., from Spanish customers and serves as an interpreter for International Department.

Specific Duties and Skills
- Performs diverse typing services requiring fundamental knowledge of company procedures and general operations, including the following:
  1. Complex statistical reports.
  2. Technical reports requiring familiarity with sophisticated nomenclature.
  3. Confidential material.
- Edits copy as typed to correct grammar and provide proper punctuation.
- Proofreads finished copy.
- Translates orders, letters, inquiries, etc., from Spanish.
- Serves as an interpreter for Spanish-speaking visitors. This requires the ability to clearly translate highly technical product specifications to customers/dealers. A knowledge of the country and customs is also an asset in working with these Spanish visitors.

Problems Encountered
- Works in centralized, high-pressure environment requiring interaction with others in group whose productivity is measured daily.
- Must follow company procedures (e.g., following standard memo, letter, and report formats).
- Must meet deadlines.

- Must decipher poor handwriting.
- Must interpret vague instructions.
- Must establish priorities as directed by supervisor.
- Must retain records as directed by supervisor.

FIGURE 13-3. (continued)

Job Title
Senior Corresponding Secretary

Responsibilities
- In Supervisor's absence, acts as back-up, including scheduling, checking, doing paperwork, working with principals, etc.
- Transcribes proficiently all kinds of dictation from central recorders on word processing equipment, consistently maintaining high productivity and meeting established deadlines.

Relationships
- Reports to Supervisor, Word Processing Center.
- Maintains frequent contact with dictators, especially during Supervisor's absence, assisting them in formatting and setting up special documents.
- Offers guidance to dictators to correct poor dictating habits and improve clarity.
- Contacts various persons and departments in regard to projects; requires tact and the ability to effectively apply knowledge of machine capability to work applications.
- Assists Supervisor with training.

Specific Duties and Skills
- Performs diverse typing services requiring fundamental knowledge of company procedures and general operations, including the following:
  1. Complex statistical reports.
  2. Technical reports requiring familiarity with sophisticated nomenclature.
  3. Extremely confidential material.
  4. Special requests of varied nature.
  5. Assists other secretaries in Center because of overall knowledge of company.
- Edits copy to correct grammar and provide proper punctuation.
- Proofreads finished copy.

Problems Encountered
- Works in centralized, high-pressure environment requiring interaction with others in group whose productivity is measured daily.
- In absence of Supervisor, supervises staff and performs other duties, such as scheduling, making necessary decisions, establishing priorities, etc.
- Must follow company procedures (e.g., must follow standard memo, letter, and report formats).
- Must meet deadlines.
- Must decipher poor handwriting.
- Must follow vague instructions.
- Must check and distribute processed documents.

d. Senior Corresponding Secretary.

Input for word processing may be handwritten, dictated, or printed copy. Word processing operators must be skilled at machine transcription. Word processing centers generally use desktop units or central dictation systems. Procedures for assigning work in word processing centers vary from one organization to another. These variations fall into two basic patterns depending on the organization's management philosophy: *work simplification* or *worker participation*. These two philosophies have the following basic differences:

1. Work simplification (authoritarian management)
   - Highly specialized work assignments.
   - Various components of the job are handled by different people. One person may input original text, another may proofread, and yet another may make revisions or corrections.
   - Random assignment of work according to specialization.
   - Principals bring all work to the word processing supervisor, who schedules and distributes it. Operators do not talk directly with principals.
2. Worker participation (participative management)
   - Diversified work assignments.
   - Each operator is responsible for all components of a job from input to proofreading and revision.
   - Each operator does all work of his or her assigned principals.
   - Principals bring work directly to each word processing operator. Direct working relationships between operators and principals are encouraged.

Well-managed word processing centers are usually very efficient and productive. Professional management and career development for staff are two major advantages of centralized office support. When not well-managed, these services often fail to achieve anticipated productivity. Under the worst circumstances, a word processing center can lead to very poor working conditions, with stressful, factory-like production, low morale, and high turnover.

Administrative support centers Under the WP/AS concept, administrative secretaries work as a team, under an administrative support supervisor, to support a group of principals. Administrative support centers are professionally managed; they provide cross-training and backup to ensure that principals receive support at all times (regardless of vacations or absences). Procedures and policies are consistent throughout the organization. AS teams may include administrative and clerical employees with a variety of skill levels. Training is provided to develop staff skills. Some AS centers include mail, messenger, and reprographic services. Figure 13-4 presents a typical job description for an administrative assistant.

FIGURE 13-4. A typical job description for an administrative assistant.

Job Title
Administrative Assistant

The Administrative Assistant provides administrative support to an assigned area and handles substantial nonroutine responsibilities.

General Responsibilities

- Thoroughly understands the mission of the assigned area and how this mission relates to company objectives.
- Knows the principal's major responsibilities and how they relate to the department mission.
- Understands related areas and is aware of company philosophy, policies, and practices.
- Uses judgment to prioritize and negotiate workload. Determines the most efficient method to accomplish work and takes the initiative to implement improved procedures within delegated authority.
- Has a thorough knowledge of the administrative computer system and uses it to carry out assigned administrative responsibilities. Seeks opportunities to use the system to improve work procedures and discusses suggestions with manager.

The Administrative Assistant is charged with the timely accomplishment of basic administrative responsibilities, additional information processing responsibilities, developing effective interrelationships, plus any specific responsibilities delegated by assigned principals.

Basic Administrative Responsibilities

- Keeps principals informed of activities and information that affect their various responsibilities.
- Processes mail daily. Uses judgment in distributing mail electronically and manually. Refers mail requiring action to proper principals after attaching reference material or noting system document numbers. Maintains follow-up and acts as liaison in follow-up as directed by principal. On own initiative, prepares routine correspondence for manager's signature.
- Keeps filing current. Logs hard copy mail on administrative system daily; monitors system log of electronic mail. Understands and adheres to current legal record retention schedules.
- Answers telephones promptly and courteously, relaying messages on a timely basis.
- Checks voice mail message queue frequently. Responds promptly to callers as appropriate.
- Secures travel reservations and advances. Ensures that expense accounts are accurate and submitted promptly.
- Checks time cards weekly to ensure that they are signed, coded, and submitted on time.
- Schedules meetings without conflict and alerts principals of commitments. Maintains calendars for designated principals.
- Identifies proper source for ordering supplies. Maintains an adequate stock of supplies at all times.
- Maintains current and well-organized desk procedures.

FIGURE 13-4. (continued)

- Uses Word Processing Center for majority of typing and verifies the accuracy of all documents prepared for principals. Coordinates with word processing personnel to ensure satisfactory turnaround time.
- Selects appropriate reproduction methods: self-service copier, central copy service, or graphic services. Uses good judgment to select best method for document transmission: electronic mail network, standard mail, facsimile, or wire services.
- Verifies accuracy of all work prepared by others for principals.

Information Processing Responsibilities

- Assumes responsibility for tracking and follow-up on all administrative details in adequate time to meet deadlines.
- Independently assists in execution of administrative details by answering inquiries and requesting, summarizing, and consolidating information.
- Intercepts and handles calls whenever possible to assist principals.
- Independently prepares reports required for principals. Gathers and corroborates data into presentation materials as needed. Learns to use the capabilities of the computer system effectively to research information and summarize details into clear, concise reports.
- Alerts Word Processing Center about anticipated peak workloads and advises manager of any problem areas. Coordinates transmission of documents back and forth between word processing and administrative systems. Edits and revises documents or refers them to the principal for review (either on the system or hardcopy printout, as preferred by the principal).

Interrelationships

- Cooperates with other department members and develops a spirit of teamwork and cooperation.
- Projects a positive, service-oriented attitude and develops positive rapport with principals.
- Help others during peak workload situations or provides back-up support for others.
- Assists in training less experienced administrative personnel.

Delegated Responsibilities

- Relieves principals of administrative details. Suggests improved procedures and offers to assume responsibility for additional tasks that could be delegated by the principal.

Although word processing centers have been implemented widely, administrative support centers are seldom implemented as they were originally conceived. Administrative support secretaries in centers were seldom able to develop a rapport and close working relationship with principals that enabled them to anticipate needs. Although managers may have difficulty articulating what makes a secretary indispensable, research indicates that anticipating requirements and producing exactly what is needed, with minimum explanation, are prized secretarial skills. Whatever the reason, decision makers at top levels were seldom willing to give up their secretaries in the name of progress. Instead, secretarial jobs were modified to reduce typing responsibilities, and the number of secretarial positions was decreased. The title "administrative assistant" is sometimes used instead of "secretary." Only senior-level managers are entitled to secretaries, while middle-level managers and professionals share administrative or departmental secretaries and use the services of word processing centers. Most administrative secretaries still have typewriters to handle small typing jobs and special tasks like labels, envelopes, and forms.

As the price of technology has come down, the cost incentive for creating large word processing centers has decreased. Office systems and microcomputers have made word processing widely available to professionals and managers as well as secretaries and other clerical personnel.

Paraprofessionals

The number of paraprofessional positions has increased in recent years. Paraprofessionals are high-level administrators such as paralegals (or legal assistants), medical assistants, and customer service representatives. Paralegals perform varied duties: searching and checking public records, preparing probate inventories, assisting with tax returns, contacting clients for information, conducting interviews, drafting wills, deeds, and trusts, and making arrangements for depositions and hearings—to name a few. Medical assistants handle a variety of patient-care responsibilities in addition to clerical functions. Customer service representatives manage customer accounts, such as insurance policyholders or bank clients. Such service includes a variety of clerical information processing. Paraprofessional jobs require a good understanding of the business and its products, as well as information processing.

Paraprofessionals are often customers' primary contact with an organization. Automation can provide better access and control of essential information, document management, and other time-saving features that offer new opportunities to improve customer service.

Clerical Accounting Personnel

Accounting clerks, working primarily with figures, perform in such areas as payroll, general ledger, accounts payable and receivable, and cost accounting. In small offices, accounting clerks may do all the bookkeeping, with an outside accountant verifying their work periodically or annually. Automated accounting and spreadsheet programs offer many opportunities for improving productivity.

General Clerical Staff

General clerical workers have the most diverse job descriptions of any support category. This group encompasses data-entry personnel, insurance claims processors, shipping clerks, order-entry clerks, receptionists, clerk-typists, and many other specialized positions (which vary depending on the nature of the business).

The Systems Concept of Office Support

The *systems, or total support, concept* of office support views the office as an interrelated system of information processing activities designed to support both the management and operation of the enterprise. All functions, even when organized as separate departments, are viewed as interrelated: typing, administration (such as filing, handling mail and telephone, researching information), replication and distribution, records management, data processing, and communications. The term *support system* suggests a planned structure for integrating all support services under centralized supervision and control. This type of support system provides the necessary coordination among various support personnel and promotes a team approach. The objective is to optimize the total work flow.

The support system concept recognizes that many office employees throughout the organization must create and manipulate the same information and databases. For example, word processing operators may type individualized form letters to large groups of customers whose names and addresses are stored in a centralized computer. The marketing vice-president's secretary may maintain a third copy of the same list of names in a card index for quick reference. Regional sales offices may each keep lists of customers in their region, and sales personnel may maintain yet another copy of these lists for their own use. Advances in communications and networking technology make it possible to minimize such duplication of effort by improving integration among systems.

As organizations move toward integrated systems, simple standalone word processing is becoming a thing of the past. Analysts focus instead on *document processing*, that is, how documents are created, reviewed, distributed, presented, and stored across the organization. Whereas word processing principally supports only text creation and editing, document processing takes into account the additional tasks of producing, communicating, and filing written communications. Document processing offers integrated, compatible tools that improve the organization's productivity, quality, and image.

In reality, the systems concept can be complex, especially in large organizations. The concept has been applied more often for WP/AS than for reprographics, records management, telephone systems, and mail services. Integrating the functions in clerical support and administrative services usually crosses departmental lines in large organizations. Such integration requires top-management support. At the very least, it requires that top management designate a senior manager with responsibility for coordinating all information management within the organization.

To define system requirements, the systems analyst must consider the overall work flow as well as departmental procedures. Personal work styles and the need for flexibility to meet the changing demands of a dynamic work environment must also be considered. The best way to design systems is to involve users. The rest of this chapter discusses word processing and other applications for clerical and administrative personnel.

DOCUMENT PROCESSING APPLICATIONS

Document processing is the use of computer technology to produce documents. Word processing has replaced the typewriter for most document applications, which range from short, informal memorandums and general correspondence to complex technical manuals requiring extensive use of formulas, tables, and footnotes.

When analyzing document processing needs, the analyst must distinguish between high-volume production requirements, general secretarial use, heavy authoring needs, and casual use by professionals and managers. Only then can the appropriate word processing software be selected. For example, the requirements for high-volume document production are far more demanding than for general secretarial or casual use. Therefore, high-volume document production is often handled by specialized personnel in word processing centers.

Word Processing Software

Hundreds of word processing programs are available on microcomputers, minicomputers, mainframes, and dedicated word processing systems. Word processing software offers a broad range of basic editing and advanced and optional features. Prices range from under $100 for some microcomputer software to thousands of dollars for mainframe systems. Word processing software varies in ease of startup, learning, use, performance, and versatility. The suitability of a word processing system depends on the major applications for which it will be used. A word processing program adequate for the occasional user would not be appropriate for the production word processing operator. Diversity and flexibility usually come at the cost of ease of learning and use.

Word processing applications will be discussed in the following order:

- Basic word processing features
- Document editing features
- Document filing/retrieval
- Document composition and automation (glossary)
- Text storage (library)
- Spell checking
- Readability analysis
- Print/photocomposition
- Document creation
    - Dictation
    - Shorthand
    - Optical character recognition (OCR)
    - Direct word processing input

Basic Word Processing Features

Word processors differ in the way documents are created and printed. These differences may represent tradeoffs in function and ease of use, or sometimes just personal preference. Some of the important tradeoffs are explained in this section.

Page-Oriented Versus Document-Oriented Systems

Word processors may be *page-oriented* or *document-oriented*. Page-oriented documents maintain only one page of text in active memory at a time. By "saving text" at the end of each page before beginning the next, loss of data is minimized in the event of a power failure or equipment problems. Moving from one page to another is slow, however, because each page must be stored and the next page recalled into memory.

Document-oriented word processing programs, on the other hand, retain the entire document in active memory, limited only by memory size or program limitations. Scrolling from page to page is much faster than with page-oriented word processors, which is a real advantage when editing long documents. The operator must remember to save text to storage periodically because if a problem occurs, all text or edits entered since the last save instruction will be lost. Operators can lose hours of work if they fail to save the document periodically.

Word Processing Programs Versus Text Editors

Word processing programs display text on the VDT screen formatted as it will look when printed. Thus "what you see is what you get" (WYSIWYG). With text editors, on the other hand, inputting the text and formatting it for printing are done in two separate steps. Especially when they are accustomed to using a typewriter, most people find the formatted display of word processing easier to use. For a skilled operator, however, a text editor can be faster because format can be indicated by keying two- or three-character codes rather than setting up the format on the screen.

Editor/formatter programs, especially on the mainframe, usually offer print format flexibility at the expense of ease of use. These programs have a number of advantages for creating large, complex documents such as manuals, texts, and manuscripts. Page numbering, hyphenation, and generation of figures, tables, footnotes, tables of contents, and indexes are handled by the formatter program. For example, if a new table were added to page 20 of a 200-page manuscript, the formatter would automatically renumber all subsequent tables as the text is formatted. Using a word processing program, the operator would have to go back to renumber all the tables.

As a side note, the entire text for this textbook was created on IBM PCs, using the IBM Professional Editor and the Script/PC print formatter. The table of contents, figures, tables, and footnotes were generated automatically by instructions embedded in the text. After review and editing, the floppy diskettes were sent to the publisher, and the entire text was input into the publisher's phototypesetting machine. Only special typesetting codes needed to be added; most of the Script formatting codes for the microcomputer printer are the same on the phototypesetter.

Document Size Limitations

Word processing programs have different size limitations for total number of characters (bytes) and number of pages. For most office correspondence and reports, size limitations pose no practical problems. For manuals or other large documents, however, size limitations are an important consideration. To handle large documents, each chapter or unit might have to be stored and printed as a separate document, which sometimes can cause problems in sequencing page numbers, tables of contents, or footnotes if programs do not have sufficient flexibility.

Command Keys Versus Function Keys and Codes

Word processing commands, such as copy, move, or delete, may be entered in one of three ways: (1) command keys, (2) program function keys, and (3) instruction codes. Command keys, which are labeled with the various editing features, are easiest to use and are usually found on dedicated word processors such as the Wang system shown in Figure 13-5.

Other word processing programs use function keys alone and in conjunction with shift, control, and alternate keys. Many popular microcomputer word processing programs, such as Multimate and OfficeWriter, use this approach. Decals or templates for the keyboard are usually provided to help the operator remember the correct key sequences. Control and alternate keys also may be used with the standard keyboard characters. For example, with AppleWriter, "Control" plus the "I" key turns the Insert mode on, and the same key sequence turns it off.

FIGURE 13-5. Command keys on a Wang word processor.

The third method, usually found in text editors, uses instruction codes, which may be embedded in the text or keyed on designated edit lines. For example, to move a block of text using the IBM Professional Editor program, the operator defines the block of text by keying "MM" on the edit lines, to the left of the first and last lines of text to be moved, and then presses the Enter key.

Defaults

Defaults refers to options that are automatically preset by the word processing program unless they are changed by the user. Defaults make it easier to get started with a program by limiting the options the new user has to be concerned about. As the user gains experience, default settings can be modified to meet the needs of various applications. (Default settings are widely used in software programs and are not limited to word processing.)

Standard Editing Functions

Editing refers to entering (creating) or changing text on the display screen. Most word processing software packages provide several basic functions for entering and revising text. Although the keys or procedures for the editing functions vary, the functions themselves are consistent across products. This section discusses editing functions common to most word processing programs. Subsequent sections discuss the many available variations, advanced features, and options.

Cursor movement functions The cursor is the symbol on the display screen that marks the current entry point. Word processing programs provide the user with command keys, function keys, and codes to move the cursor in documents:

1. *Character by character, line by line.* The cursor keys move the cursor one position at a time in any direction, corresponding with the directional arrow on the cursor key.
2. *Go to page.* The user indicates the page to which the cursor is to be moved, which can be any page in the document.
3. *Page up and page down.* The user can move *directly* from one page to the next, forward or backward.
4. *Word right or left.* The cursor can be moved directly to the beginning of the word to the right or left of the current cursor position.
5. *Beginning/end of line.* The cursor can be moved directly to the first or last character on the line on which it is positioned.
6. *Horizontal scrolling.* The user can scroll the cursor (and screen display) horizontally beyond the normal 80-character width for wide documents.
7. *Status line.* A line at the top or bottom of the screen displays information

such as document name, page number, line number, and column position of the cursor. Program prompts may also be displayed on this line.

Other basic editing functions The following basic editing functions are commonly provided in most word processing programs, although their availability may vary from one program to another:

1. *Strikeover.* A character or symbol in a word processing document may be replaced by simply rekeying another character.
2. *Word wrap.* As words are keyed, they automatically "wrap around" at the end of the display line. There is no need to use a return at the end of a line, as required with a typewriter.
3. *Insert.* An insert key or command lets the user add a character, word, or several paragraphs at any point.
4. *Delete.* A delete key or command allows the user to eliminate any number of consecutive characters.
5. *Copy.* Text can be copied from one location to any other. "Copy" duplicates the original text at the desired location.
6. *Move.* Text can be moved to any location in a document. Unlike "Copy," "Move" deletes text from the original location and relocates it.
7. *Block manipulation.* The user can manipulate multiline blocks of text for operations such as copy, move, and delete. Blocks of text are marked on the display screen with highlighting or block beginning and ending markers.
8. *Column manipulation.* The user can manipulate columns of numbers or text as blocks for operations such as copy, move, and delete. Column manipulation differs from block manipulation in that the rectangular block of text does not have to extend to the margins. This feature can be a great time saver for certain applications but is available only in more powerful word processing programs.
9. *Automatic line centering.* Text can be centered automatically between the right- and left-hand margin; no calculation or backspacing is necessary.
10. *Underlining.* Printed text can be underlined. Underlining may be designated by inserting special codes, using the underscore key to underline text on the display screen after it is keyed, or using a special underscore command as text is keyboarded.
11. *On-screen underlining.* Text underscoring can be displayed on the screen.
12. *Boldface.* Characters will appear thicker and darker than normal print.
13. *Onscreen boldface.* Boldface text can be displayed on the screen.
14. *Italics.* Text can be printed in italics (if the printer can print italic).

15. *Erase underlining or boldface without retyping.* The user can delete underscores or boldface without retyping the text.
16. *Choice of font types.* The user can select (usually from a menu of font types) the type style for printing a document. A few programs display different fonts on the screen; most just print different styles.
17. *Choice of point sizes.* The user can select (usually from a menu) the point size for printing a document. A few programs display different font sizes on the screen, but most only print different sizes.
18. *Superscripts/subscripts.* Characters can be printed one-half or one-quarter space above (superscript) or below (subscript) a line of type. A few programs can display superscripts and subscripts on the screen.
19. *Special characters/symbols.* The user can select special characters or symbols, such as math symbols or foreign-language characters.

Formatting functions

Formatting controls the arrangement of text on the display screen and the printed copy. The following formatting functions vary in operation and ease of use from one word processing program to another:

1. *Format line.* A special line to designate tabs, the right-hand margin, and vertical line spacing.
2. *Page breaks.* The user can designate where to end a page.
3. *Conditional page breaks.* The program automatically begins a new page when more than a user-specified number of lines are keyed.
4. *Global pagination.* Automatically renumbers pages, usually after insertion or deletion of text or changing the number of text lines per page.
5. *Widow/orphan control.* A global formatting feature that, for appearance, keeps the first line of a paragraph from being printed by itself at the bottom of a page (a widow) or the last line of a paragraph from being printed by itself at the top of a page (orphan). Some programs let the user specify the number of lines.
6. *Top and bottom page margins.* The user can select the top and bottom margins for printing text.
7. *Tab stops.* The user can specify the settings or select the interval between tabs. Tabs indent the first line of a paragraph or enter text in columns at tab stops.
8. *Automatic paragraph indent.* After the user keys a return, the first line of the next paragraph is indented.
9. *Automatic tab indent.* All lines of text are automatically left-aligned at the tab indent marker until the user keys a return; alignment then resumes at the left text margin.

10. *Decimal tabs.* Numbers are placed in a column so that the decimal points are aligned. A decimal is assumed to be at the end of a string of numbers or letters when no decimal point is keyed. Thus decimal tabs can also be used to right-justify columns of text or figures without decimal points.
11. *Automatic reformatting.* When the user changes the margins or tabs or inserts or deletes text, all text on the page is automatically realigned.
12. *Global reformatting.* The user can change the margin and tab settings for all pages in the document (instead of page by page).
13. *Hard spaces (required space).* The user can specify that certain spaces inserted in text should not be deleted if reformatting is performed. This keeps a portion of text together on a line, such as a name or date.
14. *Automatic hyphenation.* The program will hyphenate words that cross the right margin of the text. This is done by specifying the length of a *hyphenation zone.* Hyphenation is automatically revised when text is reformatted. Generally, this feature may be turned on or off at the user's discretion. The user may also modify the hyphenation dictionary to add or change words.
15. *Independent on-screen columns.* The user can create two or more columns on the screen, independently of each other. Text that is added to or deleted from one column does not affect other columns.
16. *Multicolumn formatting.* The program can print text in multiple column format (as in a newspaper), reformatting as necessary.
17. *Justification.* Justification programs can be used to format the margins of text in different ways.
    - *Block-justified text.* The program can display or print straight left and right margins for an entire document.
    - *Left-justified text.* Text is displayed or printed with a straight left margin and an uneven right margin (customary typewritten appearance). This is usually the default format.
    - *Right-justified text.* Text is displayed or printed with a straight right margin and uneven left margin.
    - *Microjustification.* The program can vary the distance between characters and words, using fractions of spaces rather than whole spaces. Spacing is based on the number of characters on the line rather than on the size of each character (as in proportional spacing).
    - *Section justification.* The user can specify sections of text to be block-justified. The remainder of the document is displayed or printed in left-justified text (or the default format).
    - *Proportional spacing.* Text can be printed with proportionally spaced type (variable-width characters) if the printer being used also supports proportional spacing. (A proportional space daisy wheel is required for an impact printer.)

Search-and-Replace Functions

The search function allows the user to find any word or character in a document. The search begins wherever the cursor is positioned and proceeds forward to the end of the document. Some programs also allow searching backward. The replace function finds specified words or characters and replaces them with other words or characters.

Search is useful, especially in long documents, for locating specific material in the text. Replace is very helpful for editing when one word needs to be changed for another throughout a long document (e.g., replacing "secretary" with "administrative assistant"). It can also save time as a typing shorthand. For instance, if "Superintendent of Documents, Washington, D.C." must be typed numerous times, the operator may type "SD." When finished, the operator simply uses the replace feature to find every occurrence of SD and replaces it with "Superintendent of Documents, Washington, D.C."

Options for search and replace functions include the following:

1. *Ignore case of letters.* The search command will ignore the case of letters. For example, specifying "from" will find "from," "From," and "FROM." (This is the default for some programs.)

2. *Case-sensitive (conditional) search.* The user can indicate whether or not the program should ignore upper- or lower-case letters during a search.

3. *Wild card search.* Wild cards are symbols that indicate that only other characters in the string need be matched. The program will substitute for a special character, usually ? or *, during search. For example, "n?t" will find "not," "net," and "nut." Or "thought*" will find "thoughts," "thoughtful," and "thoughtless." This feature is useful when the user doesn't remember the exact spelling of a word or for finding multiple occurrences.

4. *Search for partial word.* The user can specify a portion of a word during a search. For example, "for" will find "for," "forget," "forward," "form," and others.

5. *Conditional replace.* During the search and replace process, the program will stop at each occurrence of the specified word to let the user indicate whether it should be replaced.

6. *Global search and replace.* During the search and replace process, all occurrences of the specified word will be replaced automatically.

7. *Headers and footers.* Headers and footers are text that automatically prints at the top (header) or bottom (footer) of each page of a document. Headers and footers are used for titles, headings, page numbering, etc., and typically have the following options:
   - *Maximum lines per header or footer.* This is the maximum number of lines that can appear in a header.

- *Left- or right-justified headers or footers.* The user can specify that the header or footer print on the left or right side of a page. (Some programs allow only one of these options.)
- *Centered headers or footers.* The program can center the header or footer on a page, automatically or as an option.
- *Headers and footers on even or odd pages.* The user can specify that a header or footer be printed only on the even or odd pages.

Document Printing

Document printing is controlled by the word processing software. The program must include specific instructions (Printer Action Table or PAT) for the model being used. Word processing program documentation usually lists the printer models that are supported by the software. The options may vary from two or three to hundreds of models. Sometimes the vendor will modify the software, or provide instructions for the user to do so, for a specific printer model.

If a sheetfeeder is used with the printer, a separate set of instructions (Sheetfeeder Action Table or SAT) must be available for the word processing software. SAT options include the following:

1. *Maximum characters per line.* The user can specify the maximum number of characters that can appear in a single line on a printed page.
2. *User-specified paper length.* The user can specify the length of the paper to be used in printing.
3. *User-specified number of copies to print.* The user can specify the number of copies to print.
4. *Printer can pause at end of page.* The program can pause at the end of a page and resume printing when prompted by the user. This function is usually used to insert a new sheet of paper for each page when printing on single sheets (rather than continuous paper).
5. *User-specified page to start printing.* The user can specify the page of the document to be printed first.
6. *User-specified page to end printing.* The user can specify the page of the document that will be printed last.
7. *Automatic page numbering.* The user can have the program generate consecutive page numbers as the document prints.
8. *User-specified page to begin numbering.* The user can select the number that will be assigned to the first numbered page.
9. *Include or join files.* At print time, the user can instruct the program to include other disk files within the document being printed or to join other files to the end of the original document. Page numbering is thus continuous, treating the series of files as a single document.

10. *Print queuing.* The user can specify a series of different documents to be printed one after another.

11. *Printer support sheetfeeders.* This feature allows the user to control paper sheetfeeders and to select bins.

12. *Delayed printing.* The user can queue documents to begin printing at a specified time.

13. *Interrupt printing at any time.* The user can temporarily or permanently end the printing process.

14. *Continue printing from point of interruption.* Following a print interrupt command, the user can instruct the printer to continue from the place it stopped.

15. *Print spooling.* The user can edit one document while the program is printing a different one. Spooling is accomplished by allocating a portion of memory to hold the print file so the user can create or edit a different file (document).

16. *Automatic envelope printing.* Some programs allow the user to print an envelope, using the address at the beginning of the letter. The program will pick out the address and print it in standard format.

17. *Embedded printer codes.* The user can insert (embed) commands in the text that will be interpreted when the printer prints the document. Some programs have only special print functions (such as boldface or italics).

Merge Printing or Mail Merge

Merge printing, or *mail merge,* combines a primary file and a secondary list file to produce any number of copies of the primary file with appropriate variations of the list file. The primary file consists of permanent information such as a form letter, and the list document contains variable information such as names and addresses. Merge printing thus automates the production of form letters or other documents. It can also be used to print envelopes and labels.

Merge printing options include the following:

1. *Merge printing with list file.* The user can use the program to merge a list file containing variables (such as name, address, dates, dollar amounts, or other information) into a primary file to produce a series of individualized documents. The data file must have been created within the word processing program or within the manufacturer's family of software.

2. *Conditional merge printing (decision processing).* The user can specify selection criteria to be applied during a merge. For instance, the user

might want letters to be addressed only to accounts that are more than 60 days overdue.

3. *Merge printing with text reformatting.* When text is merged into a document, it can be reformatted automatically to conform with a specified format.

4. *Merge printing from ASCII file.* The program can accept merge data in an ASCII (American Standard Code for Information Interchange) format. The merge list file can be created by another program—a database program, for instance—as long as it is in the correct ASCII format.

5. *Merge printing from keyboard (key procedures).* This function allows the user to enter list data from the keyboard as the merge printing executes, as opposed to accepting such data only from a previously created file. This is useful for fill-in-the-blank forms or small numbers of form letters.

Document Filing/Retrieval Functions

Most word processing programs also provide various functions for filing and retrieving processed documents:

1. *Document summary screen.* A document summary screen is a special page that provides relevant information about a document. It is usually the first screen to appear when a document is created or selected. It may contain information such as document identification number, name, author, operator, number of pages, comments, key words, creation date, modification dates, and the number of characters in the document.

2. *List of files (document names) from within program.* The user can obtain a list (index) of files (documents) stored on a disk from within the word processing program. On some systems, the list may include additional information, such as author name, operator name, creation date, or special notes.

3. *Document search.* The user can search for a document by selected criteria such as document name, author name, operator name, creation date, or key words.

4. *Delete files.* The user can delete files from within the program.

5. *Rename files.* The user can rename documents without leaving the word processing program and without recopying the file under a different name.

6. *Automatic file back-up.* When the user begins to re-edit a document, the program automatically creates a copy of the original file and saves it. This feature ensures that the most recent copy of the file is always available if the user decides to discard current editing changes.

7. *Copy files from within the program.* The user can copy files from one diskette to another or between a hard disk and diskettes. Users may duplicate working copies of files or remove sensitive files from the system for storage in a safe place.
8. *Save-to- and retrieve-from-archive diskettes.* The user can back up to or restore files from an archive diskette. An archive diskette stores files in condensed format (not readable until restored). They are generally used to create back-up (duplicate) copies of all files and may also be used to save infrequently used documents (conserve memory space).
9. *Save block of text to disk.* The user can mark and save segments of the working file to separate disk files.
10. *External copy (append or include files).* The program allows the user to insert (append) contents from a second or disk file into the file that is being created or edited.
11. *Supports directories (pathnames).* Microcomputer word processing programs are compatible with the hierarchical file management system in PC DOS Version 2.0 and later versions.
12. *Document conversion.* The user can convert word processing files to formats needed for other word processing programs. Usually, a different procedure is needed for each conversion (e.g., Multimate to Wang, Wang to Multimate, or Volkswriter 3 to IBM's Revisable-Form-Text DCA).
13. *Password protection.* The user can assign passwords to documents to control access.

Spell Checking

Spell checkers provide a dictionary for verifying the spelling of all words in a document. During spell checking, the program matches all words in a document against its dictionary and identifies all words for which no match is found. Most programs allow users to add words to the built-in dictionary or to create one or more separate user dictionaries to supplement the built-in dictionary.

Spell checkers may be separate programs or integrated into the word processing program. When integrated into the program, spell checking can be activated from the editing mode. Separate programs require exiting the document and invoking the spell checking program, which generally requires switching disks on microcomputers without a hard disk.

Spell checking capabilities vary among word processing programs. Some not only locate misspellings but can suggest phonetically similar alternative spellings ("fonetic" would produce "phonetic"), correct transpositions ("siad" becomes "said"), catch repeated words, and verify capitalization and punctuation.

The speed and efficiency with which spell checkers verify text and correct errors vary among programs and are determined by the search algorithms and memory management schemes the program employs. The spell checking features found in most programs include the following:

1. *Number of words in built-in dictionary.* The number of words in the spell-checker dictionary file ranges from 20,000 to 170,000 for most programs.
2. *Maximum words added to a dictionary.* The user can add a limited number of words to the built-in dictionary file or a user-created dictionary.
3. *Displays misspelled words in context.* The program displays a potentially misspelled word in the context of the text, rather than only the word.
4. *Suggests correct spelling.* The program provides "guesses" for the spelling of words identified as misspelled.
5. *Spelling corrections made while in checker.* The user can correct misspelled words as they are identified by the spell checker rather than returning to the text to make corrections.
6. *Single-word checking.* During editing, the program allows the user to check the spelling of a word, using the spelling checker as a dictionary.

Advanced and Miscellaneous Functions

Some word processing programs provide additional advanced functions to meet various specialized needs:

1. *List processing.* Items typed in list format can be sorted alphabetically or numerically and in ascending or descending order. The user may designate one or more sort fields (criteria). The sort field width (up to 255 characters), the number of fields (up to 16), and the maximum number of lines that can be sorted at one time (up to 32,000 lines) vary among programs. Some programs can sort and combine multiple documents into one result document. The results of the sort may be stored in a new document (preserving the originals) or written over an existing document. Specifications of a sort operation can be saved and recalled in order to review, modify, or reuse them.
2. *Text storage and recall (library or boilerplating).* The user can create and store text with a one- or two-character identification code and recall it into any document. This feature is useful for creating files of frequently used paragraphs and phrases that can be added to text in any file. In writing contracts, for instance, standard paragraphs may be created and stored and later recalled and assembled in any order to compose a specific contract. The length and number of library entries allowed by the word processing software are two important variables.

3. *Readability analysis.* Readability analysis evaluates the readability of any word processing document. The results of the analysis provide the Flesch and Kinkaid grade-level reading equivalents for each paragraph, each page of text, and the entire document. Kinkaid is the standard for evaluating a document's legal readability.
4. *Mathematical calculation.* The user can perform mathematical calculations such as adding, subtracting, multiplying, dividing, computing percentages or subtotals, using constants, or crossfooting (summing rows and columns simultaneously).
5. *User-defined macro procedures.* The user can designate a key to represent a series of keystrokes that perform several commands at once.
6. *Windows or split screen.* The user can divide the screen into "windows" that allow different portions of text to be viewed and edited at the same time.
7. *Edit more than one document at a time.* The user can display and edit two or more documents on the screen at the same time.
8. *In-text footnotes.* The user can specify text to be printed as footnotes on the same page.
9. *End-of-document (chapter) footnotes.* The user can specify text to be used as footnotes that will automatically be printed at the end of the document or chapter.
10. *Index or table-of-contents generation.* The user can instruct the program to automatically create an index or table of contents based on chapter headings or key words and phrases.
11. *Foreign-language capabilities.* The user can access alternative character sets such as foreign-language characters and symbols for screen display or printing.
12. *Documents may be larger than system memory.* The size of the document is not limited to the RAM memory of the microcomputer or intelligent terminal. To accomplish this, portions of the document are swapped to and from the disk, using the disk drive as additional memory.
13. *Program editor.* The program's features allow the user to create and edit computer programs. Such features usually include the nondocument mode (or turn word-wrap off) and the production of standard ASCII files without special characters.
14. *Preference menu.* The user can change defaults and tailor options within the program. Changes may be temporary or permanent (and stored).
15. *On-screen help.* The user can at any time press a key to obtain help or reference information. The help menu guides the user to the desired information. Context-sensitive help brings the user to the appropriate

feature for the function being performed on the display screen. A keystroke exits the help mode and returns the user to his or her place in the document.

16. *On-screen tutorials.* Interactive on-screen tutorials provide the user with step-by-step instructions and exercises on how to use the various program features.

17. *Note function.* The user can enter reminders of instructions within a document. The notes will appear on the screen, but will be printed only if the user chooses. An entire page may be designated as a note that will not print.

18. *Automatic paragraph numbering.* An automatic paragraph number generator sequentially numbers chapters, sections, and subsections of documents and creates an optional table of contents. The original document remains unchanged while a new output document is generated with the numbered paragraphs and table of contents. Various numbering schemes and paragraph levels are supported. This feature is useful for reports, manuals, books, or legal briefs that require sequentially numbered chapters and paragraphs.

19. *Calculator function.* This feature performs many functions of a hand-held or office calculator. The calculator adds, subtracts, multiplies, and divides any number and is accurate to 13 digits. It also may perform powers and roots of numbers. The user can produce an output document for editing or printing the calculations.

Print/Photocomposition Capabilities

A word processing application that saves considerable time is the conversion of word processing text directly into camera-ready copy, without rekeying the text onto a phototypesetting machine. Word processing text can be converted into phototypeset copy (with the aid of special software) for printing on large, high-speed laser printers, such as the Xerox 9700. The special typesetting commands in the text are interpreted by the software and converted to phototypeset copy on the laser printer.

Software also is available for microcomputers that enables text to be produced in near-typeset quality on desktop laser printers. These desktop publishing programs allow the user to combine word processing text with artwork and graphics, arrange it on a page, and print it on a desktop laser printer. The programs vary in complexity and flexibility. While some programs display the copy on the screen as it will appear in print (WYSIWYG: what you see is what you get), others format the final document during printing. Programs have various limitations vis-a-vis the microcomputers, laser printers, and word processing software with which they will work. As discussed in Chapter 10, desktop publishing software has been a real boon for preparing in-house newsletters, announcements, flyers, programs, training materials, and other forms of low-cost printing.

As the foregoing discussion indicates, word processing software offers many features and variations. Although the distinctions may not be obvious to the novice, they can be critical to the efficient and effective use of word processing software. Office systems analysts must fully understand the significance of the various options for specific applications.

DOCUMENT CREATION

Several options are available for document input or creation. Documents may be transcribed by a word processing operator from shorthand or dictation equipment, copied from printed or handwritten material, or composed directly at the keyboard. Text may be input by optical character recognition (OCR), conversion from data files, or computer input microfilm (CIM). Devices may soon be available that can convert speech directly into written words (see Chapter 9).

Dictation and Transcription

Dictation and transcription systems (described in Chapter 5) save time for both principals and support personnel. When principals use dictation systems, they can author documents any time and any place without tying up the time of a stenographer. Dictation can be done in the car, on airplanes or trains, in a hotel room, at home, or in the office. With dial-up dictation units, principals can call in from anywhere in the world to dictate information or instructions. Support personnel can have the transcribed copy ready for the principal's signature when he or she returns to the office. The support staff's workload can be balanced more evenly.

Secretaries and administrative assistants may also use dictation in word processing centers to compose routine correspondence. To take minutes in meetings, secretaries may use dictation units designed for recording telephone and conference conversations. Secretaries do not even have to be present at the meeting; they can compose and type the meeting minutes as they listen to the proceedings on a transcribing unit.

Modern dictation systems are easy to use and provide many options to assist both the dictator and transcriber. Dictation features include marking the beginning and end of documents, special instructions, guides to judge document length, and flagging rush documents. The latest digital units provide more flexibility for editing and revising text than earlier analog systems.

Transcription management systems enable transcribers to determine how much dictation is on the system, scan special instructions, and identify and select priority documents. Some systems identify who dictated what and which transcriber has it, assign dictation to the next available operator, and print out management reports. Transcription management systems are valuable tools for managing document production in large word processing centers.

Modern dictation equipment also serves specialized applications, which ease the work of clerical personnel. For example, dictation units are used for order entry in sales and catalog businesses, bill payment, banking, and patient admissions in hospitals. Tied in with terminals or microcomputers, dictation equipment can be used to record telephone messages or send verbal or written messages to other users. Support personnel can create a message slip (from a telephone window) to leave a text or voice message for busy or no-answer phone calls. In either situation, the system supplies the information it knows, such as time, date, and name and number of sender.

Despite the advantages of machine transcription, many businesspeople still prefer face-to-face shorthand dictation, even though it is considered less efficient. Shorthand is face-to-face dictation by an originator to a secretary or stenographer who uses a special notation system (Gregg and Pitman are the most common) to record the information. The use of shorthand for dictation has declined in recent years due to improved dictation equipment, word processing centers, and the trend for authors to key documents directly with word processing software.

Principals who prefer face-to-face dictation often use such sessions to discuss business matters with their secretaries. Dictators may give secretaries the necessary information and instruct them to create the document themselves. Generally, however, machine dictation is recommended over shorthand for the following reasons:

1. Machine dictation is more cost effective because it requires the time of only one individual.

2. Any word processing operator can transcribe machine dictation whereas it is difficult for an operator to transcribe someone else's shorthand.

3. Unlike a secretary, a dictation machine can always be available, even when the user is away from the office.

4. Oral dictation interrupts the secretary, but machine dictation does not.

New work group dictation systems are available to meet the needs of small *strategic business units*. A fast-growing concept, these close-knit teams demand local secretaries rather than a remote word processing center. A work group dictation system allows multiple users to dictate into a system at the transcriber's desk. Several people can dictate at the same time, including telephone callers, even while the secretary is transcribing. No cassettes need to be carried back and forth between principals and secretaries, and no bulky desktop units sit on the users' desks.

For example, one secretary supports a work group of 15 engineers who travel frequently. They dictate reports immediately after they visit clients, often from hotel rooms or airports. This would be impractical if they had to wait for the secretary to stop transcribing before they could dictate. Transcribed material goes immediately to upper management for review. When the engineers call in again, questions can be answered immediately.

Dictation is especially effective for short, well-formatted material such as memos and letters. Authors and transcriptionists require appropriate training in methods and techniques to ensure effective use of the technology. Dictation and transcription guidelines are summarized in Figure 13-6.

FIGURE 13-6. Guidelines for dictation and transcription.

1. Gather your thoughts.
2. Pause whenever you are interrupted or gathering your thoughts.
3. Make a short outline of the subject to be dictated.
4. Insert commas and periods.
5. Completely spell out unique names.
6. Edit as you dictate.
7. Handle your dictation as soon as possible. Keep passing your complete dictation to your secretary.
8. If unsure about your dictation, tell your secretary in the beginning that it is a "*rough draft*."
9. Use your cue alert at the end of each unit of dictation. This allows your secretary to locate something in an emergency and also provides him/her with information concerning how much dictation is on each tape.
10. Use the double cue alert to make special instructions for the letter.
11. Before dictating, indicate what it is that you are about to dictate and any pertinent information the secretary requires before he/she starts typing. For example, if it is a chart with columns, indicate the number of columns and how you want the page to be set up before you dictate the information.
12. Use the *equipment.* It will save you a tremendous amount of time.
13. Always be considerate. Remember, someone is listening to you dictate.

Additional tips to make transcription easier for the secretary:

1. Imagine yourself listening and transcribing your own dictation and consider what you need to know and when you need the information.
2. Whenever a deviation in the standard format is necessary, notify the transcriptionist in advance. Remember that *what you say is simultaneously being transcribed.*
3. Give advance notice for margin changes, indentions, columns, or special tabular formats.
4. Always make clear notations of all corrections or revisions prior to the change.
5. To differentiate between *text* and *instructions,* use appropriate voice inflections and pauses, and address the transcriptionist by name, if possible. For example, "By the way, Joan, that last sentence should be in quotes," or, "Oh, Paul, underline that entire phrase."
6. Remember that you are really talking to a person! You're allowed to make mistakes or changes.

Optical Character Recognition

Optical character recognition (OCR) systems electronically scan data from paper and convert it to digital format for direct input to a computer (see Chapter 5). OCR provides a practical alternative to keying for entering printed or typed text into a computer. OCR systems, which scan a page in 15 to 25 seconds, can do in 2½ minutes what would take a typist an hour. Thus OCR input can save considerable time. For example, manuals can be scanned into a word processing system to be updated and stored on floppy disks or hard disks. OCR can also solve incompatibility problems. Text created on one word processing system can be printed out and scanned into another word processing system.

In addition, offices that use paper filing systems or micrographic storage systems can scan documents in as they are needed instead of retaining duplicate copies on magnetic storage.

Although OCR systems cannot yet produce error-free copy, they make fewer mistakes than the average typist. Some vendors claim their standard for error is 1 in 300,000 characters. A more realistic estimate is that OCRs make two mistakes per page, which compares very favorably with five errors per page for the average typist. There are 1400 characters on a typical double-spaced page, 2800 on a single-spaced page.

DOCUMENT MANAGEMENT

Integrated document-handling systems, operating on local communications networks, can help office managers to streamline work procedures. *Document management* refers to a systems approach to handling complex documents. It entails managing all steps in preparing and producing documents from their creation to subsequent editing, formatting, composition and makeup, printing and reproduction, distribution, presentation, and storage. This approach encompasses four elements:

1. Integrating the various activities that go into composing documents.
2. Reducing the number of steps required to produce complex documents.
3. Distributing the documents electronically to both local and remote recipients.
4. Presenting documents in the most appropriate medium: letter-quality printing, composite form with graphics, publication-quality output, Videotex, or other electronic display.

Information managers are just beginning to recognize the importance of document management and the unique problems associated with it. Dwight F. Ryan, president of Xerox Corporation's Business Systems Group, pointed out that the production of documents is centered in work groups. Documents are the medium for transmitting useful information and frequently are the only tangible products that knowledge workers have to show for their labor. Document creation generally moves from the bottom of an organization upward. Typically, documents are authored by staff workers, then submitted to management for review and approval. As they make their way up the management hierarchy, their format often changes. Documents tend to become shorter and more polished. As they are revised, they may be combined with graphics and images and printed in various formats.

The objective of document management systems is to streamline the movement of decision documents among the people who provide input, editing, or review. Thus communications capabilities are critical to document management. Despite hardware and software advances, however, many products are incompatible with existing systems. Ensuring the compatibility of workstations, peripherals, and networks is key to document management.

Text-Retrieval Systems

Text-retrieval systems (TRS) are a cross between word processors and database management systems. Figure 13-7 presents a comparison of text-retrieval and database management systems. The use of text-retrieval systems for general business applications is fairly recent, although these software packages have been around for over 20 years. Arthur J. Tobias, an expert on the use of text-retrieval systems, has written the following:

> Full-text retrieval systems can efficiently access the entire text database. The dozen or so TRSes on the market vary in capabilities, but a common core of features can be identified. By nature, they are menu-driven, user-oriented on-line mainframe systems that can work with, but should not be confused with, word processors. Their function is to enter, index, retrieve, display, and print documentary information. The most advanced systems can store millions of records, search entire databases in seconds, and display retrieved data in variable formats, either predetermined or user-specified.[1]

FIGURE 13-7. A comparison of text-retrieval and database management systems.

In a superficial way, relational database management systems (DBMS) and text-retrieval database systems are very much alike. Both offer users unstructured ways to access data that may or may not be structured. But there's a big difference in the form of the information that exists within the respective databases.

In a relational DBMS, information tends to be numeric, while in a text database or retrieval system it is more often word-oriented, though neither is necessarily exclusively so. Typically, however, information retrieved from a relational DBMS might be a corporate financial statement, while in a text-retrieval system the information would likely be contained in an annual report-type statement.

FIGURE 13-7. (continued)

Aside from the similarity of purpose, however, text-retrieval and database systems are quite different from DBMSes, relational or conventional. In a relational DBMS, the database consists of a collection of tables, or relations, composed of rows, or tuples, and each row contains columns, or fields. (The terms *table, file,* and *relation* are interchangeable, as are the terms *row, record,* and *tuple* and the terms *column, field,* and *attribute.*) Data stored within a relational database tends to be numeric, though character strings, or even a few words, are sometimes used.

The table is the only data structure a relational DBMS user comes in contact with. Through a variety of access methods—including menus and custom or prepackaged screen forms, but most often a high-level, English-like query language such as IBM's Structured Query Language (SQL)—the user can request related groups of records one set at a time. In hierarchical or network DBMS models, data is retrieved one record at a time.

In text-retrieval systems, data is stored in the form of documents, some of which may be separated into sub-databases by general subject matter. A science text database might be divided into physics, biology, or chemistry, for example. In most cases, the software automatically generates an index of every searchable word in a newly filed document. This index, sometimes called an *inverted file,* resembles the index at a back of a book. What constitutes a searchable word is determined by either the user or the index. The text database system almost always screens out so-called "noise words," such as "and," "a," and "the."

A third and separate file, called a *postings file,* acts as the pointing mechanism between the full-text document and its index of key searchable words. This file lists the location of each searchable word in that document. Users retrieve documents by asking the system for desired key words or phrases. These could be the subject of the document, the author, or the date of publication. Sometimes the text database system can retrieve documents on the basis of root words or word approximations, although this may vary depending on the sophistication of a particular product.

Text-retrieval system users have a wide choice of how their queries will be answered. The system displays a list of all documents containing the desired key words, the complete document, the line or lines in which the key words appear in each document, or the context of each occurrence of the desired key word.

Information in a text database is "flat," according to both relational DBMS and text database vendors, meaning there are no underlying relationships between different files in a text database nor between the indexes of key words for each document. A postings file does not point to occurrences of the same key words in other files in the database, only to the particular file it is attached to. In a relational DBMS, by contrast, direct and indirect relationships often exist between the fields in one record and the fields in another.

Another difference worth noting is that text databases tend to be much larger than many traditional relational DBMSes and thus tend to use greater amounts of CPU cycles.

Early TRS users were generally institutions such as state governments, libraries, and the legal and medical professions. In the commercial sector, the first industries to recognize the utility of TRS were either highly regulated, such as utilities and transportation, or subject to statutory, safety, and contract requirements, such as the chemical, pharmaceutical, defense, and nuclear industries. The Georgia state legislature began using Data Retrieval Corporation's text-retrieval systems in early 1970 for tracking legislation. Robert Crowe, project coordinator and manager of the computer services unit responsible for legislative tracking, said "the job of keeping up with and reporting the changes to the legislature would be unthinkable without the assistance of a text-retrieval system."[2]

The Travelers Insurance Company, which adopted Information Retrieval's Alter package in 1982, used it first on a pilot basis for its Laramis (legislation and regulation tracking) program in conjunction with contract management. Today, Travelers uses TRS for a wide variety of applications that require online updating and viewing of information. Travelers plans to develop a completely integrated electronic information management system in its 3000-member information systems department. Automated text retrieval, reporting, and distribution are an integral part of the plan.

The main objective of text-management systems is high-volume reference information for administrative and decision making functions. Whereas word processing focuses primarily on the creation of immediately usable text, TRS provides storage and rapid retrieval. Figure 13-8 illustrates the text-retrieval process.

SECRETARIAL AND ADMINISTRATIVE APPLICATIONS

A variety of software tools are available to aid secretaries, administrative assistants, and paraprofessionals. Not everyone agrees on the usefulness of some of these tools. When analyzing the needs of these personnel, office systems analysts must pay careful attention to *how* things are done, not just *what* is done. Work procedures often reflect the work styles of the managers and professionals with whom support staff work. Time saved through office automation enables administrative personnel to take on more of the paperwork and quasi-clerical duties formerly handled by management, thereby improving productivity of the principals as well.

Secretarial and administrative applications will be discussed in the following order:

- Handling visitors and scheduling appointments
- Arranging meetings
- Handling telephone calls
- Tracking and follow-up
- Processing mail
- Making travel arrangements
- Secretarial typing

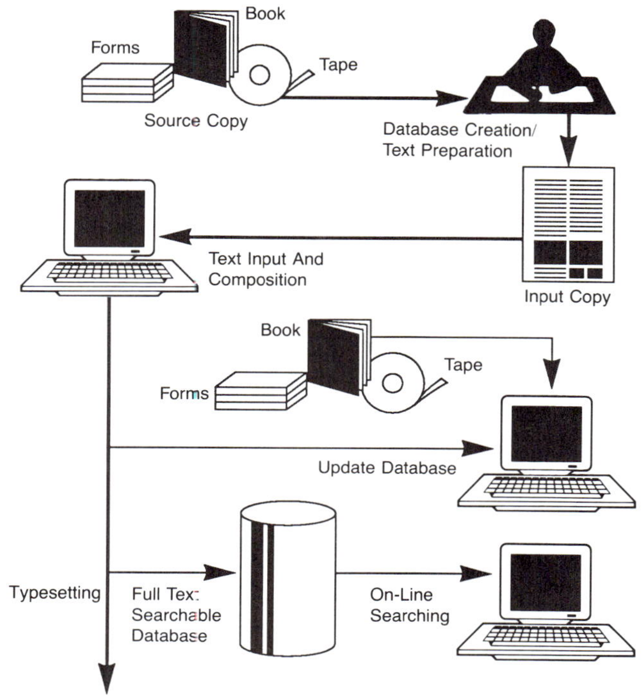

Text-retrieval systems provide a comprehensive path from initial data search to publishable document in a user-friendly language.

FIGURE 13-8. **The text-retrieval process.**

Handling Visitors and Scheduling Appointments

Electronic calendars can save time and provide better control over scheduling appointments. When both the principal and the administrative assistant schedule meetings, they always view the same up-to-date calendar. The old problem of two versions of the calendar—one on the principal's desk and one on the secretary's desk—is eliminated. The administrative assistant who maintains calendars for several principals can access all the calendars from his or her workstation and is freed from cluttering the desk with several different calendar pads. The ease with which the user can flip from one person's calendar to another's varies, however, among systems.

Most calendar systems offer daily, weekly, monthly, and annual views. The user may schedule appointments by date, time, and place. The appointment entry may include other information, such as descriptions and agenda items. Calendar systems include privacy and security features that specify who may access and update the calendar. The calendar may be viewed on the display screen or printed out.

On most systems, making an entry on the daily calendar automatically updates the weekly and monthly views. Looking for information is also easier with electronic calendars. To check an appointment, for example, the administrative secretary simply keys in the name of the visitor and the automatic search locates the date and time, eliminating the need to flip through pages.

By using a properly configured portable computer with a modem to dial into the office system, individuals can check their calendars from home or while traveling. This may be rather limited because of equipment incompatibilities, but vendors are working on a voice-response feature to enable a user to dial up the calendar from any telephone. The new unit would convert calendar entries to audio mode so that the user could check appointments from any telephone in the world.

To work effectively, calendar systems require integration among systems. In small organizations or work groups that share an integrated system, calendar systems provide maximum functionality. Functionality across computer systems, however, is often limited.

Arranging Meetings

An administrative secretary may often spend an hour or more setting up a meeting for six or eight high-level managers. Using the meeting scheduler feature of an electronic calendar, however, the secretary could schedule the same meeting in five minutes. The meeting scheduler checks the calendars of all invitees and provides a list of mutually convenient dates. Secretaries schedule meetings on the calendars of the principals for whom they have access and send invitations to the others by electronic messaging. A calendar system should enable the secretary to notify participants of the meeting time and place, as well as list the participants and the purpose of the meeting, and request confirmations. One message is sent electronically to all participants. The meeting scheduler eliminates telephoning individuals (or their secretaries) to determine dates and trying to schedule a meeting convenient to everyone. Cancellations and reschedulings, a common occurrence, can also be accomplished quickly and easily.

The meeting scheduler can also schedule conference rooms and other facilities, equipment, or groups. The conference room can be assigned a calendar on the system in the same way as individuals. When the secretary enters the name of the room, the scheduler searches the calendar of the conference room for open times. Some systems incorporate information on seating capacity, location, and equipment to select and schedule the appropriate room.

Handling Telephone Calls

Another time-consuming task that can be improved with automation is handling telephone calls. A computerized directory makes locating numbers easy. The user simply keys in the individual's last name, and the computer brings up the telephone number. If the user cannot remember the exact spelling, the user can key in the first few characters, and the computer will return a list of possible names. The computer can even be programmed to dial the number when the telephone is connected through the terminal.

Digital telephone systems provide many features that save time and make communication easier. If a line is busy, the system will automatically keep redialing and *call back* when the call goes through. Frequently called numbers can be programmed into the system and *speed dialed*. Two or three callers can be connected for a conference, or the telephone can be placed in the speaker mode for everyone to hear the conversation. Calls can be *call forwarded* to another location so that important calls will not be missed. A signal indicates that a second call is waiting when individuals are already on the telephone.

In addition, phone-mail systems increase the usefulness of the telephone. If the call is not picked up after, say, three rings, the caller hears a greeting that offers the option of leaving a detailed voice message or being transferred to the operator. By leaving a voice message, the caller can feel confident that the recipient hears it exactly. A caller may dial phone-mail directly and put a message in the recipient's phone mailbox at any time.

When recipients check their phone mailboxes, they can listen to the calls in order or scan through them, listening only to selected calls. Messages can be saved, forwarded, or deleted. When calls are forwarded, commentary can be added. If a caller wants to word a message very carefully or convey the same message to several persons, it can be recorded and sent by indicating the correct extension(s).

Tracking and Follow-up

Tracking and following up on activities or documents are important in almost every office. "Keeping track" means knowing if something was received, what needs to be done with it, what was done with it, and where it is now. These tasks usually require a *logbook*, a systematic record of progress or operation. Logs may be used for mail, messages, resumes, orders, visitors, invoices, and meeting agendas—to name just a few. A *tickler file* is a type of log that itemizes tasks that need to be performed on a given date. Deadlines and reminders are arranged in chronological order and can be retrieved at a future date.

Logbooks and tickler files can be handled with computers software. Tasks can either be recorded in narrative or be noted with upcoming due dates. Who is to be responsible for tasks and procuring background documents can also be noted on a tickler file entry. The user simply calls up the tickler files for printing or display.

The list processing feature of word processing software, spreadsheet programs, or database programs can also be used to create tracking and followup systems. Low-priced software for microcomputers, such as the Reminder System from Campbell Services, allows users to maintain a schedule of appointments and meetings, to-do lists, personal items, birthdays and anniversaries, and any other lists. (Items are always displayed or printed in list form.) Reminder notes on such systems can be reviewed, sorted, and searched. Sample screen displays of an automated tracking and follow-up system are shown in Figure 13-9.

FIGURE 13-9. An automated tracking and follow-up system is easier to maintain and provides better control than manual methods.

a. Computer screen display for adding information to a follow-up system.

```
VIEWING: □Del▮ to delete this record.     □F9▮ to Edit
         □Esc▮ to return to main menu.    □F7▮ for table view.

                      THE FOLLOW-UP            Record #    1
                         SYSTEM

 CLIENT NAME:   Adams                 Mary             M
(Last,First,MI)

 AGENT NAME:  Smith            John          CSR NAME:  Jones
(Last,First)                                (Last Only)

              POLICY NUMBER:  1 111 333

       DATE FILE ORIGINATED:   8/09/88
             FOLLOW UP DATE:   8/30/88

        REASON PENDING CODE:  SURR
             REASON PENDING:  Surrender of policy

         LAST ACTIVITY DATE:   7/23/88
              LAST ACTIVITY:  memo to agent
```

b. Computer screen display of follow-up report showing items overdue.

8/09/88 OVERDUE FOLLOW-UP DATES REPORT AS OF 8/23/88 Page 1

Agent: Smith, John

Client Name	Policy Number	Origin Date	Follow-Up Date	CSR	Reason Pending Code/ Reason Pending
Susan A Brown	4 222 444	8/09/88	8/23/88	Jones	OWNR Owner change
Phil Green	2 888 999	8/09/88	8/23/88	Jones	RETCK TM check returned
John M Paul	8 555 666	8/09/88	8/23/88	Jones	TM Check for form
Mary N White	1 666 777	8/09/88	8/23/88	Jones	NAME Name change

Processing Mail

When mail arrives in a small office or is delivered to a department or executive office in large companies, administrative personnel are responsible for sorting and distributing it. Practices vary considerably, from simple sorting to formal tracking. Mail for knowledge workers and supervisory managers may be delivered to their desks unopened. For managers and executives, mail is generally opened and sorted. Secretaries or administrative assistants may be authorized to handle all routine correspondence, using their discretion in selecting mail to be brought to the attention of the executive.

Spreadsheets, databases, and specialized tracking programs have greatly reduced the time and tedium of maintaining summary mail logs. Mail logs generally list each item of incoming mail, its distribution, and disposition. Some organizations log every piece of incoming mail (usually only first-class mail) and track it to its final disposition on a central mail-logging system. Not only has automation decreased the time and effort for maintaining these logs, but electronic search and retrieval enable a secretary to locate an item in seconds.

Making Travel Arrangements

Administrative secretaries can access reservation services by a dial-up connection through a modem. They can check airline schedules and make reservations directly on the system, thereby saving considerable time. Large companies often have their own in-house travel bureaus, with the full services of the online systems of commercial travel services. The former may even be operated as company profit centers, earning the standard commissions paid to outside travel agencies.

Secretarial Typing

Originally, word processing equipment was installed in dedicated centers. As costs have come down, however, word processing terminals or microcomputers with word processing software are commonly installed at secretarial workstations.

If secretaries do not have a word processor, they frequently use electronic typewriters, which meet the need for short letters, memorandums, and envelopes. For forms, electronic typewriters are more efficient than personal computers or dedicated word processors because typewriters are paper-handling devices but microcomputers are not. It is not uncommon for secretaries to have microcomputers *and* typewriters. Companies should carefully consider workstation policies that result in multiple devices.

Electronic typewriters offer cost-effective solutions for applications with light typing requirements, where word processing would be overkill. Most electronic typewriters are basic units with upgrade paths so that an office can start with a modest investment yet follow a path for adding capabilities as the needs become apparent.

Today, some electronic typewriters have built-in calculators, spell checkers, consulting dictionaries, calendars, and multifunction calculators. Some electronic typewriters can become part of local area networks. They can also be linked through modems and telephone lines to send messages to other electronic typewriters, word processors, terminals, and corporate data centers—in the same building or across the world. Information and data sharing may also be possible between microcomputers and electronic typewriters via translation utility programs. Statistics created by a spreadsheet on a microcomputer may be integrated with a sales report prepared on an electronic typewriter.

CLERICAL ACCOUNTING AND GENERAL CLERICAL APPLICATIONS

Administrative personnel are often responsible for maintaining department budgets and tracking expenses. Spreadsheet programs can reduce the time and effort required for these duties and provide better control for tracking expenses against budgets. With the aid of spreadsheets, many other administrative and clerical tasks are now completed more effectively and with much less time and effort. Among these tasks are the following:

- Office bookkeeping
- Petty cash funds
- Expense reports
- Invoicing
- Billing
- Timecard calculations
- Bank reconciliations
- Local taxes and reporting forms
- Depreciation schedules
- Physical inventory records

Virtually any repetitive administrative task that requires itemizing information in columns and rows is an appropriate application for a spreadsheet. Most administrative assistants, secretaries, and clerical personnel welcome the challenge of setting up spreadsheets once they have had basic training in their use. Applications such as index cards, Rolodex files, notebooks, forms, and other recordkeeping aids can be handled using database programs.

SUMMARY

Clerical and administrative personnel support the primary operations of the organization and the managers and knowledge workers who perform those primary roles. Among the personnel within the clerical and administrative category are secretaries, stenographers, typists, bookkeepers, mail clerks, file clerks, order-entry clerks, word processing operators, administrative assistants, proofreaders, billing clerks, accounts receivable or payable clerks, customer representatives, inventory clerks, mail handlers, data-entry operators, bank tellers, telephone attendants, shipping clerks, and hundreds of others.

Office technologies impact virtually every job within these ranks. Many jobs have changed significantly, some have been eliminated, others added. Previous notions about who performs what work are redefined with office automation. Some of the lines between clerical and professional work have blurred.

This chapter addressed the needs of clerical and administrative personnel primarily in document processing, administrative and secretarial, clerical accounting, and general clerical applications.

Document (or word) processing refers to the use of computer technology to produce documents. Hundreds of word processing programs are available on microcomputers, minicomputers, mainframes, and dedicated systems to meet a broad range of needs. Requirements for document processing differ significantly among users. High-volume word processing is often handled in word processing centers.

Document input (or creation) may be accomplished with transcription equipment, optical character recognition, or conversion from other software. Integrated document handling systems, operating on local communication networks, and text retrieval systems serve the specialized needs of voluminous text applications, such as government legislation.

Administrative support and secretarial applications include handling visitors and scheduling appointments, arranging meetings, handling telephone calls, tracking and follow-up, budgeting and office accounting, making travel arrangments, and processing mail. General clerical and accounting applications include spreadsheets for petty cash, expense reports, invoicing, depreciation schedules, and a host of other applications.

Additional clerical and administrative applications are discussed in Chapter 14.

DISCUSSION QUESTIONS

1. List and describe the word processing features most important for the following applications:
   a. Technical manuals
   b. General correspondence
   c. Statistical reports
   d. Company newsletters
   e. Business reports and proposals
2. How do word processing requirements of support staff differ from the requirements of managers and professionals?
3. How does the concept of document processing differ from traditional word processing?
4. Shorthand as a dictation tool has limited potential in the automated office. Do you agree or disagree? Explain.
5. OCRs offer a shortcut for entering data into a word processing system. What other benefits can be attributed to OCR systems?
6. What is document management? What is its value to organizations?
7. Secretarial and administrative applications speed the time in which secretarial work can be accomplished. List the eight applications discussed in this chapter, giving an example of how each could be used in a business office.
8. The role of secretary is changing from clerical to paraprofessional. Do you agree or disagree? Why?

APPLICATION EXERCISES

1. Survey three or four companies or offices to determine the tools available to support staff. Firms should represent the following:
   a. Financial services
   b. Retailing
   c. Government or city office
   d. University office
2. Read three reviews of the same microcomputer software in journals such as *PC Week, PC World, Software News,* or *Business Software Review.* Write an evaluation of the product, giving examples of possible administrative applications.
3. Interview two secretaries to determine which word processing software features they consider most beneficial. If appropriate, ask them how their work was done prior to using word processing.
4. Attend an office systems trade show and try (or observe) demonstrations of three word processing products. Obtain literature from the vendors. List the features identified in this chapter on the left side of a sheet of paper and the names of the three products across the top. Compare the features. Which is most appropriate for production word processing? For professional use? Why? Compare the three products.

SUGGESTED READINGS

"The Corporation: Executive Secretary: A New Rung on the Corporate Ladder," *Business Week* (April 21, 1986), pp. 74–75.

Fernberg, Patricia. "ETs Find Their Home in Tomorrow's Office," *Modern Office Technology* (September 1988), pp. 54-58.

Flanders, Frank B. "Desktop Publishing for Today's Office," *Office Systems Research Journal* (Spring 1988), pp. 31-33.

CHAPTER 14
ADMINISTRATIVE APPLICATIONS: Part 2

OBJECTIVES

After completing this chapter, the reader should be able to meet the following objectives:

- Discuss how office technologies are changing administrative services.
- Identify the major stumbling blocks in the integration of administrative services.
- Discuss the problems in managing information in digital, image, and paper formats.
- Explain how technology is changing the roles of records managers, file clerks, and staff providing mail, telephone, wire, and reprographic services.
- Understand the role of records management in the information processing cycle.
- Identify features in modern telephone systems and explain how they improve office communications.
- List the benefits of electronic forms management.
- Understand the role of mail and messenger services in the office and how automation can improve those services.

KEY TERMS

call accounting
convenience copy
distributed printing
download
electronic-key systems
facilities management
hybrid systems
key telephone systems
mail accounting systems
microfacsimile
mobile filing systems
record
records management
reprographics
rollover
rotary files
station message detail recording

INTRODUCTION

Chapter 13 covered applications for word processing personnel, administrative assistants, secretaries, paraprofessionals, clerical accounting, and general clerical personnel. This chapter continues with a discussion of applications for personnel in replication and distribution, records management, and facilities management. Replication and distribution includes telephone and wire services, mail services, reprographics, and forms control. Records management includes micrographics, optical disk applications, and networking.

Office automation technologies are helping to improve operations in all administrative services. The importance of improving coordination among administrative functions in order to create an integrated information infrastructure, is the theme throughout this chapter. After an overview of general job requirements, applications will be covered in the following order:

- Replication and distribution
- Records management
- Facilities management

General Job Requirements of Office Support

Workers whose job applications are discussed in this chapter include personnel in telephone and wire services, mail services, records management, reprographics, forms design, and facilities management.

Telephone and Wire Service Personnel

Telephone service providers play a vital role in a business office. Choosing the right telephone system is one of the most important decisions a company can make because telephone service is a major cost of doing business and affects every individual in the office. Telephone and wire service personnel include receptionists, console attendants, Telex and TWX operators, and facsimile attendants.

Mail Services Personnel

As the volume of mail has increased, so have the demands on mailroom operations. Electronic communications and distribution increase the pressure to move more information faster, both within and between organizations. Efficient, economical, dependable service has become a major challenge for mailroom personnel. Historically, mailrooms have been staffed with entry-level personnel who were expected to work temporarily in the mailroom, before moving up to better positions. Mailroom equipment and furnishings were minimal and operations were likely to be housed in the basement or some backoffice hideaway. Because mail services in large organizations handle millions of pieces of mail a month at substantial cost, the old attitude and approach are changing. Today's technology offers many opportunities to increase the efficiency and effectiveness of mail services and provide better integration with other information processing components.

The job titles of mail services personnel vary considerably among organizations. The major tasks handled by mail personnel include the following:

- Processing incoming mail
    - Receiving and opening mail
    - Sorting and time stamping
    - Distributing mail
- Processing outgoing mail
    - Collecting and sorting by destination
    - Inserting, sealing, and stamping
    - Posting mail
- Messenger services
- Express mail services
- Wire services (Telex, TWX, and facsimile)

Records Management Personnel

Records management personnel maintain information and make it available as needed. They are responsible for storing, retrieving, protecting, archiving, and purging records. (A *record* is any form of recorded information.) *Records management* has traditionally been defined as the science of managing records and information from their creation to final disposition. Records and information may be found in many forms: paper documents, computer printouts, microforms, videotapes, magnetic tapes and disks, optical disks, voice recordings, photographs, and many others.

To manage information resources efficiently, organizations must have a comprehensive program that establishes policies and procedures for storing, accessing, protecting, and purging information, regardless of format. A comprehensive program can eliminate expensive duplication of effort and optimize operations.

Large organizations generally have a separate records department, which may include an active-records supervisor, a center (inactive-records) supervisor, forms supervisor, micrographics supervisor, and clerical personnel within each function. Small organizations often do not have separate departments. The records management function may be controlled by an office manager, secretary, clerk, or accountant.

Statistics may help put the size of the task in perspective. In the United States, over a million documents are created every minute. Office workers file 180 million papers and produce 600 million pages of printout every day. In addition to hardcopies, organizations must deal with millions of tapes, disks, microfiche, and cassettes.

Paper filing systems consume a large part of a budget. It costs between $12,000 and $13,500 annually to maintain ten five-drawer vertical file cabinets (based on $20 per square foot of office space and an average clerical salary of $195 per week, plus supply costs). Seventy percent of filing costs go to salaries, 20 percent to space, 5 percent to supplies, and 5 percent to equipment. The cost of space, rent, and new construction is rising rapidly. Annual energy and maintenance costs are estimated at over $5.00 per square foot. Offsite storage costs are up to 50 percent.

Reprographics Personnel

Reprographics encompasses the various means for reproducing or duplicating information, including copying, printing, and facsimile reproduction and digital, graphic, and voice replication. Although microfilming is also used, it is generally part of records management. Reprographics personnel include phototypesetting operators, copier operators, receiving and distribution clerks, collaters, binders, and quality-control personnel. This category also includes professional/technical employees such as graphic artists, job estimators, and printing press operators.

Reprographics is a rapidly expanding field because new developments are providing lower costs, increased output, higher quality, and greater flexibility. As in other areas, the lines between reprographics and other information functions overlap. As was pointed out in Chapter 13, distinctions between word processing and photocomposition have blurred. New electronic copiers offer many capabilities formerly available only with expensive offset printing. Computer graphics and desktop publishing software are redefining the boundaries between in-house printing and end-user computing.

Forms Design Personnel

Forms design personnel oversee the creation and disposition of forms within an organization. They are responsible for approving and maintaining an inventory of all forms created or purchased. Forms control may reside in a separate department, or with the graphics or the records management department. Forms simplify and standardize the handling of recurring but variable data. Traditionally, a form is defined as a piece of paper with standard printed information and systematically arranged spaces for entering variable information. Common examples are application and order forms, invoices, credit memorandums, and bills of lading. According to estimates, 50 to 75 percent of all documents stored in records systems are forms.

The proper designing of office forms requires specialized knowledge and skill. The designer often enlists the assistance of persons performing the office work, systems analysts, and work simplification specialists. Effective forms are *simple* forms. Well-designed forms must capture all required information, make it easy to enter and use information, minimize chances for errors, and reduce the cost of printing and using the form. Office systems technologies assist with designing, storing, distributing, updating, and controlling forms.

Facilities Management Staff

Facilities management plays an integral role in the design of office space and workstations. *Facilities management,* as defined by the Library of Congress, is the process of coordinating the physical workplace within the principles of administration, architecture, and the behavioral sciences. According to the International Facility Management Association, "Facility management coordinates the physical workplace with the people and work of the organization. It combines the best management practices with the most current professional and technical knowledge to provide humane and effective work environments."[1] Facilities personnel include building service managers and space planners and designers. Technologies such as computer-aided design and databases save time and enhance services.

REPLICATION AND DISTRIBUTION

Advances in communications technologies and electronic publishing are leading to more integration among the formerly separate functions of reprographics (printing, copying, and graphics) and distribution (mail, telephone, and wire services). These information processing functions are vital to every office. To optimize information management within an organization, replication and distribution must be integrated within the total system. Management cannot optimize these separate functions until it optimizes the total system.

Reprographics

Systems analysts play a vital role in the design of electronic printing systems. This idea is revolutionary because, in the past, reprographic systems were not very integrated. Modern electronic composition systems, however, accept text from other systems electronically and thereby eliminate the need for rekeying. These systems also merge text and graphics and offer a variety of type fonts and sizes, as well as extensive design, formatting, and pagination features. While changes are occurring in the basic printing process, the greatest changes are in feeding, sorting, finishing, delivery, and communications. These areas affect electronic composition (what you print), ease of use (how easily you print), and communications (how you distribute what you print). In other words, the critical variables are system design, software, and function. The printing process, of course, must be flexible and of good quality.

Computerized nonimpact printing technologies, such as laser-xerography, ink-jet, magnetography, and ionography (see Chapter 7), have had the greatest impact on reprographics. The high speeds and resolution of these printers, coupled with powerful automated composition, make them extremely valuable tools. They have greatly improved printing applications, volumes of work, and turnaround time.

Intelligent copier/printer systems (IC/Ps) such as the IBM 6670 Information Distributor pictured in Figure 14-1 can reproduce from digital signals as well as hard copy. Other examples are the Xerox 9700 and Wang's Intelligent Image Printer. Documents stored digitally on a computer can be

FIGURE 14-1. The IBM 6670 Information Distributor (Electronic Communicating Copier).

sent directly to the copier for reproduction of as many copies as desired. This means that a worker can create a document, view it on the display screen, and print 50 copies in one easy step. If a long, complex document is being copied or communicated, a user can interrupt the processing to do another task, and the original task will resume automatically. IC/Ps may be located near the computer or can be connected by an electronic network to a computer across the country. Some experts predict growing demand for electronic communicating copiers:

> The stand-alone dumb copier is slated to become integrated and intelligent. It will still make lots of plain-paper copies that look like what is made now, but many of the images will have originated elsewhere. Many of the images will have been composed nearby or elsewhere, and will appear in hard copy form for the first time on the ECC. There will still be plenty of locally made copies, but there will also be many delayed copies, the electrical representation having been stored in, and later retrieved from, an electronic file cabinet.[2]

Another rapidly growing application is computer-based graphics. Graphics software that was originally developed by major computer-aided design/computer-aided manufacture (CAD/CAM) companies for industrial use is beginning to find its way into the office. The electronic typesetting industry also has provided important software "understanding" that has been applied to the office in word processors and office information applications. Desktop publishing is one such innovation.

Today, carbon copies have all but disappeared, even though the old "cc" continues to be seen at the bottom of letters. Some have suggested the term *convenience copy* for the old term *carbon copy,* since copies today are generally made on a machine or sent electronically. Even when an organization has an electronic mail system, it cannot be used to send copies of attachments that are not stored on the computer. These paper documents can be sent electronically, however, by facsimile machines (see Chapter 8). Until recently, facsimile machines were reserved for long-distance transmission of documents when time was of the essence. As prices tumble and capabilities increase, however, facsimile machines have more widespread applications.

Collating copiers, laser printers, and desktop publishing have had a major impact on the reproduction of documents. The old mimeograph, Multilith, and ditto machines have been relegated to basement storage or museums, along with carbon paper. Accessories such as document feeders, sorters, large-capacity paper cassettes, and finishers streamline copying. Today's copiers can reduce or enlarge images, add color, edit, and combine and reposition images while retaining the master document in its original form. A scanner converts the original image to digital signals, which can be manipulated. Cutting and pasting, creating layouts, and revising documents can be done right at the copier.

Large, high-speed copier/duplicators now handle many jobs that were formerly done on offset presses by in-house departments. These copier/duplicators can easily handle multiple-page documents requiring 10 to 100 copies and provide automatic collating and stapling. Coupled with the creation and composition capabilities of desktop publishing, these copier/duplicators meet diverse needs. Moreover, in-house publishing shops with electronic equipment can handle complex, high-quality printing jobs that were formerly sent outside to commercial printers.

When assessing reprographic needs, office systems analysts must also consider users' needs for accessibility and convenience. Small organizations with high-volume copying needs generally have one centrally located copying department. In large organizations, copier/duplicators may be distributed in several locations (perhaps one on each floor). Self-service copiers may be located in convenient areas throughout the building. Distributed copy centers minimize the time that users walk to and from the copy center or send copy back and forth through internal mail.

Controlling Copying Costs

The availability and capabilities of copiers have sometimes led to excessive reproduction. Some organizations have found that the machine tally exceeds 100 copies a day per office worker. Obviously, nobody reads this much information. Some organizations have therefore instituted controls to restrict copying. Another approach (perhaps more realistic) is to make it so convenient to "print on demand" that office workers will avoid making copies "just in case." Eventually, as electronic storage and distribution of information becomes more widespread, even the use of "convenience copiers" may decrease because an electronic copy can be available to anyone with a terminal whenever it is needed.

Distributed Printing

Distributed printing is sending information electronically to be printed at the recipient's location. Distributed printing is recommended for any organization that routinely distributes printed information from a central computer, whether it is a mainframe or microcomputer. Distributed printing provides more control, lower costs, faster distribution, and more efficient and flexible printing.

According to the trade literature, the term *distributed printing* refers to at least three different printing environments: (1) printers on a communications line, (2) centralized host to distributed host, and (3) local area networks.

Printers on a Communications Line

Printers may be connected to the host computer by a telephone line, coaxial cable, or other electronic link. For example, the Oregon Legislature Information Systems Department linked a central computer to four small electronic printers in the administrative work areas of the Oregon State Senate and House of Representatives. The system allows legislators to receive documents several hours sooner than when printing was centralized. Document turnaround time was reduced by 25 percent, and the cost of two full-time couriers was eliminated.

Centralized Host to Distributed Host

A printer can be linked to a local computer that *downloads* information for printing from a centralized host computer. The information (print file) is transferred from the centralized host to the local computer, then printed. The receiver can also be a microcomputer, defined to the host computer as a printer. The operator can download information (the print file) to a disk and display or print it. (This is not the same as transferring files for editing; the user cannot edit a print file unless it is converted to an appropriate format.) For example, staff at a distributor's remote warehouses and sales offices might download inventory and pricing reports from the mainframe at the central office to remote microcomputers and print them on their microcomputer printers.

Local Area Networks

Distributed printing can also be provided through a local area network (LAN). As explained in Chapter 8, a LAN is a network that spans a limited geographical area, such as an office building or college campus. A typical LAN configuration consists of workstations (usually microcomputers) that are linked together to share software and data files. When a LAN is linked to a large central computer, print files can be downloaded to the LAN and displayed or printed at any of the LAN's workstations or printers.

Telephone Services

Telephone services include computerized switchboards called *private branch exchanges* (PBXs) that provide a host of new services to end users. (Many of these services have been described in previous chapters in relation to managers, knowledge workers, and secretaries.) These systems also provide features that facilitate the management of telephone services.

A PBX system is generally recommended for organizations that need the following:

- Future expandability.
- Simple station telephone handsets.
- Maximum flexibility in station instruments (dialers, modems, dedicated phones).
- Least-cost, long-distance routing.
- Economy (especially in larger systems).

The following PBX features can be used in placing calls:

1. *Camp-on.* A caller can automatically connect to a busy line as soon as the line is clear, usually activating a call-waiting tone on the called phone. The caller must hold the line until it is clear.
2. *Automatic callback.* When a line is busy, the caller can disconnect and be called back when the line is clear.
3. *Recall.* To initiate a new call, some systems include a pushbutton; in other systems, the user must briefly disconnect.
4. *Flash.* Some telephones include a flash pushbutton to activate service functions; with other systems, the user must manually flash the switchhook.
5. *Conference calling.* A caller can connect three or more parties to talk with one another on the same call. Some systems require specific optional circuits if more than three parties must be connected at the same time.
6. *Trunk queue.* If all trunks are busy, the caller is put in line for the next available trunk.
7. *Paging.* A user can access a loudspeaker using the telephone handset.
8. *Toll restriction.* Only certain users can make toll calls.
9. *Speed dialing.* Users can dial long or frequently called numbers with one or a few keystrokes. Some systems store the numbers to be dialed in the individual telephones, and others store them in the main system. Some systems store numbers for speed dialing with any type of phone.
10. *Automatic redial of a busy number.* The system continually redials a busy number until the line is free.

11. *Automatic redial of last number dialed.* Some systems save the most recently dialed number in the system's memory, allowing the user to redial with the push of one button.
12. *Hands-free dialing and monitoring.* The user hears a dial tone and ringing through a built-in speaker; the caller does not need to pick up the handset until the called party answers.
13. *Hands-free calling.* Also termed *full speakerphone operation,* the caller does not need to hold the handset.

The following features can affect the way calls are received:

1. *Call holding.* The user temporarily disconnects from a caller; the call can then be picked up from the holding phone or any other designated handset.
2. *Call transfer.* A user can transfer a call to other phones in the system. In some systems, calls can also be transferred to outside phones. Some systems allow the user to add another outside caller as a conference call only if the user stays on the line. The user usually talks with the third party *before* the transfer is made.
3. *Call forwarding.* The user can order the system to forward all calls to another extension, forward calls only if the phone is busy, or forward calls only if the line called is busy or no-answer. Some systems permit users to forward calls to phones outside the system.
4. *Dial-call pick-up.* Depending on the system, a caller can answer a nearby ringing phone, answer any phone in his group, or answer an incoming call after business hours.
5. *Call-waiting tone.* Some systems alert the called party to each waiting call. Others require a holding period or specific dialing sequence to activate the warning tone.
6. *Message waiting.* Also termed *call-waiting,* the user must call the operator to receive the message.
7. *Distinctive ringing.* Different ringing signals are provided to differentiate outside and inside calls.

The following capabilities can affect the way calls are handled by the operator:

1. *Direct-station selection.* For incoming calls, the operator does not dial the desired extension number but accesses the extension's pushbutton to make the connection.
2. *Busy-lamp field.* The operator has a field of lamps indicating busy extensions and need not dial an extension number to determine that it is busy.

3. *Automatic-call distribution.* Calls to busy departments, such as order entry, customer service, or repair, are switched to the next available open line in the order they are received.

The following features can affect the way calls are perceived by outside callers:

1. *Music-on-hold.* Music-on-hold provides a pleasant signal to callers that they are still connected and holding. Many systems are connected to a background music device or radio. Some companies play a short commercial message about their products for waiting callers.
2. *Automatic recall.* The system redials the operator or the holding extension after calls have been on hold for a specified time.

The following functions can affect the way calls are billed:

1. *Station message detail recording.* The system records data such as the numbers called and length of each call.
2. *Station message detail billing.* The system sorts and prints out information; sometimes billing capability is built in, but more often billing or accounting is accomplished by downloading data to a microcomputer or other computer for processing.
3. *Least-cost routing.* The system automatically switches long-distance calls via the lowest-cost carrier.

The following features can affect the way the system operates:

1. *Flexible station numbering.* A user can keep the same phone number when moving to a new location without a need for wiring changes.
2. *Expandability and modular construction.* As an organization grows, the phone system can be expanded.
3. *Remote system programming.* The service vendor can program extension numbers and functions from a service location.
4. *Remote trouble diagnosis.* The service vendor can diagnose system problems and provide routine maintenance service from a service location.

Available miscellaneous functions include the following:

1. *Data phones.* Data phones incorporate a data terminal with a telephone handset.
2. *Door phones.* Door phones provide security for an unsupervised entrance or exit.
3. *Paging-system access.* A user can access a loudspeaker system through the operator or from individual phones.

4. *Night-answering signal.* The system automatically routes calls to certain phones after business hours.
5. *Power-failure back-up.* The system automatically saves data and programming information during short power outages ranging from 20 minutes to 24 hours.
6. *Power-failure operation.* The system operates from back-up batteries during power outages.
7. *System accepts tone or pulse dialing.* The system can support telephones with either rotary or pushbutton dials.
8. *Direct-inward access.* Authorized users on dedicated lines dial into the system from pushbutton phones and use a code to reach extensions and system features.
9. *Automatic privacy.* Most systems prevent the operator or another caller from interrupting or listening in on a call. Some systems permit such interruption but furnish a warning tone when it occurs.

Users must identify the telephone service features that are necessary to meet their needs and ensure that appropriate telephone systems are installed and properly used. For example, not all systems can transfer an incoming call to an extension reached through a tie line. Nor do all systems provide "hunting," a feature in which a call to a busy department number is automatically routed to the next available extension in the department.

The way some systems work internally affects what they can do. For example, digital or executive instruments that are loaded with capabilities might be incompatible with a microcomputer modem or dialer.

Certain switching technologies can interfere with signals from a microcomputer modem when it transmits data. In these cases, a separate outside phone line will be needed for the microcomputer connection. If you want to use a microcomputer for data transmission, ask about interference before you buy a phone system.

The process of analyzing each function in order to categorize it will make more of an impression on you than reading someone else's list. You will have a much greater opportunity to mull over exactly how each function will work in your organization.

Looking at the capabilities and data scientifically whittles down the selection process. By putting forth the effort to categorize features and compare them with your requirements, and by using common sense, you can select a system and a vendor that you will be happy with for the life of the equipment.[3]

One of the best time-saving features for telephone service management is *station message detail recording (SMDR).* SMDR provides a list of all calls, including their origins, destinations, time and length, and the services and account or client codes used. These statistics can be fed into *call accounting* programs on microcomputers to track and analyze traffic patterns, verify charge systems, and document cases of abuse. Call accounting eliminates the need for clerical staff to sift through bills, verify calls, and allocate costs to departments or individuals..

SMDR is an especially useful management tool when it is coupled with inventory control software and traffic and utilization statistics. Inventory control software, which helps maintain inventories of equipment and services, can be purchased off the shelf, custom designed, or developed in-house by using a relational database. Organizations with thousands of telephones find that inventory control software helps them not only to keep stock of equipment but also to track its location, record moves, and identify problems. Traffic and utilization software can identify busy times of day, the use of various lines and services, and problems with facilities. Coupled with inventory control and traffic and utilization statistics, SMDR software provides better services at lower costs.

Smaller organizations generally use key telephone or hybrid systems rather than true PBXs. *Key telephone systems,* which handle up to 125 lines, are compact enough to sit on a receptionist's desk. With a key system, anyone can answer any incoming call. Everyone who wants to talk can pick up the same line to create a conference call. Transfers are made by putting the call on hold and telling the recipient, "There's a call for you on Line 6."

Hybrid systems, also called *electronic-key systems,* combine the benefits of the key systems with selected PBX features and an intercom. Hybrid systems are technically simpler, and usually less costly, for a small organization than the smallest PBX. Hybrid systems are recommended for organizations that need the following:[4]

- Instant hands-free communication
- Direct access to specific outside lines
- Push-button selection (not dial codes) on each set
- A smaller system than a PBX
- Economy

In a small office with a key telephone or hybrid system, receptionists can often handle incoming calls as well as greet visitors or do other work. Phones can be programmed to *roll over* to another telephone if the first individual does not answer. Rollover allows various staff to cover other telephones in the department without having to listen for those phones or jump up from their desks to answer them.

Mail Services

Mail services are the lifeblood of business operations and constitute a major expense. The efficiency of mailroom operations can have a major impact on both service and cost. For example, retailers such as Sears, Roebuck or J. C. Penney depend on mail services for billing and receipt of payments. A company can lose money if incoming mail is not handled quickly so that payments can be deposited the same day they are received.

Electronic mail, telemarketing, computers, and voice mail have raised expectations about the speed and accuracy of communications. Electronic systems speed up business cycles, most of which involve information. Eventually, most of that information comes out in hard copy, and it must be hand delivered. As the business pace quickens, mail usage grows. Public and private services, which guarantee one-day delivery, have stimulated the demand for efficient internal mail systems.

Mechanical and electromechanical mailing machines are being replaced by electronic equipment. Advances in electronic technology have contributed to improvements in finance, data processing, and marketing and have helped to streamline mail and shipping operations. Electronic interface capabilities permit easier, more efficient use of postage and provide greater accountability. Electronics has changed mailroom equipment in three fundamental ways:

1. *Mail accounting systems.* As postage costs have risen, the need to control expenses has increased. The equipment industry has responded by providing *mail accounting systems* that track postage expenditures by class of mail, carrier, and department. With thousands and millions of dollars spent each year by mailrooms, this information may allow a company to trim 10 to 20 percent from its postage costs and improve productivity at the same time. Intelligent mailroom systems can charge postage and express expenses to departments. Some charge-back systems provide output in report formats. One model, which sits next to the postage meter, identifies the department, the number of items sent, and the postage. Other accounting systems are even more versatile. One model resides on its own scale and prints on an 80-column printer. For example, managers can request up to 2400 reports of costs and usage, by carrier and by zone. Overnight courier rates can be programmed into the system.

2. *Efficiency and ease of use.* Technology such as electronic scales allows users to *rate-shop;* that is, it finds the lowest postage at which a parcel or letter can be sent. The savings show up in lower mailroom costs and greater efficiency.

3. *Equipment reliability.* Electronic equipment is not only more accurate than manually operated equipment, it is also more reliable because it has fewer mechanical parts to wear out and break down.

Today's mailroom facilities incorporate designs and layouts that provide efficient work environments. Mailrooms are designed for specific functions in specific areas, such as incoming mail, outgoing mail, express mail, bulk mail, and other services. Of course, sophisticated electronic equipment requires well-qualified staff, and mailroom managers must be well educated and trained.

Like all support services, mailroom operations need to be coordinated with other automation efforts. For example, credit-card companies and banks place a great burden on high-speed remittance processing and the "front end" of mailroom operations, such as mail handling, opening, and extracting.

Automation may include bar coding and presorting—of value especially to utilities, credit-card companies, banks, and other high-volume operations. Mailrooms will become more important in the system flow of incoming, internal, and outgoing document processing. Mailroom operations should not be overlooked in strategic planning for office automation. Mailroom managers should be on task forces that investigate and implement electronic mail systems (see Chapter 21).

Electronic Mail

While electronic mail (E-Mail) systems suggest paperless offices, not all electronic systems are paperless. E-Mail's major advantages over paper-based systems are speed and *direct* communications. Mail can travel from sender to recipient electronically, bypassing intermediaries such as the postal service. Of course, telephones have provided direct voice communication for decades; today, E-Mail provides a similar capability for documents and graphics.

E-Mail has many applications that save time and paper. The following are among the applications that enterprises find most productive:

1. Sending and receiving documents, such as sales proposals, memos, and directives, between a main office and satellite or regional offices.
2. Transmitting legal documents between a firm and its law offices.
3. Transmitting accounting documents, such as monthly financial statements, year-end closing, or annual report copy, for approval.
4. Transmitting orders between a sales office and factory or warehouse.
5. Transmitting shipping and receiving documents.
6. Sending payroll information to the payroll department from remote offices.
7. Transacting business between a company and its banks.
8. Sending production information between headquarters and manufacturing sites.
9. Routinely exchanging documentation between one point and another.

The most commonly used media for electronic mail are Telex, TWX, facsimile, computer-based message switching, electronic mail and message systems, and voice mail.

Telex and TWX

Telex and *TWX* (described in Chapter 8) have been widely used for over 50 years. These services, provided by Western Union, are widely used both nationally and internationally. Using teletypewriters and teleprinters, participating enterprises can send and receive messages directly to and from their offices. The sender dials the correspondent's number, receives online identification, and transmits the message. Both the sender and receiver have a printed copy of the message. These services provide delivery within minutes and are economical for short messages, both domestic and international. Messages are limited to short texts, however, and output is of low quality.

Advances in technology make these services easier to use and more flexible. Previously, secretaries typed messages that were hand-carried to teletypewriter operators who rekeyed them for transmission. Today, microcomputers and word processors with special communications software and hardware can double as Telexes to send and receive messages worldwide. The story of one user, Western Universal Mercantile, is recounted in the following case study:[5]

Western Universal Mercantile, Inc., is a company in the middle. As an importer of hard goods from the Orient, Western is positioned squarely between major corporations in the U.S. and manufacturers in the Far East.

The company was also caught in a job crunch. Expensive equipment sat idle for most of the day due to a combination of time zone differences and fear of the machine itself. But rethinking the job requirements enabled the import company to combine three office jobs on one much-used machine.

Jack J. Aizerman, financial vice-president of the New York-based importing company, points out, "We're a liaison organization. We serve as the selling agent for the overseas trading companies as well as represent them to our U.S. customers." As such, Western maintains offices in Hong Kong, Taiwan, and Korea to work with the manufacturers. Meanwhile, Western's New York sales office puts the deals together.

Generally the sole contact between buyer and seller, Western requires that communications be reliable and documented. Aizerman terms Telex "very critical" and "the only way that works."

Time is of the essence to Western. Buyers want to know if items are available, how much they will cost, and when they can be shipped. "The buyer mentality," Aizerman states, "works on an 'I-need-it-yesterday' level. He's already talked to a competitor and needs answers as soon as possible, usually within 24 hours."

At the same time, Western requires hard copy for back-up. "It's impossible to remember everything," Aizerman says, particularly when carrying on negotiations with many different buyers and manufacturers. Written records are also important: sales orders, bills of lading, letters of credit, and other documentation necessary to ship the merchandise.

Telex has been so central to Western's business that, although a multi-port RCA Mach 4T was originally installed also to do word processing, it was used solely to send and receive messages between New York and the Far East.

"People were afraid of the Mach 4," recalls Gloria Sigman, Western's office manager. "They all thought of it as a Telex machine that could be used as a word processor, rather than a word processor that could be used for Telex," she says. "Because of that, it was programmed more for Telex than for word processing."

As a result, the minicomputer remained idle between 8:00 a.m. and 2:30 p.m., when the Telex operator usually began transmitting. She continued to send messages until 7:00 p.m., with the messages received at the offices in Hong Kong, Taiwan, and Korea when they opened for business the next morning, thirteen hours ahead of New York time.

Another problem, besides idle machine time, was the prospect of the operator's being out ill or on vacation. "If the Telex operator was out sick, there were no Telex operations," Sigman reports. Instead, Western's messages were typed and sent by facsimile.

Aizerman wished for a word processor that could also send and receive Telex messages—one that could also be connected to the company's IBM System/34 computer used for sales analysis, accounting, and all other record-keeping. Enter the PC + Telex™ from ITT, New York, a system that includes an ITT XTRA™ personal computer and special communications software that enables the PC user to send and receive Telex messages worldwide. The ITT XTRA is compatible and is also linked online to Western's System/34. Of course, the PC can be used as a stand-alone computer as well.

Instead of a part-time Telex, Western now has a multifunction communicating PC that is busy most of the day. And instead of one Telex operator, the company has four, including three secretaries who think of the PC as a word processor.

The PC usually becomes a Telex machine at 2:30 pm. By that time, people have read their incoming messages, and replies are dictated into a machine and transcribed by the Telex operator. Normally, ten people in the finance, import, customer service, purchasing, and sales departments send and receive Telex messages, ranging from two lines to 90 minutes of copy. In all, the Telex traffic averages 1,000 minutes per month.

When not being used for Telex, the computer does word processing, PC work, and, when online to the System/34, data entry of sales, accounts receivable, and other accounting functions.

Besides its present functions, the system "has forced us to think about other applications," Aizerman reports. One of these is to use the PC to access data from the System/34 and, without retyping, transmit the information via Telex. Another is to link the System/34 to the Telex network. Then four other online terminals, in addition to the PC, could be used to send Telex messages.

Telex and TWX subscribers may also have direct access to Western Union's InfoMaster service, which allows the user to transmit mailgrams, telegrams, and international cables (cablegrams). InfoMaster also permits the user to distribute messages to multiple locations (without rekeying) and will store messages and retransmit them if the recipient's terminal is busy.

Facsimile

Facsimile, commonly known as *fax,* combines photocopy technology and telephone communications (as described in Chapter 8) to deliver copies anywhere in the world. High-speed systems provide economical transmission of text or graphics between offices with compatible equipment. The most important advantage of facsimile over Telex is that information does not have to be keyed into the system, thereby saving time and reducing the chance for errors. Also, unlike Telex, facsimile is not limited to text material. Practically anything can be transmitted, including handwritten copy, artwork, photographs, maps, drawings, or engineering plans.

Formerly confined to a centrally located mailroom or copy room and monitored, facsimile is gaining acceptance as an everyday tool. Historically, fax has been used for special applications. The military uses it to transmit graphs and maps, police departments fax fingerprints and mug shots around the country, the U.S. Weather Bureau transmits weather maps, and newspapers wire photographs around the world. Recently, applications have become much more diversified. New lightweight, compact units fit on desktops and can double as convenience copiers. Financial institutions often use fax to verify signatures or exchange information about transactions. Rush orders, shipping documents, and invoices can be communicated quickly and inexpensively. Facsimile is used in teleconference rooms to transmit copies of materials for discussion. An illustrative legal application of facsimile technology is described in the following example:[6]

> Because facsimile machines answer the need for quick and efficient communication, they are becoming a major part of many office systems. Shannon, Gracey, Ratliff and Miller, the largest law firm in Fort Worth, Texas, is a case in point. The firm's administrative staff has solved interoffice communications problems with fax equipment, according to Jean Wilkerson, legal administrator.
>
> In a typical workday at the firm, there is a steady flow of important legal documents. Often there isn't time to wait for the mail to deliver the documents. "We need a faster yet equally cost-effective means to transmit our documents," Wilkerson says.
>
> The firm first purchased a fax machine years ago, but three minutes per page proved to be too slow. Because it required so much employee

time to use, the firm more often used other options such as Federal Express ZapMail. "Although these options were not very cost effective, they did the job," Wilkerson says.

On taking a look at a Murata Multifax (TM) 7200, the Shannon and Gracey staff decided to give fax another try. The unit offered high-speed transmission of 16 seconds per page, automatic document feed, and automatic dialing, and it could be easily programmed to transmit without an employee in attendance.

"After the first day of using the new unit, it proved ideal for our needs. The fax is used an average of 20 times daily—sending such a large number of documents by any other means would involve prohibitive costs."

Because the firm was sending so many documents, it purchased a second machine to receive incoming messages. Mailing costs have been cut considerably, and there has been a marked improvement in office productivity. "We don't spend time worrying about important papers arriving in time," says Wilkerson. "We just program the faxes to send the documents at specific times, and we can go on to other things."

Until recently, fax has been limited to receiving documents in paper format; digital facsimile code could not be read by a computer. When additional editing or communication was required, copy had to be rekeyed, or scanned by OCR, into a word processing system. Fax can now tie in to computers, opening up new applications. Xerox Corporation's Scan'n File software package allows the Xerox Telecopier 295 to scan text and images directly to a microcomputer disk. A second package incorporates editing capabilities, permitting users to manipulate the data scanned onto the disk. Pitney-Bowes Facsimile Systems' PATH, another fax-to-microcomputer interface, can send text and graphics to a microcomputer where they can be sized, annotated, combined with a word processing document and other graphics, or edited with a computer graphics package, and then output to a printer or facsimile. Another software program, GammaFax, which is menu-driven and includes an appropriate adapter card, allows a microcomputer to both send and receive from fax machines (see Figure 14-2). A microcomputer can thus use the fax as a letter-quality printer. Fax terminals can also be integrated into LANs. There are even directories of fax users, much like the telephone directory. The *Official Facsimile Users' Directory*, published by FDP Associates in New York City, lists user companies and transmission information.

To determine a company's facsimile requirements, analysts estimate how many messages will be sent per month, average distance of station-to-station calls, average length of documents, and amount of operator time required, then calculate the cost.

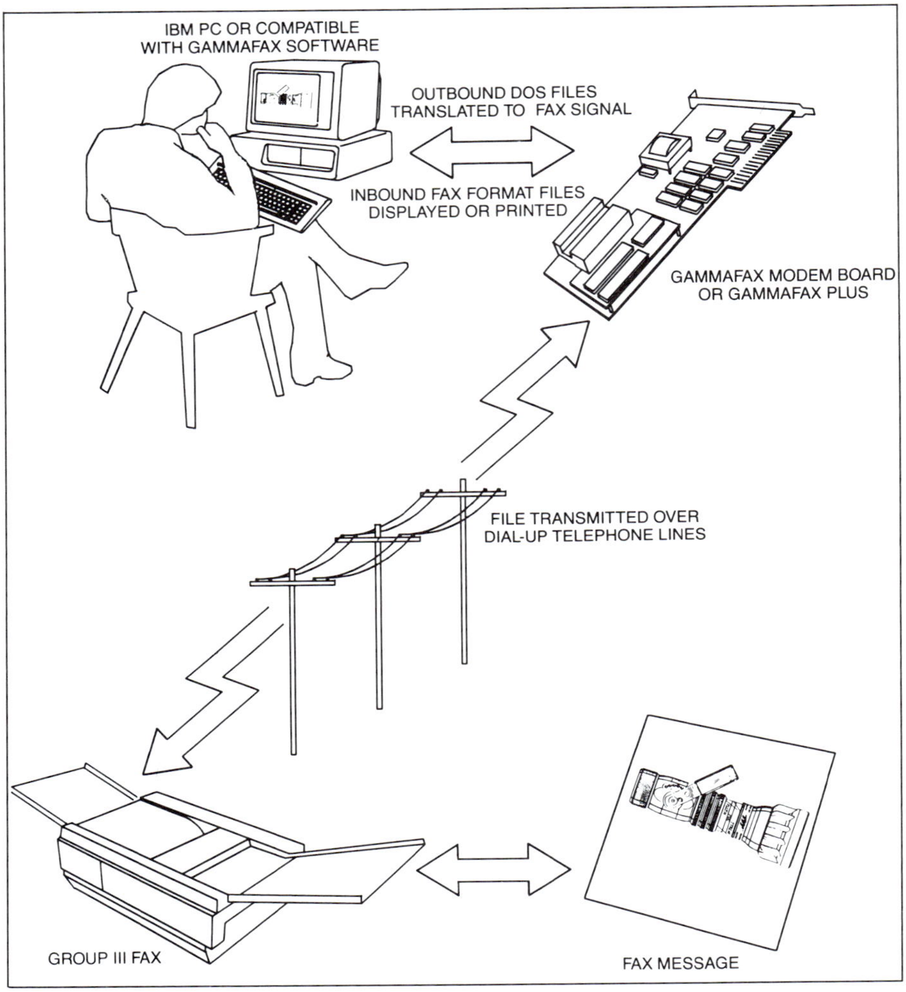

FIGURE 14-2. GammaFax software allows a microcomputer to both send and receive information from fax machines.

Computer-Based Message Switching

Computer-based message switching (CBMS) allows anyone using a terminal cabled to a mainframe or connected by a leased or telephone line to send and receive messages. Sender and receiver need not be online simultaneously. Messages are stored in a "mailbox," and the recipient may view a listing of messages, select and display messages for reading on the monitor, or print them.

Computer-based message switching is used by organizations that support a computer network of remote terminals nationally or internationally. For example, a large bank installed a computer terminal in the residence of an officer assigned to its London office for two years because his spouse did not want to leave her business to accompany him. The couple used computer-based message switching to keep in daily touch and handle much of their personal business. CBMS helped reduce the frustrations of trying to keep in touch by telephone with a seven-hour time difference and demanding business schedules.

Electronic Mail and Message Systems

Electronic mail and message systems (EMS) are a viable substitute for internal memoranda. As prices of workstations and networks tumble, EMS use is expected to grow from 300,000 systems today to over 1.7 million by 1990. Widespread use of electronic mail could significantly reduce the demand for paper-based internal mail and messenger services. Since senders tend to key their own memos and messages, electronic mail also reduces the need for dictation and typing.

Voice Mail

Voice mail reduces the time secretaries or clerical staff must spend to place and answer telephone calls and take messages (see Chapter 8). In addition to a voice-to-voice direct messaging system, digital voice mail systems like EMS can be used to broadcast information. Messages are stored and made available to anyone calling a special phone number. If necessary, messages can be updated for callers several times daily. For example, banks use recorded messages to inform callers of current rates on savings accounts. Insurance agents can call a special number at their company's home office to get up-to-the-minute rates for pension products. Several industry consultants offer their clients a voice-mail hotline (which is, in effect, an electronic newsletter). For a subscription fee, clients may call a designated number, key in an ID code, and listen to a summary of latest developments in their fields.

Some authorities, however, caution that voice mail can do more harm than good if it is used only as an answering machine:

> As a corporate manager or executive, you want your salesperson to talk to a client or a prospective customer. But what if the salesperson is on another line or away from his or her desk? Apply voice mail, right? Wrong! By providing the caller with the option of leaving (or worse, NOT leaving) a message, the company risks losing a sale without even getting a chance to talk to the prospective customer. In short, when voice mail is used only as an answering machine, it will fail to live up to the users' expectations. When it is considered the entire solution instead of a part of the solution, it will surely disappoint.[7]

Office systems analysts are only beginning to understand the types of problems that voice and electronic mail systems can solve. Generally, voice and electronic mail are viewed as complementary rather than competing communication mediums. While both media can be used to create, send, forward, append, broadcast, or delete messages, each has advantages and disadvantages. For example, voice messages are ideal for quick FYIs (for your information), one-time information notes, and inquiries. Voice mail is also more effective where inflection and emotion contribute to the meaning. Voice mail is best for short, high-priority messages. It also has the advantage of terminals (for example, telephones) in every office. Electronic messages, on the other hand, are better for lengthy, complex messages. An EMS is also effective when precise wording is important. The question, therefore, is not which medium is best but rather which is best for an organization's needs or specific applications. A combination of voice and electronic mail serves most applications.

Ultimately, voice and EMS will integrate to deliver both voice and text anywhere almost immediately. The ultimate system will offer users a choice, so that the location of the message creator may determine which system is preferred. If a person is at the airport, the most handy terminals are probably telephones. If that person were in the office with a choice of terminals, however, the message would be the determining factor. If hard copy were needed, EMS would be the choice.

Forms Management Applications

Office automation can assist forms management with creating, updating, stocking, and distributing preprinted forms. By using microcomputer graphics packages (such as MacDraw for the Apple MacIntosh), design personnel can facilitate their work. Together, designers and users can refine a form in much less time because of the ease in making revisions. Database programs aid in maintaining forms inventories.

Office personnel can design forms using word processing software such as the Wang Assistant and Multimate Advantage. These programs offer forms creation and fill-in capabilities. The application is handled as a special merge printing. The user designs and stores the required form, which can be displayed on the screen, and information can be filled in item by item, as if one were filling out a paper form. Once completed, the form and data are merged and printed simultaneously on the word processing printer. Several, even hundreds of forms can be filled out, stored, and printed together. While these capabilities are a boon to the small office, the large organization with strict forms management may have concerns about proliferation, control, and duplication of effort.

An even more promising application is *electronic forms automation*, in which forms are stored on a computer. Using the computer, design personnel can do everything they do with paper forms, only faster and less expensively. They can design, approve, revise, file, distribute, and print forms. Users can even fill them in on the computer and print a form and its data in one step.

Five steps comprise electronic forms automation: creating, managing, processing, distributing, and display/printing. All but the final step are designed to eliminate paper.

Forms Creation

Forms can be created with either a mainframe-based system or an IBM PC, AT, or OS/2 microcomputer. Some microcomputer systems use a digitizing tablet and stylus with a high-resolution graphics monitor. Mainframe systems use a command language. Both systems allow the user to see the form as it is created, making it easy to check and modify. Forms can be recalled and changed at any time. For example, when an address is changed, the new one can be on the form in minutes.

Forms Management

Electronic automation offers good control of forms. Large inventories no longer need to be maintained; forms can be printed on demand as needed. Microcomputer-based programs can store up to 5000 different forms, and mainframe-based systems can store up to 100,000. The forms management system can describe each form, the date it was created, how often it was used, when it was revised, and when it was last used. System security can control who can use or change forms, when forms are available, and what version is used.

Forms Processing

Forms can be printed blank or filled in electronically. When printed electronically, form and data are printed in one step. Forms also can be merged with information from either a central mainframe or spreadsheets, word processing, or database programs. Since data is merged with the form electronically, alignment is always exact.

Forms Distribution

Electronic distribution quickly gets forms where they are needed; they can be distributed from mainframe to mainframe, mainframe to microcomputer-based workstations, microcomputer to mainframe, or microcomputer to microcomputer. Forms need only be transmitted once and stored at the appropriate workstation. A corrected form can be transmitted in minutes. Data can be transmitted separately, or completed forms can be transmitted and printed at the destination.

Printing and Displaying Forms

Remarkable printing speeds are possible with form-specific software in the computer (rather than in the printer). Mainframe-driven printers can produce at least 120 pages a minute, while microcomputer-driven units can produce six to 20 pages a minute. These speeds are possible even when every form is different. Collated sets can be ready for distribution as soon as they print. Printing may not even be necessary; a form and its data can be displayed on a high-resolution monitor, eliminating paper handling and speeding the review process.

In the automated office, the definition of what a *form* actually is needs to be reconsidered because forms are no longer limited to paper. Data-entry screens and query and report formats for database management systems, for example, must also be considered forms. The same basic principles of good form design should be followed whether forms are printed on paper or reside on the computer (see Figure 14-3). Much would be gained if programmers consulted forms design personnel when creating data-entry screens, since the productivity of data entry personnel is significantly affected by the design of the data entry screen. For instance, if a data-entry screen is designed to correspond with the form from which data is obtained, then data can be keyed in much faster.

FIGURE 14-3. Basic principles of forms design.

1. Use standard paper or card sizes. In a legal office, you probably have numerous forms that are 8½ by 14 inches, although the use of such legal-size forms is beginning to diminish. In a business office, you have many forms that are 8½ by 11 inches. Forms to be stored in a card file would probably be 3 by 5 inches or 4 by 6 inches.
2. Use a title, a form number, and a date. The title clearly describes the purpose of the form, the form number aids in forms inventory and storage management, and the date facilitates periodic revision of the form.
3. Make the lines and spaces compatible with standard typewriters and printers if the forms are to be totally or partially typewritten.
   a. Lines should be spaced in ⅙-inch or ⅓-inch increments.
   b. Information requested should be aligned vertically, making it easy to tab from one part of the form to another.
   c. Descriptors (the words or phrases that tell what information to insert) should be on the line or just above the line so that they are not hidden by the typewriter.
4. Use terminology that all users will understand.
5. Reduce the need for writing or typing as much as possible by using boxes for check marks (√) or crosses (×) and by preprinting all information that does not vary from person to person.
6. Leave writing or typing space equal to the amount of information that is requested. For example, address information typically requires at least two lines.
7. The form should be designed with the user in mind. Put yourself in the position of the person completing the form and make sure that all needed information is requested.

RECORDS MANAGEMENT

Although the use of computer and image technologies for records management has been growing, in most organizations records management continues to be paper-based. Regardless of technology, objectives and requirements are the same: protecting information and making it available when needed.

One reason that integration of records management has been slow is that responsibility for information management is often fragmented. Various versions of information are used and maintained in different departments. The data processing department may manage online data, data tape libraries, computer output microfilm (COM), and data processing archives. The office automation department may be accountable for electronic document storage; department managers may be responsible for microcomputer applications. The records management department typically maintains paper and microfilm files. Large organizations may have one or more libraries managing additional information resources, including external online databases. In most cases, these departments operate independently.

The notion of the *paperless office* gives the impression that all records should be stored on the computer. In actuality, various storage technologies, many of which are incompatible, offer solutions for different needs. Moreover, managing data is not the same as managing records. Data consists of individual facts not necessarily related (customer name, invoice number, product prices, dates, part numbers). Data is intended to be manipulated, organized, and presented in various ways, such as reports, charts, or numerical listings. Records such as documents, on the other hand, reflect results, decisions, events, or other information. They are generally not manipulated after they are produced; rather, they are maintained as historical records or for reference. Only 5 to 15 percent of stored documents are ever referenced again. Except for frequently referenced documents, online storage is difficult to cost-justify. The idea of storing everything electronically, therefore, and letting the computer find things may be impractical.

Modern filing and storage systems can handle documents stored on a wide array of media. Such systems are designed to conserve space and use a worker's time most effectively. Image systems such as microfilm, COM, or laser disk require only a fraction of the space of paper files and provide increased accuracy and reliability. The original document or image is maintained in the file, with only copies viewed or distributed. A key issue is selection of appropriate information storage technologies: technologies that protect equipment investments yet allow records management systems to converge with new technologies. A major role of information management is to integrate text, data, and image into a comprehensive system that can transmit information over a communication network, in addition to storing, retrieving, and displaying it.

The discussion of automated records management in this section is divided into the following topics:

- Records management requirements
- Paper-based storage systems
- Micrographic applications
- Computer output microfilm (COM) applications
- Computer-assisted retrieval (CAR)
- Optical disk applications
- Networking
- Commercial records management services

Records Management Requirements

The wide variety of office technologies provides considerable flexibility for solving records storage problems. To select the appropriate system, the office systems analyst must assess the objectives and needs for an application. Requirements for implementing information management programs are similar, regardless of the technologies. If an organization already has an effective records management program, the analyst's primary job will be to evaluate alternative technologies for automating whatever components are practical. If a formal program does not exist or is inadequate, the analyst must have responsibility assigned and an appropriate records management program developed. Regardless, it is important that the analyst understand the objectives and legal requirements for records management in order to develop appropriate automation systems.

Legal Requirements

The records management system and its storage media must comply with statutory requirements pertaining to admissibility of records as evidence in courts of law or regulatory proceedings. The two major federal laws that apply to records management are the Uniform Photographic Copies of Business and Public Records as Evidence Act (UPA), passed in 1949, and the Uniform Rule of Evidence, passed in 1953 and revised in 1974. Decisions relating to legal issues of managing and retaining records should be reviewed and approved by legal counsel. Maintaining records beyond their useful and legal life, however, can waste space, time, and effort.

Classifying and Organizing Information

The most appropriate filing system for information is determined primarily by its use. There are four basic categories of usage:

1. *Active storage.* Used when users must have immediate access to information to perform their jobs.
2. *Inactive storage.* Used when users have occasional need to access information for reference, research, historical perspective, or legal

documentation. Retention of many of these records is required by law, such as medical records for patients.

3. *Archival storage.* Used when information has historical value or interest and must be stored for archival purposes.

4. *Terminal storage (destruction).* Used when information may be destroyed because it has no future reference value or its legal retention periods have expired.

Paper-Based Storage Systems

Lateral filing cabinets offer fast, easy access to paper-based documents. Unlike vertical files, every folder in a lateral file is immediately visible and can be easily extracted and refiled. Snap-in components modify shelves for other media, such as computer tapes or microfilm. Some storage units can double as partitions or counters. The predominance of paper-based records is a major challenge for organizations attempting to interface with electronic and image media.

Mechanized storage systems help bridge the gap between manual and computerized systems. *Rotary files* offer an attractive, convenient method of filing and retrieving folders, computer tapes, or microforms. The standard mechanized model provides about 260 file inches, the equivalent of three four-drawer cabinets. It has a total 1200 to 1600 filing inches, with an average reference time of six to nine seconds. At the touch of a button, it moves records to the operator. Some units can interface with computers. After keying in a name or number, the user is signaled by a red light that shows the location of the folder or tray.

High-density *mobile filing systems* save 50 to 80 percent of floorspace over open shelving and up to 300 percent over conventional drawer files by enabling users to create access aisles only when they are needed. Units may be operated manually or mechanically.

Computerized tracking and control systems are now available for all types of file systems: alphabetic, numeric, alphanumeric, subject, and others. These systems combine color-coded file folders and bar coding. By adding bar codes on file labels, folder identification is machine-readable with hand-held wands. Labels on file folders can show names, addresses, account names, primary subjects, tertiary subjects, or other identifiers. File clerks use a hand-held wand from an appropriately configured computer system to scan the bar codes for identification. Information can be read into a database containing indexing, cross-referencing, and retention information about every folder in the system. As a result, it is possible to track and control folder location and movement, log requests for folders, reserve folders, and keep records of charged-out folders.

Office technologies decrease the time and effort required to file and retrieve information, improve accuracy, reduce space, and lower the cost of maintaining records.

Micrographic Applications

Microforms meet the needs of many applications in the office, including personnel, medical, tax, and account records, to name just a few. Microfilm is also used for archival storage, storage and distribution of technical and scientific documents, and micropublishing (the publication of documents in micrographic form instead of on paper). Selecting the appropriate micrographic form—COM, CAR, microfilm, microfiche, aperture cards (see Chapter 6)—depends on several factors:

- The type of input.
- The characteristics of the stored information.
- How the information is to be used.
- The speed and ease of retrieval.
- The ability to handle the volume of work and supply hard copies.
- The frequency of updates or file changes.
- The need for security and privacy.
- Compatibility with existing office machines and equipment.
- The overall system cost.
- Legal record-keeping requirements.

These factors affect the implementation of micrographics and are discussed in more detail in Figure 14-4.

Because micrographics is not a digital form, it does not permit information to be stored or viewed on a computer. This drawback is being eliminated, however, with the advent of microfacsimile, which scans micrographic media and digitizes them at high speed. These images can be stored on optical disks, where they can be retrieved and transmitted.

FIGURE 14-4. Implementation of micrographics.

One should move well beyond the basics to design a micrographic system that will meet objectives in a way that is inexpensive and easy to use. With careful analysis of the application and exploration of all solutions, it can be done. Here are five questions the analyst should answer to narrow the choices and select the right solution:

1. *What are the objectives in implementing a micrographic system?* There are many good reasons for microfilming office documents and records. An enterprise may be looking for a back-up to valuable drawings, contracts, or other hard-to-replace records, or it may want faster, more accurate customer service. Perhaps it is microfilming files to save office or storage space or to reduce costs by making frequently used files more accessible. Clarifying specific objectives can help determine the most efficient solution for each application.
2. *What are the characteristics of the file to be microfilmed?* How many items does the file contain? Will documents require conversion before they can be microfilmed? Are additions or modifications made to the records regularly? How frequently is the file modified? How frequently must it be consulted? How much privacy and security are required?

FIGURE 14-4. (continued)

3. *What are the characteristics of the documents to be microfilmed?* A careful look at the documents to be microfilmed is the way to zero in on the most appropriate system design. Are all documents of uniform size? What are the maximum and minimum sizes of the documents? Are they in good condition? Are they clear and readable, or will they require special handling before they can be filmed? Are they paper documents, or are they computerized documents?
4. *What are the anticipated retrieval needs?* Retrieval is a key in determining the most efficient, effective micrographic system. Try to estimate the average number of retrievals per day or per week. How many individuals must have access to the files or documents? Are they all in the same department? Are they in close proximity to one another? Must the entire file be accessed or just single documents?
5. *What are the requirements for interfacing with existing systems?* Must the system be compatible with existing machines or equipment? Is all or part of the information already stored in electronic format?

Unfortunately, there is no simple formula for correlating the application to the most appropriate design. It is not as clearcut as a matrix that connects Answer A to Solution B. The office analyst must evaluate all information to develop a solution that will work best for each situation.

Computer Output Microfilm (COM)

Computer output microfilm (COM) has been used for years by data processing departments. In recent years, it has gained acceptance for office applications. COM links computer and microfilm technologies, eliminating the need for intermediary paper printouts. COM offers several advantages over paper:

- Eliminates purchasing and bursting of many computer paper forms.
- Reduces time and effort required to retrieve computer paper outputs.
- Reduces space needed to store records.
- Reduces time and effort required to handle computer-generated records.
- Reduces cost of reproducing output.

These benefits are significant, but before an analyst implements a COM project, it is essential to understand how COM operates. For example, a hookup with the computer and programs to reorganize the data and prepare it for film output are required. The analyst should be familiar with the film outputs and equipment required for each. Other important considerations are type of applications, hardware, software, systems design, cost justification, and vendor support.

The micrographics center at Irving Trust in New York City uses COM for reports and a mirror code system (bar code ID) for money transfers. It uses the system to track and backup information in the same process. All transactions are processed and encoded item by item, producing the magnetic strip that appears on the back of checks and other documents.

The microfilming, however, is still done in batches. Items are put in trays (with target cards) and sorted, and microfilm addresses are assigned to each document. This operation is typical of many large banks, but more sophisticated procedures automate the microfilming as well. Although items go through the same encoding, the computer picks up the code and *automatically* microfilms the items. High-speed item processing sorter/filmers (such as the Burroughs 9190 and IBM 3890) are becoming common.

At the Chase Manhattan Bank in New York City, COM systems produce 98 percent of all the microfilm per month. Chase began using COM in 1974 when the federal government declared that all checks must be microfilmed and stored for seven years. Prior to that, all its filming was done by outsiders. When the government made its decision, Chase purchased a COM system, and it now processes nearly 11 million frames of COM per month.

McDonnell Douglas Aircraft in St. Louis has used COM since 1963 for all health-care data processing. The system runs 24 hours a day, 365 days a year. McDonnell Douglas uses COM to put all of its clients' reports and ledgers on microfiche. Although it used a cut-fiche system until 1980, it found that roll-film recorders with bar coding were better suited to its purposes.

Computer-Assisted Retrieval (CAR)

Computer-assisted retrieval (CAR) combines filing and database management. CAR systems combine the speed of computers with a storage medium to create a record-handling system that manages every phase of a document's indexing, storage, retrieval, and reproduction. CAR systems can accommodate a variety of media, including letter- and legal-size papers, standard cards, oversize hanging files for printouts, microforms, and checks.

Computer indexing offers flexibility and accuracy in storing and retrieving information. Depending on a system's features, it speeds search and retrieval and is more accurate because of the following factors:

1. Users can search for a document under more than one index term (for example, by subject, date, recipient, or originator).
2. Users can combine index terms, or parameters, in a single search—such as all contracts (document type) since the beginning of the year (date) with ABC Corporation (vendor) related to construction of the new plant (subject).
3. Users can search for related documents on demand, based on their requirements, without predetermined decisions about how to group them for filing.
4. Users can specify chronological or numerical ranges for retrieving documents (for example, all correspondence with Innovation, Inc. between June 1, 1990, and September 1, 1990).

5. Depending on the system, users may obtain statistics about document retrieval, such as what documents the engineering department accessed most often this year and who retrieved contract files. This information can be useful for better maintenance and control of the system.

CAR systems for paper-based storage usually provide a name-to-number and number-to-name cross-index. Paper documents are filed by number and are indexed by key words on a database program. The user checks the availability and location of the file on a CAR terminal. When the location number is keyed in, the electronically controlled shelving units deliver the file to a workstation. CAR systems can also provide bar coding and automatic sorting and can file management reports.

CAR systems for microforms may be semi- or fully automatic. Semi-automatic systems locate and retrieve microforms, and the operator reads the microform on a conventional reader. Fully automated systems identify, retrieve, and display the microform as well on a special reader. Only prototype systems currently allow the user to retrieve the microform on a computer terminal. No manual intervention is necessary. In addition to convenience, the fully automated version provides greater file security because the microform always remains in the system.

Optical Disk Applications

Optical disk technology can provide the mass storage and fast retrieval demanded in today's operations. The method by which optical disk systems store and retrieve large volumes of documents is the same as in CAR systems. Both are powered by a computer. Unlike conventional CAR systems, however, optical disk systems use high-capacity, nonerasable, laser-written disks. Write-once, read-many (WORM) optical disk systems are described in Chapter 6. A basic optical digital data disk (OD^3) document management system is depicted in Figure 14-5.

A typical online micrographics CAR system costs about $175,000; a similar optical disk system costs about $500,000. The CAR system can find and retrieve a document from a storage file of 5 million records in 30 seconds; the optical system can do the same in 18 to 20 seconds.

The number of successful optical disk-based document image processing systems is growing. A survey of micrographics/records management equipment usage conducted by *Modern Office Technology* magazine revealed that 28 of the 386 respondents were using optical disk systems, and 31 other firms planned to purchase an optical disk-based system within a year.

Many records management authorities, however, still consider the application of optical disk technology to records management to be in the experimental stages. "Few nonpilot installations exist outside the design drawing/document area except in Japan."[8]

The IRS is testing a new filing, archival, image, storage, and retrieval (FAISR) system for storing income tax records. If the program is adopted,

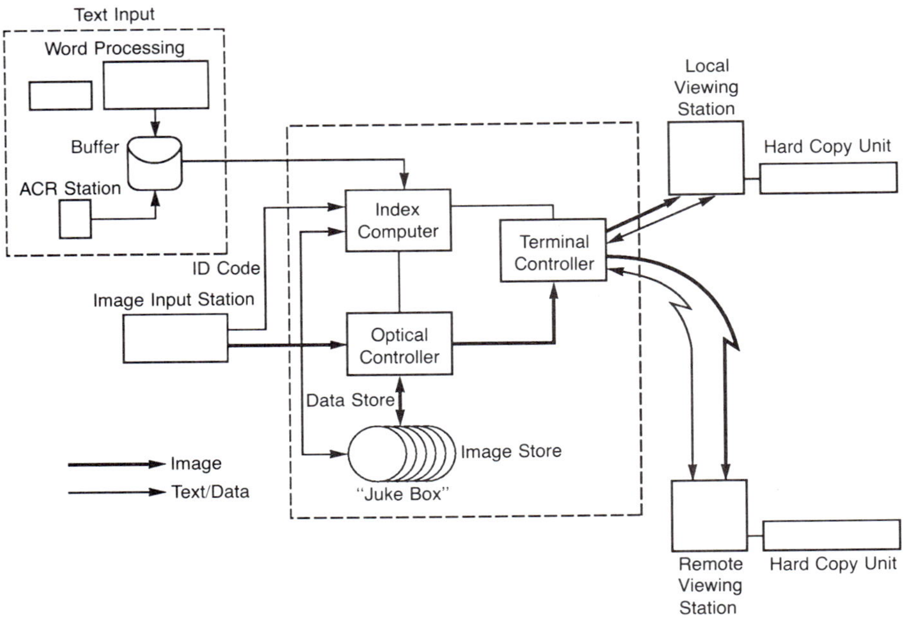

FIGURE 14.5. A basic optical digital data disk (OD^3) document management system.

original 1040 tax forms will be destroyed and all tax records will be maintained on optical disk for at least 75 years. Among the concerns are the life expectancy of optical disks (the IRS will duplicate them every ten years) and legal questions (e.g., will a document stored on optical disk stand up in court, and who authorizes destruction of the original tax forms?).

One major advantage of optical disk storage is its ability to store images. Optical disk systems convert paper documents to digital data, which gives the records manager the flexibility to pass these documents to other electronic systems. Documents can be accessed on image display terminals from both local and remote sites. Sophisticated, high-capacity networks are required to handle the quantities of data involved, however. The efficiency of the network dictates how rapidly the images can be moved from one point to another and how many users can be put on that network so a community of users can be served quickly and efficiently.

WORM (write-once, read-many) optical disks are generally considered to have the greatest potential for large document-processing applications where information is maintained primarily for historical documentation or reference. The ideal applications for WORM optical disks are environments with extremely large files, constant activity requiring immediate access, and a need for remote access. Many authorities consider WORM optical disks to be poorly suited as a replacement for magnetic hard disks and floppy disks because they cannot be written, erased, and rewritten nor easily duplicated and distributed in a timely or cost-effective manner.

Most office analysts agree that the move to optical disk will depend on several major considerations:

1. The maturity of the technology and its cost effectiveness.
2. Availability of practical systems that allow optical disks to be erased and rewritten.
3. Acceptance by the judicial system. (Some judges still refuse to accept hard copy produced from microfilm and demand the original document.)
4. Actual court cases setting precedents for optical disk acceptance.
5. Availability of low-cost, high-quality image display screens.
6. Low-cost, high-capacity communication networks.

Although nonerasability is frequently cited as a drawback of WORM technology, some authorities view it as an advantage. Nonerasability ensures that documents cannot be inadvertently erased or altered, thus protecting original evidentiary documents. Nonerasability also provides an audit trail. If changes are made, the original document is always available for reference.

Networking and Records Management

Networking, or linking computers together electronically, is the basic requirement for making records easily accessible. Networking is used for all media; whether images are stored on microfilm, magnetic disk, or optical disk is irrelevant.

Current record management systems use computers to store and retrieve information *about* microfilmed documents. They do not, however, allow the user to view the actual document (invoice, check, or order form) on the display screen. Microfilm stores documents very efficiently, but how does a company move them from Office A to Office B across the country, or even within the building? The answer is that networks that are presently able to move data eventually will be able to move images as well.

Images require substantially more space to store digitally than data. A one-page word processing document takes approximately 3KB or 4KB, whereas just one image may require 200KB to 300KB. Most image applications were impractical with floppies or hard disks, but the new optical disks have sufficient storage capacity to handle them. Likewise, an extremely high-capacity network system is required to transmit image applications. It is only a matter of time, however, until cost-effective networks with the capacity to handle images are available.

Commercial Records Management Services

Offices are turning to independent vendors to store inactive records. These services offer low-cost storage and free up valuable floorspace. The growth of commercial records management has been fostered by automated systems. By using computer databases, they maintain detailed indexes of stored materials. The materials are stored in random order, and the index finds the location when material has to be retrieved. The index can be maintained on whatever level of detail the customer requires: by individual document, file folder, groups of related files, or storage box. Obviously, the greater the detail, the more time and work to file the material and the higher the cost.

One such company, Bekins Records Management, uses a sophisticated telecommunications system (called the Safekeeper) to provide clients more control than with in-house records storage. Bekin's customers use a personal computer connected by a modem to Bekin's mainframe in each of six market areas. As much information as a customer chooses to give the company can be entered into the system and cross-referenced under several headings to ensure easy access. The system is safeguarded by a sophisticated password code at three levels: company, department within the company, and individual within the department. The firm also offers microfilm conversion. A copy goes to the customer, and the original film is stored in the firm's humidity- and temperature-controlled vault.

FACILITIES MANAGEMENT

Both the requirements and methods of facilities management, though changing rapidly with technologies, must be coordinated with office automation and administrative services. Facilities departments are directly involved in wiring and cabling for electronic equipment. It is essential, during renovation or new construction, to plan wiring and cabling for electronic equipment. Most forward-thinking enterprises include comprehensive communications and cabling designs in their planning.

An important goal of modern design is flexibility. Open floor plans, movable walls, and modular furniture enable organizations to reconfigure office space to meet requirements. Modular furniture allows planners to tailor workstations to the needs of workers or jobs. Many furniture systems include sound-absorbent panels that house channels for wiring electronic equipment.

The approach by TRW when constructing its 1.5 million square foot office illustrates the benefits of a coordinated effort. The facility manager and the director of office automation worked together in creation of the building. The team was known as the "operating review committee." Its charter, as the first level of executive management, was to judge and decide on technical and user-generated requirements. In this capacity, the facility manager and the director of office automation defined the users' work requirements and recommended ways to meet them. The result was a flexible facility, designed from the inside out, that provides a productive work environment and can accommodate technological changes. Key considerations included flexible workstations, clustered working spaces, productivity enhancements (incorporated in the workstation), networking, reduced clutter, and heavy orientation toward mini- and microcomputer office automation.

Office automation also includes new tools for space design and facilities management. Computer-aided design (CAD) software helps the designer lay out floorplans for office space and arrange workstations, equipment, plants, and other furnishings. Microcomputers with appropriate graphics packages, such as the MacDraw package for the Apple MacIntosh, are suitable for many drawing applications.

Many companies are installing computer-based management systems to maximize space and other facilities. Facilities departments use spreadsheet and database software to estimate and monitor costs. Planning professionals anticipate the availability of national and international databases of comparative cost figures. Such databases will enable a facilities department to run "what-if scenarios" and tests of reasonableness. Managers can get answers to such questions as, "What is a reasonable cost per square foot for maintaining a computer facility in the Denver area?"

Even facilities management functions such as maintenance or corporate transportation benefit from microcomputer tools. One insurance company, for example, uses spreadsheets and database packages on a microcomputer to maintain flight scheduling and maintenance records for its corporate helicopters.

SUMMARY

Administrative services personnel apply office technologies to improve support. This chapter discussed applications for replication and distribution, forms control, records management, and facilities management.

Advances in communications technologies and electronic publishing are leading to integration among the formerly separate functions of reprographics (printing, copying, graphics) and distribution (mail, telephone, wire services). The need for intermediaries to perform some of these services is decreasing as users gain capabilities for sending and receiving documents electronically.

Telephone and wire services are merging with other communications technologies, enabling staff to offer many new features, customize services to requirements, and handle higher volumes. Administration of new, sophisticated systems is aided by monitoring tools for incoming and outgoing calls, least-cost routing, built-in accounting (to allocate charges to each telephone on a system), and other features for monitoring and controlling operations.

Office technology tools assist in creating, updating, stocking, distributing, and using preprinted forms. The most promising application is electronic forms automation, which eliminates the need for paper during the intermediary steps, until form and data are printed together in the final step.

Although the use of computer and image technologies for records management has been growing, many organizations are still paper-based. Even paper-based file systems, however, benefit from the new technologies. Computers provide alternatives for creating records databases so that paper documents can be stored randomly. Tabs on folders can be scanned electronically, to track their use and to aid in filing. One of the major drawbacks to image storage systems, such as microfilm, is the need for special reader/printers. Newer optical disk storage systems provide access to stored information on image display terminals from both local and remote locations.

Facilities management must be coordinated with office automation and other administrative services. Space planners and other personnel take advantage of technologies such as computer-aided design software in laying out floorplans for office space and arranging workstations, equipment, and furnishings.

DISCUSSION QUESTIONS

1. What are some of the problems in managing information in various formats: digital, image, and paper? How are these problems addressed?
2. What factors are increasing the demands on mail services? How are mail service staff responding?
3. List five benefits of electronic forms management over manual paper-forms management.
4. The term convenience copy should be substituted for the old term carbon copy. Agree or disagree? Why?
5. What is facilities management? How does office automation impact the facilities management staff?
6. What is distributed printing? What advantages does it offer?
7. Today's telephone systems are really specialized computers. Discuss.
8. List six features of office telephone systems and explain how they save time and money.
9. What is the difference between a PBX and a key telephone system? Give an application for each.
10. What are the three fundamental ways in which electronics have changed mailroom equipment? What effect have they had on mailroom operations?
11. The text lists nine electronic mail service applications. Which medium would be most effective for each of the following applications: Telex, TWX, facsimile, CBMS, EMS, or voice mail? Why?

12. Electronic mail service and voice mail are complementary technologies. Explain.
13. What advantages does the computer offer over manual systems for storing and retrieving information?
14. What are COM and CAR? How are they similar? How are they different? What are two appropriate applications for each?
15. How will advances in networking technology facilitate and assist records management?
16. Why would a firm use a commercial records management service?

APPLICATION EXERCISES

1. Peruse records management advertisements and articles in several office automation magazines, then compare the features of alternative technologies. Recommend equipment for the following types of organizations and justify your recommendations:
   a. A large bank
   b. A small real estate firm
   c. A law firm
   d. A large insurance company
2. Visit the mailroom on your campus and arrange for demonstrations of some of its newest equipment. Discuss with personnel how mailroom services have changed over the past ten years. How has new equipment affected the volume of mail they can handle, the cost of handling mail, and the types of services they provide? What new equipment is planned in the next few years? What benefits will it provide?
3. Contact your local Association of Records Managers and Administrators (ARMA) and arrange to have the class attend one of its meetings, or request that a member visit the class to discuss automated records management systems.

SUGGESTED READINGS

ARMA Standards Program: Guidelines for Alphabetic Filing Rules (Prairie Village, Kan.: Association of Records Managers and Administrators, 1985).

ARMA Standards Program: Guidelines for Records Management Job Descriptions (Prairie Village, Kan.: Association of Records Managers and Administrators, 1985).

Fernberg, Patricia M. "Technology's Stamp Is on the Mailroom," *Modern Office Technology* (August 1986), pp. 38–57.

Lippin, Paula. "Facsimile: New Technologies, New Applications," *Modern Office Technology* (March 1987), pp. 72–78.

Ricks, Betty R., and Gow, Kay F. *Information Resource Management* (Cincinnati: South-Western Publishing Co., 1984).

Rosen, Arnold; Feretic, Eileen; and Bahniuk, Margaret Hilton. *Administrative Procedures for the Electronic Office* (New York: John Wiley and Sons, 1984).

Thursland, Arthur L. *Administrative Support: Economic Justification for Office Automation* (Willow Grove, Pa.: Association of Information Systems Professionals, 1984).

Waegemann, C. Peter. *The Handbook of Record Storage and Space Management* (Westport, Conn.: Greenwood Press, 1984).

PRODUCTIVITY: The Impact of Automation on Work

PART 4

Parts 2 and 3 addressed the technical environment of office work: hardware and software. Part 4 turns to organizational and behavioral issues and the impact of automation on work and productivity. Translating the capabilities of office technologies into tangible and intangible operating benefits affects an organization on many levels: individual tasks and work procedures, job design, organizational structure and culture, and the quality of work life. Technology is an important productivity tool, but it is not the only factor or perhaps even the most important factor in creating productive work environments. How the organization uses *technology is as important as which technology is selected. Thus managerial decisions about the organization's goals and the actions of people in using technology to achieve those goals play as large a role as the technology itself.*

Part 4 presents considerations for effectively using office automation and end-user computing technologies to achieve business goals. It emphasizes the need to evaluate technologies on the basis of their potential for changing the way people work, not simply as a means of automating the tasks they are currently performing. Integrating automation into the office is viewed as a process of managing innovation and change, not simply managing technology. Productivity is viewed as a process of creating efficient, effective office work environments.

Chapter 15, "Measuring Productivity: Cost Justification," asks the question, "Can productivity be measured?" Although experts do not agree on an answer to this question, the chapter offers methods currently used by business organizations to cost-justify office automation expenditures.

Chapter 16, "Ergonomics," addresses issues related to the interfacing of people and technology. It describes how the physical environment of office automation should be designed to help people work productively. Concerns affecting the safety, comfort, and overall well-being of the user are discussed. The chapter is divided into two major sections: "Equipment Design" and "Workplace Design."

Chapter 17, "Job Design," stresses the relationship between job design and productivity. In designing systems, technologists often overlook the systems' impact on job design. This chapter focuses on adapting technology to people rather than forcing people to adapt to technology. Job design methodologies that foster productivity are described under the premise that it is people *who are productive, not systems.*

Chapter 18, "Organizational Change," presents strategies for change from an organizational perspective. The introduction of new technologies and systems often requires organizational and work changes to achieve the intended results. Implementers of office automation play major roles as agents of change. Organizational change is a learning process that must be carefully managed. The chapter summarizes major theories of organizational change and presents methodologies for implementing technological change in organizations.

MEASURING PRODUCTIVITY: Cost Justification

CHAPTER **15**

OBJECTIVES

After completing this chapter, the reader should be able to meet the following objectives:

- Define the term *productivity.*
- Explain the difficulties in measuring office productivity.
- Differentiate between direct and indirect productivity measurement.
- List and discuss specific approaches to cost-justifying office automation expenditures.
- Describe four techniques used to develop standards.
- Given a specific situation, develop a plan to cost-justify office automation expenditures.
- Use accepted accounting techniques to calculate the costs of office automation.

KEY TERMS

productivity
hard dollar
soft dollar
direct productivity measurement
indirect productivity measurement
standard
historical data
employee logs
work sampling
stopwatch measure
return on investment (ROI)
cost displacement
payout period
value added
shadow functions
quality of worklife (QWL)
depreciation
salvage value
leasing
renting
total-life-average method

INTRODUCTION

Jack Oplinger of the Diebold Group has said that "the driving force for office automation is based on the realities of the cost of management today." As any manager knows, a firm can use one or a combination of the following strategies to improve its profits:

1. Double its sales volume. (This approach is obviously difficult.)

2. Increase the price of its products. (This approach may decrease total sales volume.)
3. Improve productivity.

The subject of this part of the text is *productivity.* Productivity is generally seen as a means of increasing the "bottom line" profit of organizations. Because of the enormous investment organizations make in both people and tools, increasing productivity has become a national goal. Moreover, while productivity in farming and manufacturing tends to make significant increases year by year, productivity gains in the office are nonexistent, minuscule, or unmeasurable.

The July 30, 1975, issue of *Business Week* reported that industrial productivity had increased 90 percent in the previous decade but office productivity had increased only 4 percent. *Business Week* also pointed out that capital investment in the average industrial worker was $25,000, whereas for the office worker it was between $2000 and $4000. These figures suggest that corporations could benefit from investing more in their office workers. It is difficult, however, to compare the productivity figures of factory workers with those of office workers. As will be outlined later in this chapter, the productivity figures of industrial and office workers are derived in completely different ways.

Economists frequently cite the shift from a blue-collar (industrial) work force to a pink- (clerical) or white-collar (managerial or professional) work force as the chief reason that overall U.S. productivity is on the decline. This trend makes capital investment in office workers even more important. The Bureau of Labor Statistics estimates that 63 percent of the work force is white collar, and experts expect that figure to climb to 95 percent by the year 2000. Therefore, much effort is spent defining and measuring productivity in the office, as that is where the majority of the population is—and will be—employed. The formula for productivity is simple:

$$\text{Productivity} = \text{Output} \div \text{Input}$$

The application of this formula, however, requires an ability to identify and measure inputs and outputs. This is a simple mathematical exercise when applied to factory work. For example, a productivity measure of 50 workers, each of whom earns $10 an hour and works 4 hours with raw materials worth $500 to produce 200 widgets, each worth $60, can be computed as follows:

$$\text{Output} = (200 \times \$60) = \$12{,}000$$
$$\text{Input} = (50 \times \$10 \times 4) = 2000 + (\$500) = 2500$$
$$P = \$12{,}000/2500 = 4.8$$

In this case, to show an increase in productivity only requires showing that workers produced more (or the same number of) widgets with less input (fewer workers, fewer hours, fewer materials).

To show a productivity increase in the office is not so simple. First, it is difficult to determine what constitutes input and output. Is the secretary's output the number of letters typed, the number of phone calls handled, or the number of travel plans completed? What is the output of the manager or professional? The number of meetings held, the number of phone calls completed, the number of reports produced, or what?

Even if definitive numbers can be established, they may not measure productivity. When ten reports are prepared during a week instead of two, it does not necessarily mean that the worker was more productive. It simply means the worker produced more reports. Unlike factory output, it is difficult to say that the extra reports contributed to the bottom-line profits.

Office automation has the potential to increase productivity because it enables work to be done faster and/or more easily. The debate continues as to whether this efficiency justifies the cost of office automation. As the supervisor of the worker who produced the eight unnecessary reports knows, efficiency is not a true measure of effectiveness, or productivity.

The question that challenges office automation planners is not only how to measure productivity but how to assign a dollar value to any productivity improvement. Such numbers (values) are important because the individuals who decide whether to buy office automation technologies often must cost-justify the expenditure. Cost justification is a way of saying that by purchasing such-and-such equipment, we'll increase productivity by *X* amount, and that translates into a savings of $*X*. Companies investing in office automation expect a return on their investment.

The crux of the problem of assigning dollars to productivity is how to apply hard dollar figures to soft dollar savings. *Hard-dollar* figures are actual values of productivity gains in dollars and cents. Office automation's worth, however, is frequently measured in *soft-dollar* savings—some intangible value. For example, measuring the worth of an expert system or an ergonomically designed workstation is an art as much as a science.

Planners are realizing that office automation's biggest payoff is likely to come from improving the productivity of the manager, not the word processing operator. A productivity improvement of 20 percent for a $60,000-a-year manager will affect profits much more quickly than a 20 percent productivity improvement of a $20,000-a-year operator. As indicated earlier in this chapter, the driving force for office automation expenditures is the need to streamline organizational management.

This chapter begins by discussing strategies that automation planners are using to measure and assign dollar values to the productivity of office workers. Following an overview of productivity measurement, approaches to measuring the dollar value of productivity improvement are discussed. The chapter concludes by offering accounting techniques for computing cost savings. These techniques may aid the planner in establishing a return-on-investment (ROI) figure for office automation expenditures.

MEASURING OFFICE PRODUCTIVITY

Office worker productivity may be measured directly or indirectly. Direct measurement requires that output be measurable. Indirect measurement may involve the development of standards for operative personnel or for subordinates' output for managerial personnel.

Direct Productivity Measurement Techniques

While direct measurement of managers and professional employees is considered impossible, direct techniques can measure the output of some clerical workers. In such instances, direct techniques include counts of output (for example, number of lines typed per hour or pages produced per hour).

Such productivity measures were used in early word processing centers not only to control output but also to compute operators' salaries, promotions, and raises. Used as a salary measure, such measures added a "piecework" approach to the office, making office work much like factory work. Such direct productivity measurements were not popular with most workers and led to increased stress and job dissatisfaction.

Given that direct measurement was not a success (in fact, it often led to *decreases* in productivity), indirect measurement is frequently substituted for direct methods, even in instances where the output is measurable.

Indirect Productivity Measurement Techniques

Indirect productivity measurement techniques for operative employees typically depend upon the development of work standards. For measuring the productivity of the manager or professional, indirect techniques include productivity based on the work of subordinates or total output of the department.

Productivity Measures Based on Standards

A *standard* is a minimum output expectation of a given job. Standards are measurements by which performances can be compared. Standards are generally applicable to measuring productivity in work with the following characteristics:

- The work is highly repetitive.
- The work is highly consistent among workers.
- The work consists of tasks that are measurable in terms of time.
- The work typically has measurable output.

For measuring the productivity of the manager, indirect techniques include measuring productivity based on the work of subordinates or the output of the department. For clerical and administrative staff, however, specific measures have been developed: historical data (past performance), employee logs, work sampling, and stopwatch measures. The most recent addition is employee-developed standards.

Historical data The use of historical data for standards development is undoubtedly the oldest and most popular technique, perhaps because of its simplicity. Historical standards establish that productivity is increasing, remaining the same, or decreasing, by comparing output (quantity of work, profits, sales, etc.) of one period (for example, month, quarter, year) with output for another period. Because of seasonal fluctuations (an accounting firm, for example, is likely to be busier in March and April than in other months because of the tax season), users of the historical approach must choose the most appropriate comparison measures.

Historical data is often used effectively to measure changes in the output of a given department before and after automation. Pilot studies, whereby equipment is tested for productivity improvement, typically incorporate a "before" and "after" measurement based on historical data. This technique should be applied cautiously, however. Although office automation has the potential to increase productivity, people's productivity may temporarily decrease when they first begin using a new system. Therefore, measurements should be taken *after* the users are comfortable with the system and have adapted to the new work procedures.

Employee logs The office automation planner may find it useful to establish what tasks office workers do on a daily basis. For example, knowledge workers may spend an hour a day photocopying, placing incomplete phone calls, or other tasks that do not contribute to their productivity. Work logs, such as the time survey sheet or log in Figure 15-1, may be used to establish standards for key tasks at a specific level. A work log is a form that lists time periods—sometimes in 10- or 15-minute intervals, sometimes in intervals of two or three hours—on which the employee records activities. Logs can be used to create standard activities and outputs that are indicative of performance in a given position. Supplementing this data is an estimate of how much time would be spent in those activities *after* automation.

In a study reported in *Datamation* magazine, Sassone and Schwartz described a two-part procedure that measures activities by a "Work Profile Analysis," together with a computer simulation they call the "Hedonic Wage Model."[1] The Hedonic Wage Model puts an actual dollar-and-cents value on individual tasks. This procedure, which explains how to put a dollar figure on data from logs, requires the planner to first identify employee classifications (manager, administrator, senior professional, junior professional, technician, and secretary). An average (or actual) hourly wage is determined for the employee. In addition, specific tasks are assigned certain values for certain classifications. Then, individuals in these positions are asked to log their activities. When activities are classified according to the value of the activity and applied to the wages received for the activity, it can be determined if employees are doing what the company pays them to do. Moreover, as shown in Figure 15-2, this procedure can be used to determine the post-implementation benefits of new technologies.

TIME SURVEY SHEET																	
NAME						POSITION						DATE					
DEPT.						SUPERVISOR									SUMMARY		
TIME	CODE		TIME	CODE		TIME	CODE		TIME	CODE		TIME	CODE		CODE		TIME
8:00			10:00			12:00			2:00			4:00					
8:05			10:05			12:05			2:05			4:05					
8:10			10:10			12:10			2:10			4:10					
8:15			10:15			12:15			2:15			4:15					
8:20			10:20			12:20			2:20			4:20					
8:25			10:25			12:25			2:25			4:25					
8:30			10:30			12:30			2:30			4:30					
8:35			10:35			12:35			2:35			4:35					
8:40			10:40			12:40			2:40			4:40					
8:45			10:45			12:45			2:45			4:45					
8:50			10:50			12:50			2:50			4:50					
8:55			10:55			12:55			2:55			4:55					
9:00			11:00			1:00			3:00			5:00					
9:05			11:05			1:05			3:05			5:05					
9:10			11:10			1:10			3:10			5:10					
9:15			11:15			1:15			3:15			5:15					
9:20			11:20			1:20			3:20			5:20					
9:25			11:25			1:25			3:25			5:25					
9:30			11:30			1:30			3:30			5:30					
9:35			11:35			1:35			3:35			5:35					
9:40			11:40			1:40			3:40			5:40					
9:45			11:45			1:45			3:45			5:45					
9:50			11:50			1:50			3:50			5:50					
9:55			11:55			1:55			3:55			5:55					

ACTIVITY CODES

A = Administration	S = Supervising
C = Collating	O = Out, away from job
B = Photocopying	T = Typing
M = Mimeographing	V = Vacation
P = Proofreading	X = Nothing to do

FIGURE 15-1. A time survey sheet or log.

Work sampling Work sampling is perhaps the most time-consuming of all the standard development measures. Work sampling is based on the statistical laws of probability. The technique requires the office systems planner to observe workers on a random basis and to log their activities at irregular intervals. Statistics tell us that with enough random observations, accurate estimations of the time employees spend on given activities can be computed. Moreover, work sampling is often regarded as much more reliable than asking workers to list how much time they spend in a given activity. Many people find keeping logs to be tedious and time-consuming, interrupting their normal workflow. Work sampling puts the burden on the planner.

Stopwatch measures The use of a stopwatch to develop work standards is applicable to only a limited number of office tasks. The procedure requires a worker to complete a given task, such as data entry or photocopying, while the activity is being timed. The average rate of completion typically becomes the standard by which work is measured. While the stopwatch has limitations for on-the-job measurement, its use may expand as

EXAMPLE BENEFIT CALCULATION FOR MANAGERS

Work Category	Implicit Value (Hourly)	Initial Hours*	Final Hours**	Value
Management	$83.99	600	700	$ 8,399.00
Specialist Professional	$65.11	320	400	$ 5,208.80
Routine Professional	$48.75	260	300	$ 1,950.00
Administrative	$41.15	320	300	($ 823.00)
Clerical	$20.90	140	100	($ 836.00)
Nonproductive	0.00	360	200	$ 0.00
TOTALS		2,000	2,000	$13,898.80

*Pre-Office Automation
**Estimated Post-Automation

FIGURE 15-2. Cost-justifying office automation: Anticipated values of employees' increased productivity through office automation.

automation planners compare ease of use of one copier (for example) with another. If workers using one copier can complete the task more quickly than by another, speed can be a criterion for selecting a copier.

Employee-developed measures Perhaps the most futuristic approach to the development of standards, and the approach that is often the most successful, is allowing employees to determine what is productive. In many organizations (General Electric is an example), task forces and project teams customize productivity measures. As will be discussed in Chapter 18 on "Organizational Change," involving employees at any and all stages related to the acquisition and implementation of new techniques and technologies is desirable.

A final note on standards In short, standards have limited applicability to office work unless they are developed with the participation of the employees themselves. This is particularly true of managerial and professional staff. Workers at all levels are likely to rebel when factory-like measures are applied to their performance. Only when employees are involved in developing the standards does real acceptance occur. The greatest application of such measures, however, may be the before-and-after evaluation of new office automation technologies. Such techniques are often used in cost-justification measures, discussed later in this chapter.

Productivity as a Measure of Subordinates' Output

A final indirect technique is to measure the productivity of a manager by measuring the results or output of his or her employees or department. In other words, when departmental output or productivity goes up, the manager is given credit for the increase. When the manager's department or subordinates are productive, the manager is seen as productive. While not a scientific measure, this technique serves as an incentive for managers.

COST-JUSTIFICATION APPROACHES

As explained in the introduction to this chapter, applying a hard-dollar figure to the soft-dollar savings of office automation is not easy. Traditional cost-justification approaches based on the output/input model are difficult to apply to office automation expenditures because automation's worth is often an "added value" to the worker or enterprise. Today, however, most organizations require office automation expenditures to be cost-justified to ensure that the investment in technology will yield hard-dollar savings. Both top managers and office automation planners consider such figures necessary for cost-justification, especially in the following areas:

1. Preparing a budget and developing long-term office automation plans.
2. Ensuring that office automation fits into the organization's long-term business objectives.
3. Developing a "contract" for organizational commitment of long-range expenditures.

Cost-justification approaches often employ some of the same techniques used in establishing standards, resulting in many of the same problems, particularly unreliability. A cost-justification figure is considered reliable if the figures are the same when the process or approach is repeated. Because of the "people element" in the productivity formula, however, reliability is not common.

In developing cost-justification figures, the automation planner must choose an approach applicable to the situation. When established approaches do not work, the planner must be innovative and develop an original strategy. There is no right or wrong methodology, just *appropriate* methodology.

Approaches for cost justification fit into one of three categories: (1) return on investment, (2) value added, and (3) the cost of doing business.

Return on Investment

The theory behind return on investment (ROI) is simple: the cost of office automation is charged against the gains obtained from the technology. ROI is based on the premise that one can measure the "before technology" costs and compare them with the "after technology" costs. Two strategies are used in this category: (1) cost savings and (2) cost displacement.

Cost Savings

The principle of cost savings is also simple: the cost of the proposed equipment will enable the organization to do the same work at less expense. Because the new equipment may be easier to use or require less maintenance, less power, etc., the purchase "justifies itself." For example, suppose a company is considering purchasing a new photocopying machine. Using a cost-savings approach, the company's present copier expenses are compared to the projected expenses of using a new copier:

Existing Copier		New Copier	
Monthly maintenance fee	$120	Monthly maintenance fee	$ 50
Monthly supplies and toner	$200	Monthly supplies and toner	$100
Monthly depreciation costs	$100	Monthly depreciation costs	$200
Monthly down hours	20	Monthly down hours	0

The result of this cost comparison shows that the new copier at $350 a month and no downtime hours would be less expensive than continuing to use the existing copier at $420 a month and 20 hours of downtime.

Another way to look at cost savings would be to show, for example, that electronic mail would reduce postage and paper costs, space, and mail room activities. Another example would be to show that an electronic filing and retrieval system would save paper and space. Space costs can be significant; it has been estimated that the space cost of a four-drawer filing cabinet can cost more than $20 a month. Such hard-dollar savings can be incorporated into the cost-justification figures.

Cost Displacement

Traditionally, office automation was justified in terms of cost displacement or cost avoidance. Using a $20,000 word processor, a typist could do the work of three typists, thus reducing personnel costs by two workers. In the 1960s and 1970s, office automation *was* word processing. Most planners justified the expense by decreases in the number of secretaries. If secretaries were paid $20,000 per year (including fringe benefits), the purchase of a word processor would displace personnel expenses of $40,000.

Interestingly enough, as the number of secretaries was reduced, much of the clerical work of proofing, copying, and "gophering" was inadvertently offloaded onto managers and professionals, who were paid two or three times as much as the secretaries. Thus cost displacement strategies must be applied cautiously to avoid achieving savings in one area at the expense of another. Productivity is increased only by improving the effectiveness of the entire system.

Value-Added Techniques

Value-added techniques put a dollar figure on the value of work done by automation by making one or more of the following determinations:

1. Determining the activities that were done by automation that could not have been done if the technology had not been available.
2. Determining how much more work was done as a result of the technology.
3. Determining how much the quality of output increased as a result of using new technology. (For example, were better or more timely decisions made because information was more accurate or more quickly compiled?)

Figure 15-3 illustrates a cost-justification based on added value for a local area network. Two techniques of assigning dollar amounts to the value of work done, using office automation, are shadow-function and quality-of-worklife measures.

FIGURE 15-3. Arguments for establishing the added value of a local area network.

A local area network would provide the following advantages:

1. The ability to share information that is stored in another location.
2. The ability to transmit information and data throughout an organization.
3. The ability for more than one person to perform work concurrently on a specific application.
4. The ability to standardize on hardware and software, such as MSDOS or Lotus 1-2-3.
5. The ability to transmit data more quickly than by traditional methods such as telephone lines.
6. The ability to integrate functions.

Shadow Functions

*Shadow functions are everyday activities that are not part of the job but are integral to its completion. For example, how much time is spent trying to find a misfiled document? How much time is lost playing telephone tag? How much time is lost reconveying messages when a telephone message is written on a notepad and then transferred to another document? It has been estimated that the average executive loses approximately two hours a day in unproductive work. The following is a hypothetical breakdown of those two lost hours:

7	unscheduled interruptions, each lasting 8 minutes.	= 56 minutes
6	letters or memos, each taking 5 minutes to give instructions, proofread, and sign.	= 30 minutes
16	phone calls that transfer information from one medium to another (for example, writing a note from a phone call), each transfer taking 1 minute.	= 16 minutes
10	document searches, each taking 20 minutes.	= 20 minutes
Total time spent on tasks unrelated to the job.		= 122 minutes

The office automation planner establishes the value of the executive's time and then applies that hourly rate to time consumed by tasks not related to the job to calculate the cost associated with those shadow functions.

Application Transfer Team

Another, somewhat similar approach to cost justification has been used by IBM for years. To help potential customers identify the type and amount of technology desirable, its Application Transfer Team approach requires that workers estimate the time they spend on specific tasks such as writing, reading, looking for files, or answering the telephone. Gains are measured by calculating the time saved by performing these tasks more efficiently.

For example, suppose planners find that a professional employee spends an hour a day in telephone tag (You call me, I'm not in; I call you back, you're not in; you call me back, I'm not in—and so on). Justifying an electronic mail system could be based on the time savings that the system could offer.

When a National Science Foundation (NSF) office investigated the productivity of four executives and their secretary, it found that the executives had display terminals at their workstations and portable terminals for use at home, and the secretary had a terminal and a letter-quality printer for word processing. The NSF researchers then listed 16 categories (reading, proofing, creating documents, etc.). With this activity list in hand, the executives estimated the number of hours they worked on each task, the number of hours the tasks would have taken *without* the technology, and the activities they would not have been able to complete had the computerized tools *not* been available. In their average work week (34.5 hours), three-eighths of executive time was spent preparing written documents, one-half on other types of communications, and one-eighth on miscellaneous activity. The NSF researchers concluded that office automation had improved their productivity by 22 percent and secretarial productivity by 33 percent. These figures are consistent with other studies that used similar methodology.

Payout Period

Related to cost displacement is an approach that shows how long it will take an investment to pay for itself, or "break even." Assume that the yearly cost of a secretary is $20,000. If the analyst determines that one word processing operator can do the work of three secretaries, then the payout period for a word processing system costing $10,000 would be calculated as shown in Figure 15-4. As illustrated, the system could pay for itself in only three months.

- Yearly cost of two new secretaries = $40,000
- Cost of one word processing system = $10,000
- Payout period = 40,000/10,000 = 1/4 year or 3 months

FIGURE 15-4. Payout period and cost justification for a word processing system.

Quality of Work Life Approaches

Value added can also be determined by assessing the quality of worklife. Are workers, with technology, able to do routine activities with ease, thus freeing them for more creative, more rewarding activities? If so, office automation has made a contribution to their quality of work life (QWL).

Figure 15-5 is a "Productivity/Satisfaction Survey" used by a major vendor to determine if office automation has affected both the worker's perceived self-productivity and job satisfaction. Typically, respondents report that factors that contribute to productivity are the same as those that contribute to job satisfaction. The problem remains, however, regarding how to put a dollar figure on QWL. Suggestions include determining that turnover rates are lower when employees have automated tools, or developing a measure of the quality of decisions and increased ease of planning. Another measure is establishing that *better* employees were attracted to the organization because of the technology.

FIGURE 15-5. **A productivity/job satisfaction survey used to assess the impact of office automation.**

PRODUCTIVITY/SATISFACTION SURVEY

Below is a list of work situations that may increase PRODUCTIVITY. Pick the eight that are most important to your own productivity. Rank them from 8 (most important) to 1 (least important). Write rankings to the left of items in the "P" column.

Pick the eight items you feel are most important to your personal on-the-job SATISFACTION. Rank them from 8 (most important) to 1 (least important). Write these rankings in the "S" column.

Then indicate the degree to which you experience each situation as an effect of using the Office Automation System by circling a number in the right column. Larger numbers indicate more effect. Judge the degree of effect independently from the importance you attach to each item.

			Effect of Automation				
P	**S**	**Work Situation**	**High**				**Low**
____	____	Faster reaction to problems/ opportunities	4	3	2	1	0
____	____	Improved quality of work	4	3	2	1	0
____	____	Increased control over operations	4	3	2	1	0
____	____	Decrease in time needed to do work	4	3	2	1	0
____	____	Better personal organization	4	3	2	1	0
____	____	Reduced interruptions	4	3	2	1	0
____	____	Reduced time spent on clerical tasks	4	3	2	1	0
____	____	More creativity	4	3	2	1	0
____	____	Reduced mistakes	4	3	2	1	0
____	____	Clearer communications	4	3	2	1	0

FIGURE 15-5. (continued)

____	____	More rapid communications	4	3	2	1	0
____	____	Increase in accuracy of data	4	3	2	1	0
____	____	Increase in amount of data	4	3	2	1	0
____	____	Improved access to needed data	4	3	2	1	0
____	____	Reduced waiting for information	4	3	2	1	0
____	____	Data in more understandable form	4	3	2	1	0
____	____	Improved decision making	4	3	2	1	0
____	____	Better planning	4	3	2	1	0
____	____	Faster reaction to problems/ opportunities	4	3	2	1	0
____	____	Improved quality of work	4	3	2	1	0
____	____	Increased control over operations	4	3	2	1	0
____	____	Timely completion of work	4	3	2	1	0
____	____	Additional work undertaken	4	3	2	1	0
____	____	Less overtime	4	3	2	1	0
____	____	Less waiting for work	4	3	2	1	0
____	____	More job satisfaction	4	3	2	1	0
____	____	Increased motivation to work	4	3	2	1	0
____	____	Cost reduction	4	3	2	1	0
____	____	Other ____________________	4	3	2	1	0
____	____	Other ____________________	4	3	2	1	0

Average amount of time you use office automation per day: Hrs. ____ Mins. ____

Compared to the way you used to do your work, how much time does the System save you on an average daily basis? Hrs. ____ Mins. ____

How does using the system save you time?

In general, your saved time is spent doing what?

Does using the System have any negative effect? If yes, please explain. Yes ____ No ____

	High				Low
Rate your overall degree of satisfaction with the System.	4	3	2	1	0
Rate your degree of comfort with the System.	4	3	2	1	0

Check your job classification:

___ Secretary/Clerical
___ Professional
___ Manager
___ Supervisor
___ Director, V.P., G.M.
___ Other __________

PLEASE ADD COMMENTS ON THE BACK OF THIS SHEET. THANK YOU.

The Cost of Doing Business

This third and final argument for persuading managers to invest in office automation is quite simple: the organization cannot go on without it! In some cases, one or more of the following situations may exist:

1. The task to be done cannot be done without technology.
2. The technology improves customer service.
3. The technology gives the organization a competitive edge.

These arguments have been discussed in previous chapters and may be the route that office automation justification will take in the future: showing an impact on the very nature of the business, or showing that office automation offers increased profit (better customer service typically produces repeat customers, which equals more sales, which equals more profit), or increasing the organization's share of the market (providing faster and better performance as a result of more timely, more accurate information).

In any case, the approach the office automation planner chooses to ensure top-management support of technology expenditures must conform to the corporate climate, cash flow, and organizational needs.

SELECTED ACCOUNTING TECHNIQUES

Office automation planners have been quite innovative in estimating the cost benefits of office automation; the following tactics have been borrowed from accounting practices and may be helpful in developing cost-justification figures: (1) depreciation, (2) salvage value of replaced equipment, (3) purchasing versus leasing/renting, and (4) total-life averaging.

Depreciation

The accounting concept of depreciation spreads the cost of equipment over its expected life. Depreciation may be likened to rent expense; in other words, the cost of equipment is expensed over a period equal to its expected life. Two approaches are straight-line depreciation and sum-of-the-year's digits.

For example, assume that a $25,000 system with a salvage value (worth) of $5000 at the end of its useful life (5 years) is to be depreciated. A straight-line formula for establishing this depreciation expense is illustrated in Figure 15-6. If straight-line depreciation is used, the expense of $4000/year may be more justifiable than the much larger $25,000 figure.

Original cost of equipment − Estimated disposal value ÷ Years of useful life = Depreciation

Example: A $25,000 piece of equipment with a salvage value of $5,000 and an expected life of 5 years can be "expensed" as $25,000 − $5,000 ÷ 5 = $4,000 yearly depreciation expense.

FIGURE 15-6. An example of the straight-line method for computing yearly depreciation.

Because the value of technology often declines rapidly in its initial years, an alternative depreciation technique is sum-of-the-year's digits. Figure 15-7 shows how this same expenditure could be "expensed" by the sum-of-the-year's-digits method. Note the higher figure for the first year's cost. Showing a larger savings in the early years is an acceptable accounting technique and may make a stronger argument.

Choosing one of these (or other) depreciation methods depends on the organization's accounting policies and government regulations. (In developing cost-justification figures, however, one needs only to determine if the high or low cost figure adds more to the cost-justification plan.)

- 1 + 2 + 3 + 4 + 5 = 15

The depreciation figures, then, could read as follows:

- Year 1 (5/15 × 20,000) = $6600
- Year 2 (4/15 × 20,000) = $5400
- Year 3 (3/15 × 20,000) = $4000
- Year 4 (2/15 × 20,000) = $2600
- Year 5 (1/15 × 20,000) = $1400
- Total $20,000

FIGURE 15-7. **An example of the sum-of-the-years-digits method for computing depreciation for a $20,000 expenditure over five years.**

Salvage Value

Salvage value, or the value of the equipment being replaced, is often overlooked when cost figures are developed. For example, if the office automation planner can trade in or sell existing equipment, the value of the existing equipment can decrease the price of the new equipment. In the previous example, the expected salvage value of the equipment to be purchased was accounted for; in this case, the market value of the existing equipment is used to reduce the current cost of the proposed equipment.

Purchasing versus Leasing or Renting

Purchasing is buying equipment outright. *Leasing* is a contractual agreement to use a piece of equipment for a given amount of time. *Renting* is buying the use of it for an unspecified time. Often, it makes good business sense to lease or rent equipment rather than purchase it outright. In addition to decreasing immediate, out-of-pocket expenses, leasing or renting provides the following advantages:

1. It puts responsibility for upkeep and repairs on the manufacturer or dealer.
2. It protects against product obsolescence; when a newer or better model comes on the market, it's easier to upgrade.
3. It spreads the cost of equipment over its useful life to the organization; there is no need to develop life estimates.

Deciding whether to purchase, lease, or rent office automation hardware requires the office automation planner to compute depreciation costs. Advantages of ownership, which may include tax benefits, must be weighed against the advantages of renting or leasing.

Total Life Average Method

The total life average method for justifying office automation expenditures involves summing all expenses related to purchasing and operating a piece of equipment into one figure. That figure is then divided by the estimated life of the equipment. The total includes all costs, including interest (if the money is to be borrowed), opportunity costs (loss of income if the money had been invested elsewhere), and salvage value, as well as all operating costs.

Such figures could be prepared for the costs of the existing equipment and compared to the costs of the proposed equipment. Decisions whether to purchase could be based on the comparison of the alternatives.

SUMMARY

Productivity is difficult to measure in an office environment because output figures are difficult to establish. Even when numbers can be applied to output, the productivity formula (P = O/I) does not consider quality or effectiveness of output. The question of the usefulness of productivity measures remains unanswered.

Despite their limitations, productivity measures are used to cost-justify office automation expenditures. Productivity measures may be direct or indirect. Direct measures involve measuring input and output, such as numbers of reports, numbers of lines typed, and so on. Indirect measures for operative employees typically revolve around the need to establish work standards for repetitive work. Such measures provide a basis for worker evaluation. In addition, a growing use of such figures is for equipment evaluation: Can the same task be done more quickly on X machine than on Y machine? Indirect measures for managers are the productivity or output of their department or employees within the department.

Once productivity has been measured, the challenge is to assess its dollar value. Such figures are often the basis for "selling" top management on the desirability or need for new equipment. While it appears that business is evolving to the point where technology is simply "the cost of doing business," office automation planners need cost-justification figures to help them prepare budgets that include office automation in the long-range plans of the organization and ensure commitment for long-range expenditures.

Approaches to cost-justifying office automation expense are categorized as (1) return on investment, (2) value added, and (3) cost of doing business. A planner, using an ROI technique, shows how new equipment can reduce the cost of a task or application. Value-added techniques show how the value of the output was increased by the new technology. Cost of doing business is the simplest, most futuristic technique: use of technology is *the* way to do the task. Choosing an appropriate technique requires careful analysis of the situation, including the organization's history, needs, and cash flow.

Not to be overlooked in cost-justifying technology are accounting techniques for developing reliable cost calculations. Such techniques include but are not limited to depreciation, salvage value, purchasing versus leasing/renting, and total-life averaging.

In short, cost justification of office automation is an inexact process. The productivity of office workers at all levels of the organization is difficult to measure by the output/input model. Productivity is much more than a simple formula because it includes a human variable. The analyst may rely on time-tested accounting techniques to justify expenditures. Until the day when office automation is regarded as just another tool, comparable to the telephone and pencils and paper, cost-justification techniques will be required.

DISCUSSION QUESTIONS

1. What is productivity? Why is it so difficult to measure the productivity of office workers?
2. Discuss the role of standards in determining the productivity of clerical employees.
3. Can the productivity of managers be determined by the productivity of their subordinates? Discuss the implications of this measure on the role of managers.
4. To justify the purchases of the following technologies, what approach might the office systems analyst take? Defend your answers.
   a. A local area network
   b. A laser printer
   c. An expert system
   d. A voice mail system
   e. A speech recognition system
   f. A top-of-the-line microcomputer
   g. An enhanced graphics monitor
5. Give examples of "shadow functions" other than those described in this text.
6. Assume you, the office automation planner, have determined that your organization could benefit from a $100,000 voice mail system. Of the accounting techniques described in this chapter, which would you use to calculate cost savings? Using this $100,000 figure, show how you would use the technique. You will need to develop your own figures for other variables required in this exercise.
7. If cost justification is so difficult, why do most organizations require it? Are there any benefits to office automation planners? Discuss.

APPLICATION EXERCISES

1. Interview an accounting professor for his or her views on what's appropriate for cost-justifying office automation expenditures. What techniques does the professor offer that expand on those in this text?
2. Write a report comparing Japanese with American views of workers' productivity.
3. As a class project, each student should interview a person who has recently begun using a new office automation technology. How pleased is the person with the new technology? Does he or she view it as a productivity enhancer? If so, in what way? Compare the results of your interview with what your classmates found. Are answers consistent? Why? Why not? Is the length of time a person has been using the technology important in the response?

SUGGESTED READINGS

Allen, Leilani E. "Measuring Productivity in the Automated Office," *Administrative Management* (December 1986), pp. 41–43.

Boone, Mary, and Meyer, H. Dean. *The Information Edge: Measuring Profits from Office Automation Tools* (New York: Holt, Rinehart and Winston, 1987).

Byrne, K. E. "Office Automation: Productivity Through Organizational Development," *Proceedings of the Seventh Annual Office Systems Research Conference* (Bowling Green, Ky.: Office Systems Research Association, 1988), pp. 1–9.

Schwartz, A. Perry. "Keeping Time and Measuring Productivity," *Information Center* (May 1987), pp. 45–47.

CHAPTER 16

ERGONOMICS

OBJECTIVES

After completing this chapter, the reader should be able to meet the following objectives:

- Define the terms that describe the video display terminal (VDT) screen: *glare, flicker, bezel,* and *character quality.*
- Explain what to look for in determining VDT character quality.
- Discuss color options for the VDT.
- Summarize both sides of the VDT radiation danger issue.
- List six terms that describe the ergonomics of keyboard operation.
- Describe the application of AMCO-PACT in the automated office.
- Discuss the relationship between lighting and worker productivity.
- Offer at least three solutions to alleviating noise in the automated office.
- Discuss the relationship between workstation design and office worker productivity.
- Suggest how office workers who use a VDT can improve their posture.
- Explain the impact of reach and viewing distances on workstation design.
- Give several examples of territoriality in the office.
- Explain why socialization patterns must be considered in office design.
- Explain the relationship of productivity to personal space, backs and sides, eye contact, privacy, and status.

KEY TERMS

ergonomics
resolution
pixel
character resolution
character cell
glare
contrast
reflection
flicker
refresh rate
American Simplified Keyboard
AMCO-PACT
candela
lumen
lux
reflection factor
articulation index
decibel
anthropometrics
territoriality

bezel
matrix density
contrast
key roll
QWERTY keyboard
socialization
human factors
radiation
font

INTRODUCTION

Ergonomics, also referred to as *human factors* or human engineering, is based on the Greek words *ergon,* which means work, and *nomos,* which means natural laws. Regardless of terminology, everyone knows that improving the way people act with their work environment and technology is important.

Ergonomics can be applied to all types of work. As a science, it began during World War II in the design of airplane cockpits. Pilots needed to have the most frequently used instruments within easy reach or sight and to have easily adjustable controls. Applications of ergonomic principles have spread to the automobile, the factory floor, the automatic teller machine, and now the automated office. Ergonomic principles apply to any situation where individuals and technology merge. During the past two decades, emphasis has been primarily on product design, drawing upon the sciences of anatomy, physiology, and psychology.

Ergonomic issues surfaced in the office environment as workers expressed concern about safety and comfort. Business has a stake here, too: increased productivity. Ergonomic design demonstrates the organization's concern about workers' health and safety. Most importantly, it provides a productive environment that may increase job satisfaction.

This discussion of ergonomic principles is organized around a conceptual systems model of productivity. Figure 16-1 depicts the areas of technology, procedures, and human needs as distinct circles, each of which can stand alone as a factor that either increases or impedes productivity. For any task, an optimum technology exists. However, when a technology is imposed without regard for procedures and/or human needs, it is not used to its optimum potential.

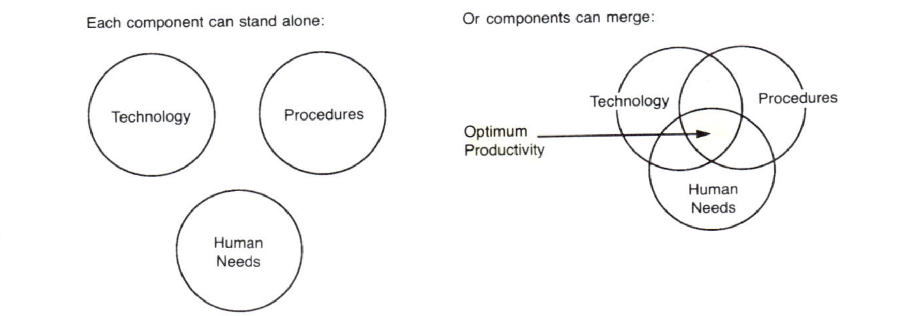

FIGURE 16-1. **A systems approach to productivity.**

The discussion of ergonomic principles related to office automation is divided into two main categories: equipment design and workplace design. In discussing ergonomic concerns, an overriding theme is human needs in relation to doing work.

Figure 16-2 is a picture of Ralph carelessly violating several important guidelines for using computers. What is wrong in this photograph? List the problems before you read the descriptions of the six major problems. This "pretest" is designed to introduce you to some ergonomic principles.

FIGURE 16-2. What is wrong in this picture?

How many things are wrong in this picture?

Here's an exercise you might want to try out on some of your IC's users (or the IC staff, for that matter). Take a good look at the photo of "Ralph" who is working at his PC. Can you tell what's wrong in this photograph? A recent IBM press release listed six possible problems.

The card table supporting the PC probably isn't steady enough to prevent harmful movement or vibration. Use a sturdy desk or table—or better yet—a desk designed specifically for computer equipment.

The radiator generates heat that could damage the equipment. Make sure the work space is well ventilated and away from direct heat sources.

FIGURE 16-2. (continued)

The open window will ventilate the room, but it also allows dust, heat, and humidity to damage the internal components of the computer. Keep the PC away from open windows and sunlight.

Ashes from a cigarette or from the kind of stoogie that Ralph smokes can interfere with the read/write heads in the disk drive. If you must smoke, blow it away from the unit and place your ashtray away from the computer.

Drinks spill. The keyboard might be damaged if Ralph's coffee cup falls off of the monitor. Crumbs from his donuts can have a similar effect on the machine's internal components.

The surface of Ralph's diskette is going down for the final count. If he hasn't scrambled his data yet, he probably will. The paper clip, his fingers, or the ballpoint pen he's using to write on his diskette could all damage the sensitive material that the disk is made of or interfere with the PC's ability to read the data. And there's not a disk envelope in sight.

Those are IBM's suggestions. Given that IBM is a hardware vendor, it's not surprising that all of its hints concern the health and happiness of the hardware. Here in the office, we think we've located a few things Ralph could do for his own comfort and peace of mind.

There is no documentation near the workstation (such as it is). Keep it handy. When a problem arises, it's maddening to hunt down documentation that "floats" around the office or to fetch a manual that's stored down the hall.

Ralph's chair doesn't look as though it was designed for style or comfort. He might be more comfortable (and more productive) in a different chair. This may sound like a minor point, but little things make a difference.

The light hanging from the ceiling probably creates glare on the screen. Use low-intensity light or provide rear or side lighting out of the line of sight.

EQUIPMENT DESIGN

Manufacturers have been interested in ergonomic principles for decades. IBM, AT&T, and Xerox, for example, have developed large research divisions to integrate ergonomic features into their products. Identifying the need for health and safety standards, the Human Factors Society has developed guidelines in the United States. Europe, however, is the frontrunner in acknowledging the need for standards and enforcing them. In particular, the Scandinavian countries are known for stringent guidelines and strict enforcement.

It also makes good sense for equipment purchasers to be aware of what constitutes well-designed equipment. As a potential user or purchaser, the reader should be aware of ergonomic factors relevant to equipment selection. Manufacturers are continually updating and revising their products based on what is known about ergonomics. The intent of this section on equipment design is to share some basic principles of ergonomics.

This discussion of technology is limited to the visual display terminal (VDT) and the keyboard. Although the VDT and the keyboard are sometimes combined, they are usually separate units. As separate units, equipment bulk decreases and the flexibility of user positioning increases. Computer manufacturers realize the need for user flexibility, and nearly all VDT units manufactured today have detachable keyboards.

Typically, the VDT selected is a product of the computer company; customers who buy an IBM computer usually buy IBM keyboards; and customers who buy Digital Equipment Company (DEC) computers usually buy DEC keyboards. However, the VDT is a computer peripheral, and many options are available.

What are the distinguishing features of VDTs? How can products be compared? This chapter limits its discussion to the CRT-VDT. Other display monitors are on the market, such as LCD, gas plasma, and so on—but the vast majority of displays used in business today are CRTs.

The Visual Display Terminal

The reader may want to review Chapter 5, which describes visual display screens in technical terms. The visual display terminal (VDT) is perhaps the instrument most frequently cited as causing stress, discomfort, and even danger in an automated office environment. As a user, as a manager supervising users, or as an analyst, it is important to be up-to-date concerning VDT comfort and safety. Once the facts are known, the user/manager can make informed judgments regarding safety and ease of use. Specific attributes to be discussed here are size, glare and reflection, flicker, bezel, character resolution, and radiation.

Size

The size of the screen is the first feature to be considered. The screen must be large enough for the user to easily distinguish characters. Most CRT displays used today are 12-inch screens (measured diagonally) offering 80 columns across and 25 rows down. For desktop publishing, screens are typically 19 inches with 66 rows down to allow an entire page to be seen. High-end screens may be 24 inches and are usually purchased by publishing departments.

Footprint is another term used to describe the size of the *entire* VDT (not just the screen) and is described in square inches. If limited desktop space is a problem, footprint is an important variable.

Glare and Reflection

Perhaps the factor most critical to user comfort (and perhaps safety) is the ability to see the screen clearly and without strain. *Glare* is light that comes through the VDT; glare can often be reduced by adjusting screen contrast. Reflection is light from the environment deflected off the screen. Both can be problems for the user. However, just as the causes are different for glare and reflection, so are the solutions.

Anyone who has sat with his or her back to a sunny window while using a VDT has probably experienced reflection, not glare. VDT surfaces reflect light from the sun as well as light from the immediate environment. Reflection causes discomfort and can result in eyestrain.

Polarized screens allow less diffused light (or glare) to penetrate from the VDT; however, such screens do little to reduce reflection. Research remains unclear as to the effectiveness of glare-reducing devices. Much of their benefit is ascribed to the positive attitude workers develop when they see that their employer is trying to make the workplace more comfortable.

Reflection and glare can be reduced in many cases by simply closing the blinds or adjusting the lighting so that no *direct* light hits the screen. In other cases, repositioning the VDT so that light originates behind or perpendicular to the screen works well. When such solutions are not possible, swivel devices, hoods, and visors may be used. An operator using a swivel/tilt mechanism such as the one shown in Figure 16-3 can position the VDT to decrease glare and reflection. Acrylic lenses that fit over light fixtures are another solution. Swivel devices, hoods, visors, and lenses are low-cost solutions to the reflection problem.

To determine the source of a reflection, one could position a mirror in front of the VDT. The source reflected in the mirror may be a white copier across the aisle or, as one operator was surprised to discover, the white shirt he was wearing!

FIGURE 16-3. The Honeywell Tilt Terminal Base.

Flicker

As the pixel grid increases in size, the need for a faster, more powerful deflection, or refresh rate, also increases. The image on CRTs, like the image on televisions, is the result of electron charges sweeping by a dot of phosphor on the screen, causing the dot to momentarily glow. The dot must be recharged for the image to remain on the screen. When the dot fades before it is recharged, a flicker is the result. Most images are recharged at high rates (about 65 times per second or more), and this frequency, or *refresh rate,* keeps users from noticing the flicker.

To address this problem, some displays employ interlaced scanning. Interlacing works by dividing the screen into odd- and even-numbered lines. The eye integrates, or "interlaces," the screen. The result is that there are no sharp images. If the user sees a "ghosting" afterimage, it is the result of interlacing. High-resolution screens are often described as "non-interlaced" and provide clear and stable characters.

There is no evidence that flicker affects productivity, but it can be an annoyance. The Human Factors Society has warned that manufacturer claims of "flicker-free" CRTs should be supported by controlled experiments. Flicker-free to one person may not be flicker-free to another.

Bezel

Webster's dictionary defines *bezel* as (among other definitions) the slanting faces of a cut jewel. *Bezel* describes the tendency for the VDT to be clearer in the middle than at its margins. Like a well-cut jewel, the screen is brightest in the middle. For ease and comfort of viewing, VDT characters must be straight and even. "Pincushioning" occurs when a character in the middle of the screen appears higher than characters closer to the margins.

Character Resolution

What is resolution? How is it measured? For years, the sole measure of character resolution or display clarity was the number of pixels on the screen. A *pixel* is a dot of momentarily glowing phosphor. Displays are made up of thousands of pixels. While the number of pixels is important, the size of the pixel and the number of dots in the character cell must also be considered.

As a general rule, the smaller the pixel and the larger the character cell, the better the display image will be. Most displays offer a 1 mm pixel size, but pixel size can be as small as .25. A character cell is the number of pixels allotted to each character, for example, 9 × 14, 8 × 8, or 7 × 9. In comparing displays with identical character cell sizes, however, the size of the pixels in that character cell must also be compared.

Pixel and character cell sizes remain a popular way of identifying resolution, but it is more accurately described by including character size and shape, matrix density, contrast, and color as variables.

Character Size and Shape

When one reads a book, one reads it not by looking at individual letters or words, but by perceiving the words as part of a larger unit—a phrase or a sentence. Therefore, if the letters are too large on a VDT screen, the user will have difficulty reading the screen. Likewise, if the characters are too small, the reader is not able to recognize their outline or shape, and thus the word. Ergonomists agree that displays with 80 characters across are the most desirable. However, screens with 40 or fewer characters may be appropriate in the same situations.

Character shape relates to the printing term *font* (described in Chapter 7). For ease of reading on a VDT, complex shapes should be avoided. For example, the user must be able to differentiate *1* and *I*, *B* and *8*, *C* and *G*, and *D* and *O*.

Matrix Density

Matrix density, which is also a printing term, describes the amount of space between characters and lines. As with character size and shape, on a VDT the spacing between characters affects readability. The Human Factors Society recommends a between-character spacing of one stroke width (or one pixel) and between-line spacing of two strokewidths. These sizes are illustrated in Figure 16-4.

FIGURE 16-4. Recommended between-character spacing and between-line spacing.

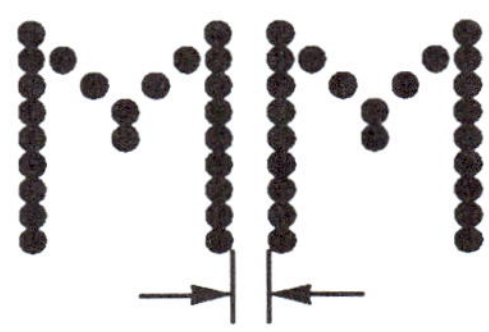

a. Between-character spacing: A minimum of one stroke width or pixel, whichever is greater.

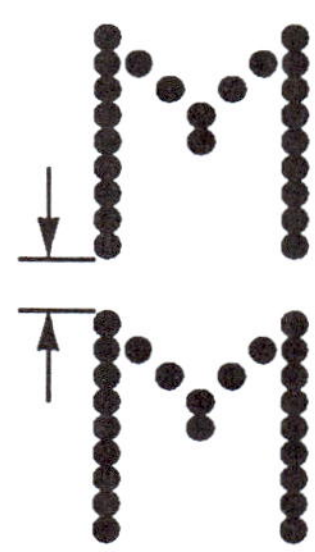

b. Between-line spacing: A minimum of two stroke widths or pixels.

Contrast

Contrast is the difference in luminance between a character and its background. On most VDTs, contrast can be controlled. The premise is that a screen with high contrast is easy to read because the characters are distinguishable. Most VDTs have a control knob by which the user can regulate contrast. One can choose between displays of dark characters on a light background (negative contrast) or light characters on a dark background (positive contrast).

Advantages of positive contrast displays are (1) less reflection and (2) the overall lighting in the office can be higher. Although negative contrast displays are generally considered superior to positive displays, they may require a higher refresh rate and more pixels to be effective.

Color

Monochrome (one-color) monitors are available in amber, green, or gray. Readers who have used VDTs probably have a color preference. The question remains, though, which color is best? Most research concludes that yellow text on an amber background is easiest to see, because (1) an amber background brightens the viewing area, increasing contrast and lessening glare, and (2) yellow is at the middle of the visual spectrum, minimizing problems with other light.

While the amber screen is touted as the most appropriate for viewing text, green and gray are acceptable. Experts concur that the preference of the user is the key to color selection. Notable exceptions are saturated blue on a dark background (this combination tends to hinder character resolution), saturated red and blue or red and green (this can cause chromostereopsis), and red (some people have difficulty seeing the color red).

It is well accepted that, for graphic applications, color adds to the user's enjoyment of the perception of the screen. The number of colors that can be used effectively on a VDT is related to the application. For alphanumeric screens, experts recommend using no more than four colors on the screen at one time with a maximum of eight colors for the total system. This is because most people cannot discriminate among more than eight colors at one time. Color must be used judiciously, or it can interfere with the user's understanding of information. For text editing applications, character resolution on color VDTs is usually inferior to that on monochrome displays.

Efforts to standardize the "best color" for VDTs have been debated (and findings revised) for years. While most early research was conducted in Europe (Scandinavia, in particular), in recent years the need for standards for ergonomics has surfaced in the United States. Some of these standards have been codified as the American National Standard for Human Factor Engineering of VDT Workstations and have been incorporated into this text. IBM's Systems Application Architecture (SAA) Common User Access (CUA) User Interface Screen Design standards, which some experts believe will become an industry standard, include detailed recommendations for using color on various types of VDTs.

The screen design test in Figure 16-5a assesses many principles of VDT readability, such as character size, spacing, and ease of use. Take this test and compare your answers with those presented in Figure 16-5b.

Radiation

Concerns have been raised about health hazards from radiation emitted by VDTs. Similar concerns were raised in the 1960s about radiation from color TV sets. The electron gun inside the VDT shoots electrons at a high speed, irradiating the screen and emitting radiation. Whether the level of radiation is sufficient to pose health hazards has been the subject of considerable debate.

Experts differ about the safety of VDTs, and research findings are mixed. Most federal agencies contend that the VDT is safe because its radiation emission levels are well below safety standards. Dr. J. Donald Millar, Director of the National Institute for Occupational Health and Safety (NIOSH), testified in hearings before the House Subcommittee on Health and Safety of the Committee on Education and Labor:

> Although no national standard has been established for extremely low frequency (ELF) radiation, measured levels from VDTs have been found to be less than those emitted by hair dryers, irons, and other typical household appliances. All forms of radiation measured were at levels well below those documented in the scientific literature as necessary for causing adverse biological effects. These data indicate that the radiation shielding that is already an integral part of the VDT equipment is adequate in protecting the worker against the radiation produced by the machine.[1]

While overwhelming evidence supports the safety of the VDT, the verdict is still out on the effect that VDT radiation may have on the user. The process that forms the characters on a VDT also creates a pulse, a regular pattern of very low frequency (VLF), nonionizing radiation. Although the level of the VLF radiation emitted by displays falls below levels set by the government, many people are concerned that these levels are not strict enough.

Concerns have arisen partly because of the reports of miscarriages, still births, and birth defects among VDT users (see Figure 16-6). In addition to these 'cluster pregnancy' reports, a case-controlled study of 1,583 pregnancy outcomes in Northern California found that women who used VDTs more than half the workweek during the first three months of pregnancy were more likely to suffer miscarriages than those doing other types of office work.[2]

SCREEN DESIGN TEST

Instructions:

One of the sets of screens (A or B) below has a number of deficiencies which will cause significant losses in productivity. Can you identify the set?

Compare the Data Entry and corresponding Inquiry Screens in each set. Check (√) the answer that best describes your opinions concerning the two sets of screens. Answers are presented on the reverse side for your convenience.

QUESTIONS

Which screen set:	A Screens	B Screens
1. Requires more time to locate information?	☐	☐
2. Requires more time to enter data?	☐	☐
3. Generates more entry errors?	☐	☐
4. Requires more documentation?	☐	☐
5. Requires more training time?	☐	☐
6. May create morale problems?	☐	☐
7. Is used and sold more easily?	☐	☐
8. Yields higher productivity?	☐	☐

To use Screen Set B repeatedly throughout the day may require a total of 10 minutes more than to use Screen Set A. Over one years' time, what will the unproductive time cost (assuming 100 users) for:

9. A clerical person ($10/hr. with overhead)

   ☐ a. $1,000 ☐ c. $30,000
   ☐ b. $20,000 ☐ d. $40,000+

10. A middle manager ($40/hr. with overhead)

    ☐ a. $4,000 ☐ c. $80,000
    ☐ b. $40,000 ☐ d. $160,000+

11. Which of these sets of screens would you prefer to buy, use, or sell?

    ☐ Set A ☐ Set B

SCREEN SET A

DATA ENTRY SCREEN A

```
ACCUMULATED TRANSACTION FILE (ATF) UPDATE

************ Enter the following Transaction data ************

       Entered by: _ _ _
              DDA: _ _ _ _-_-_ _ _ _ _ _
              TIC: _ _ _
             Date: _ _/_ _/_ _
              Amt: _ _ _ _ _ _ _ _ _ _ _ _._ _
         Serial #: _ _ _
             Addr: _ _ _ _
               SI: _ _
 Description Code: _ _ _

Press S/R to continue
Press PFI to end session
```

INQUIRY SCREEN A

```
              ACCUMULATED TRANSACTION FILE (ATF) REPORT

DDA: 0000-0-000123    File Date: 021682   Curr Bal: 1,614,609.44    Page: 1
Type: Commercial Div  Stmt Date: 012982   Stmt Bal: 2,600,140.23      BR: O
Stat: Open              OD Date: 052179   Coll Bal:   990,974.00-  Ret #: 0

*******************************************************************************

T/C   DATE     AMOUNT      SERIAL #  ADDR  SI  DESCRIPTION   SCREEN BAL

055   020182       100.00     -       -    -   Credit Memo   2,600,240.23
055   020182   110,325.93     -       -    -   Credit Memo   2,710,566.16
006   020182        85.00     1       -    -   Deposit       2,710,651.16-

006   020182       130.07     1       -    -   Deposit       2,710,781.23
006   020182       195.00     1       -    -   Deposit       2,170,976.23
006   020182       206.66     1       -    -   Deposit       2,711,182.89

006   020182       382.00     8       -    -   Deposit       2,711,564.89
006   020182       908.83    15       -    -   Deposit       2,172,473.72
006   020182     1,226.42    17       -    -   Deposit       2,713,700.14

PRESS S/R TO CONTINUE

PRESS PFI TO END SESSION
```

SCREEN SET B

DATA ENTRY SCREEN B

```
ACCUMULATED TRANSACTION FILE (ATF) UPDATE

ENTERED BY_ _ _DDA_ _ _ _ _ _ _ _ _ _ _ _T/C_ _ _
DATE_ _ _ _ _ _AMT_ _ _ _ _ _ _ _ _ _ _ _SERIAL #_ _ _
ADDR_ _ _ _SI_ _DESCRIPTION CODE_ _ _

ENTERED BY_ _ _DDA_ _ _ _ _ _ _ _ _ _ _ _T/C_ _ _
DATE_ _ _ _ _ _AMT_ _ _ _ _ _ _ _ _ _ _ _SERIAL #_ _ _
ADDR_ _ _ _SI_ _DESCRIPTION CODE_ _ _

ENTERED BY_ _ _DDA_ _ _ _ _ _ _ _ _ _ _ _T/C_ _ _
DATE_ _ _ _ _ _AMT_ _ _ _ _ _ _ _ _ _ _ _SERIAL #_ _ _
ADDR_ _ _ _SI_ _DESCRIPTION CODE_ _ _

ENTERED BY_ _ _DDA_ _ _ _ _ _ _ _ _ _ _ _T/C_ _ _
DATE_ _ _ _ _ _AMT_ _ _ _ _ _ _ _ _ _ _ _SERIAL #_ _ _
ADDR_ _ _ _SI_ _DESCRIPTION CODE_ _ _

ENTERED BY_ _ _DDA_ _ _ _ _ _ _ _ _ _ _ _T/C_ _ _
DATE_ _ _ _ _ _AMT_ _ _ _ _ _ _ _ _ _ _ _SERIAL #_ _ _
ADDR_ _ _ _SI_ _DESCRIPTION CODE_ _ _

PRESS S/R TO CONTINUE; OR INITIATE END OF SESSION
```

INQUIRY SCREEN B

```
              ACCUMULATED TRANSACTION FILE (ATF) REPORT

DDA   0000-0-000123      FILE DATE  021682 CURR BAL  1,614,609.44   PAGE   1
TYPE  COMMERCIAL DIV     STMT DATE  012982 STMT BAL  2,600,140.23     BR   O
STAT  OPEN                 OD DATE  052179 COLL BAL    990,974.00- RET #   0

T/C DATE   ITEM AMOUNT SERIAL NO ITEM ADDR SI - DESCRIPTION -  SCREEN BALANCE
055 020182      100.00                        CREDIT MEMO        2,600,240.23
055 020182  110,325.93                        CREDIT MEMO        2,710,566.16
006 020182       85.00         1              DEPOSIT            2,710,651.16-
006 020182      130.07         1              DEPOSIT            2,710,781.23
006 020182      195.00         1              DEPOSIT            2,170,976.23
006 020182      206.66         1              DEPOSIT            2,711,182.89
006 020182      382.00         8              DEPOSIT            2,711,564.89
006 020182      908.83        15              DEPOSIT            2,712,473.72
006 020182    1,226.42        17              DEPOSIT            2,713,700.14
006 020182    1,524.50        26              DEPOSIT            2,715,224.64
006 020182    4,671.69         1              DEPOSIT            2,719,896.33
006 020182    5,039.24        59              DEPOSIT            2,724,935.57
006 020182    5,373.42        73              DEPOSIT            2,730,308.99
006 020182    5,730.81        63              DEPOSIT            2,736,039.80
006 020182    9,199.42        38              DEPOSIT            2,745,239.22
006 020182   10,350.00        47              DEPOSIT            2,755,589.22
006 020182      567.40        29              DEPOSIT            2,756,156.62

MORE:  PRESS S/R TO CONTINUE; OR INITIATE END OF SESSION
```

FIGURE 16-5. Screen design test and answers. a. Screen design test.

ANSWERS

1. B — Form too congested — difficult to isolate elements.

2. B — Extra time required to identify specific elements.

3. B — More errors, since information is not organized in a meaningful pattern.

4. B — This set of screens has been designed without consideration for human factors principles.
   Greater documentation development time, expense, and pages.
   This set of screens will consume unnecessary user search time.

5. B — Again, human factors have not been considered.
   Increased training development time and expense. This set of screens will require more hours of training to bring people to proficiency.

6. B — Screens that are difficult to use increase the frustration and stress an employee experiences. When this happens morale, absenteeism and turnover rate will become problems.

7. A — When a system's screens, documentation and training have been designed in accord with good human factors principles, it will be easier to sell.

8. A — The system designed with people in mind will use and improve productivity through:

   a. Quicker entry and retrieval
   b. Fewer errors
   c. Reduced maintenance and other user support costs
   d. Less initial training and ongoing support
   e. Higher group morale

9. $42,000 — $10 x 10 min. x 5 days x 50 weeks x 100 people =
   $10 x 1/6 hr. x 5 days x 50 weeks x 100 people = $41,666

10. $168,000 — $40 x 10 min. x 5 days x 50 weeks x 100 people =
    $40 x 1/6 hr. x 5 days x 50 weeks x 100 people = $166,666

    Multiply these figures for additional users, additional screens and additional years of system life and the costs become staggering.

It's not too difficult to recognize the difference between good and bad screen design. Can you identify the human factors principles that should guide your development efforts?

ASA's Business Information Systems staff of Human Factors Experts can assist you with

- Screen Design
- Program Documentation
- User Guides
- Job Aids
- Training
- Total System Design

FIGURE 16-5. b. Screen design test answers.

The researchers in the California study could not determine that the cause of the miscarriages was the VDT, but they did identify a statistically significant association. They concluded that more research needs to be done because little is known about VLF radiation. They also explained that poor working conditions could be responsible, not simply the VDT.

Company City (Date)	Job	Outcomes VDT	Non-VDT
Sears-Roebuck/ Dallas, TX (5/79-6/80)	Financial records processing clerks	2 miscarriages 4 full-term	5 miscarriages 1 premature birth 8 full-term
Toronto Star/ Toronto, Ontario (5/79-5/80)	Classified ads processing clerks	4 birth defects	3 full-term
Air Canada/ Montreal, Quebec (2/79-4/81)	Part-time ticket agents	7 miscarriages 6 full-term	No data reported
Defense Dept/ Marietta, GA (10/79-10/80)	No data reported	3 birth defects 7 miscarriages 5 full-term	No data reported
Defense Dept/ Marietta, GA (10/80-10/81)	No data reported	14 full-term	No data reported
Pacific Northwest Bell Telephone/ Reston, WA (7/80-12/81)	No data reported	2 birth defects 1 still born	No data reported
Solicitor General Offices/Ottawa, Ontario (4/79-4/82)	No data reported	4 miscarriages 1 premature 2 respiratory diseases	1 full-term
Surrey Memorial Hospital/ Vancouver, British Columbia (1978-82)	Accounting department clerks	3 miscarriages 1 birth defect 1 premature 1 bronchitis/ full-term 1 full-term	No data reported
Old City Hall, Toronto Ministry of Attorney General (1980-81)	Clerks Secretaries	10 miscarriages 9 full-term	No data reported
United Airlines/ San Francisco, CA (1984)	Airline reservation clerks	23 miscarriages 61 full-term	No data reported
Southern Bell Telephone/Atlanta (3/81-9/83)	Telephone operators	7 miscarriages 15 full-term	26 miscarriages 159 full-term
General Telephone/ Alma, MI (1983-84)	Telephone operators	12 miscarriages 2 still births 3 premature 15 full-term	No data reported
Library/ Aarhus, Denmark	No data reported	8 miscarriages 2 full-term	No data reported
Dept of Public Employees/ Runcorn, England (1974-82)	Full-time VDT operators	8 miscarriages 4 still births 12 malformations	No data reported

FIGURE 16-6. Reported cases of reproductive system outcomes in various computer-mediated workplaces by work site and job.

VDT users have also expressed concerns related to frequent visual and musculoskeletal strains and discomfort, including eye fatigue, irritation, blurred vision, and pain or stiffness in the neck, shoulders, back, arms, wrists, and hands. The National Institute of Occupational Health and Safety (NIOSH) has pointed out that these effects are most prominent among VDT operators who engage in the following activities:

- Engage in repetitive VDT work with little opportunity for variation.
- Spend long, uninterrupted periods at the VDT.
- Undertake VDT work requiring intense, visual concentration.

According to NIOSH, user complaints were often related to glare, poor illumination, and poorly designed workstations.

The Keyboard

Ergonomics of keyboard design can be described in terms of (1) operation, (2) key pressure, (3) feedback, (4) design, (5) profile, and (6) finish and shape.

Operation

Operation describes the process of keyboarding, or entering data into a system. Manual typewriters require that the operator hit one key at a time; if a key was depressed before the previously depressed key returned, jamming occurred. Although key jamming is not a problem on computer systems, the concept of "key roll" should be understood.

Key roll describes the system's ability to accept a single key. If one were to uniformly hit many keys in rapid succession and the system could accept those keys strokes in rapid succession, the result would be key roll. No keystroke would ever be lost because the system would accept each key as soon as it was depressed. Thus keyroll could make a big difference in accuracy, and the electronic keyboard is capable of keyroll. The system can keep up with even the fastest or most sporadic typist.

Key Pressure

Key pressure is the energy required to depress the key. The reader who has used a manual typewriter remembers the relatively large amount of energy required. Electric typewriters reduced that problem; the electronic keyboard has all but eliminated it.

How much pressure is best for a keyboard depends upon the operator. Typically, the more efficient the operator, the lighter the touch. Moreover, many keyboards can be "sensitized" so that only minimum pressure is required for data entry.

Auditory Feedback

"Click" is the sound one hears and equates with knowing that the character has been entered. Research has shown that users need an aural stimulus when keyboarding, and the click serves as reinforcement. Many keyboards enable the user to control the volume of the click by a special button or an option provided by the software.

Design

Keyboard design is important. Alphanumeric and/or special-function keys that are frequently used should be within easy reach. Keys that make major changes should be in a position where they will not be struck accidentally. Most keyboards are designed for right-handed users. When a ten-key pad is part of the keyboard, for example, it appears on the right-hand side. Left-handed users could benefit from a detachable ten-key pad. The keyboard should be detachable; the user should have the flexibility to move it for efficient keying. A movable keyboard enables the operator to place it at an angle or whatever location is most comfortable.

The standard typewriter layout is termed QWERTY for the first six letters of the top row of alphabet keys (see Figure 16-7). The QWERTY keyboard was designed to separate keys in the mechanical type basket, and their awkward placement served the purpose of *slowing typists down* to avoid jamming.

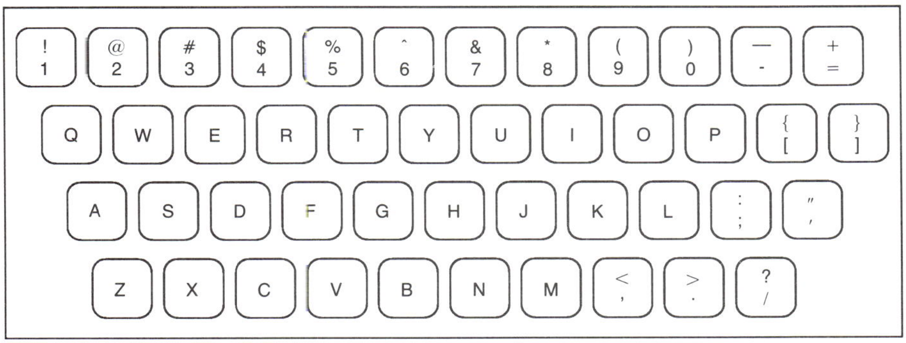

FIGURE 16-7. The QWERTY keyboard.

The QWERTY keyboard is now being seriously challenged as a standard by the Dvorak or American Simplified Keyboard (ASK) shown in Figure 16-8. In the ASK, the most frequently used keys are located in the "home row." Although controversial, the ASK layout has been demonstrated to be more efficient than the QWERTY layout. ASK users have recorded speeds up to 162 words per minute on 60-minute tests. In speed tests, the user of the ASK almost always outperforms the QWERTY user.

FIGURE 16-8. **The Dvorak or American Simplified Keyboard (ASK).**

Because QWERTY users are reluctant to change, the use of ASK has been hampered. With computer keyboards, however, ASK can challenge QWERTY because simple programming can change a traditional keyboard into an ASK and back again. This enables the same keyboard to be used by both a QWERTY and an ASK typist.

Profile

Profile refers to the thickness or height of the keyboard. Early typewriter keyboards had a stair-step profile; in other words, rows of keys were arranged in a manner that required touch typists to move their fingers from the centered "home row" up or down to other rows. Today's keyboards are much flatter. Experts do not recommend one profile over another. The best profile is the profile the user prefers.

Finish and Shape

The key itself offers tactile feedback. The operator should "feel" when the key is accepted. Tactile responses are considered more reliable and timely than audible feedback; therefore, the finish and shape of keys are important factors.

Keys are typically struck at an angle; for this reason, they generally have a matte finish and a bowl shape. The matte finish offers not only a nonslick surface for the operator, but less keyboard glare. Keys are often dish-shape to allow the fingertips to rest in the "dish." On many keyboards, the shape is more profound in the home row keys than on other rows. This gives the user more tactile feedback—confirming without looking, that one's fingers are on the home row. In addition, some keyboards have grooves on the *f* and *j* keys (for index fingers on the QWERTY layout) to provide even stronger tactile feedback. Figure 16-9 reports on litigation related to the design of keyboards. Repetition strain injuries (RSIs) are physical injuries that result when the same motion is repeated continuously.

FIGURE 16-9. Keyboards blamed in liability suit.

More than two dozen Mountain Bell employees have filed a product liability suit against a keyboard manufacturer, claiming that poor design caused or contributed to an outbreak of repetition strain injuries (RSIs). Daniel Recht and Daniel Reilly, the attorneys for the workers, believe their lawsuit is the first to seek compensation for RSIs caused by VDT work.

To date, more than 140 cases of RSIs have been reported among roughly 500 directory assistance operators at two Mountain Bell offices in Denver, CO. Sherry Kreis, executive vice president of Communications Workers of America (CWA) Local 7777, which represents the operators, charges that the keyboards, along with non-adjustable furniture and poor lighting, caused the injuries.

In a citation issued by the federal Occupational Safety and Health Administration (OSHA) on December 31, 1987, Mountain Bell was advised to replace the keyboards and to educate the employees about carpal tunnel syndrome—an RSI. The citation, which charges the company with "causing, aggravating, or precipitating" a variety of RSIs, was issued under the general duty clause of the occupational safety law. John Gonzales, a spokesperson for Mountain Bell, told *VDT News* that the company is contesting the charge.

The type of keyboard at issue, called Version 2, is made by Computer Consoles, Inc. (CCI) and has an alternative key configuration known as Dvorak. Before the Version 2 keyboards were installed, the workers used IBM units with traditional QWERTY layouts (named after the top row of lettered keys).

Recht and Reilly maintain that the incidence of RSIs "increased dramatically" with the introduction of the Version 2 keyboards.

Pat Emigh, Mountain Bell's Director of Information Services, does not agree that the keyboards were to blame for the injuries. "We replaced the keyboards primarily to meet business—rather than ergonomic—objectives," she said, referring to the need for new software and a compatible keyboard. An engineer at CCI refused to comment.

Reilly told *VDT News* that ergonomics experts will study the shape, height, width, general layout and pressure ratio (the amount of pressure required on a key) of both the Version 2 keyboards and CCI's updated Version 3 keyboards. He would not reveal the names of the experts. The lawsuit, which was filed in October, is now in the discovery phase.

Overall, Mountain Bell is spending more than one million dollars on the two offices. Emigh told *VDT News,* "We have done extensive remodeling and have received favorable feedback in general from the employees." It is unclear exactly how much money was spent on ergonomics and how much on new software.

The most important improvement has been the introduction of Version 3 keyboards, which are thinner and "have a much softer touch," according to CWA's Kreiss. "Overwhelmingly, the majority of the employees love the new equipment," she said, but pointed out that there are still some minor adjustments to be made. Kreiss expects the incidence of RSIs to decrease.

Mountain Bell management consulted with ergonomics experts and architects before installing the new, completely adjustable workstations, ergonomic chairs, sound absorbent panels and indirect lighting. The company has also painted the offices in "cool, soothing colors," Emigh said.

The CWA's national office is targeting RSIs as a major occupational health issue. David LeGrande, the CWA's occupational health and safety expert in Washington, D.C., is currently distributing an RSI fact sheet and questionnaire to CWA locals. After the union newspaper featured a major article on RSIs in a recent issue, 300 members suffering from RSIs called LeGrande for more information.

WORKPLACE DESIGN

The Facility Management Institute projects that by 1990 there will be one terminal for every three workers; the World Bank estimates one terminal for every worker. Regardless of whose figures are accurate, terminals in the workplace are having a major impact on facilities planning. This section begins with a short history of the workplace, after which today's workplace will be described, including space planning, lighting, acoustics, air quality, and color.

History

Office work has traditionally involved information creation, storage, retrieval, and dissemination, and the nature of office work has not changed. The tools used to do that work have changed dramatically, however, and with those changes have come fundamental changes in the design and features of the workplace.

The traditional office was paper-based, with filing cabinets, writing desks, lighting, and even chairs conducive to paper processing. The traditional office had row upon row of clerical workers, with higher-status managers and supervisors in enclosed offices around a large, central office area. Often described as a "bullpen," this arrangement worked well for the paper processing operations of the day. Moreover, because the paper documents were often transferred from one worker to another, such an arrangement was effective. Facilities management had a simple job of purchasing standard desks and lighting and tended to avoid concerns of noise pollution and aesthetics.

In the "automated office," which is not entirely paper-based, however, the process of entering and processing data by computer makes new demands on the environment. For example, desks that are the proper height for writing are not the proper height for a keyboard. Lighting that was appropriate for row upon row of desks does not fit the needs of an individual using a VDT. In addition, the noise of printers, copiers, and keyboards has put new acoustical demands on the workplace. Today's office must accommodate a wide range of new tasks and tools.

Because computer processing has changed the way work is done in the office, facilities management has assumed new dimensions and a new role in the automated office environment to ensure worker health and safety and to improve productivity.

While facilities managers today may also be charged with the purchasing, design, and maintenance of the exterior building, the discussion here will be limited to the interior building. Discussion of the workplace will be divided into two sections: the macro environment, which includes office layout, lighting, acoustics, air quality, and color, and the micro environment, which is the individual workstation.

Office Layout

Office layout is both a science and an art. Despite specific guidelines, the facilities planner must do more than follow the principles of layout. The tools, the work, and the individual worker must be considered. To better explain the relationship among technology-driven, work-driven, and people-driven design, considerations related to office design as they pertain to each of these driving forces are discussed.

The AMCO-PACT Model of Office Layout

Office layout centers around the need for efficient space utilization and is best described through the AMCO-PACT model of office layout developed by George R. Terry (see Figure 16-10).[3] The AMCO-PACT approach is a

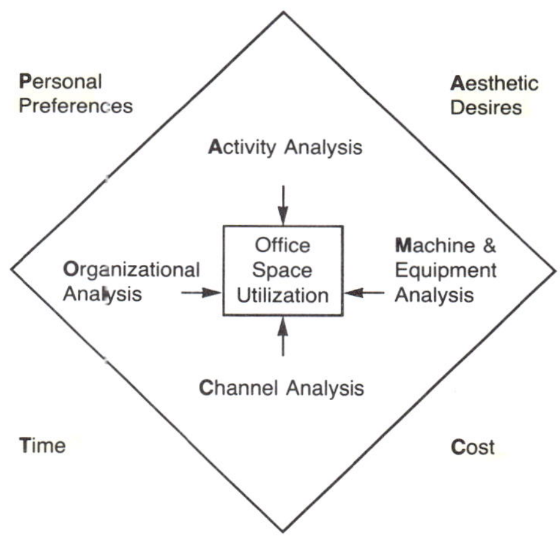

FIGURE 16-10. The AMCO-PACT approach to office layout.

short way of showing the relationship among people-driven, technology-driven, and work-driven office design. The letters in AMCO refer to the following aspects of office layout:

A = *Activity analysis* Activity analysis is the means of examining just what work is being done in the office. What specific tasks are being done? Who works with whom? How much room is needed to do a specific task? What problems currently exist? Figure 16-11 shows an office designed to support a professional worker in a variety of different tasks. The reader should note the wide variety of seating and work surfaces in this workstation.

In addition, activities specific to the automated office must be supported. Specialized activities have unique space and location needs, such as the need for training rooms, small and large conference rooms, copying and printing rooms, teleconferencing rooms, word processing centers, and film and microfilm handling rooms. Rooms for each activity must be given special design consideration.

FIGURE 16-11. An office designed with a wide variety of seating and work surfaces to support a professional worker in performing diverse tasks.

M = Machine inventory Machine inventory is the process of determining which equipment/technologies are used to perform office tasks, as well as those expected to be used in the future. How many machines are being used? What are they? How large are they? What is the type/size/shape/number of technologies to be added to the workplace?

C = Channel analysis Channel analysis is the process of accounting for power, communications, and ventilation needs. Planners agree it is easier to design a new office building than to redesign a building to accommodate new technology. What are the electrical channels, telephone lines, and conduits? What will be needed to accommodate new technologies?

O = Organizational analysis Organizational analysis is the process of determining space allocation and design, based on the size and nature of the work force. How many people need to be housed in a given facility? What is their work level—how many clerical workers, managers, supervisors, and vice-presidents? Who needs to communicate with whom? What are the identified work groups?

In many respects, AMCO describes the *ideal* space allocation, but office layouts must often be designed under less than ideal conditions. The second half of the model, PACT, outlines the restrictors—concerns that can undermine or preclude the best space allocation plan. The letters in PACT refer to the following aspects of office layout:

P = Personal preference Personal preference relates to the need to consider individual needs and desires. Who likes to work with whom? Who cannot work with whom? Who smokes? Is anyone handicapped? What do people want or need to do their work properly?

A = Aesthetics Aesthetics refers to the sense of beauty and harmony. With regard to space allocation, what is the most pleasing way to group workers? Where can partitions be placed so that they are not perceived to be obstacles? Can a sense of design be maintained?

C = Cost Cost is often referred to as "the universal regulator." What will the design cost? The ideal design is not possible if funds for its construction are not available.

T = Time Time refers to how long the design will remain in effect. Is the building rented on a short-time lease? Will the organization be in these headquarters indefinitely? Obviously, the more permanent the time factor, the more care and cost should go into space allocation.

In short, an office layout should facilitate human interaction, proper use of technology, and the work process. People need to be close to those with whom they work and the tools they use to do their job. The layout should help, not hinder, the work process.

Lighting

Lighting can directly affect productivity. In laboratory experiments, employee speed and quality of output increase as lighting is improved. Older workers, who respond quickly to better light, typically need more and better light to compare in speed and quality of output to younger workers.

The visual environment is important not only to worker productivity, but also to worker health and safety. It is perhaps in lighting that the needs of the workplace have changed most dramatically with regard to office automation, especially in regard to VDT use. The problem is compounded when lighting must support a variety of tasks, including the VDT. Tasks such as writing or sorting require a high level of lighting. The general rule is that there must be enough light to do the task at hand, and it must contribute to the task being done, not heed it.

Technical terms that describe lighting include *candela* (cd), a measure of light intensity; *lumen* (lm), a measure of light radiation; *lux* (lx), a measure of the illumination that is actually seen; and *reflection factor* (p), the measure of the capacity to reflect light. These measures are important. The addition of a VDT to a work environment dramatically changes lighting requirements. To avoid glare and strain in a stress-producing environment, experts recommend the following:

- Provide low ambient (general) lighting and increase task-ambient (task-specific) lighting.
- Provide ambient lighting that originates from areas other than the ceiling.
- Build lighting into the workstation.

The Haworth Triambient Lighting System shown in Figure 16-12 incorporates all of these recommendations. Note that both the ambient and task lighting are built directly into the workstation.

FIGURE 16-12. The Haworth Triambient Lighting System.

Sound

Just as the visual environment has changed with office automation, so has the acoustical environment. Office workers and designers should know the terms that are used to measure sound. For example, the articulation index (AI) is the acoustical level at which people can work without being distracted by outside conversation. AI ranks speech intelligibility from 0.0

to 1.0. At an AI of 0.0, one cannot understand anything a person is saying in a normal voice; at 1.0, everything anyone says in a normal voice is intelligible. Bolt, Beranek & Newman, a Boston-based acoustical consulting firm, reported that an AI level over 0.5 means that the noise level in the office is "out of control." In such a situation, everyone would be able to hear everyone else's conversations.

The decibel (dB) is a measure of the loudness or intensity of a sound. The following are the decibel ratings of some common sounds:

- The human voice, 50-60 dBs; when shouting, 80-90 dBs
- Daisy wheel printer, 73-75 dBs
- Laser printer, no measurable noise
- Two electronic typewriters, 68-73 dBs
- Large, quiet office, 46-52 dBs
- Copying machine, 55-70 dBs

Acoustic control is necessary in an office. As explained in Chapter 7, a printer can add as many as 80 dBs to an already noisy office. According to NIOSH, continuous exposure to that high a noise level can damage the ear. Characteristics of sound include absence, frequency, adaptation, and variety.

A total *absence* of sound can be as disturbing as too much sound. *Frequency,* as used here, refers to the regularity of sound: a constantly humming printer as opposed to a printer with many starts and stops. *Adaptation* refers to the ability to adapt to new sounds. *Variety* means that throughout the day different pitches, tones, and decibels are needed.

Solutions to the problem of noise are not easy to implement. Nevertheless, noise reduction falls into three broad categories:

1. *Sound-absorbing materials.* Add sound-absorbing materials (such as cloth) to wall partitions. Absorb the sound of footsteps with carpeting; it can absorb 10-30 percent of the sound that hits it. Use ceiling boards or tiles of soft, absorbent materials to improve the AI index.

2. *Sound-masking systems.* Dormitory students, rather than complain about the noise their neighbors are making, often resort to the "fan technique." They turn on a fan, which makes a humming noise, which in turn masks the disturbing sound. The same principle can be applied in the office. "White sound," a gentle humming, is used in many buildings to mask unwanted sound. Music is another sound masker. The productivity of routine clerical workers typically goes up when music is piped into an office. The impact of music on other workers depends upon the work and the individual.

3. *Office layout.* Wall partitions actually block sound, and heights of 5 feet are effective noise reducers. Another sound-reducing practice is to isolate noisy equipment from work areas. For example, impact printers can be kept in a room by themselves or encased in special furniture, as shown in Figure 16-13.

FIGURE 16-13. Dual workstations with an acoustical printer cabinet to reduce noise levels.

Air Quality

The comfort and safety of an environment are dependent upon temperature, air movement, and cleanliness. Facilities managers often refer to air quality as HVAC (heating, ventilation, and air conditioning).

Office temperatures, if not regulated by legislation (ordinances in some cities limit temperature to 68° F in the winter and 78° F in the summer), are regulated by personal preference. In one office at any given time, a number of individuals will be either too hot or too cold. (This phenomenon has a lot to do with body weight.) No specific temperatures are recommended for VDT use, but the American Society of Heating and Ventilating Engineers recommends a temperature of 74–78° F in the summer and winter, with a humidity level of 40–50 percent in the summer and 30–40 percent in the winter.

Of special note is the fact that a personal computer can generate about the same amount of heat as a person. Therefore, as the number of computers rises, so do the demands on an organization's existing cooling and electrical systems.

An important but often overlooked air circulation problem is static electricity build-up. Static electricity is not only a discomfort but can actually erase data on magnetic disks. Stories exist of personal computer users who were unable to determine why their data continually 'disappeared' from their disks. Static electricity was the culprit.

Air quality includes cleanliness—how clear the air is of pollutants. For health and safety, copier toners, cleaning fluids, and other chemicals should be handled carefully. There is also the issue of smoking. How one feels about it is almost 100 percent related to whether one is a smoker or not. Nonsmokers complain of smell and eye irritation when working near a smoker. When ventilation systems are appropriately used, such problems are minimized.

Colors and Textures

Color and texture add aesthetic appeal to an office and can actually boost worker morale. The appearance of an office is known to affect workers' emotions, senses, and thought processes. Colors also affect perceptions of temperature; for example, blue is regarded as a cooling temperature, pink as a warming temperature. Colors can also create an atmosphere that is either conducive or not conducive to work. Textures add a dimension of visual feeling, as shown in the following example:

> When faced with a controversial discussion over production schedules, an engineer arranged to hold the meeting in a room that was predominately pink rather than in the wood-paneled conference room. The soft tones of the meeting room were later credited with having calmed the executives, to the point where the engineer not only resolved the production problem but was complimented for her handling of the potentially explosive situation. The same engineer, however, did not do so well in selecting the color for the word processing center. Her selection of orange, which she felt would be uplifting, was found to have the opposite effect. The room was quickly repainted to a more appropriate light green.

The National Paint and Coatings Association reports the following current trends in office colors: "Hues range from warm blues and greys through shades of lavender, yellow, rose, and soft beige. Bright accent colors on such things as doors, pillars, lamps, and the proverbial in/out box range from intense hues of reds and blues to terra cotta and turquoise."[4] Designers today are not conforming to strict one-color schemes. An office may include several of the above colors and be aesthetically pleasing. The office may also include more "touchable" materials. Systems panels, for example, that were once metallic have materials that provide a wide range of texture, as well as sound absorption.

The relationship between color and lighting has been researched extensively. Generally, the softer the color, the more light is reflected. The darker the color, the more that light is absorbed. Walls or partitions covered by soft-color materials add light as well as sound absorption.

The Workstation

As part of a master plan to improve and update their facilities, executives at Merck & Company surveyed employees to find "satisfaction gaps" and managerial attitudes and requirements regarding their environment. Data was categorized into three factors: factors related to job effectiveness, factors of personal importance, and factors related to the importance of employee input. An excerpt from the employee questionnaire is shown in Figure 16-14, and the results of the survey are shown in Figure 16-15.

FIGURE 16-14. An excerpt from Merck & Company's employee survey to evaluate work environment.

EMPLOYEE QUESTIONNAIRE

1. Please indicate your level of satisfaction with your current workstation for each item listed below on a scale of 1 (very dissatisfied) to 5 (very satisfied).
2. Then rate each item on its importance to you personally and for overall job effectiveness on a scale of 1 (unimportant) to 5 (very important).

	Workstation Satisfaction Rating	Importance	
		To You Personally	For Job Effectiveness
Ability to adjust work surface to sort your work requirements	( )	( )	( )
Ability to concentrate without noise and other distractions	( )	( )	( )
Access to other areas and departments	( )	( )	( )
Machines and/or reference materials within easy reach	( )	( )	( )
Access to equipment and materials you work with	( )	( )	( )
The opportunity to stretch and move about during the day	( )	( )	( )
Comfort of your chair	( )	( )	( )
A place where you can go to relax	( )	( )	( )
Conversational privacy	( )	( )	( )
Adequate heat, air conditioning, and ventilation	( )	( )	( )
Lighting of your work surface	( )	( )	( )
Overall workspace surface	( )	( )	( )

The top ten factors related to job effectiveness:	The top ten factors related to personal satisfaction:	The top ten conditions related to the importance of employee input:
1. Lighting of work surface.	1. Lighting.	1. Temperature.
2. Ability to concentrate.	2. Ability to concentrate.	2. Privacy.
3. Suitability for work to be done.	3. Adequate heating, ventilation, and air conditioning.	3. Chair.
4. Overall appearance of desk.	4. Safety.	4. Desk or work surface.
5. Adequate heating, ventilation, and air conditioning.	5. Comfort of chair.	5. Desk location.
6. Adjustable surface.	6. Suitability for work to be done.	6. Lighting of work surface.
7. Size of work area.	7. Overall appearance of desk.	7. Storage space.
8. Access to tools, equipment, and materials.	8. Size of work area.	8. Decorations.
9. Materials easily reached.	9. Conversational privacy.	9. Floor/wall covering.
10. Safety.	10. Storage for personal items.	10. Color scheme.

FIGURE 16-15. Results of the Merck & Company employee survey.

Lighting and the ability to concentrate were found to be most important both to job effectiveness and personal satisfaction. Of the decisions employees wanted to make regarding their workstations, temperature was number one; color was least important.[5]

The designer of a *workstation,* an individual's work area, applies all design considerations on a micro level—after examining what work is being done. A task analysis will show the major work activities. Once a workstation is classified as paper-, VDT-, telephone-, or people-driven, the facilities planner begins to work, taking into account both anthropometric concerns and social and psychological concerns.

Anthropometric Concerns

Anthropometrics measures the size and proportions of the human body. Applied to workstation design, anthropometrics is used to evaluate body movement. Examples include posture, reach, and viewing distances.

Posture Musculoskeletal disorders accounted for 20–25 percent of workmen's compensation claims from 1973 to 1983. Unfortunately, because data regarding age and occupation of these workers is not available, it is very difficult to estimate the impact of office automation on musculoskeletal disorders. However, it is known that VDT operators are more likely than other workers to complain of neck pains, stiffness, cramps, and numbness in the back, neck, shoulder, arms, and hands.

Research into why VDT users have more musculoskeletal complaints than other workers has taken the following variables into account: age, existing disorders, and visual data, including near-sightedness, presbyopia, and whether or not individuals wore bifocals while using the VDT. It has also studied the way a worker interacts with the environment—the keyboard (hand), chair (body), and screen (eyes)—as well as the repetitiveness of the task, the length of time spent at tasks, and the physical constraints. Significantly, however, research that found musculoskeletal disorders among VDT users also indicated that the VDT was viewed from an unsuitable angle, the keyboard was too low or too high for proper keying, the chair and desk were unsuitable or of incorrect height, or the work area did not allow sufficient movement.

One disseminator of such research, the U.S. Office of Technology Assessment (OTA), reports insufficient evidence to demonstrate a cause-and-effect relationship among characteristics of the automated office and musculoskeletal disorders. Rather, the OTA explained, aches and pains are often more the result of environmental factors.

Experts concur that good posture contributes to worker well-being. While no *best* posture exists, good working posture is natural and relaxed as the computer user changes positions throughout the day. Figure 16-16

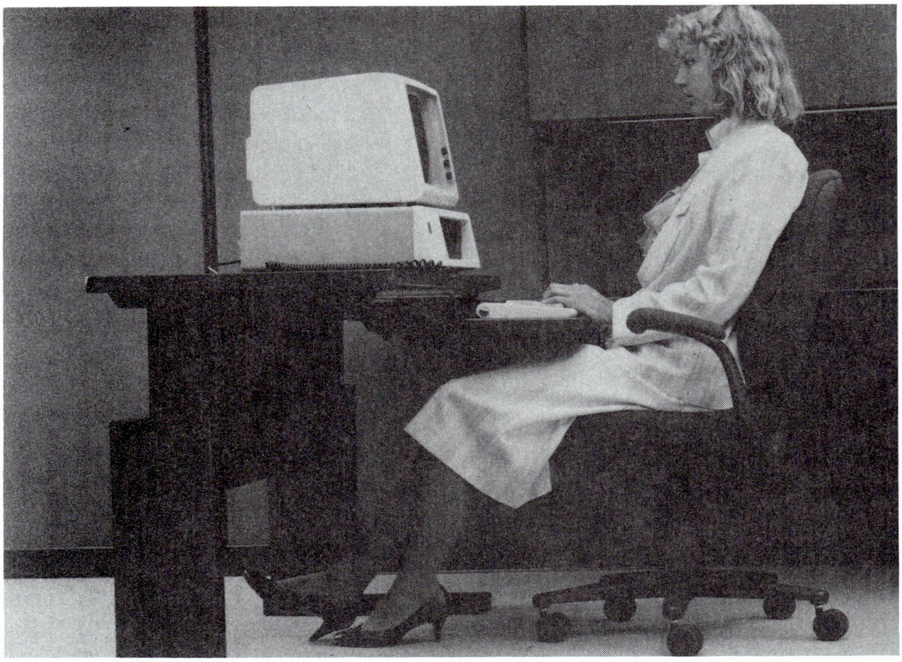

FIGURE 16-16. A workstation that provides a variety of seating positions.

shows a computer workstation that allows this flexibility. The following recommendations can help alleviate musculoskeletal disorders:

1. Use detachable, movable keyboards and adjust table heights for their use. An example of an adjustable keyboard shelf is shown in Figure 16-17.

FIGURE 16-17. An adjustable keyboard shelf.

2. Never bend your neck more than 20 degrees. When entering information from hard copy, use a copystand that is eyelevel with the monitor or directly in front of you.

3. Keep upper arms at a 90-degree angle to your forearms.

4. Keep a 105-degree angle between your trunk and thighs; use a chair that tilts slightly forward and supports your back. Chairs should be padded and covered with an absorbent fabric.

5. Position thighs parallel to the floor when feet are flat on the floor. If your feet do not reach the floor, use a footrest.

These and other proper seating guidelines for using VDTs are illustrated in Figure 16-18. Figures 16-19 and 16-20 show some "do's and don'ts" with regard to proper workstation design.

Reach and viewing distances An efficient workstation provides effortless access to needed tools so that a seated worker can reach all tools without excessive stretching or getting up. For example, a secretary should be able to get letters and envelopes from a printer without having to stand. A manager who uses a personal computer frequently should have it within arm's reach.

Workplaces are often designed with use of the keyboard/VDT as the primary task. However, this is not always the case. For example, a manager may use a computer only minutes a day. In that case, having the VDT in the prime work area would not be the best arrangement. Again, a primary reason for task analysis is to determine what "drives" the workstation—what driving force(s) should be accommodated.

FIGURE 16-18. Proper seating guidelines for using VDTs.

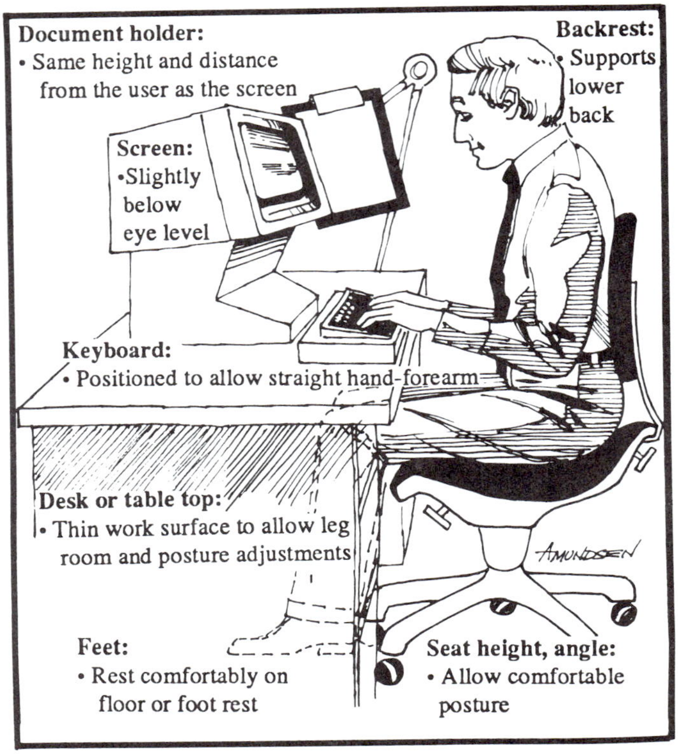

Desks need to be not only the appropriate size for the task but also the appropriate height. A desk that is right for writing is not the same height as a desk for keyboarding. Desks should have a matte finish, rather than a shiny one, to avoid VDT reflection.

Experts recommend the following guidelines for selecting the height of desks and tables:

1. Standard height is 30 inches for writing and 26 inches for keyboarding.
2. The height should provide sufficient legroom.
3. The desk or table should be adjustable, and adjustments should be easy to make.
4. Table legs should be located so that the user's knees are not immobilized.
5. Edges and corners of tables should be rounded.
6. Terminal tables should be a size and shape appropriate for the VDT. Likewise, printer tables should be of a size and shape appropriate for printing.
7. When necessary, furniture should accommodate special wiring needs (see Figure 16-21).

FIGURE 16-19. Good workstation design provides adjustable seating with lower back support, screen and document holder at same height and eye distance, and easily adjustable chair and VDT equipment for maximum comfort and efficiency.

FIGURE 16-20. In poor workstation design, seating cannot be adjusted and provides little lower back support. User must bend and twist neck to see documents because no holder is provided, and few adjustments can be made to achieve a comfortable working posture.

FIGURE 16-21. Systems furniture accommodating wiring needs.

Behavioral Concerns

The AMCO-PACT model points out that the design of workplaces cannot ignore the human element. The workplace is people-driven, not machine-driven. In designing workstations, the facility planner must be aware of some basic principles of human behavior: territoriality, personal space, "backs and sides," eye contact, privacy, status, and socialization.[6]

Territoriality The tendency to "make our mark" on a space is known as *territoriality.* Students in classes where no seat has been assigned typically choose the same seat at every class meeting. At exercise classes, participants tend to take the same place at every class. Typically, when someone is in the seat or position normally taken, the individual who has been displaced finds himself or herself a bit unsettled. The same is true when people go to the doctor's office and leave for only a minute: when they return, they expect to take the same seat, perhaps having left belongings in the seats designated "theirs."

Territoriality can also be applied to the office. Workers need a place to call their own, and an office or a desk is "theirs"—at least until the end of the day or shift. Workers also like to place their own memorabilia around their work area—pictures, flowers, calendars—things that designate "Betty's desk." In designing an office, the facility manager would do well to arrange for such ownership. In fact, organizations that restrict the type or amount of personal artifacts at a workplace always meet with resistance. On the other hand, because of open designs, security of belongings is an important issue.

Personal space Personal space depends upon many factors, including occupation, ethnic background, sex, and age. A blue-collar worker, for example, is much more comfortable than a bank president on a crowded bus. A salesperson is typically more outgoing and will stand closer to a client than individuals in other occupations. In our society, it is also more acceptable for females than for males to stand close together. The younger the person, the less space he or she requires.

Personal space has been divided into zones as follows:

- *Zone 1: Intimate distance* (up to 18 inches apart). Zone 1 is reserved for people we want to be close to—friends, family members, spouses, children.
- *Zone 2: Personal Distance* (18 inches to 4 feet away). Zone 2 is within an arm's reach and is reserved for friends.
- *Zone 3: Social distance* (4 to 12 feet away). Social distance is the zone in which much business is conducted. A desk is typically 3 to 4 feet wide, and the addition of a chair on either side increases this space. Zone 3 distances are enough to be considered formal.
- *Zone 4: Public distance* (12 to 25 feet or more). Individuals attempting to communicate in Zone 4 must raise their voices and, depending upon obstacles, may not be able to see each other. If one wishes, one can avoid individuals who are in Zone 4.

What do these zones have to do with workstation design? From an evaluation of zones, it may be concluded that one needs a workspace large enough to ensure that one's personal space is respected. Also, designers should avoid overcrowding; too many workers in a given area either force people to become temporarily friendly or deny them needed space.

"Backs and sides" The most desirable location in any building is the corner room, where a person is protected from interference from two sides and is able to minimize contact. Restaurant goers typically gravitate to a corner window; if a corner window is not available, they will choose a window seat. Only when the restaurant is full will they select a center table, and then they will most likely choose the table farthest from other diners.

What can be learned from "backs and sides"? The most desirable offices are in the corner of the building and along the outside walls. Desks in a landscaped building are often positioned so that the worker's back is to the hallway, which most people find unpleasant. Designers should consider workers' needs to be "flanked" on at least two sides and have their backs "protected." Figure 16-22 illustrates these principles. Note the location of the desk in each of the three offices.

FIGURE 16-22. Desk positions in office design.

Eye contact An overgeneralization is that New Yorkers dislike looking strangers in the eye and that people in the Southwest distrust anyone who does *not* look them in the eye! At any point where eye contact is possible, some sort of barrier needs to be developed if that contact is not necessary or desirable. This is why workers with desks facing each other have difficulty working. This is why partitions that are less than 5 feet high are often unacceptable. Many people require visual privacy. Depending upon the task being done, efforts should be made to ensure that such privacy is provided.

Status A status symbol is a possession regarded as a sign of rank. Following is a partial list of office "status symbols":

- A large office has more status than a small one.
- A leather chair has more status than a cloth one; a chair with five casters and an armrest has more status than a three-wheeled chair with no arms. (Figure 16-23 illustrates the wide range of available office seating.)
- An office with a window has more status than an office without one.

- Dark woods imply more status than light woods or metals.
- Enclosed offices have more status than open offices.

The facility planner must always take workers' status into account when designing offices. Many large organizations have developed standards that apply to various levels of workers. In other words, workers at each level are "assigned" a specific size of office, a specific type of chair, and a specific size and kind of desk. Facilities planners claim that such policies enable them to address status concerns more effectively.

Within the guidelines established by policies, facilities planners frequently allow individuals to pick and choose among furnishings and office layouts. Such options, they explain, enable each workstation to reflect the needs of individual workers.

Socialization When new systems are planned and designed, care should be taken not to disrupt workers' social interactions. Systems have failed because VDTs were stationed in areas or at angles that eliminated or discouraged worker interaction. The socialization needs of workers must be considered.

FIGURE 16-23. A wide range of office seating is available for different needs and tasks.

SUMMARY

Concern about productivity as well as the health, safety, and comfort of workers in the automated office has led to increased interest in ergonomics, the study of the natural laws of work. Ideally, workers in an automated office should be in an environment that fosters good work habits, combining design and use principles that balance technology, procedures, and human needs.

Health problems in the automated office include eye fatigue and strain, musculoskeletal disorders, fatigue, and stress. Such problems are often attributed to the VDT—to glare, flicker, bezel, and character quality. Another concern is radiation. Research tells us that radiation does not exceed safe levels; but the jury is still out.

Ergonomic principles apply to the design of keyboards. How the systems accept or enter keystrokes, the pressure required, tactile and auditory feedback, keyboard design and profile, and key finish and shape—all affect ease of use.

The workplace has changed dramatically as a result of office automation. Traditional principles of office layout and design are no longer applicable, or not as applicable as they once were. AMCO-PACT, a model layout for the automated office, balances the ideal with real-life restrictions.

In addition to layout, lighting, sound, air quality, and color have an impact on worker productivity, health, and morale. Bright colors, for example, are typically cafeteria, not workplace, colors. Optimum lighting for a VDT is not the same as lighting for other tasks, such as writing or sorting. A noisy printer can add 80 dBs to an office, making conversation or concentration difficult. The VDT adds as much heat to a room as body heat from a worker, and this has an impact on an organization's HVAC requirements. Color schemes also impact productivity and worker morale.

Finally, the workstation, an individual's work area, must be examined from both a technical and a human perspective. It is known, for example, that a good chair promotes good posture, that the proper table height can relieve musculoskeletal disorders, and that a detached keyboard allows individuals to adjust their sitting positions, which is especially important for individuals who must sit at a desk for hours on end.

It is also known that people behave in predictable patterns. Issues of territoriality, personal space, backs and sides, status, and the need for socialization also have an impact on good, effective workstation design.

In short, worker productivity, health, and comfort can be addressed through ergonomics. Applications of principles already known, and still being developed, can have a very positive outcome for the organization and the individual.

DISCUSSION QUESTIONS

1. What is ergonomics? What is the relationship between ergonomics and office worker productivity?

2. The VDT is frequently accused of causing eyestrain and fatigue. Why? What are some solutions?
3. Assume you are the supervisor of a small word processing center. One of your employees is pregnant and has asked if it is safe for her to continue working. What is your response? Suggest several ways in which you might resolve this concern.
4. You've investigated microcomputers and have limited the choice to models offered by two vendors. The major difference in the hardware, it appears, is the keyboard. Compile the list of criteria you would use in comparing keyboards.
5. Discuss the impact of automation technologies on facilities planning and design.
6. Many companies are enforcing no-smoking policies. Discuss how air pollutants impact office automation technologies.
7. Differentiate between glare and reflection.
8. If you were choosing between a monochrome and a color terminal for the following applications, which would you choose? If color, which color(s) would you choose?
   a. Word processing
   b. Spreadsheets
   c. Graphics
   d. Electronic mail
9. Discuss the social and psychological considerations important to workstation design. Have you seen evidence of these considerations outside the office? Describe your experiences.
10. Many states and cities are passing legislation and statutes regulating the office environment. Discuss the pros and cons of such laws.

APPLICATION EXERCISES

1. Examine the workspace of an individual who works with a personal computer and then interview the individual to determine what he or she does and the person's major concerns with the workplace. Redesign the work area so that it is more ergonomic. Prepare both a minimalist ($300) and an ultimate (money-is-no-problem) solution.
2. Visit a showroom where VDTs are displayed and compare them. Then write a short report, using the vocabulary in this chapter, to compare the VDTs.
3. Use the library to prepare a report on U.S. legislation relative to VDT safety.

SUGGESTED READINGS

Central Organization of Salaried Employees in Sweden. *VDT Work the Right Way* (Stockholm: Bratts Tryckeri AB, 1987).

Ericsson Information Systems. *Ergonomic Principles in Office Automation* (Stockholm: Adaptus AB, 1984).

Galitz, Wilbert O. *The Office Environment* (Willow Grove, Pa.: American Management Society, 1984).

Grandjean, Etienne. *Ergonomics in Computerized Offices* (London: Taylor and Francis, 1987).

International Business Machines Corporation. *Systems Applications Architecture (SAA) Common User Access (CUA) User Interface Screen Design* (Armonk, N.Y.: IBM Corp., 1988).

Sauter, Steven L.; Chapman, L.; and Knutson, Sheri J. *Improving VDT Work* (Madison, Wis.: University of Wisconsin Board of Regents, 1985).

CHAPTER 17
JOB DESIGN

OBJECTIVES

After completing this chapter, the reader should be able to meet the following objectives:

- Discuss the need for job redesign.
- Differentiate between task analysis and job analysis.
- Identify various approaches by organizations to design jobs.
- Recognize that office automation results in changes at the organizational, work group, and individual levels throughout the organization.
- Explain the major characteristics of motivating jobs.
- Identify dimensions to consider when designing jobs.
- Choose appropriate techniques for redesigning jobs.
- Appraise the way organizations are using technology to redesign jobs.

KEY TERMS

authority
accountability
computer-mediated work
job
job design
job enlargement
job enrichment
responsibility
sociotechnical job design
two-factor theory of motivation
quality of work life (QWL)

INTRODUCTION

Job design is "the formal and informal specification of tasks that are performed by employees, including expected interpersonal relationships and task interdependence. Ideally, the needs and goals of both employees and the organization are taken into account in job design or redesign."[1] The term *job design* suggests a systematic process for determining the content of a job. It implies that the content, interdependencies, and personal relationships of a job are carefully thought out to accomplish organizational goals. In fact, not all jobs are the result of job design. Often jobs evolve haphazardly. Every time a manager assigns work or gives instructions, job design occurs. Likewise, when analysts design office information systems, jobs are affected. Consciously or unconsciously, many factors influence the design of jobs.

This chapter considers the impact of technologies on the design of white-collar jobs in the office. It focuses on new opportunities to create jobs to meet both organizational and individual needs in line with changing work values. The chapter begins with the nature of jobs and the need for design. Five major approaches to job design and their theoretical foundations are presented. The chapter then explores the close relationship between technology and job design. It concludes with a discussion of technology as a catalyst for job redesign and presents methods that take advantage of technology to redesign jobs that are more motivating and productive.

WHAT IS A JOB?

A job is generally organizationally defined. A formal description legitimizes the position and defines the tasks, responsibility, authority, accountability, role in the organization, and pay scale for the person in each job. A job consists of a set of specific *tasks:* preparing a budget, typing correspondence, writing a computer program, conducting meetings, writing reports, supervising employees, appraising performance, hiring staff, analyzing financial trends, evaluating market data, teaching job skills, or forecasting sales. The tasks that make a job may change over time. The group of tasks may be purposefully designed or may have evolved through trial and error.

Associated with a job are certain responsibilities, authority, accountability, and roles. *Responsibility* defines the obligation to carry out assigned tasks. Whereas the tasks define the what, responsibility spells out the where, when, and how. *Authority* refers to the rights or power granted the jobholder to carry out assigned tasks and responsibilities. It may range from a clerk's right to requisition office supplies to a supervisor's right to hire, train, evaluate, and fire staff or an executive's right to approve multimillion-dollar budgets and projects. *Accountability* refers to a personal liability to perform a job according to predetermined standards or requirements. Jobholders are accountable to their immediate superiors as well as to others who are affected by their behavior. For example, corporate attorneys are accountable not only for performing the tasks assigned by their supervisors, but for performing all work according to professional legal standards.

A job's *role within the organization* refers to how or where a job fits into the work flow, the interdependencies among tasks and jobs, relationships with others, and the perceived status or prestige that a job has in comparison to other jobs inside or outside the organization. For most individuals, a job provides more than a livelihood; people identify with their jobs and derive gratification from them. The job defines a role within the work process and the social structure; it is the point of articulation among the individual, the technology, and the organization. Thus it is not sufficient to talk about how office automation affects individual tasks. Automation affects the entire job: the set of tasks, the responsibility, the authority, the role in the organization, and the self-perception of the employees.

THE NEED FOR JOB DESIGN

To fully capitalize on automated systems, people must be motivated to achieve high-quality work. Motivation is an internal psychological process, which is directly affected by the design of the job itself. The full benefits of automation cannot be realized without the support of the people who use the systems. A new computer system, even if it has the capacity to double output, may yield only a slight increase in productivity if people do not understand it, fear its impact, or see no benefit for themselves.

Technology always forces change in job responsibilities, task content, and human interactions. It often brings change in organizational structure and culture as well. Studies in the United States and Europe have shown that when organizations ignore "people issues," new systems result in poorer job designs. Poor job design threatens the well-being and performance of white-collar workers. Thoughtful design, on the other hand, can enhance both productivity and quality of work life. Thus to achieve the full benefits of automation, analysts must address the issues of job design as well as systems design.

When analysts and decision makers design systems and select equipment, they often fail to consider how their choices will alter the tasks people perform. Decision makers mistakenly assume that selecting the "right" technology is the most important part of improving productivity in the office. Considerable evidence to the contrary suggests that technology often affects productivity less than good job design does.

Despite its known value, job design is seldom a part of systems design. Analysts often consider job design outside their responsibility, or they assume employees will intuitively apply technology. Thus job design is left to department managers, who usually have little control over it. In most large organizations, job design is the responsibility of human resource or industrial engineering departments.

The result of ignoring these issues is that systems designers frequently design jobs unknowingly. Consequently, changes may be haphazard and ignore worker motivation and job satisfaction. Even when attention is given to *human factors,* designers often concentrate on such technical aspects as ease of use, lighting, and furniture, rather than on the workers' job tasks. Designers need to look carefully at the characteristics of the jobs being changed or created when computerized systems are introduced. They should know the elements of job and systems designs that meet social as well as technical objectives.

Much of the problem lies in the way systems analysts typically design and cost-justify new technology. They try to justify equipment costs by reducing operating costs—which usually means cutting salary expenses by designing systems that minimize skills. In the process, they may ignore worker motivation and job satisfaction. Usually such jobs are narrowly defined, and production goals and controls are set by supervisors with little or no participation by employees.

This narrow approach to job design may limit opportunities for users to benefit from the full capabilities of new systems. Computer systems analysts are often not aware of job design issues. Consequently, their expectations about people who will be using newly designed systems are often inconsistent with the way the systems are actually designed. For example, in one case researchers found that while analysts acknowledged the importance of worker satisfaction and motivation and expected workers to be capable and skilled, the system they developed was appropriate for only very low-level, repetitive jobs.

Computer systems analysts appear to be caught in a dilemma. They know their technical systems; they know their users. Yet it is difficult to apply knowledge of how people work to the technical side of systems development. Pressure to meet deadlines can override serious attempts to address the needs of people. If computer systems are to succeed, systems analysts must reconcile traditional development methods that often conflict with the objective of giving people tools to do their jobs.

AN HISTORICAL PERSPECTIVE ON JOB DESIGN

Job design cannot be isolated from other factors, such as organizational structure and management style. Organizational structure is defined by the pattern of relationships and activities reflected in an organization chart. Management style is reflected in the decisions of senior managers relating to the organization's goals and strategies and the role of technology and people in achieving them. Over the years, various philosophies about how to organize and manage work have guided management decision making. These schools of thought and their implications for designing and managing work in organizations are summarized in this section.

Preindustrial Jobs

Prior to the Industrial Revolution, work was characterized by craftspeople who took pride in the artistry of their labor. The medieval guilds represent one of the earliest forms of industrial organization. True craftspersons were expert at all aspects of their trade. Skills were learned through many years of apprenticeship by people who knew the business from beginning to end.

Organization of work in many small businesses and offices can be characterized as preindustrial. Each worker is essentially a craftsperson who exercises discretion in a multitude of tasks. Many entrepreneurs and workers are attracted to small businesses because of the craftspersonlike, preindustrial atmosphere.

Industrial Era Jobs

During the Industrial Revolution in the early 1900s, the concept of scientific management emerged. First applied by Fredrick W. Taylor to manufacturing, the concept was later applied to the office. Scientific management—sometimes referred to as industrial engineering—introduced the *rationalization* of jobs. That is, a complex process was analyzed and divided into simple tasks that could be performed quickly and efficiently. Workers were assigned a single task or narrow range of tasks, which resulted in routine, repetitive jobs. The idea was that workers could master single-task jobs quickly, at low cost to the company. Such a division of labor was believed to be the best route to high productivity.

The success of scientific management depends on authority to maintain direction and control. Work is closely supervised and economic incentives, such as piece-rate pay, motivate workers. The organizational structure is hierarchical, with top-down authoritarian management.

In the office, scientific management yields clerical jobs that are divided into narrowly defined, routine segments with measurable outputs. Workers are differentiated into functional groups, such as mail sorters, distribution clerks, typists, proofreaders, and file clerks. Each group has its own supervisor and is responsible for an identified step in a transaction. Documents related to transactions flow from one functional area to the next, from one "out box" to the next "in box," receiving incremental processing at each stop.

Industrial-style offices were ideal for the introduction of computers because the work process had been analyzed and each task identified, isolated, and standardized. Certain tasks could be automated by the computer's ability to process batches of calculations. Many manual tasks remained, however, such as preparing data for the computer or distributing computer output.

When word processing technology was introduced, many large organizations seized the opportunity to rationalize document processing. Word processing centers applied the principles of specialization and work measurement to typing. Some even implemented piece-rate pay. Some detractors charged that the office of the future was becoming little more than a re-creation of the factory of the past.

Professional and managerial jobs are not immune to scientific management. These jobs can also be analyzed, and the routine, predictable tasks can be stripped away. Two researchers in California noted that underwriting, the main professional occupation in the insurance industry, has been increasingly rationalized. At one firm, this was done by splitting off the lower-level functions and assigning them to a newly created clerical position called *underwriting technical assistant*. Remaining professional positions were divided into specialty categories.[2]

The assembly line structure in many manufacturing and clerical operations attests to the influence of scientific management thinking on job design and organization. Although scientific management offers efficiencies of scale for highly routine office work, it has some disadvantages. As pointed out in a report by the Office of Technology Assessment (OTA), organizational structures based on scientific management have problems dealing with *exceptions* or nonroutine situations, and they are usually not efficient for customized service. Some experts have also noted that industrial-style offices are susceptible to long-term growth in overhead costs. For example, to deal with error detection and correction, extra steps must often be added, making the process longer and more unwieldy.

Generally, no employee has all the information needed to correct an error, so mistakes may persist or build on one another. Papers might cycle the system several times before they are corrected. When work is processed in production line fashion, quick, accurate customer service is difficult to provide.

For example, OTA reported that issuing an international letter of credit at one bank required 23 steps, performed by 14 workers over a three-day period, and generated stubs and carbon copies to be stored in a number of locations. When customers called, they had a difficult time finding the worker with the right information to answer their questions. Moreover, if a customer wanted a transaction modified, the whole process had to start over again.

The typical approach of automating job steps without considering the entire flow of work can be counterproductive. It overlooks the constraints created by unautomated processes, which may result in new bottlenecks. It optimizes tasks, but not necessarily the overall work flow. It focuses on expediting existing procedures rather than inventing new procedures to capitalize on technology.

Under top-down, authoritarian management, information flow is slow, restricted, and selective. Managers often hear only what their subordinates want them to hear, and subordinates may relate only what makes them look good. Critical information may be withheld rather than passed upward, distorting vertical communications. Horizontal communications, among peers, are often minimal.The disadvantages of scientific management have led workers and theorists to advocate a people-oriented approach to the division of labor in the postindustrial era.

Postindustrial Jobs

During the 1920s and 1930s, a *human relations school of thought* examined the dynamics of interpersonal relations in the workplace. Researchers found that what people did in their jobs, and the way they did it, had a distinct psychological impact. Studies concluded that an extensive division of labor, by creating physical and mental fatigue, could hurt productivity. The human relations movement also emphasized the influence of the work group on productivity. Researchers demonstrated how norms and standards established informally by work groups defied management practices. Piece rates actually reduced overall productivity, when older workers guarded their know-how from new, young workers. Moreover, when work groups with high production standards were closely supervised, the group resented the intrusion, which also hurt productivity.

During the 1960s, Douglas McGregor related the behavior of individuals in organizations to management practices. He proposed that the way one treats individuals in an organization directly influences their productivity and how they feel about their jobs. He designated the commonly accepted practices of scientific management, with their reliance on authority to maintain direction and control, as Theory X management. McGregor then proposed an alternative view of people and work, which he termed Theory Y, which advocates participative management based on self-control and integration. According to McGregor, integration is "the creation of conditions such that the members of the organization can achieve their own goals best by directing their efforts toward the success of the enterprise." The underlying assumptions of Theories X and Y are summarized in Figure 17-1. According to McGregor, the way one designs jobs and manages people depends on one's management philosophy.

Assumptions of Theory X

1. The average human being has an inherent dislike of work and will avoid it if he possibly can.
2. Because of this human characteristic of dislike of work, most people must be coerced, controlled, directed, and threatened with punishment to get them to put forth adequate effort toward the achievement of organizational objectives.
3. The average human being prefers to be directed, wishes to avoid responsibility, has relatively little ambition, and wants security above all.
4. The best way to motivate people is to use a "carrot and stick" form of compensation. Salary and benefits are a reward to entice people to perform jobs that are inherently boring and offer little intrinsic motivation or satisfaction.

Assumptions of Theory Y

1. The expenditure of physical and mental effort in work is as natural as play or rest.
2. External control and the threat of punishment are not the only means for bringing about effort toward organizational objectives. People will exercise self-direction and self-control in the service of objectives to which they are committed.
3. Commitment to objectives is a function of the rewards associated with their achievement.
4. The average human being learns, under proper conditions, not only to accept but to seek responsibility.
5. The capacity to exercise a relatively high degree of imagination, ingenuity, and creativity in the solution of organizational problems is widely, not narrowly, distributed in the population.
6. Under the conditions of modern industrial life, the intellectual potentialities of the average human being are only partially utilized.

FIGURE 17-1. Assumptions about human work performance in Theory X and Theory Y.

APPROACHES TO JOB DESIGN

Subsequent research has expanded upon McGregor's ideas and focuses on job content and design. These views, which have led to attempts to break out of the simplification and standardization of scientifically engineered jobs, include job enlargement, job rotation, job enrichment, job characteristics theory, sociotechnical approaches, and quality of work life programs.

Job Enlargement and Job Rotation

Job enlargement expands jobs to include a variety of similar tasks. On a production line, this might mean that a worker does several assembly steps instead of just one. In an office, a typist might sort mail and file documents, rather than type all day.

A job rotation approach, on the other hand, moves workers from one job to another rather than changing the tasks that make up the jobs. Job rotation is often used to train workers so that they are exposed to a variety of jobs. In this way, greater scheduling flexibility and back-up coverage for absent employees are provided. Job rotation also upgrades the skills and promotability of workers.

Job enlargement and rotation expand jobs horizontally, not vertically. That is, these techniques do not necessarily provide workers with more control over their environment. The concepts assume that workers want more diversification in their jobs and will welcome the opportunity to do more or different kinds of tasks.

Although the techniques of job enlargement and rotation can be useful, results are mixed. Some workers appreciate the increased variety while others perceive it as just more boring tasks. It may interfere with the daydreaming or chit-chat with which workers cope with boring jobs. Sometimes management views job enlargement or rotation as a way of getting more work out of fewer workers.

Job Enrichment

While job enlargement approaches expand jobs horizontally, *job enrichment* refers to vertical expansion, including a planning or control task (or both) in a job that previously included only operating tasks. The objective is to give workers control over their jobs from beginning to end, or at least over a segment, so that they experience their tasks as a more meaningful whole. The term frequently encompasses both horizontal and vertical expansion. Job enlargement and job enrichment are based on the theory that employees are motivated by factors that meet psychological needs for achievement, self-fulfillment, recognition, responsibility, advancement, or challenge.

Job enrichment approaches are closely associated with Herzberg's *two-factor theory of motivation*. Herzberg argued that job content contributes significantly to worker motivation and job satisfaction. He identified workers' motivation and satisfaction by asking managers and workers to cite times when they felt exceptionally good or exceptionally bad about their jobs. Factors that were the source of good feelings he called *satisfiers* or *motivators*, and factors that were the source of bad feelings he called *dissatisfiers*. The motivators that produced the most long-lasting, positive attitudes included the following:

- The work itself.
- Responsibility in the job.
- Opportunities for achievement in the job.
- Advancement (for a job well done).

The major dissatisfiers included the following:

- Company policy and administration.
- Supervision.
- Salary.
- Interpersonal relations.
- Working conditions.

Herzberg said that dissatisfiers played only a *hygiene* role. He theorized that while organizational efforts to improve supervision and working conditions were capable of keeping employees from being *unhappy,* they could not make them feel positive about their work and hence willing to work harder. Thus, according to Herzberg's two-factor theory, the hygiene role addressed by management and unions did not attack motivation/job satisfaction at its heart. In contrast, according to Herzberg, the factors that he identified as motivators are related to the design of the job and can directly influence a worker's motivation and satisfaction. One set of factors could reinforce another but could not be addressed at the exclusion or expense of the other.[3]

Job Characteristics Theory

In the mid 1960s two researchers, A. N. Turner and P. R. Lawrence, made a significant contribution to job design methodology. They identified six task dimensions: variety, autonomy, required social interaction, opportunities for social interaction, required knowledge and skill, and responsibility. The dimensions are known collectively as *requisite task attributes.*[4]

Other studies followed. The view that has had the most impact on job-design research was suggested in 1975 by Hackman and Oldham, whose theory and measuring instrument, the Job Descriptive Index, is derived from earlier research as well as from their own studies. Hackman and Oldham identified five *core job dimensions* that influence motivation and satisfaction:[5]

1. *Skill variety* is the degree to which a job requires different activities—a number of skills and talents.

2. *Task identity* is the degree to which a job requires completion of a whole and identifiable piece of work, that is, doing it from beginning to end with a visible outcome. For example, it is more meaningful to an office employee to handle all orders, billings, and inquiries from a designated group of customers than to type invoices all day long.

3. *Task significance* is the degree to which the job has substantial impact on other people, within the organization or in the world at large. Employees who type labels for medicines and drugs are likely to perceive their jobs as more significant than workers who type labels for file folders, even though the skill levels may be comparable.

4. *Autonomy* is the degree to which the job provides freedom, independence, and discretion to the individual in scheduling the work and in determining the procedures. In highly autonomous jobs, the quality and quantity of work depend on an individual's initiative and efforts instead of on regulations, quotas, and supervision. By building more autonomy into jobs, large organizations can address one of their greatest weaknesses: lack of accountability. A common example in clerical operations is the requirement that the manager sign every document that goes out of the department. Why not allow the individual who does the major part of the work sign the documents, thereby assuming responsibility for their accuracy?

5. *Job feedback* is the degree to which required activities provide the worker direct and clear information about the effectiveness of his or her performance. It is much more effective if workers obtain direct feedback than if their supervisor evaluates results for them. Clerical operations are especially inclined to use too many *checkers* (such as proofreaders) rather than having employees verify the accuracy of their own work.

Sociotechnical Approaches

Sociotechnical approaches to job design integrate the social needs of workers with technological requirements. Technical systems influence the characteristics of the social (or people) system through the allocation of work roles and the relationships between tasks that are dictated by the technology. The performance of the organization is believed to be a function of the interface of the social and technical systems.

Sociotechnical approaches advocate changing the focus of work design, from adapting people to technology to adapting technology to people. The objective is to design jobs that optimize relationships among technology, people, and the needs of the organization. Unlike the previous approaches, which emphasized designing jobs for individuals, sociotechnical approaches focus on designing tasks for semiautonomous work groups. By participating in the group's decisions, workers attain a sense of personal worth and achievement from the group and the relationships within it. The motivational value of these relationships is important because social needs outweigh achievement needs for 60 percent of the work force.

Quality of Work Life (QWL) Programs

Quality of work life may be defined as the degree to which workers can satisfy their personal needs through their work. Quality of work life affects the health, well-being, job satisfaction, and productivity of employees. QWL programs emerged in the 1970s as a means of involving workers in problem solving groups to make jobs more satisfying and productive. These programs are an effective way to implement workplace innovations and measure outcomes.

The QWL movement, which is based on the sociotechnical concept of work design, grew out of European experiments with semiautonomous work teams in manufacturing plants. In the manufacturing sector, QWL programs were spurred by declining productivity in the United States and increased global competition.

QWL programs are not necessarily related to technology, although the framework and methods are appropriate for implementing technology-related work changes. The characteristics of QWL programs are summarized in Figure 17-2.

- Achieving sustained commitment from management to an open, nondefensive style of operation that sincerely encourages employees to speak up regarding problems or opportunities. (A related element is providing practical means for members of the work force to participate in refining and implementing promising suggestions.)
- Establishing a work environment that encourages continuous learning, training, and active interest regarding both the job and the product or service to which the job contributes. (Such an environment enables an employee to use and develop personal skills and knowledge, which in turn affects involvement, self-esteem, and the challenge obtained from the work itself.)
- Making the job itself more challenging by structuring it so that an individual (or work team) can self-manage and feel responsible for a significant, identifiable output if that kind of responsibility is desired.
- Providing opportunities for continued growth; that is, opportunities to advance in organizational or career terms.
- Training supervisors to function effectively in a less directive, more collaborative style.
- Breaking down the traditional status barriers between management and production or support personnel. Achieving an atmosphere of open communication and trust between management and the work force.
- Providing not only feedback about results achieved and recognition for good results but also financial incentives, such as shared cost-savings, where feasible.
- Selecting personnel who can be motivated, under appropriate conditions, to genuinely care about striving for excellence in task performance.
- Evaluating and analyzing results, including failures, leading to revised efforts toward improvement.

FIGURE 17-2. Characteristics of quality of work life programs.

A systems approach to the relationship between office automation and quality of work life reveals a number of patterns. Figure 17-3 shows the framework used by the U.S. Office of Technology Assessment to analyze these relationships. The core relationships are among the organization, technology, and individual. The arrows indicate patterns of association, not necessarily causal relationships.

FIGURE 17-3. Office characteristics that contribute to an individual's quality of work life.

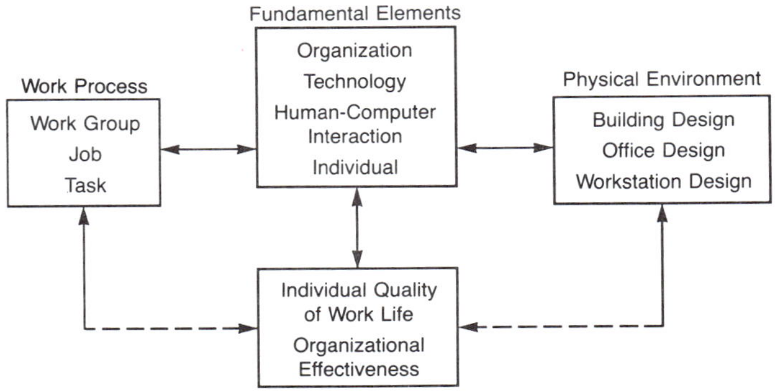

Summary of Job Design Approaches

Declining U.S. productivity in the late 1970s focused attention on the success of Japanese participative management. In his best-selling book, *Theory Z,* William Ouchi challenged the traditional American premise that specialization increases productivity. Ouchi compared the productivity of U.S. firms practicing American-style scientific management to the productivity of U.S. firms practicing Japanese-style participative management. His findings demonstrated that Japanese-style management, with low specialization, achieved higher productivity than American-style management with high specialization. Moreover, Japanese management led to higher-quality output, according to Ouchi. American managers believe that quality is achieved through testing and control. Japanese managers, on the other hand, believe that quality comes from inviting workers to continually refine product design and manufacturing processes. Ouchi found the Japanese style to be more effective.

Despite decades of experience with alternative techniques, authoritarian management still prevails in most American organizations. It is a major premise of this text, however, that new information technologies render authoritarian management inappropriate in the office—if it was *ever* appropriate—and at the same time enable organizations to move toward participative management styles by designing jobs that involve workers in setting goals and standards, solving problems, and making decisions related to their work.

The concepts described in this section underlie much of the research and practice of job design and organizational change. Job characteristics and sociotechnical theories are the bases for many intervention processes used by organizations to move from authoritarian forms of management to participative styles. Some of these procedures, appropriate for white-collar jobs, are discussed in the section "How to Design Effective Jobs."

THE RELATIONSHIP BETWEEN TECHNOLOGY AND JOB DESIGN

The impact of technology on white-collar jobs goes beyond changes in tasks. Ultimately, technology can lead to changes in the work process, quality of work life, and organizational structure and culture. Automation changes jobs in several ways:

1. Procedures for completing tasks may change. When tasks are taken over by an automated system, jobs (or portions of jobs) may be eliminated. Workers must be retrained to do the new jobs, reassigned, or let go.
2. When jobs are modified due to the addition or deletion of tasks, boundaries between jobs may change as tasks are transferred from one job to another. Sometimes these changes are accompanied by changes in job titles, descriptions, or compensation (but not necessarily).
3. Automation creates new tasks, required to support the system or related to new products or services. Existing jobs may be redesigned to incorporate these new tasks, or new jobs may be created. For example, the position of administrator may be created to operate an integrated office system, assign passwords, perform daily backup, troubleshoot problems, and so forth.
4. Technology may lead to the creation of new tasks not previously possible, practical, or cost effective. New capabilities may create opportunities for new products or services.

To understand the effects of technology on tasks, jobs, work process, and organizational structure, consider the following four results related to the introduction of a microcomputer with word processing and spreadsheet software in the office of a manager and secretary.

First, the way some tasks are accomplished may change; new skills will be needed and old ones eliminated. If the manager decides to use the microcomputer to author documents, creating them will require different skills than writing them in longhand. Previously important skills, such as the manager's dictation and the secretary's shorthand and transcription, may seldom be used.

Second, the process that governs the interactions of author, secretary, and other people to produce documents may change. The secretary now may do only the final formatting and printing of documents. Documents that are filed electronically are no longer sent to records management. If the manager uses electronic mail for intercompany correspondence, the secretary and mail services may be left out of the process entirely.

At some points, technology allows for choice rather than mandating change. For example, the microcomputer could be given to the secretary rather than the manager. The manger might continue to dictate documents that the secretary would transcribe and edit using word processing. Thus the computer becomes a substitute for the typewriter. The relationship between manager and secretary, and the flow of work, might have altered only a little, with only the secretary needing new skills. Another alternative would be to sever the relationship completely; the secretary might be reclassified as a word processing operator and moved to a newly created pool to key and correct drafts for many authors. This alternative goes beyond changes in task and job design and requires a change in the structure of the organization.

Third, new technology may introduce new steps and new tasks. For example, a microcomputer introduces the need to make backup copies, to design and use an electronic filing system, and to manage disk space or diskette storage. Decisions about these tasks, whether they will be handled by all users, by secretaries, by a systems administrator, or by some combination, will affect the work process.

Fourth, the availability of the technology will enable the manager and secretary to do new tasks that were not practical before. For example, if the secretary maintains the old card file of clients on the microcomputer, it becomes practical to send personalized letters to hundreds of clients using the merge printing feature of word processing.

Thus with even this simple example one can see how changes at the level of the task, job, work process, and organization could take place as a result of new technology.[6]

Work Integration and Work Differentiation

When there is too much work for one person, division of labor may be necessary. Once tasks are divided among two or more employees, the work process governs their relationship to the partially completed product. The tasks that make up the work process might be combined in any number of ways. Alternatives for combining tasks may be viewed as a continuum from the most integrated to the most differentiated.

Figure 17-4 shows five possible steps along this continuum for a word processing office. In the most integrated work, authors do their own authoring. They have complete responsibility for all steps in the process and total control over the end product. On the opposite end of the continuum, the most differentiated situation is where authors send work to a centralized word processing pool. Operators have specialized tasks; some key in text, some proofread, and some make corrections. Within these extremes might be a one-to-one relationship between author and operator, or relationships among a team of authors and one operator. This approach might focus on all stages of work for a group of authors.

The basic concept of work integration or differentiation applies regardless of the level of technology. The technology in the example just cited could just as easily have been typewriters or quill pens. The popular perception that advanced technology fosters differentiation and fragmentation is not necessarily the case. The image of office automation as a centralized word processing or data-entry pool is unfortunate. Although computerization has often been associated with fragmentation, other

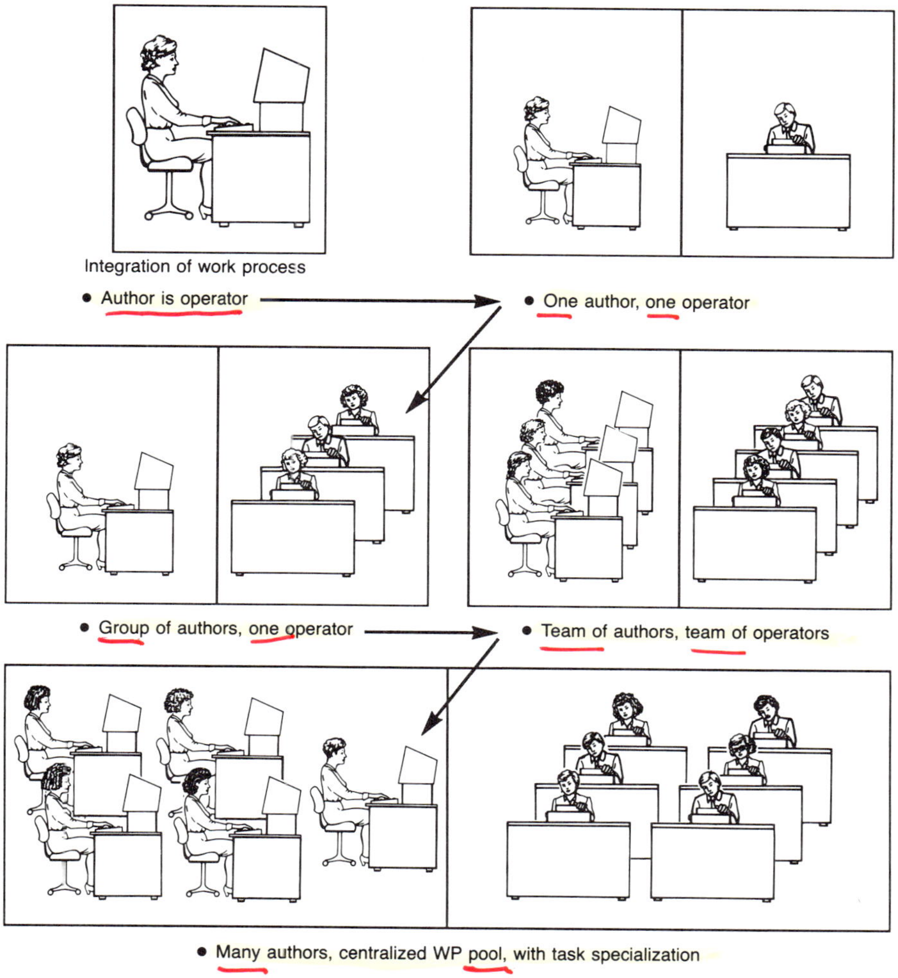

FIGURE 17-4. Possible variations of work process for word processing.

forces also have been at work. The result depends more on the job design philosophy than on the technology. In fact, office technology offers many possibilities for reintegrating work processes.

Computer-Mediated Work

Two characteristics of computer jobs are (1) that the machine makes work more abstract and (2) that the machine alters the worker's relationship to the task. The new relationship is sometimes referred to as *computer-mediated,* which means that a person accomplishes a task through the information system rather than through direct contact with objects.[7]

Workers experience tasks as more concrete when the tasks involve manipulation of objects, as in pottery making or carpentry. Manipulation itself is a form of feedback (the object "feels right"). Machines remove workers as a direct source of energy, but workers still have contact with the objects of their labor. With computers, however, workers get only indirect feedback through the symbols on the screen. "Very often, from the point of view of the worker, the object of the task seems to have disappeared 'behind the screen' and into the information system."[8]

Thus computers have made information processing more abstract. From the perspective of the office worker, when information is in physical forms that can be touched and manipulated—such as cards, letters, reports, and invoices—it appears more concrete. When information is processed on the computer, however, many of these objects disappear. The office worker is confronted with intangible information, which is manipulated in invisible ways inside the computer.

Coping with Computer Logic

The computer easily handles quantitative data, but qualitative judgments are difficult to program. Consequently, when computer systems are designed, qualitative aspects are either quantified or lost. A programmer defines correctness of data in terms of formal computer logic. Thus formal correctness can become more important than the relevance of the information. Judgment is replaced by computer logic, and errors become difficult to detect and correct.

Computers have become easier to use, but they still require codes and procedural commands. Even though the commands resemble English, computer languages are logical and precise whereas comprehension of natural language is somewhat intuitive. If words are spelled phonetically, for instance, most people recognize the intended words and the message is communicated. For most people, learning to think in a way that parallels computer logic is not trivial. It requires thinking and performing steps in the precise order dictated by the logical sequence built into the software.

The difference between how most people go about finding information in a file folder or reference book, in contrast to a computer database, illustrates the point. When physically searching for information, most people rely on intuitive aids. They recall that it was in a red volume, it was near the back, the page was torn, or it was on the second shelf. If searchers recall terminology inaccurately or misspell a term, they will probably find what they are looking for anyway. These memory aids are *not* available in computer databases; there are only names, precisely defined by computer logic. Searchers must use the right key words, in the right relationship, or the results will be faulty. (AI natural-language interfaces may eventually reduce these problems, but the technology is still a long way from general application.)

One consequence of computer-mediated work is that it becomes more difficult to exercise judgment over it. This is true for both routine clerical jobs and complex professional jobs. These comments of a bank auditor illustrate the point:

> The job of auditing is very different now. More imagination is required. I am receiving data online. I don't go to the branches if I don't want to. I don't see any books. What do I audit in this situation? I always have to be thinking about what is in the system. I may be auditing, but it doesn't feel like it.[9]

The computer has also introduced new complexity in data. The auditor can compare branches, according to criteria, and search out new relationships in the data. To do this, however, the auditor must develop a theory of the auditing process. A conceptual framework is needed to guide the auditor through the mass of information. Theoretical insight and imagination are the new keys to effectiveness. By creating a medium where imagination is more important than experience-based judgment, information technology challenges old procedures. In this auditing process, for example, planners are not automating the old, but inventing the new.

Worker Frustration

Another consequence of computer-mediated work is that it can induce feelings of frustration and loss of control. "Computer mediation of simple jobs can create tasks that are routine and unchallenging, while demanding focused attention and abstract comprehension."[10] People who are action-oriented, rather than abstract thinkers, find computer-mediated work frustrating and stressful. Those who shift from conventional procedures to computer-mediated work feel this stress most acutely. It is impossible, however, to forecast how people will adapt to the abstraction of work over the long term.

Altered Social Structure

Computer-mediated work alters the social structure of an organization. The workstation itself can become the individual's primary focus of interaction. "This focus can lead people to feel isolated in an impersonal situation."[11] The importance of communities in the workplace has been widely recognized. Jobs that isolate people at computer workstations can lead to social problems.

De-skilling versus Enhancing Jobs

Perceptions differ over whether automation is de-skilling or enhancing office jobs. *De-skilling* means using the computer to direct, control, and pace work so that the required level of skill is reduced and knowledge, judgment, and decision making are minimized. *Enhancing* means expanding the scope and level of responsibility by using technology to reduce routine, repetitive tasks and provide access to information and resources.

Many organizations that process large amounts of standardized data have elected to use automation to de-skill tasks, enabling lower-paid employees with minimum skills to process more data in a given time. Sorting rules, decision trees, and analytical processes can also be built into computer processes and software packages as a means to de-skill professional tasks. This approach can create factory-like offices, which often reduce job interest and satisfaction and increase stress.

On the other hand, automation can enhance jobs by relieving people of routine, repetitive tasks. Simple tasks can be integrated into fewer, broader jobs so that the worker has a better sense of the purpose and outcome of the work. Information systems can also give a worker access to knowledge that could previously be obtained only through advanced education. This allows a nonprofessional worker to take over interesting tasks that were previously considered the work of the professional. For example, clerks can use computerized databases to search for information that formerly only a lawyer, doctor, scientist, or Ph.D. in archeology would have known about. Some organizations are deliberately using office automation to upgrade and enhance work at all levels. As a result, they can sometimes develop a flatter institutional structure and reduce the costs of management.

Changes in Organizational Structure and Communications

When the work process changes, the organizational structure, which defines the relationships among jobs, can also change. Changes may result in revisions in the formal organization chart or may simply alter communication patterns or power relationships among groups or departments. Changes in organizational structure may take place immediately, as part of the planned system changes, or may evolve over time as the enterprise gains familiarity with the technology and its capabilities.

For example, some organizations that acquired word processing technology created administrative support centers and word processing centers. These centers drastically changed reporting relationships and were accordingly incorporated into the formal organization chart. This contrasts with the way many organizations have acquired microcomputers. Individuals or departments have typically purchased microcomputers with little formal planning. Gradually, office systems departments evolved to coordinate microcomputer acquisition and technical support.

Several changes in organizational structure and communication patterns have been attributed to automation. For instance, adoption of centralized computers created a tendency for organizations to centralize control. On the other hand, the adoption of departmental microcomputers has led to decentralization of decision making. End-user computing has put new power in the hands of local departments, since one source of power is control over resources. It has also been suggested that the widespread use of integrated office systems reduces the need for middle managers and will lead to a flattening of organizational pyramids.

Many of the organizational implications of integrated office systems are related to changes in communication patterns because communication is a major part of white-collar jobs. Electronic mail systems open new avenues of communication, which may bypass former information gatekeepers. Perhaps of greater significance will be wider availability of information databases. Senior managers will have immediate, direct access to data formerly filtered to them in summary reports. Knowledge workers will have the Library of Congress at their fingertips. Another consequence of communication technologies is ability to disperse office activities geographically. Information can be consolidated in centralized computers while access and processing can be decentralized any place in the country or the world.

Observers have noted interesting changes in the boundaries between clerical and professional and between clerical and managerial positions. Some researchers have referred to this redistribution of labor as the *clericalization of professional work* and the *professionalization of clerical work.*[12] The most prominent trend is the shift of keyboarding tasks when professionals and managers acquire workstations. Individuals who would never have typed in the past begin using word processing to author documents, and the time that clerical workers spend keyboarding original documents decreases. Sometimes secretaries are bypassed completely, or their involvement may be limited to revising, formatting, and printing. All of these effects of office technology are not inevitable. Changes in functions and shifts in power can be attributed as much to the characteristics of the organization and its management strategy as to the characteristics of the technology.

Technology as a Catalyst for Job Redesign

Efforts of American companies to improve office productivity through the application of technology have again focused on the key role of people in making technology pay off. According to a special report on the response of management to the human factors of automation,

> American managers are finally learning what the Japanese discovered years ago: The solution to fading competitive ability, sluggish productivity growth, and poor quality cannot be found in the mythical black box of a miraculous technology. To realize the full potential of automation, leading-edge companies are integrating workers and technology in *sociotechnical* systems that revolutionize the way work is organized and managed. . . . This is an immensely important trend, one that is producing a new model of job design and work relations that will shape the workplace well into the 21st century.[13]

Combining job redesign with implementation strategies for automated systems provides new opportunities to rethink the way work is organized.

Due to the influence of scientific management, work in most American corporations is structured along functional lines. The work of individuals and departments is divided according to function, such as invoicing, billing, accounting, typing, filing, shipping, and so forth. Functional organization optimizes each task and function separately. Optimizing individual functions, however, does not guarantee that the overall operation will be optimized. In fact, such segregation of functions often leads to situations where various parts of an operation are working at cross-purposes. Efficiencies in one area of the organization can be negated by bottlenecks in others. The interests of clients can get lost in the cracks between functional areas.

Because system designers seldom addressed job design issues, most early office automation applications were implemented in ways that maintained old, functional lines of organization, often compounding weaknesses. Anticipated productivity improvements were never realized because technology created new bottlenecks in the old work flows. In some of the worst cases, disgruntled workers resisted the technology or failed to use it effectively because of inadequate training. Today, progressive enterprises are applying the concepts of job redesign, turning technological changes into opportunities to rethink old forms of work organization in light of current and future objectives.

This change in orientation has been referred to as *electronic integration*. Instead of attempting to optimize each task and function separately, system designers can employ electronic integration to optimize a whole procedure. For example, they might focus on improving customer service or marketing. Electronic integration is possible because the technology allows (1) the integration of information from many sources and (2) distribution of information to many locations.[14]

The previously mentioned example of the bank where 23 steps were required to issue a letter of credit provides an excellent case in point. Under the old system, each worker performed one or two steps in processing all letters of credit. Under the revised process, each worker, with the aid of a computer workstation and a client database, performs *all* the necessary steps in processing letters of credit for a particular set of clients. The database contains all information related to their accounts. The service worker is the single contact between the customer and the bank for corrections or inquiries.

The capabilities of an integrated client service system at a major insurance company are shown in Figure 17-5. With microcomputers on their desks, client service representatives have word processing, spreadsheet, and administrative systems at their fingertips. In addition, they have direct access to the company's database of policyholder information. They can answer telephone inquiries, send written replies, check policyholder information (such as loan balances or current cash value of policies), make policy changes (such as address or beneficiary changes), issue special

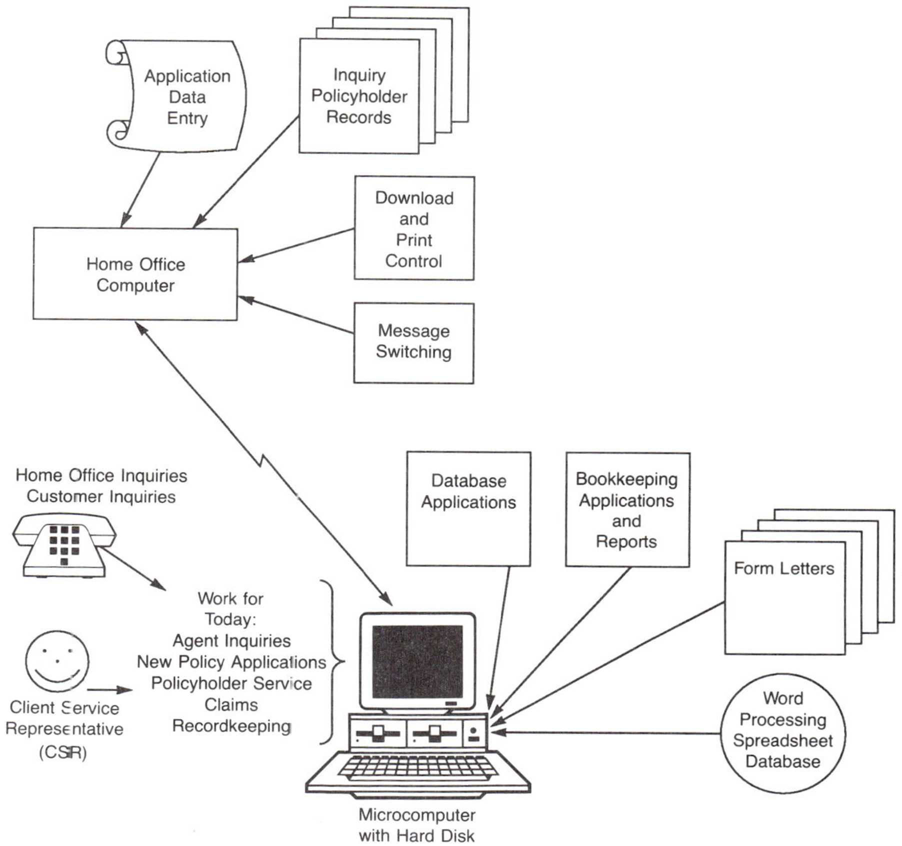

FIGURE 17-5.
An integrated client service system at a major insurance company.

statements, and much more. Most importantly, electronic integration has changed the focus of the job from processing paperwork to serving clients, or, in other words, from efficient paperwork to effective client service.

Electronic integration can be used to design jobs that give workers a variety of tasks and, at the same time, allow them to understand how the job contributes to the department or enterprise. This gives workers greater autonomy and responsibility, and contributes to job satisfaction and productivity. Electronic integration can also design a decentralized team approach to the division of labor. Some insurance companies have integrated workers who formerly were organized by function into teams that service a specific market. For example, they have created small teams of raters, underwriters, and clerical workers for specific product lines. Organizing them in teams, rather than isolating them in functional groups, allows greater understanding of the production process and facilitates communication.

When designing automated systems, analysts should remember that job design influences productivity more than technology does. Without well-thought-out design, chances are that new systems will reinforce functional organization rather than invent integrated ones. In fact, system designers often strive to tailor new technology to the existing organization to avoid disrupting the work environment. When job design is overlooked, however, important opportunities to make technology pay off may be missed.

THE REDESIGN OF JOBS

When people find their jobs motivating, they feel good about themselves and the work they do. They do not have to be cajoled or forced to perform their work; they strive to do their jobs well because they find good performance rewarding and satisfying. They are "turned on" to their work, rather than motivated solely by external (hygiene) factors, such as compliments from the boss or a paycheck.

In a book called *Work Redesign*, Hackman and Oldham describe a methodology for designing jobs that people can perform effectively and find rewarding and satisfying. Their approach is based on a combination of behavioral and sociotechnical systems that emphasizes the importance of individual differences and the need to analyze the requirements of each organization. They focus on the actual work that people perform, and they emphasize the distinctions between designing work for individuals and designing work for groups.

Characteristics of Motivating Jobs

Jobs that people find motivating have three characteristics:

- Workers have knowledge of the actual results of their work.
- Workers have responsibility for the results of their work.
- Workers experience their work as meaningful.[15]

Other measures that relate to job design—although they are not, strictly speaking, characteristics of the job—include the following:

- Growth satisfaction, or the degree to which the employee believes the job provides opportunities for personal growth and development, and
- Growth need, or the strength of the employee's desire for growth and personal development.

These two measures indicate how an employee will respond to a job with high motivating potential. These characteristics of motivating jobs relate directly to the five core job characteristics described previously under "Job Characteristics Theory." Figure 17-6 illustrates the role of motivating job characteristics in a work effectiveness model.

Designing Jobs for Individuals

When redesigning jobs for automated office systems, analysts should focus on job dimensions to encourage employees to work hard and perform well of their own accord rather than out of fear or in response to harassment by

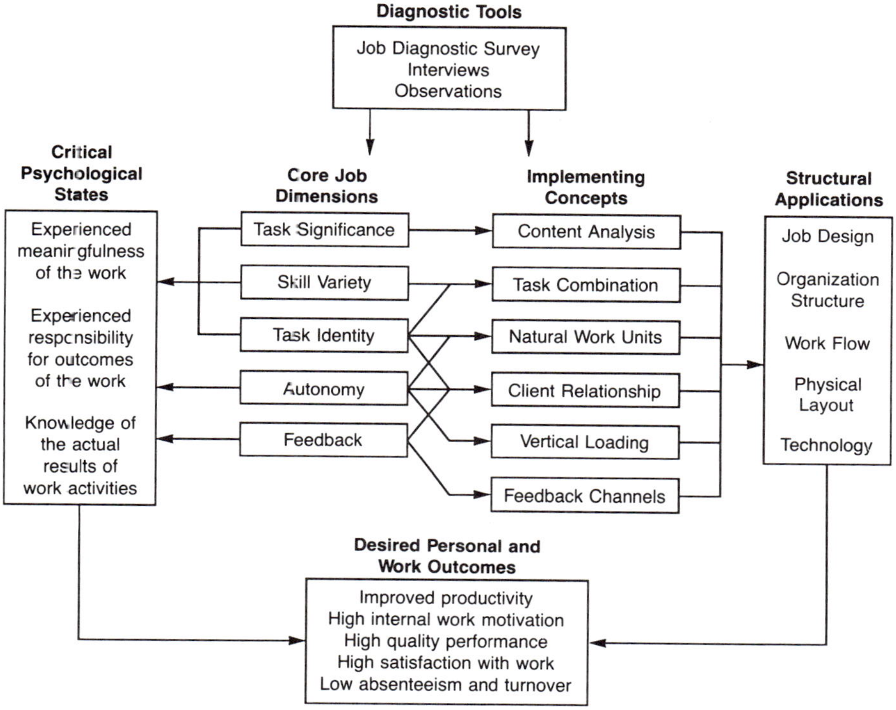

FIGURE 17-6. **The work effectiveness model.**

supervisors. Hackman and Oldham recommended the five following strategies for redesigning work. Each of these strategies directly addresses one or more of the five core job dimensions:[16]

1. *Task combination.* Task combination puts fragmented job tasks into new job modules, combining all the tasks required for a given piece of work. Computers can reduce many repetitive tasks, making combination more practical than it was with manual systems. A complete job module increases skill variety and task identity and generates challenge and responsibility for the worker. There may be times when task combination is constrained for organizational or technical reasons. For example, enterprises may want to keep internal auditing separate from other processing.

2. *Forming natural work units.* Forming natural work units, in conjunction with task combination, provides further opportunities for task identity and significance. A *natural* work unit refers to grouping tasks in a logical or inherently meaningful way. Natural work units are organized according to groups of customers, type of transactions, geographical distribution, or any other arrangement that makes good sense to those

performing the work. For example, a customer service representative might handle all contact with clients in the Chicago area rather than handling work randomly as it comes into the department.

3. *Establishing client relationships.* When natural work units are formed around specific groups of clients, it may be possible to put the employee in direct contact with the clients and give them continuing responsibility for managing relationships with them. *Clients* may be customers of a firm, other individuals or departments within an enterprise, or other *publics* of the enterprise. An effective client relationship provides direct contact between client and employee, clearly establishes criteria for evaluating the quality of the product or service, and provides a regular channel for relaying feedback directly to the worker.

   Enabling employees to establish direct relationships with clients can improve jobs in three core dimensions. Feedback increases when workers get direct praise or criticism from persons who receive the work. Skill variety increases because establishing client relationships requires interpersonal skills in addition to task-specific skills. Autonomy also increases because individuals have personal responsibility for managing their relationships with clients.

4. *Vertically loading jobs.* Vertical loading pushes down responsibility and authority formerly assigned at a higher level, thus giving employees more control over their jobs. Vertical loading can be accomplished in many ways. Controls can be removed to give employees more discretion in planning, scheduling, and checking their work. The job can be broadened by adding more difficult tasks. Workers might consult with others in the organization, rather than immediately calling the supervisor; give technical advice; author their own reports; interview job candidates; or perform other appropriate tasks. Jobs can also be vertically loaded by granting new authority, such as discretion to set one's own goals to accomplish a specific short-term objective.

5. *Establishing feedback channels.* Feedback channels should give workers direct, immediate, and regular information about how well they are performing their jobs. It is generally more effective for employees to learn about their performance directly, by doing the job, than to rely on a supervisor as their main source of feedback. Direct job feedback is usually more immediate and private, and it increases the employee's sense of control over the job. In most instances, establishing feedback channels involves removing barriers or blocks that insulate employees from information about their performance. Establishing direct client relationships (discussed previously) is one of the most effective feedback channels. Other examples include returning documents to the same word processing operator for revisions and corrections, rather than randomly, or moving quality control close to the workers.

While the implementing concepts are mutually reinforcing, each can be a separate action strategy. Other possibilities also exist for redesigning jobs. The five areas outlined by Hackman and Oldham, however, address some of the most common problems associated with job design. They are intended as guidelines for generating ideas about how jobs might be improved rather than as hard and fast rules. In order to work, these principles must be implemented in a supportive organization. Work redesign must have the full support of the managers affected by it or the intended results will be diminished, if not thwarted.

Designing Work for Self-Managing Groups

Although the same principles apply, designing work for self-managing groups is more complex than designing work for individuals. It requires addressing not only issues of motivating individuals but group dynamics as well. The focus is on the overall task of the group rather than on tasks of members.

Self-managing work groups may be defined as "intact (if small) social systems whose members have the authority to handle internal processes as they see fit in order to generate a specific group product, service or decision."[17] These groups also may be referred to as *autonomous* or *self-regulating work groups.* Self-managing work groups include task forces set up to solve specific problems, decision making committees, and many kinds of management teams.

Criteria for Group Effectiveness

The three criteria of group effectiveness identified by Hackman and Oldham include the following:[18]

1. The work of the group meets or exceeds organizational standards of quantity and quality. If the work of the group is not acceptable to those who receive and use it (reports that are inaccurate or untimely), the group cannot be considered effective.

2. The group experience contributes to meeting the personal needs of members. Sometimes groups develop patterns of interpersonal behavior that are destructive to the well-being of members. If most members find that their experiences in the group frustrate their needs, and block them from achieving personal goals, it would be hard to argue that the group is a successful social unit.

3. The social process in carrying out the work maintains or enhances the capability of members to work together on subsequent tasks. Some groups operate in ways that destroy their integrity. That is, the group "burns out" in the process of performing the task. Even if the product is acceptable, a group cannot be considered successful if it generates so much divisiveness and conflict that members are unwilling or unable to work together on future occasions.

Hackman and Oldham also identified three *intermediate* criteria of team effectiveness:[19]

1. The level of *effort* that group members bring to bear on the task.
2. The amount of *knowledge and skill* group members apply to the task.
3. The appropriateness of the *task performance strategies* used by the group in doing its work.

Designing Work Groups

An additional consideration in designing work for groups is the composition of the group. Hackman and Oldham recommended the following characteristics for a work group:[20]

1. The group should include members who have high levels of task-relevant expertise.
2. The group should be large enough to do the work, but not much larger.
3. Group members should have at least a moderate level of interpersonal skill in addition to their task-relevant skills.
4. The group membership should strike a balance between homogeneity and heterogeneity.

Implementing and managing work groups is far more complex than designing jobs for individuals. Self-managing work groups generally have a much greater impact than individual jobs on the organizational structure and management climate. Supporting and sustaining work groups without the commitment of top management is highly improbable. Some tasks are so large or complex, however, that they can be accomplished only by groups. Nevertheless, if given a choice, the systems analyst should use individual rather than group strategies, unless the latter are significantly superior and the management climate is highly supportive.

Analyzing Opportunities for Work Redesign

Before undertaking any job design or redesign project, the analyst must assess the situation and ask such questions as the following:

- Is there a need or opportunity for job design?
- Is job redesign feasible for the unit?
- Which aspects of the job can benefit from improvement and which are fine as they are?
- How receptive will employees be to change and how will changes fit with their needs and skills?
- How will changes fit with the rest of the organization?
- What opportunities for innovation are offered by the new technology?
- How should the affected employees be involved in the process?
- Are individual job redesign strategies appropriate or is the task large or complex enough to require group strategies?

When jobs are designed in conjunction with technological change, it is also important to keep in mind that innovations not initially apparent may emerge as workers gain experience with the technology.

Tools and methods that analysts can use to answer these questions include consultants, organizational mission statements, observations and interviews, survey instruments, work flow analysis, and workspace design.

Consultants

Consultants who specialize in organizational behavior and job redesign can be an excellent resource for the office systems analyst. Consultants can offer objectivity, an outside perspective, and methods and assessment tools for diagnosing job redesign opportunities. (More information about working with consultants is provided in Chapter 22, "Implementation.")

Mission Statement of the Work Unit

A *mission statement* defines the purpose of the organization or work unit. If such a statement does not exist, the analyst should ask the manager of the unit to write one. The objective is to state the *single* reason why the organization exists. A well-designed organizational structure should establish one main purpose for each unit, and secondary goals should be directly related to the primary purpose.

Armed with a clear statement of a work unit's mission, the analyst can then determine the extent to which current procedures support that mission and whether the organizational structure is consistent with the mission.

Work Flow Analysis

Before redesigning a job, the analyst should determine precisely what tasks are being done in the work unit and what purposes they serve. It is helpful to draw work flow diagrams similar to the ones in Figure 17-7. (Details on how to draw a flowchart are provided in Chapter 21.)

Roy W. Walters and Associates, Inc., a consulting firm that specializes in job design, offers several suggestions for using work flow analysis. How does each employee get the work, and where does it go next? How do separate tasks relate to one another? Are all current tasks really necessary? Can any tasks be eliminated? For example, are reports prepared that are not used? Could reports be prepared less frequently? Is all the information in the reports needed, or would a more concise report serve just as well—or perhaps better? Should any tasks be added? Should additional information be included or current information be replaced?

FIGURE 17-7. Work flow diagrams of a clerical operation.

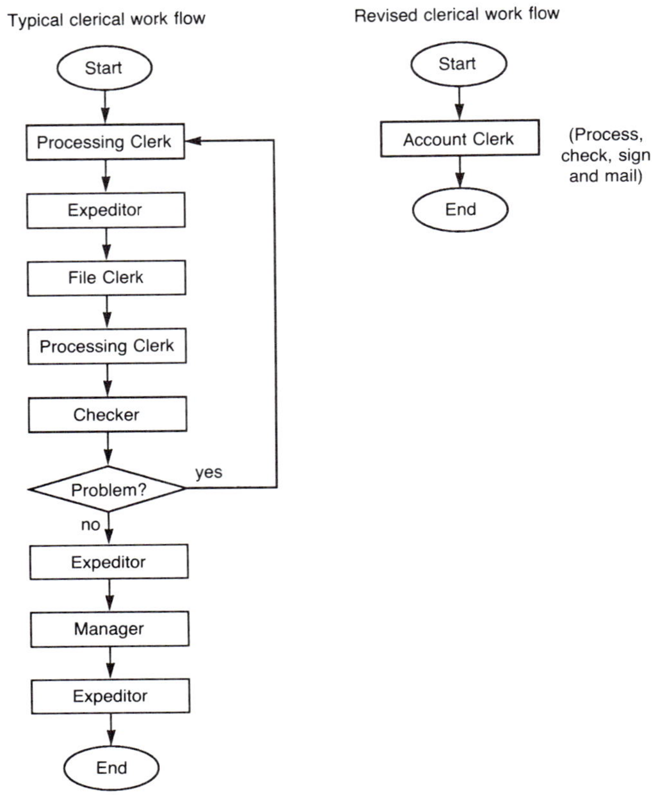

Observations and Interviews

The analyst's observations of the work unit and knowledge of the new technology to be implemented are key to understanding the opportunities for job redesign. The analyst should also solicit the observations of knowledgeable senior management about the unit's operation. Individuals familiar with similar operations in other enterprises can also provide valuable insights.

The employees in the work unit are a key source of information and can provide valuable insights into work procedures, problems, receptivity to change, and ideas for improving the work.

Analysts should not overlook the *clients* of the work unit as a valuable source of information. Clients include other departments or individuals within the enterprise who receive output from the unit, as well as consumers of the enterprise's products or services. It is important to determine how the client defines a superior service or product.

To gather information, the analyst can use either formal or informal interview techniques. Keep in mind, however, that interviewers should spend 80 percent of their time *listening*. (Interview techniques are summarized in Chapter 22, "Implementation.") Interviews and observations should provide information about the unit's mission, detailed work procedures, efficiencies and inefficiencies of the work flow, who makes decisions about work, who evaluates work, and how the unit relates to other organizational units. The analyst should be sure to assess the perceptions, attitudes, and feelings of employees about their jobs and the organization.

Survey Instruments

The analyst can develop or purchase survey instruments to obtain detailed information about the jobs that are candidates for redesign and the skills, needs, and motivations of the employees who staff the positions.

One such instrument was developed by Hackman and Oldham to gauge the degree to which each core-job dimension exists in a given job. This Job Diagnostic Survey (JDS) asks objective questions to measure the core dimensions and subjective questions to measure employee attitudes about work, such as job satisfaction, motivation, and personal growth. The JDS should be completed only by incumbents of the jobs in question. A copy of the JDS, with instructions and scoring information, is available in Hackman and Oldham's book, *Work Redesign*. An additional instrument, the Job Rating Form (JRF), surveys other individuals.

Physical Layout

The physical layout of a work unit should support the work flow. When jobs are redesigned and work flow is changed, the physical layout must also be redesigned.

When work was redesigned in the administrative departments of a large insurance agency, creating the new position of client service representative (the example previously referred to in the section "Electronic Integration"), the entire work space was also redesigned. A new workstation was ergonomically designed to provide room for a microcomputer, printer, client files, reference materials, personal items, and work area. The workstation area was designed in a "U" shape to facilitate the work flow and provide convenient access to necessary materials. Sound-absorbing panels created privacy, reduced disruptions, and housed electrical cables and wiring.

FINAL COMMENTS ABOUT JOB DESIGN

The major goal of work design programs is to organize work and assign responsibility for completing tasks in a way that creates jobs that workers will find motivating and satisfying. When job design principles are coupled with technological innovations, enterprises have new opportunities to rethink the way products and services are produced and delivered:

> Using technology to create routine jobs which can be easily performed with minimum training constrains the capabilities of both technology and people. The greatest potential of office technology in the long-run derives from the computer's capacity to enhance human capabilities. Just as humankind has historically used the lever to amplify the physical strength of the body, we can now use the computer to extend the thinking and creative power of the mind. . . . Those organizations which learn to use technology to unleash and capitalize on people's creative potential will have a tremendous competitive advantage.[21]

By this point, every reader must be impressed by the number of factors that affect the way work is organized and managed, which is precisely the reason why organizations do not undertake these projects more often. Theories can only serve as aids in planning design strategies; no blueprints detail how changes should be implemented. Using technology to redesign jobs is largely uncharted territory. It takes skilled, knowledgeable analysts, working with human-resource personnel and department management, to implement effective job design changes. Analysts must be sensitive to the many factors that affect the way change activities evolve and be prepared to deal with them (see Figure 17-8).

SUMMARY

Job design plays a vital role in making technology pay off. To achieve the full benefits of automation, office systems analysts must address issues of job design as well as systems design.

Technology invariably forces changes in job responsibilities, task content, and human interactions. Whether technology enhances or diminishes the roles of people in accomplishing organizational goals is primarily a function of job design and management decisions.

Technology has affected white-collar work in a number of ways. Automation takes over some tasks completely, replacing jobs in whole or in part. Jobs are modified when automation eliminates, adds, or shifts tasks. Automation also creates new jobs when new tasks are required to support systems or are generated by new opportunities. Computers make work more abstract and alter the worker's relationship to tasks. In some instances, jobs have been deskilled while in others they have been enhanced. When the work process changes, the organization's structure, which defines the relationships among jobs, can also change.

The influence of "scientific management" is still prevalent in most organizations today, as their production line methods and functional

FIGURE 17-8. The changing approach to organizing work.

WHAT MANAGEMENT ASSUMES ABOUT WORKERS

OLD WAY Worker wants nothing from the job except pay, avoids responsibility, and must be controlled and coerced.	**NEW WAY** Worker desires challenging job and will seek responsibility and autonomy if management provides the opportunity.

HOW THE JOB IS DESIGNED

OLD WAY Work is fragmented and deskilled. Worker is confined to narrow job. Doing and thinking are separated.	**NEW WAY** Work is multiskilled and performed by teamwork wherever possible. Worker can upgrade whole system. Doing and thinking are combined.

MANAGEMENT'S ORGANIZATION AND STYLE

OLD WAY Top-down military command with worker at bottom of many supervisory layers; worker is expected to obey orders and has no power.	**NEW WAY** Relatively flat structure with few layers; worker makes suggestions and has power to implement changes.

JOB TRAINING AND SECURITY

OLD WAY Worker is regarded as a replaceable part and is given little initial training or retraining for new jobs. Layoffs are routine when business declines.	**NEW WAY** Worker is considered a valuable resource and is constantly retrained in new skills. Layoffs are avoided if possible in a downturn.

HOW WAGES ARE DETERMINED

OLD WAY Pay is geared to the job, not the person, and is determined by evaluation and job classification systems.	**NEW WAY** Pay is linked to skills acquired. Group incentive and profit-sharing plans are used to enhance commitment.

LABOR RELATIONS

OLD WAY Labor and management interests are considered incompatible. Conflict arises on the shop floor and in bargaining.	**NEW WAY** Mutual interests are emphasized. Management shares information about the business. Labor shares responsibility for making it succeed.

organizations bear witness. Work redesign concepts are based on participative management philosophies and sociotechnical systems.

The objective of a work design program is to organize work and assign responsibility for completing tasks in a way that creates jobs workers will find motivating and satisfying. Major characteristics of motivating jobs are autonomy, skill variety, task identity, task significance, and feedback from the job itself. Five strategies for designing jobs are combining tasks, forming natural work groups, establishing client relationships, vertically loading jobs, and establishing feedback channels.

Technology is a catalyst for redesign programs that provide new opportunities for helping people work more productively and creatively. Redesigning work is a complex process, but the payoff for those who succeed can be extremely high.

DISCUSSION QUESTIONS

1. Define *job redesign.* Discuss the importance of job redesign in the automated office.
2. Differentiate *task analysis* from *job analysis.*
3. Trace the development of approaches to job redesign from the preindustrial organization to participative management.
4. Technology changes the very nature of work. Discuss. Offer examples of how a computer can change the way work is done in an office.
5. Hackman and Oldham have done pioneering work in job redesign, offering basic strategies for implementing work design. For each of these strategies, explain how a marketing manager's job could be redesigned.
6. How do jobs typically get designed? How should they be designed?

APPLICATION EXERCISES

1. Ask a secretary who has recently begun using a microcomputer how the job has changed, then compare your answers with classmates. How do the responses compare?
2. Interview a manager or professional who has recently begun using a microcomputer. Ask for a summary of how the job has changed as a result of the computer. Compile your answers with comments. How do your findings compare with those of classmates?

SUGGESTED READINGS

Hackman, J. Richard, and Oldham, Greg R. *Work Redesign* (Reading, Mass.: Addison-Wesley, 1980).

Hunt, John W. *Managing People at Work* (London: McGraw-Hill Book Company-United Kingdom, 1979).

Ouchi, William. *Theory Z: How American Business Can Meet the Japanese Challenge* (Reading, Mass.: Addison-Wesley, 1981).

U.S. Congress, Office of Technology Assessment. *The Automation of America's Offices* (Washington, D.C.: U.S. Government Printing Office, December 1985).

ORGANIZATIONAL CHANGE

CHAPTER

18

OBJECTIVES

After completing this chapter, the reader should be able to meet the following objectives:

- Explain the relationship between technology and change.
- Explain why organizational change is a learning process.
- Identify important considerations for implementing technological changes.
- Describe the three phases of the change process.
- Identify major causes of resistance to change in an organization and explain how a manager or systems analysts can avoid them.
- Explain the office automation implementer's role as a change agent.
- Diagnose pressures for and resistance to a planned technological change.
- Design a plan for implementing a technological change.

KEY TERMS

change agent
driving forces
force field analysis
organizational change
people variable
restraining forces
structure
task variable
technology variable

INTRODUCTION

The American Management Association estimates that large corporations undergo one major reorganization at least every two years. This unprecedented rate of change has affected the business office in many ways. Office automation is both a reaction to change, as offices strive to cope with new demands, and the precipitator, as new technologies introduce change. The objective of this chapter is to summarize some of the important aspects of change that relate to automation in the business office. Designing automated systems for the office is as much about change as it is about technology. Whether technology is used as a catalyst for innovation or to replace existing equipment, implementing new technologies may require changes in skills, work procedures, work flow, jobs, or even organizational structure. In recent years, almost every piece of equipment in the office, from the telephone to printing presses, has been updated to incorporate new computer and communications technologies. It would be shortsighted indeed, however, to think of automation only in terms of technological change. Many important considerations for successful change are behavioral rather than technological. Office automation and end-user computing are, first and foremost, about changing the way people work. Office employees must change their behavior to use new technologies effectively, and changes in behavior often do not come automatically. Thus it is not sufficient for office systems analysts to be technical experts; they must also be effective agents of change.

PLANNING FOR ORGANIZATIONAL CHANGE

New technology, especially of the magnitude of office automation, implies organizational change. Although the ability to adapt to and implement change is widely recognized as a necessity, behavioral scientists are just scratching the surface in understanding how to implement change in organizations.

Actually, change occurs continually in organizations. Many of these changes are *unplanned,* occurring at random or spontaneously. Unplanned changes may be disruptive, such as a strike, or beneficial, such as a machine breakdown that leads to a good idea for new procedures. Such unplanned changes constantly take place in personnel, work methods, routine office procedures, the locations of desks or machines, and many other day-to-day activities. Many of these changes seem small when taken individually, but in total, they add up to much of the improvement and progress of the organization.

Changes on a much larger scale, which were the exception prior to the 1960s, now occur more and more frequently. Whereas in the past change was viewed as an evolutionary process, today change often verges on the revolutionary. The relatively passive philosophies of managing change are no longer appropriate. Change strategies must be planned. *Planned organizational change,* which is the intentional attempt by an enterprise to alter the status quo, refers to a set of activities designed to alter the behavior or job tasks of individuals, groups, or the entire organization. Planned changes may be reactive or proactive. They include major technological changes as well as sweeping organizational changes that affect many divisions and levels at once.

Planned change has both a technical and a social aspect. The technical aspect of change refers to modification of physical routines. The social aspect refers to the way those affected by change think it will alter their relationships in the organization. Research indicates that the social aspects of change play a greater role than the technical aspects in determining the extent to which changes are accepted or rejected.

Because of the complex interrelationships between variables, it is easy for even the most carefully conceived plans to produce unanticipated consequences. Some changes are implemented smoothly while others raise havoc. Resistance is as likely to arise for small changes as for large ones. To dismiss resistance with the cliche that "people resist change" is shortsighted. The key to managing change is understanding its dynamics and the true nature of resistance.

Change brings both threats and opportunities. How one views it often depends upon one's perspective at the time. Managing organizational change involves understanding the variables and their interdependencies, creating a climate for learning, recognizing new power distributions, and handling complexity, ambiguity, and uncertainty. These and other important aspects of change are discussed in ensuing sections.

Successful and Unsuccessful Change

What is successful change? How do we know when change is successful or unsuccessful?

Planned organizational changes seldom fail completely, but on the other hand, few succeed entirely, either. Most changes take longer and cost more than expected. They sometimes exact a heavy toll on employee morale and managerial time and emotion. Sometimes plans are abandoned because of strong employee resistance or because the managers feel unprepared or unable to implement the changes successfully.

Whether or not a change may be judged successful depends on how well it accomplishes the major objectives. Planned organizational change requires changes in employee behaviors. An organization cannot implement technological changes unless its members learn to use the technology and behave differently in their relationships to one another and to their jobs.

For example, when an office introduced an automated calendaring and messaging system, the four project managers, twelve analysts, and secretary were told that they should use it. The analyst demonstrated its operation for everyone. The manager, implementor, and a few others were enthusiastic; the rest "went along" and started using the system. After a few weeks, use began to decline, and the manager took no action. A few weeks later, when the manager and implementor returned from vacation, the system had fallen into complete disuse.

Ultimately, organizations either prosper or fail because of their employees' behaviors—the things their employees do or fail to do. To succeed, changes must be supported by those affected by them. People must be motivated to make the change happen and achieve the intended objectives. The most elegant technological system may fail to improve productivity, whereas a less than ideal system may perform beyond expectations with supportive users.

Technology Brings Change

Information technologies are shaking up the business office. The changes cross traditional boundaries and upset traditional ways of thinking. The impact of the electronic revolution extends far beyond the way people perform tasks; it affects how people organize and communicate. The following example of an office without secretaries is a case in point:

> At the six-year-old Software Publication Corporation in California, no one, not even the president, relies on support staff to screen calls, arrange schedules, or type memos. All 115 employees have a personal computer and printer on their desks. A voice mail system handles all telephone messages and an electronic mail system delivers interoffice correspondence.[1]

Organizations must learn to deal with the impact of computers on work and management. Peter F. Drucker, a noted management authority, was quoted as follows in the *Wall Street Journal:*

> Both factory automation and office automation require changes in job design, in the organization and flow of work and in organizational relationships. . . . To be effective, office automation requires fairly radical changes in work flow, job design, job relations and staff. . . . The shift to knowledge work as the center of gravity of the work force will altogether force us to rethink the traditional organizational structure.[2]

Many organizations that have achieved less than anticipated productivity gains from office automation are looking beyond technology for solutions. A movement is emerging to improve the design of jobs and tasks, the organization of work itself, and the general approach to planning and implementing technological change. According to John L. Burch, "This movement, including macroergonomics, sociotechnical systems, decision support, organization theory, and other trends in management science, links software and hardware ergonomics, systems design and resource management, and strategic business planning."[3]

Historically, technology has always brought change. More precisely, technology has always been a means through which *people* have been able to implement change. Organizations must learn to coordinate technology, organizational structure, and business planning to manage change. The office systems analyst must assume a major burden of responsibility for change, along with managers.

The Office Automation Implementer as Change Agent

A change agent is an individual or team responsible for designing and introducing a change, such as a new office system. The change agent plays an important role as a *champion* who promotes and shepherds new ideas into action. A change agent must translate the vision of how things could or should be into step-by-step plans for reaching the envisioned goals.

The change agent may be an outsider, such as a consultant, or someone from within the organization with an outsider's perspective, such as a new manager, an employee with ideas, or a systems analyst. It is often difficult for someone who is familiar with existing operations (an insider) to break out of the bounds of an organization's culture, politics, and traditions. Change usually requires someone with a fresh perspective, someone with a vision of how things could be.

As change agents, office systems analysts must work closely with others in the organization. Seldom are analysts in a position to make all the decisions or command all the resources to implement new systems. Neither analysts nor managers are likely to have direct control over all the organizational dimensions that are important to successful implementation of a new system. Some organizational dimensions are subject to more direct managerial control and change than others. Systems analysts, however, must understand why changes do or do not occur in the desired directions.

When new systems do not meet expectations, failures can seldom be attributed to technical inadequacies. Failures generally result when systems analysts neglect to consider the impact of new systems on people and the organization. Thus it is important for the analyst to understand the role of a change agent and the change process. The systems analyst who understands the dynamics of change can be a powerful catalyst for helping managers achieve technological changes.

Important Considerations in Technological Change

Several considerations affect the success of technological change, including the following:

1. *The ability of employees to conceptualize change.* Some people find it very difficult to conceptualize change on an organizational or even a departmental level. If the planned change is complex or difficult to comprehend, the problem will be even more acute. When people have a problem conceptualizing change, they tend to become preoccupied with methods and means rather than ends.

2. *Employees' readiness for change.* An individual's readiness for change has to do with preparedness to entertain differences, ambiguity, and uncertainty. Employees must be ready both intellectually and emotionally.

3. *Employees' capacity for change.* Some individuals have a higher tolerance for change and uncertainty than others.

4. *Individual differences.* Individual differences in learning styles will determine to some extent the effectiveness of information about a change. The three basic learning styles are cognitive, behavioral, and affective. Individuals are not necessarily limited to just one learning style, but there are combinations that each prefers. The individual with a cognitive learning style responds to a logical presentation—what changes are planned, how, and why—but might become very frustrated with experiential exercises to create readiness for change.

5. *Environmental uncertainty and complexity.* When the environment is stable and predictable, people are reluctant to change. When it becomes uncertain and confusing, however, people accept change

more readily as they strive to stabilize the situation. If uncertainty and complexity become too great, however, learning can be impeded.

6. *Change is always more difficult than it appears.* The greater the number of people and departments, the more complex and harder to implement the change will be.

7. *Organizational structure.* Organizational structure and corporate culture affect the introduction of new ideas. The structure defines jobs, lines of authority, responsibility, and accountability and controls the flow of information. The strict emphasis on hierarchy or authority in bureaucratic organizations, for example, encourages employees to provide only positive feedback regarding their jobs. Employees generally avoid giving negative feedback that might reflect poorly on them. Thus valuable information that might help an organization identify needed changes or opportunities may never surface. The more bureaucratic the organization, the more filters information must pass through to reach the top.

8. *The distribution of power.* Novel ideas and uses of resources can upset the power relationships in an organization. People may perceive changes as a threat to their power and influence. Power in most organizations is achieved by access to vital information or resources, and the politically astute manager often controls others by manipulating this access. Even when new ideas are in the organization's best interest, they may never be implemented if they threaten the existing power structure. The power of the initiator of change in relation to the power of individuals who are affected by the change will influence the type of strategies that will be effective.

9. *The experience of the change agent.* The amount of time and effort required to introduce changes depends on the knowledge and experience of the change agent. In some instances the change agent may be the expert who orchestrates the change. Under other circumstances, the change agent assumes the role of adviser who directs the efforts of the experts responsible for implementing the change.

10. *The risks involved.* The greater the threat to organizational performance and survival if the situation is not changed, the greater the pressure will be to make changes arbitrarily and quickly. The more people involved in a change effort, the longer the implementation.

11. *Required resources.* The implementation of most changes requires budget dollars and staff resources. Even though an enterprise wants to implement change, plans may have to be compromised, postponed, or scrapped because of insufficient resources. For example, four departments may submit automation proposals for budget approval, but executives may approve funding for only two, or they may approve all four at a level below the estimated costs, forcing cuts in plans.

These are only some of the considerations that may affect the success or failure of technological changes. Clearly, some rationale for understanding the dynamics of change in organizations is needed to develop strategies for implementing changes.

MODELING THE DYNAMICS OF CHANGE

Systems analysts often have difficulty understanding situations that involve change. Anticipating how individuals may react to a new office system, for example, is difficult. Theorists offer various explanations that can help analysts visualize how a proposed system might impact a group of employees and what steps need to be taken to gain their support. This section begins with a systems model for change and then presents two theories proposed by sociologist Kurt Lewin for analyzing the dynamics of change.[4]

A Systems Model of Change

The systems model of change identifies four interacting variables that must be considered when planning change in an organization: people, structure, tasks, and technology.[5] Although this text focuses on technological change, any of the four variables may serve as the primary focus for change efforts.

People Variables

People variables refer to personalities, values, attitudes, skills, performance, and motivations that individuals bring to their jobs. People are an organization's most valuable resource for accomplishing business goals, as well as the major force pressing for or resisting changes. New technologies may affect the number of people and kinds of skills needed to perform the work of the unit, reward systems, working relationships with peers and supervisors, and job satisfaction. Changes may also upset the way individuals meet personal and professional needs. Valued employees may suddenly feel inadequate when skills and experience acquired through years of dependable service are rendered obsolete by new technologies.

Structural Variables

Structural variables refer to the system of responsibility, authority, and communication within an organization. These variables determine how work units are organized, how groups relate to each other, and who reports to whom. Structure also determines how decisions are made, leadership is characterized, and communications are handled. Each organization has its own structure, which reflects its management style, corporate culture, and power relationships. New technology may alter role responsibilities, reporting relationships, span of control, hierarchical levels, and decision making authority. Experience demonstrates, for example, that when electronic mail and message systems are introduced, communication patterns change.

Task Variables

Task variables refer to the actual types of work that are performed in the work unit. Are the tasks simple or complex, repetitive or varied, standardized or unique? Some tasks (such as stuffing envelopes) are highly standardized, simple, and repetitive. Other tasks (such as designing a new mailer envelope) are creative and complex. The way that tasks are combined into jobs determines how independent, interdependent, or dependent relations among departments are in an organization.

Strategies for changing task variables focus on the job performed by the worker. When new technologies are introduced, the nature of tasks usually changes. Thus, in practice, it is difficult to make technological changes without also making task changes that affect job design. Some tasks may be eliminated, new ones added, others modified, and responsibilities shifted. Strategies for redesigning white-collar jobs are discussed in detail in Chapter 17 on "Job Design."

Technological Variables

Technological variables refer to the tools and methods used to accomplish work and solve problems. Of course, the office systems analyst is primarily interested in applying computer technologies for the processing of office work. What office technology should be selected and how should it be used? The technological approach is based on the pioneering work of Frederick Taylor and the scientific management movement. Specialists in work processes and methods, or industrial engineers, are trained in planning and measuring units of production. Traditional systems analysis techniques used to design computer systems have grown out of this approach.

Application of the Systems Model

As illustrated in Figure 18-1, these four variables are highly interdependent; change in one variable impacts one or more others as well. Because technological changes cannot be implemented without affecting one or more of the other variables, decision makers must understand all variables before disturbing any one. The systems model of change provides a framework for understanding these interrelationships. Methods for applying the concepts of the systems model of change to office automation are discussed in more depth in Chapter 17 on "Job Design" and Part 5 on "Planning and Implementing Office Systems."

By being aware of the impact on other variables, the systems analyst can avoid resistance or other problems that could jeopardize the anticipated benefits. The successful implementation of new technology depends on *identifying and planning* needed changes in one or more of the other three variables as part of the project. Indeed, as will be discussed in more detail

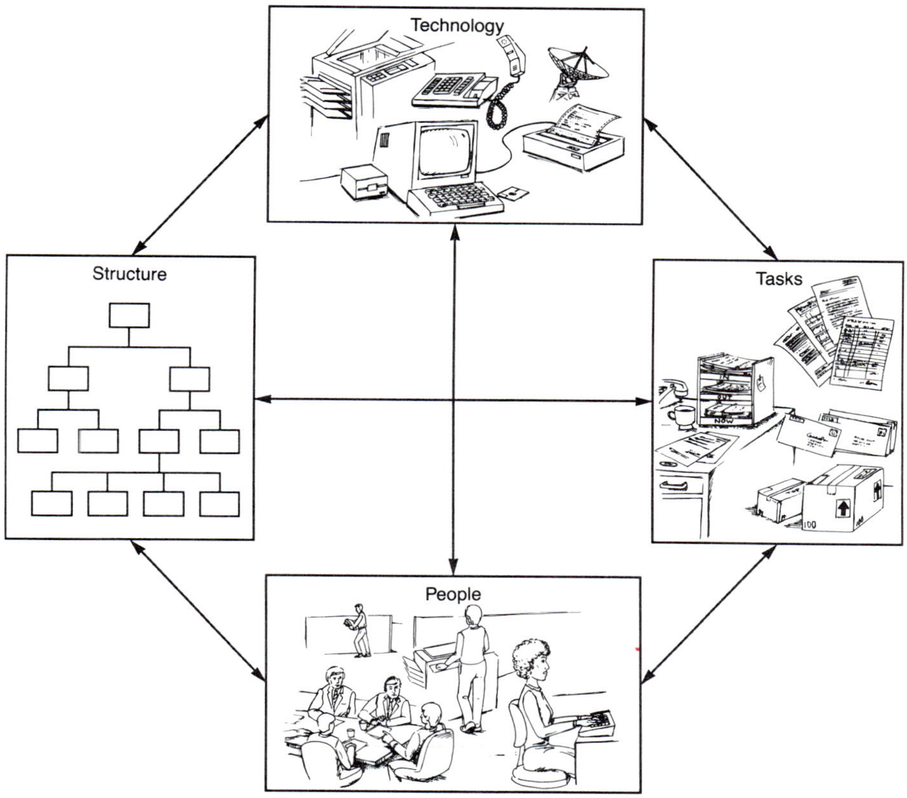

FIGURE 18-1. A systems model of change: The interrelationship of variables.

in Chapter 19, "Strategic Planning for Office Systems," a firm can use technology as a catalyst to increase its own competitive advantage. The four variables of the systems model provide a good framework for examining change alternatives.

Analyzing the Dynamics of Change

Analyzing the dynamics of a planned technological change can become very complex because of the large number of variables. Building on his systems model of change, Kurt Lewin developed one of the most widely applied methods for conceptualizing change. His theories of force field analysis and change stages are a useful framework that systems analysts and managers can use to plan strategies for implementing new technologies.

Force Field Analysis

Lewin envisioned change as a dynamic process, rather than an event, characterized by forces working in opposite directions. The existing situation can be considered a state of equilibrium, resulting from a balance of these forces pushing against each other. According to Lewin, organizations are pressured by various internal and external forces. *Driving forces* encourage change, growth, and development whereas *restraining forces* resist change and encourage stability and the status quo. The framework of the model in Figure 18-2 shows the organization in terms of a field force analysis of the four variables (people, structure, task, and technology) of the systems model of change.

FIGURE 18-2. Force field analysis.

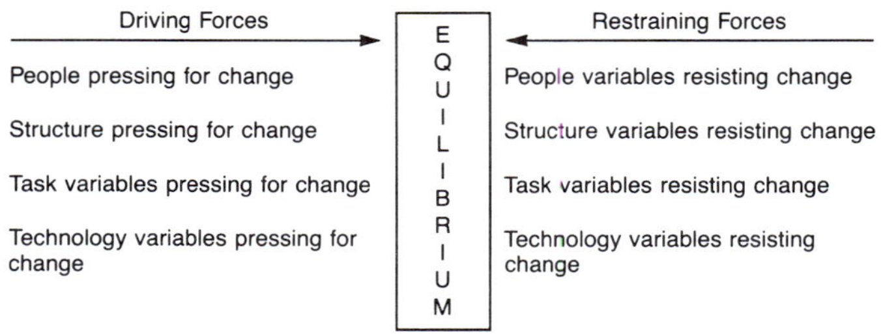

The analyst can use this model to help understand the relevant forces in a planned change. The model may also help analysts identify the factors they can influence and those they cannot. To implement a new office system, the change agent must modify the equilibrium of forces in one of three ways:

- Increase the pressures for change.
- Reduce the pressures resisting change.
- Alter the direction of a force (turn a resistance into a pressure for change).

The natural tendency is to increase the pressures for change. At least initially, however, it is often preferable for action planning to reduce the restraining forces rather than increase the driving forces. Increasing driving forces without decreasing the restraining forces can sometimes stimulate new forces resisting change or create excessive stress—like blowing up a balloon until it pops. In other words, analysts must be sensitive to the pressures for and against change and how they interact. Otherwise, the analyst may encounter unanticipated problems or results when implementing a project, or employees may revert to former practices as soon as driving pressures are relaxed. The most effective way to make technological changes is to identify possible forces of resistance and reduce or eliminate as many as possible. After an action plan has been formulated, the analyst is ready to proceed with implementation.

The Three Phases of Change

Implementing planned organizational changes should be thought of as a learning process through which people modify their behavior. An important part of Lewin's theory suggests a three-step process for guiding and managing change: unfreezing, changing, and refreezing.

1. *Unfreeze phase*. Unfreezing is the process of relaxing people and creating readiness for learning. It involves creating an awareness of the need to change, challenging previous beliefs or practices, removing barriers to change, and emphasizing the benefits of change.
2. *Change phase*. The second phase is the period when learning occurs and attitudes are changed. It involves the search for new information or learning new skills. It moves people toward new behavior patterns. This is the phase where individuals acquire the skills to use new systems, adopt new procedures, and change work flows and working relationships to meet goals.
3. *Refreeze phase*. The refreeze phase consolidates new behaviors after they have been tried and confirmed. The refreezing period ends when new behaviors are integrated into the organizational norms and individuals' routines and work styles.

These phases represent a learning curve similar to the one depicted in Figure 18-3.

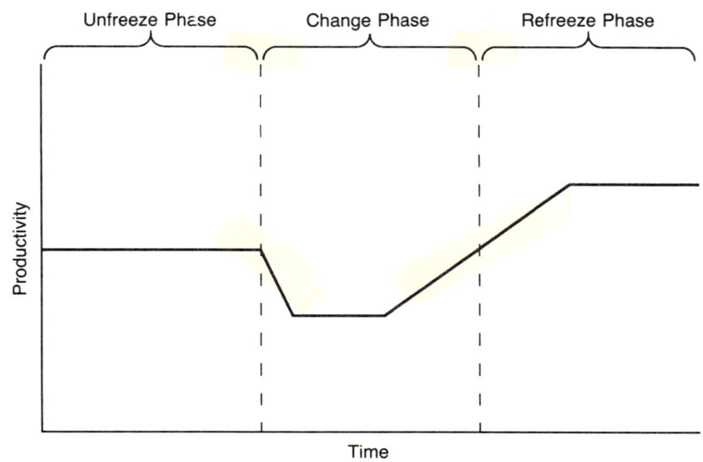

FIGURE 18-3. The learning curve for introducing office technologies.

To illustrate Lewin's three-stage learning model, the reader should consider the process of implementing microcomputers into an accounting department. A force field analysis of an accounting department is shown in Figure 18-4.

1. *Unfreeze phase.* To introduce the project to the accounting staff, the manager discusses the difficulties of meeting monthly and year-end deadlines for filing reports and the amount of overtime required to get the job done. No additional staff positions are approved for the current year, and everyone agrees that working overtime has become a drag. She talks about some ideas for using microcomputers that she has heard from peers at professional meetings and read about in accounting journals. She encourages other staff to share what they have heard or read, pro and con. She summarizes some of the potential benefits to the department from microcomputers, then proposes that the department work with an office systems analyst to identify applications and appropriate hardware and software. She invites the staff's ideas and suggestions during the process.

2. *Change process.* After discussing the project with the manager, the office systems analyst arranges demonstrations of microcomputer applications used in other areas of the company. The analyst explains that the demonstrations are intended to start people thinking about possible applications in their own areas. The analyst works with the department to identify required reports, the major steps in their preparation, where their data comes from, and where they should be sent when completed. Working closely with the manager and staff, he develops work flow diagrams. During the two-month analysis, several staff make suggestions, work groups discuss the ideas and make recommendations, and several suggestions, including one to consolidate two work teams and eliminate some intermediary reports, are included in the final recommendation.

   The project is implemented according to plan. The department starts with six microcomputers; staff attend training classes and then begin to set up the less complicated reports on microcomputers. The manager brings in temporary help to free staff time for learning and applying their new skills. Proposed changes are implemented in phases as staff acquire more skills, ending with the consolidation of the two work teams.

3. *Refreeze phase.* Staff are encouraged to develop their microcomputer skills. Six additional microcomputers and software are purchased. Some suggestions are revised as they are implemented, and one suggestion is scrapped. Several new ideas evolve. At year end, all reports are produced on time, with only 20 percent of the overtime required the previous year.

Pressures for Change →	EXISTING SITUATION	← Resistance to Change
Increased volume of work		People accustomed to old procedures Need to learn new skills Threats to social system
Need to avoid adding staff		Managers fear losing some of their control over information
Vice-president enthusiastic about results in other companies		Managers concerned about security of microcomputer systems
Projected 10–50% time savings for target applications		Jobs must be redesigned to incorporate new tasks; some clerical jobs will be eliminated
		Some old mainframe systems will be made obsolete by new microcomputer systems

FIGURE 18-4. Force field analysis of an accounting department.

DIAGNOSING RESISTANCE TO CHANGE

Before the analyst can develop a plan for implementing a project, it is essential to understand the sources and reasons for resistance to change. Organizations implement changes to become more effective. The individuals affected by the changes, however, often view them from another perspective: how the changes will impact their jobs.

Resistance may manifest itself subtly, as indifference, excuses, complaints about related matters, absenteeism, or tardiness. Often, resistance is more overt, such as reduction in output, outright complaints and objections, resignations or transfers, chronic quarrels, hostility, work slowdowns, or strikes.

The successful change agent needs to recognize these symptoms and determine *why* individuals are resisting. Following is a list of reasons why individuals sometimes resist planned changes. When analysts recognize the legitimate concerns that underlie worker resistance, they can address them directly to build confidence in the project and gain worker support.

Reasons for Resistance to Technological Innovations

Many concerns affect people's attitudes toward change. Some of the most important are discussed briefly in this section.

Social Uncertainty

Often, employees do not resist technological change as much as the social changes that it brings. People need to interact with others at work. When changes disrupt social patterns or isolate employees, employees resist. For example, when one company upgraded clerical workstations with new, ergonomically designed furniture that doubled the workspace and provided privacy and features that almost matched those of professional workers, some clerical employees complained. Space design personnel were dismayed. The nature of the complaints revealed that the clerical employees were accustomed to sitting in clustered work groups, which allowed them to chat as they worked. The chatter broke up the monotony of their routine. The new furniture incorporated high, sound-proof panels that isolated the employees, both physically and visually. The boredom of their tasks soon got on their nerves.

New technologies can disrupt worker relationships with superiors when close working relationships, such as that between a secretary and manager, are altered. Technology might also decrease workers' autonomy. For example, when changes in work procedures require close supervision or training to master new skills, highly proficient workers, who normally require little direct supervision, may react negatively to their loss of independence, even if it is only temporary.

Limited Perspective

Once people develop a mindset, they tend to respond to ideas and suggestions within that framework. They selectively attend to and retain information that reinforces their attitudes and ignore or downplay information that, if perceived, would be incongruent with their perceptions and behavior. For example, managers enrolled in executive training programs may be exposed to various approaches for redesigning jobs to capitalize on computer capabilities. Although they may adeptly discuss such approaches in class, in their minds they may screen out approaches that are inconsistent with their own management styles. They may dismiss such approaches as good ideas for some *other* department but not applicable to their own.

Lack of Understanding

Workers are likely to resist change when they do not understand its purpose. Workers—especially those on the lower levels of the organization, who are least involved in planning changes—often do not receive the details of the project, why changes are necessary, and what the objectives are. Worse yet, they may receive much of the detail through rumors, which tend to distort facts. Under these circumstances, it is likely that distrust will build up. This distrust, sometimes labeled "fear of automation," can be avoided if users are meaningfully involved, if rumors are settled early, if training is provided throughout the project (not simply tacked on at the end), and if credibility is built by designers.

Threats to Power and Influence

When individuals perceive that new technologies or procedures may reduce their power or influence, they are likely to resist their implementation. When new office information systems improve access to information, individuals who formerly served in "gatekeeper" roles may resist the perceived loss in power and influence.

Resistance to Technical Personnel

Most technical specialists are outsiders as far as the organization is concerned. Specialists may have certain blind spots and faulty attitudes because of preoccupation with the technical aspects of new ideas. Change agents must demonstrate that theirs is a service (helping) role, rather than purely technical. If the change agent builds credibility, it becomes possible to work cooperatively to achieve mutually agreed-upon goals and resolve problems.

Users Consider Costs to Outweigh Benefits

Employees will accept change more readily when benefits clearly offset the costs of change. In the eyes of users, costs are measured not only in dollars but also in terms of the time and effort required to learn new systems, the pressures of initial loss in productivity, frustrations in working out the glitches of a new system, and many other concerns discussed in this section. Cost savings and productivity increases are benefits to *management*, but what are the benefits to the employees? Will they receive a raise? Recognition? Grade-level increase? Increased responsibility? Better opportunity for advancement? Improved working environment?

Fear of Failure or Inadequacy

Workers frequently have spent years developing the skills that make them proficient. When new systems threaten to make these skills obsolete, they are likely to resist. Rather than welcome the opportunity to learn new skills, they may fear that they will be unable to cope. Suddenly, the skills that have provided job security are no longer sufficient. Instead, workers are faced with the need to learn new procedures and methods and establish new working relationships.

Moreover, many workers find computers intimidating. Until recently these "magical" machines have been protected behind the locked doors of computer centers and attended by technical wizards. If workers are suddenly confronted with computers on their desktops and their job depends on using them, they may wonder if they are capable of learning them, or fear they will break them if they push the wrong button. Many people are far behind technology and feel inadequate when faced with simple technologies, let alone a computer. From the perspective of the intimidated worker, the computer creates problems rather than solving them.

Loss of Control

Many people perceive computers as devices that control their behavior rather than as machines that *they* control. Thus computers are seen as a threat to their autonomy. The idea of "big brother watching" can give workers a sense of powerlessness, so that they sometimes develop pathological symptoms, such as anxiety, depression, or even violence.

Feelings of Insecurity

Most people become anxious when faced with a new situation, whether the change is seen as good or bad. Anxiety stems from unknown factors that may require new responses. Rules, policies, and procedures frequently become habits, and people rely on them for both guidance and protection. These habits provide a feeling of security. Habits also promote productivity when they allow workers to attend to routine chores without having to think about them or make decisions about what or how to do things. Change frequently disrupts the security of work habits.

Threat of Economic Loss

Any change that threatens to eliminate jobs or decrease work hours usually meets with resistance. Even promises to provide retraining may not reduce the concern. Changes that affect career ladders and promotional opportunities may likewise meet resistance.

In Figure 18-5, the various forces creating pressures for and against technological change in the office are depicted within the framework of Lewin's force field analysis model.

FIGURE 18-5. Forces creating pressures for and resistance to technological change in the office.

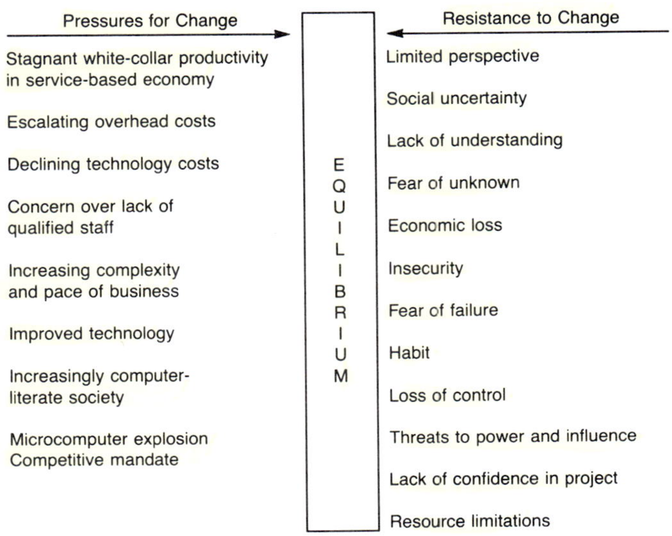

OVERCOMING RESISTANCE TO CHANGE

With potential resistance to planned changes identified, the change agent can plan appropriate strategies to reduce or avoid resistance. The key variable is the *people* involved. Individuals react differently to change. Determining which strategy or combination of strategies is most appropriate depends on the type of change, the time involved, situational factors, type of resistance anticipated, and sources of resistance. The strategies that change agents select for implementing changes also may depend somewhat on their management styles. The following six strategies can be used to overcome resistance to change:[6]

Education and Communication

Employees should be informed about changes before they are introduced. Education can help reduce resistance by helping people understand the need for and the logic of a change. Education can involve one-to-one discussions, presentations to groups, and memos or reports. Video tapes or broadcast voice mail messages can also be effective. Education and communication are especially appropriate when resistance is based on inadequate or inaccurate information. It is especially important for employees to be well-informed when their help is needed to implement changes. An effective educational program requires time and effort. If the change agent and resisters do not have a good working relationship, it is unlikely that resisters will believe what they hear.

When new skills must be learned, adequate training and support are important. Education should start early and continue throughout a project. Implementers should not tack education on at the end of the project.

Participation and Involvement

When people are involved in designing and implementing changes, they are more likely to feel committed to making the changes work. Participation can generate new ideas and alternatives not considered by designers. Participation has its limitations, however. If the process is not carefully managed, employees may feel resentful when all their ideas cannot be implemented. Participation does not lend itself to problems that require quick solutions.

Facilitation and Support

Managers or change agents can help reduce resistance by being supportive. They can listen to concerns, provide emotional support, give employees time off after a demanding period, and provide training in new skills. Facilitation and support are especially helpful for overcoming fear and anxiety. It is all too easy for managers to overlook these causes of resistance or dismiss them as silly or irrelevant.

Negotiation and Agreement

Another way to reduce resistance may be incentives to employees for compliance with the change. For example, management might give employees higher wage rates in return for work procedure changes. Negotiation is especially appropriate when it is clear that one group is going to lose out because of a change. Negotiations are usually required when new technologies create changes in work procedures for union workers.

Manipulation and Cooptation

In some cases, especially if changes are urgent or other methods have not worked, change agents may resort to manipulation or cooptation. They may selectively control who gets information, present only information that is favorable to a change, or create a false sense of urgency. Another technique is giving an individual a favorable role in design and implementation to gain their influence (cooptation). Of course, managers or change agents risk their credibility when they resort to manipulating people.

Explicit and Implicit Coercion

Finally, if managers have sufficient power, they may resort to forcing people to accept change by threatening them with discharge, poor promotional opportunities, or transfers. Coercion is risky because people resent forced change. Moreover, as soon as coercive pressures are decreased, individuals will likely revert to their former methods or behaviors. If changes must be made quickly, however, in some cases a manager may have little choice but to use coercion. In addition, if changes are going to be very unpopular regardless of how they are implemented, an arbitrary decision may be appropriate.

Each of these six strategies for overcoming resistance to change may be especially effective or ineffective in particular situations. The advantages and drawbacks of each strategy in various situations are summarized in Figure 18-6.

MANAGING THE CHANGE PROCESS

People are vital to the success of office automation projects. Poorly conceived projects that have the support of staff can succeed. By the same token, well-conceived projects that are resisted by employees can fail. People can sabotage a project even while seeming to cooperate. The following sections discuss several important considerations for managing the human dimensions of the change process.

Participation

Participation is frequently recommended as the solution for overcoming resistance to change. In reality, however, participation is not always practical, and pseudoparticipation can lead to more problems. It is important to avoid pseudoparticipation as a guise for true problem solving. To be effective, participation must address specific concerns or causes of resistance, and management must be prepared to accept and implement solutions arrived at by participants.

Participation is more than the mechanical act of asking one's opinions or taking part in discussions. It is a feeling that people's opinions are respected because the people themselves are respected. In general, it is advisable to involve managers and employees in planning and implementation. Change agents should also encourage open, two-way communication.

Incentives

Change agents can provide incentives that encourage individuals to use new systems. An incentive could be a measurement and reward system to encourage change. Measurement incentives, however, must be imple-

Approach	Commonly used in situations	Advantages	Drawbacks
Education + communication	Where there is a lack of information or inaccurate information and analysis.	Once persuaded, people will often help with the implementation of the change.	Can be very time-consuming if lots of people are involved.
Participation + involvement	Where the initiators do not have all the information they need to design the change, and where others have considerable power to resist.	People who participate will be committed to implementing change, and any relevant information they have will be integrated into the change plan.	Can be very time-consuming if participators design an inappropriate change.
Facilitation + support	Where people are resisting because of adjustment problems.	No other approach works as well with adjustment problems.	Can be time-consuming, expensive, and still fail.
Negotiation + agreement	Where someone or some group will clearly lose out in a change, and where that group has considerable power to resist.	Sometimes it is a relatively easy way to avoid major resistance.	Can be too expensive in many cases if it alerts others to negotiate for compliance.
Manipulation + co-optation	Where other tactics will not work or are too expensive.	It can be a relatively quick and inexpensive solution to resistance problems.	Can lead to future problems if people feel manipulated.
Explicit + implicit coercion	Where speed is essential, and the change initiators possess considerable power.	It is speedy and can overcome any kind of resistance.	Can be risky if it leaves people mad at the initiators.

FIGURE 18-6. Methods for overcoming resistance to change.

mented with caution. It is important to avoid creating undue pressure or making people feel that they are constantly under electronic surveillance. Measurement systems that enable employees to monitor their own progress can be effective.

Peer leaders can be allies for implementing change. Work-group leaders who demonstrate a capacity to handle change, are adept at learning the technology, and are enthusiastic about the project can be identified. However, peer leaders can be obstacles if they selfishly guard their new-found skills or have little patience for teaching others.

Mastery of technology should be a criterion for advancement. It should be included in the formal evaluations to ensure that employee efforts are recognized and rewarded.

Gaining Management Support

Management support is critical to the acceptance of change. Managers must convey their support through actions as well as words. Subordinates can read between the lines if support is limited to verbal approval rather than changed expectations, actions, and recognition from managers. Many managers underestimate not only the variety of ways people react to change but also the ways they can influence individuals and groups during change. Executives can be effective at staff meetings where change is discussed by shifting attention from schedules, technical details, work assignments, and so forth and focusing on resistance and receptiveness to change.

Evaluating Change

The most difficult step in the change process is evaluating results. Because change is complex and comprehensive, it is difficult to isolate specific causes and effects. When changes take place over a period of time, other events might also influence results. Moreover, the process of collecting information about results can bias the findings. Some of the difficulties of measuring results of technological change were discussed in Chapter 15, "Measuring Productivity."

Evaluation is an important element of the refreezing phase of change. It provides information about the costs and benefits of a change, and it offers opportunities to make modifications over time. Evaluation provides valuable feedback for making adjustments in the systems, methods, work flow, or intervention strategies. Neglecting evaluation (the refreezing phase) can result in changes that are abandoned or incompletely implemented. It is very important, therefore, to have ways of verifying that changes have accomplished the intended results.

SUMMARY

The introduction of new technologies always brings change, and organizational change is a learning process that must be managed. Thus the implementer of office technologies must function as a change agent.

Some of the variables that affect change include the ability of employees to conceptualize change, readiness for change, individual differences, environmental uncertainty and complexity, the number of people involved, the formal structure, distribution of power, knowledge related to change, and the stakes involved.

The systems model of change and Lewin's force field analysis theory can help systems analysts understand the forces that affect change in an organization. To be successful, systems analysts must employ strategies to create readiness for change (unfreezing); implement the needed modifications in tasks, structure, people, and technology (changing); and provide reinforcement, support, and modifications as necessary to sustain the momentum of change (refreezing). Improper refreezing results in changes that are abandoned or incompletely implemented.

Resistance is a frequent by-product of change and may be indicative of problems with the change itself, the change strategy, or the implementation procedures used by the change agent. Sources of resistance are often related more to social issues or the methods of implementing changes than to technical aspects of the change. Sources of resistance include social uncertainty, lack of understanding, resistance to technical personnel, lack of confidence in the project, fear of failure, loss of control, feelings of insecurity, fear of the unknown, or economic reasons.

Change agents commonly employ a number of strategies to avoid or reduce resistance, depending on its source. Strategies include education, participation, facilitation, negotiation, manipulation, and, as a last resort, coercion.

By effectively managing the change process, the office systems analyst can avoid unforeseen problems or consequences when new computer systems are introduced and can help ensure that technology is used efficiently and effectively.

DISCUSSION QUESTIONS

1. Why is the office systems analyst a change agent?
2. "The more things change, the more they stay the same." Discuss this statement in light of the information in this chapter.
3. What differentiates successful from unsuccessful changes? What advice would you offer an office systems analyst in planning for organizational change?
4. Describe the three phases of Lewin's change process. Give an example of this process.
5. List barriers to successful change, then discuss why it is important for an analyst to be aware of these barriers before beginning a systems implementation.
6. Assume your university is implementing a voice-mail system. Design a plan for implementing this technology.

APPLICATION EXERCISES

1. Read case studies of successful implementation in journals such as *The Office Systems Research Journal* and trade magazines such as *Datamation, Modern Office Technology,* and *Information Center.* Using Lewin's theory, explain how each system was implemented (unfreeze, change, refreeze).
2. Interview an office systems analyst or consultant for examples of two successful and two unsuccessful (or less successful) office automation implementations. Identify factors that led to successful or less-than-successful implementation.

SUGGESTED READINGS

Fallik, Fred. *Managing Organizational Change: Human Factors and Automation* (Philadelphia: Taylor and Francis, 1988).

Kanter, Rosabeth Moss. *The Change Masters* (New York: Simon and Schuster, 1983).

Lawrence, Paul R. "How to Deal With Resistance to Change," *Harvard Business Review* (January-February 1969).

Schrank, Robert (ed.). *Industrial Democracy at Sea* (Cambridge, Mass.: Massachusetts Institute of Technology Press, 1983).

PLANNING AND IMPLEMENTING OFFICE SYSTEMS

PART 5

As explained in Part 4, a major purpose of office automation is to improve office effectiveness. Part 5 discusses concepts, methodologies, and tools an office systems analyst might employ in assessing how work is currently accomplished, designing new systems to improve the work process, implementing new systems, and then determining if the systems are operating as intended. An umbrella term for the application of systems concepts to the study of office operations is office systems analysis.

Chapter 19, "Strategic Planning for Office Systems," gives an overview of the impact office automation is having on the way organizations and their employees—at all levels—conduct business. Technology is viewed as a catalyst for innovation and productivity improvement. The emerging business strategy of using technology to gain a competitive advantage is introduced. Consideration is given to how organizations foster innovative use of technology. The chapter includes guidelines for developing strategic plans for office systems technologies.

Chapter 20, "Office Systems Analysis: Frameworks," begins with an overview of systems theory, then applies that theory to conceptual approaches and frameworks applicable to studying office activities. This chapter provides a frame of reference for subsequent chapters.

Chapter 21, "Office Systems Analysis: Assessment and Design," offers a perspective on the first two stages of office systems analysis, then discusses "how to's"—how to research, report, and evaluate current systems with an eye to developing new systems.

Chapter 22, "Office Systems Analysis: Implementation and Evaluation," reviews specific implementation strategies. Implementation must be a carefully managed process that addresses all aspects of putting a system into operation: site preparation, equipment installation, conversion of procedures, training, technical support, and problem resolution. To be successful, a system must be used: how the new technology is introduced into the office is often the major reason for ready acceptance or early rejection. Evaluation is the final step in systems analysis: How effective is the new system? Techniques appropriate for evaluating the effectiveness of office systems are discussed.

Chapter 23, "Implementation: Management Issues," addresses the management of computers in the work place from the business perspective. The spread of computing from technical data centers to office desktops has introduced many new opportunities and issues for business managers. Chapter 23 addresses pressing management issues: establishing policies for office automation and end-user computing, identifying and automating high-value applications, controlling access to information, protecting the integrity and confidentiality of data, addressing legal issues, and others.

Chapter 24, "Implementation: Human Resource Requirements," addresses important issues of managing people in the automated workplace. The more productive coordination and accomplishment of work made possible by information technology can potentially improve every aspect of business performance. An environment of change demands the continual development of employees. Training and supporting a white-collar work force in the use of computers are pressing needs in today's business office. Labor-management relations must be addressed. Learning to learn in an environment of change and ambiguity demands new skills. The training function must be prepared to adapt quickly to changing opportunities and requirements.

STRATEGIC PLANNING FOR OFFICE SYSTEMS

CHAPTER

19

In 1513, Niccolo Machiavelli made the following observations about the difficulties involved in creating any new system:

> There is nothing more difficult to plan, more doubtful of success, nor more dangerous to manage than the creation of a new system. For the initiator has the enmity of all who would profit by the preservation of the old institutions and merely lukewarm defenders in those who would gain by the new ones. The hesitation of the latter arises in part...from the general skepticism of mankind, which does not really believe in an innovation until experience proves its value.[1]

OBJECTIVES

After completing this chapter, the reader should be able to meet the following objectives:

- Understand the relationships between technology and innovation.
- Discuss the use of technology to deliver products and services.
- Give examples of how industries have used technology to gain a competitive advantage.
- Identify organizational characteristics that foster innovation.
- Explain the role of office automation in corporate strategic planning.
- List the benefits from adequate planning.
- List reasons why organizations fail to plan adequately for automation in the business office.
- List possible consequences of inadequate planning.

KEY TERMS

catalyst
competitive weapon
innovation
mission statement
policies
programs
procedures
strategic planning
synergy

INTRODUCTION

Innovation is a two-edged sword; it is both applauded and feared. While organizations acknowledge the value of new ideas, corporate cultures (in actuality) seldom foster and reward innovation. New technologies, like new ideas, bring both threats and opportunities. Office automation offers new opportunities for improving the way organizations and their employees—at all levels—perform work and provide products and services. It also poses threats to the status quo and the quality of work life. To take advantage of the opportunities and avoid the pitfalls, decision makers must carefully integrate technology with business operations and goals. Capitalizing on new opportunities requires foresight, careful planning, and good management.

The purpose of this chapter is to help the reader understand how office automation fits into the overall goals of an organization. After a discussion that defines innovation, the chapter offers two models that describe how technology is assimilated in organizations. If technology is used for predefined tasks only, creativity and potential opportunities are lost. Technology is not only a means of improving internal operations, but also a means of increasing competitive advantage. The chapter concludes with an overview of how to plan for office systems.

In reading this chapter, the reader should keep in mind that innovation theory borrows from ideas discussed in previous chapters regarding change and productivity. These ideas are only reviewed here. The reader should read this chapter with a view to seeing how the need for productivity and change affect innovation and creativity.

OFFICE AUTOMATION BRINGS BOTH THREATS AND OPPORTUNITIES

The opportunities afforded by office automation are a recurrent theme throughout this text. The following quote aptly summarizes the perspective of office automation proponents:

> The single most important development in the work of information technology over the past ten years is the progress of technological capabilities in the office. . . . [Office technologies are a] catalyst of change which is beginning to revolutionize the managing of corporate operations. The big investment remains in large central computers, but the *real opportunity* for differential performance improvement rests with machines in the workplace and the new capabilities they offer.[2]

Not all impacts of technology have been beneficial, however. Poorly planned applications of office technologies have produced some of the following *undesirable* results:

- Factory or assembly line approach to office work.
- Routine, boring jobs.
- Displacement of people.
- Reduced autonomy for employees.

- Tasks structured to the lowest level of human ability.
- Output volume as the only performance variable over which individual workers have control.
- Excessive monitoring of work.
- Social isolation or lack of social support in the work place.
- New problems as employees attempt to gain some control over their work environment (such as union representation).
- Poorly designed work areas, resulting in discomfort or health hazards.
- Stressful work environments.
- Low job satisfaction, high absenteeism and turnover.

These undesirable consequences of office automation often result when decision makers ignore the potential impact of newly designed systems on individual workers and the organization. Negative consequences also may result from inexperience with the technology, inadequate planning, lack of foresight, excessive focus on short-term benefits, or management practices insensitive to employee welfare. Whatever the reason, planners and analysts should not overlook the personal and organizational impact of new systems. In the long term, ignoring these issues not only lowers the quality of work life, but productivity as well.

Moreover, economists have challenged the belief that computers improve productivity. According to one estimate, white-collar productivity stands just about where it was in the late 1960s. Office computers are often used inefficiently or sit unused much of the time. For example, one study of office automation in an organization of slightly over 100 people revealed that although the system appeared highly used at 88 percent capacity, most of the 60 terminals were merely logged on to the main menu. On balance, only 28 percent of the capacity of the system was used at any time for any function during the two-day evaluation.[3]

These negative results cast a shadow over office automation and raise important questions for analysts and decision makers:

- What factors make the difference between successful and unsuccessful implementations of office automation?
- Why do some companies achieve substantial productivity gains while others do not?
- Why does much of the computer capability often go unused?

Researchers and practitioners find three recurring themes in the success stories:[4]

1. Work is done differently from the way it was done in precomputer days.
2. Achieving results takes time.
3. Getting results requires a leader, an *innovator*.

These findings suggest that office automation technology in itself is not sufficient: it *must* be coupled with innovative changes in the way work is done, and these changes go far beyond the task level. Innovations such as these are difficult to achieve, as reflected by the quotation at the beginning of this chapter. Few prescriptions for success are available. The office systems analyst can start by looking more closely at the process by which organizations assimilate technology.

THE INFUSION OF TECHNOLOGY: DESCRIPTIVE MODELS

To apply technology innovatively, one must understand how it is assimilated into the work environment. This section presents two models describing its infusion in organizations. These models provide a useful framework for the practitioner by clarifying interrelationships among people, tasks, and technology.

OTA Model of Technology Infusion

At the request of the U.S. Senate Committee on Labor and Human Resources and the House Committee on Education and Labor, the U.S. Office of Technology Assessment (OTA) studied the consequences of the rapid growth in the use of information and communication technologies in offices. In conducting this study, OTA used a simple conceptual model that was developed by Joseph T. Coates. Depicted in Figure 19-1, the model

FIGURE 19-1. The OTA model of technological change.

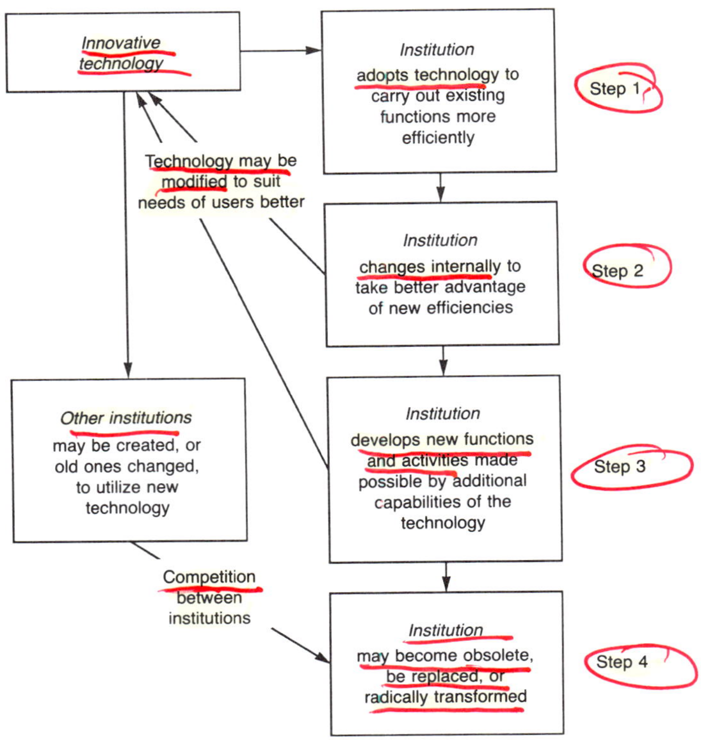

provides a useful conceptualization of the process organizations use to adopt and apply new technologies.[5]

According to the OTA study, when organizations adopt new technology, three kinds of effects are likely, including *substitution, adaptation,* and *transformation.*

Substitution

Initially, there are direct substitution effects at both the task and organizational levels. New technology replaces an older technology or human labor, or both. Word processors and computers replace the typewriter, bookkeeping ledgers, and payroll systems. Other communication systems augment telephones. These changes have effects on productivity, size of work force, job content, workers' skills, and other variables. These effects are perceived as good or bad depending on one's perspective and interests.

When technology is seen as substitution, institutional structures, culture, operating procedures, and management expectations still reflect the old workflow and work process. Tension may result because the characteristics of the new technology and/or the requirements for its use are different than what existed before the new technology was implemented. Until this tension is resolved, the full benefits of the substitution are not realized, and productivity may even fall. Many organizations see technology as a new way of doing the same things.

Adaptation

Gradually, the institution, deliberately or unconsciously, by plan or by trial and error, begins to adapt to new ways of doing things. This stage may include, for example, formal reorganizations, shifts in power relationships, adjustments in responsibilities, or changes in the way workers are recruited and compensated. Two kinds of problems, however, may arise in this stage. If significant changes are made quickly and arbitrarily, they may meet resistance from those who lose power or are uncomfortable with changes in the status quo—especially when people do not understand the reasons for the changes or have not participated in the decisions. On the other hand, if adaptations are not planned, those affected may undergo a long period of frustration and inefficiency before they discover what changes are necessary.

Transformations

The third kind of effects, transformations, is possible because new technologies have entirely new capabilities that the organization may use to develop new activities, products, or services. For example, computers offer not only a more efficient way to do mass mailings but also to target mailings to special customers and track the results. Thus new, potentially more effective activities replace the old.

Some enterprises, as soon as they computerized, began to offer new services. This round of effects may bring about the restructuring of an industry or a mix of industries. Financial services, for example, used new information systems to overcome legal boundaries between banks, insurance companies, brokers, and other elements of the industry.

Organizations that fail to adopt new technology, even when it becomes the norm among competitors, risk eventual obsolescence and failure. For example, mail order businesses that have not automated customer services are in serious trouble.

The feedback loop in OTA's Model of Technological Change is important. Ongoing development of technology is shaped by the market and the demands of users. New businesses emerge that specialize in innovative use of the technology or in helping other firms use it.

Day's Five Stages of Office System Evolution

A second model, developed by L. H. Day of the Diebold Office Automation Group, provides a somewhat different perspective on the assimilation of office automation. Day's Five Stages of Office Systems Evolution focus on how an organization moves from isolated tools to integrated systems. Like the OTA Model of Technological Change, Day's model characterizes the assimilation as an evolutionary process:[6]

1. *Conception.* Individual tools, like word processing, facsimile, or distributed data processing, are judged to be inadequate. There is recognition of the need to support knowledge workers directly with integrated tools.
2. *Initiation.* Planners look beyond cost displacement applications and implement the first value-added office systems pilot. Studies are initiated and requirements for a pilot determined. Implementation begins.
3. *Contagion.* Integrated office system pilots are implemented (and evaluated) to improve the work of professional, multifunction clerical, managerial, and executive personnel.
4. *Consolidation.* Full operational systems are implemented to consolidate many developments in the contagion stage.
5. *Creative evolution.* Integrated systems are developed that are inherent in the plans to improve services, meet objectives, expand markets, and revise the mission of the organization.

Notice that the emphasis shifts in several ways in the progression through Day's stages:

1. From using new technologies as a replacement for old technologies or people to using new technologies for changing the way work is done.
2. From isolated applications to integrated systems.

3. From an emphasis on clerical applications to an emphasis on managers and knowledge workers.
4. From a focus on individual tasks to a focus on the objectives and mission of the organization.

Understanding this pattern can help the OA planner to determine where the organization currently is and what action plans need to be put in place to move the organization forward.

USING TECHNOLOGY: OPPORTUNITY

Progression through the stages of technological innovation is not automatic. Many organizations are still in the substitution or conception/initiation stages of technological development, merely substituting new technologies for old. Progression beyond that point can be a painful learning process. Organizations may need to adapt their internal structures in ways that encourage employees to change the way they work. Work procedures and standards may need to be changed, patterns in the flow of work altered, reporting relationships changed, jobs redesigned, and performance criteria revised. Executives may need to make changes in the organization's culture: its business philosophy, management style, and departmental relationships. Changes of this magnitude are easy to talk about but very difficult to accomplish. They are rare in large institutions. As discussed in Chapter 18, changing the behaviors of hundreds or thousands of people is complex, slow, and usually requires the intervention techniques of outside consultants.

Although some pioneers in office systems and end-user computing recount stories of the spontaneous creation of innovative applications, there are as many tales of equipment collecting dust. Analysts would be short-sighted indeed to assume that plugging in the right equipment is sufficient. That is precisely what happens in most organizations, however. Typically, analysts assess the business needs, recommend an equipment configuration, and, if the project is approved, install the system, arrange initial training, and then walk away.

Department managers are often mystified when new equipment is not used as anticipated. After all, the systems analyst identified a long list of appropriate applications, and staff members attended classes. A flurry of excitement followed the first few applications. Months later, however, everything seems to have reverted to business as usual. Where does the department manager turn for help?

Placing a computer on an employee's desktop does *not* automatically lead to improvements and innovations. Employees who embrace the technology and quickly fly on their own are the exception rather than the rule. Note that in the office automation models, contagion or transformation are later stages in the evolutionary process. Prior to reaching these stages, the organization went through a learning period. To use technology creatively, individuals must reach a "critical mass" of know-how and experience. Without appropriate training, support, and guidance, this critical mass may never be achieved amid the pressures of everyday work. Until individuals understand the potential opportunities and benefits, they have little incentive to expend the time and effort required to learn the technology. Moreover, these efforts must be supported by an environment that fosters initiative and rewards innovation. Otherwise, the efforts of even the most innovative employees can be easily thwarted.

Innovative use of technology must be nurtured and managed. Skilled office systems analysts must be innovators who can provide leadership through the stages of technological development. To succeed, analysts must understand how technology can contribute to improving operations and meeting business goals.

The study of office automation disuse cited earlier revealed that "overshadowing all of the specific complaints from staff members was a sense of a lack of direction and commitment to the development of the system as an integral part of the company. The perceptions varied about the purpose of the system and the goals governing its use."[7] Apparently, technology often focuses too much attention on itself and not enough on how it is supposed to improve a unit's ability to accomplish its mission. New technologies can actually *increase* the level of effort required to get a task done and divert concentration from the task itself. People use technology only when they view it as essential to carrying out their main responsibilities or goals.

An office systems team must bring together the technical resources, business expertise, and management decision making essential for innovative application of technology. This implies not only that systems analysts must work closely with decision makers, but that executives must become more knowledgeable about technology. To recognize new opportunities, executives do not necessarily have to know how the technology works. They need to understand, however, how to use it. Executives must focus on using office technologies strategically to meet two corporate business goals:

1. To improve productivity by
   - streamlining information processing, improving accuracy and timeliness, and eliminating unnecessary duplication of effort;
   - contributing to more effective use of information, enabling decision makers to put their finger on *the right information at the right time;* and
   - adapting technology to people so that it increases the effort focused on business goals and reduces the effort required for supplementary chores.

2. To gain competitive advantage by
   - creating innovative products and services and
   - creating new delivery systems in the marketplace.

Strategies for improving productivity and gaining competitive advantage are discussed in the next two sections.

Technology as a Catalyst for Improving Productivity

The ultimate image of the office of the future may still be hazy, but the trends are clear. The most significant productivity improvements have been achieved by using technology to change the way people work. Successful companies are adopting innovative work practices that get the most out of technology:

> It is becoming evident that advanced computer technology calls for radical change in traditional practices. New technologies are being used as a catalyst to institute major changes in the way jobs are designed and organizations are managed....The old idea that a manager's main function is to control workers is replaced with the concept that a manager should encourage employees to use initiative.[8]

Because productivity increases do not result just from the speed of computer processing, the pertinent questions become: How can the office systems analyst facilitate innovation and shorten the learning curve? What are some of the successful techniques used by innovators? What kinds of work changes need to be made?

Replacing Old Procedures

For systems to become productive, automated procedures must *replace* manual procedures, not continue them. Old procedures must be eliminated when new ones have been learned. In practice, replacing the old with the new is not as simple as it may appear. For example, employees who are not yet confident of their computer abilities may cling to old, manual procedures to verify computer output or as a back-up "just in case" something goes wrong with the computer. Employees may receive inadequate training, or resist the intrusion from outside, or may have insufficient motivation to change ingrained habits and practices.

Eliminating Work

Whenever possible, work procedures should be scrutinized *before* they are automated. Usually this means looking at the overall workflow in an organizational unit instead of just individual tasks. Analysts should look for opportunities to simplify or eliminate work. This is a departure from the typical approach of identifying applications and recommending hardware and software based on existing tasks.

Japan's experience with high-technology robots illustrates the dilemma. In retrospect, the Japanese discovered that in some cases they had programmed the inefficiencies of former technologies into their robots. They overlooked opportunities to streamline old procedures before automating them. For example, a different assembly sequence might be called for, or a robot might be able to perform two or three tasks simultaneously that would need to be done one at a time if they were performed manually.

Synergy between Technology and People

Many of the most innovative improvements result from the synergy of linking people skills and technology. Analysts should devote as much time to analyzing the tasks and procedures that are to be performed by people as they do to the tasks and procedures to be automated. All too often jobs are created by default, rather than by design, when new technologies are brought into the workplace. People need to be part of the design, not tangential to it. The ultimate objective should be a synergistic relationship between people and technology that will attract capable employees and encourage them to achieve their fullest potential and process information in the most efficient and cost-effective manner.

Task Combination

With the aid of technology, one individual may be able to handle a job from start to finish that formerly had been broken down into several steps performed by different people. Such task combination can reduce duplication of effort and improve coordination. For example, Monsanto redesigned previously separate jobs into *vendor account representative* positions, giving employees responsibility for all ordering and servicing for a specific group of customers. Many tasks in transferring work from one department to another and checking work in between departments were eliminated. Most importantly, the vendor account representatives took pride in servicing *their* customers. (Redesigning jobs and workflow was discussed in detail in Chapter 17, "Job Design.")

Changing Office Roles

Analysts should not limit solutions to those that fit existing job roles. For example, professional and managerial use of word processing requires changes in clerical roles. With decreased time spent on word processing, secretaries can do a wider variety of tasks. These changes will alter jobs and career ladders in many ways. According to Carolyn J. Mullins, "Secretaries and word processing operators are finding that their traditional services are less in demand, but that their job opportunities are broadening as their skills grow."[9] In several instances, organizations have found it more efficient to expand the responsibility of clerical employees in customer service and upgrade their jobs to paraprofessional levels.

Integrating Functions

Some opportunities, especially those associated with networking, require that organizations integrate functions typically managed as separate entities. For example, forms management on the computer crosses traditional lines that separated word processing, forms design, graphic services, and records management. In her book *The Change Masters,* Rosabeth Moss Kanter refers to segmentation as *the great inhibitor of creativity.* She points out that in a segmented organization, units work in isolation. Little lateral communication occurs, relationships are restrictive, and members are indifferent to the efforts and achievements of other units. Innovative organizations can seize the opportunities afforded by computer technologies to integrate functions, thus reducing the limitations of excessive segmentation and opening the door to more creative efforts.

Making Systems Analysis More Innovative

The high level of structure characteristic of traditional systems analysis does not lend itself to creativity and innovation. Structured analysis is unduly restrictive, especially with respect to the definition of problems and conceptualization of solutions. Systems analysis methodology emphasizes technically correct systems rather than usefulness of systems. Systems analysts must be encouraged to develop innovative systems, the result of analyzing a large number of alternatives.

Moreover, systems analysts generally rely on the user to explain how work is accomplished. These analysts seldom have the insight needed, because of limited business experience, to suggest new procedures. Conversely, users' inexperience with the technology limits their ability to envision how the technology can help solve problems rather than automate them. What is needed is an analyst with both perspectives. These emerging roles for office systems or business analysts are vital to the innovative application of computer technologies in the office.

Translating Problems into Opportunities

The way a problem is defined determines, to a great extent, the alternative solutions. For example, if the problem of a clerical operation is defined as escalating costs, the solutions usually focus on ways to reduce costs by using automation to eliminate jobs. If the problem were redefined as lagging revenue, the new definition suggests considerations for additional revenue to offset rising costs. Alternatives may call for investing additional dollars to help service personnel better support marketing operations.

For example, a major life and health insurer was alarmed at the escalating costs of policyholder services. Services were provided by administrative departments in each of the company's independent agencies throughout the United States. The original task force identified the problem as excessive cost and recommended reducing operating costs by consolidating service in regional units or centralizing it at company headquarters. When results of the pilot test of regional service units were reviewed, executives recognized that they were missing opportunities.

They had focused on cost reduction at the expense of quality service. The problem was redefined, and the new objectives called for more personal, responsive service in concert with the company's marketing strategies. To accomplish that objective, the company formulated a strategy to use office automation in ways that would improve service and reduce paperwork.

The ultimate solution turned a problem into an opportunity by changing the job focus from paperwork processing to customer service. The company invested $10 million to ergonomically redesign offices, put a microcomputer (connected to mainframe insurance systems) on every desk, and restructure procedures, workflows, and employees' jobs. The *payback* was achieved in the long term by avoiding staff additions as the workload increased, attracting better-qualified agents to sell products, and improving the level of customer satisfaction.

Using Technology to Gain Competitive Advantage

The idea of information as a competitive weapon emerged from growing awareness of the volume of information in today's computer systems and its value as a corporate resource. Alarmed by declining productivity and increasing global competition, many corporations seem to have picked up on the idea.

End-user computing has been credited with providing the biggest boost to the idea of technology as a competitive weapon. As long as corporate computers were locked away in data processing shops, which had months or years of backlogged requests for programming, managers rarely took advantage of electronically stored information. In the early 1980s, as managers began to manipulate data on microcomputers, they demanded more and better information. Progressive companies developed ways to give managers access to sources such as external databases that provide intelligence on competitors, markets, and inventory management systems. Putting computer power in the hands of the work force (and helping employees learn to use it) has become a catalyst for innovative applications of technology. The best ideas often come from those in close contact with the organization's tasks, products, and customers or even from the customers themselves.

Major success stories about technology as a competitive weapon, such as those about American Hospital Supply and Merrill Lynch Cash Management Accounts (CMA), have been well publicized in the business press. General Electric generated a wealth of information that helped improve old products and develop new ones by creating a toll-free hotline for customer complaints and questions. Translating information into innovative products and services is not a game for the faint-hearted, however. Payoffs are high, but so are the costs. Yet systems analysts should be aware of the opportunities and prepared to work with managers in developing business plans.

In a discussion of what he calls *third-era computing,* John F. Rockart, Director of the Center for Information Systems Research at the Massachusetts Institute of Technology, stated that new-product marketing opportunities are

> usually spotted by people on the firing line—people close to both markets and products and who have a working feel for the new information technology. Consequently, companies that do the best job of managing their end-user computing resources also have the best chance of becoming the marketing leaders of tomorrow. . . . Indeed, the long-term value of end-user computing is accelerated learning on the part of end-users. They learn more about the limits and opportunities of the technology. More important, they discover *innovative* approaches to tasks that can actually transform the nature of the job being done.[10]

In Rockart's view, the important distinction between computing in the first two eras and in the third era is the role of end-users. During the first two eras, information processing remained under the control of data processing professionals. In the third era, computers have moved out of the realm of specialists "into the hands of end-users—whoever and wherever they may be." Rockart sees no end in sight. According to research statistics, the growth rate of end-user computing is at least five times that of conventional systems. The major growth areas are word processing, business programs (such as accounting and sales analysis), electronic spreadsheet analysis, office support programs, business graphics, and writing new programs. According to Rockart, the significance of this growth "is that computing systems are rapidly becoming a part of the corporate infrastructure. Just as a society needs its highways, bridges, railroads, and airports to survive, so a company needs its 'seamless web' of computing systems." For that reason, Rockart believes that "third-era computing requires the urgent involvement of senior management in ways that first- and second-era computing never did."

Companies today realize the importance of finding creative ways to use and integrate computer technologies to retain their customers and capture new ones. For example, using information competitively is the essential strategy employed by Sears, Roebuck and Company, the nation's leading retailer, for expanding into consumer financial services:

> Sears learned the value of information several years ago when they used it to augment their service business. The strategy to follow up on appliance purchases with telemarketing calls, offering maintenance contracts and package deals, provided Sears with a powerful marketing tool that boosted their service revenues and created customer goodwill. Today, Sears has combined telemarketing, information systems, and networks to form an extremely potent strategic weapon.[11]

Innovation and creativity must be actively nurtured. Successful strategic systems are *not* a natural evolution from existing data processing operations and a tradition of investing heavily in data processing. A direct correlation exists between a strategic system's success and top management's support for creative information systems.

Strategic use of information implies a direct tie between business strategy and information systems. Thus it strikes at the heart of the way organizations do business. In their enthusiasm to use information as a strategic tool, many companies make the mistake of "moving ahead" without thoroughly researching and analyzing how the organization works. Consequently, they underestimate the structural changes needed to implement innovations. "In fact, the greatest drawback in managing information as a strategic tool may be the changes it often imposes on the way a company conducts its business and how its employees do their jobs."[12]

Researchers have identified the following characteristics of strategically successful corporations: [13]

- They understand the structure of their industry.
- They recognize the activities that have the greatest impact on strategic success.
- They use innovative and creative thinking to search for and use information for competitive advantage.
- The most competitively significant applications appear to come from a combination of top-down design and bottom-up implementation.

Another researcher has identified the following additional characteristics of the successful use of strategic information:[14]

- Strategically important systems seem to develop best in an environment of broad communication and widespread understanding of corporate strategy.
- These systems also seem to develop best in environments that facilitate and encourage the use of information technology by functional employees throughout the organization.

In summary, using information as a strategic tool is a complex challenge. Decision makers must understand the critical factors that affect the success of their business and how technology can impact upon those factors. They must also support organizational change and job redesign and encourage and reward innovation at all levels of the organization.

USING TECHNOLOGY: INNOVATION

Creativity and innovation have been studied by numerous researchers over the years. Identifying characteristics common to creative individuals has proven very difficult, and fostering those characteristics in individuals—or institutions—has proven even more elusive. Innovation in organizations has been defined as "the creation or adoption of new products, services, processes, or procedures. The capacity to innovate is central to the ability of an organization to adapt to changes in its environment."[15]

The common perception is that innovation springs from spontaneous inspiration: the light bulb comes on, and a great idea is born! According to management authority Peter F. Drucker, however, most innovations "result from a conscious, purposeful search for innovation opportunities, which are found only in a few situations." Drucker believes that "purposeful, systematic innovation begins with the analysis of sources of new opportunities."[16] According to Drucker, four major areas of opportunities exist *within* a company: (1) unexpected occurrences, (2) incongruities, (3) process needs, and (4) industry and market changes. Three additional sources exist *outside* the organization: (1) demographic changes, (2) changes in perceptions, and (3) new knowledge.

Drucker emphasizes that innovators must be sensitive to opportunities and purposeful in their attempts to capitalize on them. Innovation is attributable more to hard work than to genius. "Innovation is both conceptual and perceptual....Successful innovators use both the right and left sides of their brains."[17]

Characteristics of Innovative Organizations

A recent worldwide study reported by James Brian Quinn in the *Harvard Business Review* identified the following characteristics of small and large innovative organizations in the United States and other countries.[18]

1. *Innovation requires flexible management.* Managers need to think carefully about how innovation fits into their strategies and to structure technology, skills, resources, and organizational commitments accordingly.

2. *Innovation is an incremental process.* Quinn's research revealed that "few, if any, major innovations resulted from highly structured planning systems." Rather, "major innovations are best managed as incremental, goal-oriented, interactive learning processes." (The OTA Model for Technology Innovation describes such an incremental process.)

3. *Successful innovators attack a problem from several angles simultaneously.* They often encourage multiple efforts to address opportunities until more information becomes available. "Not knowing precisely where the solution will occur, wise managers establish the widest feasible network for finding and assessing alternative solutions. They keep many options open until one of them seems sure to win." According to Quinn, "incrementalism helps deal with psychological, political, and motivational factors that are crucial to success. By keeping goals broad at first, a manager avoids creating undue opposition to new ideas."

4. *Effective managers of innovation allow for chaos within guidelines.* In other words, managers avoid elaborate planning or control systems and manage by "setting goals, selecting key people, and establishing a few critical limits and decision points for intervention." Choosing among competing projects can be difficult, and the decision is often intuitive rather than scientific. Innovative companies also find special ways to reward innovators.

5. *Management practices in innovative companies reflect the realities of the innovation process itself.* "Innovation tends to be individually motivated, opportunistic, customer responsive, tumultuous, non-linear, and interactive in its development." Innovative companies strive to keep their plans flexible and freeze them only when they become essential for strategic purposes, such as timing.

Managers must balance the need for continuity and stability with the needs for fostering creativity and nurturing innovation. This is a tough job. Few organizations can afford to make many mistakes. Moving too aggressively can mean making costly mistakes or causing chaos; moving too slowly, on the other hand, can lead to obsolescence.

Supporting Research and Development

Although the emphasis in this text has been on designing office systems in response to identified needs, the preceding discussion on innovation points out a need to experiment and take chances. Organizations provide for such experimentation—or research and development (R and D)—in a number of ways. Often, they conduct pilot studies to evaluate solutions to a problem. Generally, potential solutions are narrowed to two or three alternatives, which are tested in the actual work environment or under simulated conditions.

In short, managers must not be too "efficient" in resource allocation; they must encourage creativity in R and D. Rapidly developing technology exceeds our understanding of how to use it. The tendency to use new technologies as substitutes for the old usually produces short-term benefits at the expense of long-term opportunities.

Large organizations that have the resources at their disposal often have internal R and D teams to experiment with the application of technologies. Some companies call these teams Advanced Technology Groups (ATGs). The flowchart in Figure 19-2 shows how one such group, the Technology Services group at Boston Fidelity Investments, operates. Boston Fidelity Investments responds to user needs and also explores "blue-sky" technologies. These groups often work closely with vendors, signing nondisclosure statements, testing new products before they are released for general sale. The company gets a product better suited to its needs, and vendors benefit from careful market testing of their products before release. Some of the products that ATG groups are looking at include artificial intelligence, supercomputing, voice recognition, data-entry alternatives, optical storage, local area networks, compact disks, voice mail, and Videotex. These R and D teams also serve as in-house technical resources for office systems analysts who develop solutions to business problems.

Many companies view research and development groups as a luxury. Even those without formal ATG groups, however, often encourage their office systems or business analysts to experiment with new technologies.

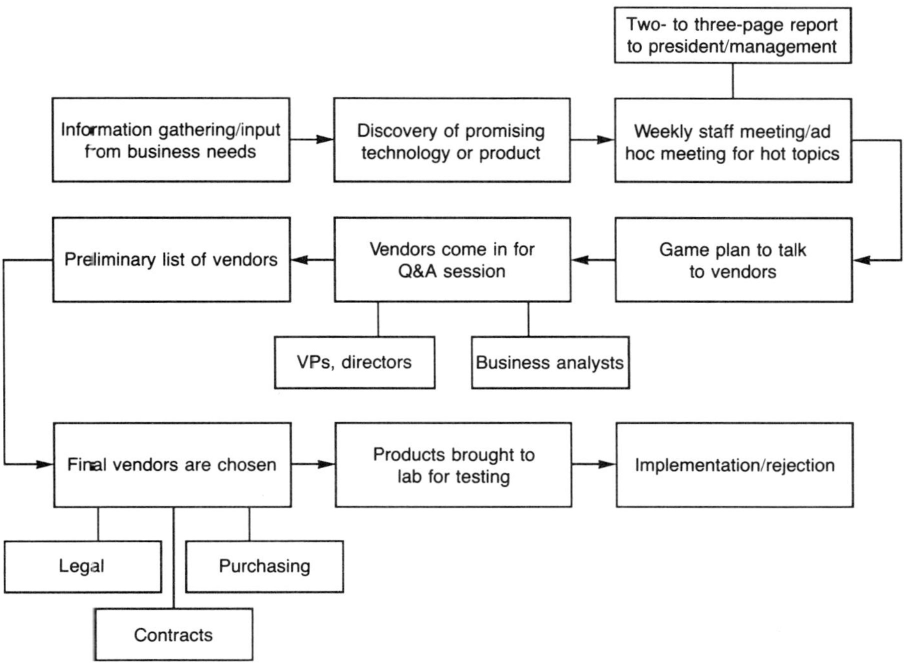

FIGURE 19-2. Boston Fidelity Investments' route to new technology.

Fidelity's technology services group responds to users' needs and also explores blue sky technology by gathering information from research organizations such as the Gartner Group, reading periodicals like *InformationWEEK,* and attending conferences on topics such as communications and AI.

If an engineer comes across an interesting technology or a vendor's idea for a new product, he can discuss it at a weekly staff meeting. If it's a hot item, he can call for an ad hoc meeting.

At the meeting, engineers decide if the new technology or product can support the strategic goals and specific objectives of the company. They outline a plan for detailed research—talk to the vendor, attend conferences, read the industry press check with the Gartner Group.

Engineers can also submit a two- to three-page report to Michael Simmons, president of Fidelity, and to managers and end users where appropriate, explaining the planned use of the technology. Several reports at several stages may be necessary to get final go-ahead.

If the research finds the technology promising, the group develops a game plan to talk to vendors. The vendors visit Fidelity, where they submit to a Q&A session with engineers. They may be joined by business analysts from the systems group, who act as a conduit, carrying information from the technical specialists to the business end users and vice versa. Business analysts, who are organized as a task force, also evaluate the financial soundness of vendors, determining, for example, whether new vendors, who are historically poorly funded, have the resources to remain in business for a year or two. No commitments are made at this stage.

During the selection-of-vendors process, which Fidelity calls "qualifying," other corporate people become involved. Directors and VPs attend to evaluate contract options—lease vs. purchase, for example—and financial and technical soundness of vendors. Purchasing managers and contract people then follow through after the initial meeting.

Fidelity whittles down the list of vendors for further discussion and more specifics. These meetings are often governed by nondisclosure rules that protect everyone involved. At this stage, the legal department becomes involved. If Fidelity plans to enter into a joint venture, which means swapping sensitive material with a vendor, the firm wants legal protection. Counsel also helps the purchasing managers, laying out the basis for a contract—whether it's a joint venture, custom-build, or straight purchase agreement.

Finally, the technology services group evaluates the products in an isolation lab, poking and prodding to see if they will stand up to requirements and vendors' claims. If they do, final purchase or lease agreements are signed and implementation can begin. If they don't, the product can be rejected. For ATGs, there's room for failure; not every project comes to fruition.

Such experiments are usually more directly tied to identified user needs, however, than are R and D projects. One consultant advises companies that cannot afford R and D groups to make better use of their end users to research new technologies. She advises companies to "employ your users and get them involved in looking at new technology. That is the most effective strategy, because they understand the business. If you give them the required amount of DP education and then set them loose to look, they'll do a much better job at finding out what works for your firm."[19]

STRATEGIC PLANNING FOR OFFICE AUTOMATION

Strategic planning for office automation has become a pressing need in recent years. Organizations have made substantial investments in office technologies, with purchases often adding up to shockingly high sums, yet often they cannot justify the benefits in terms of bottom-line profits. Moreover, these organizations are facing the need for continued expenditures to keep pace with technology in the years ahead. As the islands of technology converge (office systems, data processing, and telecommunications), managers are rethinking corporate roles and philosophies regarding information technologies. Without strategic planning, organizations miss opportunities, and gains may be limited to only immediate short-term benefits. The only way organizations can be confident that their technology dollars are invested in the right places to help maintain long-term profitability is by careful strategic planning.

What Is Strategic Planning?

Strategic planning is a process of defining an organization's major business goals and objectives. A typical strategy is for a five-year period, although occasionally firms may plan for 20 years or longer. Strategic planning's major objective is to move an organization from where it is to where management determines it should be in the future. Important questions and considerations in the strategic planning process are outlined in Figure 19-3.

Strategic planning should not be confused with project planning, which is also an important part of implementing office systems. The distinction is primarily in the objectives of these processes. Strategic planning predetermines what an organization should do. In other words, it establishes goals. The best goals for the use of technology relate directly to an organization's business goals, or strategy. Project planning, on the other hand, establishes how and when goals will be implemented. Project planning and control are discussed in subsequent chapters in Part 5.

The Strategic Planning Process

The strategic planning process is intended to meet the following objectives:

1. Determine where the organization is with regard to a certain concept.
2. Decide where the organization should be at a certain date.
3. Develop plans to achieve the desired result.

Questions	Considerations
Where are we?	Nature of business or organization Current state of development Position relative to other organizations
Where do we want to go?	Capabilities and opportunities Assumptions Issues Objectives
How will we get there?	Strategy and policy Political pressures Programs, projects, and procedures
When do we want to arrive?	Priorities Timing
Who will be responsible?	Senior-level generalist at the helm Organization
How much will it cost?	Budget Resources

FIGURE 19-3. The strategic planning process.

Planning and strategies require accurate assessments of the future: something that has proven extremely difficult. The most important thing for managers to predict is where they want the business to be in five or ten years. Of course, this prediction depends on where their industry is going, which can be equally difficult to forecast. To plan strategically for office automation, managers must also predict where the technology is going. The fainthearted give up in despair, but wise business managers make their best estimates and remain flexible enough to correct the course en route.

The following ten-step planning process is recommended by Booz, Allen, and Hamilton, a major consulting firm specializing in planning and implementing information systems:

1. *Understand business strategies.* Depending on the business, strategies may be explicit, implicit, or not fully developed. If they are not explicit, assumptions should be made for each major business unit and their reasonableness agreed to by the top managements of those units.

2. *Determine critical success factors (CSFs).* The management of each business strategy requires a series of decisions, some of which are

critical to success (e.g., making versus buying, timing of market entry, debt versus equity funding). In addition to grasping which decisions are critical, the systems planner must also understand the associated activity and resource requirements. Each activity and resource, in turn, has two sets of factors that need to be identified: one set measures activity or resource consumption (e.g., activities pending versus completed, resources available versus those consumed), and the other set evaluates how well the results (e.g., sales, plant utilization, human resource productivity, regulatory compliance) satisfy strategic objectives.

3. *Relate CSFs to information flows.* Each decision and each activity, resource, and results measurement defines a set of management information needs. These needs are invariably interrelated, and the content, timeliness, accuracy, and form of the information to be consumed should be interpreted in terms of the users and their likely analytical and decision processes. Allowance should be made for the variations in personal behavior and style that inevitably alter information consumption patterns over time. The likely sources (both external and internal) of the information should then be traced, and rudimentary flows from source to use established.

4. *Develop information technology assumptions.* Just as the formulation of a business strategy is based on environmental and economic assumptions, a systems strategy must be based on assumptions relating to the availability, price, and performance of hardware, software, telecommunications, and related materials. Most of the forecasts upon which these assumptions can be based are readily available from trade publications and technical consultants.

5. *Conceptualize information systems solutions.* This involves matching the information flows and technology assumptions in steps 3 and 4 with an ordered list of potential applications, such as described under the heading of *electronic-based solutions.* The resultant solutions that are selected must then be blended in terms of their physical (i.e., architectural) requirements. Architectural considerations relate to the physical deployment and sharing of input/output, processing, storage, and software resources and the degree to which they are made directly available to end-users and to each other through communications networking.

6. *Prioritize the solutions.* Systems solutions vary widely in terms of their importance in the attainment of business strategies, although those of lesser importance often are prerequisites for more important applications. This initial cut at prioritization should be based primarily on a qualitative evaluation of how critical each potential solution would be to

achievement of the business strategy it supports and, secondarily, on any building-block interrelationships among solutions.

7. *Determine resource requirements.* This involves sizing the potential solutions and their architecture. It also requires estimates of the people that will be needed to develop and operate the system and the cash outflow to fund both development and operation. In addition to quantity, the quality of each set of technical and human resources should be determined.

8. *Understand the available resource base.* To stimulate fresh and incisive thinking about needs and solutions, the planning process intentionally has been structured up to this point to avoid the issues of technical, human resource, or funding availability. However, the pace of any practical plan has to recognize and strive to make maximum progress within availability constraints, and the purpose of this step is to identify these constraints. The scope of this assessment should include the quality as well as the raw capacity/quantity of the existing technical and human infrastructure within the organization.

9. *Time-phase the solutions.* The priority sequencing of solutions was largely determined in Step 6. Now the solutions must be paced to the quality and capacity of development and operational resources available, plus those the organization can justify adding in the future. Many businesses undermine their strategic interests by taking an unnecessarily narrow view of their ability to fund and support beneficial systems projects. They often limit themselves by artificial year-to-year ceilings on computer and office equipment spending, rather than looking at the broader trade-offs from the perspective of cumulative ROI and strategic management effectiveness.

10. *Define the management process.* In the past, too many thickly documented, long-range systems plans have wound up gathering dust. This is usually due to the absence of any strategic relevance. But often, a plan's "death" has been preordained by the simplistic assumption that processes were adequate to support new systems solutions. Evaluating information systems to the decision support level requires systems executives to upgrade their own organization, feasibility, development, and operations techniques. And these new techniques should be defined within the plan. For example, if managerial/professional productivity is the rationale for new office systems, the plan has to come to grips with the knotty issue of how to quantify productivity at these levels. Furthermore, as new systems affect end-user involvement in the planning, development, and operational processes, fresh questions arise.

Who Should be Responsible for Strategic Planning?

Strategic planning is usually a responsibility of upper-level managers. Often, high-level staff personnel, directly accountable to senior management, are responsible for relevant research and recommendations.

In practice, however, not all planning for office automation is strategic, nor is it always done at top levels. N. Dean Meyer, an office automation consultant, cautions that office automation planning must do more than predict technologies. It also must forecast business needs, the broader business environment, the pace of organizational change, staff support requirements, and investment strategies. Thus office automation planning should not be done by staff groups alone.[20]

The question of who should plan depends, in part, on the scope of the planning. Is the organization large or small? Will planning apply to the entire organization, one division, or one department? Is planning within the organization primarily centralized or decentralized? Strategic planning must be adapted by each organization to its own needs.

The most effective office automation plans generally are originated by and involve upper-level managers. Strategic planning, involving technology for competitive advantage, is generally of a magnitude that can be authorized only at top levels. Often, it exceeds the scope of office systems technologies and calls for integrating office systems, data processing, and communications.

Strategic planning for office automation is not easy. Firms frequently hire consultants to provide direction. Information technologies can appear bewilderingly complex. Many enterprises do not have the staff or organization to pull key players together to develop a cohesive company strategy for using information technologies. A consultant can fill this critical role.

The ability of most businesses to assimilate and apply office technologies lags far behind the opportunities, a strategic void that can be critical. Senior executives often feel that they should receive more benefit from technology investment, but few are able to articulate how those benefits should be achieved. Here again, a consultant can show companies how they can use technology to support and augment their business goals, both currently and in the future.

A consultant can provide an unbiased, outside perspective to balance the concerns of management. Involvement of both technical and business people is essential for planning a strong, practical approach to strategic information systems. A consultant can bring together the information systems managers (who understand the potential of the technology) and the line managers (who know the business).

The Strategic Plan A strategic plan for office automation forms the basis for determining which applications should be addressed in what order. It should help executives answer basic questions concerning information systems activities: Are there competitive opportunities in my industry that office automation can help implement? Is the company spending its office automation budget effectively on the appropriate applications? Are the leadership and organization for office automation systems appropriate for the role information now plays in the enterprise? What applications will produce the greatest business benefits? To develop a strategic plan for office automation, planners must study the organization's long- and short-term business needs.

A strategic plan for office automation and office systems should include the following tasks:

1. *Support the business goals defined in the corporate strategic plan.* In overall management planning, information systems are tools that can help an organization implement its business strategies. It is easy to lose sight of the role information systems play in the organization, and to plan as if they were an end in themselves. Focusing on business objectives defined in the corporate strategy helps to keep information systems planning in proper perspective.

2. *Respond to management concerns and changing business requirements.* A plan must be sufficiently flexible to take advantage of new opportunities or address unexpected problems.

3. *Coordinate with overall information systems or information management planning.* Regardless of whether OA is part of the IS organization or has a separate reporting structure, plans and programs must be complementary and compatible. In an increasing number of organizations, information systems managers play a major role in strategic planning. According to a 1985 report, "More and more companies realize they can't chart their corporate futures without gauging the effects of information, office, and communications systems on products, services, and internal operations."[21]

Once formulated, strategies are written in report format and submitted for management approval. Figure 19-4 illustrates the table of contents from the five-year office automation strategy developed by a major insurance company. Generally, someone from the planning team makes a formal presentation to management, using slides or other appropriate graphics to help focus attention on key points. Clear explanations of objectives, business justification, recommendations, costs, and benefits are vital to gaining support. Top-management approval of the office automation strategy is a key step in obtaining commitment to office automation programs.

FIGURE 19-4. Table of contents of an office automation strategy document.

Table of Contents

Putting the Strategic Plan into Action

Putting strategic planning into action requires mission statements, policies, programs, projects, and procedures. A mission statement is a clearly delineated statement of the major goals and objectives of the office automation systems department. Policy, which is the strategy in written words, reflects guidelines developed by top management regarding major issues. The following is an example of a policy for the implementation of office automation:

> The Office Systems Department's policy is to provide the overall framework and strategy for five-year development of an office network that balances the needs of individual users and departments against the overall corporate needs and objectives. Within that framework, we will provide as much flexibility as possible.

Programs put policies into effect. *Programs* refer to the series of efforts needed to follow through on the policy. *Projects,* the next level of activity, serve the objectives of programs. Several projects may be needed to implement one program. The most precise, measurable unit of activity is *procedures,* specific methods for accomplishing work activity.

Policies, programs, projects, and procedures are needed to support the short-range tactical plans of the organization. The following examples of this hierarchy are based on the office systems policy:

Example of a Program

- Replace the existing corporate telephone voice system (Private Branch Exchange or PBX) with a new digital Computer Branch Exchange (CBX) system that is capable of handling both voice and data communications.

Examples of Projects

- Install new CBX and connect all current telephones to the system.
- Pilot-test a voice-mail system.
- Establish data communications through the new CBX for microcomputers to provide users with access to data stored on the mainframe computers.

Example of a Procedure

- All microcomputer users who require access to mainframe data will submit a request form, authorized by the vice-president of their division, to the Office Systems Department.
- To aquire access to the voice mail system, all users should develop their own four-digit codes and request a password from the system manager.

SUMMARY

Innovation is a two-edged sword: it is both applauded and feared. While organizations acknowledge the value of new ideas, corporate cultures seldom foster and reward innovation. Technologies, like new ideas, bring both threats and opportunities. Chapter 19 discusses some of the many opportunities that office technologies offer. Capitalizing on technology to improve productivity and quality of worklife is complex and challenging. It requires foresight, careful planning, and good management.

The incorporation of technology into the work environment is an evolutionary learning process. Two conceptual models of technological change were presented. The Office of Technology Assessment's (OTA) Model of Technological Change, developed by Joseph Coates, describes the process in three stages: substitution, adaptation, and transformation. L. H. Day of the Diebold Office Automation Group offers a five-stage model: conception, initiation, contagion, consolidation, and creative evolution. The major opportunities offered by new technologies are associated with their potential for transforming offices into more efficient and effective workplaces.

Transforming organizations requires innovative approaches to business needs. When technology is used innovatively, it offers new opportunities for managing information. Office automation planners and analysts are challenged to design systems that capitalize on technology for productivity improvement and competitive advantage. Organizations that succeed will reap benefits in improved products and services.

Innovation is the creation or adoption of new products, services, processes, or procedures. Capacity to innovate is central to the ability to adapt to changes in environment. Innovation is both perceptual and conceptual, and can be attributed more to hard work than to genius. A worldwide study revealed the characteristics that innovators have in common: flexible management, attacking problems from several angles simultaneously, allowing for chaos within guidelines, and freezing plans only when necessary.

Without strategic planning, organizations miss opportunities and often gain only immediate, short-term benefits. Strategic planning is a process of defining major business goals and objectives for an organization. It identifies action required to move an organization from where it is to where management determines it should be. A strategic plan for office automation should support the goals defined in the corporate strategic plan. Strategic plans are translated into action through policies, programs, projects, and procedures.

DISCUSSION QUESTIONS

1. Define the term *innovation.* Why is it a "two-edged sword"?
2. What is the relationship between technology and innovation?
3. List some negative impacts of office automation. Give an example of each.
4. What do the two models of technology infusion show about its assimilation in organizations?
5. The text makes a number of suggestions about using technology as a catalyst for productivity improvement. Why do you suppose these approaches are not more widely used?
6. List characteristics of companies that have successfully used technology as a competitive weapon. What do these characteristics suggest about their management style?
7. What is strategic planning? Why is strategic planning for office automation important?
8. Who is usually responsible for strategic planning in an organization? Why would responsibility reside at that level?
9. How are strategic plans put into action in an organization?

APPLICATION EXERCISES

1. Working with a group of classmates, identify an office, small business, or other organizational unit with which you are familiar and brainstorm ideas for using technology to change it. How would such changes alter the way products or services are provided? How would they improve productivity? How would they affect employees' jobs? Which ideas do you think would be most profitable? Summarize your recommendations to share with the class.

2. Identify an office automation application at your college or a local business that you feel is innovative. In what way is it innovative? Who thought of the idea? How was it implemented? What technology is involved? Were the changes implemented when the technology was installed or afterwards?

3. Using current literature such as *Business Week* or trade publications (see list at end of text for suggestions), give examples of how industries have used technology to gain competitive advantage. What was required to turn the idea into action?

SUGGESTED READINGS

Bowen, William. "The Puny Payoff from Office Computers," *Fortune* (May 26, 1986), pp. 20–24.

Buday, Robert, and Tom Ewing, eds. "The Strategic Use of Information: Seizing the Competitive Edge," *Information Week* (May 26, 1986), pp. 26–72.

Drucker, Peter E. *Innovation and Entrepreneurship: Practice and Principles* (New York: Harper and Row, 1985).

______."The Discipline of Innovation," *Harvard Business Review* (May–June 1985), pp. 67–72.

Ewing, Tom, ed. "Building Corporate Strategy around the Personal Computer," *Information Week* (February 17, 1986), pp. 27–56.

Kanter, Rosabeth Moss. *The Change Masters* (New York: Simon and Schuster, 1986).

McFarlan, F. Warren. "Information Technology Changes the Way You Compete," *Harvard Business Review* (May–June 1984), pp. 98–103.

Quinn, James Brian. "Managing Innovation: Controlled Chaos," *Harvard Business Review* (May–June 1985), pp. 73–84.

Shirley, Steve (interviewed by Eliza G. C. Collins). "A Company Without Offices," *Harvard Business Review* (January–February 1986), pp. 127–136.

OFFICE SYSTEMS ANALYSIS: Frameworks

CHAPTER

20

OBJECTIVES

After completing this chapter, the reader should be able to meet the following objectives:

- Understand the systems concept and how it can be applied to office systems and office systems analysis.
- Explain the purpose/role of a conceptual view of office systems analysis.
- Differentiate among the various conceptual approaches to office systems investigation.
- Identify five frameworks appropriate to office systems analysis.
- Decide which framework of office systems analysis works best in a given situation.

KEY TERMS

system
subsystem
suprasystem
open system
closed system
boundary
environment
entropy
interface
throughput
feedback
systems analysis
office systems analysis
office systems
organizational communication approach
functional approach
information resource management approach
quality-of-work-life approach
pilot test
office systems cycle

INTRODUCTION

Office work consists of observable activities such as reading, writing, filing, keyboarding, and talking on the phone. It may also be functional tasks such as accounting, marketing, or operations management.

This chapter is designed to give the prospective office systems analyst an overview of models that might serve as a framework for a study of office work (both definitions) and how it could be done more effectively with automated tools. First, fundamental concepts are outlined. Second, conceptual approaches that office systems analysts follow in assessing, designing, implementing, and evaluating office activities are explained. The chapter concludes with a variety of frameworks for the entire analysis process, including a variation of *action research,* and the framework this text will follow as it offers specific how-to's on office systems analysis.

GENERAL SYSTEMS CONCEPTS

Before office systems can be discussed, it is appropriate to understand what constitutes a system. The following definitions of *systems* and *systems analysis* will lead into definitions of *office systems* and *office systems analysis*.

A Systems Definition

Systems concepts have wide applicability. Consider these various definitions of what constitutes a system:

> Systems are any set of components which *could* be seen as working together for the overall objective of the whole.[1]

> A *system* is a particular linking of interrelated and interdependent components having a facilitating effect, or an intended facilitating effect, on the carrying out of one or more processes.[2]

As used in this text, the term *system* expands on these definitions: *A system is a set of separate but interrelated components (people, technology, and tasks) that process input (data, raw materials) into desired output (reports, guides, memos, etc.) to reach an identified objective.* The following examples of systems will help to clarify this definition.

Examples of Systems

Good examples of systems abound: a computer system, the respiratory system, a car's exhaust system, a school system, a political system, an economic system. Each system is made up of distinct, identifiable components, or parts, and a change in any part has a direct effect on the operation of the system. In addition, one system can be a *subsystem* of another system, or a *suprasystem* of another. Systems can be technical or social.

One example of a technical system is a microcomputer, which consists of a keyboard, disk drives, systems unit, and monitor. This system may include additional hardware, such as OCR devices and printers. When this microcomputer is networked with other microcomputers via a local area network, it may be considered a *subsystem* of the local area network *suprasystem*.

The word *system* is also used to describe social/work systems. The office itself is considered a system that inputs, processes, outputs, distributes, and uses data to support the operations of a business. An office is people, technology, structure, and tasks. It is these work systems that the office systems planner analyzes.

Systems in operation are described by the input/output-processing model. The microcomputer system is inputs (keyboard, OCR, facsimile, etc.); processing (manipulation of data/words); and output (monitor, printer, memory). When any part of this microcomputer system is "down," the system cannot do its work.

Systems Characteristics

Systems—both technical and social—can be identified by their characteristics. In this section, selected systems characteristics are listed and defined, and the terms that describe them are then discussed in terms of their relationship to office systems.

Open and closed systems Systems are often described as either *open* or *closed.* These terms refer to whether or not the system is affected by activities outside its boundaries. If a system is open, it is greatly affected by occurrences that are not under its control; if a system is closed, it is *not* affected by occurrences outside itself. It is difficult, however, to imagine a *completely* closed system.

Inputs and outputs *Inputs* and *outputs* are the energies that go into and come out of the system, respectively.

Throughput *Throughput* is the process of transforming input into output.

Boundary *Boundary* is the term for the area that separates one system from another. A system is *bounded* by everything controllable by the systems analyst and important to its operation.

Environment A system's *environment* is anything outside the boundary that has an impact on the operation of the system but which the systems analyst cannot control.

Entropy *Entropy* (pronounced *n-tro-p*) is a tendency toward disorder. The more closed a system is, the more it is subject to entropy.

Interface The *interface* is the point at which systems meet and interact, transferring the output of one system into the input of another.

Feedback System output is measured against evaluation criteria, or standards. Information comparing what was produced or provided with what was *expected* to be produced or provided is *fed back* into the system as input.

Systems Analysis

The systems characteristics discussed above are basic to an explanation of systems analysis. Open and closed systems do not always operate (process or throughput) as intended (entropy). The source of the problem may be within the system's boundary, environment, or interface. Feedback is the means for identifying that something is amiss. Systems analysis is the process of determining what the problem is and attempting to fix it. Systems analysis is not conducted by taking apart the entire system. Rather, systems are analyzed by examining discrepancies between expected outputs (the standard) and actual outputs.

For example, if one considers the human body as a system, the process by which a doctor diagnoses an illness (entropy) can be considered systems analysis. If one goes to the doctor with a headache, the doctor considers that headache as output. Rather than operate immediately (go into the system), the doctor asks questions about inputs and outputs (When did the headache begin? Does it occur frequently? What seems to trigger it?). Diagnosis may result in a prescription, and if the prescription does not work, the individual returns to the doctor for more advice and another remedy is suggested; and so the process, which is a form of systems analysis, continues. Hopefully, the system (body) itself will not need to be operated upon.

FUNDAMENTAL OFFICE SYSTEMS CONCEPTS

The term *office systems* is used in a variety of ways. Some vendors use it to describe their word processing hardware; others use it to describe more integrated hardware and software products. In other words, the definition varies greatly from vendor to vendor.

The term *office systems* is also used in a larger context, to describe all the support activities of an organization. Care should be taken to ascertain which meaning is relevant. *Office systems* may also be considered a subsystem of the larger business system, which is itself part of the organization suprasystem.

An Office Systems Definition

Figure 20-1 shows the business system to be comprised of distinct functional subsystems such as accounting, finance, production, sales, etc. The mission of each function is to support business objectives. The functions overlap, but *office systems* is common to all of them.

FIGURE 20-1. The business system.

In this text, *office automation* and *office systems* are often used interchangeably. However, *office systems* typically describes office automation in the larger organization. In other words, *office systems* is a generic term that describes the subsystem responsible for office automation.

As Figure 20-2 shows, office systems are composed of subsystems. True to the definition of a system, support services such as word processing, data processing, reprographics, or facilities management all work together for the completion of the common goal of office automation. Organizations vary in the degree to which each subsystem outlined in Figure 20-3 is a distinct, separate entity. The *coordination* of all such subsystems is what makes office automation truly office systems.

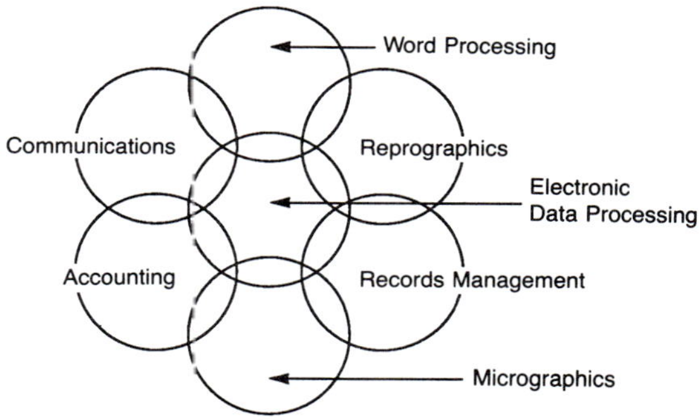

FIGURE 20-2. Subsystems of the office system.

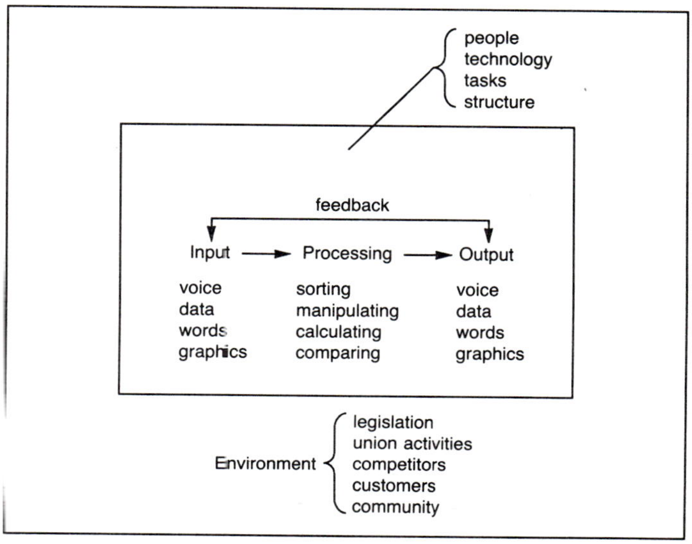

FIGURE 20-3. The office as an open system.

Using a processing definition, office systems—as Figure 20-3 shows—is an open system, constantly affected by its environment. The office does not exist in isolation; legislation, union activity, and even a transit strike could impact operations. The boundary of an office system is the scope of activities the office systems analyst is able to affect, and the system itself, within that boundary is definable inputs, processing, and outputs.

Office Systems Analysis

Figure 20-3 also shows that the office system is made of people, technology, tasks, and structures that together make the system work. Using systems analysis as a basis, the analyst studies operations of the system by examining its input and output. When feedback indicates that the office is not operating correctly (the desired output is not received), a systems study begins.

For example, if it is determined that three days is too long for processing a purchase order, the office systems analyst would begin asking questions (much like the doctor in the earlier example) to determine why and where the delay is occurring. The analyst in this case could examine the steps the purchase order takes, interview people who are doing the processing, or initiate other means to determine where the problem lies. The analyst, then, is applying systems analysis concepts in examining office activities.

The preceding example of a purchase order is a very simple illustration of systems analysis. Office systems analysis typically goes beyond making a single process more effective because the office systems analyst is analyzing business systems to apply office automation technologies to identified problems. The objectives of office systems analysis go far beyond trying to make a single process (purchase order handling) more streamlined or word processing more efficient; the goal is to make the business more *effective*.

Office systems analysis differs from data processing analysis in that the former is appropriate for unstructured office work. Data processing analysis is appropriate for well-defined, structured processes. However, as previously discussed, both office systems analysts and data processing analysts rely on systems concepts to guide their investigations.

CONCEPTUAL APPROACHES TO OFFICE SYSTEMS ANALYSIS

Conceptual approaches to office systems analysis are the overall views that the office systems analyst takes as he or she examines the office automation needs of the organization or individual worker. Tapscott grouped the approaches or investigations into five categories: (1) organizational communications, (2) functional approaches, (3) information resource management, (4) decision support systems, and (5) quality of work life.[3]

As the categories indicate, conceptual approaches define the *what* that is to be investigated: communications patterns, jobs, etc. No single approach is the best. The analyst chooses the approach (or approaches) that works best in a given situation.

Organizational Communications Approaches

Using an organizational communications approach, a systems analyst examines how individuals in the office communicate. The logic is that if communication is good, individuals are able to work well. The goal is to provide end users with office automation tools that enable them to access the information they need, to communicate more efficiently, and to increase the quality or timeliness of the information needed to make informed decisions.

Functional Approaches

As the term implies, *functional* approaches examine office functions. The emphasis is on *functions,* not tasks. Office automation should help the worker do his or her job better, not merely make a task easier. *Task* is an activity that enables the *function* (job) to be done. For example, entering data into a spreadsheet is a task; accounting is a function.

Another example of a task is typing. When word processing was introduced, the typing task was enhanced. In a functional approach, the secretarial function, *not* the typing task, would be examined to determine the types of support tools required to make the secretary more efficient.

Information Resource Management Approaches

Using an information resource approach (IRM), the analyst regards information as a resource of the organization, to be managed much like any other resource—money, people, materials, facilities. By quantifying the value of the information resources of an organization, analysts can attempt to ascertain where and how this resource can be used effectively.

When an organization considers information a resource, it looks for ways to enhance the use or value of that information; in other words, it uses an *information resource management approach.* For example, American Airlines used an information resource management approach in its development of the Advantage Program. With its rich database of customer names and addresses, American used its existing system to create a program that tabulates the number of miles a customer flies. Such data enables American to offer "bonus" flights or "upgrades," based on the number of miles flown, because records of customers' flights are relatively easy to establish and maintain. (Other airlines have followed American's lead.)

Decision Support Systems Approaches

Decision support systems (DSS) approaches examine office activities from the standpoint of quality decisions. The objective of any study to assess office automation needs is to determine end users' needs for automation that could aid them in their decision-making processes. Emphasis here is on the *quality* of decisions.

Decision support systems are typically used by upper-level management. These managers often need to make important decisions quickly. In some organizations, such as banks or brokerage houses, delay of a day or even an hour can mean a difference worth thousands of dollars. When an organization attempts to aid the decision making process by installing new technologies, it is using a decision support approach.

Quality of Work Life Approaches

Quality of work life (QWL) approaches include disciplines such as economics, psychology, sociology, industrial relations, engineering, and systems theory. QWL approaches look at the nature of the work being done, worker motivation, and job design. Because office automation (as explained in previous chapters) alters the way people work, a QWL approach focuses on opportunities to improve workers' job satisfaction and productivity by providing meaningful jobs in a supportive work environment.

The QWL approach promotes worker involvement and satisfaction. When employees feel that the organization is doing all it can to provide a healthy work environment and enable workers to make meaningful contributions to the organization's goals, they are typically more productive and have greater job satisfaction. When it is applied appropriately, office automation has immense potential to improve QWL. The organization that begins an office automation study with workers' motivation and satisfaction as its rationale is using a QWL approach.

All five approaches can be used to explain why an organization decides to automate. More often than not, the approaches overlap in that QWL is improved by office automation tools that enable a job function to be done better. Likewise, when functions are improved, so are communications channels. The value of identifying a conceptual approach is in establishing a frame of reference for the analyst to *begin* the investigation.

FRAMEWORKS FOR OFFICE SYSTEMS ANALYSIS

The theoretical approaches just described are related to the perspective from which an office systems analyst begins a systems study. Frameworks are also theoretical, but they deal with models of processes—steps to follow in investigating office activities. Hirschheim noted that few formal frameworks exist and that "those which do exist tend to be either too simplistic, unworkable, misguided, or some combination of these."[4] Although no process model is perfect, an office systems study needs a framework. Following is an overview of four selected frameworks that are used today to examine office activities: Tapscott's User-Driven Design, Pava's Sociotechnical Design, Hammer and Zisman's Approach for Planning, and Lewin's Action Research.

Tapscott's User-Driven Design

Tapscott organized office systems design around three phases: the prepilot phase, the pilot phase, and the operational phase. Essential to the process, the user and the user environment are input at all phases. Also critical is the use of a pilot or "test" application of any proposed system. The following is a summary of the activities at each stage:[5]

Prepilot systems phase The *prepilot systems phase* includes an organizational scan, diagnosis, and pilot systems analysis.

The *organizational scan* determines whether an organization should begin a formal office study. The analyst uses activities such as discussions with top management and interviews with all office employees and also analyzes secondary sources, including organizational charts, planning documents, and corporate objectives.

The *diagnosis* attempts to determine where office systems may improve the effectiveness of an organization. At this stage, a questionnaire is frequently sent to key employees to discover improvement areas, such as communications, human resource utilization, or administrative support.

The *pilot systems analysis* employs several methods to determine the feasibility of an office systems solution. At this time, a feasibility report is prepared, which includes prospects, costs, and ways to undertake pre- and postpilot evaluations.

Pilot system phase The *pilot system phase* is actual construction and operation of the pilot project. The pilot system is monitored, and user feedback is obtained through interviews and observation. This data is used to refine the system.

Operational phase The *operational phase* implements the permanent solutions agreed upon based on the results of the pilot installation. The system continues to be monitored, post-test evaluations are made, and any additional requirements are identified. Cost-justification measures are also computed at this time.

Pava's Sociotechnical Design

Sociotechnical (social and technical) is a term that defines office systems as having two components: technical design, which involves identifying various job tasks and technology, and social design, which involves identifying people with their various roles and behaviors. The sociotechnical design concept developed by Calvin Pava differentiates routine office work from nonroutine office work. According to Pava, traditional sociotechnical analysis is not amenable to nonroutine office work because office workers frequently handle several tasks at the same time. Pava also explained that nonroutine office work involves work without clear-cut solutions.

Using a case study approach to identify steps to systems analysis, Pava revised the Norwegian Industrial Democracy Experiment (NIDE) of the 1960s to develop frameworks for designing systems for (1) routine office work, (2) nonroutine office work, and (3) routine *and* nonroutine office work. Because the emphasis of this text is on nonroutine office work, only this latter framework is briefly discussed here. The method assumes that the office systems analyst, or *consultant*, leads the process through the following steps:

Step 0: Mapping the target system Identify the work, the major issues, communications patterns, and "key players" who should be involved in the system design.

Step 1: Entry, sanction, and startup Obtain top management approval and establish a design team. The consultant works more *for* the design group than *with* the design group.

Step 2: Initial scan Facilitate the team in reaching a consensus on mission; identify important factors to consider; and trace major historical, social, and physical features of the organization and/or unit being examined. Team members agree on the "big picture."

Step 3: Technical analysis Set major goals, analyze the component activities of office work, and apply them to major functions or the work to be done.

Step 4: Social analysis Identify the people who will be using the system, list their views on automation, identify individuals with divergent views, and identify those who can help mediate differences.

Step 5: Work system design Establish the responsibilities of the team, identify corporate policies that support group activities, and determine ground rules for problem solving.

Step 6: Approval and enactment Obtain upper management approval, describe the proposed design to the organization, and modify the design as necessary. Arrange to have people trained.

Hammer and Zisman's Approach for Planning

Earlier, in 1979, Michael Hammer and Michael Zisman offered a detailed and specific framework composed of the following steps:

Step 1 Conduct a functional analysis of the office's operations, identifying the procedures being performed and their purposes.

Step 2 Construct a specification of existing procedures.

Step 3 Analyze these specifications for inefficiencies and bottlenecks.

Step 4 Redesign the procedures in the context of existing office structures and the analysis of Step 3.

Step 5 Identify the critical steps of the new procedures and abstract the fundamental issues in their implementation.

Step 6 Specify the objectives and the functionality of the system to be designed, guided by the results of Step 5.

Step 7 Design and implement a system to meet these objectives.

Step 8 Develop an introduction path for the system.

Step 9 Install the new system.

Step 10 Enhance and maintain the system.

Action Research

In the late 1940s, Kurt Lewin outlined an Action Research approach that describes a very practical tactic for problem solving. While the Action Research design is applicable to several diverse applications, its common-sense approach to problem solving provides a very practical, easy-to-use framework for systems analysis.

The Action Research model is made up of four stages:

Stage 1: Assessment The investigation of the current state of the problem.

Stage 2: Design The creation of an intervention targeted at modifying the existing state of the problem.

Stage 3: Implementation The installation of the intervention designed in the second stage; and

Stage 4: Evaluation The assessment of whether or not the intervention had a positive impact on the problem.

The Action Research approach requires that people who are involved with the problem—people who work or live in the context in which the problem exists—are key to the problem-solving process. Another feature of the Action Research design is that the evaluation stage eventually becomes the assessment stage. Applied to office automation, this continuous cycle of assessing, designing, implementing, and evaluating is termed the *office systems cycle*. The office systems cycle is depicted in Figure 20-4.

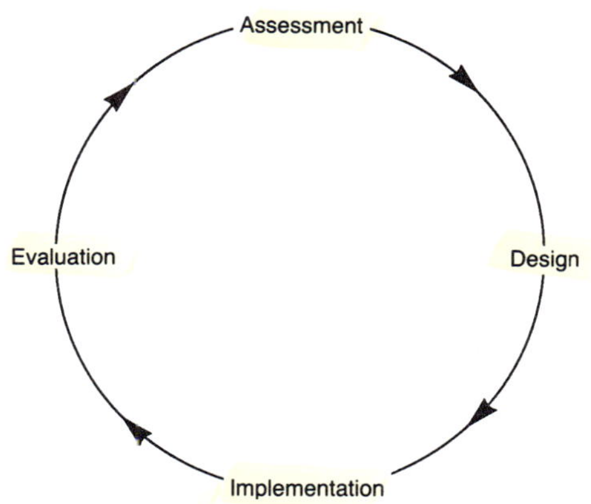

FIGURE 20-4. The office systems cycle.

Figure 20-5 depicts a framework for systems analysis based on the Action Research approach. It identifies the four stages and outlines the activities of the systems analyst in each stage. Frequent review of Figure 20-5 will help the reader to understand each stage of office systems analysis and how activities at all stages are important to the success of office systems analysis.

FIGURE 20-5. Action research framework for office systems analysis.

ASSESSMENT	Determine	How to initiate
	Select	Who should conduct
	Develop	Plan for study
	Use	Appropriate tools
	Inform	Everyone who may be impacted
DESIGN	Analyze	Data from analysis
	Sell	Chief decision maker on ideas
	Write	Request for proposals
	Evaluate	Vendor responses
IMPLEMENTATION	Plan	Strategies and dates
	Know	Your product and its users
	Choose	High-visibility pilots
	Train	All users
EVALUATION	Monitor	Continuously, all products
	Revise	When necessary

It is expected that each office systems analyst will use parts of these frameworks in establishing investigation strategies appropriate for a given organization and a given project. Organizations vary in size, and projects vary markedly in scope. The analyst who "does it right" will have established a framework—or plan—at the initiation of the study.

SUMMARY

This chapter provided an overview of theory related to office systems analysis concepts and frameworks. Because of the expense, importance, and complexity of office automation, danger exists in planning for it on an ad hoc basis. Office automation implemented on an ad hoc basis may solve a particular problem, but the solution probably will not have considered the overall information needs of the organization or addressed compatibility issues.

The first part of this chapter outlined general systems theory. A *system* is a set of separate but interrelated components that process input into desired output. A system may be a subsystem of a larger suprasystem and may itself have subsystems. Systems may be either open or closed, depending upon the degree they are impacted upon by events outside their boundaries. It is difficult to conceptualize a truly closed system since even the most closed system is affected by what happens in its environment. Systems have a tendency toward disorder; the more closed a system, the more likely that entropy will result. Interface, the region between systems, is responsible for the transference of one system's output as the input for another system. Systems analysis is based on feedback—knowledge that the actual system output is not what is expected.

Systems can be defined by a description of their sub- and suprasystems, or by an input-processing-output model. As part of the larger business system, office systems is that function responsible for the support activities of an organization. Its subsystems may include word processing, reprographics, records management, communications, database management, decision support, administrative support, or other office functions. Using the input-processing-output model, office systems are composed of definable input, processing, and output. Application of systems analysis theory to office operations is termed *office systems analysis.*

Next, this chapter described the approaches that office systems analysts use to examine the value of office automation: ways to improve the communication processes, ways to enable jobs to be done better/faster, ways to put dollar figures on the value of information, ways to determine that better decisions are made due to office automation, and ways to improve the quality of work life of employees. All five approaches may be used to some extent by office automation analysts. However, a good systems analyst needs to understand these approaches—understand that a variety of ways of looking at an office exist—as he or she begins an office systems analysis project. While no one approach is right for every situation, sometimes an investigation calls for more than one approach.

This chapter then described frameworks for the systems analysis process. Four frameworks were outlined: (1) Tapscott's User-Driven Design, which rests on the need for users to be involved with office automation planning at all stages; (2) Pava's Sociotechnical Design, which offers six steps for analyzing nonroutine office work; (3) Hammer and Zisman's Approach for Planning, which identifies tasks within the stages, including procedures specifications and systems maintenance; and (4) Lewin's Action Research, which is considered a logical approach to problem solving. While appropriate to many disciplines, action research has applicability to office systems analysis. Its four stages—assessment, design, implementation, and evaluation—require collaboration of all individuals who will be affected by any new system. In addition, action research emphasizes that office systems are cyclical in that the evaluation stage of one project becomes the assessment stage of another.

DISCUSSION QUESTIONS

1. What is a system? Give an example of a system and describe it, using the systems components listed in this text.
2. What is an office system? What can the term mean to vendors? What is the relationship of office systems to office automation?
3. How does office systems analysis compare with traditional data processing systems analysis?

4. A conceptual approach to office systems analysis is simply a way of examining office activities. Explain the rationale for each of the following approaches. Is only one approach used by an analyst in initiating an office systems study?
   a. Organizational communications
   b. Functional
   c. Information resource management
   d. Decision support systems
   e. Quality of work life
5. How does a conceptual approach to office systems analysis lead to a framework for office systems analysis? This text offers four frameworks. Of what value are these frameworks to office systems analysts?

APPLICATION EXERCISES

1. Interview two systems analysts and ask what their jobs entail and how they go about office systems analysis. Which approach or approaches do they follow? Can each approach be labeled? Compare responses from your interviews with classmates' findings.
2. Put yourself in the role of an office systems consultant. You've just been called in by a major company to manage an office systems project. Make a list of the questions you will need for your first meeting.

SUGGESTED READINGS

Hammer, Michael, and Zisman, Michael. *Design and Implementation of Office Information Systems* (New York: Exxon Enterprises, 1979), pp. 1–43.

Hirschheim, R. A. *Office Automation: A Social and Organizational Perspective* (New York: John Wiley and Sons, 1985).

McLeod, Raymond, Jr., and Jones, Jack William. "A Framework for Office Automation," *MIS Quarterly* (March 1987), pp. 87–104.

Pava, Calvin. *Managing New Office Technology: An Organizational Strategy* (New York: Free Press, 1983).

Tapscott, Don. *Office Automation: A User-Driven Method* (New York: Plenum Press, 1982).

OFFICE SYSTEMS ANALYSIS: Assessment and Design

CHAPTER

21

OBJECTIVES

After completing this chapter, the reader should be able to meet the following objectives:

- Identify appropriate person(s) to conduct an office systems study.
- Choose appropriate means of gathering data for assessment.
- Design an interview guide, questionnaire, and observation guide.
- Prepare a flowchart to describe work processes.
- List the components of a feasibility report.
- Understand the role of the request for proposal (RFP).
- Compare vendor responses to RFPs with a view to selecting appropriate hardware and/or software.

KEY TERMS

primary data
secondary data
flowchart
interview guide
questionnaire
observation guide
time log
document log
work sampling
feasibility report
request for proposal

INTRODUCTION

Office systems *assessment* is the approach used to examine office work to identify problems or opportunities to improve efficiency and effectiveness. *Design* is developing new ways to alleviate those identified problems. *Implementation* is the process of introducing the new systems to the workplace, and *evaluation* is the process of examining those new systems to ensure that they are operating as intended. This chapter details tools and methodologies that an office systems analyst might employ in the first two stages: assessment and design.

In its early days, office automation was equated with word processing. Word processors were typically given to workers to increase the speed at which typing tasks could be accomplished. Analysis tools such as typing logs, and even hand and motion studies, were used for justification of word processing centers. Although the typing task was streamlined, inefficiencies in other areas of the secretarial function frequently caused automation to create as many problems as it solved.

Even today, office systems are sometimes designed without any type of system assessment. When an organization gives a personal computer to its mid-level managers, for example, that organization has frequently not yet identified all prospective uses. Moreover, it is possible that the organization has given a manager the computer without regard for how it fits into the overall information processing plans of the organization. Such an approach is indicative of the initiation stage of office automation.

Because of the expense, complexity, and need for office automation, experts agree that a more formal approach to identifying need areas should be taken. Office automation is no longer a luxury; this costly resource can improve worker productivity, morale, and the overall operations of an organization. Formal planning is desirable not just because of the expense, but also because office automation changes how people work. It can alter well-established job descriptions and patterns of doing work. For such reasons, office automation should not be an ad hoc solution to a problem.

While Chapter 20 concentrated on theoretical approaches to office systems analysis, this chapter concentrates on practical approaches: how to assess and how to design office systems. Assessment and design are the first two stages of the office systems cycle, and the first two steps of the Lewin Action Research Framework. The chapter will be subdivided into two main sections: assessment and design. Assessment involves determining how to conduct an office systems investigation, including the creation of information-gathering instruments. Design involves analyzing and using collected data, including writing a feasibility report and a request for proposal (RFP), and how to evaluate vendor responses.

ASSESSMENT

In the early 1960s and 1970s, office automation *was* word processing, which simply automated the typing task. In the past ten years, however, businesses have come to regard office automation as a resource, as its purview has expanded across functions and up and down the corporate structure. Therefore, corporations are looking to see how office automation can aid the knowledge worker, as well as the clerical worker, in their job functions—not just tasks.

During the assessment stage of an office systems study, business requirements are defined. Office work is identified and described and inventories of current technologies are logged. In other words, the "state of the office" is assessed, with an eye to just how desirable it might be to change the way work is accomplished.

Most office automation projects, especially in large organizations, are considerably smaller in scope than analyzing the entire organization's needs. Organizations that "do it right," however, have an office automation strategy document that addresses organization-wide needs (see Chapter 19). This strategy provides the overall framework within which smaller projects are designed.

Project planning, which is discussed here and in Chapter 22, is different from strategic planning. Comprehensive projects may address the needs of one department (e.g., analyze the needs of the Law Division and implement an integrated office system for support). Most projects, however, are more focused. Projects such as the following make up the majority of projects addressed by office systems analysts:

- Developing a microfilm system to reduce paper files for processing claims and other transactions.
- Putting microcomputers in real estate regional offices with communications capabilities with the home office.
- Providing the marketing research department the ability to access mainframe-based data and perform statistical analysis.
- Analyzing work flow for the vice-president of a regional service unit to recommend where time could be saved by using microcomputers with word processing, spreadsheets, database applications, and so forth.

Initiating an Office Systems Study

The primary reason an office systems study is initiated is that a problem exists (e.g., reprographic service is poor or costs of providing customer service must be reduced) or an opportunity is identified (e.g., electronic mail). It is impossible to generalize exactly how office systems investigations are started. In some organizations, anyone can initiate an office systems study; in other organizations, a more formal approach is required. Procedures for initiating a systems study depend, of course, on the individual organization—its size, organizational culture, and how office systems are organized and controlled within the organization. Given these restrictions, an office systems study could be initiated by any of the following:

- A request from an individual.
- A request from a department.
- A directive from top management.
- An observation from within the office systems department.

Conducting the Needs Assessment

Like the question of who initiates an office systems study, the question of who should conduct the needs assessment is dependent upon the particular organization. In organizations with an office systems department/division, the office systems analyst is typically the project leader, charged with determining the study strategy. In many instances, others are called upon to assist in the needs assessment: a vendor or an outside consultant. In nearly all cases, however, an office automation task force is recommended.

The Vendor as Investigator

Most office automation equipment manufacturers (vendors) have a staff for client consultation. Sometimes for a fee, sometimes for no fee (assuming the organization buys the vendor's line of equipment), a manufacturer will offer advice or even conduct the needs assessment. Typically, highly trained, experienced vendor analysts can help an organization identify tasks and functions where automation can make the worker more efficient/effective.

With a thorough understanding of how to conduct a needs assessment, vendor representatives may be in a good position to assess the current situation and design a new system. An obvious outcome is that the needs assessment will result in a recommendation that the organization buy the vendor's goods. While not denying that the vendor may have a good solution, such an approach does negate the possibility of choosing another vendor's solution that may be equally desirable or less expensive. Vendor studies also tend to focus on problems for which the vendor has a solution and to ignore office problems that their technology cannot solve. For example, a word processing vendor may not notice or attend to a phone system deficiency.

Despite such drawbacks, organizations with an extremely good opinion of a given vendor often choose to have its representatives conduct or assist in the needs assessment. Deciding to be a single-vendor organization has potential payoffs in terms of discounts, service, and (typically) elimination of compatibility problems. Organizations with an "approved" vendor list may not have a choice but must select from a given vendor's solutions. In such situations, vendors are the most appropriate choice for systems assessment.

The Outside Consultant as Investigator

An organization may determine that it needs outside, independent assistance in developing an automated office. It may not have personnel with the required expertise or enough time to devote to the project or may simply want fresh views on how it operates. In such a case, the organization may choose among thousands of consulting firms and individual consultants to aid in the automation project. Usually, consultant-aided projects are large in scope. Guidelines for selecting an outside consultant include the following:

- Choose the *right* consultant.
- Know what you want the consultant to do.
- Work closely with the consultant at all stages of the project.
- Make time available for people in your organization to work with the consultant.
- Ensure that the consultant "follows up" once the plan is in place.

The office systems analyst or manager charged with working with the consultant must first choose the best person for the job. Picking up a directory of consultants and choosing one at random is risky. Choosing the right consultant may mean getting recommendations from others who have done similar projects, or perhaps using that directory but having the prospective consultant offer names and phone numbers of previous clients. Not to be overlooked is the need to select an individual or firm with whom the project leader can work. Personality and working styles are two factors to consider, as the project leader and the consultant will be working very closely together.

The next task is to ensure that the consultant has whatever is needed to conduct the assessment. Primary, of course, is a detailed understanding of exactly what the problems appear to be and, very important, what the outcome of the investigation should be. Ancillary to the investigation are office space for the consultant and clerical assistance. The wise office systems manager will choose a consultant with a "track record" of success and will give that person (or firm) all the support needed to conduct the assessment.

Continuous monitoring, discussion, and feedback are desirable throughout the study. The adage that work expands to fit the time allotted for it can be very applicable in the consultant/client relationship. Keeping communications channels open throughout the process is a part of good project management.

The best consultant is involved with the project at all stages and monitors the project as it is implemented and then evaluated. Such follow-up on the part of the consultant shows professionalism and interest. Moreover, such a consultant is available to help change strategies or plans if necessary.

The Office Automation Task Force as Investigator

Workers need to participate in decisions that affect them; their jobs and how they conduct those jobs are of vital concern. Because people are more apt to adjust to change when they have played a role in creating that change—as well as because no one knows better what is being done than the person doing the work—organizations typically begin large-scale investigations by establishing an office automation task force. This task force works under the leadership of the office systems analyst, perhaps in conjunction with an outside consultant or a designated vendor.

The task force leader (sometimes referred to as the project leader) is typically the office systems analyst/manager. The leader should choose individuals who represent the major users of any new system. In selecting members of the office automation task force, Larry Penwell, a systems planning specialist for General Electric, recommends that the analyst ask himself or herself the following questions:

- Who is pushing for the change?
- Who stands to lose from any change?
- Who are key organizational players?
- Who has power to designate dollars toward the project?

The individuals who are described by answers to these four questions are likely candidates for the office automation task force. In addition, it is recommended that the force be made up of representatives from as many types of jobs and departments as possible. Members of the task force should have interest in serving on the task force and have the time to devote to the project. Because of the desirability of top-down support for an office automation project, all highly ranked individuals should be included.

Getting the right mix of individuals on the task force is important to the success of the project. This same team may have responsibility for implementation, and implementation (discussed in Chapter 22) requires strong coordination and good communications skills. The task force itself is not a closed committee; it shares the team's ideas with others in the organization. The media it uses may be informal meetings or even newsletters. Ideally, the communication is two-way; team members disseminate information and gather information and ideas from nonmembers to take back to the task force meetings. In short, task force members should be able to work well together and communicate well.

The task force or investigation team also needs to understand the organization as a whole. What does it take to make the organization productive? How can this be measured? How could office automation contribute to the overall mission of the organization? What is the mission of the unit? How will the project contribute to meeting the mission? Once the task force has struggled with these questions, it can begin to measure or assess what is happening. The business requirements and goals for the project should be clearly defined. Once the project sponsors and investigators are in agreement about expectations, work can begin.

Project Management

The first step of office systems analysis is to identify the problem or opportunity area and the scope of the problem. With the decision to begin such a study, the office systems manager/analyst, in conjunction with (perhaps) an outside consultant and/or task force, plans the investigation.

Perhaps the most difficult question facing the office automation team is "How long will the project take?" Developing a realistic estimate of time for completing an office systems analysis is essential to the planning. To develop a timetable, the planning team must establish the activities for investigating the problem (e.g., if questionnaires are to be used, time is needed for development, distribution, and recording). With an overview of activities, the team is in a position to estimate time needed to complete the project, as well as detail where the investigation should be at any given time.

Figure 21-1 is a hypothetical timetable developed by an office automation team. Determining a timetable can rest heavily on team consensus, intuition, expert opinions, and historical data (how long did such a project take the last time?). The amount of time required depends on the scope,

Task	Time Allowed
Prepare formal study approach.	2 weeks
Obtain top-management approval.	1 week
Explain project to those who may be affected.	1 week
Develop assessment tools.	2 weeks
Validate assessment tools.	2 weeks
Train study teams.	1 week
Collect data.	3 weeks
Compile and analyze data.	3 weeks
Develop feasibility report.	2 weeks
Present feasibility report to top management.	1 week

FIGURE 21-1. Timetable for an office systems project.

complexity, and urgency of the project. Once these are developed, the analyst can chart the timetable on Gantt charts such as the one in Figure 21-2, preferably using project management software.

The timetable is translated to these two media as follows. The Gantt chart compares the time the team expects each step in the project to take with the time it actually takes to complete the step. In addition, the Gantt chart shows a frequent overlap of steps; often, work begins on the next step before the current step is completed. The chart, a visual cue, can help the project manager (and team members) stay on schedule.

Project Name		Jan					Feb				March				April				May
Phases	S/C*	2	9	16	23	30	6	13	20	27	6	13	20	27	3	10	17	24	1
Prepare formal study approval.	S	■	■																
	C	X	X	X															
Obtain top-management approval.	S		■																
	C		X																
Explain project to those affected.	S			■															
	C			X	X	X													
Develop assessment tools.	S				■	■													
	C					X	X												
Validate assessment tools.	S						■	■											
	C																		
Train study teams.	S								■										
	C																		
Collect data.	S								■	■	■								
	C																		
Compile and analyze data.	S										■	■	■						
	C																		
Develop feasibility report.	S												■	■					
	C																		
Present feasibility report to top management.	S														■				
	C																		

*S = Scheduled; C = Completed

FIGURE 21-2. A Gantt chart for project management.

Project management software is available from several software developers. Like the Gantt chart, this computer-generated chart offers a visual cue to keep the project on target and on the timetable. A project mapped out on project management software is shown in Figure 21-3.

FIGURE 21-3. A timetable for an office systems project using project management software.

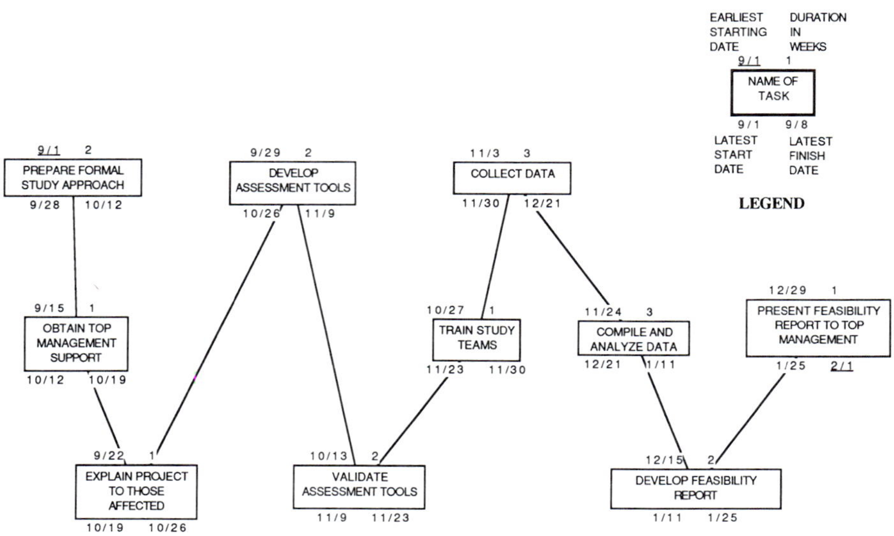

Information Gathering

Techniques to make an office systems investigation more a science than a guessing game are the same techniques used by any scientific investigation. Sources of data are described as either primary or secondary. Primary data reflects first-person accounts (eyewitnesses); secondary data is reports of those accounts. For example, a letter written by a president is a primary source document; an eyewitness report of an event is also a primary source document. When these documents are recorded by a reporter, however, the reporter's account becomes secondary data.

The office systems analyst can choose from a variety of research tools for the investigation. Following is a discussion of secondary sources and seven popular categories of primary sources. These research techniques are offered as examples only; it is the analyst's job to determine which are appropriate in a given situation. In selecting a methodology, the analyst considers the scope of the problem, the potential impact on the organization, and the urgency of the problem. Data collected at this stage is analyzed in the next stage, design.

Secondary Sources of Information

Secondary information that is found in books, journals, files, and so on may provide invaluable information about a specific problem. Any data that is not collected directly by the user is considered secondary.

Appendix 2 contains a list of journals and magazines that may aid the analyst in an office systems investigation. For example, case studies or results of research projects in the *Office Systems Research Journal* explain how a similar problem was solved in another organization or by someone else. Announcements and critiques of new products published in journals such as *Administrative Management* or *Datamation* help identify new office systems opportunities. Information exchange articles in the *Words* journal of the Association for Information Processing or the *Journal of Systems Management* published by the Association for Systems Management can provide the analyst with new ideas and contacts for learning how particular problems can be solved.

Equipment and Human Resources Inventory

It has been said that you cannot get where you are going if you do not know where you are. This axiom is also true when beginning an office study. Vital to any comprehensive analysis is identifying the organization's current technological and human resources.

In organizations within or just beyond the expansion stage of office automation, listing resources may not be an easy task. One department may have numerous IBM products; another may be using Wang products; yet another may be using a collection of IBM PCs, Apple MacIntoshs, and several other vendors' products. Identifying current technologies is important to future analysis and direction, particularly where equipment compatibility and user preferences must be considered. The inventory list can be referred to in future phases of the study.

Human resources should also be inventoried. Job responsibilities and skills should be identified for employees who will be affected by the new system. A list of individuals with technical skills will also be valuable when it comes to actually designing and implementing new office systems.

The Flowchart

A flowchart is a graphic description of work activities. While the technology and human resources inventories describe tangibles, the flowchart describes the process. The flowchart typically takes a standard form, using specific symbols that describe the activity being examined. A wide variety of templates exists for this purpose. Most flowcharts, however, use symbols that conform to those developed by the International Organization for Standardization (ISO).

To speed the flowcharting process, computer programs or preprinted forms may be used to describe office activities. Flowcharts actually sketch out how work is currently accomplished. With such a picture, the office analyst can determine if work is being accomplished in the most efficient way. Figure 21-4 depicts a flowcharting template, and Figure 21-5 is an example of work that has been flowcharted with ISO symbols.

Other means of describing work processes may also be used. For example, narrative descriptions are sometimes used instead of symbols. Steps in the work process are described in narrative words or text that identify who, when, where, and how an activity is being performed.

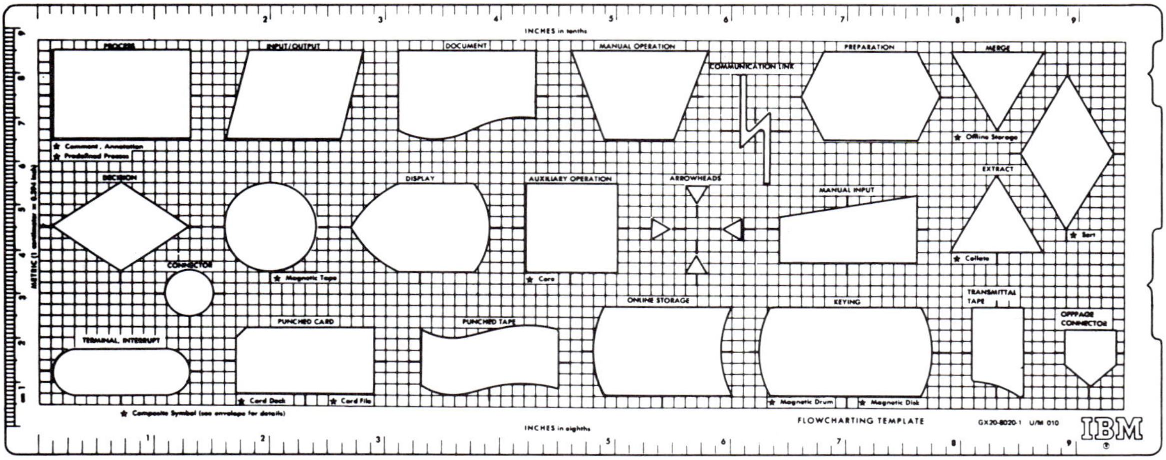

FIGURE 21-4. An IBM flowcharting template based on ISO standards.

Interviews

Interviews are face-to-face meetings between an information giver and an information gatherer. Before beginning any interview, the analyst needs to know the kind of information being sought. Interviews are most beneficial when the analyst can determine who is in the best position to provide the needed information.

Interviews can be *open* or *structured.* In open interviews, which are exploratory in nature, the analyst asks questions that require a small number of interviewees to explain processes, offer opinions, or forecast needs. When many individuals are interviewed about the same topic, or when specific data is needed, interview guides are recommended.

Interview guides are pre-established questions that guide the interviewer. A structured interview guide helps ensure that everyone is asked

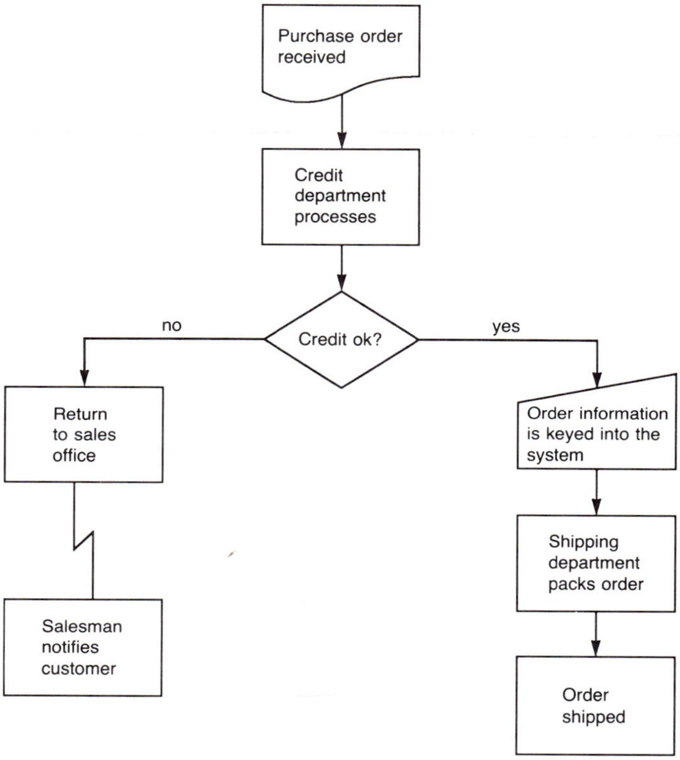

FIGURE 21-5. An example of work that has been flow-charted using ISO symbols.

the same questions. The interview guide standardizes data collection and makes responses easier to compile and compare. It also improves the reliability of the investigation because it ensures that all respondents are asked questions in the same order and the same words.

To develop a good, reliable, and valid interview guide takes skill and practice. Figure 21-6 offers some tips for developing an interview guide. Figure 21-7 presents a hypothetical situation for which an analyst constructed an interview guide. The interview guide that the analyst developed for this situation is shown in Figure 21-8. Before examining the analyst's interview guide, the reader should formulate five questions that would be appropriate for this situation.

In solving problems, analysts frequently need to gather information from both managerial and support personnel. Figure 21-9 is an interview questionnaire designed for managers; Figure 21-10 is an interview questionnaire designed for support staff. Any system to be developed must be appropriate for everyone whose work it may affect.

FIGURE 21-6. Tips for developing an interview guide.

1. Know the kind of data that is needed.
2. When appropriate, ask for "yes" and "no" responses.
3. Word questions so that they are easily understood.
4. Attempt to keep the interview guide short.
5. Always be prepared for explanations of answers.
6. A final question should always be an "open" question. For example, "What other information regarding this subject would you like to share?"

FIGURE 21-7. A hypothetical situation requiring development of an interview guide.

Situation: It has come to the attention of the office systems analyst that users are not satisfied with the way reprographics are currently managed. Users are reporting long turnaround times from the central Reprographic Center and very long lines at "quick copy" locations [sites with small copiers for making one or two copies].

FIGURE 21-8. The analyst's Reprographic Center interview guide.

QUESTIONS FOR MANAGERS

- Who does your Quick Copy?
- How many times a day do you require this service?
- How many minutes a day do you spend on this service?
- How many copies are needed on an average job?
- Who fills out the form to be sent to the Reprographic Center?
  ☐ Yourself ☐ A support person
- Are you pleased with the quality of work done in the Reprographic Center?
- Are you satisfied with the turnaround time from the Reprographic Center?
- Can you suggest ways to improve service?

FIGURE 21-9. An interview questionnaire designed for managers.

MANAGER QUESTIONNAIRE

Personal Background

1. How long with company?
2. In what capacities?
3. In this job?
4. How many people work for you?
5. Organization chart (ask for one).

Department Background

1. What key services does your department provide to your company?
2. Specifically, what key functions does your department do now?

FIGURE 21-9. (continued)

3. What changes do you predict for your department over the next five years (volume, growth, strategy)?
4. What are your personal goals for this department, and what do you watch (key indicators) to monitor your department activities?
5. What have been the key bottlenecks you've faced in getting your department's work done (timeliness, quality, information)?
6. What ideas have you had to break these bottlenecks? Have you tried any? With what results?
7. Would you give me an overview of how your department is organized (organization chart)? Could you indicate the key individuals and their responsibilities?
8. How does your department relate to other departments in the company, particularly in information flow (in and out)?
9. What are the key products of your department (reports up, out, and within; budgets; lists; etc.)?
10. Do you have peaks and valleys of work effort?

Manager Work Style Background

1. What information do you need to know to get your job done (within and outside your department)?
2. How do you get this information now?
3. Any problems in getting the information you need when you need it?
4. What are the causes of these problems, and how would you want this changed?
5. Is there any information you want that you haven't asked for because it would take your secretary or staff too much time to pull together manually?
6. Many managers report that they are faced with time wasters such as waiting for a person to answer a phone, not getting a party called, waiting for a meeting to begin, waiting in line to use equipment, or searching for a missing document. What time wasters do you face?
7. How much time do you lose on each of these during an average week?
8. How frequently must you coordinate with others in the company to schedule meetings or other activities? How do you generally go about scheduling things that depend on coordination with others?
9. Could you see any benefit to your organization having a centralized filing system in which information would be stored electronically and accessed via terminals? If yes, what benefits? Who should have access to it?
10. What are your personal work style preferences (writing, communicating, managing)? Describe how you schedule your work time, meetings, etc.

Automation

1. Do you know of any frustrations your secretary has in meeting your department's needs? How do you think this system might change that?
2. If you could design an ideal automated support for your job, what features would it have? (Show list of features.)
3. Is there anything else you think would be helpful to us in preparing this group for the introduction of automated support?

UNISYS CONSULTING GROUP

FIGURE 21-10. An interview questionnaire designed for support staff.

OFFICE SYSTEMS SUPPORT
PERSONNEL QUESTIONNAIRE

NAME: ______________________ TITLE: ______________________

DEPARTMENT: ______________________ PHONE: ______________________

MANAGER: ______________________ DATE: ______________________

How many people do you support? ______________________

How long have you been with the company? ______________________

How long have you worked in this position? ______________________

1. If you were to describe what you do at work to a friend, what would you say about your job responsibilities?
2. Of the following general task categories, how do you distribute your time?

Typing	____%
Filing and retrieving information	____%
Answering phones, placing calls, transmitting messages	____%
Scheduling meetings	____%
Composing reports, calculating budgets, editing and/or analyzing material	____%
Other administrative support tasks (mail, update calendar, organize work, etc.)	____%
Average number of telephone calls per week:	____

3. Do you have peaks and valleys in your workload? If so, please describe them and relate them to a project or product where you can.
4. Of all the things you do, what specific project takes you the most time?
5. Of all the things you do, what task wastes the most time?
6. Of all the things you do, what task is most frustrating to you, and why?
7. List all the suggestions you have for getting your work done faster, better, and/or with less frustration for you.
8. Do you have any experience using automated office systems?
9. Check the following features and functions of an automated system you think you would use in your work:

☐ Filing and storing information	☐ Scheduling meetings
☐ Mailing information within your department	☐ Leaving electronic messages
☐ Mailing information throughout your company	☐ Processing forms
☐ Producing and editing text	☐ Using directories
☐ Calculating	☐ Taking notes
☐ Creating line drawings (charts)	☐ Accessing data processing
☐ Keeping calendars updated	☐ Sorting information
	☐ Mailing to lists of people

10. Is there anything else about your work that would be useful for us to know in planning this system installation?

UNISYS CONSULTING GROUP

While a well-constructed interview guide is important, the skill of the interviewer is also important in collecting data. Interviewing skills are perfected with practice. It is important for the interviewer to remain as objective as possible; the tone in which a question is asked, for example, can lead the interviewee to respond a particular way. Also, when more than one interviewer is collecting data using the same interview guide, special training may be needed to establish the procedure and tone to be used in the interview.

The telephone interview Telephone interviews, though conducted by phone, are designed to collect the same kinds of information as an in-person interview. Typically, telephone interviews are conducted when the interviewer and interviewee are at distant locations. Telephone interviews are appropriate for "quick questions" or when a survey needs to be completed quickly. A drawback is that interviewees usually do not elaborate on telephone inquiries to the same degree that they might if the interview were conducted in person.

Questionnaires

A written or printed questionnaire is used when information is needed from a large sample of people or when time and expense do not permit personal interviews. Questionnaires can be completed by respondents at their leisure. Unlike a personal interview or telephone call, respondents can place the questionnaire in a to-do stack and respond at a more convenient time. However, therein lies a disadvantage. Because it can be lost or viewed as unimportant, response rates for questionnaires tend to be low.

Nevertheless, the office systems analyst can use the following suggestions to ensure that (1) the questionnaire is well designed and (2) that respondents fill it out honestly and (3) return it:

1. Have a strong opening paragraph or a cover letter with the questionnaire that explains the purpose of the survey. If appropriate, explain how the respondent can learn of the results.
2. Keep it short! The shorter the questionnaire, the more likely it will be completed and returned. Rather than place it in a to-do pile, the recipient of a one-page questionnaire may fill it in on the spot.
3. Make the questionnaire as easy to complete as possible. When appropriate, ask dichotomous (two-choice) questions (yes/no, male/female, etc.) and offer checklists. Example:

   Static electricity can be a problem at my workstation. Yes No

4. Word forced-choice questions so that they are easy to understand. Example:

   Which of the following projects should be begun first?
   ☐ A spelling checker for the mainframe
   ☐ An electronic indexing system for manual and desk files

5. Use ranking questions when preferences are solicited. Example:

   On a scale of 1 to 4, rank the following word processing software features for their potential value to your work (1 = most potential; 4 = least potential):

   ☐ Spelling checker
   ☐ Footnote capabilities
   ☐ Search and replace
   ☐ Thesaurus feature

6. Intensity-scale questions and answers reflect the degree of positive or negative feeling. Example:

   Rate these proposals from 1 to 7 based on the following scale:
   1 = Something we absolutely should *not* do
   4 = Neutral
   7 = Absolutely necessary

Install a voice message system	1	2	3	4	5	6	7
Initiate a company-wide calendaring system	1	2	3	4	5	6	7
Begin projects using desktop publishing	1	2	3	4	5	6	7

7. No matter how structured the questionnaire, it should end with an unstructured, open-ended question. Examples:

   What issues relative to improving the word processing center has this survey failed to address?

   Do you have suggestions for ways in which office automation could aid you in your job?

   What other services from the Information Center would be helpful to you in performing your job?

Figure 21-11 presents samples of structured and unstructured questionnaires for beginning an office systems study. Figure 21-12 presents questionnaires on activity distribution, resource utilization, and document preparation that are used to gather more specific data about employees' needs and work habits.

TYPING QUESTIONNAIRE

1. Who does your typing for you?
   a. School facilities: Dept. secretary ____% Student labor ____%
   b. Own resources: Spouse ____% Paid assistant ____% Myself ____% Other ____%
   c. If you use your own resources, what kinds of documents are typed? Letters ☐ Exams ☐ Research papers ☐ Articles ☐
   d. If a typing resource were readily available, would you use it for any of the typing now done by your own resources? ☐ Yes ☐ No

2. How do you create work that is typed?
   Longhand ____% Shorthand ____% Machine dictation ____%

3. How frequently do you need to have typed items revised or retyped? Never ☐ Rarely ☐ Occasionally ☐ All the time ☐

4. Do you ever wish you could revise finished material but do not because of a deadline? ☐ Yes ☐ No

5. How long does it take to get your items typed?
   Less than 1 day ☐ About 2 days ☐ More than 2 days ☐

6. Are you satisfied with the appearance of the documents leaving your office? ☐ Yes ☐ No

7. Do you ever send out original repetitive letters? ☐ Yes ☐ No

8. Do you send out form letters with fill-ins? ☐ Yes ☐ No

9. Do you compose letters that might include standard or stock paragraphs? ☐ Yes ☐ No

10. Is there work you wish you could do but can't because of your workload? ☐ Yes ☐ No
    If yes, would this work generate additional typing? ☐ Yes ☐ No

11. Do you originate documents that require printing? ☐ Yes ☐ No

12. Would you like to discuss your typing requirements with the Word Processing Consultant? ☐ Yes ☐ No

Please include any additional comments on the reverse of this questionnaire.

UNISYS CONSULTING GROUP

FIGURE 21-11. Sample questionnaires for beginning an office systems study.

a. A structured questionnaire.

FIGURE 21-11.

b. An unstructured questionnaire.

DEPARTMENT PROFILE

The purpose of this profile form is to help Office Systems gain a preliminary understanding of your department's goals, strategies, and the work it performs. Your answers will help us to understand how automated systems will support your department's business objectives. This profile form is to be completed by the department manager and returned with an organization chart. The information gathered on this form will be used to focus and supplement personal interviews. You may use the reverse side of this form, if more space is needed.

1. What does your department do (i.e., mission, charter)?
2. Name up to five key functions your department performs.
   a. d.
   b. e.
   c.
3. List up to five key departments, groups, and/or individuals with whom your department regularly communicates or shares information.
   a. d.
   b. e.
   c.
4. What are the key goals for your department for the next two years?
5. What are the key strategies for achieving these goals?
6. What factors, internal or external, could prevent you from achieving these goals?
7. What suggestions do you have for how automation might assist your department in achieving these goals?
8. What changes do you expect your department to face over the next two years?

UNISYS CONSULTING GROUP

FIGURE 21-12. Questionnaires for gathering specific data on employees' needs and work habits.

a. An activity distribution questionnaire.

ACTIVITY DISTRIBUTION

Please estimate the average number of hours per week (to the nearest .25 hours) that you currently spend in the following activities. In terms of the importance of your time to department goals, also indicate any activities where you feel you should spend more time or less time, by circling M or L.

Activity	**Hours**	**More? Less?**
Composing textual materials (longhand)	_____	M L
Composing textual materials (dictation)	_____	M L
Composing textual materials (keyboard)	_____	M L
Filling out forms	_____	M L
Reading letters, memos, notes	_____	M L
Researching, reading reports & documents	_____	M L
Reviewing correspondence & documents for approval	_____	M L
Reviewing forms	_____	M L

Attending meetings (formal & informal)	_____	M	L
Incoming mail handling	_____	M	L
File handling	_____	M	L
Searching for information	_____	M	L
Copying/sorting/collating	_____	M	L
Having telephone conversations	_____	M	L
Calculating	_____	M	L
Typing	_____	M	L
Using a computer terminal	_____	M	L
Engaging in analysis, thinking, decision making	_____	M	L
Touring, inspecting	_____	M	L
Travel	_____	M	L
Other ______________________	_____	M	L
Other ______________________	_____	M	L

UNISYS CONSULTING GROUP

FIGURE 21-12. (continued)

RESOURCE USAGE

How frequently do you use the following information sources in your work?

	Daily	Weekly	Monthly	Under Monthly
Your own personal files	1	2	3	4
Documents from others	1	2	3	4
Department files	1	2	3	4
Journals/periodicals/books	1	2	3	4
Microfiche files	1	2	3	4
Computer printout reports	1	2	3	4
Computer database (company's)	1	2	3	4
Computer database (subscriber)	1	2	3	4
Company directories	1	2	3	4
Activity schedules of others	1	2	3	4
Other (specify)	1	2	3	4
Other (specify)	1	2	3	4
Other (specify)	1	2	3	4

How frequently do you use the following methods to prepare drafts?
(Please indicate your most preferred method with a check mark.)

	Prefer				
Handwriting	1( )	1	2	3	4
Your personal typing	2( )	1	2	3	4
Dictating	3( )	1	2	3	4
Other (specify) __________	4( )	1	2	3	4

UNISYS CONSULTING GROUP

b. A resource usage questionnaire.

FIGURE 21-12.

c. A document preparation questionnaire.

DOCUMENT PREPARATION

Estimate the average number of typed pages you generate in a week: ______

Estimate the percent of typewritten material you generate that
(a) contains significant amounts of text from other documents: ____%
(b) is sent to someone for review or approval: ____%
(c) is sent to five or more people as drafts or in final form: ____%
(d) is sent to each of the following classes of recipients:
within department ____%
other department at local office site ____%
at other company site ____%
outside company ____%

Estimate the average number of typed pages you receive in a week: ______

Estimate the percent of the materials you receive that originate from
within department ____%
other department at local office site ____%
other company site ____%
outside company ____%

UNISYS CONSULTING GROUP

Observation

Observation is perhaps the oldest method of problem solving. Assessment by observation may be as simple as sitting down with a word processing operator and identifying instances in which features could aid the process or as complex as designing a schedule in which the investigator completes numerous random observations of workers and their activities.

Time or Document Logs

Logs are recordings (loggings) of activities. Depending upon the activity examined, the log may be classified as *time* or *document*. For example, time logs are used in determining how much time an executive spends using a personal computer during the day. Time logs may also be a listing of the number of times a day a worker makes a phone call. Document logs are typically used to determine the number and type of documents a worker processes during a given period.

Figure 21-13 is an example of a document log and instructions for its use; refer to Chapter 15 for an example of a time log.

TYPING VOLUME LOG

Name ______________________ Date ______________________

Department ______________________ Supervisor ______________________

Operator Number	Document Number	Document in	Deadline	Document Code	Author	Input Type	Service Class	Number of Pages	Number of Lines	Typing in	Typing out	Time Spent Typing	Document out	Turnaround Time
1 2	3 5			6	7 9	10	11	12 14	15 18			19 22		23 26

Fill all fields to left with zeros.

Right justify all numbers in fields

Times are in minutes.

Operator Number = 01 – 99

Document Number = 001 – 200

Document Code & Input Type = A – Z

FIGURE 21-13. A document log and instructions for its use. a. A document log.

FIGURE 21-13.

b. Document log instructions.

HOW TO USE THE DOCUMENT LOG

1. Use a new sheet every day.
2. Fill in your name and today's date.
3. Fill in the columns as follows:

Operator # – Leave blank.

Doc # – Starting with "1," assign each document a number as you start it. Do not return to "1" until the end of the survey period. When a document you typed previously is returned, *do not* assign it a new number; use the original number every time it is returned.

Doc In – Date and time document arrives from originator.

Deadline – Deadline requested.

Doc Code – List one of the following codes to represent document type:

M = Memo	I = Internal Miscellaneous
F = Form	S = Statistical Report
L = Letter	N = Narrative Report
R = Repetitive Letter	A = Manuscript
E = Exam	O = Handouts/Class Outlines

Author – Initials of author.

Input – Form in which you received document:

M = Machine Dictation	I = Self-authored
L = Longhand	R = Retype
S = Shorthand	F = Standard Format, Stored

SR (Service Requested) – N = Normal
R = Rush
C = At typist's convenience

 # pp – Number of pages produced.

 # Lines – Number of lines produced.

Typing In – Date and time typing started.

Typing Out – Date and time typing terminated.

Total Time – Actual amount of time spent typing. This should be the difference between the previous two columns, less interruptions.

Doc Out – Time document was returned to its originator.

Turnaround – Difference between *Doc Out* date and *Doc In* date.

Work Sampling

Work sampling is an examination of system outputs to determine if the outputs are needed and, if so, if they are of acceptable quality. An analyst uses work sampling techniques, for example, to determine needed word processing features. In other words, letters, memos, and reports (outputs of the system) are examined to determine if advanced editing features would be helpful. Quality of output can also be examined (Are new printers or other type fonts needed?). Work sampling can be as easy as examining 20 outputs or as complex as examining every document processed in a given period (e.g., one week or one month).

The analyst or office automation task force chooses one or any number of techniques appropriate to the problem/opportunity being investigated. Knowing the kinds of information needed to make informed choices leads the task force in selecting appropriate methodology. Figure 21-14 charts the advantages and disadvantages of six primary data collection instruments.

Technique	When To Use It	Advantages	Disadvantages	Results
Flowchart	Process of doing work is taking too long or appears to be ineffective.	Provides graphic description of work.	May also need to interview key people to chart a process.	Identification of work delays, unnecessary storage, and transportation.
Interview Guide	Scope of problem is small. Opinions of key personnel are vital.	Requires top-level involvement. Quantitative results.	Time-consuming. Skilled interviewers required. Interviewees not always available.	Identification of organization's needs. Applications. Areas needing more study.
Questionnaires	Scope of problem is large.	Less time-consuming than interviews. Skilled interviewers not required. Quantitative results.	Paper-intensive. Analysis is difficult. Limited accuracy. Writing good questions is difficult. Words are inexact.	Identification of department needs. Applications.
Observation Guide	Scope of problem limited to a given department or location.	Skilled interviewers not required. Quantitative results. Only way to collect some information.	Time-consuming. Requires careful planning. Measures only overt acts.	Identification of individual and department needs. Applications.
Time or Document Log	Quantitative measures of work activities are required.	Skilled interviewers not required. Quantitative results.	Time-consuming, disruptive, inaccurate. Follow-up interview often required.	Identification of quantity or type of work performed. Applications.
Work Sampling	Problem is identifiable as quality of output.	Skilled interviewers not required.	Subjective results. Time-consuming.	Identification of department or unit needs. Applications.

FIGURE 21-14. **Advantages and disadvantages of six investigation techniques.**

DESIGN

Design entails analyzing the results of the assessment stage and applying work requirements to available technologies. Keeping in mind the problem to be solved, data is analyzed with a view to how new technology can benefit the organization (or its workers). This text breaks design into the following four steps:

1. Evaluating data.
2. Writing the feasibility report.
3. Writing the request for proposal.
4. Evaluating vendor responses.

Evaluating Data

In tabulating and analyzing data, the office automation task force relies on problem solving skills. Office systems are implemented not just because of what the technology can do, but because the technology fills an identified need. Data must be compiled from whatever gathering methods were used and then be coded and tabulated. The findings of the investigation are the basis on which the problem will be solved. Given this information, the analyst may ask any—or all—of the following questions as a framework for analysis:

1. *Who* performs each procedure within the system? Why is this person doing the activity? Should someone else be doing it?
2. *What* is being done? Exactly what procedures are followed? Why are they used? Often, procedures are followed for years and no one knows why. Is the procedure needed at all?
3. *Where* is the work done? Why is it done in this location? Could it be better done somewhere else?
4. *When* is the procedure done? Is it done at an appropriate time? What are the delays in getting work done? Is this the best time?
5. *How* is the procedure performed? Could it be done in a more efficient manner? Would additional training or technology enable the procedure to be done better, more cheaply, or more efficiently?

The results of this analysis are a response to the initial problem. If a technology solution (opportunity) is appropriate, the analyst prepares a feasibility report. This report is prepared for upper management, who determine if the solution is workable and cost effective.

Preparing the Feasibility Report

The feasibility report is a rough estimate of the kinds of technology needed and approximate costs. The feasibility report indicates the benefits to be derived from application of the technology to the identified needs/opportunities. It includes any data necessary for the decision maker to make an informed choice. An approved feasibility report is, in essence, a contract between the design team and top management. For this reason, details, including the proposed solution, estimated time frames, estimated cost figures, and an overall project plan, should be included. While the feasibility report is typically not highly technical, it needs to provide adequate data to enable the decision maker to make one of three choices:

1. Approve the project.
2. Mandate further investigation or alternative design.
3. Terminate the project.

Writing the Feasibility Report

The feasibility report may be developed with the following structure:

1. Management summary.
2. Description of the present system.
3. Description of the analysis.
4. Description of the proposed system.
5. Cost/benefit analysis.
6. Conclusions and recommendations.
7. Appendices.

The report should follow writing principles applicable to any clear, concise business report. Writing clearly and concisely includes avoiding jargon. To understand how easy it is to use big words to say very little—or nothing at all, examine Figure 21-15.

FIGURE 21-15.
The Systematic Buzz Phrase Projection.

Column 1	Column 2	Column 3
0. Integrated	0. Management	0. Options
1. Total	1. Organizational	1. Flexibility
2. Systematized	2. Monitored	2. Capability
3. Parallel	3. Reciprocal	3. Mobility
4. Functional	4. Digital	4. Programming
5. Responsive	5. Logistical	5. Concept
6. Optional	6. Transitional	6. Time-phase
7. Synchronized	7. Incremental	7. Projection
8. Compatible	8. Third-generation	8. Hardware
9. Balanced	9. Policy	9. Contingency

The procedure is simple. Think of any three-digit number and then select the corresponding buzzword from each column. For instance, number 257 produces "systematized logistical projection," a phrase that can be dropped into virtually any report with that ring of decisive, knowledgeable authority. No one will have the remotest idea of what you're talking about, but the important thing is that they're not about to admit it.

Figure 21-16 is a summary of an actual feasibility report addressing the feasibility of implementing word processing in a school of business. Note that the study provides an overview of the problem, a summary of how the investigation was conducted, findings, conclusions, and recommendations, as well as a section for other considerations and the recommended next step.

The next step involves selecting the most appropriate configuration of equipment. At this point, the office systems analyst (or office automation team) writes the request for proposal.

Writing the Request for Proposal (RFP)

Assuming that upper management decides to continue the project, the office systems analyst (and team) is in a position to find the best configuration of equipment among many vendors. The request for proposal (RFP) identifies organizational needs. Sent to appropriate vendors, the RFP calls for them to address the identified needs with specific products and their costs.

Evaluating Vendor Responses: Hardware

Vendor selection is more than establishing that a specific vendor has a solution to the identified need at the lowest cost. To facilitate the vendor selection process, criteria should be listed, including "functionality, service support, financial strength, contract terms and conditions, product reliability, maintainability, availability, research and development activities, and adherence to industry standards."[1]

Figures 21-17 and 21-18 are forms that organizations use to evaluate vendors' responses to RFPs for office automation. Such a form could be filled out by one individual in a small organization or by any number of individuals in a large organization. The forms are useful in selecting vendors because ratings can be quantified and compared.

Evaluation of the selected vendor's responses may also take the form of pilot installations. A pilot installation is a test application of the product in a given location. In this case, users confirm that the product is either acceptable or unacceptable. As an alternative, or in addition to a pilot installation, users may be asked to evaluate hands-on operation of various products. In such a case, users play a very important role in product selection.

Evaluating Vendor Responses: Software

The evaluation of responses to RFPs for software can follow a structure similar to that used in evaluating hardware. Ascertaining that proposed software solutions actually address identified needs is the first step. Once that determination is made, comparison of vendor products should not be on a "lowest cost" basis alone. Other considerations are ease of use, compatibility with chosen hardware, vendor training options and support, clarity of manuals, cost of licensing, and the personal preferences of users.

FIGURE 21-16. **A summary of a feasibility report.**

MANAGEMENT SUMMARY

I. Introduction

The School of Business Administration (SBA) appointed a word processing task force and arranged for the services of a consultant. The consultant, working with SBA Coordinator, Mrs. Regan, conducted an advisability/feasibility study to determine if, generally stated, the implementation of word processing equipment and/or procedures could allow SBA to improve clerical/administrative support.

II. Study Method

The SBA secretarial/clerical support kept document logs and time ladders for a four-week period to document their activities. The analyst and coordinator tabulated the logs, analyzed them, and developed recommendations. In addition, they conducted interviews and addressed work flow issues.

III. Findings

Approximately 90 percent of SBA typing could be handled more efficiently with word processing equipment. Largest applications are manuscripts, letters, examinations, repetitive letters, and statistical and narrative reports. Rush work was frequent enough to require that some excess capacity be built into the recommendation.

IV. Conclusions and Recommendations

The recommendation is to service the entire SBA with a centralized word processing center using a minicomputer central processing unit (CPU) with six workstations, two high-quality printers, one high-speed printer, and two Correcting Selectrics. The report also provides some alternative recommendations. Full-time operators for the workstations will be additional staff positions.

V. Additional Considerations

Some consideration should be given to compatibility of a word processing center with our present computer center and the potential for compatibility with possible future word processing centers at other locations on campus. In addition, the requirements for dictation equipment and staffing should be considered.

VI. Next Steps

The next step is the selection of a vendor and the development of exact equipment configurations and costs. Upon acceptance of equipment recommendations, implementation begins, including submission of purchase order, appointment of word processing staff, development and communication of procedures, training, equipment installation and testing, work phase-in, and reevaluation of equipment in terms of original objectives.

FIGURE 21-17. A form for evaluating a vendor's response to an RFP for office automation.

OFFICE AUTOMATION VENDOR SELECTION

Vendor ______________________________

Name of Evaluator______________________________

Signature of Evaluator ______________________________

Date of Evaluation ______________________________

Please rate each vendor on the following criteria. The overall rating for each criterion should be between 5 (highest) and 1 (lowest). Brief comments would also be useful.

Rating

1. Proposer's understanding of the scope and magnitude of the work to be accomplished, as evidenced by the proposal. ________
   Comments:
2. Qualifications and experience of the Proposer's assigned personnel. ________
   Comments:
3. Proposer's ability to provide the service and system features required. ________
   Comments:
4. Quality of hardware/software configuration. ________
   Comments:
5. Flexibility and longevity of proposed system. ________
   Comments:
6. Ability of the Proposer to initiate and complete the project within the time frame specified in this RFP. ________
   Comments:
7. Prior experience of the Proposer in providing systems of similar scope and complexity. ________
   Comments:
8. Quality of technical support. ________
   Comments:
9. Quality of training and maintenance programs. ________
   Comments:
10. Total cost of the proposed contract. ________
    Comments:
11. Compliance with other terms, conditions, and provisions of the RFP. ________
    Comments:

Overall Comments: Total ________

VENDOR COMPARISON FORM Rank the three vendors 1 to 3 on each criterion; tie scores are allowed.			
	Vendor A	Vendor B	Vendor C
Ease of operation	1	2	1
Communication capability	1	1	1
WP/DP dual function	1	1	1
Special needs*	1	2	3
Technical requirements	1	1	1
Vendor support (reputation)	3	2	1
Experience with proposed system	1	3	2
Growth/adaptability	1	1	1
Cost (Rental)** (monthly)	($2393) 2	($2637) 3	($2131) 1
TOTAL	12	16	12

*Special needs include high-quality print, proportional spacing, super and subscripts, and special characters.

**This is the rental price on the basic system with compared optional features. The final rental figure may vary somewhat depending on the final configuration of optional equipment selected.

FIGURE 21-18. **A vendor comparison chart: Nine key factors for comparing and selecting vendors.**

SUMMARY

The purpose of this chapter was to describe how an analyst might undertake the first two stages of the office systems analysis process: assessment and design.

Once the problem is identified and the scope of the investigation set, the next step is to decide who should lead the study. Often, the analyst will appoint an office automation task force to aid in the investigation. Often, too, an analyst or task force can benefit from the expertise of an outside consultant (or even an equipment vendor) in the investigation.

The project team's first step is to define business needs and objectives. The next step is to plan the approach to solve the business problem. Once the study methodology is set, the team estimates how much time the study will take. Using Gantt charts or even computer programs, the analyst establishes timelines that will guide the project to completion.

The success of the project is dependent upon the value of the information obtained in the assessment stage. Choosing appropriate assessment tools—flowcharts, interviews, questionnaires, observation guides, work sampling—is important. Using assessment tools effectively mandates that they be well prepared and tested before actual use.

In the design stage, the office systems analyst/team applies appropriate solutions to identified problem areas. These solutions are described to top management in a feasibility report that outlines the need for the study, how the study was done, and what the study team recommends. Included are specific recommendations as to categories of equipment, number of units, and cost benefits. The chief decision maker will determine whether it is feasible to continue the project.

Once the feasibility report is approved, the next step is to find the vendor with the best solution. The request for proposal (RFP) outlines the organization's requirements in detail and asks that vendors respond with a description of appropriate technologies, cost, and other considerations deemed important (such as training).

Selecting the best solution—be it hardware or software—requires the team to determine which vendors have addressed the identified need and to then rank the vendors as to suitability. At this point, checklists that compare vendor responses are useful tools.

A thorough assessment and workable design are vital to successful office automation. Implementation and evaluation are discussed in the next chapter.

DISCUSSION QUESTIONS

1. Who is the best person to conduct an office systems analysis?

2. Given the following situations, how would you plan to collect data? Which instrument(s) would be most effective? Support your answer.
   a. A large New York City organization wants its divisional vice-presidents to be able to communicate electronically.
   b. A book company in the Midwest wants to update its sales force on new books and services.
   c. The claims department of an insurance company can't keep up with the number of telephone calls it receives each day.
   d. The costs of printing and distributing the *Employee Manual* are going up. What are the alternatives to having it published outside the company?
   e. Long-distance telephone bills doubled last month. What should be done?

3. Assume you are assigned to write a questionnaire to determine people's desktop publishing needs.
   a. Write one ranking question.
   b. Write one intensity-scale question.
   c. Write one open-ended question.

4. If you were to ask, "What type of word processing do you prefer?" what answers might you receive? Rewrite the question to get the response you are looking for.

5. Getting company employees to agree to sit for an interview or complete a questionnaire is frequently difficult. List some ideas for getting them to participate in your investigation.
6. What is a feasibility report? Who prepares it? Who reads it? What are its major subsections?
7. What is a request for proposal (RFP)? What are its major subsections?
8. How would you go about comparing the proposals you've received from five vendors?

APPLICATION EXERCISES

1. Using one of the examples in Discussion Question 2, draft an interview guide, questionnaire, or observation form that you might use in collecting the needed information.
2. Use flowchart symbols to trace the way grades are processed at your university, beginning with the student handing in the final exam.
3. Select an actual office automation problem and solve it. Choose problems from your university, your job, or even your personal information processing requirements.

SUGGESTED READINGS

Kalow, Samuel J., and Ercole, Rosa. *Office Systems* (Englewood Cliffs, N.J.: Prentice-Hall, 1984).

Katzan, Harry, Jr. *Office Automation: A Manager's Guide* (New York: American Management Association, 1982).

Lieberman, Mark A.; Selig, Gad J.; and Walsh, John J. *Office Automation: A Manager's Guide for Improved Productivity* (New York: John Wiley and Sons, 1982).

Stallard, John J.; Smith, E. Ray; and Reese, Donald. *The Electronic Office: A Guide for Managers* (Homewood, Ill.: Dow Jones-Irwin, 1983).

OFFICE SYSTEMS ANALYSIS: Implementation and Evaluation

CHAPTER

22

OBJECTIVES

After completing this chapter, the reader should be able to meet the following objectives:

- Describe the role of implementation and evaluation in the office systems cycle.
- List steps an organization could follow as a guide to implementing new systems.
- Given a situation in which new technologies are planned, suggest strategies for their implementation.
- Identify major facility changes that must be considered in preparing a site for new technologies.
- List ten ways to conduct an office systems evaluation.
- Develop an equipment feature analysis form, an interview guide, and an attitude questionnaire appropriate for office systems evaluation.

KEY TERMS

implementation
planning document
pilot installation
prototype installation
evaluation
barriers

INTRODUCTION

Technology planners must remember that technology is useless unless it is used. The best-designed office system in the world will have no value to the organization if users are not convinced of its value, are not motivated to use it, and are not adept in its use.

Chapter 21 presented an overview of strategies related to assessing and designing automated office systems. This chapter continues the office systems cycle by offering practical strategies related to office systems *implementation* and *evaluation*. The strategies are based on the concepts and theories outlined in Chapter 18 ("Organizational Change") and Chapter 20 ("Office Systems Analysis: Frameworks"). "Organizational Change" discussed the impact of change on organizations and the people in those organizations. "Office Systems Analysis: Frameworks" reviewed systems concepts and frameworks for office systems analysis.

The office systems cycle illustrates the difficulty of putting definite beginning and ending points on any phase of office systems analysis. Many of the strategies to be discussed here were begun in the assessment or design stage. Moreover, even if the strategies were not actually begun, they were planned prior to the date on the plan that said "Implementation" or "Evaluation."

This chapter is divided into two main sections: implementation and evaluation. After an overview of the role and importance of an implementation plan, the first section discusses the steps involved in implementing a project.

The second part of this chapter discusses specific how-to's with regard to evaluating office systems once they are in place. Evaluation is a critical step in the office systems cycle. The results of an evaluation are often the input necessary to begin the entire investigative cycle again (see Figure 22-1).

FIGURE 22-1. The office systems cycle.

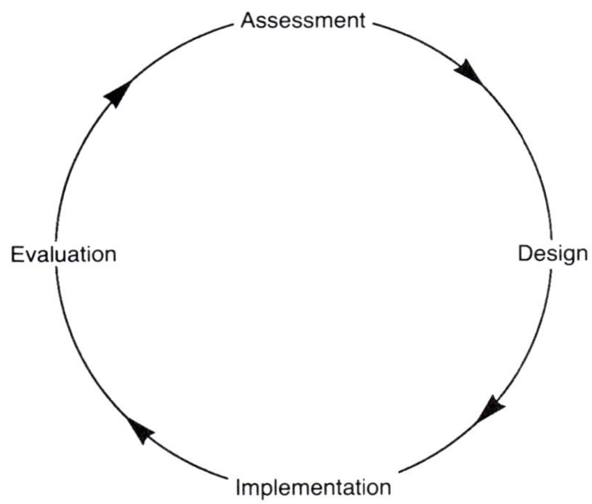

IMPLEMENTATION

The focus of office systems implementation is twofold: people and facilities. People who will be using the system need to be eased into it, which means being aware of how the system will affect their jobs. It also means being comfortable with using the system. The technology itself mandates changes in the physical workplace. Technology may require special lighting, cooling, or ventilation. It needs a physical location—and proper furniture—to support it. This change in work behavior and facilities can result in crisis if not managed properly.

The key to successful implementation, therefore, is to plan the work and to work the plan.

Whenever technology is added to the workplace, people's work and workplace change. An implementation plan may be simple (e.g., to coordinate delivery and installation of a replacement copier on the third floor) or large (e.g., to install microcomputers on every desk in the loan department).

Steps for Successful Implementation

Chapter 18 discussed several theories dealing with organizational change. This section is more pragmatic; it presents techniques that are based on these theories and applicable to introducing new office automation technologies to users. Following are a number of office automation implementation strategies that have met with success in many organizations. These steps work best in organizations where the following conditions are present:

1. The organization has a history of involving workers in making decisions that affect their jobs.
2. Office systems is an identifiable business function that supports other business functions in the organization.
3. Office automation is viewed as a continuous process, not a one-shot remedy.

The following section provides a step-by-step guide to the major items that may need to be accomplished in a typical office systems implementation. Since no two projects are the same, these steps need to be adapted to the requirements of each project.

Step 1: The Planning Document

A planning document is a written explanation of expected changes and exactly when and where the proposed changes will take place. The plan should identify all activities and tasks to be completed and should specify how long each activity/task will take, as well as target dates for completion. In developing a planning document, the analyst must have detailed delivery information from the vendor as well as biographical and personality-related information about individuals in the organization. The implementation plan is customized to an organization.

The analyst must meet with all individuals charged with implementing the new technology, getting their commitment to perform given activities in the required timeframe. The planning document may be in narrative form, or a Gantt chart (see Chapter 21), or any other descriptive format. It should explain the structure for the entire implementation, eliminating any surprises for implementers or employees. It is, in effect, a public relations document. Outlining what is happening, why it is happening, when it will happen, and the impact the technology will have on everyone is vital to the communication process. The communication process, in turn, is integral to ready acceptance of change.

Successful implementation mandates that the planners and those to be affected by office automation know what is—and what will be—happening in the future. Such communication is a key tenet of successful implementation.

In addition, the planning document serves as a buffer between plans for the change and the actual change. People need advance time to evaluate the impact of the technology and adjust to the idea. Providing this document well ahead of implementation is highly recommended.

Step 2: Staff the Project

As discussed in Chapter 21, the office automation task force is a select group of employees representing user departments, upper management, office systems employees, and others who help the analyst plan and complete the office systems study.

That same task force (or, if appropriate, a newly appointed group) can aid the analyst in implementing and then monitoring implementation strategies. The very creation of a task force is, in essence, an implementation technique. The more people who are involved in planning, who actually participate in the change, the higher the likelihood of acceptance of the final product. The office automation task force's role in implementation may be planning, coordinating, and communicating the project's goals to the user community and top management.

Duties of the task force may include the following:

1. Planning the implementation process.
2. Coordinating dates, times, and places with systems vendors and users for specifics on delivery and use.
3. Determining the demands of the technology on workplace facilities.
4. Writing and disseminating status reports on the progress of implementation.
5. Interfacing with the office automation task force (if the two groups are different).

The implementation team should appoint several subcommittees whose members may be delegates from each department or section to be affected by the new technology. A subcommittee member aids in the coordination plans of physical facilities (discussed later) as well as the communication process. The implementation team should meet regularly with these members.

Step 3: Select Pilot and Prototype Installations

While pilots and prototype installations are part of the design stage, they can also be considered an implementation strategy.

A *pilot* is a planned and managed installation of office automation support that serves as a model for providing the same support in a larger scope (e.g., the organization). A *prototype* is also a planned and managed installation of office automation. Unlike the pilot, however, a prototype is a test in a self-contained area, with no plans for expansion.

Pilot tests are an assessment strategy when used as a field test of the quality and usefulness of the products being considered for adoption. Pilots are an implementation strategy in that results from the test can be used to diagnose learning problems and acceptance of the technology by its users. Such information can be very valuable to the project manager or task force in determining appropriate implementation strategies. Sites for pilot installations should be carefully selected. The following are some rules of thumb:

1. *Choose a site with high visibility.* The pilot installation is a "trial run" of the automation. Placing the new technology in a department or area where people see it, use it, and talk about it has ramifications for its large-scale implementation: "Yes, we've been using electronic mail for six months; everyone is using it!"

2. *Choose a site with a high likelihood of success.* Selecting a locale where the installation has a high success probability—where users are enthusiastic about the technology or where its success can be calculated by a large return on investment—is recommended. "Desktop publishing saved the Personnel Department $200,000 the first quarter!"

In short, a well-planned pilot installation can play a key role in design and implementation.

Guidelines for choosing prototype applications likewise include selecting applications with a high potential for success. A prototype installation will often change the way people work, even if it is scheduled for a short period of time. Removing prototype technology that appears not to be the best solution to automation planners requires the same care as installing it. One planner whose prototype failed said, "Removing the prototype word processing system from the department was worse than curing people of a drug addiction! No one wanted to return to their former way of doing work, yet the system itself wasn't living up to expectations."

Pilot and prototype installations are both test sites, and test site success is always dependent upon meeting technological standards and user acceptance.

Step 4: Manage and Control the Project

Managing and controlling implementation are the role of the implementation task force, which must create a document that includes the activities, tasks, and subprojects that must be accomplished. Specific responsibilities are assigned to team members for tasks such as hardware and software installation and training. A detailed checklist is very useful for identifying all tasks and time estimates for completion, milestones that must be reached, and the required completion date for each task. Just as the office automation task force had a plan for project management, so must it have a subplan for implementation. Written plans are prepared not only for team members, but for subcommittee members as well. It is advisable to have a written description of the role of each committee member in the implementation plan—and how that role contributes to the overall goal.

Management and control of an implementation project involves continually following up with everyone involved in the project, from vendor to committee member. Meetings should determine not only that the project is on target but also identify any problems that may arise.

Step 5: Prepare the Facilities

Critical to effective implementation is proper site preparation. Before a new system can be installed, the implementation team must ensure that facilities are appropriate for the new technologies. The planner needs to ensure that the equipment is (1) installed correctly, (2) installed conveniently, and (3) installed to contribute to comfortable, safe employee use. Safety and correctness were discussed in Chapter 16, "Ergonomics," and security is discussed in the next chapter, but some key points are reviewed here.

Correct installation Correct installation requires the equipment to be put into place, keeping in mind power needs, space needs, and other conditions such as humidity and security. Installation may require physical alterations in buildings. In some instances, walls must be knocked down or put up. Air conditioning requirements, especially those of minicomputer systems, must be evaluated. Also, wall configurations or high wall panels can impact air flow and ventilation.

Furniture and storage needs must also be addressed. New furniture must be assembled and set up, wiring must be installed, and telephones moved. New furniture must be placed conveniently, as well as near appropriate power and lighting sources. Supplies will need to be stored; the new copier will need paper and toner. Where will these supplies be? Where will computer supplies such as disks, printer paper, ribbons, printwheels, backup disks, and other needed items be stored?

For example, a local area network installation requires cable wiring. The cables, in turn, must meet fire and safety regulations applicable to the building in which the LAN is installed. In addition, a "closet" (or closets) must be identified as a site for the multifunction access unit. Security issues (discussed in detail in Chapter 23) must also be addressed. If, for example, new microcomputers are part of the LAN installation, how will the organization address theft-protection concerns? In short, getting the physical site ready for installation mandates that the planner prepare for such technological demands.

Convenient installation Convenient installation, though related to correct installation, has physical demands that are coupled with practical, usable designs. For example, the planner who intends to install "quick copiers"—small photocopiers—throughout the organization needs to consider not only where they can be installed in keeping with their technological demands, but also where they can be installed *to meet the needs of users*. Copiers placed in the middle of a busy office can be a source of aggravation for employees located near them—not only from added traffic, but the individual closest to them is often considered the resident expert on their operations. However, copiers need to be conveniently located so that users can easily access them.

Comfortable and safe installation Comfortable and safe installation mandates not only that the equipment be technologically aesthetic and properly installed, but also addresses ergonomic concerns (see Chapter 16). Comfortable installation may require new or adapted furniture to ensure ease of use. The traditional desk was not designed to accommodate a personal computer. Printers do not work well on a standard table (e.g., where does the form-feed paper come from? Where do completed sheets fall?). In other words, facility planning should be addressed prior to installation and should be completed before the equipment arrives.

Step 6: Obtain and Install the System

The analyst should verify that all hardware, software, and required documentation have been ordered. It is also important to verify that special supplies such as cables, power-surge controls, wire management systems, and the like are ordered. Sometimes systems do not arrive with these necessary extras. Getting technicians to install the cable requires advance planning, so that cables and other supporting devices are in place when the system arrives. If part of the system, telephone service must also be arranged.

Installation includes setting up and testing all equipment. The amount of time will vary, of course, depending upon the complexity and scope of the system. All software must be installed and tested. Minicomputer systems may have a "burn-in" period before they can be used. Problems should be resolved and stability of the system verified before it is used.

Systems arrival is another challenge. Who keeps inventory of goods that have arrived? Which box goes to which floor, to which workstation? What should be done with the refuse? Where should documentation be placed? What about employees who may not be at their desks on arrival day? Work goes on, but delivery of the technology can disrupt the entire work process. Without security measures in effect, how will the systems be secured?

Step 7: Install Security Measures

Security measures include both protection of equipment and access to software. For example, will the minicomputer be in a locked room, or will it be accessible to everyone? Usually, the systems administrator has access to system and administration programs. Who else needs access? How is backup provided in the administrator's absence? Other security considerations are discussed in Chapter 23.

The systems administrator needs the list of authorized users, along with the applications they will be authorized to use. Some users may have only "read" access, whereas others are authorized to both "read" and "write" to files and applications. *Read* means that one can access files but cannot make changes (*write*).

Step 8: Develop Applications

Requirements for new applications will have been identified during the assessment stage. The task force will need to confirm all applications with related user groups and management. Plans and schedules to design and implement applications must be established. Which applications must be ready for initial installation and which need to be phased in later? Does work need to be converted from manual systems or other computer systems? Who will do this work, and how? Is documentation available or does it need to be developed? Who will assist personnel with using or developing applications?

The task force (or an appointed committee) should arrange periodic meetings with users to review the implementation of new applications, get their ideas, and encourage "ownership" and acceptance of the application.

Step 9: Deliver Specific Training Requirements

Perhaps the most important implementation strategy for new technologies is a strong training program. Study after study has shown that applications that a user understands and can apply with expertise to the job at hand are the applications that are most used. A manager, for example, who knows nothing of word processing is not likely to use word processing. Likewise, a secretary who does not understand spreadsheets will not use spreadsheets. While these two examples are simplistic, the point is clear: effective, creative use of new technologies mandates user expertise.

The planning team, the vendor, user departments, and even top management must decide on the right mix of training strategies: orientation seminars, product demonstrations, systems training, applications training, and so on. Because of its importance to the success of office automation, training has a separate chapter in this text, Chapter 24.

Step 10: Establish Functional Procedures

Work procedures may have been redesigned in the design stage; however, the introduction of a new system does not result in automatic acceptance of the system or the new work procedures. During the transition phase, it is generally a good idea to run "tandem" activities. That is, work is done under both the old and the new systems concurrently. This allows for not only a comparison of systems but also for modification.

While there is a push for new administrative procedures to mirror the new system, caution should be exercised to minimize the overload caused by too many new activities at the same time. Administrative procedures, while important to modify, should follow implementation of the new system until the bugs have been worked out.

Other functional procedures include establishing who is to be responsible for the maintenance and repair of the system. It is also desirable to write procedures for ordering supplies. Establishing departmental or unit responsibility for operation of the new system is important.

EVALUATION

Evaluation is the fourth and final phase of the office systems cycle. It is often difficult to determine where the evaluation stage stops and the assessment stage begins again. These stages overlap in organizations with a long history of office automation studies.

The crux of evaluating office automation technologies is determining if the technologies met their objectives. Why were the technologies installed? To improve the quality and quantity of written documents? To provide management with more information—or more timely information—on which to base decisions? To speed up order handling? Evaluation always involves knowing the original objective of the technology. That objective serves as a standard by which to say "Yes, the technology has met our expectations" or "No, the technology is not working out as we expected." Preestablished methodologies for evaluation also enable evaluators to be more objective.

Office systems evaluation must address the following questions: Who should do the evaluation? When should it take place? How should it be done? After these questions are addressed, they are followed by a discussion of specific evaluation strategies such as the following:

- Equipment feature analysis
- Personal interviews
- Company files
- Attitude questionnaires
- Communications audits
- Work-time measurements
- User competency testing
- Participant observation

Who Should Do the Evaluation?

Whether planned or not, system evaluation is done by everyone who has contact with the system. The CEO who uses the new phone system, the vice-president who reads the report that was published using desktop publishing, the secretary who uses electronic calendaring to schedule appointments, the customer who receives an order—all are potential evaluators of the system. The overall responsibility of formal evaluation, however, rests with the office systems analyst or task force that implemented the system. The analyst or team is charged with determining the evaluation strategy and carrying it out. Users may be one source for providing evaluation data.

When Should Evaluation Take Place?

In essence, informal evaluation of new technologies is constantly taking place. From the day the technology is introduced, its users are critiquing its value. The office systems analyst, however, must have taken evaluation needs into account in the initial planning of the systems study. Supplemental evaluations may be necessary if, for example, a problem exists in implementation.

Before the technology is evaluated for usefulness and before users are rated on job performance using the new technologies, however, a nonevaluative period should have elapsed. How long this period should be depends upon the complexity of the application. A nonevaluative period allows users to be exploratory, to make mistakes, to correct them, and to continue using the technology.

Such a period is also important for gaining an understanding of the value of the technology. At first, work may be done more effectively with the old tools. Users need time to learn to use and appreciate the new technology, and the new technology needs time to become an accepted tool. In short, any new work tool or process should be given adequate time to have an impact on work before evaluation begins.

While no exact time can be offered here, evaluation should be well-planned. The analyst determines when evaluation should take place, depending upon the complexity of the technology and the rate at which users incorporate it into their work processes. Thus a formal evaluation may take place any time after the technology becomes part of work.

How Should Evaluation Be Done?

The evaluation process should facilitate understanding of what new technology has done for the individual and the organization. The evaluation will be less threatening if it is conducted as if it were the assessment stage of the next cycle. Changing the terminology from evaluation to assessment is not only less threatening to users but may be appropriate because evaluation techniques are the very same techniques described in Chapter 21 (observations, interviews, questionnaires, etc.).

Evaluation is both a science and an art. The evaluator must select the most appropriate data collection tool and then design an instrument that follows accepted techniques and determine what to do with the resulting data. A questionnaire designed with no view of what to do with the data that will result is pointless. Data collection techniques must also be administratively feasible, which means that while interviewing all users may be desirable, time and personnel constraints must be taken into account. The process of understanding and reporting primary data is a science/art that can be learned and is polished with every project.

Evaluation Strategies

The following strategies, which are offered strictly for illustration, have worked for various organizations. As explained earlier, any assessment tool described in Chapter 21 may also be used for evaluation. The office systems analyst chooses from among these strategies, or even develops original strategies to determine if the new system or technology is performing or being used as planned.

Equipment Feature Analysis

Equipment feature analysis involves creating a list of the features of the new technology that differentiate it from other technologies. Users can rate the features as *mandatory, desirable,* or *optional.* Specific features could also be rated as operating *slowly* or *fast.* The analyst can develop a composite score for the equipment by giving a numerical value to the ratings and adding up the columns. For example, the feature rating form in Figure 22-2 could be used to evaluate word processors.

User Interviews

Interviews with users, which can provide information regarding the effectiveness of the technology, may be open or tightly structured. They are a means of finding out what's good and what's not so good about a system. Interviews allow the analyst to evaluate the planning and implementation as well as the actual operations of the technology.

FIGURE 22-2. A feature rating form for word processors.

	Use Frequently (10 points)	Use Moderately (5 points)	Never Use (0 points)	Total
Spell check				
Mail merge				
Footnote generator				
Headers				
Footers				
Table of contents				
Columns				
Pagination				
Total Value				

Company Files

One reason an organization implements office automation is to improve workers' quality of work life (QWL). As discussed in Chapter 20, office automation has the potential to improve motivation and job satisfaction. A review of company records may provide the analyst with data regarding turnover rates, personnel evaluations (did individual or department productivity go up?), or even attendance. Improvement in any of these items may be attributed to the technology available to the worker.

Attitude Questionnaires

Rather than assess the technology itself, the office systems evaluator may assess individuals' attitudes toward that technology. While company files may provide hard data regarding the effect of the system on work, a questionnaire can offer information regarding attitude and worker acceptance of the technology. Again, to be effective, new technologies need to be used. If the individual who uses the technology feels it is of little value to him or her, chances are that it *is* of little value.

Communications Audit

A conceptual communications approach to office systems analysis was identified in Chapter 20. Office systems are sometimes implemented to improve communications within an organization, and a communications audit can determine if the new technology facilitated more or better communications among employees. A communications audit is a form that shows who, when, and how many communications were made with others in the organization. Although a communications audit is a time-consuming endeavor, an analyst who can show that a system actually improved communications within a company has verified a valuable benefit of the system.

Work-Time Measurement

Work-time measurement simply compares the before-technology time involved in doing a task with the after-technology time for the same task. Time savings, as discussed in Chapters 15 and 21, can show substantial cost savings (benefits) to the organization.

Cost Comparisons

An important measure that should be addressed in any evaluation report is a comparison of expected versus actual costs of the system. Such comparisons give little information about the effectiveness of a new system, but they can show that costs were reasonable or that a value is obtained when the operating costs of the current versus the previous system are compared. Figure 22-3 presents an example of a cost comparison report.

	Cost Savings Summary		
	Proposed	**Actual**	**Variance**
Centralized Annual Operating Costs	$212,711	$227,122	+$14,411
Decentralized Annual Operating Costs	193,429	192,853	576
Annual Savings	$ 19,282	$ 34,269	$14,987
Development Costs	$ 12,320	$ 14,080	+$ 1,760
One-Time Equipment Costs	4,000	4,245	+ 245
Total First-Year Development Costs	$ 16,320	$ 18,325	+$ 2,005
Payback	10.2 mos.	6.4 mos.	– 3.8 mos.

FIGURE 22-3. A typical cost comparison report.

User Competency Testing

If individuals who were expected to use the system can use it to its fullest, chances are the system is a success. If it can be determined that users can use its features to their advantage—or have created even more ways to use it than originally outlined—the evaluator can assume a high degree of system success.

Participant Observation

A specially trained worker who monitors new technologies is the final evaluation method to be discussed here. A person who is working in the system is often in the best position to determine its effectiveness. Such an approach may conjure up images of spying and spies; however, the purpose of the observer is to evaluate the technology, not necessarily the workers. This observer may be an outsider or a regular employee who simply fills out a technology-use observation form.

Why Some Systems Fail

Systems fail more often because of poor planning than because of hardware or software problems. The following is a list of reasons why some office automation projects fail.[1] These barriers are divided into organizational, people, implementation, and technological barriers. Note that these barriers to successful office automation can occur at any phase: assessment, design, implementation, or evaluation.

1. *Organizational barriers.* Top management or the office systems planners
   - based decisions on short-term goals/earnings,
   - failed to understand the potential for improved operations,
   - failed to understand productivity/cost-benefits, and
   - wanted benefits without costs.
2. *People barriers.* Users of the office system
   - resisted change,
   - wanted more control over selection of technologies or how they were to be used,
   - did not understand how office automation changed their jobs, and
   - did not learn to use the technology adequately.
3. *Implementation barriers.* Implementers of the office system were
   - unsure of user requirements,
   - sought "ultimate" solutions,
   - lacked planning expertise, and
   - did not understand the anxiety of employees toward change.
4. *Technological barriers.* The technology itself was
   - too complex to learn to use,
   - incompatible with other technologies in the organization,
   - based on media incompatible with existing media,
   - wide open to security problems, and
   - not given adequate or appropriate space in the office.

Identifying potential problems related to management, users, implementers, and the technology itself can be of value to the office systems evaluator in diagnosing why things went wrong. For example, finding that a system is not being used may be attributed to any of these barriers. Identifying and correcting the problem (barrier) is of utmost importance to systems success.

SUMMARY

This chapter offered how-to's related to office systems implementation and evaluation, the last two stages of the office systems cycle. Steps relative to installation needs and evaluation strategies were offered as examples of techniques the automation planner could consider in developing plans for implementing and evaluating new technologies.

A planning document outlines the implementation plan. Knowing what technology will be delivered when and to whom is key to communications. Communications relieves surprises, thereby contributing to user acceptance.

The office systems task force may continue as the implementing team or appoint a new group to oversee the implementation. Pilot and prototype installations allow users to test the technology themselves. The task force must manage and control the project, setting goals and time frames.

Preparing the facility includes ensuring correct, convenient, and safe installation. The physical installation requires ensuring that the correct hardware and software arrive and are installed at the proper location. Installation also requires preplanning in seeing that cabling and electrical needs have been addressed. Security and training measures should begin (discussed in detail in the next chapter).

All applications should be phased in gradually, allowing systems to become part of the work pattern. New functional procedures should be established.

Evaluation strategies should be well planned, well executed, objective, verifiable, continuous, and feasible and should result in useful information. Evaluation leads into the next step in the cycle, assessment. In addition, because the planner learns from errors, evaluation findings may mean that the next project has a higher likelihood of success. Keeping users involved at all stages also helps ensure system acceptance.

Equipment feature analysis forms allow an evaluator to determine the use (and desirability) of expensive or additional features of the new technology. Information in company files can tell the evaluator if the technology has had an impact on employee performance. Attitude questionnaires can determine what people think of their technologies; if the new system is highly regarded, chances are it is operating as expected (or better!). Work-time measures compare the before and after times for completing specific tasks. Cost comparisons contrast expected technology costs with actual technology costs. While these figures do not necessarily indicate quality performance, they can show that the system is operating as planned.

The implementation and evaluation strategies offered here are examples of how these processes have been completed in the past. From this discussion, the reader should see that all four stages of the office automation cycle are never really done and forgotten. While the stages are identifiable, what is done at any stage has an impact on the other stages—an impact identifiable even for future, yet-unthought-of projects.

DISCUSSION QUESTIONS

1. List the ten steps offered as an approach for office systems implementation. Why is implementation considered the key to a system's success?
2. Given the following implementation sites, develop a project management plan. Describe the resources needed to do the implementation and estimate a time frame for the site.
   a. A large community college has a new telephone system: new operating procedures, new telephone numbers, new handsets.
   b. A government office plans to install a local area network that will connect department heads on five floors.
   c. The corporate headquarters of a large manufacturing organization is offering personal computers to all its employees.
3. What is the role of evaluation in the office systems cycle? Why is it frequently difficult to distinguish the evaluation phase from the assessment stage?
4. If you were charged with evaluating the systems identified in Discussion Question 2, what questions would you need to ask yourself before you developed an evaluation strategy and timetable?

APPLICATION EXERCISES

1. Interview at least three people who are using office automation at their workplace. How were they introduced to the technology?
2. Write an item for a company newsletter detailing the benefits of the voice-mail system that is scheduled for implementation in three months.
3. Prepare a written questionnaire for evaluating an organization's personal computers. What will you be evaluating, the technology itself or acceptance and use of the computers?

SUGGESTED READINGS

Bair, James H., and Mancuso, Laura. *The Office Systems Cycle* (Palo Alto, Calif.: Hewlett-Packard, 1985).

Sokol, Tom. "Office Automation System Case Study," *Proceedings of the Office Systems Research Conference, March 20–22, 1987* (Bowling Green, Kentucky, 1987), pp. 93–94.

IMPLEMENTATION: Management Issues

CHAPTER 23

OBJECTIVES

After completing this chapter, the reader should be able to meet the following objectives:

- Identify critical factors for managing and supporting office systems and end-user computing.
- Identify major policy issues for office systems and end-user computing.
- Describe steps managers should take to provide adequate security for office computers and data.
- Explain why backup of computer data is important and how data can be protected.
- Identify legal issues about which managers should be aware.
- Describe steps managers should take to ensure the accuracy and reliability of user-developed systems.
- Explain the role of auditing in protecting computer resources in the office.

KEY TERMS

back-up
copyright
data encryption
documentation
site-license agreement
volume-purchase agreement
virus

INTRODUCTION

Developing and managing end-user computing resources and office information systems have become high priorities for managers. Issues that were previously of concern only to managers of technical data processing departments have become general concerns in the workplace.

Many procedures that monitor and control information processing in the "paper office" are no longer adequate in the new world of electronic information processing. On the other hand, the controls and procedures used in technical data processing centers may not be practical in a decentralized office. New techniques must be developed and implemented. The solutions, of course, will vary from one situation to another, but guidelines can help.

Managers must be informed about the risks and issues involved with office computers. Otherwise, they may not recognize problems until after disaster strikes. When new technologies are introduced, it takes time for end users to understand their full implications, the risks as well as the opportunities.

Issues and concerns for managers discussed in this chapter fall into six major areas:

1. *Policy issues.* What policies should managers establish, and how should these policies be communicated? How do managers integrate information systems policies into an organization's overall policy? What auditing procedures should be established to ensure compliance with corporate policies?

2. *Physical security of hardware and software.* How do managers protect computers and disks from theft and physical damage?

3. *Data security and confidentiality.* What safeguards should be taken to protect data that is stored on diskettes and hard disks? How can organizations protect information stored on mainframe computers from unauthorized access or use by microcomputers or other office terminals?

4. *Accuracy and reliability of information.* How can managers be sure that data developed with spreadsheets, databases, and other user programs is accurate and reliable? What kind of documentation is needed, and who develops it and keeps it up-to-date?

5. *Legal issues.* What risks and liabilities are an organization and its managers exposed to in connection with the use of office automation? For example, who is liable when employees make unauthorized copies of software?

6. *Appropriate use of information technologies.* How do managers identify and automate high-value applications? How do they avoid wasteful proliferation of hardware and software?

This chapter discusses a variety of resources, products, and services that managers use in dealing with these issues. This chapter also includes a discussion of auditing procedures, data-protection and encryption products, hardware security products, and others. The most viable techniques, however, are practical guidelines and good management practices.

POLICY ISSUES

Policies established by top management are a first step toward showing employees that computer-related risks are an important corporate concern. Senior management is often too busy running the business to address these risks until a serious problem arises. Even organizations that have established security and disaster-recovery plans for their centralized data processing operations may overlook the risks and issues of managing computers in the office environment.

Policies for office automation and end-user computing vary among organizations according to their corporate cultures. Policymakers generally have similar goals, however, including the following:

- Avoiding incompatible hardware and software.
- Minimizing duplication of effort.
- Avoiding unnecessary spending.
- Coordinating office automation and end-user computing with corporate data processing.
- Coordinating office automation and end-user computing with corporate strategy.
- Providing adequate protection for corporate resources.

The manager who wants to address these goals needs a corporate policy. The key steps for establishing a policy for end-user computing include the following:[1]

1. *Develop acquisition guidelines.* Centralize buying as much as possible; large transactions can save money and secure better maintenance terms.

2. *Take inventory.* Sudden costs must be known and evaluated before any *de facto* standards are set; the installed base will obviously affect policy decisions and future acquisitions.

3. *Develop hardware and software standards.* Standards will facilitate the sharing of resources and the porting of development work (transferring an application developed on one computer to another).

4. *Establish return on investment standards (ROI) and schedules.* Some users require this type of cost/benefit analysis, and return-on-investment standards (sometimes also referred to as *payback*) will assist them in evaluating and justifying hardware and software investments.

5. *Establish maintenance, housekeeping, and security standards.* Poor machine and data maintenance can be expensive. These standards should describe proper hardware care and how to physically secure the machine.

6. *Develop legal guidelines for hardware and software use.* Large sums of money may be at risk if legal issues are ignored. Novice users may be unaware of copyright restrictions on some software, and corporations have been sued for violations of these laws.

7. *Establish periodic policy reviews.* Microcomputer technology changes so quickly that a solution defined today may not be cost-effective tomorrow.

Management should be proactive in *avoiding* problems. Preventive measures should include a written policy statement that identifies all computer and information resources as significant assets. The intent of an information policy should be to encourage care and concern by making employees accountable for unauthorized acts involving computer and information resources. The policy statement should clearly state the company's position on unauthorized copying of software and should be distributed to all employees who have access to information resources. Figure 23-1 presents a typical policy statement on the use of corporate information resources.

FIGURE 23-1. A typical policy statement on the use of corporate information resources.

Computer Software Resources

Growing numbers of company employees and associates use computer software resources in connection with their jobs. Such resources are crucial company assets that make our tasks easier and enable us to perform our jobs with greater accuracy and efficiency. Many employees are not aware of the legal duties that accompany the use of computer software, however. Often, people do not realize that unauthorized copying or disclosure of software has a costly impact.

When software has been developed here at the company, unauthorized taking or copying of that software obviously diminishes the value of a company asset. When software is used under license from an outside supply firm, improper duplication or disclosure deprives that firm of revenue, ultimately raising costs for the customer community. More importantly, whether software resources are developed in-house or licensed from a vendor, unauthorized copying or disclosure is illegal.

Consequently, the Company has issued the following Policy Statement on Computer Software Resources. It is the responsibility of every employee and associate who uses or has access to software resources to adhere strictly to this policy.

Policy Statement on Computer Software Resources

The computer software resources are assets of the company that are vital to our operation. Such resources may be exclusive company property or may be proprietary products used under contractual license from program supply firms. Either way, software is a valuable commodity that the owner is entitled to protect. Consequently, whether using software owned exclusively by the company or software licensed from program supply firms, it is the responsibility of every employee and associate to prevent destruction, misuse, or misappropriation of such resources.

This policy has two components. First, the unauthorized copying or reproduction of any software program, program documentation, or related material is strictly prohibited. This policy also prohibits using any program, program documentation, or related material, or any copy thereof, for personal purposes or making such materials available to anyone outside the company.

Reproducing computer software without authorization may constitute an improper taking of a company asset or may violate the terms of a license agreement into which the company has entered. The money paid for proprietary products generally represents a license fee for the use of one copy. It

FIGURE 23-1. (continued)

does not represent an authorization to make unlimited copies. More importantly, unauthorized duplication of software violates U.S. Copyright Law. Civil damages can be as much as $50,000, and copyright infringement can qualify as a federal misdemeanor punishable by up to $10,000 in fines or up to one year's imprisonment. Consequently, this policy must be strictly followed.

Second, employees and associates must make every effort to maintain and protect the integrity of confidential data contained in software programs, program documentation, and related materials. Employees and associates must not disclose this data and must take reasonable precautions to see that it is not left in the open or haphazardly discarded.

Computer software resources may constitute confidential material or trade secrets entitled to legal protection. Software license agreements often require the company to treat software resources as confidential. The unauthorized disclosure of software materials could thus create legal liability. Therefore, this policy must also be strictly regarded.

Violation of the above policy may result in disciplinary action, including termination, where appropriate. Employees or associates with questions concerning the policy should contact the head of the Computer Security and Contract Administration Department.

Organizations can also help establish personal accountability by having employees sign *confidentiality covenants*. By signing such a document, employees agree not to disclose any proprietary information or to misuse corporate computer resources to which they have access. These covenants also acknowledge that failure to comply with company information policies will result in disciplinary actions.

Acquisition Guidelines

Managers must balance needs for encouraging innovative application of technology against wasteful spending, duplication of effort, or incompatible equipment. Many managers have sufficient budget control to purchase office hardware and may be tempted to circumvent corporate procurement procedures. If the equipment meets the department's needs and the purchase can be cost-justified, why not?

One reason "why not" is that such ad hoc equipment purchases may be incompatible with other corporate hardware, thereby limiting future options. Regardless of whether an organization maintains strict or flexible controls, managers should be aware of the issues relating to hardware and software acquisition. Understandably, vendors often portray personal computing to end users as effortless and immensely beneficial and understate the risks, pitfalls, and problems. Shortcomings of products are generally not evident until the novice gains experience. Users often learn the limitations of hardware or software too late, when they discover that if they had only bought another product, it would be able to do what they wanted.

Such practices often mean higher costs because organizations usually have volume discount purchase agreements. Managers should recognize that there are many trade-offs in computer products in terms of price, performance, and features. Selecting appropriate hardware and software can be time-consuming and fraught with problems. The immense diversity of products means that novices may select incompatible hardware or software. This can lead to costly mistakes that preclude the transfer of data between systems or greatly increase the complexity of supporting, aiding, or training users. In-house technical resources may not support nonstandard hardware and unique software, thus forcing the department to go outside for more expensive services.

Another reason that technology should not be purchased ad hoc is that options may be overlooked that limit or increase the equipment's use for applications other than the one for which it was originally justified. Managers should seek the advice of knowledgeable office systems analysts when considering the purchase of computer devices for their departments. Experienced analysts, whether in-house or outside consultants, can save managers valuable time, money, and frustration. Moreover, they can often cite considerations or opportunities not apparent to managers who have limited experience with the technology.

PHYSICAL SECURITY OF HARDWARE AND SOFTWARE

Physical security involves avoiding potential threats and deterring anyone with intentions to steal or tamper with equipment or information. Managers are responsible for protecting valuable equipment and files. What does the manager do when two microcomputers "turn up missing" on Monday morning? How did the spreadsheet software and manual disappear?

A list of all office computer hardware and software and their serial numbers should be kept in a safe location, and physical inventories should be made regularly. A signed authorization should be required for all hardware and software that is taken into and out of the office building. Devices should be adequately insured.

Avoiding Damage

Appropriate work space should be set aside for microcomputers and other office systems to safeguard the equipment. The analyst should assess possible environmental hazards such as heat from direct sunlight or rain from windows that might be left open. Proper electrical outlets and wiring should be provided. Cables and wiring should not be exposed where employees may trip over them or accidentally snag them, bringing everything crashing to the floor.

Spilled liquids are a major cause of damage, and beverages and other liquids should be kept away from hardware and software. Liquids can leak into electrical circuits or damage diskettes. Smoking should not be allowed near computers and stored diskettes. Smoke lays a deposit on sensitive disks and driveheads, shortening their useful life and increasing the danger of losing data.

An especially insidious threat to data and programs is posed by the recent outbreak of computer viruses that have been planted by disgruntled programmers. A computer virus is a self-perpetuating set of instructions that spreads by inserting copies of itself into other files. Extremely hard to detect, the virus is introduced by an infected program (especially games) or, commonly, a file that is downloaded from a commercial bulletin board. The virus is intended to destroy data and can ultimately destroy all information on a computer system.

Employees should also be cautioned about handling storage media. Since floppy disks store data magnetically, they should not be placed next to a telephone; the ringing device is sufficiently magnetic to rearrange bits and bytes. Extreme temperature changes can also affect floppy disks. If floppies are transported from one location to another in temperatures below 40° Fahrenheit, they should be given a few hours to return to room temperature before they are used. Users must avoid touching recording surfaces, and disks should always be stored in their protective jackets in a place where they will not gather dust. Staff should be instructed to write on labels *before* affixing them to disks, or at least to use felt-tip pens. Labels should never be erased; erasure bits can find their way into the disk jacket and damage the diskette. Techniques for handling floppy disks were discussed in Chapter 4.

Managers must also provide for routine computer maintenance. One individual may be assigned to keep track of all microcomputers in the area, or various individuals may be responsible for different devices. Disk drive heads must be cleaned periodically, but vendors differ in their recommendations on frequency. Because each cleaning removes material from the head, managers will want to avoid unnecessary cleanings. Drive heads may need to be realigned periodically, which is a job for a service technician, not office staff. Power surge protectors are also an inexpensive precaution against damage to equipment or software from electrical power fluctuations.

Managers should also be aware of the need to protect computer hardware and software from static electricity during dry winter months. Humidifiers, carpets that resist static buildup, and antistatic sprays and mats are resources that managers should consider.

Protecting Software (Back-Up)

What does the manager do when an inexperienced word processing operator inadvertently deletes stored text that required three weeks to capture? What happens when the new office systems administrator mistakenly deletes the directory containing all the department's automated form letters? Data stored on the computer must be protected from modification, destruction, and disclosure. Diskettes are vulnerable to loss and accidental erasure. To ensure that data are not lost, backup systems are required.

Back-up refers to duplicate copies of electronically stored data. In computer centers, data is routinely backed up, and two or more copies of all data files are maintained in different locations. Copies of critical information are often stored in specially constructed vaults at a site separate from the computer center. These procedures serve much the same purpose as records management departments.

Office automation and end-user computing have greatly increased the volumes of data that are electronically stored within departments instead of in carefully managed data or records centers. In the automated office, managers must take responsibility for establishing procedures to protect data files created and stored in their departments. Copies should be maintained of all work stored electronically. Managers should follow these guidelines:

1. Accountability for back-up should be clearly assigned. If a departmental computer or LAN is used, a system administrator can be assigned to perform back-up each night. With standalone workstations or microcomputers, individuals should be held accountable for backing up their own files. Responsibility for back-up of all departmental files, however, should be specifically assigned.
2. Back-up diskettes should be stored in a secured location, not at random in individual desks.
3. Back-up diskettes should be clearly labeled and dated.
4. At least two back-up copies of critical data should be maintained. If a problem occurs during the back-up process and both the original and the back-up are damaged, a second back-up copy is then still available. When multiple back-up copies are maintained, they are usually updated on alternate days. For example, on Day 1, Back-up Copy A is updated; on Day 2, Back-up Copy B is updated; on Day 3, back-up is made to Copy A again; on Day 4, to Copy B; etc.

Because electronic storage is very reliable, it is easy to become complacent about electronically stored data. In the absence of strict procedures, people tend to become careless about maintaining up-to-date copies of their work. When problems occur, however, as they invariably do, reconstructing lost information can be time-consuming and expensive. Figure 23-2 presents additional strategies for safeguarding data through better back-up procedures.

Naming Conventions

Managers may need to establish standards for naming data files and storing data on floppies and hard disks. When left to the whim of individual users, it may be difficult or impossible for someone else to locate information. At the very least, hours of valuable time can be wasted finding the correct files or directories. The importance of a systematic approach to naming and storing information becomes more apparent when departmental LANs are used. All employees who create, research, and request information must talk the same language, or considerable time and effort can be wasted locating information.

Tactics for Achieving Better Back-Ups

1. Although it is initially difficult to enforce, make a policy that microcomputers with internal hard disks will not be purchased without also purchasing a streaming tape or external hard disk as a back-up. If an existing back-up unit is not currently being used to capacity, it may be designated for back-up in lieu of a new unit.
2. External fixed hard disks should be subject to the same policy. For removable hard disk units, a purchase may be made as long as at least one other removable disk is available as a back-up and at least one other drive unit is available as a back-up.
3. Organizational policy should clearly indicate what types of data and programs need (a) no back-up, (b) secure on-site back-up, or (c) on-site *and* off-site back-up.
4. Every staff person who will be using a microcomputer should be required to attend training classes on back-up management procedures. Training should cover the use of hard and floppy disk systems and provide instruction on how to make and store back-ups of programs and data.
5. The Data Security Office should be readily available to consult on questions about whether and how to make and store back-ups for microcomputer applications.
6. Supervisors should be required to perform periodic audits on microcomputer back-up activities. The data security officer should perform regular checks on the supervisors' audit records.

FIGURE 23-2. Tactics for achieving better microcomputer back-ups.

DATA SECURITY AND CONFIDENTIALITY

How does a manager guard against an employee's copying confidential trade statistics onto a diskette and taking them to a new job? What happens when a storage box of diskettes containing vital information disappears? How does the manager deal with the uneasy feeling that someone has been using the microcomputer on his or her desk, where all the department personnel and salary information is stored on the hard disk?

Data security and the confidentiality of data in computers and data banks are continuing concerns. Office automation increases these concerns because it provides wider access to data and to devices for manipulating it. Desktop computers are linked to other computers, providing access to multiple computers from each device. Small computers are seldom monitored or guarded.

Office automation presents two distinct security problems. The first is protecting mainframe data from unauthorized access by microcomputers either inside or outside the organization. Insiders who gain access to specific information or inadvertently damage files are perceived to be a greater threat than outside "hackers." The second security issue is the problem of protecting information stored on microcomputer floppy and hard disks, whether developed by users or downloaded from mainframe data.

End users may be less informed than computer professionals about the requirements of confidentiality for client and employee data. Control of databases is often separated from responsibility for their integrity and reliability. The same level of control is usually not built into microcomputer applications as is built into mainframe data-entry systems. Yet stored information may be used and updated by novices unfamiliar with many of the software features. Moreover, office automation enables work to be done away from the office—at home, in airplanes, hotels, or client offices—which increases the risk of loss, damage, or theft.

It is extremely difficult to safeguard diskettes. Data disks are easily lost, stolen, destroyed, or copied. Thus the potential for computer system abuse has increased as microcomputers and other diskette-based office systems have proliferated. Of course, theft or misuse of sensitive data has always been a threat, even before computers. Before the growth of end-user computing, however, it was more difficult to conceal large piles of paper or large computer tapes. It took time to hand-copy, type, or even photocopy pages of information. Today, individuals can copy a wealth of information onto diskettes in a few minutes and walk out of the company with it in their shirt pockets.

Managers must carefully assess the company's exposure. They must identify what it is they need to protect and the possible threats. They must determine how much time and expense are warranted and establish appropriate measures. Suggested tactics for protecting sensitive microcomputer data are presented in Figure 23-3.

FIGURE 23-3. **Tactics for better protection of sensitive microcomputer data.**

Tactics for Better Protection of Sensitive Data

1. Establish a clear organizational policy on what types of data are to be considered sensitive. As a matter of policy, ensure that every sensitive data set has a designated custodian to bear responsibility for its safekeeping.
2. Establish a policy that no sensitive information may be stored in a file, either temporarily or permanently, on a fixed hard disk. All sensitive information is to be recorded either on specially colored floppies or on specially designated and distinctly marked removable hard disks.
3. Ensure that a locked area or cabinet is available for all media containing sensitive information. Access should be possible only for the data custodian. Arrange this either by individually controlled locks and keys or by using a centrally secured data library.
4. Place microcomputers in private offices for work with sensitive data.
5. Encourage the use of encryption for sensitive data files.

ACCURACY AND RELIABILITY (INTEGRITY) OF INFORMATION

What does a manager do when the individual who developed a BASIC software program, used regularly for processing department information, is promoted to another department or leaves the company? Who is responsible when a monthly report, produced with a computer spreadsheet, is inaccurate because a formula was inadvertently altered? Whose figures does the executive accept when department managers show up at a meeting with three different versions of divisional sales results maintained on their microcomputers? These are just some of the questions and issues related to the accuracy and reliability of computer information.

Problems arise in part because of the complexities of computer programs and the difficulties involved when one person tries to figure out the logic of a program developed by someone else. These problems can be significantly reduced when computer programs are adequately documented.

Documentation

Documentation is a detailed, written explanation of how a computer program works. It details the programming logic, variables, formulas, processed data (and where it comes from), and any other items pertinent to the creation and use of the program. Documentation is usually contained within a program and also in supplementary reference documents (referred to as *run books*).

If a spreadsheet or a program is used by someone other than the individual who created it or is intended for departmental information (rather than individual calculations), thorough documentation is essential. Without documentation, it is extremely time-consuming for anyone other than the program originator to modify or correct it. Documentation also serves as a tool for verifying the correctness of a program or reconstructing it if disks containing the program are destroyed or damaged. A good technique for documenting spreadsheet programs is to print out all the formulas used to create the program. Most spreadsheet software provides this option.

Verifying the Accuracy of Computer Programs

Professional programmers are well aware that many errors and problems can creep into computer programs, and they realize that errors are difficult to detect. While the structured design and programming methods of technical data processing departments minimize risks, department managers need to be aware of potential problems and see that programs developed by their staff are adequately tested and verified.

In the rush of everyday business, it is easy for new microcomputer users to overlook the importance of extensive testing and verification. Managers and users must be made aware of the risks and taught appropriate procedures. The Association of Computer Users recommends that before any program is put into full use, it be run concurrently with the existing, manual system. Good programming helps a user discover errors.

Accounting programs with audit trails or database management systems that will reject letter input where there should be numbers (and vice versa) help keep input errors to a minimum. For number-crunching applications, users should calculate the number of entries and batch totals before data is entered in the computer. These item counts and totals can be used to verify the accuracy of the data and determine if errors were made as the data was keyboarded into the program.

Managers should cross-train personnel to do each other's jobs in order to prevent the operation from coming to a stop when a microcomputer user is sick or on vacation. Job rotation can help keep skill levels up, as well as provide employees opportunities to review each other's work. Dividing responsibility for various phases of computer operation increases the chance that one user will detect another's errors.

Reliability of Spreadsheet Results

Managers must insist on careful testing and validation of all calculations performed on the computer. An error in a single formula or a mistyped figure can easily produce inaccurate results in computer spreadsheets—just as they do in manual calculations. Actions that a manager can take to establish controls include the following:

1. *Establish controls to verify the accuracy and integrity of spreadsheets.* Examples include independent reviews, walkthroughs, and parallel runs. (A *walkthrough* checks the program logic by manually doing each step in the program in the programmed sequence.) The accuracy of spreadsheets can be verified by comparing results against the same calculation done manually. Old manual reports can be used for test data, or duplicate calculations can be performed.

2. *Carefully document all spreadsheets.* Documentation should include data prepared, programs used, department of origin, and other relevant information. Print out and verify the accuracy of all formulas used in the spreadsheet.

3. *Remind individuals that they are accountable for their work.* "The computer made a mistake" is not an acceptable excuse.

Managers can get assistance from the computer to help verify and document the accuracy of spreadsheets. Software packages such as The Spreadsheet Auditor from Consumers Software, for documenting Lotus 1–2–3 spreadsheets, are available. The Spreadsheet Auditor helps verify formulas, makes notations about cell entries, provides interactive error checking, and prints documentation. For additional recommendations on improving the integrity of microcomputer data, see Figure 23-4.

Tactics for Improving the Integrity of Data

1. All customized microcomputer programs should be validated and certified for accuracy.
2. All corporate databases, whether stored on micros, minis, or mainframes, should have user-accessible date and time fields to indicate the last time the database was modified.
3. All microcomputer output should be clearly marked with date and time of production. If the report draws upon any external database, the report should note that database's date and time stamp.
4. All analytical data reports done on microcomputers should have independent validations of data input and embedded formulas. Analytical models are to be checked for conceptual accuracy as well as clerical accuracy. The checkers should initial the reports and note the date and time.
5. As a matter of policy, no corporate decisions shall be made on the basis of any microcomputer-based data unless they meet all the conditions set above.

FIGURE 23-4. Tactics for improving the integrity of microcomputer data.

Guidelines for Information Systems Security

One computer expert has summarized major threats to information system security in the list shown in Figure 23-5. Types of security threats are listed in the left column, and the two right columns differentiate between intentional acts of malice and human error or naturally caused accidents.

Disasters and vandalism (Items 1 and 2 in Figure 23-5) that damage equipment or software are risks to microcomputers just as they are to large systems. Disaster recovery planning for microcomputers is not taken as seriously, however, because losses are likely to be much smaller and easily rectified. In comparison to mainframe or minicomputer systems, microcomputers are inexpensively replaced and applications can be transferred with little difficulty to other equipment.

Items 3 through 6 in Figure 23-5 represent cases where information is compromised either by unsystematic error or total loss. The key to solving these problems is the maintenance of adequate back-ups.

Items 7 and 8 represent situations in which systematic error is entered into data through incompetence or criminal intent. The controls against these threats are primarily quality-assurance checks, audits, division of responsibility, and the like.

Items 9 and 10 represent threats of disclosure of sensitive information. Controls involve taking care to secure information behind physical and logical locks.[2]

FIGURE 23-5. Threats to information system security.

Threats to Information System Security

	Human Error and Natural Accident	**Acts of Malicious Intent**
Physical resource damage	1. Disasters	2. Vandalism
Random information modification	3. Mistakes	4. Pranks and nuisances
Destruction of information	5. Erasure	6. Sabotage
Systematic information modification	7. Incompetence	8. Fraud and embezzlement
Disclosure of confidential information	9. Exposure	10. Data theft

LEGAL ISSUES

Who is responsible when a company's microcomputer is damaged in an accident while an employee is transporting it home? An employee decides to market a software program she developed at home on the company's microcomputer. She uses the program on her job, but developed it primarily on her own time at home. An employee claims that a fire in his home was started by a short circuit in his company's microcomputer, brought home from work. Bob's four-year-old son destroyed the program disk for the database package that the department just purchased for $500. Bob brought it home to finish a project that was due the next day. Clearly, office automation has raised a number of legal issues and concerns for business managers.

Defining Corporate versus Personal Data or Programs

An important measure that organizations can take is to establish clear policies on the ownership of programs or data created on company time or equipment and to require employees to sign covenants before being assigned to development projects or authorized to borrow equipment. Whether strict measures are warranted depends, of course, on how sensitive or important information is to the company.

Unauthorized Copying of Software

Software copyrights limit the rights of purchasers to copy or modify software programs. Making multiple copies of software to distribute in an office is a clear violation of most copyright agreements. Besides being unethical, violating copyrights subjects the organization to liability suits from software vendors. Notable examples include a multimillion-dollar suit by Lotus Development Corporation against a company that allegedly made illegal copies of 1-2-3, and a suit by MicroPro International Corporation against a subsidiary of American Brands, accusing it of making unauthorized copies of WordStar and other programs. Other such incidents have also been publicized.

The right to copyright software was established by the Software Act of 1980, which modified the federal Copyright Act. When software programmers (or others) obtain a *copyright,* they retain the exclusive right to reproduce or modify their software. Thus others are prohibited from copying or modifying. A copyright grants five exclusive rights:

1. The exclusive right to make copies.
2. The exclusive right to distribute copies to the public.
3. The exclusive right to prepare "derivative works."
4. The exclusive right to perform the work in public. (This mainly applies to plays, dances, etc., but could also apply to software.)
5. The exclusive right to display the work in public (such as showing a film).

Software is often sold under licensing agreements that may be more or less stringent than the copyright laws. It is common to see a warning on a package of program diskettes that the purchaser read all terms and conditions carefully *before* opening the package, because opening the package constitutes acceptance of such terms and conditions. Often these agreements stipulate (among other conditions) that use of the program is restricted to one machine, and the purchaser is requested to provide the serial number of the machine when returning the software registration form (which is required for ongoing support from the manufacturer). It is not yet clear to what extent these licensing agreements are valid and under what circumstances they will stand up in a court of law. Some states have passed, or are considering, laws to make such agreements valid.

Many users object to copyright restrictions or licensing agreements on the grounds that they encumber legitimate uses of software. For example, it is not clear whether making a copy of a software program on a hard disk violates the copyright. Even if the first copy is legal, what about copies created during routine back-up of the hard disk? Some software manufacturers prevent the user from copying the program diskette more than once. Thus if the hard disk fails, the user would not be able to recopy the program onto the hard disk a second time. These restrictions may also interfere with regular back-up of the hard disk. Corporations and other large software purchasers have been pressuring manufacturers for site-licensing (discussed later in this chapter) and other agreements that would better meet their needs. Office systems analysts and managers should monitor these legal issues and keep them in mind when negotiating with software vendors.

Managers can take several steps to help control unauthorized copying of software. First, the organization should establish a clear policy forbidding unauthorized copying of software. The policy should establish penalties for infractions and should be published and disseminated to all employees.

Employees should be educated regarding the rules and restrictions for copying software. They should be reminded of the ethics of unauthorized copying and the corporation's exposure to legal action.

Some companies make software available on the mainframe computer through contractual arrangements with vendors that allow it to be used on any personal computer connected to the host computer. This reduces the use of application programs on floppy diskettes, which are easily copied.

Hardware and Software Contracts

When managers have the autonomy to sign hardware or software purchase contracts, they should be aware of possible pitfalls or problems. A well-drawn contract should specify the rights, duties, and obligations of the seller and purchaser. It should also meet the following objectives:[3]

- Specify all sales claims and promises in writing.
- Establish the time frame within which these claims should be carried out.
- Clarify the performance of the system or services the vendor will provide.
- Specify the price of the product or service.
- Specify how payment should be made.
- Describe the kind of product or service provided.
- State any provisions that allow the purchaser to reject the product or service if it fails to perform to standard.
- Identify the forum that has jurisdiction in the event of litigation.
- Spell out any penalty or cancellation clauses, and when they come into play.
- Clarify responsibility for installation and maintenance of the equipment and for training in-house personnel.

Managers should check with their legal departments before signing computer hardware or software contracts.

Site Licensing

Some vendors offer site-licensing arrangements that can help organizations reduce their exposure to illegal copying. Site-licensing arrangements can also reduce the order, reorder, and program-upgrade headaches that come with buying volume copies of software. Two categories of site-licensing arrangements are offered by various vendors:

1. *Full site-licensing agreements,* which allow users to duplicate the program disk and documentation in-house.
2. *Volume-purchasing agreements,* which offer pricing discounts based on the number of copies ordered.

Site-licensing agreements may offer additional benefits, such as technical support, newsletters, or training. Some plans incorporate clauses that limit an organization's liability for unauthorized copies to the retail price of the copies duplicated.

Preventing Unauthorized Access to Data

Unauthorized access to data in any interstate computer system or federal government computer is a federal crime. The Computer Fraud and Abuse Act (PL99–474) was signed into law October 16, 1986. Under the new law, first offenses are punishable as a misdemeanor or felony, depending on the circumstances, with up to five years' imprisonment; and second convictions carry jail sentences of up to ten years. Prior to its passage, institutions had little recourse against "hackers," except to expose them. Institutions hope that the law will be a deterrent to would-be hackers. Its impact will be tested when the first cases are prosecuted and results are publicized. The burden of proof in prosecution is on the holder of the data.

APPROPRIATE USE OF INFORMATION TECHNOLOGIES

Managers are often concerned—if not quite suspicious—that resources are being wasted on frivolous activities. Experience indicates, however, that managers have reason to be more confident about the application of end-user computing tools. End users—whether professionals, managers, knowledge workers, sales staff, or secretaries—are busy people. They use computers to obtain a direct, quick, and pragmatic benefit to getting their jobs done. Given a choice, few employees persist in applications that are inefficient or make their jobs more difficult. Nonthreatening activities, such as computer games, music, or nonbusiness programs, can be good ice-breakers and learning experiences for novice users. Experimentation should be encouraged. When given an opportunity, individuals who work with information on a daily basis often come up with excellent ideas for saving time and effort. Managers who involve their employees in solving problems or generating cost-saving ideas are usually amply rewarded.

Managers should look for opportunities to change or eliminate procedures, not just speed them up. One of the most effective ways of doing this is to evaluate the impact on an entire work flow before automating individual tasks. Employees—especially those on a clerical level—may lack the perspective or authority to change work methods beyond their own assignments. The manager must provide the broad perspective or appoint task forces to explore options and make recommendations.

Every department has its strengths and weaknesses relative to the organization's competitors or goals. The department that is looking for a starting point should use technology to emphasize its areas of strength that also have importance to the organization as a whole. Capitalizing on strong points can give an organization a competitive advantage.

For decision makers seeking to boost organizational performance in meaningful areas through end-user computing, the logical first step is to look at the way managers or professionals spend their day. They usually perform a wide variety of functions, only some of which are high-value activities. If you give managers or professionals tools that enable them to spend 10 percent more time on high-value work, you enhance their value to the company. Adequate training, technical support, and guidelines for end-user computing and office systems are the best ways to ensure that high-value applications are identified and addressed during the long learning curve. These points are discussed in more detail in the next chapter.

RESOURCES, PRODUCTS, AND SERVICES

A variety of resources, products, and services are available to help provide adequate control of technology in the office. Managers must assess the risks and determine how much effort and expense should be spent to provide adequate protection. The answer to the question, "Which product should I buy?" depends on how much protection is needed. Managers must also assess how much convenience and accessibility they want to trade for protection and security.

Auditing Procedures for Office Automation and End-User Computing

The auditing department is an important ally in helping managers establish control procedures to ensure the proper use of information systems. Auditors can help a manager in several ways:

- Designing control systems and procedures for managing information flow.
- Stipulating specific requirements for documentation, control, and systems access.
- Developing audit trails that document personal responsibility for actions taken.
- Reviewing procedures for meeting requirements and ensuring that they are met.

Harry B. DiMaio, Director of Data Security for IBM, argues that security and audit procedures should be concentrated on applications rather than hardware or systems software. According to DiMaio, the question should not be "How do I protect a PC?" or "What security do I need on a shared logic office system?" Instead, managers and auditors should focus on requirements for specific applications. According to DiMaio, the following directions and questions would be more appropriate: "Describe the applications." "What is the nature and value of the information?" "Who is involved in the process?" "Where does the information come from and where does it go?" "At what point in the process can I attest to its integrity?" "How are we using the microcomputer or shared logic system?"[4] Organizations must make a clear statement about the importance of information security and auditing controls.

Hardware and Software Security Devices

Several products and services that address office security needs are available. This section provides a sampling of some of the types of products that offer solutions. A comprehensive discussion is not intended.

Security Systems

Many devices are available to secure computers to work surfaces or lock them so as to control access. One such device, Anchor Pad's PC Sentry, attaches to a microcomputer and works like an ignition key. It allows control over who is using a computer, at what times, and for what purposes. It is limited to physical access, however. Once the user has turned the computer on, it does not control applications or data.

Several security products are designed to control access to software. One type of system uses a *logon floppy disk,* which is inserted in the B drive of the microcomputer after the disk operating system is inserted in the A drive. A systems administrator or supervisor must program the logon with identification codes for all authorized individuals. The latter must provide an identification code and password before using the system. These disks can be impractical, however, when many occasional users share the same microcomputer.

Another type of security system comes on a circuit board and is plugged into one of the microcomputer's expansion slots. Again, users must provide their correct identification code and password. Although board-based products provide the tightest form of control, many microcomputer users do not want to give up the expansion slot for the security circuit board. These products may work with only certain models of microcomputers.

Some software-based products control access to the hard disk but do not prevent users from working with floppy diskettes—unless, of course, the microcomputer has no floppy drive. While some of these products are designed only for specific models, other products work with almost any MS or PC-DOS microcomputer system. They are virtually hardware-independent, and some offer file encryption. A few can also prevent access to a hard disk when a microcomputer is booted from a floppy diskette.

One product is now available in both board- and software-based versions that are completely compatible. Called *Secure!* and *Secure! PS,* it protects selected files but does not interfere with regular microcomputer use. Users who wish to access a secured file, however, must provide the correct identification (ID) and password, or they will get only garbage. It is permissible to share protected files and transport or transmit them between protected microcomputers.

Data Encryption

The products described above are designed primarily to prevent access to devices or software. Data encryption goes a step farther by making information unintelligible even if it is accessed. *Data encryption* uses a mathematical algorithm to scramble data. Two types of data encryption are the public-key type and the Data Encryption Standard (DES). DES, developed in the early 1970s by IBM and adopted by the National Bureau of Standards in 1976, combines two operations called *substitution* (replacing information) and *transposition* (scrambling information). These two operations transform *plaintext* or *cleartext* into *ciphertext*. The person who deciphers the encrypted text uses the same key that encrypted the data to reverse the substitution and transposition process. The algorithm for DES encryption has 64 bits, 56 of which are active bits, and 8 are used to detect errors in transmission. Public-key encryption works with two keys for each user: a public encryption key and a private decryption key. The user keeps the private key to decrypt messages sent by anyone who has a public encryption key. The two keys are mathematically linked, but it is not feasible in terms of time and energy to figure out from the public key what the private key is. DES-based encryption is the most widely used, although many experts favor the public-key method and predict increased use.

Available products include *PC Lock II* and Pathway Design's *pcPATH/Encryption*. One drawback of encryption systems is that they are not automatic. To access an encrypted file, the user must activate a decryption program, and provide the correct key or password. When finished using the file, the user must re-encrypt it. If the user is running an application and wants to access an encrypted file, it is necessary to exit the application program, decrypt the file, and reenter the application program. Encrypted files can also present problems in copying or backing up diskettes.

Micro-Mainframe Links

Micro-mainframe links pose a major concern for security. The most widely used forms of protection are call-back devices. Located either before or after the modem at the host computer, the call-back unit intercepts the sign-on attempt when a user dials in. When the user keys in a personal identification code or password, the call-back unit scans its directory for the user's code and the call-back telephone number. The device disconnects the caller and immediately calls back the phone number corresponding to the user's password. If the caller is a legitimate user, he or she will again know the password. If the caller is not a legitimate user, the mainframe computer will usually not find a microcomputer connected to the telephone when calling back.

Dial-in call-back devices offer security at a reasonable cost and are considered to be hacker proof. They are also cheaper than leased lines, which are considered the most secure. A disadvantage of call-back devices is that costs are multiplied with call-backs, and the host site must absorb the costs of transmission. The popularity of call-forwarding has introduced a flaw in dial-back systems. The call-back device knows it dialed the correct number but has no way of detecting if its dial-back was forwarded somewhere else. Call-back devices are also inefficient for applications where the user must travel.

Among the newest devices are hardware and firmware security systems that prohibit unauthorized access to single computers or all workstations on a shared-resource host, LAN, or data communication network. To use the computer system, individuals must have a security access card, which looks like a thick credit card. One such product from Security Dynamics called *ACE* (access control encryption) contains a microprocessor, a two-year lithium battery, and a band of liquid crystal display readouts across the top (see Figure 23-6). The read out flashes a four- to eight-digit code that changes every 60 seconds. When the authorized user dials up the computer from a microcomputer or other terminal, he or she types in his or her memorized PIN (personal identification number) and the display code blinking at the moment on the card. The computer matches that figure against its calculation of the number displayed on the card before it gives the user access to the computer's files.

FIGURE 23-6. Security Dynamics Corporation's Access Control Encryption device.

A similar device is the Card Reader/Verification Port Protection Series, manufactured by Codercard. The Codercard system provides authorization, software protection, DES encryption, and file security. A workstation user's Codercard contains a tamper-proof microprocessor, encoded with a unique ID number and a complex series of algorithms. After the user's ID is validated, software determines the level of permission and time limitations. If an ID is not validated, access is denied, and the Codercard, with the host software, can automatically report exact times and locations of attempted security breaches, whether inside or outside the company.

The authorized data distributor (ADD) is another product designed to work alone or in conjunction with micro-mainframe links to reduce data inconsistencies and improve security. ADD stands between the microcomputer user and the corporate database and acts as interpreter, sentry, and translator for the user's data needs. ADD consists of a data extractor that acquires data from internal and external files and translates it into a common format. The ADD data loader then provides tailored data files to microcomputers based on predefined requirements. Among the advantages of the ADD approach, according to one software reviewer, are security, certified and accurate data, vendor and software independence, flexibility in growth, and efficiency in data transmission.

SUMMARY

Now that computers have moved into the office environment and onto desktops, responsibility for managing their use falls directly on business managers. Often, in their enthusiasm for new-found opportunities, managers have overlooked risks and responsibilities. Unless they are informed about the issues related to managing end-user computer resources and office systems technologies in the workplace, they may not recognize potential problems until disaster strikes.

Policies established by senior managers are an important first step toward showing employees that computer-related risks are a legitimate corporate concern. Policies can foster an attitude of care and concern by making employees accountable for unauthorized acts involving computer and information resources. Policy statements should be distributed to all employees and should clearly state the company's position regarding unauthorized copying of software.

Acquisition guidelines must be established to avoid incompatible hardware and software, duplication of effort, and unnecessary spending. Equipment must be protected against damage, loss, or theft. Regular back-up procedures are required to safeguard electronically stored data against accidental loss. Standard procedures for naming and storing files save time and effort. Managers also need to protect sensitive data against unauthorized access, tampering, or copying.

Without strict procedures in technical data processing departments, errors in end-user-developed programs may go unnoticed. A dangerous tendency is to accept detailed computer analyses without adequate verification. Managers must establish procedures to ensure that data produced and stored on departmental computers is accurate and reliable.

Among the legal issues raised by office automation are ownership of employee-developed programs, prosecution from infringement of copyright laws, purchase and licensing arrangements, and responsibility for damage to hardware and software. Policies and guidelines are needed to minimize risks.

Several resources and services are available to help provide controls for managing technology in the workplace. Auditors help assess risks and exposures as well as recommend procedures to protect corporate resources and comply with corporate policies. Various products, such as locks, logon programs, encryption programs, and security access controls, help secure hardware and software resources against unauthorized use.

Managers and employees need adequate guidelines and technical support to translate business needs into computer solutions. A long learning curve is involved as nontechnical personnel gain experience in applying new computer tools. Managers must be aware of both the opportunities and the related risks to manage office computing resources effectively.

DISCUSSION QUESTIONS

1. What is the purpose of policy statements? Who writes them? Who follows them? Why are they important to the office systems analyst?
2. Summarize the issue of data security in an automated office.
3. What is meant by the term *back-up?* Why is back-up often ignored by computer users?
4. Why is documentation considered a data reliability issue?
5. What options are available to the manager who wants to audit microcomputer operations?
6. Identify legal issues related to microcomputer software about which managers should be aware.
7. List steps a manager can take to help control unauthorized copying of software.
8. Describe three devices that secure data access in micro-mainframe links.

APPLICATION EXERCISES

1. Compose a policy statement that addresses legal concerns related to microcomputer operations.
2. Review computer catalogs to determine the types of security devices on the market.
3. Assume you are a manager who has hired a college student (who has never worked on a computer) for a summer job. The job entails updating records on the microcomputer. Role-play the introduction to computer orientation you will give the student, but limit it to care of the computer and care of magnetic disks.

SUGGESTED READINGS

Findlay, Douglas. "Don't Wait Until You Get 'Burned,'" *Administrative Management* (March 1988), pp. 16–22.

Microcomputer Security in Your Business (New York: Ernst and Whinney, 1986).

Zonderman, John. "Corporate Managers Tackle Security," *PC Week* (March 13, 1984), pp. 37–45.

IMPLEMENTATION: Human Resource Requirements

CHAPTER **24**

OBJECTIVES

Upon completing this chapter, the reader should be able to meet the following objectives:

- Understand the importance of training in implementing computer systems.
- Understand the design of training programs that meet project goals.
- Apply the learning theories of andragogy and pedagogy in developing training strategies.
- Select appropriate methods for analyzing training needs.
- Recognize the benefits of well-planned training programs.
- Develop performance criteria for training programs.
- Choose appropriate methodologies and media for training programs.
- Establish criteria for evaluating training programs.
- Discuss the impact of office automation on career opportunities for women.
- Summarize labor relations issues resulting from the advent of new technologies.

KEY TERMS

andragogy
computer-based training (CBT)
interactive video
pedagogy
performance objectives
teletraining
training
training needs analysis

INTRODUCTION

Chapter 24 expands on the human side of office systems implementation. People can make or break a system. Even the most technically advanced system may fail if people do not understand how to use it. People will learn to overcome deficiencies if they understand how the system will help them work more effectively. According to Alexia Martin, office systems analysts should strive to "improve productivity and worker satisfaction through harmonization of people, the organization, and the technology."[1] When implementing technologies into the office, systems analysts should address human resource requirements on both a micro or individual level, as well as the macro or organizational level.

The micro level requires that planners pay attention to worker differences, including values, rewards, autonomy, identification with job results, work and communication styles, privacy, and need for training, support, and information. The macro level requires that planners pay attention to managerial issues and concerns, including incorporating office automation plans with company goals, "selling" top management on the value of office automation, ensuring that job descriptions and pay scales are commensurate with new systems, and addressing the concerns of minority workers and unions.

This chapter is divided into two main sections. The first section covers training issues and expands on requirements for effective use of technology by individual employees. The second section covers personnel issues and expands on some issues already identified, with special emphasis on the concerns of office support workers, including equitable pay, part-time and temporary work, and unions.

Individual and organizational issues can be discussed separately, but they are interrelated. By addressing individual workers' concerns, organizational concerns are also addressed. Office systems analysts must ensure that people not only have the right tools to do their jobs, but that they understand how the equipment fits in with their jobs and the company's overall objectives.

THE WALL STREET JOURNAL

ADDRESSING THE NEEDS OF THE INDIVIDUAL WORKER: TRAINING

The number of new office systems hardware tools and software applications continues to expand geometrically. The key to ensuring that new technologies are used effectively is adequate training.

As used in this text, *training* is a teaching/learning process whereby individuals acquire new skills and concepts that enable them to perform their jobs more effectively. A fine line exists between training and education. The term *training* is typically used when the learning outcome is directly applicable to the job. *Learning* should be measurable in terms of performance improvement. *Education,* on the other hand, refers to long-range development of the individual, with outcomes that are not necessarily measurable or directly applicable to a task. A good way to keep the correct perspective is to differentiate between driver's education and driver's training (in the former, you learned the rules of the road; in the latter, you applied them).

According to the U.S. Office of Technology Assessment (OTA), the need for white-collar workers to acquire office automation skills is critical because of the following factors:[2]

- At least 75 percent of adult workers for the year 2000 are already in the labor market. The majority of those who must be trained and educated to use office technologies are adults past the stage of secondary education.
- Office automation technologies have the potential to affect the lives of more people than any other type of computerized technology, since office workers now outnumber manufacturing workers.
- Employment trends show a continual change in skill requirements. This means that adults must frequently be retrained to use the new technologies and adapt to changes in occupations and the work environment.

To design an effective training program, one must know not only what people need to learn but also *how* they learn. To be an effective trainer, one must not only master the subject being taught but also know appropriate methods of delivering that knowledge and know-how to the trainee.

This section provides an overview of how the office automation analyst or planner can ensure that training is for the *right* things and done the *right* way. Beginning with an outline of how adults learn, the chapter takes a systems approach to training: determining what training is needed (assessment), then formulating programs (design), as well as methods of instruction (implementation). Implementation includes media—traditional and electronic—that can help people learn to use new systems. The chapter concludes with suggestions that office systems trainers can use to assess the results of training projects (evaluation).

Applying Learning Theory

Andragogy and *pedagogy* refer to how people learn. *Andra* comes from the Greek word *andr,* which means "man, not boy." *Peda* comes from the Greek word *paid,* which means "child." Both words use the Greek suffix *agogus,* which means "leading." In short, andragogy is *student-directed* learning, and pedagogy is *teacher-directed* learning.

As a theory, pedagogy originated with early monks who recorded common characteristics among children learning basic skills. Andragogy developed much later in Europe, and the term was introduced in the United States in the 1960s by Malcolm S. Knowles. The assumptions and process elements used in these two learning theories are diagrammed in Figure 24-1. Knowles emphasized that the two models can coexist. The task

Assumptions About	Pedagogical	Andragogical
Concept of the learner	Dependent personality	Increasingly self-directed
Role of learner's experience	To be built on more than used as a resource	A rich resource for learning by self and others
Readiness to learn	Uniform by age-level and curriculum taught	Develops from life tasks and problems
Orientation to learning	Subject-centered	Task- or problem-centered
Motivation	By external rewards and punishments	By internal incentives, curiosity

Process Elements	Pedagogical	Andragogical
Climate	Tense, low trust Formal, cold, aloof Authority-oriented Competitive, judgmental	Relaxed, trusting Mutually respectful Informal, warm Collaborative, supportive
Planning	Primarily by teacher	By learners and facilitator mutually
Diagnosis of needs	Primarily by teacher	By mutual assessment
Setting of objectives	Primarily by teacher	By mutual negotiation
Designing learning plans	Teachers' content plans Course syllabus Logical sequence	Learning contracts Learning projects Sequenced by readiness
Learning activities	Transmittal techniques Assigned readings	Inquiry projects Independent study Experiential techniques
Evaluation	By teacher Norm-referenced (on a curve) With grades	By learner-collected evidence validated by peers, facilitators, experts Criterion-referenced

FIGURE 24-1. The assumptions and process elements of the pedagogical and andragogical learning models.

to be learned and the individual's learning style dictate whether a pedagogical or andragogical approach should be used in the design and delivery of a training program. For example, how would you prefer to learn each of the following?

- To use a new desktop publishing system
- To be oriented to a new job
- French history
- To improve your writing
- The technical aspects of local area networks

Responses to this question reflect a combination of both pedagogy and andragogy. How the reader responds to the questions reflects his/her own particular background and learning preferences. While French history may best be learned by the lecture method (using elements of pedagogy), desktop publishing may require a problem-solving approach (using elements of andragogy).

The following are selected principles of andragogy and their implications for developing effective office automation and end-user training strategies.

Learning Is Not Its Own Reward

Children learn for reasons quite different from adults. Adults are not motivated by gold stars or good report cards; they want a learning outcome that they can put to use. Because human behavior is directed in relation to goals, adults learn best when they have a specific use for the knowledge or skill being taught.

Therefore, office automation training strategists should remember that their students (adults) prefer practical, hands-on training sessions over general, theory-oriented classes. The best way to motivate individuals to learn a spreadsheet software package, for example, is to show them how they can apply it. Otherwise, trainees will probably learn very little.

Adult Learning Is Integrative

Unlike the child, the adult learner brings a wide variety of knowledge and experiences to the learning situation. Adults learn best when they are able to integrate new ideas with what they already know. Moreover, if the information conflicts with what the learner "knows" or "values," learning is more difficult. Therefore, the office training strategist should build on what the trainee already knows.

For example, when teaching word processing to typists, the trainer should compare how a word processing technology operates with how a typewriter operates. In a word processing class for knowledge workers, compare the advantages of word processing over handwritten drafts. The trainee's previous experience also influences the training methods that should be employed. In general, the more proficient trainees are with software, the easier it will be for them to learn another software package.

In addition, "value judgments" must be considered. Because office automation changes how work is processed, the adult learner should know *why* the technology is used, as well as how to use it. In this case, *value adjustment* means understanding why work that has been done a specific way in the past will no longer be performed that way. Trainees will accept change more readily when they know why the change is taking place.

Adult learners also want more control over their learning experiences. Instructors should consult with trainees about curriculum content. Such an approach gives trainees opportunities to contribute to course content as well as methodologies that fit their learning styles.

Practice Must Be Meaningful

Repetition for repetition's sake does not produce a substantial learning effect. However, if repetition has meaningful results, learning can take place. This principle is borrowed from the work of E. L. Thorndike, an early leader in developing learning theory, who was opposed to meaningless drill. A related premise is that adults tend to be slower in some psychomotor tasks than children. Adults compensate for this by being more exact; they make fewer trial-and-error ventures and fewer errors.

Therefore, rather than have trainees work on textbook drills, the office automation trainer should have them "practice" on actual work in the learning environment. A similar suggestion is that trainees apply what has been learned "back at the desk" as an assignment or, in the language of training, as *pre-work* for the next learning session.

Because they tend to learn psychomotor skills more slowly (a tendency that increases with age), adults should be given every opportunity to proceed at their own pace. In many instances, self-paced learning materials such as computer-assisted instruction can support self-paced learning. Some organizations, such as Apple Computer, give their employees a computer to take home, enabling learning to take place in the privacy of the home rather than in the office or classroom.

The foregoing principles are background to the remainder of this chapter. They will be drawn upon in subsequent pages, as they have relevance to training program identification, design, delivery, and evaluation. Figure 24-2 summarizes significant considerations for teaching computer skills to adult learners.

How to Teach Microcomputer Skills

Although the Training Program is primarily self-study, there may be occasions when a trainee will have a question about a microcomputer-related matter, and you will be called to the terminal to help answer the question. Here are a few pointers to keep in mind at that time:

1. Telling is not teaching. Learning microcomputer skills requires practice.
2. Be aware that most people feel hesitant about using a computer for the first time. They may feel threatened, insecure, anxious, and intimidated. Assure them that there's a lot to learn, but it's not too difficult when taken one step at a time.
3. The learner should always sit at the microcomputer while you explain steps or procedures.
4. Keep your hands off the keyboard. When helping people correct a mistake, explain how to undo the mistake as well as the correct steps to follow. Don't do it for them!
5. Remember that adults learn by reasoning, not rote. Explain *why* as well as *how.*
6. Don't forget that everyone makes mistakes, and that mistakes can be quite instructive.
7. Don't be afraid to admit that you don't know the answer. Use the hotline for support.

How to Manage Training in Your Office

1. Keep in mind that training is a matter of priorities. Your staff must find the time to train during the week, and you should be available as needed.
2. Encourage your staff to spend a minimum of two to three hours a week on the Training Program.
3. Point out to your staff that they need to have realistic expectations about this program. It takes time and practice to learn microcomputer skills. Tell them to think of the time spent as an investment that will begin to pay back many benefits after a few weeks of effort. Be aware that productivity will probably go down, but they will recognize the benefit of their efforts after a few weeks. Plan on a person taking ten times as long to get a letter out the first time!
4. Some managers have reported good results from letting their staff work on the program during the evenings or on Saturdays.
5. Keep in mind that good teaching is more like coaching than lecturing.
6. Be aware that change is a learning process. Individuals must learn new procedures and skills to replace old procedures and habits. This takes time.
7. Finally, recognize that resistance to change is often a response to the way changes are implemented rather than disapproval of the change itself. Change always brings both threats and opportunities. When confronting change, it's natural to feel somewhat insecure.

FIGURE 24-2. Computer training guidelines. These suggestions were developed by the training group for a large field office automation project and printed in the manager's overview of the project's training program.

Analyzing Training Needs

All training projects begin with research, whether it is described as needs analysis, needs assessment, performance analysis, or task analysis. Whatever term is used, the goal is to determine what must be learned and how that learning can best take place. A training program may be initiated as part of the implementation of new systems or in response to ongoing job requirements.

Identifying skills and knowledge required in a training population (an organization, department, work group) is difficult. It is critical to determine precisely what features, skills, and knowledge the user needs to learn about using the technology to do his or her job. The problem is more acute when one tries to match a training design with the needs of a wide range of users with various backgrounds and motivations.

Needs analysis can be described by using a system's input-processing-output model. In a given job, the individual responds to job demands, and work is completed as a result. Knowledge of results goes back to the worker in the form of feedback (see Figure 24-3). The training specialist must determine if training could result in improved performance, what training would be required, and how it should be delivered.

FIGURE 24-3. Systems model of training needs analysis.

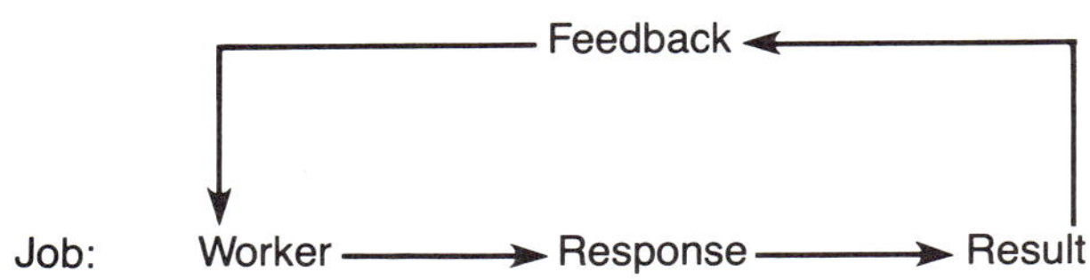

The first premise the training specialists work with is that a problem exists: feedback to the worker shows that the result was not as expected. Next, the training specialist determines what caused the unexpected result (poor performance). Once the cause of the poor performance is identified, corrective steps can be taken.

Not all performance problems call for a training solution. Other job-related factors, such as faulty equipment, unclear procedures, or poorly designed work flow, could be causing the problem. In such cases, the solution is not the training specialist's responsibility. However, if it is determined, for example, that an accountant is having difficulty producing timely reports because she cannot use advanced functions on her spreadsheet package, training *is* the solution.

Training is also required when new equipment or procedures are introduced. Training strategies in this case are included in the implementation plan (see Chapter 22). In such a case, training is not a reaction to a problem but an implementation strategy for acceptance of the new technology or procedures.

The importance of careful needs analysis, especially for first-time users of computer systems, cannot be overemphasized. The mistake that implementers of new computer systems make most frequently is to cram everything about operating a system into a training program at the time of implementation and then walk away, believing that users are prepared to use the system effectively. Unfortunately, this type of training is often more a demonstration of system capabilities than skill development. This approach might be appropriate for an experienced computer user who is learning a new system or software package, but it is not effective for first-time users. More often than not, such an approach leaves first-time users overwhelmed, discouraged, and ill-prepared to begin using the system. The likely result is that they will return to their jobs not knowing where to begin. Individuals who have a great deal of initiative find technology fascinating, and if they have sufficient time they will pick up the class notes and computer manuals and learn on their own. Most people, however, will feel pressured to catch up on work that accumulated while they were in class for several days. They will try to use the computer, flounder, and then return to doing their work in the usual manner, with the good intention of learning to use the computer as soon as they catch up on their work and can spare the time. By the time they return to the computer, however, they will have forgotten 80 to 90 percent of what they learned in class. They will make excuses for not using the computer and, unless compelled by a superior, will probably use it only minimally or not at all.

In determining what needs to be taught, some key questions must be asked:

- Who needs to use the systems?
- What is the current level of user expertise?
- If individuals have computer experience, how much of this experience can be expected to apply to the new system?
- What do users need to learn to do on the system?
- Do all users need to learn the same applications, or do requirements vary?
- Which applications will individuals start with?
- Which applications will be used most frequently?
- Which applications have the greatest potential for increasing effectiveness or saving time?
- Have all applications been identified, or will more be added in the future?
- How much can individuals be expected to learn during initial training?
- What skills and applications will be taught after initial training and over what time period?

Needs Analysis Tools

Assessing training needs—answering questions such as those listed above—can be done a number of ways. The most frequently used techniques are observations, interviews, focus groups, questionnaires, and critical incidents. Techniques related to using these tools were discussed in Chapter 21. Figure 24-4 is a summary of their advantages and disadvantages with regard to training needs analysis.

Techniques	Advantages	Disadvantages
Observation	Firsthand view of situation	Time-consuming
Personal Interviews	Interviewees carefully chosen	May require a large interviewing staff
Telephone Interviews	Less expensive than personal interview. Can be monitored and evaluated. 80–90% of those called usually agree	Not everyone is good at telephone interviews; subtle body language is missing
Focus Groups	Offer fairly reliable access to ideas and attitudes of a work group	May be difficult to schedule; require strong group leader
Questionnaires	Can reach a large audience at a limited cost; recipient can fill one at his/her leisure; offer anonymity to respondent; do not need a large staff to administer	Difficult to design; nonresponses can diminish cost savings; possible bias; long turnaround; not sure the right person completes; requires statistical treatment
Critical Incident	Objective	Data collection may not be complete; easy to overlook positive outcomes

FIGURE 24-4. Advantages and disadvantages of various investigation techniques for training assessment and evaluation.

Data gathered from an assessment study provides answers to the following questions:

- Why are current systems not being used?
- Who could benefit from training?
- What are users' current and desired level of expertise on a given system or application package?
- Which systems require additional training support?
- Which application packages need to be taught?
- Which skills and features need to be taught for a particular application package?

- How much training is needed?
- How much time could employees have to train?
- What tasks must employees be able to perform when training is completed?

To illustrate the value of a needs assessment, Figure 24-5 provides an excerpt from a completed report. Of all the steps in the training process, needs assessment is the most frequently overlooked—and the most important. The remainder of the process—design, delivery, and evaluation—is worthless if the *right* skills are not taught to the *right* people for the *right* systems.

FIGURE 24-5. Excerpt from an assessment report.

Even those who are using the microcomputer do not use some of the most fundamental features of the software. For example, one clerk was not familiar with centering in word processing. One secretary did not know how to type a document directly within the word processing document screen; she thought she needed to use a key procedure to create a document. A new clerk had developed two applications in a spreadsheet package but did not know basic skills like erasing a cell, inserting rows and columns, or copying and moving cells.

One clerk learned the word processing system, but after setting up letters she was unable to get them to print. She ended up doing the work all over again on the typewriter. She has not used the microcomputer since then and is reluctant to go back to it, even though the other clerk is using the microcomputer and is very enthusiastic.

The result is that people are spending inordinate amounts of time developing even the most straightforward applications, thus negating any potential time savings. They experience frustration in developing the applications, and results are sometimes undependable because they don't have the basic understanding or skills to assess or resolve the problems themselves.

Designing Successful Programs

With data from the assessment in hand, the training designer should be able to identify skills and concepts that need to be taught, those individuals who should receive training, how much training is needed, and who should be responsible for the instruction.

Performance Objectives

The training designer develops a training program by first identifying expected outcomes. These *performance objectives* (also known as *course goals, learning objectives,* or *behavioral objectives*) define what the trainee is expected to do as a result of the training. These objectives become the basis for developing a sound training program as well as evaluating its effectiveness. After all, how can people know what route to take or that they have reached their destination if they don't know where they want to be? The point is that training should relate directly to expected job performance.

In his 1962 research-based book, *Preparing Objectives for Programmed Instruction*, Dr. Robert Mager made a profound point: The best training programs tell both trainee and trainer what the learner should be able to do, under what conditions, and with what degree of competence. Specifying learning by objectives makes training accountable. The approach also gives learners knowledge "up front" about what is expected of them, relieving anxiety and confusion. Chester Delaney, Vice-President for Human Resources of Chase Manhattan Bank, has observed that the use of performance objectives keeps "the focus of training on learning rather than teaching and on job enablement or mastery rather than on the mere statement or coverage of content."[3]

According to Mager, a learning objective consists of three factors: (1) the condition, (2) performance, and (3) criteria. For example, given LOTUS 1-2-3 software (condition), the trainee should be able to prepare a department budget (performance) with no errors (criteria). Or, given a rough draft of the monthly sales report (condition), the trainee should be able to prepare a usable document to include at least two graphs (performance) with no mistakes (criteria).

Some training experts believe that the time frame for successful completion of the task should also be identified up front. After all, if one can prepare a budget or sales report but takes three weeks to do so, the usability of the performance objective is compromised.

Writing performance objectives Despite their importance, many trainers hesitate to write performance objectives because they find the task difficult and time-consuming. Why do trainers find it difficult to write objectives? Several reasons have been identified:

- Writing itself is difficult for most people.
- Skill is involved in choosing the right words and identifying the proper amount of qualification and quantification.
- Objectives are only as good as the standards for the task being taught. What if no standards exist?
- Trainees often come to the learning experience with various levels of skill. How do you develop a goal common to all?

Despite such difficulty, performance objectives *can* and *should* be written. A useful guide in developing a list of performance objectives is a Taxonomy of Educational Objectives. A taxonomy breaks instructional objectives into levels of mastery called *domains* and offers a listing of action words appropriate to each level (domain). Examples of action words to describe learning outcomes include the following:

1. *Cognitive domain:* defines, names, states, distinguishes, infers, changes, computes, demonstrates, diagrams, categorizes, revises, compares, concludes, and interprets.

2. *Affective domain:* asks, describes, uses, tells, writes, completes, reads, arranges, relates, acts, listens, performs, solves, uses, verifies.
3. *Psychomotor domain:* assembles, builds, cleans, composes, fixes, manipulates, starts, uses, connects, identifies, demonstrates.

Selecting Training Participants

Selecting the "right" training participants occurs in the assessment stage. Perhaps the most important rule is that the trainees selected for the learning activity should have a "need to know." In other words, they should be able to apply the skills they are going to learn directly to their jobs.

Another consideration is how workers should be grouped for the training. It is not always practical to group people solely on their need to know. Other considerations are the current skill level of trainees, their organizational level, and the skill level required (performance objectives). For example, putting novice and advanced spreadsheet software users together to learn a newly adopted version of the software is not recommended. Grouping individuals with different learning objectives also poses problems. Some individuals may need a thorough working knowledge of all software features while others may need just a general overview of capabilities and applications. Also, when managers and subordinates are grouped together for the same learning activity, an even split of managers and subordinates is suggested.

Selecting Training Instructors

Office automation training may be done by the vendor or a vendor's agent, by an outside consultant or firm, or by an internal trainer. A discussion of advantages and disadvantages of each of these approaches follows.

The vendor as trainer Most office automation equipment and software manufacturers include training in their customer support offerings. Vendor training can range from a demonstration of how to use a printer to a five-day seminar on local area networks. Training is often included in the vendor's proposal to sell and install the new system. It is expected that the vendor has the most expertise in using its products, and a vested interest in ensuring that the equipment is used effectively.

IBM, for example, offers a multitude of courses on topics such as word processing, system administration, and local area networks. IBM's courses are offered at various instructional levels, from novice to highly technical. Some IBM courses are for-fee, others are free. Typically, a vendor provides basic training for one or two people at no charge. Courses for additional persons or for advanced skills are available on a fee basis. In addition, while courses are sometimes offered at the customer's site, many courses are available only at the vendor's facility.

Some vendors have developed training courses and materials that can be purchased by the customer for in-house trainers. In effect, a vendor may offer purchasers a course to "train the trainer." In addition, vendors often offer tutorials, reference manuals, or other learning aids for their products. Wang, for example, offers an interactive videodisk program called WILS (Wang Interactive Learning System) to teach word processing.

Most hardware and software vendors, such as WANG, IBM, Lotus, and Ashton-Tate, have customer "hot lines." Using a toll-free number, purchasers can call for online, expert assistance. The use of such hot lines is not intended for training, in the true sense of training; rather, it offers support for problem resolution. In addition, vendors often establish user groups. For example, the International Society of Wang Users (ISWU) is a forum that promotes communications among Wang users. Members of ISWU discuss problems and opportunities related to Wang equipment.

In a presentation to the Office Automation Society International (OASI), consultant John W. Meroney listed the following possible drawbacks to vendor training:[4]

- Limitations on the number of individuals who can be trained at no cost
- Backlogs in training schedules, causing long waiting periods
- Type of training offered
- Insufficient instructor time provided
- Lack of adequate follow-up

The outside consultant as trainer An outside consultant is typically used when an organization does not have the expertise or resources (time, staff, materials) to develop a training program for an identified need. When an organization chooses an outside consultant to conduct the training, frequently that trainer was involved in the initial needs assessment. At other times, the assessment was done internally, and a consultant is hired to develop a program to address the identified training needs.

When choosing an outside training consultant, the planner should follow the same advice offered in Chapter 21: check the reputation of the consultant, ensure that the consultant knows what outcomes are expected, and continually follow up with the consultant, including continuous evaluation of the classes being conducted. In short, the learning experience remains the responsibility of the training planner.

The outside institution as trainer Many organizations offer tuition reimbursement programs to employees who take job-related courses or attend seminars outside the organization. In such cases, the training planner has virtually no control over course content. Institutions generally publish performance objectives and content outlines, however, which the training planner can use to select courses or seminars that fit the overall training strategy for learning new systems or applications. Figure 24-6 is a description of a typical course offering.

REVISED

Data Communications I:
An Introduction to Concepts and Systems

A thorough understanding of data communications has become mandatory for information processing professionals. This seminar guides you through the maze of equipment, techniques, and services available and provides a solid foundation in the technology.

Benefits include:

- How to apply the terminology and operating concepts of the data communications field to your environment.
- How to deal effectively with vendors, carriers, purchasing agents, and members of your own organization.
- How to determine network interfaces and compatibility issues.
- How to convert user and organizational needs into operational systems.
- Understand what is available today and which products and services best fit your environment.

Who Should Attend:

EDP, teleprocessing, telecommunications and data communications systems analysts, planners, vendors, decision makers, and anyone who needs to develop or improve expertise in data communications systems.

Course Outline

An Overview of Data Communications
- Evolution
- Quantifying and fulfilling needs
- Application and traffic categories
- Performance categories
- System components and interrelationships

Concepts and Definitions
- Codes—ASCII, EBCDIC
- Asynchronous/synchronous
- Parity, Checksum, CRC
- Full and half-duplex
- Switched vs. private line
- Analog vs. digital transmission

Terminals
- Keyboard printer (TTY)
- CRT (VDU or VDT)
- Batch/RJE
- Intelligent
- Personal computers

Modems
- Synchronous and asynchronous modems, acoustic couplers, limited distance modems
- Independent suppliers
- Supervisory channels for remote diagnostics and control
- Interface standards (RS232, RS449)

Common Carriers
- FCC and state regulations
- AT&T divestiture
- BOCs
- The carriers and offerings

FREE: Your choice of Datapro Reference Volumes for post-seminar support information. (See inside front cover for details.)

Telephone Switched Network
- Elements and organization of the switched network
- Performance
- Turnaround delay
- Pricing aspects
- WATS
- ISDN

Private Line Services
- Narrowband to wideband
- Analog voice grade channels; two-point and multipoint four-wire vs. two-wire; effect of modem turn-on delay
- Performance
- Dataphone Digital Service (DDS)
- T1 and T45 Services
- Pricing

Packet Switching Networks
- Value-added and intelligent data networks
- Circuit/message/packet switching concepts
- Packet network operation
- Public data networks (Telenet, Tymnet, BOCs)

Introduction to Protocols
- General; varieties; standards, control characters
- PC (TTY, XModem, X.PC)
- BISYNC (2780/3780/3270)
- SDLC, HDLC
- X.25

Multiplexing and Concentration
- Basic time division multiplexing
- Statistical multiplexers
- Remote concentrators

Satellite Communications
- Concepts; the path, earth stations, satellites, transponders, propagation delay, performance
- Satellite service suppliers

Network Architectures
- Concepts
- ISO seven layer model
- IBM's Systems Network Architecture

Course Leaders

Gary Audin
Harvey Hershkowitz
Les Haentzschel
Tom Abramofsky

LOCATIONS	DATES
New York	August 11-13
	September 15-17
	October 15-17
	November 17-19
	December 10-12
San Francisco	August 18-20*
	October 20-22*
	December 8-10*
Washington DC	August 18-20*
	October 20-22*
	December 3-5*
Chicago	August 4-6
	November 5-7
Atlanta	August 4-6
	November 17-19
Boston	September 22-24*
	November 19-21
Hartford	August 25-27*
Orlando	October 27-29*
Philadelphia	October 20-22
Los Angeles	September 22-24*
Denver	October 27-29

* EXPENSE SAVER—Seminar dates noted with an asterisk (*) are delivered back-to-back with companion course, *Data Communications II*. See page 5.

To Register
For complete enrollment information see inside back cover. For instant registration, call our toll-free number or complete the registration form.

1-800-DATAPRO
(that's 1-800-328-2776)

Your registration will be confirmed immediately.

FIGURE 24-6. A typical course offering of a training vendor.

The major disadvantage of courses provided by outside institutions is that they are general in nature, and trainees must sift through the information to select what applies specifically to their job environments. They must also take the initiative to acquire practice on the job and apply the skills they have learned.

On the other hand, when trainees go outside the organization for training, they have opportunities to exchange ideas with others. It is this aspect that persuades organizations to sponsor employee participation in institutions such as the Office Systems Research Association, the Association for Information Processing Professionals, or the Association for Systems Management. Of similar value are organizations for trainers, such as the American Society for Training and Development.

The internal trainer Internal trainers may work full-time at training or be practitioners who have part-time training responsibilities. Trainers often develop expertise in certain areas of instruction—for example, word processing, database management, graphics—and plan and conduct all courses in their specialty. Many large organizations have extensive internal training programs to meet business, technical, and office computing needs. (The role of the information center in training and supporting end-user computing was discussed in Chapter 11.)

An internal training staff typically assures the organization of good, consistent training. Most important, it provides efficient training because programs can be tailored to specific business needs or project objectives. In addition, large organizations can provide internal training at a low cost per trainee. However, trainers may become too narrow; they may determine that their expertise is always needed, or (like some teachers) they may become too rigid in their plans.

Advantages and disadvantages, as well as cost, must be considered by any training manager. For example, for special requirements or small organizations it may be less expensive to hire a $1000-a-day expert to conduct the training than pay an internal trainer to learn the content, plan, and deliver the course.

The Training Plan

Plan the work and work the plan. Planning the training experience entails knowing what needs to be taught and to whom. The complexity of the material or skill to be learned and the abilities of the trainers are taken into account as the designer puts together an instructional program and follows it through to completion.

The designer should also ensure that the training program is given adequate time and priority. Technology is often underused because practitioners do not know how to use it to the fullest. Braverman, Castle, and McKee attributed underuse of technology in an organization they studied to shortcomings in the training program.[5] Dissatisfied users complained that insufficient time was spent in training, course content was too complex, and training manuals were too difficult to understand.

The users surveyed by Braverman and colleagues reported a need for training that was more practical than theoretical and for training that focused on how they could *use* the system. Users suggested follow-up training sessions, users' groups, and a newsletter for sharing ideas.

Time Frames for Training

Determining adequate time for training requires knowing what needs to be taught (content complexity) and the needs of trainee group. How quickly can this group be expected to learn? Must they maintain production while they are learning, or can they be excused from job responsibilities for the duration of the training? Will management excuse trainees for whatever time the trainer feels is adequate, or only for a few hours or days? Is it reasonable for trainees to absorb all the content at once, or do they need time to apply skills on the job as they are learning? In all instances, the complexity of the learning and background of the trainee should be considered.

Delivering Training Programs

Experts agree that the best way to learn to use office automation tools is through hands-on experiences: to learn by doing. Experts also agree that interactive learning experiences contribute to learning; in other words, the learner is not passive but an active participant. It is also a given that most people learn best in a one-on-one, face-to-face situation with an instructor with whom they can easily communicate, asking questions and proceeding at their own rate of speed. Unfortunately, one-on-one training is seldom a practical training strategy because of the time it takes and the cost involved. Many available alternatives, however, can provide satisfactory results when properly planned and executed.

The following discussion of training methodologies describes each training technique, with examples of its effective application, and discusses advantages and disadvantages. The discussion proceeds from traditional methodologies, such as the lecture, to computer-based instruction, including interactive video.

Lecture

"Lecture only if you must." This advice is frequently offered by people interested in training results. Lecture is a traditional classroom approach to learning and usually involves an individual trainer giving information to a group of trainees. The trainees typically listen and take notes in an effort to understand and remember the information. The following example illustrates the use of lecture as a method of training delivery:

> Company DEF, with a network of personal computers in place, trained its supervisory people on new software designed to report performance appraisals. The new system could tabulate scores and help the supervisor identify recurring problems or trends. It could also plot an employee's progress from quarter to quarter. Because the system needed to be operable within two weeks and because the supervisors were centrally located at the organization's headquarters (which had a training room equipped with microcomputers), lecture, combined with demonstration, was deemed the most appropriate mode of training delivery.

Advantages and disadvantages The advantages of the lecture are that such a learning experience is easy to establish, trainees are familiar with the technique, and it is an effective way to disseminate information to large groups of people very quickly. On the other hand, unless the lecturer provides ample opportunity for trainee interaction, the lecture is a passive activity. Research has shown that when individuals leave a lecture, they retain only 25 percent of the material to which they were exposed. A week later, that figure drops to 10 percent. A number of variables, of course, dictate how much is remembered, such as the skill of the lecturer, the number and type of visual aids, and the interest/applicability of the information.

Generally, lecture is not an appropriate way to teach computer skills when individuals are expected to go back to the job and perform. They cannot be expected to remember detailed sequences of keystrokes without adequate opportunity to practice. Lecture can be effective, however, when it introduces relatively easy procedures to experienced computer users and is supported with handouts that provide operational details. It also may provide an appropriate overview to individuals who need to be aware of system capabilities but will not actually operate the system. It is usually more effective, however, when it is combined with a demonstration.

Demonstrations

Demonstrations involve an experienced user showing a prospective user how to use the new technology, typically on a one-time-only basis. The following example illustrates the use of demonstration for training:

> Company EFG installed a new Dynamo copier in its General Office. Renee Gittings, EFG secretary, is trained to use the copier through demonstration by a knowledgeable Dynamo salesperson. Taking her time, the Dynamo salesperson shows Renee how to load paper, sort, stack, reduce, enlarge, copy both sides, use color, and even make slides. As the demonstration continues, Renee is also shown how to change the toner and respond to problem codes. Renee listens and then repeats the demonstration with the salesperson in attendance.

Advantages and disadvantages When the demonstrator is training an individual who has had experience with the technology, learning new features or new ways to use familiar features may not be a problem. In other words, when the technology is neither novel nor complex, simple demonstration may suffice. Often, however, simply showing someone how a piece of technology operates is not enough; having the trainee repeat the demonstration can better assure that learning took place.

A demonstration may be inadequate, however, if it is hurried or if the trainee cannot "keep up" with it. If Renee were a novice copier operator, the demonstration might not have been enough. Chances are that, even now, Renee may refer to the manual when she enlarges a document or changes the toner.

Workshops

Workshops are training sessions in which the trainer guides the trainees to solve mutual problems or use technology more creatively. In a workshop situation, trainees learn and use skills through hands-on exercises, in which they can also learn from each other. The following example illustrates the use of workshops to deliver training:

> Patricia Medrano calls her training staff together to discuss how best to teach users to access the DIALOG database, to which the organization has just subscribed. Patricia explains the problem to her staff, a group of professional trainers, who discuss the issue and decide on the approach for training executives and secretaries in using the utility.

Advantages and disadvantages Advantages to using a workshop approach to training are that the real-life problem is addressed by individuals with a vested interest in its solution. When participants are knowledgeable about a range of potential solutions, each participant can contribute to solving the problem. A primary caution in workshop training is that participants should be of relatively equal background or expertise. Moreover, it is the skill of the trainer that, typically, determines its success or failure. In this case, group-leading abilities are mandatory skills.

Coaching

Coaching has long been recognized as the most effective way to learn. It entails one-on-one, face-to-face interaction between trainer and trainee. In such a situation, trainees get immediate, personalized feedback throughout the learning experience, as well as proceed at their own rate of learning. The following example illustrates the use of coaching to deliver training:

> When John England began his new job as manager of the loan department at City National Bank, he needed to learn how to use the bank's customer databases. Because the databases were online and available for verifying customer records, they would be an asset for John. John's supervisor spent an afternoon with him going over access codes, key words, and what to do when problems arose. John's intensive training enabled him to learn the system easily and quickly.

A special application of coaching is the *hot line*, which is run by the systems or information center trainer. Users who are teaching themselves software packages call the trainer on the hot line to ask questions or discuss problems and possible solutions.

Advantages and disadvantages One-on-one training is the most effective but also the most costly method of training delivery. Its effectiveness stems from direct interaction between trainee and trainer, so that concerns and problems are addressed immediately. The trainee does not have to spend time learning manuals or by extensive trial-and-error approaches. It is often difficult to justify monopolizing the time of a trainer with one person when, in a classroom situation, a trainer can teach 10 to 15 people. Coaching may be the best approach, however, in selected situations, such as for executives and specialists whose time is limited and expensive, for highly specialized applications or skills, and for resolving problems.

Print-Based Manuals and Tutorials

Manuals, which are also referred to as *system documentation*, are a written description of how a system operates and are a vital component of any system. Manuals are valuable reference resources for experienced users, but they are seldom good learning tools for the novice. Manuals for off-the-shelf software sometimes include tutorials, or written descriptions of how to use the software. These tutorials can be used in initial training efforts. Understanding them may be difficult for the novice, however. As a training tool, paper-based tutorials are of value primarily to experienced computer users who want to learn new software programs. The following example illustrates the use of manuals as a training tool:

> The office automation task force has determined that the corporate and divisional offices should use an updated package, Spreadsheet IV. Currently, all employees use either Spreadsheet III or Superspread I. Because all prospective trainees are proficient with a spreadsheet package, corporate training has determined that users will be expected to learn Spreadsheet IV on their own, using a manual.

Advantages and disadvantages Because a reference manual is comprehensive, individuals may need to know a system before they can even understand how to use the index. This is because programmers are often more concerned with what the program can do than in being able to explain how to use it. On the other hand, an experienced user can often use a manual to teach him or herself on a "need-to-know" basis. Extensive training programs for the experienced user are often not necessary.

While well-written documentation does exist for some programs, manuals are rarely recommended for initial training. Only if the manual is accompanied by an interactive tutorial and a very motivated learner are manuals effective for training novices.

Audio- and Video-Based Training

Today in many bookstores, audiotapes and videotapes sit on shelves alongside the books. While such media are not in contention to replace books, they are alternative forms for information dissemination. Audio- and videotapes sometimes supplement paper-based training manuals. Some trainees consider such media more personal than a book; others explain that audio or visual cues illustrate or explain things in a manner that a book cannot. Whatever the reason, the use of such media for training is growing. The following example illustrates the use of audio- and video-based training delivery:

> Company RST has just installed workstations on the desks of its mid-level managers. Although the managers have been using personal computers for some time now, they are suddenly introduced to a wide range of new applications, including database management. The organization has in stock a number of video players, and its approach to training is to lend a video player and training video to any manager who requests it for a period of one week.

Advantages and disadvantages Audio and video add a human element to self-paced training. Video goes a step beyond audio in providing visual information—demonstrations and examples that aid the learning process. In addition, such media enable trainees to learn at their own pace and convenience. Besides the problem of ensuring high-quality audio and video learning packages, there are other problems, such as keeping the trainee's interest. Also, quality training programs are expensive to produce or buy. Costs to produce an in-house, application-specific video, for example, may range from $5,000 to $75,000. Prices for ready-made videos typically begin at $200.

Computer-Based Training

Computer-Based Training (CBT) refers to a variety of techniques that use the computer as a training medium. *Training* magazine reported that 46.4 percent of organizations responding to its questionnaire used some type of computer-based training. Various terms are associated with different types of computer-based training:

- PI = Programmed Instruction
- CAI = Computer-Assisted Instruction
- CMI = Computer-Managed Instruction
- CBI = Computer-Based Instruction
- IVD = Interactive Video Disk

This alphabet soup of terms describes learning activities that involve a computer. PI and CAI are often used interchangeably and refer to instruction delivery. CMI refers to management of the training process, CBI refers to delivery and student management, and IVD usually refers to delivery.

Programmed Instruction (PI) PI originated with B. F. Skinner in the early 1950s. Skinner theorized that for effective learning, students must be constantly reinforced. Media for such experiences were either books or teaching machines. The book or teaching machine took the student, step by step, through learning activities (similar in many ways to print-based tutorials, mentioned above). When students completed an exercise, they turned to the next page or frame and immediately knew whether or not their answer was correct. When the answer was incorrect, the correct answer was explained, or the student was directed to review and then attempt to answer the question again. Teaching machines, such as PLATO (Control Data Corporation) and AIS (McDonnell Douglas Corporation), require customized terminals and software.

Computer-Assisted Instruction (CAI) CAI expands on PI principles. An important difference is that CAI does not require special hardware. The first CAI programs ran on mainframe computers. Today, CAI programs can run on mainframes, minicomputers, and microcomputers. For example, microcomputer software vendors sometimes supply a learning diskette with their software. The learning diskette, or tutorial, offers various degrees of interaction between the trainee and the computer. Using a tutorial, the individual completes a series of lessons on the computer, which provides directions and practice in using the software. Some tutorials include companion paper-based exercises and instructions. Information centers often use CAI to teach end-user computer skills. Companies such as Interactive Training Systems (ITS) specialize in developing end-user CAI programs. Tutorials are available on topics such as Intro to DP for End Users, Intro to Data Communications, Using SAS, Using TSO, Basic JCL, Using FOCUS, Using RAMIS, Using PROFS, and a variety of others.

Computer-Managed Instruction (CMI) CMI systems manage the instructional process. They keep class rosters, trainee profiles, class schedules, test scores, and so on. CMI systems aid the process, but do not actually provide the instruction.

Computer-Based Instruction (CBI) CBI systems, on the other hand, typically combine PI, CAI, and CMI. CBI systems can be used for testing, instruction, and/or keeping student records. They can generate, administer, and score tests. Many CBI programs have built-in pre- and post-tests. CBI can be used for drills (repeated practice), tutorials (discussed earlier), or simulations (models of how something works).

CBI systems can also keep student records (employing CMI principles). For example, Ernest and Whinney's Interactive Computer-Based Training Program generates progress reports on individual students. Figure 24-7 illustrates a sample report that was generated by Ernest and

SABER ADMINISTRATION SYSTEM

Lesson Description	Course Status	Start Date	Last Date	Total Answers	Correct Answers	Percent Correct	Current Page #	Time Spent in Course	Control Number
John Jones, Social Sec. No. 289-27-8084									
EDP CONCEPTS - FINAL TEST	complete	03/14/86	03/14/86	169	109	64%	157	0h 37m 21s	104
EDP CONCEPTS FOR BUSINESS MOD 1	complete	03/10/86	03/14/86	65	56	86%	36	4h 31m 2s	104
EDP CONCEPTS FOR BUSINESS MOD 2A	complete	03/11/86	03/11/86	19	14	74%	286	0h 59m 25s	104
EDP CONCEPTS FOR BUSINESS MOD 2B	complete	03/11/86	03/14/86	50	40	80%	95	2h 32m 3s	104
EDP CONCEPTS FOR BUSINESS MOD 3A	complete	03/14/80	03/14/86	30	28	93%	77	2h 54m 32s	104
EDP CONCEPTS FOR BUSINESS MOD 3B	complete	03/11/86	03/14/86	38	28	74%	121	1h 45m 28s	104
EDP CONCEPTS FOR BUSINESS MOD 4	complete	03/12/86	03/14/86	35	26	74%	9	3h 57m 39s	104
EDP CONCEPTS FOR BUSINESS MOD 5	complete	03/12/86	03/14/86	38	23	61%	0	2h 22m 15s	104
EDP CONCEPTS FOR BUSINESS MOD 6	complete	03/13/86	03/14/86	45	39	87%	191	2h 43m 6s	104
EDP CONCEPTS PRE-TEST MOD 1	complete	03/10/86	03/11/86	21	8	38%	14	0h 19m 34s	104
EDP CONCEPTS PRE-TEST MOD 2	complete	03/11/86	03/11/86	31	28	90%	16	0h 6m 49s	104
EDP CONCEPTS PRE-TEST MOD 3	complete	03/12/80	01/12/80	29	10	34%	17	0h 8m 21s	104
EDP CONCEPTS PRE-TEST MOD 4	complete	03/12/86	03/12/86	25	7	28%	11	0h 5m 7s	104
EDP CONCEPTS PRE-TEST MOD 5	complete	03/12/86	03/12/86	10	6	60%	10	0h 10m 6s	104
EDP CONCEPTS PRE-TEST MOD 6	complete	03/13/86	03/13/86	17	8	47%	14	0h 36m 30s	104
Jack Smith, Social Sec. No. 258-44-7726									
EDP CONCEPTS - FINAL TEST	complete	03/12/86	03/12/86	171	143	84%	32	0h 46m 29s	104
EDP CONCEPTS FOR BUSINESS MOD 1	complete	03/10/86	03/10/86	61	57	93%	579	1h 32m 34s	104
EDP CONCEPTS FOR BUSINESS MOD 2A	complete	03/10/86	03/12/86	23	17	74%	0	0h 37m 22s	104
EDP CONCEPTS FOR BUSINESS MOD 2B	complete	03/10/86	03/12/86	54	45	83%	0	0h 54m 16s	104
EDP CONCEPTS FOR BUSINESS MOD 3A	complete	03/11/86	03/12/86	29	24	83%	481	1h 23m 39s	104
EDP CONCEPTS FOR BUSINESS MOD 3B	complete	03/11/86	03/12/86	38	34	89%	453	1h 12m 23s	104
EDP CONCEPTS FOR BUSINESS MOD 4	complete	03/11/86	03/12/86	35	31	89%	413	1h 49m 35s	104
EDP CONCEPTS FOR BUSINESS MOD 5	complete	03/11/86	03/12/86	39	38	97%	487	2h 32m 29s	104
EDP CONCEPTS FOR BUSINESS MOD 6	complete	03/12/86	03/12/86	47	42	89%	589	1h 26m 10s	104
EDP CONCEPTS PRE-TEST MOD 1	complete	03/10/86	03/12/86	21	12	57%	14	0h 17m 45s	104
EDP CONCEPTS PRE-TEST MOD 2	complete	03/10/86	03/12/86	31	22	71%	16	0h 11m 5s	104
EDP CONCEPTS PRE-TEST MOD 3	complete	03/11/86	03/12/86	29	17	59%	17	0h 15m 35s	104
EDP CONCEPTS PRE-TEST MOD 4	complete	03/11/86	03/12/86	25	15	60%	11	0h 8m 47s	104
EDP CONCEPTS PRE-TEST MOD 5	complete	03/11/86	03/12/86	10	3	30%	10	0h 7m 58s	104
EDP CONCEPTS PRE-TEST MOD 6	complete	03/12/86	03/12/86	17	12	71%	14	0h 7m 50s	104

FIGURE 24-7. Sample reports from Interactive Computer-Based Training Program.

Whinney's Interactive Computer-Based Training Program. Note that the reports provide information regarding not only where John Jones and Jack Smith are in the training program, but also how well they are doing.

A second example of CBI is the ForceTen Management System. The advertisement in Figure 24-8 says that this CBT program performs needs analysis, offers course resources, plans and delivers instruction, and even evaluates the trainee's progress.

FIGURE 24-8. An advertisement for the ForceTen Training Management System.

ForceTen Training Management System

Computer-based training at its best.

The ForceTen Training Management system is the most effective and comprehensive training support tool available. It includes

- identification of current skills and required skills;
- maintenance of a comprehensive course library;
- course planning, budgeting, and scheduling;
- tracking trainee progress and monitoring responses for course evaluation.

Find out more. Call or write:

ForceTen Enterprises, Inc.
180 Atwell Drive
Rexdale, Ontario
(416) 675-3720

Plus, a powerful authoring system featuring

- "what you see is what you get" approach to building frames;
- course evaluation through trainee feedback;
- interactive video disk or videotape;
- a mouse to avoid extensive keying and facilitate the creation of graphic images;
- color graphics library of user-created images;
- character set library of user created special fonts, mathematical symbols, foreign language letters;
- seven response types, including parsed free form through the use of an extensive thesaurus.
- additional customer services available upon request.

Interactive video disk Interactive video disk combines the capabilities of video with CAI and comes in two formats: laser disk and videotape. The disk provides more capability and flexibility than tape. Resembling a shiny record, one side of a laser disk can hold 54,000 images and be accessed randomly. If these images are "full motion," this translates to approximately 30 minutes of playing time. In addition, the laser disk is capable of stereo sound. Alternatively, the two sound channels can be used individually, to give the user a choice, for example, of a Spanish or an English sound track. Pioneer's Industrial Laser Disc Player is shown in Figure 24-9. *Interactive videotape* is similar to the video disk; however, to access frames, the user must "scroll" through the tape, without the ease of random access.

FIGURE 24-9.
Pioneer's Industrial LaserDisc Player.

Many interactive video systems use a diskette to store the computer programming, with only the video and audio on the videotape or laser disk. In this way, the CAI and CMI can be modified easily and inexpensively. To run interactive video requires a computer, CAI/CMI software (on a diskette or loaded on the system disk drive or hard disk), a video cassette player or laser disk player, and appropriate cabling.

Traditional PI and CAI instruction offers linear programming. *Linear* means that lessons proceed in a straight line; everyone in the learning experiences goes through the same set of learning activities. The interactive video disk and tape, on the other hand, allow users to skip activities that (based on their responses) they have mastered. This means it is unlikely that any two people would complete the instruction the same way. The following example illustrates the use of interactive video disk and tape:

> "The screen was part of a computer terminal, but the show on it was more like Miami Vice than Lotus 1–2–3. I was still tapping my foot to the theme music when I saw a picture of an office door with the sign 'Richard Benjamin—VP for Marketing,' and the words, 'Go right in. Mr. Benjamin is expecting you.' "[6]

Advantages and disadvantages Computer-based training systems conform well to several principles of learning:

- Trainees are able to proceed through the lesson at their own pace.
- Training is time-independent—trainees need not adhere to a rigid time frame.

- Training is done independently of an instructor; only one person's time is used.
- Training can be "as-needed."
- Although computer-based media vary in interactivity, the learner is always active in the learning process.
- Many computer-based media offer audio, video, or manuals.

The list of drawbacks to computer-based training typically begins with its expense, which is closely followed by its "lack of personal touch." Expenses begin with the costs incurred for the following to develop a CAI program:

- Authoring system (the computer software needed to design the system).
- Content expert (the expert in the subject matter to be taught).
- Instructional design expert (the person who understands learning theory and how it is applied to the skills and concepts being taught).

Costs increase with the development of an interactive video disk program with expenses for the following:

- Authoring system (same as above).
- Content expert (same as above).
- Instructional design expert (same as above).
- Script writer (the person who writes the audio and video sections of the disk).
- Film/video producer, actors, actresses (individuals who produce and perform in the production).
- Pressing the laser disk (costs involved with producing the disk itself).
- Laser disk player.
- Computer and CAI software.

Obviously, expenses can be high. Video disks are often cost-justified, however, by showing per person or "marginal" costs. Per person costs spread the expense of production over the number of trainees expected to benefit from the training. Marginal costs are the expense of adding a trainee—in other words, the expense, once the disk is produced, to train yet another person. Other disadvantages include the necessity that the trainee often operate more than one piece of equipment and the scarcity of well-written, job-applicable, off-the-shelf programs.

The Computer as Instructional Tool

Products such as Executive Computers' "Electronic Transparency" enable the trainer to project computer images onto a screen to be viewed by an entire class. When used in this way, the computer is an instructional aid not only for teaching computer skills but as a means of showing graphics, maps, outlines—anything that can be projected. Computer programs such as IBM's Storyboard enable the instructor to add color and movement to classroom illustrations.

Job Aids

Job aids were discussed in detail in Chapter 9, "Artificial Intelligence." Job aids involve the use of expert systems to incorporate training for new users or provide guidance for handling exceptions in computer software and are growing in popularity. Job aids can provide natural-language prompts for data entry, which can be bypassed after the operator becomes familiar with the system.

Not all job aids use expert systems, however. Another type of job aid is online help for micro- and mainframe computers. For example, microcomputer programs like MultiMate word processing and Lotus 1–2–3 have built-in "help" programs that are context-specific. When "Help" is pressed, the computer takes the user directly to the correct procedure, based on what the user is doing.

Job aids are also available for mainframe computers. For example, a large insurance company recently introduced several new data-entry screens for application processing. The company developed an in-house tutorial (using the ADROIT authoring system) to teach client service representatives (CSRs) to use these screens. The tutorial runs on the microcomputer. The mainframe data-entry system includes help screens, which are coordinated with the tutorial (they were developed by the same team). When CSRs have questions about what data to enter in a field or what command to use, they press a function key and the system takes them to the appropriate help screen. Pressing the Escape key brings them back to the entry screen just where they exited.

Teleconferencing

Teleconferencing equipment was described and explained in Chapter 8, "Communications Technologies." When teleconferencing equipment is used to deliver instruction, the process is known as *telelearning* or *teletraining*. Teletraining is the medium of choice when a dispersed group needs identical training on a timely basis. It eliminates the time and expense of trainees or trainers traveling to various locations. The teleconference may be audio only, or it may be enhanced by pictures delivered via slow-scan (much like slides) or via computer graphics or electronic blackboards. The teleconference may be full video (much like TV) or be conducted via a computer (a computer conference). The following example illustrates the use of teleconferencing for training delivery:

> The Massachusetts Mutual Life Insurance Company uses audio teletraining as part of its strategy for training and supporting microcomputer users in its field offices across the country. Teleconferences are used to introduce software changes, discuss problems, share ideas, and even to walk users step by step through new applications. Detailed documentation and illustrations to aid in training are prepared and mailed in advance to conference sites.

Advantages and disadvantages Because of improved networks, telelearning holds much potential as an instructional medium. With teleconferencing, learning is human-interactive; students learn with a live instructor. To be effective, the instructor who uses teleconferencing must be very well prepared. For example, course materials such as handouts or outlines must be forwarded to the instruction site prior to class (unless a facsimile system is available). Moreover, because time frames are strictly set, beginning and ending on time is more important than in the typical classroom.

Cost may or may not be a drawback. In its simplest form, the cost of a teleconference is the cost of a phone call. However, depending upon the type and quality of equipment, a video teleconferencing site can cost $10,000 to $100,000 for equipment alone.

Checklist for Choosing Training Methodology

No standard solution for meeting training needs exists. The trainer must choose from a variety of methods and media. Moreover, the trainer will probably use a variety of methodologies, not only one solution. The following checklist can be used to help choose the "best" method.

- How many people must be trained? Where are they located?
- What is the current level of trainee expertise?
- How complex is the learning?
- How soon do people need to be trained?
- What methodologies have been successful in the past?
- What facilities are available?
- Are any training materials available or must they be developed?

Evaluating Training Programs

Evaluation is an integral part of ongoing training. Its methodology should be established in the design process and be directly related to the performance objectives. In examining approaches, the training designer should look at the who, what, where, when, and why of training evaluation.

Who Should Be Evaluated?

The answer to this question is directly related to *why* training is conducted. Is the purpose to evaluate the performance of the trainer or the trainee? Many end-of-training evaluations are "opinionnaires" of trainees' perceptions of the learning experience. Other evaluation forms, such as written or performance tests, are used to evaluate progress. One chooses a technique based on who is being evaluated.

What Should Be Evaluated?

Again, why is training being conducted? Is the purpose of the program to increase worker productivity? Improve morale? Enable trainees to use a new software package? After the why is answered, evaluation may be of productivity, attitude improvement, or software expertise. Each option mandates a different approach to training evaluation.

Where Should Evaluation Take Place?

Where is the most appropriate place for evaluation? In the training room? Back at the desk? Where can the evaluator best establish that learning has taken place?

When Should Evaluation Take Place?

How frequently should trainer/trainee/course evaluation take place? Every day? Every week? At the midpoint? At the end of the program? Two weeks later? A month later? Six months later? Longer? Again, depending upon the why of training, the timing will vary. For example, worker productivity may be measurable only after the trainee has had time to apply the new skills or concepts on the job. On the other hand, determining if a trainee has mastered spreadsheet skills, for example, can be accomplished at the end of the training session through an application exercise. One of the most effective forms of evaluation for computer skills is *progress checks*, which require trainees to master and apply skills to complete cases or exercises that represent actual job requirements.

Figure 24-10 illustrates different forms used to determine trainees' reactions to their training experiences. The first form could be used at a midpoint in the training program, or it could be reworded to solicit *daily* evaluation. The second and third forms would be appropriate at the conclusion of a training program. The fourth form solicits information regarding trainees' evaluations of courseware used in the course. The final form addresses trainees' perceptions of their own performance in a video teleconference training class.

FIGURE 24-10. Typical training evaluation forms.

TRAINING PARTICIPANT REACTION FORM

–Midpoint Evaluation–

At this point in the training program, you understand the purposes and procedures of your classroom experiences. Please take a few moments now to share your reactions with me. I will use the information from these forms to make the remaining sessions as valuable to you as possible. Complete the following sentences:

1. To date, the topics I have valued most in this program are
2. To date, the topic(s) I have valued least in this program are
3. The method of instruction I prefer is
4. The method of instruction I least prefer is
5. The next time the instructor teaches this material, I suggest
6. The instructor should emphasize the following in the next sessions
7. I suggest we discontinue doing
8. Overall, this program has been

INSTRUCTOR EVALUATION FORM

Date: __________

Please rate the instructor you had for this course.

	Low				High
Knew the subject matter	1	2	3	4	5
Comments:					
Enunciated clearly	1	2	3	4	5
Comments:					
Was well prepared and organized	1	2	3	4	5
Comments:					
Involved students in discussion	1	2	3	4	5
Comments:					
Signaled transitions between topics	1	2	3	4	5
Comments:					
Periodically reviewed topics	1	2	3	4	5
Comments:					
Chose proper vocabulary	1	2	3	4	5
Comments:					
Had an appropriate appearance	1	2	3	4	5
Comments:					

FIGURE 24-10.
(continued)

WORKSHOP RATING SHEET

Participant # ______

Rate each of the following on a five-point scale:
1 = Disagree strongly
2 = Disagree
3 = Neutral
4 = Agree
5 = Agree strongly

1. ______ Presentations were well organized.
   Comments:

2. ______ Trainer used appropriate visual aids and used them well.
   Comments:

3. ______ Trainer chose appropriate methodology for instruction.
   Comments:

4. ______ Trainer knew the subject matter.
   Comments:

5. ______ Entire course design was appropriate for skills/concepts.
   Comments:

6. ______ Trainer's overall presentation style was good.
   Comments:

Topics/activities most valuable:

Topics/activities least valuable:

FIGURE 24-10. (continued)

COURSEWARE EVALUATION FORM

Following is a list of courseware used in this session. Please rate each category as to its overall quality as well as the overall impact it may have had on your subject comprehension or class enjoyment.

Quality Scale:

n/a	throw away!	poorly done	neutral	nicely done	superb!
0	1	2	3	4	5

Comprehension Scale:

n/a	confused me!	of no help	neutral	of some help	of great help
0	1	2	3	4	5

Textbook: Quality: ______ Comprehension: ______
Comments:
Handouts: Quality: ______ Comprehension: ______
Comments:
Slides: Quality: ______ Comprehension: ______
Comments:
Videotape: Quality: ______ Comprehension: ______
Comments:
Pictures: Quality: ______ Comprehension: ______
Comments:
Electronic Blackboard: Quality: ______ Comprehension: ______
Comments:
Computer Graphics: Quality: ______ Comprehension: ______
Comments:

EVALUATE YOUR PARTICIPATION

Were you prepared for this session? Had you read the assigned materials *before* class today? (Yes/No/Comments)

Did you refer to any written materials (text, handouts) during the class session? (Yes/No/Comments)

Did anyone come in late or leave your group before the class concluded? If so, was the entrance/exit disturbing?

How many times were you "on the air" during this class session?

Were there times when you wanted to ask a question or make a comment but could not? (Yes/No/Comments)

Did you feel that there was enough time for questions and interaction? (Yes/No/Comments)

Other Education and Support Strategies

In addition to training for new systems and other identified business needs, organizations may offer various other educational programs to promote and support the effective use of computers in the workplace. Some of the most commonly used are discussed in this section.

Office Automation Fair

"The [insert the name of your state] State Fair is an opportunity for [insert the nickname that describes people in your state, e.g., Hoosiers] to display their latest developments—agricultural, industrial, technological—to the rest of [insert the name of your state again]." This is also the purpose of an office automation fair.

Such a fair may be similar to a state fair or national conference, such as the annual Federal Office Systems Expo (FOSE) in Washington, D.C., or the annual INFO show in New York City. Both FOSE and INFO feature many technologies; vendors are invited to display their latest hardware and software developments. Both groups also feature seminars or talks by office automation leaders on issues relevant to office planners and users (e.g., standards, implementation, training, forecasts). Such fairs provide an opportunity for information sharing.

Likewise, an office automation fair held in an organization can be a forum for information sharing. On a less grandiose scale, a company-based fair can provide an opportunity for the office automation group (under whatever title it goes) to display hardware and software that are available to end users. In addition, a seminar, presentation, or even roundtable discussion can increase user acceptance of new technologies. Such forums also provide an opportunity to communicate to office automation planners individual needs and concerns.

Advisory Council

An advisory council is a select committee that offers advice and council to the office systems analyst or task force regarding technology and information-related concerns. An advisory council is typically created "after the fact." With the new technology in place, a council may monitor the implementation of the current project and perhaps help the systems analyst develop new products or identify training requirements. Like any advisory council, it is composed of individuals at the upper levels and in user departments who have a vested interest in the success of the project. Success of the council rests, in large part, upon its membership and the ability of the office systems analyst to listen and respond to its suggestions.

Newsletters

Newsletters and internal newspapers (often called *house organs*) are part of the organizational culture of most large companies. Newsletters are typically written and disseminated by a human resource department and offer updates on company policies, news about business performance and company events, and personal notes about employees (promotions, transfers, marriages, etc.).

The office systems analyst can use such newsletters to disseminate information about plans, new products, an upcoming fair, users' groups (discussed later), and so on. As an alternative, many office systems groups write and disseminate their own newsletters. Either way, a newsletter can be a very effective way to reach everyone in the organization with news of automation plans, new products, training programs, and "success stories" where office automation has been well accepted. The front page of a typical office systems newsletter is shown in Figure 24-11.

Internal Consultants

In Chapter 21, guidelines for selecting and using external consultants were offered. *Internal consultants* play a similar role but are full-time employees of the organization. An internal consultant is available to company employees on an ongoing basis to aid with information processing needs. Consultants perform a variety of roles. They may provide technical expertise to office systems or business analysts, provide planning expertise to managers, or fulfill other high-level roles. They may also aid end users in applying automation technologies to their jobs or departments. The internal consultant offers an individualized support that is often of extreme importance to implementation. He or she may work within the office systems department or be a member of the information center staff.

Information Center

The information center is a focal point for supporting the use of computers by nontechnical personnel. The center is a place where users can go for help in learning new programs or developing new applications. An information center usually offers a "hot line" for quick response to questions or problems. The information center can provide the tutoring and expertise users need in applying new computer technologies on the job. Employees who know where to get additional training and help in using technologies are less resistant than employees who feel left on their own.

User Groups

User groups are informal groups of users of computers or other technologies who meet to exchange expertise, experiences, and problems. Members are typically highly motivated and skilled individuals who want both to share and learn techniques related to technology. User groups were first formed by microcomputer users who were developing ways of working

PLEASE ROUTE TO:
NAME MIP

OFFICE SYSTEMS

A BIT XTRA

THE OFFICE SYSTEMS NEWSLETTER JUNE

HAPPY SUMMER !!

In addition to our regular features, this month's Newsletter brings you several articles worthy of note. See page 13 for an updated index of articles through June of 1986, which you may wish to detach and place in the front of your *Bit Xtra* binder for easy reference. On the back page is our third Quarterly Training Calendar, complete with instructions for course registration. Page 10 features details of Mass Mutual's PC Employee Purchase Plan, for those of you who are thinking of purchasing a home computer. And on page 4 you will find an updated list of Service Phone Numbers, another helpful reference to copy or clip & save.

WANTED:

PROJECT ESTIMATORS

Office Systems is evaluating a project estimator software package called SPQR/20. The package provides a full range of estimating projects capabilities on a Wang/IBM PC. If you do large scale project estimations, *we need you!* We are looking for volunteers to try the package and give us their opinions on its estimation capabilities. If you are interested in looking at SPQR/20, please contact Gayle Rediker, ext. 3949.

FIGURE 24-11. The front page of a typical office systems newsletter.

more effectively with their computers and wanted to exchange information with other users. Often, one person had both expertise to share and questions to ask. The solution: meetings of experienced users.

Many cities have metropolitan users' groups, and organizations may sponsor members. What is becoming more prevalent, however, is that organizations sponsor user groups within the organization. Often over "brown bag" lunches, users discuss successes and problems. User groups are extremely motivational in fostering not just more use of new technologies, but more creative uses.

Professional Organizations

Professional organizations such as the Association of Information Systems Professionals (AISP), the Association for Systems Management (ASM), and the Office Systems Research Association (OSRA) provide a source for information processing personnel to learn about new developments in information processing and what is happening nationwide and in their communities. Such "networks" enable individuals to participate in seminars, presentations, and conferences on topics related to effective technology application. This "networking"—meeting others with similar concerns, problems, and new ideas—offers many benefits: "In my organization, we did it this way. . . ." A complete list of information processing professional organizations appears in Appendix 1.

ADDRESSING THE NEEDS OF THE ORGANIZATION: PERSONNEL ISSUES

As pointed out in the introduction of this chapter, office systems analysts should be aware of the macro concerns related to implementing new technologies. Chapters 19 through 22 emphasized the need to coordinate office automation with company goals and objectives. This section, "Personnel Issues," is a selected (not an exhaustive) overview of concerns related to the clerical work force: labor-management relations and women's issues.

Labor-Management Relations

Only a small minority of the office work force belongs to unions. In fact, the Bureau of Labor Statistics reported that only 6 percent of executive, administrative, and managerial workers belong to unions. Moreover, only 14 percent of clerical workers belong to unions, and about 17 percent more are covered by union contracts. Increased mechanization, however, tends to accelerate the growth of unions. When workers are concerned about job security, wage and salary structures, quality of work life, and the very nature of their work, they often turn to unions for support.

The National Labor-Management Relations Act guarantees the rights of workers to bargain with management. This Act is based on the premise that workers can organize to ensure that employers do not infringe upon their rights. Because office workers are typically unorganized, they may find themselves unrepresented. A report published by the U.S. Office of Technology Assessment made the following observations:

> While some labor contracts contain clauses concerning automation, negotiation about the decision to automate is not construed as mandatory by either the NLRB [National Labor Relations Board, the group charged with oversee-

> ing the Act] or the courts. However, it also is not clear that management has an absolute right to automate. The employer does have the right to determine equipment needs and the size of the work force, and can change the nature and scope of the business, but only if it does not affect contract terms and conditions of employment. Technology bargaining has become a focus of the collective bargaining process and the extent of employee rights and employer prerogatives is decided on a case-by-case basis by NLRB and the courts.[7]

District 925 is a nationwide office workers' union formed by the Service Employees International Union and by 9-to-5, a branch of the National Association of Working Women. This group addresses job security, job quality, wage and salary concerns, and other related issues.

Women's Issues

Office automation is an issue among women's rights organizations because of the large percentage of women in the lowest-paid positions. The Bureau of Labor Statistics reports that clerical workers are mostly female (79 percent of all secretaries, stenographers, and typists) and a third of all female workers are office workers.

In "Differential Experiences of Men and Women in Computerized Offices," Barbara A. Gutek and Tora K. Bikson reported that when businesses introduce new technology into the office, men have greater control over the technology than women, greater autonomy in its use, and, as users, gain more from their experiences than women gain.[8] Gutek and Bikson attributed this pattern to the fact that women tend to be in less influential positions than men, and thus their pattern of computer use reflects their lower status. This conclusion was supported by the following findings:

- Women are more likely than men to say that their use of computers has become a *routine* part of their work. Over three-quarters of the women, compared to about 60 percent of the men, said their use of computers was very routine.
- Men and women were equally likely to have used computers in previous jobs and to use them in their current jobs.
- Women spend about half of their working day at their terminals. Men more frequently use their terminals to communicate with others than do women.
- More women than men said that learning to use the computer was mandatory. While men and women were equally likely to have taken formal training courses, women were more likely to receive on-the-job training. Overall, support staff were more pleased with their training than were managers and professionals; women rated their training higher than did men.

Office automation has changed many clerical jobs. Skills are upgraded, and secretaries are often editors or copywriters rather than typists. This differential, however, has not had much impact on increasing job opportunities and earnings. Many employers believe that additional training on new technologies is payment in itself. A woman still earns 68 cents to every dollar a man earns.

Pay equity is a simple concept that advocates equal pay for equivalent work. Equitable pay is an important issue for female clerical workers. What is the value of a clerical worker's actual contribution to the work that is performed in an office? The Women's Bureau has defined the value of clerical workers, particularly secretaries, as "invisible labor." This labor involves making expert judgments, mediating conflicts, reassuring and guiding customers, and so on. Clerical workers such as bank tellers and reservation clerks are often the first people to meet clients and must often solve problems quickly. These cognitive and interpersonal skills, which are rewarded at the managerial level, are often unrecognized and undervalued at the clerical level.

But while the concept of equitable pay is easy to understand, its application is very difficult. Most formal proposals for developing pay equity figures are based on the ability to rate the value of a specific job to the overall mission of the organization. The State of Washington, a leader in developing pay equity programs, conducted one of the first pay equity studies in the early 1980s. That study produced very interesting findings, and a sample of the data is shown in Figure 24-12. The data shows, for example, that the predominantly male position of truck driver was rated 97 evaluation points and earned a monthly salary of $1493. The predominantly female position of secretary, however, was rated more than double the truck driver's evaluation points (197 to 97) yet was paid less monthly salary ($1122).

The introduction of new technologies changes jobs and the skill levels of people in those jobs. Therefore, the office systems analyst should be aware of the need to re-evaluate wage and salary structures, as well as job descriptions, and to develop career ladders.

SUMMARY

Technology is useless until it is used, and using it requires training. Training for office automation encompasses needed skills, understanding why the technology is used, and how to apply it on the job. Training is different from education in that training results are directly applicable to the job.

Training for office automation will increase in importance as users are trained and retrained to use new technologies, as the use of computer workstations grows, and as the number of workers employed in offices continues to increase. Moreover, employment trends show that skill requirements will continue to change.

Benchmark Title	Evaluation Points	Monthly Prevailing Rates[1]	% Female Incumbents
Warehouse Worker	97	1286	15.4
Truck Driver	97	1493	13.6
Laundry Worker	105	884	80.3
Telephone Operator	118	887	95.7
Retail Sales Clerk	121	921	100.0
Data Entry Operator	125	1017	96.5
Intermediate Clerk Typist	129	968	96.7
Highway Engineering Technician	133	1401	11.1
Word Process Equip. Operator	138	1082	98.3
Correctional Officer	173	1436	9.3
Licensed Practical Nurse	173	1030	89.5
Automotive Mechanic	175	1646	0.0
Maintenance Carpenter	197	1707	2.3
Secretary	197	1122	98.5
Administrative Assistant	226	1334	95.1
Chemist	277	1885	20.0
Civil Engineer	287	1885	0.0
Highway Engineer 3	345	1980	3.0
Registered Nurse	348	1368	92.2
Librarian 3	353	1625	84.6
Senior Architect	362	2240	16.7
Senior Computer System Analyst	384	2080	17.8
Personnel Representative	410	1956	45.6
Physician	861	3857	13.6

[1]Prevailing rates as of July 1, 1980. Adopted state rates for midpoint of ranges, October 1981.

FIGURE 24-12. A comparison of salaries and evaluation points for selected sex-segregated positions in the state of Washington.

Basic to knowing how to train is knowledge about how people learn. This text reviewed two popular approaches to learning: pedagogy and andragogy. While the terms' roots are related to the age of the learner, the terms refer to strategies applicable to teaching. Pedagogy refers to learning experiences that are structured and in which the instructor has most of the responsibility for the learning. Andragogy, on the other hand, is learner-directed training and requires the learner to be responsible for learning.

Four stages in training program development were discussed: needs analysis, program design, delivery, and evaluation. Needs analysis is considered the most critical stage. Identifying what needs to be learned by whom should be determined up front. In short, training should be for the *right* things for the *right* people. To conduct a needs analysis, the training program developer can use interviews, questionnaires, observations, critical incident methods, or focus groups. The purpose of such inquiries is to determine if training could result in improved performance.

With knowledge of who needs to learn what, the next step is to identify how and where the training should be delivered. Should the vendor, an outside consultant, an outside institution, or an internal trainer conduct the training? Choosing the *right* instructor depends on time, in-house expertise, company requirements, and budget (always!). The correct mix of trainees is also important. It is suggested that trainees be grouped according to skill levels and work groups. In designing training programs, the best time frame needs to be identified: when should training take place, and how much time should be allotted to training delivery?

The value of clear, concise training objectives is paramount. Knowledge of expected outcomes in behavioral terms, or identifying what the trainee should be able to do as a result of the program, keeps the program on track and provides a basis for training evaluation.

Delivery of training programs also relates directly to what and who needs to learn. Choices include lectures, demonstrations, workshops, coaching, print-based tutorials, audio- and video-based training, and a range of computer-related instruction, including programmed learning, computer-assisted instruction, computer-managed instruction, computer-based instruction, and interactive video. Two additional delivery methods, job aids and teleconferencing, are also available.

Experts agree that the choice of delivery method depends upon the complexity of the skill and knowledge to be learned, the current expertise of the learner, how many people need to be trained on a system, the time frame for learning, and individual learning styles. With answers to these questions, the training designer can choose one or a variety of methods for doing the training.

Evaluation answers the question, "Did the training program do what it was expected to do?" Evaluation may assess the trainer's or the trainee's performance; it may be done at the time of training or six months later. The trainer or a supervisor may do the evaluation. Evaluation findings should be used to assess learning and to provide feedback to the training designer on the appropriateness of the instruction for future programs.

In short, the key to getting people to use office automation is to ensure that they get adequate training. *Adequate* means that training is for the *right* things, is allotted adequate time and priority, is conducted in the right way, and is continuous (it never ends!).

Organizations also employ a variety of other educational strategies to support office systems and end-user computing. Among the more commonly used educational strategies are office automation fairs, newsletters, user groups, internal consultants, information centers, and membership in professional organizations.

Several other global issues must also be considered when organizations implement new technologies. These include personnel issues such as labor-management relationships, equal rights, and pay equity.

DISCUSSION QUESTIONS

1. Discuss the role of training in implementing computer systems in the office.
2. Distinguish between andragogy and pedagogy. Which of the two learning approaches is generally more appropriate for office systems training programs? Why?
3. List six training principles that should be applied when designing training programs for office automation and end-user computing.
4. What is the purpose of training needs analysis? Why is it the most critical step in designing training programs? What are some of the key questions to be asked when assessing training requirements for a new computer system installation in the office?
5. What are performance objectives? Why do trainers often find them difficult to write? What purpose do they serve?
6. What alternatives do organizations have when selecting instructors to conduct training programs? Discuss the advantages and disadvantages of each.
7. What alternatives do organizations have for delivering training programs? Give an appropriate training situation for each alternative.
8. What is the purpose of training evaluation? Why is it important? How does evaluation relate to training objectives?
9. Name six educational strategies commonly employed to promote and support office automation and end-user computing. What purpose does each serve?
10. Why is office automation an important issue among women's rights organizations?
11. How can labor-management relations affect office automation efforts?

APPLICATION EXERCISES

1. Select a microcomputer software program, such as a spreadsheet, database, or word processing package. Conduct a needs analysis among your classmates and design a training program to teach it to them, including a means for evaluation. Conduct a training session to teach the first part of your program, introducing the software to the class, and have the class evaluate the training.
2. Investigate the training program for office systems and end-user computing provided through the computer center (or other facility) on your campus. Interview the director or an instructor in the program. What courses are offered? How are the courses taught? How was the appropriate content for courses determined? Evaluate the program in light of what you learned in this chapter.

3. Visit an office, or talk with someone you know who works in an office, to find out about the training programs offered in his or her organization for office systems and end-user computing. Obtain samples of course offerings, internal newsletters, or other information about the program. Has your interviewee participated in any of the computer training programs? How does he or she evaluate the experience? Summarize your findings in a report or organize them for presentation to your classmates. Compare your findings with the findings of other students.

4. Obtain tutorial software programs for popular microcomputer packages (it is usually permissible to copy these). Try them out and evaluate their effectiveness in helping first-time users learn to use the software programs.

5. Research articles on women's rights organizations and office automation. What are the main issues and concerns that they raise? What benefits do they see? Summarize your findings in a brief report to share with classmates.

SUGGESTED READINGS

Atre, Shaku. *Information Center: Strategies and Case Studies, Volume 1* (Rye, N.Y.: Atre International Consultants, 1986).

Galitz, Wilbert O. "Humanizing Office Automation: The Impact of Ergonomics on Productivity," *Training* (Wellesley, Mass.: QED Information Sciences, 1984).

Gery, Gloria. *Making CBT Happen: Prescriptions for Successful Implementation of Computer-based Training in Your Organization* (Boston: Weingarten Publications, 1987).

Goldfield, Randy J.; Epstein, Leslie B.; and Cushing, David. "Training Strategies for the Interactive Office," *Education & Training Exchange* (Summer 1984), pp. 9–13.

Perry, William E. *The Information Center* (Englewood Cliffs, N.J.: Prentice-Hall, 1987).

Spinner, Robert J. "Wired for Training: The Teletraining Site," *Data Training* (May 1985), pp. 26–30.

U.S. Department of Labor, Women's Bureau. "Women and Office Automation: Issues for the Decade Ahead" (Washington, D.C.: Government Printing Office, 1985).

PART

AUTOMATING THE OFFICE: Epilogue

6

In the press of everyday business, one needs to step back occasionally to see how things have progressed and to look ahead to see in what direction they are moving. In the fast-paced world of technology, people easily become so enmeshed in technical complexities that they lose sight of practical goals.

This text has attempted to present a balanced perspective of technology and its application in the office. Historical commentaries were provided as necessary to help the reader understand the effective use of technology. Chapter 25, "Trends and Future Directions," the final chapter, looks to the future. It outlines trends, issues, and opportunities related to office systems and end-user computing. The future directions of office automation are organized around three major topics: technology, the workplace, and personnel.

TRENDS AND FUTURE DIRECTIONS

CHAPTER **25**

OBJECTIVES

After completing this chapter, the reader should be able to meet the following objectives:

- Identify trends related to technology, the workplace, and personnel likely to dominate office automation in the next decade.
- Explain the term integration, offering examples of technologies that will be integrated in the next decade.
- Differentiate between word processing and desktop publishing and explain how they are expected to merge.
- Give three examples of collaborative work tools.
- Summarize the arguments for and against telecommuting.
- Describe a satellite work center.
- Summarize how office automation will have an impact on clerical workers, professional workers, and technology-related professionals.

KEY TERMS

integration
vertical solutions
collaborative work tools
group authoring software
face-to-face meeting facilitation services
telecommuting
satellite work center
job sharing
temporary service industry

INTRODUCTION

In 1986-87, Wohl and Associates found computer penetration rates of 35 percent, or about one workstation for every three workers. The Office of Technology Assessment (OTA), Washington, D.C., has predicted that by the mid-1990s nearly every office will have at least one computer. As the ratio of computers to users increases, computers will ultimately be as common as telephones. Depending upon the industry, some experts predict a ratio of 1 to 1, meaning one computer for every worker, by the year 2000. This ratio may soar even higher. Some workers today have already reached a ratio of 3 to 1; they have a computer in their office, one in their home, *and* a portable computer!

A variety of factors influence the absorption rate of technology, including economic conditions, the resources required to implement the technology, and the time required to recover the necessary investment.

This text has emphasized that office systems and end-user computing are an ongoing process. The increasing capacity of the computer chip, storage media, and communications technologies makes the mastery of this new field very challenging. As businesses automate, then upgrade their technologies—as corporate America moves from the initialization to the maturity stage of office automation—the opportunities and the issues facing the office systems analyst will change.

The rate of technological change has been staggering. Consider that it took

- 50,000,000 years to develop the alphabet, then only
- 5,000 years to develop the printing press, then only
- 500 years to develop the television, and then only
- 50 years to develop the microcomputer.

Given this pace of technological advances, one can be overwhelmed with information regarding new technologies. The office systems analyst must be continually learning and relearning. *Relearn* does not mean "learn more"; it means adapting to new information. It also means being exceptionally flexible. Today's technologies and solutions may not be appropriate for tomorrow's office. It is not easy to substitute new knowledge for old knowledge. However, this continuous learning-relearning process cannot stop.

Attempting to describe future trends and opportunities for office automation is difficult, if not impossible. However, this chapter attempts to outline some trends, issues, and opportunities facing office systems analysts in the coming decade. Understanding and dealing with these concerns can result in realizing the potential of office automation and end-user computing. These future directions are organized around three major topics: technology, the workplace, and personnel.

TRENDS IN TECHNOLOGY

The infusion of technology into business is changing the focus of office automation—hardware and software—from supply to selection. The issue will no longer be deciding whether or not to automate but rather deciding *which* automation tools will provide the best solutions. The increasing availability of technological options for office systems and end-user computing will make choices more complex. In addition, the challenge facing those who have invested heavily in office automation will be how to justify the purchase of new systems and what to do with existing, now-obsolete systems. Following is a discussion of selected technology-related trends and opportunities.

Integration

Traditional bureaucratic barriers separating personnel and departments within large organizations are expected to weaken. Electronic information systems will globally link operations and support better coordination among people and activities. The ability to move and share information, as opposed to only storing it, is expected to become a key factor in national and international competition. Future developments in technology will center on integration between hardware, software, functions, and people.

Integration between Hardware

Hardware integration is a key issue because approximately 1600 vendors are manufacturing products that are not necessarily compatible. The Corporation for Open Systems (COS), a group of major U.S. vendors and users (based in Virginia), is promoting the interconnectivity of computers through the Open Systems Interconnect (OSI) model. Some OSI standards, such as the X.25, have been widely accepted. Specifically, COS is testing two forms of electronic communication:[1]

1. Store and forward electronic mail applications, including development of the X.400 standard.
2. File transfer software and access methods, permitting the real-time exchange of computer-based data.

Integration between Software

More integration of capabilities within and between software packages can also be expected. One result may be the demise of general-purpose software. Today's integrated packages typically are excellent for only one application, and other applications are considered *add-ons* to the main program. Software developers are designing packages that integrate top-of-the-line spreadsheets, word processing, databases, and graphics capabilities. The Yankee Group, a Boston-based research group, predicted that within five years word processing software will be replaced by these integrated packages, which bundle word processing with other applications or with vertical (industry-related) software such as airline/hotel reservation systems and order or insurance claims processing.

In addition, programs that can translate documents from one word processing or spreadsheet package to another will offer end users more flexibility and control over how they do data processing or text editing. A spreadsheet created by a Lotus 1-2-3 user or a document created in WordStar, for example, can be used or edited by someone who works exclusively with Supercalc or WordPerfect.

IBM's recent announcement of the Personal System/2 and its proprietary operating system, OS/2, poses new questions about interconnectivity and the sharing of software. Will the increased capabilities of the new system be enough to persuade offices to trade their systems and software in on new solutions?

The OS/2 operating system jointly developed by IBM and Microsoft has some advantages over MS/DOS. For example, OS/2 can handle large applications because it has a memory capacity up to two megabytes, whereas MS/DOS is limited to 640K. In addition, OS/2 is very fast. It also will allow *multitasking*, which means that a user can run more than one applications package at a time.

With multitasking capabilities, a user could create a spreadsheet on Lotus 1-2-3, call up a database on dBase IV, and, while waiting for the database search, play Space Invaders. OS/2 has also advanced communications capabilities. To be used on older equipment, however, OS/2 requires costly hardware adjustments. OS/2 is designed to take advantage of the 16-bit architecture of the 80286 chip and the 32-bit architecture of the 80386 chip.

Departmental use of minicomputers will grow, creating integrated, tiered systems of microcomputers, minicomputers, and mainframes. Many applications formerly done on mainframes will be relegated to departmental minis, and larger and larger applications will be shifted to microcomputers. An issue that office systems specialists will need to address is how to allow mainframes, minis, and microcomputers to operate as one system, as part of a corporate network.

Such a network will also allow personnel to communicate with each other more efficiently and effectively. For example, personnel in units on the factory or shop floor, in administrative offices, and in research laboratories or engineering departments will be able to work more closely together. Time and distance will be less serious problems as telecommunications capabilities increase and become easier to use.

Vertical Solutions

The applications software discussed in this text have been, for the most part, horizontal solutions to information processing. The term *horizontal* means that a package is adaptable to any one of several different industries, businesses, or individuals. *Vertical* solutions, as described in the previous section, are software applications that are appropriate for only one specific industry.

Software solutions will become more vertical than horizontal—in short, more tailored to specific industries. An example of a vertical solution is software that has been developed for the newspaper industry. The word processing, pagination, and communications needs of writers, editors, and publishers are identifiable and distinct from the needs of a manufacturer. Therefore, software developers have designed specific software packages to meet the needs of specific types of work in the newspaper industry. Similarly, accounting packages have been developed to meet the needs of small real estate offices. Moreover, these packages have been integrated with other programs used for sales, rentals, and bank financing.

More for Less

Both hardware and software will continue to offer more power at less cost. Artificial intelligence software coupled with more powerful computers on the desktop will provide more features and greater ease of use. Software will increasingly adapt to the way people work in the office instead of the other way around. End users, not technical specialists, will drive the features and options that vendors will offer in tomorrow's market. When corporate executives, knowledge workers, sales and marketing personnel, and administrative staff ask for solutions to business problems, vendors will listen and rush to provide them.

The Merging of Word Processing and Desktop Publishing

Word processing and desktop publishing are distinct applications today. Word processing is typically associated with day-to-day text processing; desktop publishing is associated with text and image processing that results in publications that were previously prepared in a print shop. Word processing and desktop publishing will merge as (1) software developers offer combined programs and (2) the user becomes adept at using the technology.

In response to user demands for professional-looking output, software developers are offering word processing programs that have many of the features associated with desktop publishing. Examples include column layout, control over word spacing, multiple point sizes, a variety of fonts, and the ability to combine graphs and charts from other programs into the body of a word-processed document. Users do not want a two-step process that separates text creation from text production.

The second reason that word processing and desktop publishing are expected to merge is that many users are adept at the former and consider themselves competent to produce print-quality documents. Moreover, the features of word processing, including spell-checkers, grammar checkers, and style editors, offer users additional confidence that their documents are professional.

Desktop publishing is frequently cited as "the next" software addition in many organizations. In a 1987 study of 661 office automation executives, Walter Kleinschrod reported that 93 percent of respondents were using word processing, 89 percent were using spreadsheets, and only 30 percent used desktop publishing. As shown in the survey results in Figure 25-1, however, the use of desktop publishing is expected to grow rapidly: 38 percent of respondents indicated that they plan to add desktop publishing within two years.

As desktop publishing becomes commonplace, expectations of what constitutes acceptable documents rise. The standard for newsletters and bulletins, as well as the letter and memo, is going up. At the same time, the costs of producing such communications go down, which could mean more and better communications.

FIGURE 25-1. Desktop publishing: The next big software addition.

Software Application	Percent of Respondents Planning To Add by 1990
Desktop publishing	38
Graphic representation	30
Electronic mail/messaging	28
Artificial intelligence (AI)	26
Expert systems	22
Natural language systems	14
Spreadsheet analyses	23
Decision support	19
File management	19
Word processing	19
Computer-aided design (CAD)	17
Account processing	11
Scientific analyses	8
Other	4

Collaborative Work Tools

Most managerial work involves the input of more than one person, and organizations operate as departments, units, committees, and task forces. Office automation tools such as word processing or spreadsheets have traditionally supported a person working alone, for a single purpose. To address the needs of group work, new work tools are being developed that facilitate groups, not just individuals. Following are three examples of group-oriented tools: group authoring software, group decision support systems, and face-to-face meeting facilitation.

Group Authoring Software

Reports are typically the result of group work. Usually, one person in a department or committee is assigned the task of drafting the report, which is then circulated to others to add to, delete, or clarify. A paper document, with notes in the margins and between lines, is routed back to the originator, who prepares the final document.

Group authoring software is an add-on package to the group's word processing software. The originator drafts the document (memo, report), using an agreed-upon word processing package coupled with the group authoring software. The originator then shares the document with others via a local area network or by physical transfer of the data disk. The features of group authoring software allow reviews, edits, additions, and so on, showing who made what suggestions. Some reviewers may be asked to edit the document directly; others may be asked to comment on the contents. Either way, the originator can determine whether reviews and edits show up on the final printed document. At least four group authoring packages are now on the market, including For Comment, Compare-Write, Red Pencil, and In Synch. The value of such programs lies not only in how much time they save or the sharing of ideas but also in whether or not they improve the quality of the writing.

Group Decision Support Systems

Group decision support systems (GDSS) help a group come to a decision. Robert Johansen of the Institute for the Future offers the following scenario of how such systems operate:

> The team has to decide. There are seven different views among the seven team members, but they have to reach one decision. The first thing they agree upon, though not easily, is how to phrase the question, how to decide what they have to decide. Next the GDSS asks them for anonymous judgments, it asks them about their own uncertainties, and it asks them to self-rate their expertise. After all the team members have entered their judgments, the system does some aggregation of the opinions and feeds back a first round set of judgments from the group. The group goes through a series of these 'rounds' until a decision is reached. The system certainly does not make the decision, but it provides an effective and efficient group decision making process.[2]

Face-to-Face Meeting Facilitation

Face-to-face meeting facilitation services are used in much the same way as flip charts and felt pens. Using a computer, a meeting facilitator records the discussion, projects key ideas or summary statements on a screen, then *organizes* the discussion. Such facilitation helps assure that the group stays on the subject and that ideas are clearly understood by everyone. At the end of the meeting, participants can take home a complete set of notes.

THE WORKPLACE

Office environment specialist Leonard Kruk has estimated that the 45 million personal computers that will be in offices by 1995 will be using flat-panel display screens. With an average volume of two cubic meters for each of these computers, "this many units, packed tightly on a football gridiron, would create a mass towering more than a third of a mile above the stadium. And that's only PCs. We have not yet introduced the printers, scanners, media files, and other 'things' of OA, to say nothing of books and paper."[3]

The furniture industry, for example, is already addressing the space needs of these technologies, which demand that the traditional office be adapted to new operating needs. Furniture manufacturers are designing flexible, movable panels with built-in shelves, cabinets, and lights. Where space is at a premium, as in Manhattan, workstation design is taking on new priorities as workers and employers realize the need for adequate space.

In addition to describing a work site, the term *office* has been stretched to cover a variety of alternatives. Office automation technologies give people the flexibility to perform their work at convenient locations and times. Although many changes in the workplace are controversial, advocates sing their praises. Managers, however, are concerned with how to manage them. While these changes are not for everyone, they offer alternatives that allow businesses to obtain the most from office automation and, at the same time, address the needs of a changing work force.

Telecommuting

Telecommuting is the concept that a person can work at home, using a terminal connected to a business computer via a telephone line. Many people—artists, writers, and self-employed professionals—work at home (see Figure 25-2). The idea that people whose main job is information processing can do their work at home has major implications.

Alvin Toffler has said that there may be as many as 15 million home-based white-collar workers by 1990. Such a prediction is high, however, and considered unlikely. Estimates of the number of today's telecommuters are much smaller. For example, The Yankee Group reports that 30,000 workers are linked full-time to their offices, and there are an additional 100,000 part-time workers. The Office of Technology Assessment, on the other hand, has estimated that only between 3000 and 5000 people are doing office work in their homes for employers. A recent survey in Sweden found only 200 full-time telecommuters in that country.

FIGURE 25-2. **With electronic media, "office work" is no longer confined within the walls of an office building. Telecommuting is one alternative work style that some workers and employers find mutually beneficial.**

From the individual's standpoint, telecommuting permits flexible work schedules; companies see it as a means of decreasing costs. Telecommuting offers the following benefits:

1. Savings to the company in the form of reduced space requirements, lower costs for employee benefits, less absenteeism, and less employee turnover.
2. Savings to the company in the form of better computer use (telecommuters often use the computer at off-peak hours).
3. Savings to the employee in terms of commuting, clothing, and lunch expenses.
4. Increased productivity where employees are paid on a piece rate or contract basis.
5. Broader pools from which to attract personnel. Benefits can accrue to both the employer and the new labor force: people who need flexible hours, who have child care responsibilities, who cannot afford the cost of commuting, who live too far to commute, and so on.
6. More employment opportunities for handicapped workers.

Telecommuting also presents some concerns, however, including the following:

1. Telecommuters may actually have *less* control over their workday; they may have to operate at times when the computer is "free" (off peak).
2. Workers may be required to lease or buy terminals and to pay telephone bills or fees for special, dedicated telephone lines; they must also provide the furniture they use.
3. Clerical telecommuters almost always receive less pay than their office counterparts; moreover, they frequently do not qualify for benefits (such as health insurance) because of their contract or part-time status.
4. Clerical telecommuters often find their workload uneven, and may work fewer hours than their counterparts.
5. Many telecommuters suffer social isolation, which may result in job dissatisfaction.
6. Telecommuting has *not* proven to be a satisfactory solution to the child care problem. Workers are finding it impossible to perform both jobs at the same time.

The AFL-CIO is attempting to ban clerical telecommuting, saying it is trying to protect workers from "electronic sweatshops." Union leaders cite exploitations of people working at home at the turn of the century, and the resulting child-labor and minimum wage laws. Union organizers also know how difficult it is to collect dues from people who work in their homes. However, telecommuting can provide benefits for both employer and employee. Telecommuting is an opportunity, but only with appropriate job design and personnel. A challenge that faces the management of office systems is how to determine the benefits of telecommuting and, if benefits are appropriate, manage a remote work force.

Satellite Work Centers

A satellite work center is a compromise between telecommuting and the traditional office. Satellite work centers are usually fully equipped facilities remote from the central office, often in suburban areas. For example, a large bank or financial company in a major city might have three satellite offices in the suburbs, allowing them to attract employees from a much larger radius.

In addition to decreasing commuting time, the satellite center makes the worker part of a group, thus addressing social and emotional needs. Companies benefit from less expensive real estate and the option to employ part-time workers for whom long commutes are impractical or unappealing.

Job Sharing

Job sharing is based on the notion of one job for two workers. The worker who needs the flexibility of a part-time job can become a partner with another such worker and, between them, share a position. In many instances, the employer offers benefits to both of them. Absenteeism is reduced and workers have greater flexibility and control.

Temporary Workers

The temporary service industry has been described as the fastest growing service industry in the United States, increasing nearly twice as fast as the GNP over the last 14 years—and faster than the computer industry. According to Norrell Corporation, a temporary-help firm, more than 750,000 people, representing 1 percent of the work force, work daily as temporaries. Ninety percent of all business firms use some form of temporary help. Many of the large agencies, such as Kelly Services, a Detroit-based firm, offer training for employees. While temporary work is often associated with clerical work, the demand for temporary computer specialists, communications specialists, and other such professionals has also been growing.

PERSONNEL

According to office automation consultant Samuel J. Kalow, "The mission of OA is not the reduction of 'headcount' among office workers. The mission of OA is to further the mission of the office, and the mission of the office is to further the mission of the organization."[4] In describing his 1987 book, *The Renewal Factor: How to Best Get and Keep the Competitive Edge*, Robert Waterman (co-author of *In Search of Excellence*) reported that the most important attribute of "renewing companies"—companies that are excellent and remain excellent—is informed opportunism. This means that information is their main strategic advantage, and flexibility is their main strategic weapon. This growth in demand for information and the reduction in labor associated with information handling are two competing trends that will affect the employment level of white-collar workers and the nature of office jobs.

The demand for information is well documented; companies that make the most of their information resources are likely to be successful. Complete information, at the right time and in the right format, is increasingly recognized as important. On the other hand, fewer people are needed to process information. According to the U.S. Office of Technology Assessment (OTA), the most dramatic substitution of technology for labor will be the elimination of data-entry work by the following:[5]

1. Interorganizational transfer of data, from computer to computer.
2. Direct input of data by optical scanning technologies, and possibly by speech-recognition technology.
3. Capture of data, at the point of origin, in a variety of ways—from bar code readers to consumer use of terminals such as automated teller machines (ATMs).

In a recent study, the OTA concluded that the most likely employment outlook appears to be a slowing down in growth in office employment over the next decade; and a decline in office employment could begin by 2000. The U.S. Department of Labor, however, is more optimistic in its forecasts, saying that the outlook for clerical positions will continue to keep pace with, or surpass, the outlook for other job categories.

Professional workers are differentiated from clerical office workers in that the former do cognitive tasks that require specialized knowledge gained through lengthy education, often with a graduate degree, or special certification or licensing. Professionals in office-oriented occupations, such as lawyers, accountants, analysts, consultants, and so on, are subject to computerization through expert systems. Information systems and data banks allow part of their responsibilities to be taken over by paraprofessionals with fewer credentials. Paralegals, for example, can do much of the work formerly done by lawyers. For the most part, however, office automation will be used by professionals as a tool. Office automation is expected to have little impact on the number of people in these occupations.

Professionals in technology- and computer-related careers will continue to be in demand. Figure 25-3 is an excerpt from the Source EDP *Computer Salary Survey and Career Planning Guide* for three types of professional positions of interest to readers of this text: Information Center/Office Automation Analyst/Decision Support Specialist; Senior Analysts, Project Leaders, and Consultants; and Computer Industry Sales Representatives. Figure 25-4 presents other job descriptions for an Information Center Analyst and an Information Center Director, plus a partial listing of information center job titles.

FIGURE 25-3. Job descriptions for three types of positions in technology- and computer-related professions.

a. Information Center/Office Automation Analyst/ Descision Support Specialist job description.

Information Center/Office Automation Analyst/Decision Support Specialist

Responsibilities: Evaluate, implement, and interconnect microcomputers, word processing products, and office teleprocessing products to allow various levels of management access to database management systems, electronic mail, query facilities, spreadsheets, and decision support systems. Establish methods and criteria for evaluation of office automation hardware and software. Function as a central source for the selection, training, and use of a wide range of "off-the-shelf" software, including 4GL products such as FOCUS, NOMAD, etc. Determine best uses of local area networks (LANs) to link microcomputers to each other and to larger computers. Provide user training and support.

New Trends: The explosive growth of microcomputer technology has resulted in a boom in the demand for office automation products designed to integrate word processing, teleprocessing devices, mini and microcomputers, and mainframes.

Office automation professionals may bear a variety of titles, including Information Center Analyst and Decision Support Specialist. In any case, the underlying purpose of the office automation professional is to provide vehicles and training for all company employees to communicate more effectively with each other and have more timely access to the information they require.

Integration of the various office automation products has been complicated by the incompatibility of the various communication architectures. As a result, people with communications knowledge in addition to mainframe and microcomputer backgrounds will be at a premium.

Past distinctions between office automation, telecommunications, and data processing will be less clearcut in the future. Also, the proliferation of personal computers will create a corresponding demand for systematic methods to evaluate and implement truly integrated office automation systems. Since these systems are and will be used mainly by nontechnical managers and analysts, there is an expanding need for skilled specialists to assist in systems definition, training, and implementation of office automation systems.

b. Senior Analyst, Project Leader, and Consultant job descriptions.

Senior Analysts, Project Leaders, and Consultants

Responsibilities: Typically responsible for user liaison, systems specification, systems design, and project control. May also supervise analysts and programmers through implementation phase and occasionally assist in programming effort. Provide key link between ultimate user and computing resource.

New Trends: Those professionals in greatest demand will possess in-depth, advanced industry knowledge in manufacturing, insurance, banking, distribution, etc., and actual information systems implementation experience involving database and data communications. Typical user assignments range from responsibility for development of stand-alone systems to high-level staff assignments in hardware/software evaluation, database administration, or long-range planning.

More organizations than ever before are providing promotion opportunities to line operating functions to individuals with intimate company and industry knowledge. Also in demand are experts who can provide necessary quality assurance through audit and evaluation of functional technology and procedures.

Continued growth of management consulting firms and computer services organizations (including facilities management) offer additional opportunities to gain diverse exposure. Likewise, high demand will continue within computer manufacturers (including micros and minis) for systems professionals to move into marketing support roles. Importance of this position level dictates a unique blend of technical, business, and interpersonal skills. Minimum requirements usually include two years systems design experience and prior programming with some specialized industry experience desired. College degree preferred; MBA or some graduate study desired.

FIGURE 25-3. (continued)

Computer Industry Sales/Technical Support Representative
Responsibilities: Provide technical support in the sales of hardware and software products and services. Duties include both pre- and post-sales support, system studies, feasibility studies, demonstrations, and technical presentations. Requires good oral and written communication skills and the ability to interface with clients and to understand their requirements.

New Trends: Demand is increasing as the number of products in the marketplace increases, particularly in the areas of database management systems, mini and micro systems, visual display units, specialty software, and custom systems. Requires the ability to assimilate new product specifications and capabilities rapidly and relate to customer requirements. Technical depth in software, hardware, or applications is needed. Career path usually leads to sales management, technical services management, or consulting.

c. Computer Industry/Technical Support Representative job description.

Information Center Analyst
Responsibilities: The Information Center Analyst will assume responsibilities in six major areas: acting as a liaison with users, providing technical expertise, presenting educational programs, assisting in the development of systems, investigating new software and hardware products, and performing administrative duties in the information center.

User Liaison: The IC Analyst will act as a liaison with the users. The responsibilities in this area include the following:

- Preparing and giving presentations to new and existing users.
- Handling ad hoc inquiries on products supported by the IC.
- Supporting users in the use of software products.
- Offering limited help for user problems with products that are not supported by the IC.
- Offering limited support for hardware and software questions and problems.
- Determining user needs for hardware and software.
- Appraising user projects in terms of the feasibility for the mainframe and microcomputer environment.
- Educating users, with the objective of product independence. Ideally, the user should know the details of product use and should only have to consult on matters of analysis.
- Performing cost/benefit analyses of IC usage.
- Acting in a professional manner.

FIGURE 25-4. Typical information center job descriptions and job titles.

a. Information Center Analyst job description.

FIGURE 25-4.

a. Information Center Analyst job description (continued).

Technical Expertise: In the area of technical expertise, the IC Analyst should have a knowledge and understanding of the IC's products for both personal computers and mainframes. The IC Analyst will also estimate the cost of projects, including CPU costs, media costs (paper, ribbons, VM IDs, disk storage, etc.), programming time, hardware costs (terminals), personnel savings, and intangibles (such as the benefits of having access to corporate data). The IC Analyst is also responsible for monitoring the CPU use of individual users.

Education Programs: The IC offers its own training courses to give users company-related examples and to maintain close contact to our users and their needs. The Analyst is responsible for the preparation and presentation of IC training courses. In the area of self-education, the Analyst must also keep current with new technology.

System Development: The IC Analyst will be responsible for system development as necessary, including problem definition, feasibility studies, system design, developing system components, and system implementation. The Analyst is expected to request help from other IC Analysts, the IC Manager, and the MIS staff (as required). After a user system has been developed, the IC Analyst will develop system documentation, standards, and a user manual to meet both user needs and technical requirements.

Software and Hardware Investigation: The IC Analyst will investigate new software and hardware products as they become available. Other responsibilities include testing new software and hardware products that will meet company needs.

Administration: The IC Analyst will fulfill the following administrative duties:
- Assisting in writing and producing the IC newsletter.
- Scheduling IC courses.
- Assisting in creating and evaluating an IC survey.
- Maintaining existing products and keeping all products at the current release level.

b. Information Center Director job description.

Information Center Director

Responsibilities: The Information Center Director is charged with supporting end-user computing and reports to the Director of Information Services. The Information Center Director will have a college degree in business, office systems, or computer science with experience in management, data processing, and computer systems, including personal computers, mainframes, and data communications systems. This person is responsible for the development, coordination, and maintenance of programs for the following areas:
- Acquisition, distribution, and installation of personal computers within the organization. This includes training, consulting, and maintenance programs for all microcomputers.
- Training and providing consulting support services for all users of mainframe IC applications.
- Evaluation of all microcomputer and IC software packages for possible acquisition.
- Development and coordination of systems to transfer data between microcomputers and other computer systems.
- Extraction of required data from corporate databases on the mainframe for user access through microcomputers and IC report-writing systems. This requires

extensive work with the database administrator to create appropriate security systems.
- Close coordination with the database administrator to define and manage the corporate data dictionary.
- Planning for all IC programs. This will involve working with data processing to determine the system capacity requirements associated with IC services.
- Active involvement in the review and approval of all computer-related capital equipment budget requests as a member of the computer acquisition review committee.
- Active involvement in the planning of all information systems projects as a member of the information systems planning committee.
- All general personnel and financial management duties associated with the position of department head.
- Long-range planning for the above programs and marketing these services to management, administration, and staff.

The Information Center Director will have the following skills:
- The management skills to design and implement programs in a manner that uses the capabilities of a highly technical staff.
- The interpersonal skills required to market the department's services to the administration, management, and staff as well as to maintain the positive image required of a service department.
- The analytical skills required to evaluate and design technically complicated programs and systems.
- The communication skills required to act as a link between a highly technical department and administration, management, and staff.

FIGURE 25-4. (continued)

Information Center Job Titles

Managers
Information Center Director
Information Center Manager
Information Center Supervisor
Manager of End-User Computing
Manager of End-User Computing and Office Automation
Manager, Special Projects
Microcomputer Support Manager
Principal, End-User Computing Support
Product Manager, Information Center
Systems Administration Manager
Supervisor, Microcomputer Support

Staff
Communications Analyst
Computer Programmer Analyst
End-User Computing Specialist
Education Consultant
Help Desk Representative
Information Center Analyst

c. A partial list of information center job titles.

FIGURE 25-4.

c. A partial list of information center job titles (continued).

Information Center Consultant
Information Center Resource Specialist
Information Center Specialist
Information Center Technical Representative
Information Support Analyst
Management Analyst Manager
Microcomputer Support Analyst
Office Automation Administrator
Problem Analyst
Product Consultant
Product Specialist
Programmer/Analyst
Systems Analyst
Technical Analyst
Technical Trainer

SUMMARY

This chapter identified trends that are expected to have an impact on office automation—technology, work environment, personnel—in the coming decade.

Technology integration, whereby dissimilar hardware and software can share files, thereby allowing users more choice in their information processing options, is a trend with much potential. Such integration allows more extensive and more flexible use of hardware and software and, at the same time, makes communications easier for work groups.

Another technology-related trend is toward more specialized information processing, referred to as vertical solutions. Unlike horizontal solutions, which meet generic needs for information processing such as word processing or spreadsheets, vertical solutions address the specialized needs of a specific industry.

Desktop publishing and word processing are expected to merge, resulting in a one-step rather than the current two-step process. As users become more adept with word processing systems and as the quality standard for documents rises, hardware and software manufacturers will work on developing the one-step process.

Collaborative tools that support the work of groups rather than single individuals in applications such as group authoring, group decision making, and meeting management will be increasingly available and used.

In the workplace, telecommuting, which offers employees greater control over their workday and fewer work-related expenses (for clothing, travel, food, and possibly child care), and which offers employers savings (in the form of lower salaries, fewer benefits, and reduced space requirements), is expected to remain constant.

A compromise with telecommuting is the satellite work center. Employees who work in such a center are part of a work group and thus suffer less from the isolation of the telecommuter. In job sharing, two workers share a single position. Such an arrangement offers flexible scheduling to workers. At the same time, employers benefit as absenteeism and turnover are typically reduced.

Personnel trends include decreases in the number of people needed to do data-entry work The outlook is good, however, for those interested in information management careers.

DISCUSSION QUESTIONS

1. Assume that you are an office systems analyst at a bank and a member of the Administrative Management Society. The upcoming AMS program involves a round-table discussion of several topics, including the office of the future. Because of your expertise, you have been chosen to lead a discussion of the technological changes that are expected in the next decade.
   a. What are the major technological trends expected?
   b. What problems may be encountered as managers in the office of the future implement these changes?
   c. Which of the trends you have outlined will (in your opinion) have the biggest impact on information processing and distribution?
2. Differentiate a vertical solution from a horizontal solution.
3. Describe the following three categories of collaborative work tools:
   a. Group authoring software
   b. Group decision support systems
   c. Face-to-face meeting facilitation
4. What is telecommuting? What are its pros and cons? Do you expect the number of telecommuters to grow in the next decade? Why? Why not? Defend your response.
5. What benefits do satellite work centers offer employers? What benefits do they offer employees?
6. Is the number of clerical workers expected to increase or decrease in the next decade? Why is this trend expected?

APPLICATION EXERCISES

1. Prepare a three-page update on one of the following: the Open Systems Interconnect (OSI) model, telecommuting, or temporary work agencies.
2. Interview the personnel director of a local business. Which positions are growing in number? Which are decreasing? Does the company employ any telecommuters? Does the company use temporary workers from an agency? Prepare a short report of your interview.
3. Assume you are an office systems analyst in the year 2000. Project a description of the trends and issues you envision for the first decade of the twenty-first century. Compare your description with those of your classmates.

SUGGESTED READINGS

DeSantiz, Geraldine. "A Telecommuting Primer," *Datamation* (October 1983), pp.214–220.

Ewing, Tom. "Ten MIS Megatrends: A Road Map for Strategic Planning," *Information Week* (Jan. 19, 1987), pp. 26–44, 72.

Howard, Robert. *Brave New Workplace* (New York: Viking Penguin, 1984).

Johansen, Robert. *Groupware* (New York: The Free Press, 1988).

Kleinschrod, Walter A. *Update 1987–88: Approaching the Automated Office* (Willow Grove, Pa.: Administrative Management Society, 1987).

Zachman, William F. *Industry Predictions: 1986/87* (Framingham, Mass.: International Data Corp., Office of Technology Assessment, March 1986).

Zachman, William F. *Industry and Technology Update: 1986* (Framingham, Mass.: International Data Corp., Office of Technology Assessment, April 1986).

OFFICE SYSTEMS ORGANIZATIONS

APPENDIX

I

1. **Administrative Management Society (AMS),** 4622 Street Road, Trevose, PA 19047.
2. **American Federation of Information Processing Societies (AFIPS),** 1899 Preston White Drive, Reston, VA 22091.
3. **American Management Association (AMA),** The American Management Association Building, 135 West 50th Street, New York, NY 10020.
4. **American National Standards Institute (ANSI),** 1430 Broadway, New York, NY 10018.
5. **American Productivity Center (APC),** 123 North Post Oak Lane, Houston, TX 77024.
6. **American Society for Personnel Administration (ASPA),** 606 North Washington Street, Alexandria, VA 22314.
7. **American Society for Training and Development (ASTD),** 1630 Duke Street, Box 1443, Alexandria, VA 22313.
8. **Association for Business Communication (ABC),** English Building, 608 South Wright Street, University of Illinois, Urbana, IL 61801.
9. **Association for Computing Machinery (ACM),** 11 West 42nd Street, New York, NY 10036.
10. **Association for the Development of Computer-Based Instructional Systems (ADCIS),** Western Washington University, Bellingham, WA 98225.
11. **Association for Educational Communications Technology (ACET),** 1126 Sixteenth Street NW, Washington, DC 20036.
12. **Association for Educational Data Systems (AEDS),** 1201 Sixteenth Street NW, Washington, DC 20036.
13. **Association for Information and Image Management (AIIM),** 1100 Wayne Avenue, Silver Spring, MD 20910.

14. **Association of Information Systems Professionals (AISP),** 104 Wilmot Road, Deerfield, IL 60015-5195.
15. **Association of Records Executives and Administrators (AREA),** P.O. Box 4259, Grand Central Station, New York, NY 10017.
16. **Association of Records Managers and Administrators (ARMA),** 4200 Somerset Drive, Suite 215, Praire Village, KS 66208.
17. **Association for Systems Management (ASM),** International Headquarters, 2457 Bagley Road, Cleveland, OH 44138.
18. **Business Forms Management Association (BFMA),** 1818 Southeast Division Street, Portland, OR 97202.
19. **Computer and Business Equipment Manufacturers Association (CBEMA),** 311 First Street NW, Washington, DC 20036.
20. **Data Processing Management Association (DPMA),** International Headquarters, 505 Busse Highway, Park Ridge, IL 60068.
21. **Institute for Certification of Computer Professionals (ICCP),** 2200 East Devon Avenue, Suite 268, Des Plaines, IL 60018.
22. **Institute of Certified Records Managers (ICRM),** P.O. Box 8188, Prairie Village, KS 66208.
23. **International Federation for Information Processing (IFIP),** IFIP Secretariat, 3 Rue de Marche, CH-1204, Geneva, Switzerland.
24. **International Micrographic Congress (IMC),** 13388 Hammons Avenue, Saratoga, CA 95070.
25. **Life Office Management Association (LOMA),** 100 Colony Square, Atlanta, GA 30361.
26. **National Office Products Association (NOPA),** 740 Investment Building, Washington, DC 20005.
27. **National Records Management Council (NAREMCO),** 60 East 42nd Street, New York, NY 10017.
28. **Office Automation Society International (OASI),** 15269 Mimosa Street, Suite B, Dumfries, VA 22026.
29. **Office Microfilm Management Association (OMMA),** AMS Building, Willow Grove, PA 19090.
30. **Office Systems Research Association (OSRA),** Dr. John Stallard, Executive Director, College of Business Administration, 501 Grise Hall, Western Kentucky University, Bowling Green, KY 42101.
31. **Office Technology Research Group**, P.O. Box 65, Pasadena, CA 91102.

32. **Professional Secretaries International (PSI),** Publication Office and World Headquarters, 301 East Armour Boulevard, Kansas City, MO 64111–1299.
33. **Society for the Advancement of Management (SAM),** American Management Associations, Inc., 2331 Victory Parkway, Cincinnati, OH 45206.
34. **Society for Information Management (SIM),** 111 East Wacker Drive, Chicago, IL 60601.

OFFICE SYSTEMS PUBLICATIONS

APPENDIX

2

1. ***Administrative Management,*** The Automated Office, Ltd., 1123 Broadway, New York, NY 10010.
2. ***AEDS Monitor,*** Association of Educational Data Systems, 1201 Sixteenth Street NW, Washington, DC 20036.
3. ***AOC Market Guide on Office Automation Systems,*** One Bala Plaza, Bala Cynwyd, PA 19004.
4. ***ARMA Records Management Quarterly,*** 4200 Somerset Drive, Suite 215, Prairie Village, KS 66208.
5. ***Advanced Office Concepts Newsletter,*** One Bala Plaza, Bala Cynwyd, PA 19004.
6. ***Agricultural Computing,*** Doan Publishing Company, 11701 Borman Drive, St. Louis, MO 63146.
7. ***Apple Magazine & Catalog,*** 10260 Bradley Drive, Cupertino, CA 95104.
8. ***The Balance Sheet,*** Marketing Department, South-Western Publishing Co., 5101 Madison Road, Cincinnati, OH 45227.
9. ***Business Computer Digest,*** 1076 Boca Entrada Boulevard, Boca Raton, FL 33433.
10. ***Business Computers Systems,*** Cahners Publishing Company, 221 Columbus Avenue, Boston, MA 02116.
11. ***Business Education Association Journal,*** Business Education Association of Metropolitan New York, Business Education Program, New York University, 239 Greene Street, New York, NY 10003.
12. ***Business Education World,*** 1221 Avenue of the Americas, New York, NY 10020.
13. ***Business Week,*** McGraw-Hill, Inc., McGraw-Hill Building, 1221 Avenue of the Americas, New York, NY 10020.

14. ***BYTE,*** BYTE Subscriptions, P.O. Box 590, Martinsville, NJ 08836.
15. ***Classroom Computer Learning,*** Peter Li, Inc., 2451 East River Road, Dayton, OH 45439.
16. ***Color Computer News,*** P.O. Box 1192, Muskegon, MI 49443.
17. ***Communication Briefings,*** P.O. Box 587, Glassboro, NJ 08028.
18. ***Communications News,*** Harcourt Brace Jovanovich, Inc., 124 South First Street, Geneva, IL 60134.
19. ***Comp-U-Fax,*** 505 Busse Highway, Park Ridge, IL 60068-3191.
20. ***Compute,*** P.O. Box 5406, Greensboro, NC 27403.
21. ***Computer Decisions,*** Hayden Publishing Company, 10 Mulholland Drive, Hasbrouck Heights, NY 07604.
22. ***Computer Industry Update,*** P.O. Box 681, Los Altos, CA 94022.
23. ***The Computer Instructor,*** 614 Santa Barbara Street, Santa Barbara, CA 93101.
24. ***Computers & Electronics,*** Ziff-Davis Publishing Company, One Park Avenue, New York, NY 10016.
25. ***Computer Products,*** Box 1952, Dover, NJ 07801-0952.
26. ***Computer World Office Automation,*** CWC Communications, Inc., Box 880, 375 Cochituate Road, Framingham, MA 01710.
27. ***Computing Newsletter,*** P.O. Box 7345, Colorado Springs, CO 80933.
28. ***Computing Teacher,*** Department of Computer and Information Science, University of Oregon, 1787 Agate Street, Eugene, OR 97403.
29. ***Concepts,*** One Industrial Avenue, Fawell, MA 01851.
30. ***Creative Computing,*** Ahl Computing, Inc., P.O. Box 789-M, Morristown, NJ 07960.
31. ***Database: New Directions in Computer Education,*** South-Western Publishing Company, 5101 Madison Road, Cincinnati, OH 45227.
32. ***Data Management,*** Data Processing Management Association, 505 Busse Highway, Park Ridge, IL 60068.
33. ***Datamation,*** Cahners Publishing Company Computer Center, P.O. Box 5211, Denver, CO 80217.
34. ***Datapro Reports on Office Automation; Microcomputers; Datapro Management of Office Automation,*** Datapro Research Corporation, 1805 Underwood Boulevard, Delran, NJ 08075.
35. ***Data Training,*** Weingarten Publications, Inc., 38 Chauncy Street, Boston, MA 02111.

36. *The DEC Professional,* P.O. Box 362, Ambler, PA 19002-0362.

37. *Desktop Computing,* Wayne Green, Inc., P.O. Box 917, Farmingdale, NY 11737.

38. *Electronic Learning,* 902 Sylvan Avenue, Box 2001, Englewood Cliffs, NJ 07632.

39. *Electronics,* McGraw-Hill Building, 1221 Avenue of the Americas, New York, NY 10020.

40. *Facilities Design & Management,* 1515 Broadway, New York, NY 10036.

41. *Glencoe Printout for Business Education,* Glencoe Publishing Company, 17337 Ventura Boulevard, Encino, CA 91316.

42. *Hufact Quarterly,* The Report Store, 910 Massachusetts Street, Suite 602K, Lawrence, KS 66044-2975.

43. *ICP Interface: Data Processing Management,* International Computer Programs, Inc., 9000 Keystone Crossing, P.O. Box 40946, Indianapolis, IN 46240.

44. *In-Cider,* Circulation Department, Wayne Green, Inc., 80 Pine Street, Peterborough, NH 03458.

45. *Infoworld: The Personal Computer Weekly,* Circulation Department, 375 Cochituate Road, Box 837, Framingham, MA 01701-9987.

46. *Information Center,* Weingarten Publications, 38 Chauncy Street, Boston, MA 02111.

47. *Information & Word Processing Report,* Geyer-McAllister Publications, P.O. Box 1129, Dover, NJ 07801.

48. *Information Industry Review,* Association of Information Systems Professionals, 104 Wilmot Road, Suite 201, Deerfield, IL 60015-5195.

49. *Information Management,* PTN Publishing Corporation, 101 Crossways Park, West Woodbury, NY 11797.

50. *Information Strategy: The Executive's Journal,* Division of Warren, Gorham & Lamont, 210 South Street, Boston, MA 02111.

51. *Information Systems News,* 333 East Shore Road, Manhassett, NY 11030.

52. *Infosystems,* Hitchcock Publishing Co., Hitchcock Building, P.O. Box 3007, Wheaton, IL 60187.

53. *Input,* 1943 Landings Drive, Mountain View, CA 94043.

54. *Inside World Management,* 20 Railroad Avenue, Hackensack, NJ 07601.

55. ***Interface,*** Stephen Mitchell, Publisher, 915 River Street, Santa Cruz, CA 95060.
56. ***Interface Age,*** 16704 Marquardt Avenue, Cerritos, CA 90701.
57. ***IT Focus,*** IEEE Service Dept., 445 Hoes Lane, Piscataway, NJ 08854-4150.
58. ***Journal of Business Communication,*** Association for Business Communication, 100 English Building, University of Illinois, 608 South Wright Street, Urbana, IL 61801.
59. ***Journal of Education for Business,*** Heldref Publications, 4000 Albemarle Street NW, Washington, DC 20016.
60. ***Journal of Information & Image Management,*** Association for Information and Image Management, 1100 Wayne Avenue, Silver Springs, MD 20910.
61. ***Journal of Information Systems Management,*** Division of Warren, Gorham & Lamont, 210 South Street, Boston, MA 02111.
62. ***Journal of Studies in Technical Careers,*** School of Technical Careers, 908 South Wall Street, Southern Illinois University, Carbondale, IL 62901.
63. ***Journal of Systems Management,*** Association for Systems Management, 24587 Bagley Road, Cleveland, OH 44138.
64. ***Management Technology,*** 11 Commerce Street, Norwalk, CT 06850.
65. ***Management World,*** Administrative Management Society, AMS Building, 2360 Maryland Road, Willow Grove, PA 19090.
66. ***Managing End-User Computing,*** Auerbach Publishers, Inc., 210 South Street, Boston, MA 02111.
67. ***The James Martin Report,*** Promotional Distribution, 219 Bear Hill Road, Waltham, MA 02154.
68. ***Microcomputing,*** Subscription Services, P.O. Box 997, Farmingdale, NY 11737.
69. ***Micro-Mainframe Line News,*** Edgetech Publishing Company, 582 Market Street, Suite 305, San Francisco, CA 94104.
70. ***Micro Magazine,*** 34 Chelmsford Street, P.O. Box 6502, Chelmsford, MA 01824.
71. ***Micro Market World,*** 375 Cochituate Road, Box 880, Framingham, MA 01701.
72. ***MIS Week,*** Circulation Department, P.O. Box 1003, Manasquan, NJ 08736.

73. ***MIS Quarterly,*** Society for Information Management and Management Information Systems Research Center, 271 19th Avenue South, University of Minnesota, Minneapolis, MN 55455.

74. ***Modern Office Procedures,*** P.O. Box 95795, Cleveland, OH 44101.

75. ***Modern Office Technology,*** 1111 Chester Avenue, Cleveland, OH 44114.

76. ***News 34/38,*** 295 East 29th Street, Suite 210, P.O. Box 5107, Loveland, CO 80537.

77. ***The Observer,*** P.O. Box 1119, Aptos, CA 95003.

78. ***The Office,*** Office Publications, Inc., P.O. Box 1231, Stamford, CT 06904-1231.

79. ***Office Productivity,*** CDM Publishing Company, Inc., 102 North Kensington Avenue, LaGrange, IL 60525.

80. ***The Office Products Analyst,*** MRSA, Inc., Dept. A., Suite 1606, 150 Broadway, New York, NY 10038.

81. ***Office Products Dealer,*** Hitchcock Publishing Company, Circulation Department, Hitchcock Building, Wheaton, IL 60187.

82. ***Office Systems,*** Office Systems Magazine, Inc., P.O. Box 1015, Southeastern, PA 19398.

83. ***Office Systems Report,*** Patricia Seybold's Office Computing Group, 148 State Street, Suite 612, Boston, MA 02109.

84. ***The Office Systems Research Journal,*** Office Systems Research Association, Dr. John Stallard, Executive Director, College of Business Administration, 501 Grise Hall, Western Kentucky University, Bowling Green, KY 42101.

85. ***Office Technology and People,*** Elsevier Publications, 52 Vanderbilt Avenue, New York, NY 10017.

86. ***Office World News,*** 645 Stewart Avenue, Garden City, NY 11530.

87. ***Officemation Product Reports,*** Management Information Corporation, 140 Barclay Center, Cherry Hill, NJ 08034.

88. ***On Communications,*** P.O. Box 1021, Southeastern, PA 19398.

89. ***Open Systems: Managing Office Technology,*** P.O. Box 1231, Stamford, CT 06904.

90. ***Output,*** Technical Publishing Company, 666 Fifth Avenue, New York, NY 10103.

91. ***PC Week,*** Customer Service Dept., P.O. Box 5970, Cherry Hill, NJ 08034.

92. ***PC Products,*** Cahners Publishing Company, 270 St. Paul Street, Denver, CO 80206.
93. ***PC World,*** PC World Communications, Inc., 555 DeHaro Street, San Francisco, CA 94598.
94. ***Panorama: A New Vision of Technology,*** Eastman Kodak Company, 343 State Street, Rochester, NY 14650.
95. ***Personal Computing,*** Hayden Publishing Company, 50 Essex Street, Rochelle Park, NJ 07662.
96. ***Perspectives in Computing,*** International Business Machines Corporation, 44 South Broadway, White Plains, NY 10601.
97. ***Popular Computing,*** P.O. Box 307, Martinsville, NJ 08836.
98. ***Profiles,*** Profiles Circulation, P.O. Box N, Del Mar, CA 92014.
99. ***Secretarial Services Today,*** P.O. Box 29203, Shreveport, LA 71149.
100. ***Seybold Report on Professional Computing,*** Seybold Publications, Inc., P.O. Box 644, Media, PA 19063.
101. ***Softalk,*** P.O. Box 60, Milford, NH 03055.
102. ***Softside,*** P.O. Box 68, Milford, NH 03055.
103. ***Software News,*** Sentry Database Publishing Company, 1301 South Grove Avenue, Barrington, IL 60010.
104. ***Solutions,*** Digital Equipment Corporation, 200 Baker Avenue, Concord, MA 01720.
105. ***T.H.E. Journal,*** Information Synergy, Inc., 7 Spruce Street, P.O. Box 992, Acton, MA 01720.
106. ***Telecommunications,*** Horizon House-Microwave, Inc., 610 Washington Street, Dedham, MA 02026.
107. ***The Secretary,*** Professional Secretaries International, 2440 Pershing Road, Crown Center, Suite G-10, Kansas City, MO 64108-2560.
108. ***Today's Office,*** Hearst Business Communications, Inc., VTP Division, 645 Stewart Avenue, Garden City, NY 11530.
109. ***Today's Secretary,*** Subscriber Relations Dept., 1221 Avenue of the Americas, New York, NY 10020.
110. ***VAY/RSTS Professional MI Systems,*** P.O. Box 361, Ft. Washington, PA 19034-0361.
111. ***VDT News,*** P.O. Box 1799, Grand Central Station, New York, NY 10163.
112. ***Words,*** Association of Information Systems Professionals (AISP), 104 Wilmot Road, Suite 201, Deerfield, IL 60015-5195.

CASE STUDIES

APPENDIX 3

Appendix 3 contains six comprehensive case studies related to office automation and white-collar productivity in major U.S. corporations. Studying these cases will help the reader relate the concepts discussed in the text to actual business situations. These cases effectively illustrate the close relationship between business goals and productivity improvement efforts, such as office automation.

Due to their comprehensive nature, these cases are not directly related to particular chapters in the text. To guide the reader, however, the following list suggests chapters that the authors feel relate most directly to the cases. To fully appreciate the organizational dynamics and application of office systems analysis concepts, most readers will find it beneficial to read the cases several times in relation to different chapters.

Case	Related Chapters
Bethlehem Steel Corporation	*1–3, 17–19, 22*
Blue Cross and Blue Shield Association	*14, 15, 16*
First Bank of Edina	*16, 17, 24*
Digital Equipment Corporation	*19, 20–24*
The Memorial Hospital System	*13, 14, 20–24*
Polaroid Corporation	*13, 20–23*

Discussion questions and projects are presented at the end of each case. The discussion questions can aid the reader in thinking about the cases or serve as a basis for class discussion. The instructor will assign projects at appropriate times to provide practical application of the concepts covered in the course. As a guide, the authors have identified related chapters in parentheses next to each activity.

These case studies are adapted from a series related to White Collar Productivity: The National Challenge, *written by the American Productivity Center, Houston, Texas, and sponsored by Steelcase, Inc. The inclusion of these cases in the text does not necessarily imply the authors' endorsement of the solutions described or that these firms, or any firms, would take the exact same courses of action today. The cases were selected to provide a broad overview of actual productivity efforts related to office automation in U.S. corporations.*

Bethlehem Steel Corp.: Office Automation and Quality of Work Life

CASE 1

THE ORGANIZATION

The American steel industry, which is synonymous with American power and know-how, dominated the world market for more than 70 years. By the late 1970s, however, American steel production captured only 20 percent of the global market. As the U.S. economy slipped into a deep recession in the latter half of 1982, the steel industry was operating at about 30 percent of its capacity.

Responding to adverse market conditions generated by declining demand and rising costs, the Bethlehem Steel Corporation initiated several productivity improvement efforts within its plants and offices. Among these were a quality of work life strategy that incorporated a more participative management style, a major thrust toward office automation, and a productivity program in the Steel Group Office that combined these directions and departed significantly from Bethlehem's traditional work patterns.

QUALITY OF WORK LIFE AT BETHLEHEM STEEL

A new human resources policy established by Bethlehem's chairman stated that employees have a right to know what is expected of them. It also indicated that rewards would be based on demonstrated competence in job performance. Future individual success at Bethlehem would depend on self-development supported by educational and training opportunities.

The quality of work life (QWL) movement at Bethlehem was a departure in the company's philosophy. Focusing on the work process itself, it sought to tap the creative and problem-solving abilities of all employees. The goal was to optimize and synthesize the personal and professional interests of its workers and the financial goals of the company.

The new policy moved the company toward greater employee participation. It was hoped that open, two-way communication between employees and various levels of management would foster an environment of mutual trust and cooperation.

OFFICE AUTOMATION AT BETHLEHEM STEEL

The need to improve productivity in the face of turbulent business conditions moved Bethlehem toward office automation systems. The increasing complexities of the steel industry made vast amounts of timely information critical. For example, a staff office within the Sales Department acted as a central depository for all competitive price reports. These reports originated in the District Sales Office, were transmitted to Product Sales for review and recommendation, and were then transmitted to the staff office to coordinate review and action by Executive Sales.

In recent years, the number of competitive price reports increased tremendously. Through extensive use of the computer, the staff office created a historical library of key competitive information from these reports. Based on this competitive information, the staff office created key reports for District Sales, Product Sales, and Executive Sales to help them manage their business. This type of office automation eliminated manual reports in all areas and increased productivity.

The move toward office automation at Bethlehem was driven by more than a desire to improve the flow of information; a second motivating force was the management's desire to reduce labor costs, which have increased a staggering 400 percent over the past 15 years.

Actually, automating manual procedures is nothing new to Bethlehem. The company is a leader in the utilization of text, voice, and data processing. At the heart of the three-phase office automation project was the goal to integrate all professionals, managers, and secretaries into an integrated office system to support a new way of conducting the company's business.

To accomplish this goal, Phase 1 established a base of secretarial workstations that were compatible with the corporation's data processing systems and allowed data to pass freely between them. In addition to word and text processing, Phase 1 implemented electronic text filing systems. After electronic filing and retrieving of documents became routine, the ability to verify spelling and perform basic mathematical tasks was also incorporated on a wider scale.

Phase 2 implemented electronic mail throughout the total corporate system and merged computerized data with text. This advanced office system was capable of calendaring, meeting scheduling, personal reminders, and electronic messaging to all directory locations.

In third-quarter 1983, implementation of Phase 3 began. This phase focused on improving manager and professional productivity. Where applicable, computer graphics, decision support systems, executive workstations, advanced voice systems, and teleconferencing were introduced or expanded.

Phase 3 provided for the total integration of office automation and data processing by 1985. The use of text and data functions for secretarial terminals, personal computer workstations with text and data compatibility, and normal data terminals enhanced with text functions provided key tools for users. These terminals had access to electronic filing, retrieval, and display as well as to corporate databases and application programs through the corporate telecommunications network. All personnel shared in the productivity benefits gained from improved information flow.

The PROS Effort: Putting It All Together

The Productivity Through Office Systems (PROS) effort of the Steel Group Sales area was the first white-collar program at Bethlehem Steel to synthesize QWL and office automation. PROS was an office automation project to improve the productivity of the 400-person sales force and their support personnel and was a major development in Phase 1. The thrust of PROS was primarily aimed at the secretarial force and created the foundation for future office automation developments.

In mid 1980, a steering committee studied the technical feasibility of automating some functions of the General Sales Office. A team examined transactions and paper flow (see Case Figure 1-1), volume and manhours

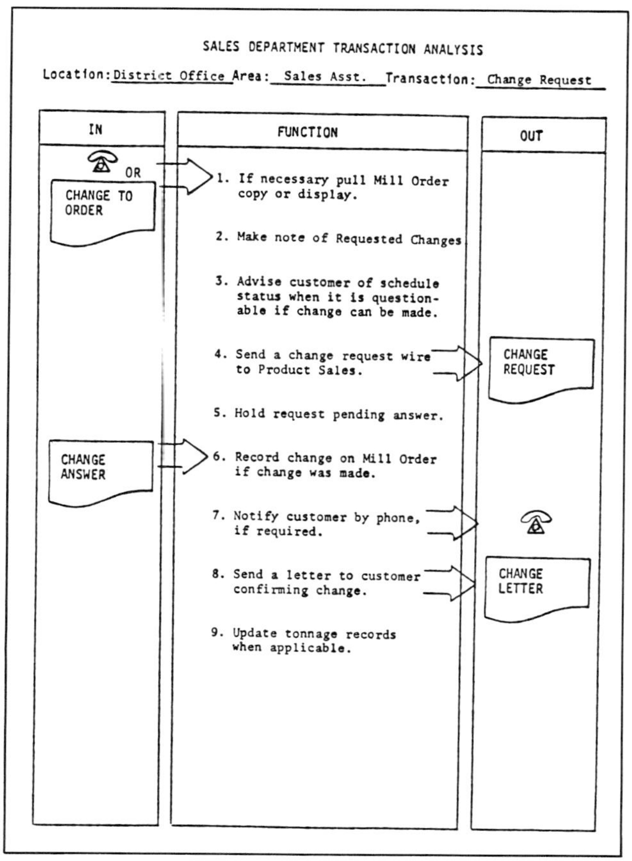

CASE FIGURE 1-1. Paper flow in the General Sales Office.

involved in these transactions, and total volume of paper flow through the Sales Department (over 10,000 pieces of paper daily). The goals and missions of the Steering Committee are shown in Case Figure 1-2. Concluding that selling steel to approximately 14,000 customers is a rapidly changing function that depends on timely information, the Steering Committee proposed a pilot project to connect the home office with one of the remote district offices.

The proposed system streamlined document dictation, preparation, revision, filing, and mailing between headquarters and field locations. It also facilitated meeting scheduling and calendar management. Approxi-

CASE FIGURE 1-2. The goals and missions of the PROS Steering Committee.

PROS Steering Committee

Our group has formed a Steering Committee to help the membership develop and accomplish our missions (reasons for existing) and goals (ways to attain the missions). The committee includes Deanne Blomstrom, Linda Bradley, Donna Ferrey, Pat McGinley, Linda Pagotto, Irene Pope, and Charlene Young. The Steering Committee developed some missions and goals for PROS and proposed them to the membership at a monthly meeting. Our total membership agreed to the following missions and goals for the PROS effort:

1. Increase office productivity.
   - Improve task effectiveness.
   - Increase CRT diversity.
   - Improve bottom-line results.
2. Gain expanded system knowledge.
   - Provide an exchange of ideas through meetings.
   - Ask for suggestions.
   - Find shortcuts, faster ways to do text functions.
3. Become "agents" for future implementation of office automation.
   - Determine what the present plan is.
   - Determine what is expected of us to help in this change.
   - After first two goals have been defined, put forth willingness and commitment to PROS.
4. Professionalism.
   - Develop acceptance of PROS.
   - Develop recognition as PROS.
   - Develop contact with outside professionals.
5. Involve management in PROS programs.
   - Invite management to attend meetings.
   - Determine management's expectations of their PROS.
   - Solicit management's input at meetings.

mately one year after the Steering Committee was formed, the $360,000 pilot project was approved by Bethlehem's sales and corporate managements.

After soliciting work samples, information requirements, and other input from the work force involved in the changes, the pilot system was implemented during the last four months of 1981. As equipment was installed and tested, training was provided to tailor the system to individual needs.

When the paperwork of the General Sales Office had been reorganized, a member of the QWL Task Force recognized the opportunity to apply employee involvement principles to the project. A PROS Task Force was set up and promptly implemented the following:

- An electronic newsletter
- Pins in recognition of the program
- Certificates of achievement
- Circulation of articles
- A suggestion box
- Coffee and doughnuts in training room
- A bulletin board
- A recognition system for ideas
- A desk name plate for graduates

As 48 "PROS" successfully completed their training in January 1982, corporate management announced its approval of the entire $2,000,000 project. The announcement confirmed the importance of the PROS effort to Bethlehem management. By the end of the first quarter of 1983, approximately 150 PROS secretaries had been trained.

The entire system connected equipment for the seven district offices to the home office installation and was completed by the fall of 1982. It included 11 cluster units, 85 CRTs, and 45 printers. In order to support the newly organized Steel Group, an additional cluster unit with 22 CRTs and 14 printers was added in early 1983. A total of 14 remote sales locations communicated with the clustered units, which tied into the corporate data network and allowed exchanges of information with other text and data systems within the company.

More than the mere implementation of a new office system, the PROS effort provided support for new applications and new working relationships. Monthly PROS meetings devoted equal time to technical and social concerns. Along with exchanging ideas on system functions and applications, meetings were devoted to team-building exercises, problem solving, stress management, and assertiveness training. Through the electronic newsletter and electronic mail, any individual could communicate with all the PROS on the system and, via distributed printing, with a growing number of interested supervisors and managers.

RESULTS OF THE PROS EFFORT

No formal productivity measures were undertaken before or after the system's implementation. By the end of 1982, however, a reduction of 31 staff was achieved, two-thirds of which was attributed to gains realized through the PROS effort. The systems development team also ranked the following as the most frequently reported impacts of the PROS effort; estimates of the improvement percentage are indicated:

- Increased output 20%
- More timely delivery 80%
- Credibility of offices improved 20%
- Work force morale improved 20%
- Task difficulty reduced 20%
- Communication facilitated 50%
- Office space more effectively used 25%
- Response time reduced 80%
- Errors reduced 5%
- Quality of service enhanced 50%

Electronic mail on the system reached a volume of 50,000 pages per month. This rapid exchange of documents in combination with word processing significantly improved efficiency. Applications were continually developed to eliminate steps in generating this information.

Typical of the time and cost savings produced by the PROS effort was the improved efficiency in handling customer requests for visits to plants or home office locations. Previously, 1,600 requests per year, with 10 copies of each request, were typed on preprinted forms. Half of these required revisions and subsequent retyping on fresh forms. Using a new form created on the PROS system, the 24,000 preprinted forms per year were eliminated. Revisions no longer required complete retyping. The requisite number of copies were printed automatically at various locations.

Another result was improved time management as business units became better able to support and coordinate with one another. Managers reported dramatic improvement in the degree and quality of support they received; support personnel reported that their supervisors' willingness to learn basic systems features allowed them more flexibility to meet new requirements. Using technological innovation in conjunction with organizational change enabled the Sales Department to moderate the tensions of staff reductions and in many cases significantly improved organizational morale.

Problems in Improving Quality of Work Life

As the PROS effort matured, it encountered occasional opposition. A special session for participants was held to address both positive and negative aspects of the effort. Positive aspects identified in this special session included opportunities to gain confidence, meet people with common problems, enhance personal growth, effectively solve problems, and speak openly in a group.

On the negative side, work tended to back up while participants attended the monthly PROS meetings. As a solution to this problem, participants could "make deals" with others to get the work done. It was felt that this process of interoffice negotiation would improve both participants' and nonparticipants' understanding of the QWL movement.

Another problem was that employees' participation in candid group discussions could backfire if confidentiality was not honored. This problem was solved by pledges to keep all group discussions strictly confidential.

A third difficulty resulted from management's suspicion that no worthwhile results were coming out of QWL meetings. To address this concern, it was decided to send the results of all QWL meetings to management. Improved communication between participants and their managers was identified as the best way to convey the results of the QWL effort.

Despite these setbacks, QWL became a growing, corporate-wide effort at Bethlehem Steel. The philosophy was expressed by the head of the Sales Department: "We are committed to encouraging a management style that fosters and supports open communication, individual initiative, recognition, personal growth, and mutual respect. The QWL process will provide structured opportunities for participation in decision making and will result in the effective utilization of our individual skills and talents. Our goal in this direction is vital to the success of our company."

CONCLUSIONS

To facilitate the implementation of QWL at Bethlehem and to avoid the conflicts encountered in the PROS effort, special assistants with problem-solving skills acted as corporate resources. These special assistants conducted awareness sessions in several Bethlehem Steel offices around the country and were responsible for keeping the QWL movement on track.

At the core of all the changes at Bethlehem Steel was the need to achieve higher productivity with a reduced staff in order to survive. While other U.S. firms may not face such formidable difficulties, the experience of Bethlehem Steel indicates the value—and perhaps the necessity—of social and technical changes in the ways organizations operate. Whether change is imposed by external conditions or proactively initiated from within organizations, active participation of employees is a critical factor for successful organizational productivity.

DISCUSSION QUESTIONS

1. Bethlehem Steel's goal was "to integrate all professionals, managers, and secretaries into an integrated office system to support a new way of conducting the company's business." Why was this integrated approach important? What other factors were important to accomplishing the results reported in the case? (Chapters 1–3)

2. Bethlehem Steel used a three-phased approach to integrate office automation and data processing. Compare these three phases to the stages of office automation development described in Chapter 2. Do you think this phased approach was an effective implementation strategy? Why or why not? If you were the systems analyst on this project, would you have done anything differently? Why or why not? (Chapters 1–3)
3. Bethlehem Steel's productivity improvement program included a quality of work life strategy that incorporated a more participative management style and a major office automation thrust. Do you think Bethlehem Steel could have accomplished the same results with either of these programs alone? How did these programs affect each other? Do you think there was any synergy between the programs? (Chapters 17–19)
4. Why do you think the Steering Committee started with a pilot system for the office automation efforts? Why was this an appropriate implementation strategy for Bethlehem Steel to use? What was learned from the pilot? (Chapter 22)

INDIVIDUAL OR GROUP PROJECT

1. Break into groups of three or four people. On the left side of a T-chart, list the results achieved by Bethlehem Steel's productivity improvement program. Then, on the right side, identify the aspects of the productivity program that you think were most important to accomplishing each result. Compare your group's responses to those of other groups. The beginning of a sample T-chart is shown below:

Result	Key Productivity Strategies
1. Increased output	1. Word processing systems. Streamlined work procedures

ROLE PLAY

1. Assume you are attending the monthly meeting of the Steering Committee. Brainstorm the potential of desktop publishing applications to both the sales force and the secretarial staff. (Chapters 7, 12)

WRITING ASSIGNMENT

1. Assume you are the electronic newsletter editor. Using a word processing package available at your institution, write a column for the newsletter summarizing the results of the PROS effort.

Blue Cross and Blue Shield: Reducing Costs through Increased Productivity

CASE **2**

THE ORGANIZATION

The Blue Cross and Blue Shield Association is the largest private health-care financing system in the world. Its domestic plans serve more than 100,000,000 people. The prepaid health care concept began during the Great Depression in response to the public's need for affordable hospital care and hospitals' need to fill beds.

Since its inception in 1935, Blue Cross and Blue Shield of Virginia has grown steadily. Currently serving 1.3 million participants, the company also acts as a government intermediary for Medicare Part A for 500,000 people. A nonprofit, nonstock corporation, members of its board of directors represent the consumer, hospital, and physician communities.

Blue Cross and Blue Shield of Virginia takes pride in its efficient management; its operating expense ratio in 1981 was the lowest in the system. Its claims processing per employee has improved 10 percent, largely due to innovative marketing, cost containment, and an effort to improve productivity.

THE PROBLEM AND THE SOLUTION

In the early 1970s, as insurance companies increasingly entered the health-care financing field, the management of Blue Cross and Blue Shield of Virginia recognized the need to reduce unit costs to remain competitive. The management determined that the Virginia Plan's operating expense ratio was unacceptable and that improved productivity was the proper means to lower that ratio. The organization was overstaffed at that time, and a number of layoffs initially reduced operating expenses. Nevertheless, the need for a comprehensive, long-range plan was apparent.

After securing an experienced consultant on staff, the management authorized him to appraise the situation and design a work measurement system to improve current productivity levels. Within six months, a work measurement program was launched. The objective of the newly created Work Management Department was "to establish methods for controlling production costs and to develop programs for reducing those costs."

To accomplish this, the Work Management Department developed a system to measure and improve individual, departmental, and corporate productivity. The system involved a means to report input and output, formulas to analyze the data, and a method for circulating and utilizing the data. For a more detailed description of the measurement system, see Case Figure 2-1.

The data was utilized in many ways. Eighty-five percent of individual performance reviews were based on the work measurement and quality control data. Staffing needs were determined on the basis of the departmental figures. Equipment needs, budget preparation, overtime justification, supervisor evaluation, production scheduling, and even new service pricing were aided by these reports.

CASE FIGURE 2-1. The work management system implemented by Blue Cross and Blue Shield of Virginia.

Work Management System

The system currently functions in the following manner: First, an informal meeting is held with managers, supervisors, employees, and Work Management analysts to discuss the program and answer questions. Each member of the "team" is then asked to complete the necessary paperwork. The workers fill out a "duty list" form. Supervisors fill out a form listing equipment, forms, and reports used in their areas.

All forms are collected and analyzed by creating a work distribution chart. A flowchart is then developed to analyze complex work flows for possible method and procedure improvements. Such improvements are suggested to management. All major tasks are observed, and procedures are established for greater efficiency and standardization.

This data is used to establish staffing requirements, standardize procedures, and set levels of performance. These are termed *engineered standards. Nonengineered standards* are those established by means of self-logging, past historical norms, and short interval scheduling (as opposed to the time study, work sampling procedure) and are used for professional or "creative" work.

In the case of Blue Cross and Blue Shield of Virginia, quality levels are an intrinsic part of the work measurement program. The Quality Control Program was initiated by the national organization to ensure consistent quality of service throughout tne plans. Blue Cross and Blue Shield of Virginia has applied the standards of the national organization to increase both the quality and quantity of work produced by its employees.

The system is essentially a random sampling of an individual's work to determine the number and seriousness of errors found. An index is used in combination with the work measurement data to determine each individual's productivity level. Together, the data constitutes 85 percent of an individual's performance review.

The system can be applied to virtually all Blue Cross and Blue Shield employees. However, the clerical staff is most directly affected. The "standards" apply mainly to routine tasks. Thus clerical workers log the duties they perform and their hours of work on standard and nonstandard time (reassignment, nonstandard duties, etc.). This information is compiled, computerized, and fed back to immediate supervisors and managers. Data is available on the performance of individuals, comparison of productivity in various departments, and company-wide productivity.

The Work Management Department consisted of a director, a manager, and six to eight analysts. They performed the following functions:

1. *Methods engineering.* Utilizing operational analysis, motion study, production schedules, value analysis, flowcharts, and work simplification.
2. *Work measurement.* Developing performance standards in cooperation with department supervisors and managers; data compilation and input and output reports.
3. *Staffing analysis.* Determining labor needs to complete work volume on a timely basis.
4. *Developing inventory models.* Developing work-in-progress models as guidelines in reducing backlogs, smoothing work flow, and improving productivity by enhancing workstation and equipment layout.

Work Measurement Results

The work measurement system netted some immediate benefits for the Virginia Plan:

1. Productivity rose 20–40 percent during the first year (see Case Figure 2-2). As a result, the operating expense ratio improved by about 27 percent during the first four years.
2. Managers and supervisors reported that they now had adequate data to evaluate employees objectively and to project needs and departmental performance.
3. Employees affected by the work measurement program were assured of relatively impartial performance reviews, equally distributed work loads, and streamlined procedures to simplify tasks.

Some employees expressed some apprehension regarding the work monitoring. To date, however, approximately 99 percent of all employees have met or exceeded the specified standard performance figures.

	1982	1981	1980	1979	1978	1977	1976	1975	1974	1973
Claims	8,500,616	7,814,644	6,745,750	6,138,791	4,877,158	4,527,107	4,024,485	3,435,985	2,666,192	1,959,879
Labor Hours Plan-wide)	2,012,225	1,903,971	1,693,191	1,487,300	1,473,070	1,435,765	1,394,335	1,336,940	1,282,270	1,225,089
Claims processed per labor hour	4.22	4.10	3.98	4.12	3.31	3.15	2.89	2.57	2.08	1.60
% Change		+ 3.03%	+ 3.00%	- 3.40%	+ 24.47%	+ 5.08%	+ 9.00%	+ 12.45%	+ 23.56%	+ 30.00%
Claims processed per employee (full time equivalent)*	7563	7365	6890	6724	5567	5246	4814	4279	3449	2857
%Change		+ 2.7%	+ 6.89%	+ 2.47%	+ 20.78%	+ 6.12%	+ 8.97%	+ 12.50%	+ 24.06%	+ 20.72%

* Excludes Membership Development

CASE FIGURE 2-2. Corporate productivity measures.

Facilities Planning: Environmental Redesign and Productivity

Work measurement was not the only direction the Virginia Plan pursued to increase productivity. Having occupied its present building for almost fifteen years, the company initiated plans to redesign workstations and enhance the professional environment.

The Facilities Planning staff worked with a work management team to redesign the work environment and purchase the necessary materials. Employee participation in the design process was encouraged. Each employee within a department that was scheduled for redesign completed a survey of suggested changes, current work flow, and equipment. Results were compiled with the assistance of the Work Management Department. The designers planned the space and presented the first draft to the department management. Once revisions were made, employees were again asked to participate.

The redesigned offices were individual workstations enclosed by colorful acoustical panels. Panel height depended on the tasks performed within the station. In addition to standard work surfaces and storage space, paper flow designs and special equipment shelves were utilized. Coordinated bulletin boards displayed each employee's photograph, announcements, job postings, and the corporate values statement.

RESULTS OF REDESIGN

Every department moving into a new systems environment showed a marked increase in productivity. Increases ranged from 3 to 14 percent within the first month and have been sustained over time. Workers reacted positively to the installation of systems furniture, citing increased storage space and more privacy as distinct improvements. Managers and supervisors reported reduced noise levels and fewer distractions. Memos sent to the Facilities Planning staff from department managers regarding the new systems environment are shown in Case Figures 2-3 and 2-4.

Steps were also taken to improve lighting conditions in many areas. The general consensus was that the existing overhead fluorescent lighting was too bright and glaring. Temporary adjustments reduced candlepower, and task lighting was utilized when possible. The Word Processing Department was the focus of an experiment to determine proper lighting for terminal and CRT use; "cool" white or blue fluorescent tubes were selected.

CASE FIGURE 2-3. Excerpts of letters to Facilities Planning Staff from managers and supervisors.

"The workstation was greatly improved by utilizing paperflow and shelving to furnish more work space and enhance efficiency. Acoustical panels were used to reduce noise levels. Productivity improvements of approximately 3.5% were achieved."

"During the three months prior to the move, the performance ratio for the micrographics unit was 81%. Since the move, productivity has increased to 87%. While there may be numerous reasons for this increase, one cannot overlook the positive effect more effective management of people and improved working conditions have had on productivity."

Inter-Office Communication

Blue Cross. Blue Shield. of Virginia

To: Roberta Tingle
Thru: Cleveland Regis
From: Jim Cohen

Date: December 1, 1982

Subject: Benefits from Microfilm Consolidation

The consolidation of Micrographics into one area has resulted in a number of benefits for the unit. The following are the major benefits derived from the move.

- The consolidation of the unit into one area has resulted in a work environment that is much more conducive to effective management. The Supervisor and Senior Clerk are able to better control and monitor the flow of work, and are more accessible to the Microfilm employees to answer questions and solve problems before they become a problem to the user. It also provides for a smoother transition between shifts with all the work in one area.

- We have recently changed our procedures for filming and data entry of Phase II CAR. We are now keying from paper and then filming the documents in the exact order they were keyed. This change has resulted in a 10% increase in throughout, as well as improved accuracy with the CAR project. By keying from paper, we have in effect eliminated the process of weekly error corrections, and through a slight change in the method of filming we have increased our filming speed and accuracy. This new process requires considerable coordination among the batcher, keyers and filmers. With the unit split in two areas it would have been much more difficult to effectively control this type of concept.

- Another positive effect the consolidation has had is to create more of a feeling of togetherness among the microfilm employees. Since the move, data entry personnel and microfilm operators are in daily contact with each other which has resulted in each having a better understanding for what the other group does. This has also resulted in more of a team effort among the microfilm employees.

- The final benefit can be attributed to productivity gains. During the three months prior to the move, the performance ratio for the Micrographics unit was 81%. Since the move, productivity has increased to 87%. While there may be numerous reasons for this increase, one cannot overlook the positive effect more effective management of people and improved working conditions has had on increased productivity.

Inter-Office Communication

Blue Cross. Blue Shield. of Virginia

To: Cleve Regis

From: Linda Caskey & Lonnie Johnson

Date: February 2

Subject: Work Manage of the Mail

A Work Management Study of the mailroom began in October and was conducted intermittently until the end of February with the major effort taking place in October. This study was conducted to find solutions to inefficiencies occurring in the mailroom in three specific areas:

1. Increasing volumes of outgoing mail were making it more and more difficult to meet the daily 4:00 p.m. deadline.
2. Double and triple handling of mail during the sorting stage was slowing down the incoming mail process.
3. Increasing postage rates mandated more efficient weighing techniques to eliminate excess postage on pieces of mail.

After reviewing our entire mail system, several problems were apparent. The design of the mailroom inhibited a smooth work flow for both outgoing and incoming mail. In addition, each mail clerk was performing every mailroom task independently, with very little specialization occurring and with minimal work scheduling. Although this independence breaks up the monotony of doing repetitious tasks, it forced the unit supervisor to be constantly preoccupied with shifting personnel to where a backlog is already in progress.

Accomplishments

Methods Improvements

After conducting a study of the mailroom work flow, a more systematic and logical means of handling the mail was proposed. This was achieved

- 2 -

by improving the layout so that incoming and outgoing mail functions will be separated to reduce delays and excessive travelling while processing the mail (see attached sketches). As a result the new design will stream-line production and improve space planning. In conjunction with this improvement several procedures and standards changes have been tested to encourage mail clerks to adopt an assembly-line approach where they will work more as a team than individually. Projected savings from these improvements amounted to 1035 hours per year or $6236/year.

Another achievement directly related to the layout changes involves replacing the lazy susan currently used for sorting the incoming mail with two through-sort mail bins. Under the present system mail is sorted in several areas, transferred into the main circular sorting bin, and transferred again into mail carts. The elimination of these scattered sorting areas and replacement of the circular mail sorting bin with the more efficient sort thru modules will isolate the mail sorting function into one area and eliminate delays and double handling of the mail. In addition to increasing sorting efficiency, these new bins were an essential element in space planning. Savings resulting from this improvement will amount to 309 hours/year or $1788/year with a payback period of .82 years.

Two electronic weighing scales were purchased to replace the fan scales, which will reduce the amount of excess postage on borderline pieces of mail and speed up the weighing process. Savings resulting from improved accuracy was $12,562/year. In addition, 112 hours/year

- 3 -

or $648/year were saved as a result of reduced labor hours spent weighing mail with the new scales. The total dollar amount saved was $13,210/year with a payback period of .28 years.

The combination of the accomplishments listed above amounted to a total savings of 1456/hours/year or $21,233/year.

Future Projects

As an effort to plan for increasing mailroom efficiency in the future, several potential projets are being explored.

Electronic Computer Originated Mail (E-Com). E-Com was researched at the time of its onset (Jan., 1982) in an effort to explore a more efficient means of generating outgoing mail, to help alleviate the growing overload of mail in the print shop and mailroom and to possibly prevent the need for additional employees in those areas in the future. E-Com is a service offered by the Postal Service which enables a computer to transmit messages to their computer by means of a telecommunications common carrier (the telephone). The post office then prints, envelopes, affixes postage and delivers anywhere in the continental U.S. within two days. The charge for the service is 26 cents for the first page, 5 cents for the second page and $50.00 annual fee.
There is potential for future consideration of the service -- the major benefits would be reduced turnaround time and the elimination of human error for outgoing mail. At the present time there is no application for this service at Blue Cross Blue Shield due to the limitations imposed by the postal service (i.e. a maximum 2 page limit and no insertion or return envelope capabilities).

CASE FIGURE 2-4. **Memos to the Facilities Planning Staff from department managers on the new systems environment.**

- 4 -

Internal Presorting - Potential savings are being lost by sending our qualifying mail to a presort service which zip sorts our mail and combines it with other company's mail in order to have the minimum volume to qualify for the reduced rate. We pay the service .014 cents per qualified presort piece of mail or.016 cents per residual piece of mail out of the total 3 cents discount on presort postage. Since an estimated 85% of our mail volume now satisfied the minimum volume specifications, there is approximately $25,000/year savings potential to be realized from presorting internally.

There are a few alternatives to be explored in this area:

1. OCR zip sort machine ($70,000) - Reads 5 to 9 digit zip codes and sort all outgoing mail internally. With this option there is also the potential to go to the 9 digit conversion to zip sort incoming mail by machine. Limitations - Zip code would have to be placed in a separate field on every envelope so the OCR can read the number. Also, the 9 - digit conversion is a long way away from the present system of opening, manually reading and sorting incoming mail.
2. Manual presort machine - operator/keyer controlled. ($40,000) The keyer reads the first 4 digits of the envelopes going through the feeder, keys in those digits and automatically is sorted - this must go through 2 sorts and could require 2 additional employees to operate. (This model was observed at U.V.B).

- 5 -

3. Obtain a software package that would allow us to presort with the computers we already have. Cost is not known. Still would need to reconstruct envelope to put zip code in a separate field to be read. Also, expensive CPU time would be involved.

These and other innovative technologies will be explored in conjunction with management in the future, as an ongoing effort to maximize productivity and cost effectiveness of mail handling operations within the plan.

cc: Ed Stover
Jerry Barnes
Ron Nash

CASE FIGURE 2-4. (continued)

OFFICE AUTOMATION: TECHNOLOGY AND IMPROVED PRODUCTIVITY

With over 1.5 million subscribers, accounting and information systems within the Virginia Plan were complex. Due to the following technological innovations, the systems began to flow smoothly:

- With two mainframe computers and access through terminals throughout the building, some departments began to use self-contained mini- and microcomputers.
- Another important factor was the increasing use of computer-assisted retrieval (CAR) for microfilm. Hardcopy (paper) storage was being eliminated, with easy electronic access to documents through CAR. The transfer of paper records to microfilm was completed in 1984.
- The firm installed a sophisticated energy-monitoring system to further reduce operating expenses. The system regulated cooling and heating, monitored energy usage, and sensed temperatures in any area of the building.
- The mailroom also experienced a dramatic increase in productivity resulting from automation and facilities planning. Initially, Work Measurement analysts studied incoming and outgoing mail flow; the Facility

Planning staff then designed a method for utilizing the space and equipment more efficiently. In addition, new equipment was added to reduce the number of manual tasks. Total savings were $21,233 per year.

- Productivity gains that result directly from automation are not demonstrated as rapidly as those that result from human resource and environmental changes. This is partly due to the training required to use automated systems. Gains are substantial, however, and more automated systems will be acquired.

AN INTEGRATED APPROACH

Blue Cross and Blue Shield of Virginia recognized the interdependence of all factors in improving productivity. Although measurement, facility planning, and automation have been mainly cited here, employee participation was encouraged with each undertaking. Work standards were set and revised based on employees' and supervisors' suggestions and were revised again after environmental or automation changes were completed. Departments worked together to reduce operating expenses.

CONCLUSIONS

Consistent measurement of individual, departmental, and corporate productivity resulted in important gains in productivity and provided a gauge for assessing the impact of other programs. Smoother work flow, more accurate staff analysis, better projection capabilities, and employees' knowledge of required output all significantly improved productivity. The use of this data also improved perceived management effectiveness. The reports were used in many decision-making areas as an objective, "hard numbers" tool.

Finally, facility planning was handled with concern not only for smooth work flow and easy equipment access but also for employees' comfort. In all decisions affecting workers, employee participation was encouraged and workers' suggestions were usually followed.

When productivity improvement efforts are integrated, team effort pays off handsomely. The Virginia Plan had a lower operating expense ratio than any other plan and has had annual productivity improvements of 3 to 5 percent for the past ten years.

DISCUSSION QUESTIONS

1. Case Figure 2-1 identifies the types of productivity measures used by Blue Cross and Blue Shield. Were these measures appropriate? How did Blue Cross and Blue Shield apply a quality measure to its standards development? (Chapter 15)

2. Why did Blue Cross and Blue Shield redesign workstations and enhance the professional environment? How did this help the company to accomplish its productivity goals? Relate your answers to the ergonomic principles discussed in Chapter 16. What results did Blue Cross and Blue Shield achieve? (Chapter 16)

3. Blue Cross and Blue Shield took a very integrated approach to productivity improvement. Could the company have achieved the same results without an integrated approach? How important do you think the role of employee participation was to the results achieved? (Chapters 1, 2, 17, 18)
4. What problems are inherent in assuming that the workstation redesign described in this case study was directly responsible for increased worker productivity? Could other factors also have been responsible? (Chapter 16)

INDIVIDUAL OR GROUP PROJECTS

1. Assume that you or your group are responsible for facilities management at Blue Cross and Blue Shield. Research modular office furniture and recommend a workstation configuration. How would you involve employees, and what types of information would you expect to obtain from them? How would it help you make your final selection? Explain the rationale for your recommendation and relate it to the ergonomic principles discussed in Chapter 16. (Chapter 16)
2. Blue Cross and Blue Shield increased its use of microfilm and computer-assisted retrieval (CAR). Use vendor equipment brochures and trade magazines or visit a trade show to investigate various types of microfilm and CAR equipment that might be appropriate for Blue Cross Blue Shield. Select the three systems that you (or your team) think would best meet Blue Cross's needs. What information would you need to make a final recommendation? Write a recommendation justifying the three alternatives you have selected for further investigation and your plan for arriving at a final recommendation. (Chapters 6, 14)

ROLE PLAY

1. Play the role of a systems analyst who has been asked by the manager of mailroom operations to investigate OCR zip sort machines and other sorting equipment. Make a management presentation to justify this investigation based on the results of improvements that have been implemented previously. Use Case Figure 2-3 for background information. (Chapters 5, 14)

WRITING/LIBRARY RESEARCH

1. Job satisfaction theories are based on the assumption that workers' needs affect their performance. Summarize the classic job satisfaction theories developed by A. Maslow and F. Hertzberg. Follow each summary with a paragraph explaining how Blue Cross and Blue Shield applied the theory. (Chapters 16, 17)

First Bank of Edina: Developing People, Services, and the Work Environment

CASE **3**

THE ORGANIZATION

The United States financial industry is undergoing unprecedented change as a result of current and pending deregulation. Bank managements are confronted with new and unique issues relating to competition, profitability, and productivity. As government constraints are eased and altered, greater attention has been directed at reducing the cost of doing business, improving services, and providing the desired appeal to the customer.

Prominent within the industry is the First Bank System, Inc., headquartered in Minneapolis-St. Paul. The system is comprised of 92 banks and trust companies with 152 offices in Minnesota, North Dakota, South Dakota, Montana, and Wisconsin. The corporation is the eighteenth-largest banking organization in the country with approximately $15 billion in assets and over 10,000 employees.

Productivity is not a new issue within the First Bank System. The corporation has a considerable history of operations analysis that provides a foundation for improvement and change, and it is intent on addressing five critical success factors, including "productive use of resources."

One noteworthy example of the corporation's efforts to ensure productive use of resources is the First Bank of Edina, a subsidiary bank located in a Minneapolis suburb. The First Bank of Edina is one of fifteen banks comprising the Twin Cities Bank Group and maintains approximately $160,000,000 in assets.

THE SITUATION

In the late 1970s, conditions within the bank were unacceptable to management. Morale was low, employee turnover was high, many employees lacked sufficient training and experience, and records and document counts were out of balance and behind schedule.

New leadership within the First Bank of Edina undertook three major approaches to improve the overall operation. Almost concurrently, several similar and potentially redundant functions were combined and restructured, inexperienced employees were cross-trained, and the physical facility was made more comfortable and attractive.

The results of the initial and ongoing changes were significant. Turnover was drastically reduced, and staffing levels decreased via attrition. The bank's management learned several valuable lessons about the process of change, the value of training and operations analysis, and employee motivation.

Management of the First Bank of Edina developed a conscious recognition of the need for improvement during 1979. Over an extended period of time, several unacceptable conditions had resulted in high staff turnover, high personnel costs, low morale, and some fundamental weakness in the development and delivery of services. Moreover, an employee survey confirmed the management's concerns about problems with temperature and humidity control as well as machinery. The clientele was provided with more than adequate service, but internal operations were suffering from a lack of control and increasing costs.

One source of difficulty was the lack of experience and training among many employees in the operations and administrative areas of the bank. Standard practice had allowed employees to train one another; over time, bad habits and incomplete information resulted. Also, supervisors were subsequently less influential in directing and guiding the day-to-day work; their knowledge of employee skill and motivation was somewhat lacking. Consequently, the staff was often unable to keep up with a flow of approximately 100 million items per day, and balance control problems emerged in savings, checking, loan, and correspondent bank accounts. Training needs became even more apparent as new products were introduced by the First Bank System and as the bank attempted to restructure.

A second source of problems appeared to be the bank's long-standing organization and structure. Work flow and item processing involved procedures and steps that, under close scrutiny, appeared to be unnecessary or repetitive. Moreover, across separate units, individual employees conducted similar duties, and staffing was subsequently inflated to ensure adequate support. Weaknesses in structure and organization appeared in several functions, including accounting, proofing, credit and commercial loans, and retail sales.

The office environment was a third source of problems. Although the customer service area was adequately appointed, the "back room" operations area suffered from uncomfortable and less than professional conditions. Temperature and humidity were not easily controlled; employees were frequently cold in the winter and hot in the summer. Furthermore, a large open "bullpen" arrangement of facilities allowed for little privacy and caused frequent distractions. In general, the atmosphere contributed to the perception that the bank operations area was an undesirable, "dead end" place to work.

THE PRODUCTIVITY IMPROVEMENT EFFORT

A conscious recognition and delineation of these three problem areas allowed new leadership of the First Bank of Edina to seek solutions. The recently appointed president and the management team took steps to resolve the three problems almost concurrently. Most of the developments were conducted in the Operations Department under the guidance of a new vice-president and cashier, but additional changes emerged in the retail area and in a small remote facility.

The problems due to inexperience and insufficient training were attacked in several ways:

1. Corporate Human Resources was asked to provide job-related training for various positions, specifically tellers and lenders.
2. Supervisors were encouraged to spend less time in their functional activities and more time in organizing and training the employees they supervised. Whereas in the past fellow employees had trained "new hires," the supervisors were now responsible for training.
3. In various work groups, cross-training enabled employees to back up each other during absenteeism or peak work periods and to check each other's work.
4. Job rotation for lenders provided a broader job exposure and more challenging assignments.

Organizational and structural problems were also addressed in several ways. Procedures for processing items were reviewed and abbreviated whenever appropriate, thereby reducing the number of steps required for proofing items. At the same time, facsimile machines enabled timely, efficient document flow within the building and both to and from the remote facility.

Whereas similar duties were previously performed by different persons or groups, the structure was changed to combine the groups and increase their responsibilities. Restructuring occurred in the accounting area. Direct and indirect sales groups were combined, as were the credit and commercial loan functions.

As a result of the structural and organizational changes, several job descriptions were rewritten and salary compensation for many employees was reconsidered. The review and analysis even led to a new position at the remote facility; typing of loan applications was identified as a separate job that would enable applications to be handled more expediently and the writers' work to be upgraded.

Finally, the changes provided an opportunity to establish reasonable measures of performance in the document-proofing area. In areas where heavy volumes of data required excessive overtime, management had few standards to determine staffing levels. The new standards indicated that two shifts of work were needed for proofing. As greater experience was achieved, employees were allowed to follow "flex time" schedules, and two shifts were no longer needed.

Problems resulting from the office environment were handled in a straightforward fashion. The bookkeeping function was moved to new quarters, thereby reducing some of the crowding, and the available space was refurbished. New carpeting, contemporary office furniture, and improved air-quality control provided a more comfortable and professional environment.

The new workstations were comprised of modular units with partitions that enhanced employee privacy and reduced noise and distractions. As the physical conditions improved, a greater interest in a professional appearance of the operations staff surfaced, and a dress code was established for all employees of the bank.

The First Bank of Edina relied on the corporate staffs for assistance in some areas of training and operations analysis. Most developments, however, were conducted by the bank's management and employees. Consequently, both management and employees understood the nature of the changes and continued to pursue new productivity improvements. Moreover, they now had "ownership" over the changes and took pride in the results.

RESULTS OF THE EFFORT

The results of these various developments ranged across several "hard" and "soft" issues and reflected improvements in both productivity and the quality of work life.

The most immediate results were in employee turnover and document processing. Within a few months of the training and environmental changes, turnover was reduced by as much as 60 percent. Over the three-year period from early 1979 to late 1982, turnover was further cut by approximately 75 percent. Similarly, the proofing of receipts was expedited, and the time required for daily balances was significantly reduced. In comparison to previous performance levels, proofing time was cut by approximately 50 percent.

The structural and organizational changes allowed work to be accomplished by fewer personnel. Except for three part-time employees, all reductions in staff were accomplished through attrition. By the second quarter of 1983, total staff had been reduced from 146 to 126. The ability to handle an increased work load with fewer employees was clearly displayed in the bank's efficiency rating. An independent bank staffing analysis revealed that overall efficiency improved from 77.8 percent in May 1980 to 93 percent in November 1982. In other words, for the amount of activity conducted across a variety of services, the bank enjoyed significant gains toward recommended staffing levels. Furthermore, the staffing levels were based on averages of several hundred banks and did not necessarily reflect a particular concern for service quality as expressed by the bank's management.

Although quality of work life is somewhat elusive and difficult to measure, it appears to have been both directly and indirectly enhanced. The reduction in turnover appeared to result from a more comfortable and professional work atmosphere as well as employees' sense of accomplishment and understanding their jobs. In the past, many employees had quit their jobs out of frustration, but employees now elected to stay with the bank. The changes also resulted in opportunities for upward mobility and new career paths. The younger staff members were more inclined to develop a long-term commitment. In general, morale appeared to improve considerably.

CONCLUSIONS

The two-year time frame and multiple developments provided several lessons and observations for the bank's management and employees. In retrospect, they referred to the following seven points:

1. In a changing dynamic environment, particularly with high turnover, there is no substitute for training. The introduction of new products, competition from aggressive area banks, and new employees with limited experience created conditions in which internal operations were slipping and the quality of service was potentially threatened. There may be other means of acquiring competent, satisfied employees, but job-related training and cross-training proved to be the most expedient means to accommodate the First Bank of Edina's unique restructuring and reorganization.

2. Redesign of structure and organization was a key to avoiding unchecked increases in employment costs. The proofing function of the bank experienced significant growth in the number of items processed; previously, the typical response would have been to hire more people as the staff failed to keep up with the work load.

3. Reconsideration of work methods and staff availability were necessary if major improvements were to occur. Similarly, reducing compartmentalization and combining the sales, loan, and accounting groups enabled staff members to cover for one another and to respond more effectively to periodic fluctuations in work load.

4. Patience was required to implement improvements effectively. Perhaps without recognizing the magnitude of the undertaking, management set forth on an ambitious effort to improve the internal operations. Several concurrent changes were mounted; even over the course of two years, resources to implement the changes were stretched thin, and few internal staff members were experienced with developments ranging from motion-time measurement (MTM) to furniture systems design.

5. Perhaps more than was anticipated, providing for employees' personal comfort and a professional atmosphere contributed significantly to employee morale and tenure. Sources of discomfort were clearly apparent and required correction, but the value gained from not only physically comfortable surroundings but tasteful, professional furnishings appeared to be even more important. Even in entry-level positions where most banks hire inexperienced, lower-paid workers, the turnover rate was noticeably checked; less time was spent in processing persons in and out of the bank's staff.

6. Most employees will support the improvements to the extent that their individual efforts are recognized. The developments were not necessarily welcomed by all employees, however. Several persons with long tenure in the bank had difficulty in changing; there was some reluctance to step beyond the security of a familiar job description. Management observed early in the course of the developments that the staff needed advance notice of the changes and periodic feedback as the developments progressed. Communication was also extended to include financial information, such as the bank's earnings.

7. Finally, properly developed and managed standards of job performance were critical for determining staffing levels and setting expectations. The bank was successful in developing performance standards for the more routine areas, and the data enabled projections for future fluctuations in work load. Managers were challenged to use the data in a constructive manner with the employees and to prevent the standards from being too closely tied to incentives.

The First Bank of Edina addressed several difficult problems and experienced the challenge of changing its employees' job designs, organizational structure, and physical work environment. Over the course of more than two years, numerous developments required corporate assistance, management leadership, and employee support and input.

The changes did not always transpire easily, and the results were not fully realized. However, significant improvements did occur. Turnover was drastically reduced, processing time was decreased, overall efficiency was improved impressively, morale appeared to improve, and the quality of customer service was maintained if not enhanced. Reflecting on the development of the effort, a vice-president of the bank observed, "We've lowered turnover, we've established good controls, and we have been able to adapt to change."

DISCUSSION QUESTIONS

1. Assume you are responsible for rewriting job descriptions. How would you begin? How would you collect information? How much time would you expect to need to complete the project? (Chapter 17)

2. This case presents a rather rosy picture of a structured change effort. Is this depiction of the change process realistic? Explain your answer and present examples from your own experience or readings. (Chapter 18)

3. Assume it is the year 2040 and that the life span of the average American is 110. What implications does this have for the training strategies of the First Bank of Edina and other organizations? (Chapter 24)

GROUP ACTIVITIES

1. Break into groups of three or four people. Present your breakdown and analysis of this case to others. Using a T-chart, identify the problems and the solutions developed by the First Bank of Edina. The beginning of a sample T-chart is shown below:

Problem	Solution
1. Overlapping job duties	1. Organizational structure changed to combine work groups

When the T-chart is completed, consider the following issues: Did the First Bank of Edina address all the problems? Do you agree with its solutions? (Chapters 16, 17, 18, 24)

2. Break into groups of three. Develop a list of as many options or courses of action as you can to solve the problem of high staff turnover. Then list the advantages and disadvantages of each option. (Chapter 24)

3. Break into groups of three. Develop a list of ten reasons or causes of a poor training program. Rank the importance of each cause and compare your group's responses with those of other groups. Are you in agreement? Brainstorm ways to prevent such problems. (Chapter 24)

WRITING ASSIGNMENT

1. Assume you are the Office Systems Manager for the First Bank of Edina and that you have been working for two weeks with the Facilities Manager to determine the office design requirements of secretarial workstations. Write a memo to the Facilities Manager summarizing your concerns about the safe and effective use of VDTs. (Chapter 16)

Digital Equipment Corp.: Office Automation and Productivity Improvement

CASE **4**

THE ORGANIZATION

Founded in 1957, today the Digital Equipment Corporation (DEC) is the second-largest manufacturer of interactive computers in the world. With 7,000 sites and 67,700 employees, it generates $3.9 billion in revenues annually.

Throughout the 1960s, DEC supplied "state-of-the art" computers to the scientific community. In the 1970s, it extended its product line to include the business market. During this latter time period, DEC's annual growth rate averaged over 35 percent. To support this rapid growth, DEC evolved into a matrix organization, with a management style reflecting a high degree of autonomy and individual responsibility.

Although office automation products and vendors have proliferated, often these systems have failed to achieve the expected gains in productivity. Recognizing the educational process required to implement these tools effectively, DEC designed its automated office systems to meet the following goals:

1. To develop an implementation method that would dramatically increase productivity.
2. To develop a perspective for expressing and measuring productivity that would improve efficiency within the context of effectiveness.
3. To support research and development for new products and marketing.

DIGITAL INFORMATION SERVICES: OFFICE AUTOMATION AND PRODUCTIVITY IMPROVEMENT

Digital Information Services (DIS) was chartered in 1978 to bring new information and communication technologies to DEC's office operations. This effort brought local office functions together into a central corporate function to provide consulting support to DEC business units. It was hoped that this consolidation would minimize error and duplication, facilitate integration, and increase the visibility and leverage of the office system function. The overall objective was to provide better support to users.

At its inception, DIS consisted of information system and telecommunication professionals. They saw their role as evaluating and implementing tools; they were mainly concerned with quantitative measures to describe the impact of this effort on the organization.

After eighteen months, human resource personnel from the Organization Development Department were added to DIS to work on "human factors." This resulted in a much broader view of the impacts and opportunities presented by technology, not only for work groups and corporations but also at a societal level. However, a significant gap in planning for these broader considerations was recognized.

As DIS evolved, so did its goals. From its original goal "to implement office automation through the introduction of modern office technology," it began working "to improve office effectiveness and job satisfaction, drawing on new technology as needed." Ultimately, it hoped "to achieve business and social goals through organizational and technological innovation." This shift in goals paralleled a growing market maturity. With informed consumers seeking specific answers to their own needs, organizational analysis and design became high priorities.

DEC Teams: Efficiency and Effectiveness

This shift of emphasis within DIS required an approach to productivity measurement that included qualitative as well as quantitative measures. Existing metrics were narrowly concerned with text output, filing time, and keystrokes per minute; more global measures were required.

One promising approach to productivity improvement within the context of improved effectiveness involved the establishment of user "teams," groups of managerial, professional, clerical, and administrative personnel who worked together to produce combined outputs. By examining outputs in the context of specific business functions, the teams supported corporate objectives; productivity was defined in terms of the functions' services. Rather than looking for incremental increases in efficiency in routine activities, substantial increases were sought by focusing on the extent to which people were doing the right thing and doing it well. This approach recognized a broad range of organizational impacts associated with new technology (see Case Figure 4-1).

CASE FIGURE 4-1. Organizational impacts of new technology.

1. Increase or decrease in employment.
2. Technical obsolescence or new career options.
3. Improved or worsened manager-employee relationships.
4. Redistribution of information; change in power structures.
5. Increased or decreased interdependence of organizational units.
6. Trends toward decentralization or centralization.
7. Constructive or destructive measurement systems.
8. Increased or decreased work schedule flexibility.
9. Increased or lessened social isolation.
10. Increased remoteness or closer touch with end result of labor.

Finally, it was recognized that prospective users needed to become more involved in the system design. To effect significant productivity improvement from the new technology, these prospective users were the people who could best match business, personal, and social needs to the available options.

Office Systems: Developing a Planning Methodology

The Office Systems Group (OSG) within DIS was responsible for the development of applications software, long-term planning of technical systems, and the development and implementation of what is called "office systems planning methodology." Their mission was to support the long-term objective of DIS "to achieve business and social goals by integrating organizational and technical innovation." Toward this end, a three-part strategy was developed in late 1981.

One strategy targeted improving the productivity of DEC line functions; a second sought to develop a set of situational measures that would be useful to line managers in assessing productivity improvement; a third freed these managers to use any automated system that was best suited to their needs. Productivity was the core of the strategy, whereas interactive systems and employee involvement were its features.

Traditional approaches are often based on product design and engineering models and often overlook human and organizational needs. The office systems team sought to design a system that would play a "consultant" role (helping clients to achieve their own goals) rather than an "expert" role (delivering finished products).

Office Systems Planning Methodology: Helping Work Groups Help Themselves

The Office Systems consulting team designed an office systems planning methodology to provide a way for work units to improve their productivity. Via organizational changes chosen by the work units themselves, it was intended to facilitate a work system's productivity improvement effort.

As described in Case Figure 4-2, the ten-step process yielded an action plan. To implement the process, a series of five workshops was designed. Called "The Productivity Improvement Series," it is described briefly in the following section and more specifically in Case Figures 4-3, 4-4, and 4-5.

When a work unit decided to purchase the series, it was requested to select a planning team to administer the ten steps. This "design" or "planning" team consisted of up to six persons from a "diagonal slice" of the work unit. A steering committee of senior managers associated with the work unit was then established. The committee was responsible for supporting the design team and approving proposals of the team and played a key role in diffusing the method to other work units.

CASE FIGURE 4-2. Office systems planning methodology.

Office Systems Planning Methodology

1. Answer questions:
   - Why are we changing?
   - What is the problem or opportunity?
   - How will we measure success?
2. Identify system boundaries:
   - What are the groups with which we are directly concerned?
3. Present system analysis:
   - Key charter demands.
   - Current work procedures.
   - People's job needs.
   - Major problem areas.
4. Determine future system model:
   - Determine critical success factors.
   - Given these, what are the key assumptions/demands?
   - Identify related key processes and information needs.
5. Identify work content needs:
   - Target description of new system.
   - Identify resources and constraints.
   - Identify technology.
6. Identify people's job success needs:
   - Identify resources and constraints.
7. Set and prioritize new system objectives:
   - Determine work content needs.
   - Determine job success needs.
8. Develop alternative strategies:
   - Organizational strategies.
   - Technological strategies.
9. Present proposal to management/steering committee:
   - Obtain approval/support.
   - Ensure that resources are committed.
10. Implementation and evaluation:
    - Develop action plan.
    - Agree on measurement criteria.

CASE FIGURE 4-3. The Productivity Improvement Series.

Productivity Improvement Series

1. Data Collection (Steps 1-2)

During this two-day seminar, the team begins defining the problems/opportunities for productivity improvement. The subject matter ranges from general to specific considerations such as the following:

- The environments interconnected with the work system affect its productivity.
- The actual purposes served by the work unit in comparison to its formal charter.
- Internal boundaries within the work unit and interdependencies across groups.
- What people seem to need to do their jobs better.

CASE FIGURE 4-3. (continued)

- Major, obvious problem areas.
- How to measure the effectiveness of the individuals and groups in the work unit.

In addition, the team obtains instruments, learns techniques, and begins to develop skills for collecting accurate and useful data about what is going on in the office. The team develops an action plan for collecting data from colleagues in the unit. In the time between seminars, a member of the Office Systems Consulting staff supports the data collection and assimilation effort by telephone, plus a day of on-site consulting.

2. Data Analysis (Step 3)
Using the data collected (from observation, interviews, and questionnaires), the team learns techniques for understanding the organizational dynamics that affect productivity. A model is presented for organizing the data (see Case Figure 4-4). This model illustrates the internal and external dynamics of the production process preventing a permanent state of equilibrium. Case Figure 4-5 illustrates the kinds and sources of data that are plugged into the model. After the workshop, the resulting "cognitive map" of the office is fed back to the originators of the data for discussion and revision. When this step is completed, the design team presents its findings to the Steering Committee to solicit comments and observations.

3. Future Systems Design (Steps 4-6)
In this session, the team learns to create a model of the future system based on the factors identified as critical to success. Team members learn to identify variances between their current system and where they would like to be. Included in the analysis are task considerations, as well as job constraints and resources in both the current and future work systems. The results of the team's efforts are again fed back to the Steering Committee and the office workers.

4. Technical/Organizational Alternatives (Steps 8-9)
This seminar focuses on the techniques and skills that enable the team to accomplish the following:
- Set productivity improvement objectives.
- Prioritize those objectives.
- Develop alternative strategies to meet organizational, technological, and social needs of the future system.

Overviews are provided on the range of options available for the redesign of the work system. After the workshop, the team may visit exemplary offices to get a better feel for the possibilities. Information gained flows into the stream of feedback that the team obtains from the work unit itself. After assessing alternatives, a design is selected that best fits social abilities and technological capabilities in light of the task requirements. It is then presented to the Steering Committee. The Steering Committee has the option of approving the design or sending the team back to the work unit with suggested design modifications. Once agreement is reached on the overall design of the new system, the team is prepared for the last workshop in the series.

5. Implementation and Evaluation (Step 10)
Based on their understanding of present circumstances and their ideas of how things will change with the new design, the teams develop an appropriate implementation plan. The workshop aims to develop skills to do this effectively and emphasizes the need for specific measurement criteria.

CASE FIGURE 4-4. Model used to organize data.

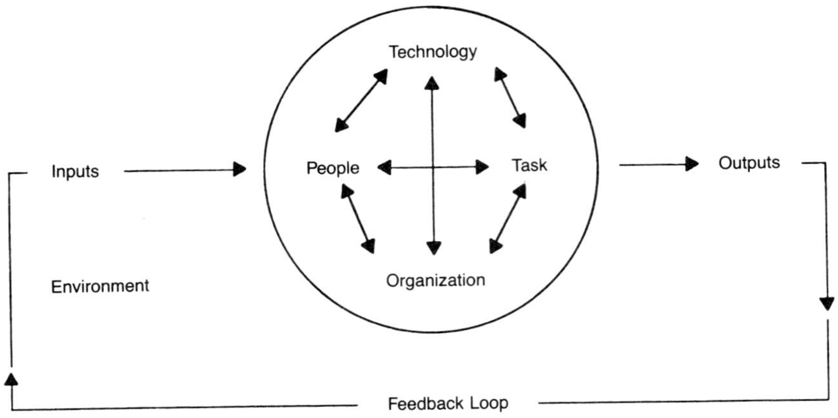

CASE FIGURE 4-5. Data overlayed on model.

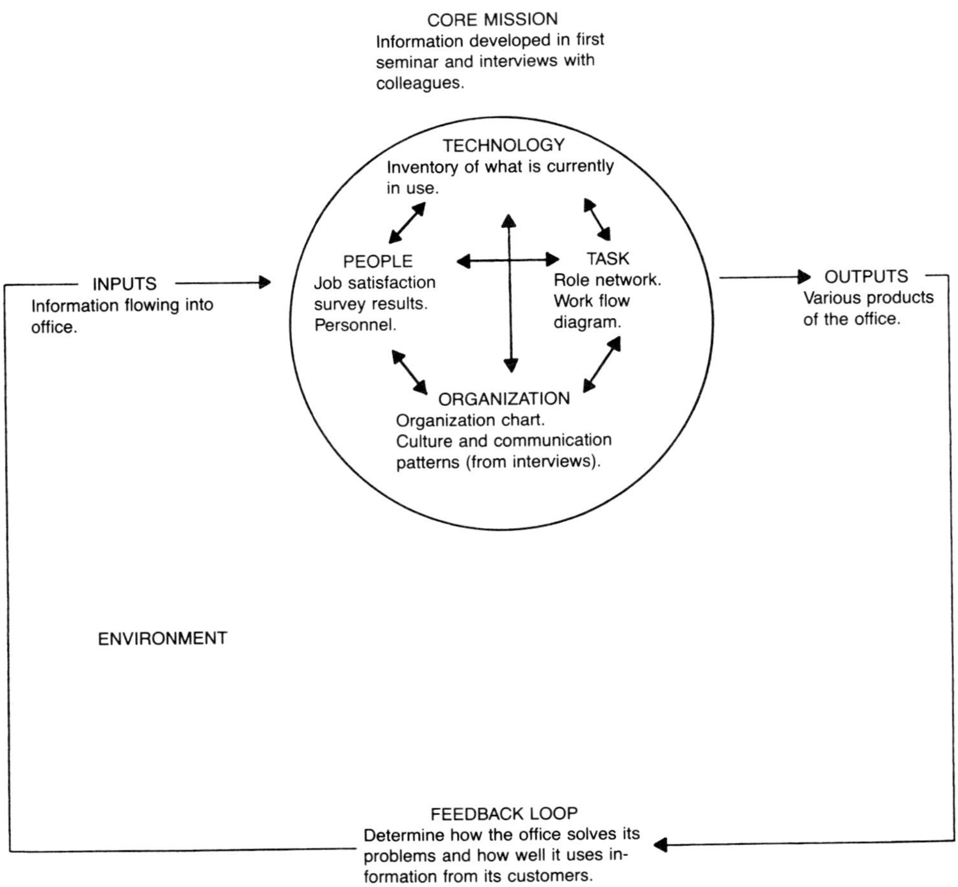

The Productivity Improvement Series: Tools and Techniques

The series of five workshops covered the tools and techniques required to manage office productivity efforts. It broke down the planning methodology into five general procedures: data collection, data analysis, future systems design, organizational and technological alternatives, and implementation and evaluation. Each workshop was a two-day program designed to help the work team implement the planning process step by step. A detailed outline of these steps appears in Case Figure 4-3.

A Pilot in Purchasing: Midstream

The Maynard Area Administrative Purchasing Department was selected as a pilot because of its proximity to Corporate Purchasing and its reputation as a healthy organization that was amenable to change. It supported 24 facilities and 11,000 people and purchased approximately $50 million worth of supplies annually for administrative support, building construction, and facilities renovation. The staff processed 30,000 outgoing documents a year (purchase orders, debit memos, shipping, and billing forms, etc.). The operations were supported by twenty terminals linked via modems to an off-site mainframe computer system and three word processing workstations.

Members of the design team were selected by management. Two people from Corporate Purchasing were chosen, one for his technical expertise and the other for his experience in group relations and organizational behavior. They were also expected to play a key role in diffusing the methodology to other purchasing departments.

Three more people were selected by the department manager: a line manager, a buyer, and a secretary. A steering committee was selected in the first workshop by determining who were the "key influencers" inside and outside the department. Five managers were identified: the Corporate Purchasing Manager, the department head, a line manager, a manager outside the department who was in charge of receiving and stocking supplies, and one within the Accounting Department.

Although the process is not complete, the design team is considering the following issues:

1. *Job satisfaction.* A survey was taken to assess employee attitudes toward their work; many believed they were able to do more. This called attention to the need to examine the relationship between peoples' abilities and their responsibilities, as well as the amount of discretion each had to complete his or her work.

2. *Work systems.* An analysis of work boundaries and key players in the external environment revealed that any given transaction had implications beyond the immediate exchange. Therefore, any reorganization within the Purchasing Department would affect working relationships with those outside, which in turn would affect internal productivity. Thus incentives for suppliers to maintain quality and support for requisitioners in planning to reduce the number of purchase orders to be processed were likely outcomes (see Case Figure 4-6).

3. *The buyer's role.* One implication of the open system analysis was the role that buyers could play in improving supplier performance. Ways to shift buyers from routine transaction processing to more proactive work, such as developing greater product expertise, eliminating back orders, and identifying goods related to research and development tax credits, were fully investigated.

4. *Measurement.* Prior to the design effort, the management asked department employees what measures of their productivity they considered appropriate. A task force of employees who were not on the design team considered several measurement areas, including quality of procurement, prices, delivery time, and bottom-line impact.

5. *Technological change.* People in the Purchasing Department began using computer-based tools. Several changes in, and additions to, the tools were considered. These included a minicomputer-based system to increase capability while decreasing response time and a more advanced telephone system.

6. Although the department adapted a modified open-office plan, the new design of the organization required further rearrangements. Workstations with ergonomically designed systems furniture were considered; these systems served as prototypes for field testing.

CASE FIGURE 4-6. Role network in a given transaction.

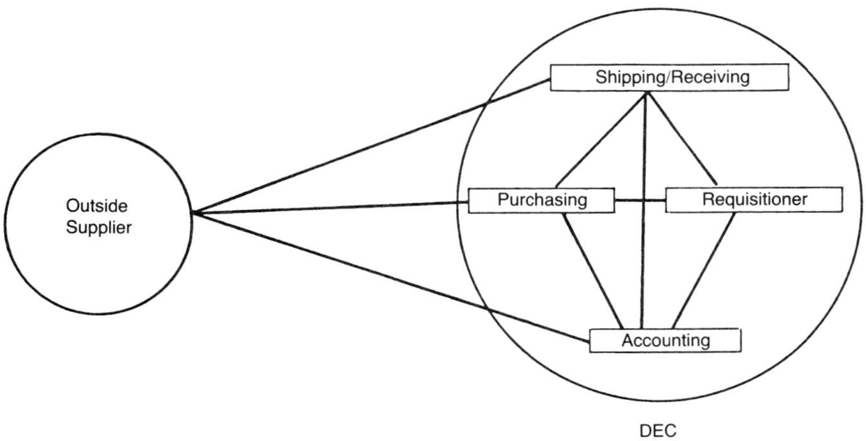

IMPACT AND RESULTS OF THE REDESIGN EFFORT

Within a few months, what started as an effort of six people became of active interest to nearly everyone within the Purchasing Department. There was satisfaction with the *process,* although the outcomes were yet to be fully realized. Specific results achieved included the following:

1. Monthly "rap sessions" between the department manager and groups of buyers and secretaries supplied the management with first-hand perspectives. These sessions also provided everyone else a first-hand glimpse of what upper management perceived to be happening and/or would have liked to see happen.
2. Individuals' roles were redefined to respond to new business needs.
3. A secretary assumed some purchasing duties, thereby enabling buyers to leverage their skills while introducing more variety into the secretary's work. Other secretaries reported that they found the workplace more interesting and, recognizing the importance of the pilot, they provided input into the process.
4. Knowing that it had insufficient internal resources, the team created "task groups," which enthusiastically addressed contingencies of the planning process.
5. Portable message units and a portable terminal were field-tested by the organization.
6. A more effective telephone system using new technology was purchased and installed.
7. A Digital Vax 11-780 computer was also installed. A high-power, interactive purchasing system was developed for the Purchasing Department.
8. Several operating procedures were modified to improve work flow and reduce the total cost of operations.
9. Systems were developed to handle high-volume/low-dollar procurements more effectively with minimal buyer involvement.
10. A career path planning program was implemented by department personnel.
11. Progress was made in defining appropriate metrics to measure performance/productivity in the department.

Eventually, redesign of the social and technical systems within the Purchasing Department reduced costs at least 20 percent and increased employee satisfaction. Overall, there was a real sense in the Purchasing Department that productivity improvement and its business had become inseparable.

CONCLUSIONS

DEC viewed the effective implementation of office automation systems as more complex than is commonly understood. DEC's innovative approach—internal groups seeking their own productivity improvement and job satisfaction by work redesign, supported by appropriate technology—was designed to enable users to inform themselves about the new technology and its potential. Closing the existing information gap between vendors and users and harnessing the coherent energy within organizations designing their own work systems was DEC's focus in this productivity improvement effort—turning what was known into what could be.

DISCUSSION QUESTIONS

1. Case Figures 4-1 and 4-2 show how DEC used the systems approach in analyzing data from its needs analysis. What is the difference between *ad hoc* problem solving and systematic problem solving? Think through this model; apply it to the decisions that must be made by your course instructor in designing a class syllabus. (Chapters 20-22)

2. What is meant by a system's *environment?* How is it determined? Using the business section of your local newspaper, list at least ten events that could be expected to have an impact on a manufacturer of office technologies, such as DEC. (Chapter 20)

ROLE PLAYS

1. Play the role of an evaluator of the strategies that DEC used in its Maynard pilot study. Use the following form to complete your evaluation. (Chapter 22)

Strategy	Was it effective?	What motivator was used?	Was it effective?

2. A key to the effectiveness of the DEC teams was that they were able to work well together to solve mutual problems. Play the role of a group of DEC trainees in a team-building class. Your group task is to design a basket using only ten strips of paper. You will have five minutes to complete this exercise.
   a. What did you learn about leadership?
   b. If your group had been composed of people at various organizational levels (e.g., managers, professionals, and clerical workers) would leadership have been affected? Would the resulting basket have been different? (Chapters 17, 18)

WRITING ASSIGNMENT

1. Write a one-page mission statement for the Office Systems Consulting Team. (Chapter 19)

Memorial Hospital System: An Integrated Approach to Improving Productivity

CASE **5**

THE ORGANIZATION

Memorial Hospital in Houston is part of the Memorial Hospital System, which consists of six facilities in Texas. Employing 1,883 people (47 exempt), Memorial Hospital admitted 26,882 patients in fiscal year 1982 (July 1, 1981, to June 30, 1982). It processed 33,462 emergency visits during the same period.

PRODUCTIVITY IMPROVEMENT EFFORT

The productivity improvement effort of Memorial Hospital involved the clerical function of the Radiology Department. The program had the following objectives:

- To provide services in a more timely manner.
- To improve the department's image, both internally among functional areas and externally with other departments.
- To reduce high employee turnover, overtime, and internal conflict.

To accomplish these objectives, two separate but complementary efforts were undertaken: new technology was installed, and performance management training was implemented. The new technology was a word processing/record management system to improve information processing capacity within the department. Approving the funds requested for the equipment, top management stipulated that the department investigate various computer systems.

After consulting with the data processing staff, the office systems analyst and the department supervisor selected a system that was compatible with the hospital's mainframe computer while meeting both department and hospital needs. Additional features of the system included its capacity for storing information and its efficient access.

Along with the implementation of the new system, the entire hospital management staff received management development training. Contracting with an external agency, the top management initiated a performance training program with the primary objective of teaching personnel how to effect very specific performance changes within their departments.

Other training objectives were to provide all management personnel with a common base of knowledge and experience for developing projects and to foster a common language to improve project planning and information sharing.

Implementation began in November 1981. All 200 supervisory staff members at all levels of management were to receive the training by November 1982.

Management Development Training

Each manager or supervisor received 16 hours of training that was provided four hours each day for four consecutive days. The training program taught them to utilize performance data and to provide feedback and positive reinforcement. It focused on specific rather than general behavior (i.e., not "reduce late charges," but, more specifically, "reduce late charges from 3 to 0 per day by July 1").

Two of the staff received special training to assist managers and supervisors with projects. These "performance managers" were responsible for reinforcing management improvements, listening to ideas, providing feedback, and monitoring the accountability structure. The performance managers attended semiannual update meetings sponsored by the consulting firm that developed the program.

The active involvement and support of top management were prerequisites to the success of the training program. Consequently, managers participated in both performance training and accountability activities.

The accountability structure was a series of activities during which ideas and the successes and failures of the management project were shared. The first accountability meeting was held one week after any given group had concluded its performance management training. At this meeting, managers presented their initial project plans, which addressed specific, measurable performance changes. Opportunities to give and receive feedback and positive reinforcement were provided at this and subsequent monthly meetings with all vice-presidents and department heads.

Each level of supervisory personnel reported performance management progress. Upon successful completion of a project, managers were awarded performance management diplomas. A manager at the vice-president level was not eligible for a diploma until 100 percent of his or her subordinates had received diplomas.

Another element of the performance management reward/reinforcement system was the "Certificate of Achievement" that was awarded to managers who attained three different department performance goals (three completed projects).

Radiology Department Clerical Functions

The Radiology Department of Memorial Hospital employed eleven people, including one supervisor, and performed three separate but interrelated functions:

1. The *reception* function entered patient information (name, doctor, birthdate, etc.) into the system to obtain X-ray numbers and charge control numbers; it also scheduled patient X-ray procedures, submitted radiology charges, provided patient X-ray numbers on request to staff, and sorted physicians' mail. The reception function employed one part-time and three full-time employees.
2. The *transcription* function transcribed patient and diagnostic X-ray information, which was placed on the patient's permanent medical record. It employed three full-time employees.
3. The *film file* function retrieved, forwarded, and stored patient X-rays and X-ray reports. It also attached transcribed reports to X-ray film jackets and distributed transcribed X-ray reports. The film file function employed three full-time employees.

The reception, transcription, and film file areas were interdependent. Film file interfaced with reception for initial references to assigned X-ray numbers. Transcription relied upon film file staff to retrieve, forward, and store the X-ray reports they transcribed, and so forth.

Before the New Technology

Before the computerized records management system was installed, the reception personnel processed patient information by typewriter onto cards and then placed the cards in coded upright files. Each request for an X-ray number required a manual search through the files. This was a very time-consuming process because the area received several hundred calls a day.

Employees also transcribed physicians' reports via the typewriter at the rate of approximately 36–38 reports per person daily. An extensive backlog existed, and often reports were not processed in time for surgery or for the scheduling of diagnostic study. This time lag in report processing had a negative impact on both physicians and patients.

In the film file area, employees spent great amounts of time responding to as many as 100 calls a day from patients, physicians, and nurses regarding missing or late reports. The film file staff also spent considerable time waiting for the reception staff to provide the X-ray numbers to check the files and respond to these requests.

The entire department was characterized by frustration and frequent complaints due to the backlog of work. This frustration resulted in low morale, high turnover, excessive absenteeism, and internal conflict.

The Turning Point

The situation began to change when a new Radiology Department supervisor was named. The new supervisor participated in the performance management training and became involved in the planning process for the new technology. Utilizing the new techniques, the supervisor was able to effect performance changes soon after the new word processing/records management system was installed. Once the system was installed and employees were trained to use it, all elements of the effort seemed to coalesce.

When the supervisor felt the employees were comfortable with the new technology, she implemented performance management projects with three distinct goals:

1. *Reception:* Using records management, eliminate late charges entirely.
2. *Transcription:* Using word processing, finalize X-ray reports no later than 6:00 p.m.
3. *Film file:* Deliver all reports to patient floors by 6:30 p.m. daily.

After collecting baseline data for each performance behavior to be changed, realistic goals were established. Data and corresponding goals were displayed on the walls in each area. Individual progress was tracked and updated on the graphs daily, providing visual feedback on each employee's performance.

Using a nonfinancial reward structure, the supervisor provided verbal reinforcement for any improved performance, which was later followed by time off, a double lunch period, and a complimentary memo placed in the personnel file for goals achieved (see Case Figure 5-1). A weekly department meeting called "Suggestion Day" provided employees with opportunities to suggest new projects and to give and receive feedback. These group discussions sustained an evolving team spirit.

Several months into the productivity improvement effort, the department supervisor received approval from the Director of Radiology to include physicians in the transcription project. The physicians, department supervisor, and transcriptionists jointly established goals for the physician function.

CASE FIGURE 5-1. A complimentary memo for goals achieved.

MEMORANDUM

TO: Jane Roberts

FROM: Word Processing Office Manager
Radiology Coordinator

This memorandum is to thank you as Employee of the Month for doing such a fantastic job and helping your Radiology Department look so good.

We really appreciate your effort and concern and hope to keep you around so that your "A, #1 performance" can be a good example for other coworkers to follow.

Nice to have you on our team!

The physicians agreed to track the quality of their dictation, to become aware of the pace and clarity of their dictation, and to note the volume of their voices when giving dictation. Their performance was charted and displayed.

The radiologists are no longer participating in the activity, but they did participate actively for several months, raising their awareness of a significant issue: modifying certain elements of their dictation style facilitated the timely transcription of X-ray reports.

RESULTS OF THE EFFORT

The dovetailing of computerized record management/word processing and performance management produced the following substantial improvements:

1. The number of transcribed radiology reports increased from a baseline of 70 per month per typist to between 95 and 121 per month per typist.
2. The average number of overtime hours decreased from 25.12 to 4.50 hours per pay period.
3. Late charges were reduced from an average of 15 per month (amounting to over $2,000) to 0 during the months of June through August.
4. The distribution of X-ray reports to patient floors became more time-effective, improving from a 7:00 p.m. distribution baseline to 5:50 p.m. by the month of July.

These productivity improvements are delineated more fully in Case Figure 5-2.

Problems

All employees in the Radiology Department were somewhat apprehensive about using the automated system. Each attended a 90-minute training session that explained and demonstrated the new system. They also practiced using the system during the session and were encouraged to continue practicing on their own until they felt proficient.

Hoping to avoid additional costly turnover, the department supervisor ensured that her staff understood the upcoming changes, learned to use the hardware, and had ample time to make the transition. Despite the supervisor's efforts, however, one transcriptionist who was normally a high performer experienced difficulty adjusting to the new system. Resisting the change, she continued to use her typewriter. Her performance lagged behind the others, keeping the group from meeting its daily production goals. Resulting peer pressure added to her mounting frustration.

Seeing a need to force the issue, the supervisor removed the employee's typewriter, setting up a "join the effort or leave the group" option. Not wishing to lose a valuable employee, but needing to maintain the group's enthusiasm over improved performance, the supervisor communicated this final option to the employee as positively as possible.

PRODUCTIVITY IMPROVEMENTS

1. **Increase in number of radiology reports transcribed**
   Baseline: Average of 70 radiology reports transcribed per typist.
   Improvements: Average number of reports per typist per month:

Month	**Typist 1**	**Typist 2**	**Typist 3**	**Typist 3A**
May	80	100	78	—
June	93	95	80	—
July	95	81	87	—
August	121	—	96	95

Note: Typist 2 terminated and was replaced in August by Typist 3A.

2. **Reduction in overtime hours**
   Baseline: For the first eight pay periods in the calendar year (January 9, 1982, to May 1, 1982), the transcription area averaged 25.12 overtime hours per pay period.
   Improvements: For the last six pay periods (May 15, 1982, to July 24, 1982), the transcription area averaged 4.50 overtime hours per pay period.

3. **Reduction in late charges**
   Baseline: Average of 15 late charges per month, amounting to $2,183.
   Improvements: Number of late charges per month:

Month	**No. of Late Charges**	**Amount**	**Month**	**No. of Late Charges**	**Amount**
February	21	$ 1,249.95	May	1	$36.00
March	20	550.60	June	0	—
April	192	10,104.20	July	0	—
			August	0	—

4. **Radiology reports to be distributed to patient floors by 6:30 p.m. daily**
   Baseline: Reports distributed after 7:00 p.m. or the next day.
   Improvements: Average distribution time of reports:

Month	**Average time distributed**
May	6:15 p.m.
June	6:10 p.m.
July	5:50 p.m.

CASE FIGURE 5-2. Results of the productivity improvement effort.

With more encouragement and support from the group and the supervisor, the employee eventually overcame her problem and became a competent performer. Despite initial apprehension, all employees soon came to greatly appreciate the new system.

Another problem related to the new technology that was not so easily overcome surfaced early in the productivity improvement effort. Although the new system was selected for its compatability with the hospital's mainframe computer and its capacity for processing and storing information, the hospital and radiology managements were unable to obtain adequate instruction on using the new system from the vendor.

The vendor's representative was relatively inexperienced, and the hardware itself was new to the vendor's product line. Although the department was able to train employees to implement basic transactions, the new system was not being utilized to its full potential.

In addition, reception employees had the time-consuming task of transferring patient information to the new system from file cards dating back to 1977 admissions; updating the records management system delayed submitting of current patient data, thus causing a backlog.

Film file employees also experienced problems with the new system because of "downtime." During downtime, film file staff could call reception staff for X-ray numbers, but the reception staff could not access that information on the terminal and therefore had to revert to the computer printouts kept in coded upright files. Thus downtime not only reinstated the former time-lag problem but also caused a new backlog of data awaiting entry into the system.

The transcription area also had problems with the new equipment. Due to performance competition within the Radiology Department (caused in part by the graphic display of performance standards), strong individual competition surfaced. With production rates substantially increased, a shortage in available work sometimes appeared. Some transcriptionists began to stockpile X-ray tapes in order to maintain their individual performance levels. One transcriptionist even collected untranscribed tapes for weeks, causing physicians and nurses to complain about missing reports they remembered taping! The transcriptionist eventually resigned. The supervisor was able to use this incident to unite the group. Employees now work to reach group goals rather than individual goals.

FUTURE PLANS

With the success of this productivity improvement effort, the Radiology Department hopes to expand its effort in the following ways:

1. A CRT terminal will be added to the film file room so that employees in this area will not need to phone reception to obtain X-ray numbers.

2. The system will eventually be programmed with identical patient and X-ray numbers, thus eliminating the need for a separate entry.

3. Remote printing of transcribed radiology reports will be available on patient floors.

4. Interface between the mainframe and word processors will provide greater information sharing and immediate access to information.

Encouraged by the efficiency and effectiveness gains of the Radiology Department, the Memorial Hospital management plans to investigate further productivity improvement opportunities within the hospital.

CONCLUSIONS

The Radiology Department enhanced its chances for success by taking an integrated approach to productivity improvement. Department management attributed the directly measurable improvements to a combination of human resource and technological factors. In all probability, the installation of word processing and record management alone would not have increased productivity within the troubled Radiology Department. The addition of computer hardware and software does not automatically ensure productivity improvement. Such technology must be coupled with attention to the "human factor" to effect sustained improvement.

DISCUSSION QUESTIONS

1. What steps might have been taken prior to the installation of the new hardware to ensure appropriate, timely vendor training? (Chapter 24)
2. Discuss alternative technologies available on the market today for performing data entry and media conversions. (Chapters 5, 6)
3. Now that word processing and information management technologies have been integrated, what do you think should be the next step of technology integration for this hospital?
4. In view of the problems that the Memorial Hospital System experienced with vendor support, discuss the importance of good vendor support for office systems. How can a systems analyst help to avoid the kinds of problems encountered by Memorial Hospital? (Chapters 20–24)

ROLE PLAY

1. Assume you are the Radiology Department supervisor. You have called the "reluctant transcriptionist" described in this case into your office. Role play a conversation in which you explain the transcriptionist's need to learn to use the new system.

INDIVIDUAL OR GROUP PROJECTS

1. Conduct a force field analysis. Social psychologist Kurt Lewin described problems as "a sea of forces in motion." Forces may be positive or negative, but at any one time the forces produce a situation of stability. Using a force field analysis model, diagram the "before the new technology" situation by adding items to the following diagram. (Chapter 18)

Driving Forces	Restraining Forces
• Backlog of physicians' reports. • High employee turnover.	• No one person responsible for records management. • Typewriter used for transcription.

2. To change the status of a problem, the forces must be diagnosed and changed. Give examples from this case in which items you listed in Project 1 above were addressed.

3. Based on the facts in this case, propose word processing and records management systems that would meet the needs of the Memorial Hospital Radiology Department. Give a detailed description of the hardware and software, including prices of recommended equipment. Identify the features that are most important to this application and explain why you are recommending your choice over other alternatives. Use vendor product publications, software and hardware resource manuals, and trade journals or visit a product trade show or specific vendors to obtain information. (Chapters 4, 13, 14, 17)

4. Based on the facts in this case, develop a detailed implementation and training plan. Include a specific, detailed listing of tasks, responsibilities, and starting and completion dates. Make up the details needed and briefly explain these assumptions in the introductory paragraphs of the report. Use the format illustrated below. (Chapters 22–24)

Task	Person Responsible	Start Date	Complete Date

WRITING ASSIGNMENT

1. Based on the data in Case Figure 5-2, prepare a report for the top management of the Memorial Hospital System to justify acquisition of the new technologies. (Chapter 15)

Polaroid Corporation: Implementing Office Automation

CASE 6

INTRODUCTION

The Polaroid Corporation became informally involved in office automation in 1978 with the introduction of the company's first word processing system. Since that time, formal methodologies and groups have been established as the capabilities of new office technologies have increased. An Office Technology Council and various user groups were created to monitor and guide this proliferation. A needs analysis methodology was developed to justify requests for purchases of new technology. A post-audit procedure was created to assess the benefits actually gained after the technology was in place. Polaroid's sense of the benefits of office automation and its perception of the effort's future direction also changed.

An Early Application of Word Processing

The corporate culture at Polaroid was a decisive factor in shaping its office automation efforts and policy. Autonomous initiatives by individuals and business units were highly valued. When the Materials Laboratory decided to acquire the company's first word processing system in 1977, there was no central authority to appeal to for permission or assistance.

The application that justified purchase of the system was the typing of materials specifications. Much of this work was being done by outside agencies and support groups within Polaroid outside the laboratory. The lab expected the system to be mainly an electronic typewriter that would improve the quality and uniformity of materials specification records. The new system exceeded expectations within the first year.

A turning point was reached about a year and a half after the system was installed. A technical manager in charge of specification administration taught himself to program keystroke sequences using one of the word processor's advanced functions. Data could then be entered, calculations automatically performed, and a report generated in only a fraction of the time and effort previously required. This success, along with the inadequate support received from the vendor to develop the new application, encouraged the laboratory to discover further extensions of the system's capabilities. With the aid of software written by in-house personnel, several databases were created that extended the lab's role as an information resource to the entire corporation.

Polaroid's many positive experiences with what some were beginning to call "office automation" and the increased demand for word processing brought out the need to coordinate efforts and share learned knowledge and skills. This need was reinforced by a staff reduction from over 18,000 employees in 1978 to approximately 14,000 by 1982. All these forces spurred Polaroid to find a way to manage its utilization of emerging office technologies.

Formation of an Office Technology Council

At Polaroid, initiatives that shape company policy often start in middle management and then rise to seek the "sponsorship" of top management. The Systems Management Division (the data processing function at Polaroid) had created a Manager of Office Systems Technology position in 1978. One of the manager's first actions was to obtain sponsorship for formation of an Office Technology Council to serve as a forum for identification and discussion of issues related to office automation. The Council was subsequently established in 1979 with politically and personally influential middle managers drawn from a wide variety of business units.

One of the Council's first actions was to create a task force to develop an Office Automation Long-Range Plan. In 1980, the task force presented its findings to the Council, including an assessment of the status of office automation in the company, a technology forecast, a long-range strategy, a tactical approach to implementation, and issues likely to be of concern to the Council. Office automation was defined as "the utilization of systems to reduce costs and enhance the effectiveness and productivity of personnel working in administrative offices."

The initial role established for the Council assumed that the principal initiatives to automate offices would come from the various business units themselves (see Case Figure 6-1). A paramount concern was placing some form of control on the proliferation of office equipment. A word processing needs analysis methodology was adopted that had been developed by the Internal Management Consulting Group prior to the formation of the Office Technology Council.

Needs Analysis Methodology

The task force's inventory of word processing systems indicated a dramatic increase beginning in the third quarter of 1979. The acquisition procedure adopted by the Council (see Case Figure 6-2) tied approval to "hard dollar" savings surfacing in the needs analysis. "Soft dollar" savings, such as time saved, were generally considered insufficient to justify a systems purchase.

The Internal Management Consulting Group did acknowledge circumstances in which the result of *not* utilizing advanced technology was more costly than the lack of hard dollar savings. One such instance occurred when a needs analysis in the Environmental Engineering Department could not determine hard dollar savings for a text processing and control system. Because the task of managing industrial wastes was an administrative nightmare and a single mistake could cost Polaroid more than the price of the system, the $15,000 purchase was approved.

ROLE OF THE OFFICE TECHNOLOGY COUNCIL

The major function of the Council is to coordinate and integrate technology and other support provided to customer organizations regarding office technology. The initial scope of the Council encompasses the following key elements:

1. Guide and direct activities relating to administrative systems reviews, planning alternatives, customer requirements, equipment evaluations, user training and education, standards of performance, and implementation.
2. Monitor, approve, and control the acquisition and performance of automated office equipment (i.e., word processing, electronic mail, and micrographics).
3. Analyze requirements based on future technologies and develop a corporate plan for their integration.
4. Act as a communications center for improved interdivisional communication on technology, methods, and problem-solving.
5. Assist users in understanding requirements, justifying needs, developing alternatives, and implementing office technology.

CASE FIGURE 6-1. The role of the Office Technology Council.

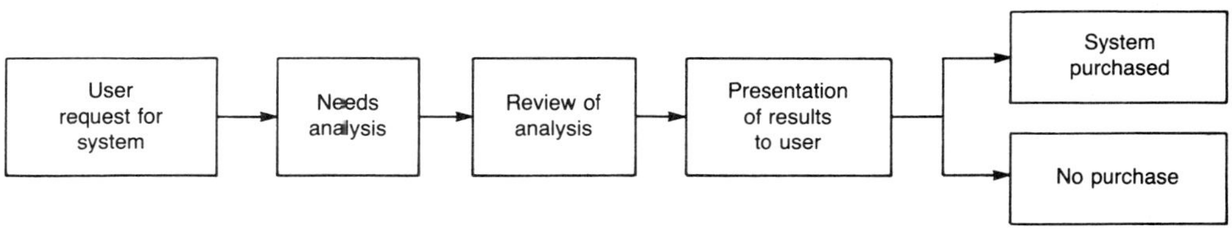

CASE FIGURE 6-2. Polaroid's systems acquisition procedure.

The needs analysis developed by the Internal Management Consulting Group involved seven steps (see Case Figure 6-3). First, an organizational scan produced a general picture of the personnel, tasks, and tools needed by a department to accomplish its mission. Data was gathered and analyzed to produce a summary of the qualitative benefits expected from the application of electronic technology. A financial analysis was then prepared estimating the previously determined savings in professional and secretarial time.

The Internal Management Consulting Group provided multiple services in five areas: finance, information, operations, personnel, and general management. As requests for word processing needs analyses increased, the Group's other priorities prevented it from meeting this demand. It therefore devised step-by-step instructions for a Word Processing Study Outline for departments to use in conducting their own needs analyses with the help of an outside consultant. The consultant reported to the Manager of Office Systems Technology but worked with the Internal Management Consultant Group on the review phase of the systems acquisition process.

CASE FIGURE 6-3. The word processing needs assessment methodology

WORD PROCESSING NEEDS ASSESSMENT METHODOLOGY

1. Orientation
   a. Determine overall mission.
   b. Develop organizational chart and assign administrative personnel to professional staff.
   c. Develop brief descriptions of individual functions.
   d. Identify major administrative needs.
   e. Determine associated costs for current operations.
   f. List all current office automation equipment.
2. Professional Activity Profile
   For each professional function in the organization, describe in detail the work activities that represent the content of each job.
3. Administrative Activity Profile
   For each secretarial, clerical, and administrative function in the organization, describe in detail the work activities of each job.
4. Administrative Reporting
5. Detailed Document Work Load
6. Word Processing Benefits Summary
7. Financial Analysis Worksheet

A Broadening Perspective on Office Automation

In addition to the Office Technology Council, the Manager of Office Systems Technology fostered other semi-formal groups to facilitate office automation at Polaroid. Personal computing, micrographics, and word processing user groups were formed with representatives from various business units.

One of the first activities of the Word Processing Users Group was to establish a subcommittee to evaluate the technology's impacts on jobs, a topic of growing concern to secretaries. The subcommittee found two ways in which word processing could be implemented: one placed secretaries into pools, eliminating some secretarial positions in the process; the other added word processing equipment to the tools already available to secretaries. This study helped the Office Technology Council to establish a policy of "no jobs loss" in implementing word processing. Another forum the Manager of Office Systems Technology helped to establish was the New England Office Systems Round Table, which consisted of office automation managers and consultants in the Boston area. Participation in this group broadened the Office Technology Council's perspective.

Originally, the Council was concerned with controlling the "fad" of word processing acquisition. The Council had developed the reputation in certain areas for dampening efforts to automate offices. With its broader perspective, a new charter was created for the Council in 1981 that expressed concerns for implementation and impact evaluation in addition to needs assessment (see Case Figure 6-4).

OFFICE TECHNOLOGY COUNCIL CHARTER

The principal functions of the Office Technology Council are to plan, set the direction, coordinate, and assist the systematic and informed introduction of office technologies at Polaroid and thus optimize their benefits to the company. To carry out its mission, the Council oversees or engages in the following operational objectives:

1. Analyze company requirements for office technologies and develop corporate plans for introducing them. Recommend long-term objectives, evaluate the impact of these technologies on the company, and prioritize the technologies that Polaroid should exploit.
2. Keep abreast of the state-of-the-art in present office technologies such as word processing, personal computers, micrographics, electronic mail, computer graphics, multifunction terminals, and communication networks, as well as conduct research on technologies that are still emerging.
3. Commission pilot studies on, evaluate, and recommend new equipment and office systems. Function as an information source and problem-solving resource for potential users. Develop resources that will assist potential users in analyzing applications, justifying needs, developing alternatives, and implementing office technology.
4. Function as a communications link to keep managers informed of developing technologies and their potential for improving productivity, solving problems, and lowering costs.
5. Consistent with the Council's long-range plans, provide the framework for orderly and coordinated acquisition and application of systems and equipment. Where appropriate, provide mechanisms to monitor the financial and operational results of such acquisitions.
6. Ensure that effective, coordinated training programs are implemented for users of office technology systems and equipment.

CASE FIGURE 6-4. Expanded charter of the Office Technology Council.

Tailoring Training to Meet Specific Needs

A *total* approach to training blends equipment, procedures, and people in implementing word processing systems. In addition to formal courses, training personnel work closely with users to meet individual and business needs. The seven steps identified in the training approach are listed in Case Figure 6-5.

The Training Department recognized four specific learning phases in the training process:

1. *Basic training* on text entry, editing, and output gets users started. Vendors offer two-day off-site courses, while Polaroid's own Continuing Education School offers eight four-hour sessions that are spread over several weeks. The ideal training schedule is five two-hour sessions conducted over five consecutive days on a one-to-one basis.

2. *Directed practice* with the features and procedures to be used on the job is the next phase. Twelve hours of directed practice within a two-week time frame is ideal.

3. *On-the-job utilization* constitutes the third phase. Users are still in a slow learning mode and need to be protected from normal work load pressures. The word processor has usually replaced the typewriter by the tenth week.

4. *Effective utilization* of advanced word processing equipment is the last phase. After three months, users are checked to see how well they are assimilating advanced capabilities such as math functions, database management, advanced text editing functions, keystroke sequence programming, and telecommunications functions. Mastering the basics does not guarantee that users will develop the ability to exploit the full potential of the system, moving beyond initial cost reductions to "profit enhancement" applications.

Given the proliferation of word processing systems and the limited resources of the Training Department, the need for "last phase" training presented a dilemma. This challenge was met through providing advanced

CASE FIGURE 6-5. Procedures to ensure successful training programs.

STEPS TO SUCCESSFUL TRAINING PROGRAMS

1. Identify training needs. In a large company, these might include the following:
   - A general overview of what word processing is and what it can do.
   - Introductory, hands-on experience.
   - On-the-job training.
   - Specialized training for specific procedures.
2. Determine your objectives. What needs to be accomplished by this training? State objectives in measurable terms.
3. Investigate instructional approaches, such as the following:
   - Setting up an in-house center.
   - Using existing equipment for after-hours education.
   - Making arrangements with vendors.
   - Using facilities at local schools.
   - Consolidating your training efforts with other companies.
4. Do a cost-benefit analysis for each alternative. Costs include equipment, supplies, instructor fees, transportation, and employee time away from the job.
5. Recommend appropriate options. Give management a full recap of work, including alternatives, costs, and your recommendations.
6. Develop the program. Some firms purchase courses from consultants, but your company may wish to design its own courses. Try to involve hourly people, too, because they know the technical aspects of the job and are more likely to accept the program if they participate in planning and developing it.
7. Evaluate the program for possible improvements. How have you done? Evaluate participants' performance and then ask them to comment on the training program and suggest improvements.

courses in the Polaroid Continuing Education School and a limited amount of tailored training on a "by request" basis. New applications and new ways to utilize advanced capabilities were also shared in the various word processing user groups.

Evaluating Impacts: A Post-Audit Procedure

Monitoring the *effects* of new technology became as important to the Office Technology Council as assessing the need to purchase it. The Internal Management Consulting Group was responsible for establishing a post-audit procedure "to assess the financial and operational impact of word processing on Polaroid's office environment." An extensive data-gathering instrument was developed to be administered either by interview or as a questionnaire. Features of the post-audit technology study are listed in Case Figure 6-6.

The post audit of the Materials Laboratory indicated some interesting impacts. The calculation of hard dollar savings is depicted in Case Figure 6-7, while Case Figure 6-8 briefly describes a broader spectrum of benefits.

CASE FIGURE 6-6. Factors to be addressed in post-audit technology study.

POST-AUDIT TECHNOLOGY STUDY

1. Equipment inventory and background information: equipment, history, costs.
2. Impact on operations: changes in jobs, work, and organization of business unit.
3. Percent utilization work sample summary: purpose, size, cycle, preparation time.
4. Cost-benefits matrix: reduced time, improved quality, efficiency gains.
5. Training and technical support: needs/costs analysis, technical support evaluation.
6. Human factors evaluation: display screen, keyboard, chair, noise, lighting, etc.
7. Council and user groups: To what extent are these resources used?
8. Future of office automation: current or anticipated use of additional technology.
9. Summary and conclusion: comments and questions.

CASE FIGURE 6-7. Calculations of hard dollar savings in the laboratory.

	Professionals		Typists		
	Number	Yearly Cost	Number	Yearly Cost	Total Cost
Before introduction of word processor	2	$60,000	6	$100,000	$160,000
After introduction of word processor	3	$90,000	0	0	$ 90,000
TOTAL ANNUAL SAVINGS					$ 70,000

CASE FIGURE 6-8. Hard and soft dollar savings of benefits to the laboratory.

LABORATORY BENEFITS MATRIX

Benefit	Savings in Soft Dollars	Savings in Hard Dollars
1. Technical Documentation Dept. reduction in clerical help	—	$70,000
2. Improved turnaround time	Time saved	—
3. Improved quality	More recognition More expectations More work done	— — —
4. Increased efficiency	More work done	—
5. Job enhancement	More work done	—
6. Improved communications	Better product, less questioning	—
7. Enhanced image of department	More responsibilities, more work done	—
8. Professional appearance	More recognition, more work done	—
9. Do things where the need was not previously recognized	More work done, easier to accomplish tasks	—
10. Increased work load	More work done	—
TOTAL SAVINGS		$70,000

Applications beyond the manufacturer's recommendations and specifications had been discovered. As a result, the department that administers specifications of vendor materials and their lab-designed structures expanded its role to provide information to the laboratory and the rest of the corporation. The post-audit procedure was designed to make such learning experiences available to everyone involved with new office technologies.

THE FUTURE OF OFFICE AUTOMATION AT POLAROID

What is now clear to the Office Technology Group and others throughout Polaroid is that office technology offers a key source of leverage for improving white-collar productivity. What is *not* clear is exactly how office automation tools will come together in the "office of the future."

While the existing environment inhibited top management support for a comprehensive pilot project, the Council suspected that a pilot project would be necessary to integrate office automation capabilities. The technologies needed for such a pilot are described in Case Figure 6-9 and would cost approximately $400,000 based on current prices.

TECHNOLOGIES FOR MAJOR OFFICE AUTOMATION PILOT STUDY

1. *Multi-function terminals.* Terminals connected to a shared resources CPU capable of performing word processing, data processing, imaging, electronic mail, personal computing, and other functions at single workstations.
2. *Local area networks (LANs).* Privately owned networks offering reliable, high-speed communications channels optimized for connecting information processing equipment such as word processing, data processing, and electronic mail systems in a limited geographic area.
3. *Message systems/electronic mail.* A central system for accepting, storing, and transmitting information electronically.
4. *Filing and records management.* The use of techniques and technology of micrographics to provide the following:
   - Economical storage of records with long-term retention periods.
   - Protection of vital information.
   - A storage medium for document retrieval systems.
   - Reduction in physical size and volume of records.
5. *Intelligent copiers.* Devices to provide hardcopy output transmitting text, data, and graphics from one site to another at high speeds. These systems can perform special functions such as page numbering and two-sided copying. In addition, these devices store several different fonts or type styles from which to select, and styles can be mixed as needed within a single document.
6. *External, online databases.* Proprietary databases compiled and maintained by an outside service.
7. *Word processing.* The technology to reduce repetitive typing, minimize keyboard strokes, manipulate text, reduce proofreading by professionals, and improve the quality of typewritten documents.

CASE FIGURE 6-9. Technologies to be involved in a major office automation pilot project.

The tentative plan would be to solicit "bids" from business units interested in being the pilot site. A bid would include the charter of the organization, its location(s), a description of its key business problems, names and titles of prospective users, and expected benefits. The pilot organization would be expected to fund a portion of the pilot project's cost. Short of launching such a pilot project, the Council provided hands-on demonstrations of the various technologies to be set up at the pilot site by selected vendors.

A major thrust was in the area of personal computers, which were recognized as having the capacity to do more work at lower cost than standalone word processors could do. A survey by the Personal Computer User Group revealed that 25 percent of Polaroid's microcomputers were being used for single tasks (e.g., word processing), 25 percent for two tasks (e.g., word processing and database management), and 50 percent for multiple tasks (e.g., spreadsheets, decision support, telecommunications links with outside databases, etc.). The survey also revealed that the number of users was growing at three times the rate of installed hardware.

The history of microcomputer utilization at Polaroid is charted in Case Figure 6-10. Case Figure 6-11 presents the Personal Computer User Group's projections of future development.

CASE FIGURE 6-10. The evaluation of microcomputers at Polaroid.

Stage 1 (1979–1980) Single Task—Single User
Stage 2 (1980–1981) Multiple Tasks—Single User
Stage 3 (1981–1982) Multiple Task—Multiple Users
Stage 4 (1983–) Future Direction

CASE FIGURE 6-11. The future direction of microcomputers at Polaroid.

FUTURE DIRECTION OF MICROCOMPUTERS

1. Sophisticated operating systems
   - Multitasking capabilities/integrated applications
   - High-resolution graphics/decision support systems
   - Networking/information management
2. Public networks (The Source and CompuServe)
   - Intercompany computer conferencing
   - Information databases
     a. Dow Jones News Retrieval Service
     b. Data Resource Institute
     c. New York Times Index
3. Corporate network
   - Decision support systems
   - Computer-based messaging
   - Executive scheduling
   - Telephone/voice management
4. Local computer networks within business units

CONCLUSION

Polaroid discovered that the purchase of new equipment may not be justifiable in hard dollar savings but in certain cases may be appropriate nevertheless. The company realized that ways to improve productivity without introducing new technology can be revealed in the process of needs assessment. The audit of implemented systems assessed both the effectiveness of the needs analysis method and the learning experiences of business units that were innovating new applications.

The Office Technology Group, the various user groups, and the New England Office Systems Round Table all played significant roles in guiding office automation efforts at Polaroid as the range of new, cost-effective tools continued to expand.

DISCUSSION QUESTIONS

1. Review the historical development of office automation at Polaroid. Was its development consistent with what you might expect of a large organization? Which specific actions earned Polaroid the classification of "innovator"? (Chapters 1, 2, 17–19)
2. Classify the approaches Polaroid used in cost-justifying its initial office automation expenditures. (Chapter 15)
3. Identify the many committees and groups that the Office Systems Manager established to promote innovative uses of office automation. What other things might the manager have done? (Chapter 19)
4. In what ways is this case a good illustration of the office systems cycle in operation? (Chapter 20)
5. Assume that you are on the Office Technology Council charged with establishing future directions for office automation. What title would you give Stage 4 in Case Figure 6-10? Justify your response. (Chapter 25)
6. Assume that you are the Office Systems Manager. What would you do to ensure the *continuation* of your successes? (Chapter 18)

ROLE PLAY

1. Building on the Discussion Questions above, break into groups to discuss the future directions of office automation. Come to a consensus on the directions office automation should take. (Chapter 25)

WRITING ASSIGNMENT

1. Assume that you are editor of the Polaroid Company Newsletter. Prepare an article explaining the function and goals of the Office Technology Council.

INDIVIDUAL OR GROUP PROJECT

1. Conduct a post-audit technology study of a departmental office at your college or university (see Case Figure 6-6). Summarize benefits using the format given in Case Figures 6-7 and 6-8. Recommend additional work procedures or organizational improvements that you think could be made. Also recommend additional office automation applications that the department should consider. (Chapters 20–24)

NOTES

Chapter 1

1. *Webster's Ninth New Collegiate Dictionary* (Springfield, Mass.: Merriam-Webster, 1983), 937.

Chapter 2

1. Helen M. McCabe and Estelle L. Popham, *Word Processing: A Systems Approach to the Office* (New York: Harcourt Brace Jovanovich, 1977), 173.
2. "Special Report: Office Automation Restructures Business," *Business Week* (8 Oct. 1984), 118.
3. Ron Winslow, "Everybody with a PC," *Wall Street Journal* (16 Sept. 1985), 28C.
4. Henry Mintzberg, "The Manager's Job: Folklore and Fact," *Harvard Business Review* (July–August 1975), 49–61.
5. Blanche Ettinger and Estelle L. Popham, *Opportunities in Office Occupations* (Skokie, Ill.: National Textbook Co., 1982), 5.

Chapter 3

1. Eric R. Chabrow, "Information Strategies: Insurer's IS Sets New Policy," *Information Week* (28 Jan. 1985), 44.
2. Carl Edwards, Director of Four Oaks Institute, quoted in James Hannan, "The Strategic Approach," *Infosystems* (January 1985), 80.
3. Jeff A. Chester, "The Information Management Charter," *Infosystems* (April 1985), 30.
4. International Business Machines Corporation, "The Chief Information Officer," *IBM Information Processing* (Summer 1985), 33.
5. *Ibid.*
6. *Ibid.*, 34.
7. Dean N. Meyer, "Two Very Different Meanings to OA Strategies," *Office Automation Conference '85 Digest* (Atlanta: American Federation of Information Processing Societies, 1985), 223.
8. Adapted with permission from Addie Mattox and Janice McCollum, "How To Create a Career Path in Information Processing," *Papers and Proceedings of Syntopticon VII* (Willow Grove, Pa.: Association of Information Systems Professionals, 1980), 413–417.

Chapter 4

1. C. Evans, *The Micro Millenium* (New York: Viking Press, 1979), 4.
2. John Roach, "More Prevalent than Typewriters: Calculators," *Infosystems* (January 1985), 12.
3. "Chipping Away at Processing Potential," *Infosystems* (April 1985), 16.
4. Alan Purchase, *The Office Technologies* (Willow Grove, Pa.: Administrative Management Society, 1985), 11.

Chapter 5

1. "Bar Codes Beat Registry Delays," *Administrative Management* (June 1987), 9–10.

Chapter 6

1. Don M. Avedon, "What the Future Holds," in *Automating Your Office: Pathways to Management Success,* ed. Lou Pilla (Willow Grove, Pa.: Administrative Management Society, 1984), 139.
2. Bonnie Canning, "Records Automation," *Office Administration and Automation* (April 1984), 92–93.
3. Purchase, *The Office Technologies,* 36.
4. Linda W. Helgerson, "The Optical Disk as an Information Storage Tool," *Office Administration and Automation* (April 1985), 71.

Chapter 7

1. John Greitzer, "Printers," a supplement to *PC Week* (11 Dec. 1984).
2. Karen Keer, "Fast and Feature-Rich: The Shape of Copiers To Come," *Administrative Management* (December 1986), 20.
3. John Soat, "Do's and Don'ts of Desktop Publishing," *Administrative Management* (July 1986), 51.

Chapter 8

1. Gail Siragusa, "Voice Mail Takes Off," *Administrative Management* (April 1986), 44.
2. Adapted from Elizabeth M. Ferrarini, "Videotex: The Race To Plug In," *Computerworld Extra* (18 March 1981).
3. Lance R. Brilliantine, "Design and Selection Guide to Local Area Networks," *Administrative Management* (October 1985), 36.

Chapter 9

1. Roger C. Schank and Peter G. Childers, *The Cognitive Computer* (Reading, Mass.: Addison-Wesley, 1984), 76.
2. Peter Hillyer, "Talking to Computers," *Think* (March 1987), 49.

Chapter 10

1. Carolyn J. Mollins, "WP as a Management Tool," *Words* (August–September 1985), 12.
2. Susan F. Ehrlich, Elizabeth A. Akiba, and Vernell K. Munson, *Research Report: The Organizational Impact of Voice Store and Forward Technology* (Lowell, Mass.: Wang Laboratories, November 1983).
3. "Product Focus: Workstations: Making Executive Decisions," *Information Week* (16 Sept. 1985), 44.

Chapter 11

1. E. Mandt, "Managing the Knowledge Worker of the Future," *Personnel Journal* (March 1978), 138.
2. Robert Knight, "Financial Software Permeates Corporations," *Software News* (August 1986), 40.
3. Paul Harmon, ed. "A New Breed of Job Aids," *Expert Systems Strategies: The Monthly Newsletter for Managers and Developers of Expert Systems* (Cahners Publishing Co., March 1986).
4. Paul Harmon, "Intelligent Job Aids: The Use of Small Expert Systems in Office Automation" (Paper presented at Fifth Annual Office Systems Research Association Conference, Houston, 22–23 March 1986).
5. Isaac Asimov, "The Next 70 Years for Law and Lawyers," *ABA Journal* (American Bar Association, January 1985), 56–59.

Chapter 12

1. Robert Marinello, "Marketing in the Modern Mode," *Best Review* (April 1986), 82–84.
2. William M. Bulkeley, "Better than a Smile: Salespeople Begin To Use Computers on the Job," *Wall Street Journal* (13 Sept. 1985), 29.
3. Ehrlich, Akiba, and Munson, *Research Report*.
4. William E. Storts, "Tuning into Videotex," *Words* (April–May 1986), 16–18.
5. Gerald E. MacLean, "Taking PC Power with You," *Words* (April–May 1986), 37–38.

Chapter 13

1. Arthur J. Tobias, "Text-Retrieval Systems: What Are They and What Do They Do?" *Information Week* (1 Sept. 1986), 38–42.
2. *Ibid.*, 42.

Chapter 14

1. Nancy Sandquist, "Facility Management: A Strategic Function," *The Office* (March 1987), 41.
2. George Moreland Stamps, "Users Want Electronic Communicating Copiers," *The Office* (July 1986), 49–50.
3. Adapted from Harrison McDonald, "Telephone Selection: Everybody's Business," *Office Systems '87* (February 1987), 60–61.
4. *Ibid.*, 60.
5. "Computer Is a Real Plus," *Modern Office Technology* (October 1986), 124.
6. "Business Communications," special report published by *Industry Week* and *Modern Office Technology* (May 1986).
7. Sanford J. Morganstein, President of DYTEL Corp., Schaumburg, Ill., quoted in Lura K. Romei, "The Message is the Medium," *Modern Office Technology* (July 1986), 50.
8. David Wolf, National Systems Manager of A. B. Dick Co., quoted in "Micrographics Is No Small Business," *Modern Office Technology* (July 1986), 66–73.

Chapter 15

1. Peter G. Sassone and A. Perry Schwartz, "Cost-Justifying OA," *Datamation* (15 Feb. 1986), 83–88.

Chapter 16

1. United States Occupational Safety and Health Administration, *OSHA Oversight: Video Display Terminals in the Workplace* (Washington, D.C.: Government Printing Office, 1984), 210.
2. Marilyn K. Goldhaber, Michael R. Polen, and Robert A. Hiatt, "The Risk of Miscarriage and Birth Defects among Women Who Use Visual Display Terminals During Pregnancy," *American Journal of Industrial Medicine* 13 (June 1988):695–706.
3. John J. Stallard and George R. Terry, *Office Systems Management*, 9th ed. (Homewood, Ill.: Richard D. Irwin, 1984), 331–333.
4. "Paint Overcomes Hi-Tech 'Blahs,' " *Administrative Management* (March 1986), 49.
5. Marita Thomas, "Merck's Facilities Plan Fuses Physical, Technical, and Behavioral Factors," *Facilities Design and Management* (November–December 1983), 60–63.
6. Elaine Cohen and Aaron Cohen, *Planning the Electronic Office* (New York: McGraw-Hill, 1983), pp. 101–125.

Chapter 17

1. Don Hellriegel, John W. Slocum, and Richard W. Woodard, *Organizational Behavior,* 4th ed. (St. Paul, Minn.: West Publishing Co., 1986), 362. Adapted from R. W. Griffin, *Task Design: An Integrated Approach* (Glenview, Ill.: Scott, Foresman, 1982), 4.
2. Barbara Baran and Suzanne Teegarden, *Women's Labor in the Office of the Future: Changes in the Occupational Structure of the Insurance Industry* (Berkeley, Calif.: University of California, Dept. of City and Regional Planning, 1983), 11.
3. Frederick Herzberg, Bernard Mauser, and Barbara Block Snyderman, *The Motivation to Work,* 2d ed. (New York: John Wiley & Sons, 1967), 113–119.
4. A. N. Turner and P. R. Lawrence, *Industrial Jobs and the Worker* (Boston: Harvard Graduate School of Business Administration, 1965).
5. J. R. Hackman and G. R. Oldham, *Work Redesign* (Reading, Mass.: Addison-Wesley, 1980), 77–80.
6. Example adapted from United States Congress, Office of Technology Assessment, *The Automation of America's Offices* (Washington, D.C.: Government Printing Office, 1985), 97.
7. Shoshana Zuboff, "New Worlds of Computer-Mediated Work," *Harvard Business Review* (September–October 1982), 142.
8. *Ibid.*
9. *Ibid.*, 145.
10. *Ibid.*
11. *Ibid.*
12. Joan Greenbaum, Cydney Pullman, and Sharon Szymanski, "Effects of Office Automation on the Public Sector Workforce: A Case Study," in United States Congress, Office of Technology Assessment, *The Automation of America's Offices* (Washington, D.C.: Government Printing Office, 1985), 105.
13. John Hoerr, Michael A. Pollock, and David E. Whiteside, "Special Report: Management Discovers the Human Side of Automation," *Business Week* (29 Sept. 1986), 70.

14. United States Congress, Office of Technology Assessment, *The Automation of America's Offices,* 101.
15. Hackman and Oldham, *Work Redesign,* 72–73.
16. *Ibid.,* 135–142.
17. *Ibid.,* 164.
18. *Ibid.,* 168–169.
19. *Ibid.,* 170.
20. *Ibid.,* 174–177.
21. Elizabeth A. Regan, "Behavioral and Organizational Issues of Office Automation Technology" (Doctoral dissertation, University of Connecticut, 1982), *Dissertation Abstracts International,* 1982), 167.

Chapter 18

1. Louise Rodgers and Roxane Farmanfarmaian, "Technology Shakes Up the Organization (for Better or Worse)," *Working Woman* (November 1986), 100.
2. "Goodbye to the Old Personnel Department," *Wall Street Journal,* 22 May 1986, 30.
3. John L. Burch, "Ergonomics of Management Will Inherit the Energy of VDT Health and Safety Movement," *Report and Catalogue* (Summer 1986), 3.
4. Kurt Lewin, "Quasi-Stationary Social Equilibria and the Problems of Permanent Change," in *Organizational Development: Values, Process, and Technology,* ed. N. Margulies and A. P. Raia (New York: McGraw-Hill, 1972), 65–72.
5. H. Leavitt, "Applied Organizational Change in Industry: A Structural, Technological, and Humanistic Approach," in *Handbook of Organizations,* ed. J. March (Chicago: Rand-McNally, 1965), 1144–1170.
6. John P. Kotter and Leonard A. Schlesinger, "Choosing Strategies for Change," *Harvard Business Review* (March–April 1979), 109–112.

Chapter 19

1. Niccolo Machiavelli, *The Prince,* ed. Thomas G. Bergin (New York: Appleton-Century-Crofts, 1947), 15.
2. John J. Connell, "Catalyst of Change in Managing Office Technology," *The Office* (January 1986), 93.
3. Barbara Braverman, Thomas Castle, and Barbara G. McKee, "Snapshot of an OA System," *Information Center* (July 1986), 86.
4. William Bowen, "The Puny Payoff from Office Computers," *Fortune* (26 May 1986), 22–24.
5. Joseph T. Coates, "Aspects of Innovation: Public Policy Issues in Telecommunications Development," *Telecommunications Policy* (July 1987), 10.
6. L. H. Day, "Stages of Growth in Office Automation" (Paper delivered at the Diebold Automated Office Program, Fourth Plenary Meeting, Boca Raton, Fla., 25 Oct. 1979).
7. Braverman, Castle, and McKee, "Snapshot of an OA System," 88.
8. Hoerr, Pollock, and Whiteside, "Special Report: Management Discovers the Human Side of Automation," 72.

9. Carolyn J. Mullins, "WP as a Management Tool," *Words* (August–September 1985), 12.

10. John F. Rockart, Director of the Center for Information Systems Research at the Massachusetts Institute of Technology, quoted in International Business Machines Corporation, "End Users and Technology Combine To Extend the Range of Information," *IBM Information Processing* (Winter 1986), 5.

11. "Information Networks: A Competitive Advantage," *Modern Office Technology* (May 1986 supplement), 11.

12. *Ibid.*

13. Harold S. Bott, Jacque H. Pasino, and Jeff Hamilton, "How To Make a Strategic Move with Information Systems," *Information Week* (26 May 1986), 31.

14. Michael R. Vitale, "Strategic Systems Are No Fad, and MIS Must Lead the Way," *Information Week* (26 May 1986), 72.

15. Hellriegel, Slocum, and Woodman, *Organizational Behavior,* 580.

16. Peter F. Drucker, "The Discipline of Innovation," *Harvard Business Review* (May–June 1985), 67.

17. *Ibid.,* 68.

18. James Brian Quinn, "Managing Innovation: Controlled Chaos," *Harvard Business Review* (May–June 1985), 73–84.

19. Rita Shoor, "Micro Technology: Change Is the Name of the Game," *Infosystems* (March 1986), 32.

20. Dean N. Meyer, "Two Very Different Meanings to OA Strategies," *Office Automation Conference 1985 Digest* (Atlanta: American Federation of Information Processing Societies, 1985), 223.

21. Chabrow, "Information Strategies," 44.

Chapter 20

1. Thomas H. Athey, *Systematic Systems Approach* (Englewood Cliffs, N.J.: Prentice-Hall, 1982), 12.

2. Wendell L. French, *The Personnel Management Process,* 4th ed. (Boston: Houghton Mifflin, 1978), 33.

3. Don Tapscott, *Office Automation: A User-Driven Approach* (New York: Plenum Press, 1982), 66.

4. R. A. Hirscheim, *Office Automation: Concepts, Technologies, and Issues* (Reading, Mass: Addison-Wesley, 1985), 212.

5. Tapscott, *Office Automation*, 92–102.

Chapter 21

1. Mark A. Lieberman, Gad J. Selig, and John J. Walsh, *Office Automation: A Manager's Guide for Improved Productivity* (New York: John Wiley & Sons, 1982), 149.

Chapter 22

1. Adapted from Alexia Martin, "The Human Connection: A Strategy for Making Automation Work," *Administrative Management* (February 1982), 33–35.

Chapter 23

1. Ken Michielsen, "A PC Policy Primer: A Few Basic Rules Lend Direction to MIS Departments Supporting Micros," *IBM Innovation* (January–February 1986), 4–5.
2. Joel S. Zimmerman, "PC Security: So What's New?" *Datamation* (1 Nov. 1985), 85–92.
3. August Bequai, "A Management Guide to a Good Computer Contract," *The Office* (February 1986), 23.
4. Harry B. DiMaio, IBM Director of Data Security, quoted in Gerald E. MacLean, "Who's Guarding Your PC?" *Words* (August–September 1985), 24.

Chapter 24

1. Alexia Martin, "The Human Connection," 33.
2. United States Congress, Office of Technology Assessment, *The Automation of America's Offices*, 75.
3. Chester Delaney, "ASSBATS and All That," *Data Training* (November 1984), 11.
4. John J. Meroney, "Planning/Designing User Training Programs" (Paper presented at Office Automation Society International Conference, Chicago, 6 Sept. 1986).
5. Barbara Braverman, Thomas J. Castle, and Barbara McKee, "Implementing OA: A Case Study of Technostress," in *A Compendium of Materials from the Fifth Annual Office Systems Research Association Conference* (New York: Office Systems Research Association, 1986), 313–325.
6. James Hassett and Sheree Dukes, "The New Employee Trainer: A Floppy Disk," *Psychology Today* (September 1986), 30.
7. United States Congress, Office of Technology Assessment, *The Automation of America's Offices*, 162.
8. Barbara A. Gutek and Tora K. Bikson, "Differential Experiences of Men and Women in Computerized Offices," in *Girls, Women, and Computers*, a special edition of *Sex Roles* journal of American Psychological Association (1985).

Chapter 25

1. Erik Mortensen, "Adapting Electronic Mail to Management's Needs," *Administrative Management* (August 1987), 30.
2. Robert Johansen, "User Approaches to Computer-Supported Teams," in *Technological Support for Work Group Collaboration* (New York: New York University Center for Research on Information Systems, 1987), 35.
3. Walter A. Kleinschrod, *Update 1987–88: Approaching the Automated Office* (Willow Grove, Pa.: Administrative Management Society, 1987), 107.
4. Samuel J. Kalow, quoted in Kleinschrod, *Update 1987-1988*, 21.
5. United States Congress, Office of Technology Assessment, *The Automation of America's Offices*, 47.

GLOSSARY

accountability A personal liability to perform a job according to predetermined standards or requirements.

acoustic coupler A modulation device for transmitting and receiving data signals over telephone lines using an ordinary handset.

activity management software Software that is primarily designed to manage time and events.

administrative assistant An individual assigned responsibility for administrative tasks. *See also* **administrative support**

administrative support Information processing (nontyping) tasks assigned to specialized personnel, such as handling mail, receiving visitors, making travel arrangements, scheduling calendars, filing, composing and editing, and researching information.

advisory council A select committee that advises and counsels the office systems analyst or task force.

ambient lighting General or overall lighting.

AMCO-PACT (Activity analysis, Machine inventory, Channel analysis, Organizational analysis/Personal preference, Aesthetics, Cost, Time) An office layout model to show interaction between optimal and practical office layouts.

American Simplified Keyboard *See* **Dvorak Keyboard**

analog computer A category of computers that operate by measuring continuous values such as voltages and temperatures. Many scientific computers are analog computers.

analog signal A signal that carries voice in the form of waves.

andragogy A teaching approach that is student-directed.

aperture cards Keypunch cards with special inserts for pieces of roll microfilm.

application Use of computer technology for a particular purpose or in a special way.

applications programs Programs designed for a specific purpose, such as payroll processing or word processing.

architecture The manner in which a computer system is structured.

arithmetic logic unit (ALU) The part of a computer's central processing unit that performs arithmetic computations and comparisons.

articulation index (AI) The acoustical level at which people can work.

artificial intelligence (AI) Computer operations that emulate human thought processes.

assembler A computer program that can convert assembly language to machine language.

assembly language A means of communicating with a computer; a low-level language.

asynchronous In data communications, transmission that is controlled by start and stop elements at the beginning of each character.

attitude questionnaire A survey form to determine workers' attitudes toward a new technology.

audial feedback The sound one hears upon entering a character into a system.

audio teleconferencing Voice-only interaction between individuals at two or more sites.

audiographic teleconferencing A technology that combines audio teleconferencing technology with one or more graphics technologies, such as a facsimile machine or electronic blackboard.

authoring systems Software that uses an artificial intelligence-based "shell" for building computer-assisted instruction courseware.

authority A set of rights or powers granted to a jobholder to carry out assigned tasks and responsibilities.

automated office systems (AOS) A term used interchangeably with **office systems, office automation,** and **office automation systems.** *See* **office systems**

back-up A duplicate or copy of electronically stored data that is created to protect against loss or damage to computer software.

backward chaining In artificial intelligence software, a deductive reasoning technique, used by **inference engines,** that starts at the solution of a problem and reasons backward to the current situation.

ball element printer A printing element the size and shape of a golf ball; characters are formed when the ball strikes a ribbon at high speed. May contain up to 98 characters.

band printer A printer that uses a metal band to produce characters; the band spins at high speed and forms characters by striking a ribbon. Typically contains 48 characters.

bar codes Bars or lines of varying thickness that are read by a special scanner for direct input into a computer system.

baseband network A network in which digital signals are inserted directly onto a cable one signal at a time.

batch processing Storing and processing data from start to finish, all at once; batch processing is not interactive with the user.

baud rate The number of signal changes per second. One baud can code one or more data bits, depending on the modulation scheme and number of states. Old

300-bps modems operated at 300 baud; newer 1200- and 2400-bps modems operate at 600 baud.

bezel When used to describe a visual display terminal, the tendency of the screen to be clearer in the middle than at the margins.

bit-mapped graphics Graphics output of dot matrix printers.

blip coding In micrographics, an indexing method in which documents are manually indexed and then fed to a camera that makes a small square on the film to facilitate retrieval.

block mode graphics The graphics output that is made by repeating regular characters.

boundary In systems theory, the area that can be controlled by a system and separates one system from another.

broadband network A network that can be divided into frequencies or bands to enable a system to carry more than one type of signal at a time or in any mode.

bus network A network topology that can transfer data in more than one direction; the network has a beginning and end.

cable An electrical conductor for sending information from one site to another.

calendar management software Software for appointment scheduling and time management.

call accounting Programs that track and analyze traffic patterns of telephone calls, verify telephone charge systems, and document cases of telephone abuse.

candela (cd) A measure of light intensity.

capture rate The speed of an optical character reader; measured in characters per second.

carrier sense multiple access with collision detection (CSMA/CD) A method whereby computer devices access a network by "listening" to determine if a line is busy and then send their messages. If two devices attempt to use the same line at the same time, transmission is canceled.

catalyst A cause of activity between other persons or forces.

central dictation system A multiuser dictation system.

central processing unit (CPU) The major hardware component of a computer system. The CPU acts as the brain of a computer system and includes the internal storage unit, arithmetic logic unit, and control unit.

Centrex system Telephone exchange in which each dialer has a unique seven-digit number.

change agent An individual or team responsible for designing and introducing change, such as a new office system.

character generation Process that generates characters on a display screen.

closed system A system that is not affected by events outside its boundaries.

coated-paper copier (cpc) A copier that operates much as a plain-paper copier but requires special coated paper.

coaxial cable wires A central conductor wire that is surrounded by insulation and then covered with a copper, aluminum, or metal jacket; commonly used for television cable transmission.

code A set of specifications for data representation; another term for computer **program.**

coding Another term for writing computer programs; so called because programs are know as **code.**

collaborative work tools Technologies that are designed for use by groups rather than individuals.

communications The electronic transfer of data between computer devices.

communications technology Technology that facilitates data transfer in any form over any distance.

compact disk (CD) An optical disk for storing extremely high-quality audio, video, digital, and digitized data.

compatible The quality of being able to be used with something else.

compiler A computer program that translates a high-level language program into a machine-language program.

computer A machine that uses electrical signals to perform work. Its power is derived from its speed, accuracy, and memory capacity.

computer-aided publishing An umbrella term referring to the use of computers to integrate text and graphics for publication.

computer-assisted instruction (CAI) Courseware developed for individualized instruction using a computer.

computer-assisted retrieval (CAR) A micrographic system in which documents are retrieved with the aid of a computer. In some technologies, CAR acts as an indexing medium; in other technologies, the computer activates mechanical retrieval or digitizes a microform document for direct transmittal to the user.

computer-based message switching (CBMS) system A computer-based system that allows users to send electronic messages.

computer-based training (CBT) Training that is accomplished with the aid of computer devices, including programmed instruction (PI), computer-assisted instruction (CAI), computer-based instruction (CBI), computer-managed instruction (CMI), and interactive video disk (IVD).

computer hardware Equipment that constitutes a computer system.

computer information systems (CIS) Another term for **data processing** systems.

computer input microfilm (CIM) Microfilm that is used as input for a computer system.

computer-mediated work Work in which tasks are accomplished through the information system rather than through direct physical contact.

computer output microfilm (COM) Microform that is a direct output of a computer system; the paper stage of a document is bypassed.

computer software Step-by-step instructions that the computer follows to process data.

computer teleconferencing Interactive, nonlinear, asynchronous communications using computers.

console copier A large, feature-laden, high-quality, high-volume, high-speed copier.

continuous speech recognition systems Voice recognition systems that understand predefined words that are used in everyday vocabulary.

contrast When used to describe a visual display terminal, the difference in luminance between a character and its background.

control unit The part of the central processing unit that interprets software instructions and controls all computing activity.

convenience copy (cc) Suggested substitute for the old term *carbon copy.*

copyright The exclusive right to reproduce or modify an original work. Software copyrights prohibit copying or modifying computer software.

cost displacement A cost justification technique in which the cost of technologies is justified in terms of replacing personnel.

CSMA/CD *See* **carrier sense multiple access with collision detection**

cursor A small symbol (line, dot, or rectangle) or flashing light that indicates input positions on a visual display terminal.

daisy wheel printer A round print wheel, with spokes similar to a daisy's petals, that spins at high speed; characters are formed when the hammer strikes the print wheel against a ribbon.

data A collection of facts, statistics, or pieces of information. (Although *data* is the plural form of *datum,* in computer science *data* is generally used as a singular term.)

data communications Data transfer from computer to computer.

data encryption A data protection scheme with mathematical algorithms to scramble data. Only users with authorized keys can unscramble data to view or update it.

data processing Application of computer technologies to business operations. A systematic set of techniques for collecting, manipulating, and disseminating data to achieve specific objectives.

data processing department An organizational unit responsible for planning, implementing, and maintaining computer applications and operations.

database A collection of related records stored in a computer file, or a collection of systematically organized data on magnetic tape or disk. These records contain specific information (fields) such as names, addresses, and order or part numbers.

database inquiry A software program that enables users to interface with a database using natural language rather than computer commands.

decibel (dB) A measure of loudness or intensity of sound.

decision graphics Graphic displays that help users to analyze information.

decision modeling software Software that is designed to create and manipulate complex business models on an interactive basis without the help of professional programming specialists.

decision support systems (DSS) Computer support for management decision making.

defaults Options that are automatically set by computer software but may be changed by the user.

depreciation An accounting technique to spread out the cost of expenditures over the expected life of the item purchased.

desktop copier A convenience copier for low-volume needs that fits on a desk top.

desktop dictation unit A single-user, multifeature dictation system small enough to sit on a desk.

desktop publishing A publishing system in which a microcomputer assists in all phases of producing a finished page, from text entry to composition, layout, graphics, and sometimes reproduction. Users can design and format documents on the screen, as well as pick type fonts and sizes. Display provides a what-you-see-is-what-you-get (*wysiwyg*) presentation of exactly how the document will look when it is fed into a laser printer or sent as a completed page to a commercial printer.

digital computer A type of computer that operates by counting discrete units. Most business computers are digital computers.

digital dictation device A device that translates sound waves to digital storage for later editing and transcription.

digital signal A signal that represents discrete units to symbolize values.

direct productivity measurement A technique in which inputs and outputs are identifiable and measurable.

direct response marketing Marketing and distribution systems that appeal to consumers who are expected to place orders directly to the company without intermediaries such as salespersons or retail outlets.

disk pack An airtight container holding six or more rigid magnetic disks that is typically used in large computer systems.

distributed printing Printing that is done directly at the reader's location; includes at least three environments: printer on a communications line, centralized hosts to distributed host, and local area network.

document log A record of documents processed or handled in a given time frame.

document processing How documents are created, reviewed, distributed, presented, and stored.

documentation A written explanation of how a computer program works; provides details of programming logic, variables, and formulas used to process data and all other details pertinent to the creation and use of the program.

dot matrix printer A printer that designs a character when needles or wires strike a ribbon to produce a series of dots; the design is the matrix.

download To transfer information electronically from one host computer to another computer; to transmit text or data between compatible equipment.

driving forces In Lewin's force field analysis theory, those factors that encourage change, growth, and development.

dual-spectrum copier A copier that uses both light and heat in the copying process.

dumb terminal A terminal with virtually no editing capabilities.

duplex In data communications, a line that can send data in two directions but in only one direction at a time.

Dvorak Keyboard A keyboard layout that puts high-use keys in the "home row"; also know as the **American Simplified Keyboard (ASK).**

electroluminescent displays A visual display terminal referred to as a *projection display;* requires more energy and costs more than liquid crystal display (LCD) terminals.

electronic directory Software that maintains listings of names, addresses, and telephone numbers; some include automatic dialing.

electronic filing and retrieval software Software that searches for documents or stored information by keying selected words or subjects into a terminal.

electronic forms automation The creation, management, processing, distribution, and printing/displaying of forms on the computer.

electronic key systems Telephone systems that combine the benefits of key systems with selected PBX features and intercom; also called **hybrid systems.**

electronic mail An umbrella term that describes electronically transmitted messages or documents.

electronic notebooks Software for storing random items of information in the format of a notepad; users can easily search through items by any topic, word, or date recorded as notes.

electronic photocomposition An electronic system that creates typeset copy.

electronic typewriter A typewriter with microchip technology that allows it to perform many functions associated with word processors.

employee logs Forms used to determine the tasks done by an employee; used to determine if the employee is doing work appropriate for his or her job level and/or if office automation tools could facilitate task completion.

end user An individual who uses technology to perform work or carry out his or her job.

end-user computing The process of nontechnical business personnel performing some computer programming themselves with fourth-generation languages and application packages. The term, a spillover from technical data processing terminology, distinguishes people who *use* technology to carry out their jobs (end users) from people whose job *is* technology (e.g., programmers and analysts).

entropy In systems theory, every system's tendency toward disorder (breakdown or malfunctioning).

environment In systems theory, anything outside a system that may have an impact on the system but is beyond its control.

equipment feature analysis The process of evaluating special features of equipment to determine their value for improving productivity.

erasable disk Disk that can be written to, read, and updated.

ergonomics The scientific study of human interaction with the workplace and its tools; also known as *human factors* or *human factors engineering.*

evaluation The fourth phase of the office system cycle in which technologies are judged in terms of whether they are performing or being used as expected.

executive support systems Databases that are customized to provide "status access" to decision makers, that is, the ability to obtain information about the corporation at a glance, in graphic form, without developing computing skills.

executive workstation A terminal that integrates voice and data and is designed to provide decision makers with access to information, including corporate data, commercial online databases, electronic mail, voice mail, and other information.

expert system A computer program that uses artificial intelligence techniques to provide detailed information about a particular subject.

face-to-face meeting facilitation Services to facilitate a meeting.

facilities management The process of coordinating the physical workplace in terms of administration, architecture, and behavioral engineering sciences to maximize utilization of facilities for higher productivity.

facsimile A technology that combines photocopy and telephone technologies to transmit duplicates of paper-based pictures, charts, graphs, etc., over telephone lines.

facts In regard to artificial intelligence, the knowledge base for an expert system.

feasibility report A report prepared by an office systems analyst for upper management that outlines the desirability of a new system.

feedback In systems theory, the comparison of actual output with expected output.

feeder An accessory that feeds paper into a printer.

fiber optics A thin core of glass or plastic through which light pulses are transmitted; employs extremely fast transmission channels that can send all types of data (text, image, voice, full-motion video, etc.).

financial modeling Computer programs that use natural-language commands (a modeling language) to enter, manipulate, and calculate data.

flat database A database that maintains all data in a single file; best suited for simple applications. *See also* **relational database**

flicker The tendency of characters displayed on a visual display terminal to appear unstable.

floppy disk A magnetic data storage device of flexible plastic with a protective cardboard jacket.

flowchart A graphic description of how work is performed.

font Printer term that refers to shape or style of a character.

force field analysis A theory developed by Kurt Lewin that defines change as a dynamic process rather than a single event; change is characterized by forces working in opposite directions. *See also* **driving forces** and **restraining forces**

format The form or style in which text is printed.

formatting *See* **initialization**

forward chaining In artificial intelligence, a deductive reasoning technique used by **inference engines** that starts at the beginning of a problem and searches forward until a solution is found.

fourth-generation languages (4GL) Nonprocedural programming languages that are relatively easy to learn and use; appropriate for end users.

frequency-division/time-division multiplexers (FDM/TDM) The division of broadband technology into distinct channels for access, based on either frequency or time.

full duplex In data communications, a line that can send data in two directions at the same time.

full-motion video teleconferencing A television technology that enables users to see and hear each other.

function A role or activity that accomplishes a specific objective.

functional approach An approach to office systems analysis that attempts to improve the way work (accounting, sales, etc.) is accomplished.

gas plasma display A visual terminal display based on gas plasma; offers a sharp monochromatic graphic display.

gateway A means of connecting separate, distinct networks that use different protocols.

general-purpose computer A computer that can perform a wide variety of applications. Most business computers are general-purpose.

glare Light from a visual display terminal that makes reading the screen difficult.

group authoring software Word processing add-ons to facilitate group writing.

group decision support systems Software to help a group come to a joint decision.

hard disk A magnetic storage device of rigid metal enclosed in a sealed case.

hard dollar value Actual monetary value.

hard sectoring The process of dividing a disk by permanent holes in its hub.

heuristics *See* **rules**

high-level language A computer language that uses natural-language statements for commands.

historical data Standard by which to compare the output of individuals or departments based on past performance.

human factors engineering *See* **ergonomics**

HVAC Abbreviation for *heating, ventilation, and air conditioning.*

hybrid computer A category of computers with the capabilities of both digital and analog computers. A supercomputer is an example of a hybrid computer.

hybrid systems Telephone systems that combine the benefits of key systems with selected PBX features and intercom; also called **electronic key systems.**

icon-based natural-language query system An approach to natural-language understanding in which the computer helps the user develop a question by presenting icons (images) that represent commands the computer can understand.

impact printer A printer that uses a typebar or other striking device to transfer ink from ribbon to paper.

implement To introduce computer technology for a specific purpose or work application.

implementation The third phase of the office systems cycle; introducing new technologies into the workplace.

index In records management, the address of a particular document.

indirect productivity measurement Measuring productivity by either the development of standards or assessing the output of the department/individuals one is managing.

inference engine An expert system component that tests the rules in a knowledge base.

information A meaningful collection of data; the meaning that people attach to a related group of data; the output from processing data.

Information Age Sociological term for the current era in which over half of today's work force is performing jobs related to information processing rather than farming, manufacturing, or other production.

information center An organization that puts computer technology directly in the hands of people who are not data processing professionals; a functional unit charged with assisting end users with computer applications.

information infrastructure A network of services that keep information flowing into, within, and out of an enterprise.

information management (IM) A global term that refers to office systems, data processing, and communications; often used interchangeably with **information systems** or **management information systems.**

information processing The process of transforming information from source data, or input, into forms of information that are usable for an intended purpose.

information resource management (IRM) The use of information as a valuable resource that should be managed and conserved; the systematic management of information through organization, policy, and procedures.

information resource management approach An approach to office systems analysis that seeks to make better use of an organization's information resources.

information system (IS) Systematic procedures to create, capture, transform, interpret, reproduce, distribute, store, and make available data and information for knowledge workers and decision makers; often used interchangeably with **information management** or **management information systems.**

initialization The process of preparing a disk for use.

ink-jet printer A nonimpact printer that aims a tiny stream of electrostatically charged inkdrops at paper to create characters and images.

innovation The creation or adoption of new products, services, processes, or procedures.

integrated dictation/transcription/word processing technology A technology that provides visual feedback, in symbols, to a dictator during dictation.

integrated office systems (IOS) Computer systems that perform various office and data processing functions with a standard user interface.

integrated software Computer programs that combine applications into one package, permitting data transfer among applications.

integrated systems Systems that combine technologies such as data processing, word processing, voice, graphics, image, and communications.

integration Separate technologies working together.

intelligent copier A copier that can produce multiple copies directly from electronic input; may be capable of sending copies over telephone lines for remote site printing.

intelligent job aids Software that uses artificial intelligence to explain work processes, procedures, or quality control.

intelligent terminal A terminal with a built-in microprocessor; can be programmed to perform functions such as data editing or communications.

interactive processing Processing data in small segments over a period of time; permits frequent interchange between the user and the system.

interactive tablet Visual display terminal (VDT) input device that resembles a small blackboard; what the user draws on the tablet also appears on the VDT.

interactive video Training programs that combine computer-based training (CBT) with laser disk technology.

interface In systems theory, the region between systems or the process of transferring the output of one system into the input of another.

internal consultant An employee whose job is to provide information and support to an organization's technology users.

interpreter A computer program that translates one statement at a time into machine code for immediate execution.

interview guide A structured guide for conducting an interview.

ion printer A nonimpact printer that uses charged air molecules to create characters or images.

isolated word recognition system A voice recognition system that uses pattern-matching to understand words.

job design Formal and informal specifications of tasks performed by employees, including expert skills required, interpersonal relationships, and task interdependencies. Ideally, the needs and goals of both employees and the organization are taken into account in job design or redesign.

job enlargement Expanding a job to include similar tasks.

job enrichment Vertical expansion to include planning or control tasks (or both) in a job that was previously limited to operating tasks.

job rotation Moving workers from one job to another to provide variety in work tasks and training experiences.

job sharing Two workers sharing one job.

joystick A visual display terminal input device that resembles a gear shift; the user can move the cursor in any direction.

key pressure The amount of energy required to depress a key.

key roll In keyboard operation, the speed at which the system accepts a character.

key telephone systems A telephone system that can handle up to 125 lines; compact enough to sit on a desk; anyone can answer any incoming call.

key word indexing An electronic filing and retrieval system that enables the user to retrieve documents by specifying key words or categories.

keyboard As a verb, to enter data into a computer system via a keyboard containing letters, numbers, and special function keys.

kiosk Electronic kiosks combine video and computer technologies to provide marketing information and entry of client orders into an easy-to-use display system.

knowledge workers Office workers whose jobs require highly specialized training and education and who work primarily with information; people whose jobs require mental rather than physical work.

language-translator program Software that translates natural-language programming instructions into machine language for processing.

laser printer A nonimpact printer that uses light as its transfer medium.

leasing A means of obtaining office automation technology in which the vendor retains title to the technology and offers maintenance services; in return, the user usually pays a monthly fee for a specified time.

library programs Sets of computer instructions for frequently performed tasks.

light pen A visual display terminal input device that resembles a pen, with a light for an eraser; the user touches the VDT with the light pen to enter instructions.

line and staff Indicates whether departments in an organization have direct responsibility for operations (line) or provide ancillary services to support operations (staff).

line authority Chain of command used to carry out major goals of an enterprise, in contrast to *staff authority,* which provides support or special expertise to line authority.

liquid crystal display (LCD) A visual display terminal based on liquid crystal technologies that were first used in watches and clocks.

LISP An artificial intelligence programming language used primarily in the United States and Europe.

local area network (LAN) A geographically limited, user-owned data communications system that provides for intraoffice communication needs.

logbook A systematic record of progress or operations.

low-level language A complex computer language that uses mnemonics (three- or four-letter acronyms) to symbolize machine code.

lux (lx) A measure of illumination.

machine language A language that can be interpreted directly by the internal circuitry of a computer.

magnetic ink character recognition (MICR) A process that allows direct input of information written in magnetic, specially shaped characters; primarily used to process bank checks.

magnetic printer A nonimpact printing device that uses magnetic coil heads to attract toner to a drum to produce printed copy.

magnetic tape An auxillary storage medium on which data is stored sequentially.

magnification ratio The number of times that a microform is enlarged for viewing.

mail accounting system A system for tracking postal expenditures by class of mail, carrier, and department.

mainframe computer A large, expensive, and extremely powerful category of computer; typically operated by highly trained technical personnel.

management information systems (MIS) Used interchangeably with **information management** or **information systems** as a global term referring to office systems, data processing, and communications; sometimes used in a narrow sense as another term for **data processing.**

management support system *See* **decision support system**

market-driven development The evolution of computer technology in response to needs to solve specific problems and perform more work in less time.

matrix The space between characters and lines on a visual display terminal.

meeting schedulers Software designed to assist in setting times for meetings and notifying attendees.

meet-me bridge A communications service that connects more than two sites for a teleconference.

menu-based natural-language query system An approach to natural-language understanding in which the computer helps the user to build natural-language sentences by presenting menus of choices (option lists) that the computer can understand.

merge printing A word processing function that combines two separate files (a primary document and a secondary list document) to produce any number of copies of the basic (primary) document with appropriate variations (lists) for each copy; used to automate production of form letters or other documents.

microcomputer A desktop computer that is less powerful and less expensive than a minicomputer. Its operating system is contained on an integrated chip.

microfacsimile A very small image produced by scanning and digitizing micrographic media at high speed for storage on optical disks, where it can be retrieved and transmitted electronically.

microfiche Microfilm images that are cut and slipped into a plastic holder.

microfilm chip A small piece of microfilm with a high reduction ratio that is stored in a special retrieval device.

microfilm jacket A microform fused between two plastic sheets.

microform reader/printer A device that reads microforms and prints paper copies of microform documents.

micrographics The reduction of documents to microminiature size; includes all technologies and media.

minicomputer A smaller, less expensive, and less powerful version of a mainframe computer.

mission statement A clearly delineated statement of the major goals and objectives of a department or organization.

mixed inference In artificial intelligence, a deductive reasoning technique that starts with simple goals and incrementally reaches higher goals.

modem A device that converts computer digital information to analog signals for transmission over telephone lines and then converts them back to digital signals for use.

mouse A visual display terminal input device; the user pushes a small device on a special pad or desk surface, "clicking" it to give the system an instruction.

natural-language processing An area of research in artificial intelligence that allows users to communicate with a computer in a natural, human language.

newsletter Written communication that presents information about company policies, personnel, and events. Frequently referred to as a *house organ*.

node A point in a network where service is provided or used, or where communications channels are interconnected.

nonimpact printer A printer that produces output without the use of a typebar.

observation guide A written or printed schedule for recording observations.

office automation (OA) Computer systems designed for office applications and end-user computing. Tools under the office automation umbrella include word processing, spreadsheets, databases, fourth-generation languages, computer graphics, decision support systems, electronic mail and message systems, copiers, image processing, storage and retrieval systems, and printer technologies. Term is used interchangeably with **office systems, office automation systems,** and **automated office systems.**

office automation department A unit that is responsible for planning and implementing computer systems for office applications within an organization. May also be called an **office systems department** or the like.

office automation fair A demonstration, round table discussion, or seminar to let employees see and learn to use equipment and technologies.

office automation systems (OAS) Term used interchangeably with **office systems, office automation,** and **automated office systems.** *See* **office systems.**

office automation task force A committee charged with planning office automation for an organization.

office support *See* **support function**

office systems Term used by vendors to describe hardware and software; used in this text to describe the support activities of an organization.

office systems analysis A systematic procedure for examining an office system by identifying its procedures and required outputs.

office systems cycle The continuous, ongoing process of office systems analysis, including assessment, design, implementation, and evaluation; completion of one stage leads into another stage, with evaluation leading directly back into the assessment stage.

office systems department *See* **office automation department**

online databases Commercially marketed repositories of information stored on computers and accessed electronically by subscribers; information is developed and produced by thousands of organizations and companies throughout the world and is marketed by vendors.

open system A system that is affected by events outside its boundaries.

optical character reader (OCR) A device that electronically scans printed data or graphs and converts that data to a digital format for direct input to a computer.

optical digital data disk (OD3) A read-only optical disk; offers long archival life and extremely quick retrieval.

optical disk A disk that stores digital images or pictures of documents etched by a laser.

optical video disk A video disk for storing graphics, full-motion video, and possibly audio tracks.

organizational change Planned, intentional change to alter the status quo.

organizational communications approach An approach to office systems analysis that seeks to meet the communications needs of office workers.

organizational structure The system of responsibility, authority, and communication within an enterprise; usually reflected in organizational chart.

overhead cost The cost of doing business.

paddle A visual display terminal input device that enables users to move the cursor in two directions at the same time; used to create graphics.

parallel data transfer The transmission of data one word at a time; requires multiple wires.

participant observation An evaluation strategy in which an observer is "planted" in an office to determine the value or use of newly installed technologies.

payout period The time period required for equipment to pay for itself.

PBX *See* **private branch exchange**

pedagogy Teaching approach that is teacher-directed.

performance enhancers Software that is designed for personal time management; includes to-do lists and electronic notebooks.

performance objectives Expected outcomes of learning; what the trainee is expected to be able to do as a result of training.

personal copier The smallest category of copiers; used for extremely low-volume copying.

personal space The space a person needs to work well.

pilot installation A planned and managed installation of office automation technology to test a proposed solution to meet a specific need.

pilot test In office systems analysis, a trial of a proposed solution to meet a specific need.

pitch The size of a printed character and the spacing between characters; the larger the pitch, the smaller the character size.

plain-paper copier (ppc) A copier that operates by a camera throwing an image of the original document onto a positively charged drum.

planetary camera A stationary, manually controlled micrographics camera that creates roll microfilm.

planning document A written explanation of expected changes that outlines when and where changes will be made.

point-of-sale terminal An input device that scans data written in a special optical character recognition font for direct input into a computer system.

policies Written guidelines developed by top management regarding major organizational issues and goals.

portable dictation unit A pocket-sized basic dictation device; typically used by travelers.

principal A supervisor, manager, or other office employee for whom a secretary or administrative assistant performs work.

private branch exchange (PBX) Centralized telephone switching network used internally by most large organizations and owned by the telephone company.

procedures Specific methods for accomplishing work.

process A systematic series of actions directed at achieving a specific end.

processing programs Programs that handle system configuration, device assignments, file maintenance, and programming support; includes language translators, utility programs, and library programs.

productivity Output divided by input.

profile Keyboard thickness.

program (1) In computer systems, a set of step-by-step instructions written in a symbolic language that directs a computer to perform a specific task or series of tasks.

program (2) An organized action or effort designed to put **policies** into effect; the series of efforts needed to implement an organizational process.

programming languages Predefined sets of words and symbols that can be converted to machine language to control a computer system.

project An activity with defined goals and starting and stopping points; projects implement the objectives of **programs.**

project management software Software that automates project planning techniques; enables users to outline required tasks, estimate starting and ending dates, assign staff resources, and analyze project costs.

Prolog An artificial intelligence programming language that is popular in Japan and growing in microcomputer applications in the United States.

proprietary network A network that is a product of the vendor of specific computer systems.

prospect management software Software that maintains a directory of potential clients; prospects can be selected or qualified by any appropriate criteria designated by salespersons.

protocol In data communications, a procedure that controls transmission between devices.

prototype installation A planned and managed installation of office automation support in a limited area, with no plans for expansion.

quality of work life (QWL) The degree to which employees satisfy important personal needs through their work in an organization; the impact of work or a job upon the well-being, job satisfaction, and productivity of employees.

quality of work life approach An approach to office systems analysis that seeks the best tools and environment in which employees work.

questionnaire A written (or printed) set of questions to collect information.

QWERTY A keyboard layout named for the first six letters in its home row of keys.

random access memory (RAM) Volatile (temporary) memory that stores software programs or data during processing.

raster-scan display A visual terminal display in which the electronic beam is projected from top to bottom.

rationalization of jobs The process of analyzing a complex production process and dividing it into simple tasks that can be performed quickly and efficiently with little training.

read-only disk A prerecorded disk that cannot be updated or changed.

read-only memory (ROM) Nonvolatile (permanent) memory supplied by the computer manufacturer.

real-line processing The capability of a system to obtain data from an activity, perform computations, and return a response rapidly enough to affect the outcome.

record Any form of recorded information.

records management The science of managing records and information from creation to final disposition.

reduction ratio The relationship between the size of a source document and its microform.

reflection Light that bounces off a visual display terminal, making the screen display difficult to read.

reflection factor (p) A measure of the capacity to reflect light.

reject rate The ratio of the number of optical character recognition (OCR) errors to the number of characters read by the OCR.

relational database A database that allows users to store data in more than one file and to retrieve information from several files simultaneously. The user defines interrelationships among items by "relating" or linking data elements in one file with those of other files. *See also* **flat database**

renting A means of obtaining office automation technology in which the vendor retains title to the technology and offers maintenance services; in return, the user pays a monthly fee (no time promises).

reprographics All methods of reproducing or duplicating information, including printing, copying, facsimile, digital, graphic, and voice replication.

request for proposal (RFP) A report identifying systems requirements that is prepared by an office systems analyst and sent to vendors to obtain information on specifications, prices, etc., of vendors' technologies to meet an organization's needs.

resolution The quality of print. The higher the resolution, the higher the print quality.

responsibility Obligation to carry out assigned tasks.

restraining forces In Lewin's force field analysis, those factors that resist change and encourage stability and continuation of the status quo.

return on investment Logical business premise that an organization should obtain monetary return on monies it invests.

ring network A network topology in which all users are directly connected without passing through a central point.

robotics The application of computer technology to tasks or processes that require physical labor.

roll film A micrographics medium in which documents are captured and stored sequentially on a roll of microfilm.

rollover A telephone feature that forwards incoming calls to another number if the dialed number is not answered after a designated number of rings.

rotary camera A high-speed micrographics camera that creates roll film.

rules In artificial intelligence, clauses that stipulate ways of writing the facts; also called *heuristics*.

salvage value The value of replaced equipment.

satellite work center A fully equipped office facility in a location remote from a central office.

self-diagnostics The ability of technology to identify operational problems to users, usually by code.

serial transfer The transmission of data one bit at a time; like the telephone, it requires two wires.

shadow functions Activities that are not part of a job but contribute to completing work (e.g., "telephone tag").

shadow mask A visual terminal display in which the beam is emitted by three electronic light guns rather than a single gun, as in vector and raster-scan displays.

shared-logic word processor A special-purpose computer system that is dedicated to word processing applications; several dumb terminals share the storage and processing power of one central, or host, central processing unit (CPU).

shared-resource word processor A special-purpose computer system, dedicated to word processing applications, in which each terminal has its own local memory and software capabilities but is linked with other terminals via a local area network.

shorthand Face-to-face dictation by an originator to a secretary or stenographer who uses a special, abbreviated notation system to record the information.

simplex In data communications, a line that can send in one direction only.

site-license agreement A software purchase agreement that allows users to duplicate program disks and documentation in house.

slow-scan video teleconference A teleconference in which participants can hear and see each other; the visual medium is much like a slide show.

smart building A building designed with built-in communications facilities, such as computers, security devices, and temperature controls; also called *intelligent building*.

smart terminal A terminal with limited editing capabilities.

sociotechnological job design Job design approaches that integrate the social and psychological needs of workers with technological requirements. Organizational performance is believed to be a function of the interface between the social and technical systems.

soft dollar value Intangible values.

soft sectoring The process of dividing a disk by special codes written on the disk.

speaker-dependent system A computer system that understands words spoken by only a specific individual.

speaker-independent system A computer system that understands words spoken by any number of individuals.

special-purpose computer A computer that can process data for only one specific application (e.g., a standalone word processor).

speech recognition An application of artificial intelligence that allows the computer to recognize human words or phrases.

speech synthesis A computer's ability to respond in spoken words to input.

speed The output rates of printers and copiers.

spreadsheets Computer programs that provide a shell of columns and rows for data manipulation and calculation; users input labels, values, or formulas.

staff authority Special support or expertise to aid line authority; line authority is responsible for carrying out the major goals of an enterprise.

standalone word processor A special-purpose computer system that is dedicated to word processing applications and supports a single operator.

standard A measure against which performance can be compared.

standardized network A network that is licensed by computer system manufacturers to support their equipment.

star network A network topology in which a central unit routes messages to all intended destinations.

statements Computer directions written in programming code.

station message detail recording (SMDR) A program that lists all telephone calls, including their origins, destinations, times and lengths, and the services, accounts, or client codes used.

step-and-repeat camera A high-speed camera that updates microfiche and computer output microfilm; requires special film.

stopwatch measure A standard productivity measurement in which individuals are timed as to how long they take to perform a given task; the standard is typically the average of the measures.

strategic planning The process of defining major long-range goals and objectives.

subsystem A system that is part of a larger system.

support function An activity or service designed to help other employees perform their jobs; includes word processing, administrative support, mail services, forms design, telephone services, reprographics, records management, facilities management, and graphics services.

support personnel Employees who provide assistance to others; employees who perform support functions.

support services *See* **support function**

support system A planned structure for integrating all support services under centralized supervision and control.

suprasystem A system that includes a smaller system.

synchronous In data communications, transmission that is controlled by separating blocks of data by start and stop elements.

synergy Actions that add up to more than the sum of the parts.

syntax The rules governing the writing of statements in computer programs.

system A combination of interrelating parts that form a unitary whole that functions to meet specific objectives.

systems analysis The process of examining a system on the basis of feedback.

systems approach A perspective that views activities as part of an interrelated whole, all contributing to common objectives.

systems concept of office support A conceptualization of office work as an interrelated system of information processing to support the management and operation of the enterprise; even when they are organized as separate departments, all functions are viewed as interrelated; also called *total support concept.*

systems programs Computer programs that coordinate the operation of computer systems.

task lighting Lighting that is designed to enable a worker to perform a given task.

telecommunications Distance communications, including telephone, telegraph, and television.

telecommuting Working at home using a computer that is connected to a central business computer via telecommunications lines.

teleconferencing Communication between two or more individuals through electronic media.

telemarketing Using a telephone for marketing activities, usually with the aid of computerized databases.

teletraining Using teleconferencing equipment to deliver instruction.

Telex The international communications network of Western Union.

temporary-service industry Firms that supply businesses with temporary clerical services.

territoriality The tendency of people to "make their mark" on and lay claim to a certain space.

text-retrieval system (TRS) A cross between word processing and database management systems; designed for high-volume text storage and retrieval.

thermal copier A copier that uses heat in the copying process.

thermal printer A nonimpact device that uses heat in the printing process.

thimble printer A thimble-shaped printing element with up to 88 characters that rotates at high speed; characters are formed when the thimble strikes a ribbon.

throughput In systems theory, the transformation of input into output.

tickler files A type of log that itemizes tasks that must be performed on a given date.

time log A record of activities performed in a given time frame.

to-do lists Software for prioritizing and tracking tasks.

token passing A media access method whereby an electronic packet continually circles until it is "caught" by an intended user.

topology The arrangement of network stations in relation to each other.

total-life average method An accounting technique in which expenses related to purchasing and operating equipment are determined and then divided by the estimated life span of the equipment; often used to compare the costs of new technologies with the operating expenses of present technologies.

total support concept *See* **systems concept of office support**

touch-sensitive screen A visual display terminal screen that responds to instructions as the user touches the screen.

trackball A ball-like visual display terminal input device that is mounted on a display unit; when the ball is spun, the cursor moves rapidly across or down the screen.

tracking and follow-up Administrative tasks that maintain records of when items are received, what needs to be done with them, what was done with them, and their status at the present time.

traditional office An office where secretaries work in one-to-one relationships with their bosses; office personnel tend to be generalists as opposed to word processing/administrative support specialists.

training needs analysis The process of determining what needs to be learned and how that learning can best take place.

transcription unit A device used to listen to voice dictation and key it into a word processing system.

translation system A software program for translating written documents from one language to another; used as an aid to the translator, not as a replacement.

twisted pair wires Two pairs of plastic-sheathed copper wire twisted around each other; commonly used in telephone transmission cables.

two-factor motivation A theory developed by Frederick Herzberg that job content significantly contributes to worker motivation and satisfaction. Motivators produce long-lasting, positive job attitudes; hygiene factors, on the other hand, merely keep employees from being unhappy.

TWX The communications network of Western Union.

ultrafiche Microfiche filmed at a high-reduction ratio; requires a special reading device.

universal networks Networks with interfaces that allow dissimilar devices to attach to a common network.

user-friendly Easily learned or used by people with little technical expertise.

user group An informal group of computer users who meet to share expertise and experiences and discuss common problems.

user interface In artificial intelligence, the means by which an expert system gathers data from users about particular situations or problems.

utility programs Specialized software programs that perform specific tasks.

value added technique A cost-justification technique in which "values" such as activities, outputs, or quality are increased as a result of automation.

vector display A visual terminal display in which the electronic beam aims at the image only.

vertical solutions software Software that is designed for a particular industry.

Videotex Databases that are broadcast over television.

virus A self-perpetuating set of instructions that spreads by inserting copies of itself into other files; usually planted by disgruntled programmers to disrupt or destroy data.

vision systems A robotics application of artificial intelligence that allows computers to "see" and interpret images.

visual display terminal (VDT) A device that electronically displays text and graphics.

voice annotation A specialized application of voice technology that allows the user to record spoken comments along with a document or message.

voice mail A telephone answering system in which messages are recorded on a digital medium.

voice message system Software that allows users to create and send digitized voice messages over standard telephone systems; also called *voice store and forward system.*

voice store and forward system *See* **voice message system**

volume purchase agreement A purchase agreement that offers discounts based on the number of items ordered.

wide area network (WAN) A public network that offers data transmission services.

word-in-text indexing An electronic filing and retrieval system that allows users to retrieve documents by any word within the text.

word processing/administrative support (WP/AS) The concept of work specialization for secretaries originally conceived when word processing was introduced. WP/AS transformed secretaries from distributed office generalists into centralized teams of specialists.

word processing center A room or area housing personnel and equipment (usually word processing staff and equipment) to produce written communications systematically.

work flow The sequence of steps required to accomplish an activity from beginning to end.

work sampling The review of samples of current work output to determine areas that may need improvement.

work scheduler Software that generates work schedules for groups of employees.

workstation publishing systems Publishing systems that utilize mini- or mainframe computers, page composition software, graphics capabilities, and laser printers.

work-time measurement Comparing the time and work required to complete a specific task before and after the introduction of a given technology.

WP/AS A systems approach that employs specialists to perform specific aspects of office work. *See* **word processing/administrative support**

write once/read only disk A disk that can record but cannot update.

INDEX

FIGURE AND PHOTO CREDITS

Chapter 1

1-1, 1-2, 1-3, 1-4: Courtesy of International Business Machines Corporation.
1-5: Courtesy of The Computer Museum, Boston.
1-8a: Bruce Bliven, Jr., *The Wonderful Writing Machine* (New York: Random House, 1954), p. 51. © 1954 by Random House, Inc. Reprinted with permission.
1-8b: Courtesy of International Business Machines Corporation.
1-9, 1-10: Courtesy of The Yankee Group Seminar, "The Use of Technology To Improve Managerial Productivity" (20–21 May 1980).

Chapter 2

2-2a: Courtesy of International Business Machines Corporation.
2-2b: Courtesy of Wang Laboratories, Inc.
2-2c: Courtesy of Digital Equipment Corporation.
2-3: United States Congress. Office of Technology Assessment, *The Automation of America's Offices* (Washington, D.C.: Government Printing Office, 1985), p. 56.
2-9: Henry Mintzberg, *The Nature of Managerial Work* (New York: Harper and Row, 1973), p. 59. © 1973 by Harper and Row. Reprinted with permission.

Chapter 3

3-10: Courtesy of Office Systems Research Association.
3-13: Courtesy of Hanover Insurance Company, Waltham, Mass.; Limra International, Farmington, Conn.; Courant Corporation, Hartford, Conn.; Hamilton Standard Corporation, Windsor Locks, Conn.; Job Service of Florida, Fort Lauderdale.
3-14, 3-15, 3-16: Adapted from Addie Mattox and Janice McCollum, "How To Create a Career Path in Information Processing," *Papers and Proceedings of Syntopticon VII* (Willow Grove, Pa.: Association of Information Systems Professionals, 1980), pp. 413–417. Used with permission of the Association of Information Processing Professionals, 104 Wilmot Road, Suite 201, Deerfield, IL 60015-5195.

Chapter 4

4-2: Courtesy of Honeywell Information Systems, Inc.
4-3: Courtesy of Moniterm Corporation, Minnetonka, Minn.
4-4: Courtesy of International Business Machines Corporation.
4-5, 4-6, 4-7, 4-8: Courtesy of Maxell Corporation of America.
4-9: Courtesy of Honeywell Information Systems, Inc.
4-10: Courtesy of International Business Machines Corporation.
4-11: Courtesy of Compaq Computer Corporation.
4-12: Courtesy of Digital Equipment Corporation.
4-13: Courtesy of Apple Computers, Inc.
4-14: Courtesy of Compaq Computer Corporation.
4-15: Courtesy of Zenith Data Systems.
4-16, 4-17: Courtesy of Wang Laboratories, Inc.

Chapter 5

5-1: Courtesy of International Business Machines Corporation.
5-2: Courtesy of The Key Tronic Corporation.
5-3: Courtesy of Kraft Systems.
5-4: Courtesy of The Key Tronic Corporation.
5-5: Courtesy of Xerox Corporation.
5-6: Courtesy of CompuScan, Inc.
5-7: Adapted from Pamela Bond, "OCR: Examining the Benefits of Page Readers," *Words* (December–January 1985), pp. 34–35. Used with permission of the Association of Information Systems Professionals, 104 Wilmot Road, Suite 201, Deerfield, IL 60015-5195.
5-8, 5-9: Courtesy of Kurzweil Computer Products, Inc., A Xerox Company.
5-10: Courtesy of The First Tennessee Bank, Memphis.

5-11: Courtesy of McDonnell Douglas Information Systems Group, St. Louis.
5-12: Courtesy of Lowell Systems, a wholly owned subsidiary of S & S Electronics, Inc.
5-13, 5-14, 5-15: Courtesy of Dictaphone Corporation.

Chapter 6

6-1: Courtesy of Eastman Kodak Company.
6-2: Courtesy of UNISYS Corporation.
6-3, 6-4, 6-5: Courtesy of ALOS Micrographics Corporation.
6-6: Courtesy of Micron Corporation.
6-7: Courtesy of Canon USA, Inc.
6-8: Courtesy of Minolta Corporation.
6-9, 6-10: Courtesy of Eastman Kodak Company.
6-11: Don M. Avedon, "What the Future Holds," in *Automating Your Office: Pathways to Management Success*," ed. Lou Pilla (Willow Grove, Pa.: Administrative Management Society, 1984), p. 140. © 1984 by Administrative Management Society. Reprinted with permission.
6-12: Alan Purchase, *The Office Technologies* (Willow Grove, Pa.: Administrative Management Society, 1985), p. 37. © 1985 by the Administrative Management Society. Reprinted with permission.
6-13: Jennifer Roberts, "Newsreel of Fortune," *New York* magazine (15 Sept. 1986), p. 43. © 1986 by North America Syndicate, Inc. Used with permission.
6-14: Linda W. Helgerson, "The Optical Disk as an Information Storage Tool," *Office Administration and Automation* (April 1985), p. 49. Reprinted with permission of *Office Administration and Automation*. © 1985 by Dalton Communications, Inc., 1123 Broadway, New York, N.Y.

Chapter 7

7-1, 7-2: Courtesy of Allied Corporation.
7-3: Charles M. Williams and James A. Senn, "Introduction of Images into Automated Office Systems," *Proceedings of the Sixth Annual Office Systems Research Conference* (Athens, Ga.: Office Systems Research Association, 1987), p. 71. © 1987 by Office Systems Research Association. Used with permission.
7-4: Courtesy of Michael Camardello.
7-6: Courtesy of UNISYS Corporation.
7-7, 7-8: Courtesy of Xerox Corporation.
7-9: Courtesy of Apple Computers, Inc.
7-10: Courtesy of Xerox Corporation.
7-11: Courtesy of Hewlett-Packard Corporation.
7-12: Courtesy of CPT Corporation.
7-13: Adapted from "A Dictionary of Desktop Publishing Terms," *Administrative Management* (July 1986), p. 51. Used with permission of *Administrative Management*. © 1986 by Dalton Communications, Inc., 1123 Broadway, New York, N.Y.
7-14: Courtesy of Xerox Corporation.

Chapter 8

8-4a, 8-4c: Courtesy of Hayes Microcomputer Products, Inc., Norcross, Ga.
8-5: "The Computer-Modem Dialog," *BYTE Guide to the IBM PC* (Fall 1984), p. 245. © 1984 by *BYTE* magazine. Used with permission.
8-6: Fred Stern, *Data Communications and Networking for Personal Computers*, 4th ed. (Andover, Mass.: Digital Consulting Associates, Inc., 1982). © 1982 by Digital Consulting Associates, Inc. Used with permission.
8-11: Courtesy of NEC America, Inc., Melville, N.Y.
8-12: Courtesy of DataPoint Corporation.
8-13, 8-14: Courtesy of AT&E Systems, Inc., Portland, Ore.
8-15: Courtesy of Apple Computers, Inc.
8-16: Courtesy of Pitney Bowes Facsimile Systems, Inc.
8-17: Courtesy of Video Dial, Inc.
8-18: Courtesy of Equity Advertising Agency, New York, N.Y.
8-19: Frederick R. Feldman, "Brainy Buildings," *Impact: OA* (September 1985), p. 2. © 1985 by Administrative Management Society, Willow Grove, Pa. Reprinted with permission.

Chapter 9

9-1: Roger C. Schank and Peter G. Childers, *The Cognitive Computer* (Reading, Mass.: Addison-Wesley, 1984), p. 76. © 1984 by Addison-Wesley, Inc. Reprinted with permission.
9-2: Courtesy of Worldwide Communications Corporation, Northbrook, Ill.
9-3: Edward Foster, "Artificial Intelligence Faces a Crossroad," *Mini-Micro Systems* (May 1984), p. 123. © 1984 by Cahners Publishing Company. Used with permission.
9-4: United States Congress, Office of Technology Assessment, *The Automation of America's Offices* (Washington, D.C.: Government Printing Office, 1985), p. 134.
9-5: Courtesy of Tektronix, Inc., Wilsonville, Ore.
9-6: Robert Stevens, "Artificial Intelligence," *Mini-Micro Systems* (December 1983), p. 232. © 1983 by Cahners Publishing Company. Reprinted with permission.
9-7: Tom Moran, "Efficient Prolog Pushes AI into Wider Market," *Mini-Micro Systems* (February 1985), p. 55. © 1985 by Cahners Publishing Company. Reprinted with permission.
9-8: DOONESBURY. Copyright © 1985 by G. B. Trudeau. Reprinted with permission of Universal Press Syndicate. All rights reserved.

Chapter 10

10-1: Courtesy of International Business Machines Corporation.
10-2: Courtesy of Chang Labs, San Jose, Calif. C.A.T. is a trademark of Chang Labs, Inc.
10-4: Courtesy of Wang Laboratories, Inc.

10-7: Courtesy of Computer Associates International.
10-8: "Project Management at Magnavox," *Insight* (Winter 1985), pp. 26–27. Reprinted from *Insight* (now *CA-Insight)* magazine by permission of Computer Associates International.
10-9: Courtesy of Comshare, Inc., Ann Arbor, Mich.
10-10: "End-User Computing: Information at Your Fingertips," *Innovation Digest* (October 1986), p. 5. © 1986 by International Business Machines Corporation. Reprinted with permission.
10-11, 10-12: Courtesy of Comshare, Inc., Ann Arbor, Mich.

Chapter 11

11-1: "Business Computer Report: Engineering and Manufacturing," *Business Computer Systems* (July 1986), p. 23. © 1986 by Cahners Publishing Company. Reprinted with permission.
11-3: Courtesy of Connecticut National Bank, Hartford.
11-4: Alan D. Mazursky and Eileen Bechtold Dlugoss, *Lotus 1-2-3: A Practical Learning Guide* (Chicago: Science Research Associates, 1988), p. 138. © 1988 by Science Research Associates, Inc. Reprinted with permission.
11-7: Courtesy of Execucom, Inc.
11-10: Courtesy of Ashton-Tate Corporation. All rights reserved.
11-13: Copyright © 1988 Aldus Corporation. All rights reserved. Used with permission.
11-14: Courtesy of the Information Center Institute, a Division of Chantico Publishing Company, Inc., 3230 Commander Drive, Carrollton, Tex. Telephone (214) 250-3644. Reprinted with permission.
11-15: Barbara McLean and Bernard Peuto, "Desktop Publishing: Tools for Office Authors," *Words* (April–May 1986), pp. 27–28. Barbara McLean and Bernard Peuto are partners of Concord Consulting, Menlo Park, Calif. Concord provides consulting services to both vendors and customers in the computer-aided publishing field. Reprinted with permission of the Association of Information Systems Professionals, 104 Wilmot Road, Suite 201, Deerfield, IL 60015–5195.
11-16: Courtesy of Hewlett-Packard Corporation.
11-18, 11-19: Courtesy of Paul Harmon Associates. All rights reserved. Used with permission.
11-21: Gaile A. Swider, "Ten Pitfalls To Avoid in Information Center Implementation," *Words* (October–November 1986), p. 18. Reprinted with permission of the Association of Information Systems Professionals, 104 Wilmot Road, Suite 201, Deerfield, IL 60015–5195.
11-22: Copyright © 1987 Crwth Computer Coursewares. All rights reserved. Based on the Third Annual Crwth Information Center Survey (1987). Used with permission.
11-25: "Bestsellers Stand Their Ground in 1986," *Software News* (January 1987), p. 14. © 1987 by the Century Publishing Company, Westborough, Mass. Reprinted with permission.
11-26: Bill Dooley, "Computerization Is Beginning To Permeate the Legal Profession," *MIS Week* (3 Feb. 1986), p. 12. © 1986 by Fairchild Publications. Reprinted with permission.

Chapter 12

12-1: Len Horton, "Hosts Reach Out to Automatic Sales," *Software News* (August 1987), p. 55. © 1987 by Century Publishing Company, Westborough, Mass. Reprinted with permission.
12-3: Courtesy of Massachusetts Mutual Life Insurance Company.
12-4: Courtesy of Local Data, Inc., Torrance, Calif.

Chapter 13

13-2: Ina P. Simpson, "Changing Trends in the Secretarial Profession," *The Balance Sheet* (March–April 1983). © 1983 by South-Western Publishing Company. Reprinted with permission.
13-3: Marcia A. Anderson and Robert W. Kusek, *Word Processing Curriculum Guide* (Reston, Va.: National Business Education Association, 1982), pp. 97–98. Originally developed for the Illinois Office of Education. Reprinted with permission.
13-5: Courtesy of Wang Laboratories, Inc.
13-6: Courtesy of Dictaphone Corporation.
13-7: Phillip J. Gill, "And How Do DBMSes Fit In?" *Information Week* (1 Sept. 1986), p. 41. © 1986 by CMP Publications, Inc., 600 Community Drive, Manhasset, N.Y. Reprinted with permission of *Information Week.*
13-8: Courtesy of Data Retrieval Corporation.

Chapter 14

14-1: Courtesy of International Business Machines Corporation.
14-2: Courtesy of Gammalink Synchronous Communications, Inc.
14-3: Harold T. Smith, William H. Baker, and Marvin P. Evans, *The Administrative Manager: Principles and Strategies for the Automated Office,* 2d ed. (Chicago: Science Research Associates, 1987), pp. 103–106. © 1987 by Science Research Associates, Inc. Reprinted with permission.
14-4: Joseph Wise, "Designing the Micrographic System," *Administrative Management* (July 1986), pp. 62–63. Reprinted with permission of *Administrative Management.* © 1986 by Dalton Communications, Inc., 1123 Broadway, New York, N.Y.
14-5: Linda W. Helgerson, "The Optical Disk as an Information Storage Tool," *Office Administration and Automation* (April 1985), p. 49. Excerpted with permission of *Office Administration and Automation.* © 1985 by Dalton Communications, Inc., 1123 Broadway, New York, N.Y.

Chapter 15

15-2: Peter G. Sassone and A. Perry Schwartz, "Cost-Justifying OA," *Datamation* (15 Feb. 1986), p. 84. © 1986 by Cahners Publishing Company. Reprinted with permission.
15-5: Courtesy of UNISYS Corporation.

Chapter 16

16-2: Narrative adapted from press release of International Business Machines Corporation. Used with permission.
16-3: Courtesy of Honeywell Information Systems, Inc.
16-5: Courtesy of Applied Science Associates, Inc.
16-6: United States Congress, Office of Technology Assessment, *The Automation of America's Offices* (Washington, D.C.: Government Printing Office, 1985), p. 145.
16-8: Courtesy of Smith-Corona Corporation.
16-9: "Keyboards Blamed in Liability Suit," *VDT News: The VDT Health and Safety Report* (March–April 1988), p. 1. Copyright © 1988 by Louis Slesin. Reprinted with permission.
16-10: John J. Stallard and George R. Terry, *Office Systems Management*, 9th ed. (Homewood, Ill.: Richard D. Irwin, 1985), p. 121. © 1985 by Dow Jones-Irwin, Inc. Used with permission.
16-11: Courtesy of Herman Miller, Inc.
16-12: Courtesy of Haworth, Inc.
16-13: Courtesy of Stow/Davis Corporation.
16-14: Reprinted with permission of Duffy, Incorporated, Planners and Designers.
16-15: Marita Thomas, "Merck's Facilities Plan Fuses Physical, Technical, and Behavioral Factors," *Facilities Design and Management* (November–December 1983), pp. 60–63. © 1983 by *Facilities Design and Management*. Reprinted with permission.
16-16, 16-17: Courtesy of Haworth, Inc.
16-18, 16-19, 16-20: State of Washington Department of Labor and Industries, *Workplace Guidelines for VDTs* (Olympia, Wash.: August 1985), pp. 4–5.
16-21, 16-22, 16-23: Courtesy of Haworth, Inc.

Chapter 17

17-1: Douglas McGregor, *The Human Side of Enterprise* (New York: McGraw-Hill, 1960). © 1960 by McGraw-Hill, Inc. Reprinted with permission.
17-2: Edward M. Glaser, *Productivity Gains through Work Life Improvements* (New York: The Psychological Corporation, 1976), pp. 3–4. © 1976 by the Psychological Corporation. Used with permission.
17-3: United States Congress, Office of Technology Assessment, *The Automation of America's Offices* (Washin, ton, D.C.: Government Printing Office, 1985), p. 126.
17-4: Adapted from S. M. Pomfret, C. W. Olphert, and K. D. Eason, "Work Organization Implications of Word Processing," *Proceedings of the First IFIP Conference on Human/Computer Interaction (INTERACT '84)* (Geneva, Switzerland: International Federation for Information Processing, 1984), pp. 357–363. © 1984 by International Federation for Information Processing. Used with permission.
17-6, 17-7: Courtesy of Roy W. Walters and Associates, Inc.
17-8: John Hoerr, Michael A. Pollock, and David E. Whiteside, "Special Report: Management Discovers the Human Side of Automation," *Business Week* (29 Sept. 1986), p. 71. © 1986 by McGraw-Hill, Inc. Used with permission.

Chapter 18

18-1: Adapted from H. Leavitt, "Applied Organizational Change in Industry: A Structural, Technological, and Humanistic Approach," in *Handbook of Organizations*, ed. J. March (Chicago: Rand-McNally, 1965), p. 1145. © 1965 by Rand-McNally Corporation. Used with permission.
18-2: Kurt Lewin, "Quasi-Stationary Equilibria and the Problems of Permanent Change," in *Organizational Development: Values, Process, and Technology*, ed. N. Margulies and A. P. Raia (New York: McGraw-Hill, 1972), p. 211. © 1972 by McGraw-Hill, Inc. Used with permission.
18-6: Reprinted by permission of *The Harvard Business Review*. An exhibit from "Choosing Strategies for Change" by John P. Kotter and Leonard A. Schlesinger (March–April 1979), p. 11. © 1979 by The President and Fellows of Harvard College. All rights reserved.

Chapter 19

19-1: Joseph T. Coates, "Aspects of Innovation: Public Policy Issues in Telecommunications Development," *Telecommunications Policy* (June 1977), p. 10. © 1977 by *Telecommunications Policy*. Reprinted with permission.
19-2: Richard Layne, "Advanced Technology Groups: Can You Afford (Not) To Have One?" *Information Week* (19 Jan. 1987), p. 61. © 1987 by CMP Publications, Inc., 600 Community Drive, Manhasset, N.Y. Reprinted with permission from *Information Week*.
19-3: Courtesy of Jack W. Mynett and Associates. Reprinted with permission.

Chapter 20

20-1, 20-2: Georgia Miller, "The Basics of Office Systems," *Office Systems Research Journal* (Fall 1986), pp. 3–4. © 1986 by the Office Systems Research Association. Reprinted with permission.

Chapter 21

21-4: Courtesy of International Business Machines Corporation.
21-9, 21-10, 21-11, 21-12: Courtesy of UNISYS Corporation.
21-17: Courtesy of New York City Office of Business Development.

Chapter 23

23-1: Courtesy of Massachusetts Mutual Life Insurance Company.
23-2, 23-3, 23-4, 23-5: Joel S. Zimmerman, "PC Security: So What's New?" *Datamation* (1 Nov. 1985), pp. 89, 90, 92. © 1985 by Cahners Publishing Company. Reprinted with permission.
23-6: Courtesy of Security Dynamics, Inc., Cambridge, Mass. ACE®, Security Dynamics®, and SecurrID® are registered trademarks of Security Dynamics, Inc.

Chapter 24

Cartoon on page 684: Reprinted from *The Wall Street Journal* with permission of Cartoon Features Syndicate. All rights reserved.
24-1: Malcolm S. Knowles, *The Modern Practice of Adult Education* (New York: Cambridge Press, 1980), pp. 43–44. © 1980 by Cambridge Press. Reprinted with permission.
24-2: Courtesy of Longman Financial Services Institute, Minneapolis. All rights reserved.
24-6: Courtesy of DATAPRO, Inc.
24-7: Courtesy of Ernest and Whinney, Inc.
24-8: Courtesy of ForceTen Enterprises, Inc., Rexdale, Ont., Canada.
24-9: Courtesy of Pioneer Communications of America.
24-11: Courtesy of Massachusetts Mutual Life Insurance Company.
24-12: Helen Remick, "The Comparable Worth Controversy," in *Current Issues in Personnel Management*, ed. Kendrith M. Roland, Gerald R. Ferris, Jay L. Sherman, 2d ed. (Boston: Allyn and Bacon, 1983), p. 156. © 1983 by Allyn and Bacon, Inc. Used with permission.

Chapter 25

25-1: Walter A. Kleinschrod, "Desktop Publishing: The Next Big Software Addition," *Update 1987–88: Approaching the Automated Office* (Willow Grove, Pa.: Administrative Management Society, 1987), p. 62. © 1987 by Administrative Management Society. Reprinted with permission.
25-2: Courtesy of Hewlett-Packard Corporation.
25-3: Courtesy of Source EDP Computer Recruiting Specialists, San Mateo, Calif.
25-4: Michael Dodge, "The Working IC Professional," *Information Center* (July 1987), pp. 48–50. Reprinted with permission from the July 1987 issue of *Information Center*. © 1987 by Weingarten Publications, Inc., 38 Chauncy Street, Boston, Mass.

Appendix 3

All figures in the Case Studies are adapted from *White Collar Productivity: The National Challenge*, written by The American Productivity Center, Houston, Tex., and sponsored by Steelcase, Inc. © 1983 by Steelcase, Inc., Grand Rapids, Mich., Form Number S-380R1.

Pages 278–281: The description of the impact of a voice mail system on a furniture company's sales operations is from Susan F. Ehrlich, Elizabeth A. Akiba, and Vernell K. Munson, *Research Report: The Organizational Impact of Voice Store and Forward Technology* (Lowell, Mass.: Wang Laboratories, 1983). © 1983 by Wang Laboratories. Used with permission.

Pages 368–370: The case study of the use of portable computers by the Equitable Life Assurance Society is reprinted from Gerald E. MacLean, "Taking PC Power with You," *Words* (April–May 1986), pp. 37–38. Reprinted with permission of the Association of Information Systems Professionals, 104 Wilmot Road, Suite 201, Deerfield, IL 60015-5195.

Pages 425–428: The lists of telephone services are adapted from Harrison McDonald, "Telephone Selection: Everybody's Business," *Office Systems '87* (February 1987), pp. 60–61. © 1987 by Office Systems Magazine, Inc., Georgetown, Conn. Used with permission.

Pages 432–433: The description of Western Universal Mercantile's use of microcomputers and word processors with special communications hardware and software is reprinted from "Computer Is a Real Plus," *Modern Office Technology* (October 1986), p. 124. © 1986 by Penton Publishing Co., Cleveland, Ohio. Used with permission.

Pages 434–435: The narrative example of the legal applications of facsimile technology is adapted from "Business Communications," a special report published by *Industry Week* and *Modern Office Technology* (May 1986). © 1986 by Penton Publishing Co., Cleveland, Ohio. Used with permission.

Page 499: The description of the effects of room color on work behavior is adapted from "Paint Overcomes Hi-Tech 'Blahs,'" *Administrative Management* (March 1986), p. 49. Used with permisssion of *Administrative Management*. © 1986 by Dalton Communications, 1123 Broadway, New York, N.Y.

Pages 506–509: The discussion of behavioral issues in the workplace is adapted from Elaine Cohen and Aaron Cohen, *Planning the Electronic Office* (New York: McGraw-Hill, 1983), pp. 101–125. © 1983 by McGraw-Hill, Inc. Used with permission.

Page 548: The description of an office that functions without secretaries is reprinted from Louise Rodgers and Roxane Farmanfarmaian, "Technology Shakes Up the Organization (for Better or Worse)," *Working Woman* (November 1986), p. 100. © 1986 by Hal Publications, New York, N.Y. Used with permission.

Pages 587–589: The ten-step strategic planning process was developed by Booz, Allen and Hamilton, New York, N.Y. Used with permission.

Page 707: The narrative example of the use of interactive video disk and tape is adapted from James Hassett and Sheree Dukes, "The New Employee Trainer: A Floppy Disk," *Psychology Today* (September 1986), p. 30. © 1986 by the American Psychological Association. Used with permission.

Pages 755–811: The case studies in Appendix 3 are adapted from *White Collar Productivity: The National Challenge*, written by The American Productivity Center, Houston, Tex., and sponsored by Steelcase, Inc. © 1983 by Steelcase, Inc., Grand Rapids, Mich., Form Number S-38OR1.